AN INTRODUCTION TO GLOBAL FINANCIAL MARKETS

An Introduction to Global Financial Markets

Fifth edition

STEPHEN VALDEZ

First published 1993 as *An Introduction to Western Financial Markets*
Reprinted twice
Second edition 1997
Reprinted four times
Third edition 2000
Reprinted four times
Fourth edition 2003
Reprinted five times
Fifth edition 2007

Published by
PALGRAVE MACMILLAN
Houndmills, Basingstoke, Hampshire RG21 6XS and
175 Fifth Avenue, New York, N. Y. 10010
Companies and representatives throughout the world

PALGRAVE MACMILLAN is the global academic imprint of the Palgrave Macmillan division of St. Martins's Press, LLC and of Palgrave Macmillan Ltd. Macmillan is a registered trademark in the United States, United Kingdom and other countries. Palgrave is a registered trademark in the European Union and other countries.

ISBN-13: 978–0–230–00635–5
ISBN-10: 0–230–00635–3

This book is printed on paper suitable for recycling and made from fully managed and sustained forest sources.

A catalogue record for this book is available from the British Library.
A catalogue record for this book is available from the Library of Congress.

10 9 8 7 6 5 4 3 2 1
16 15 14 13 12 11 10 09 08 07

Printed and bound in China

Contents

Preface

The idea of a book on global financial markets came to me when I hit the problem of recommended reading for candidates coming from the continent of Europe to one of the courses run by my former company, 'Valdez Financial Training'.

Since the courses in question were about the markets in general, books called 'How the City of London Works' (or similar titles) did not exactly answer the problem. This was particularly true when we found ourselves facing audiences from the former Russian republics and from Eastern Europe.

It seemed to me that there was a need for a more general book about the global markets as a whole, as opposed to one about markets in one particular country such as the US or the UK. In any case, the financial world is becoming more integrated and global in its operations. A parochial knowledge of just one country is proving less and less satisfactory. This book seeks to answer this need.

Having said that, the book does not attempt a systematic coverage of the markets in all countries. Such a book would be far bulkier than this one and, probably, unreadable! Instead I have usually concentrated on examples from the US, the UK, Germany, France and Japan, with the inclusion in the 5th edition of a chapter on the new tiger economies of China and India. From time to time, illustrations will also be given from markets such as the Netherlands, Spain, Italy and Switzerland. The aim is not only to give a basic idea of how the markets work, but also to show the diversity of customs and practices within a common theme.

The book should prove useful for those preparing for a variety of examinations (MBA, banking, finance, economics and business studies), those working in banking and financial institutions in a support role (computer staff, accountants, personnel, public relations, back office and settlement) and, finally, staff in the many suppliers of information and computer services to the financial markets (computer manufacturers and software houses, Reuters, Thomson Financial and so on).

The first edition came out in 1993 and, while each subsequent edition has been brought up to date, it has sometimes seemed appropriate to add completely new chapters. Thus, the third edition added a chapter on European Economic and Monetary Union and this edition has, as mentioned, a chapter on China and India. In view of their growing influence, we have also included a chapter on hedge funds and private equity.

Apart from these new chapters, the fifth edition has new or expanded sections on credit derivatives, Islamic banking, the Sarbanes-Oxley legislation and hybrid bonds. The current situation in the EU following the rejection of the constitution is discussed as well as recent directives, such as the Markets in Financial Instruments Directive (MIFID). The last chapter reviews current trends.

Finally, for this edition we have introduced something new – the Companion Website – and this is explained on the next page.

Stephen Valdez

Companion Website

Books on financial markets usually involve a large number of mathematical formulae. In this case I have had the non-numerate reader in mind and, while there are references to formulae from time to time, no equations or Greek letters are give (to the relief of many!). On the other hand, those readers who are quite happy with mathematics may find this a little limiting.

For this reason, we have supplemented the 5th edition of this book with a website – http://www.palgrave.com/business/valdez – which contains analytical material on the following topics. The chapters of this book for which they are relevant are also given:

Chapter 6   The Money and Bond Markets –
Theories of the yield curve
Bond price calculation and duration.

Chapter 7   Stock Exchange –
Portfolio theory – the capital asset pricing model.

Chapter 12   Traded Options –
Option pricing.

These examples are all taken from the excellent *Finance and Financial Markets* by Keith Pilbeam, Palgrave Macmillan ISBN 1–4039–4845 and I am grateful for his cooperation. Indeed, those who are happy with mathematics might consider using this book in association with my own.

Stephen Valdez

Acknowledgements

Many organisations kindly gave permission for copyright material to be used and these were:

Association for Payment Clearing Services.
Bank for International Settlements.
European Association of Cooperative Banks.
European Central Bank.
Proquote.
Society for Worldwide Interbank Financial Communications.
Swiss Re Sigma Publications.
World Federation of Stock Exchanges.

Regarding the BIS mentioned above, I have found their staff to be exceedingly helpful and courteous in pointing me in the right direction for certain answers.

Other individuals who were very helpful include Steve Kelly of Thomson Financial Ltd. for details from the annual Thomson Extel Survey; Sandie Deane of UBS Global Asset Management for pension fund statistics; Stuart Drew for useful comments on insurance; Ashmita Chhabra of Eurohedge for hedge fund figures; Ian Tabor of Euronext.liffe for the FTSE100EDSP calculation; Richard Stevens of the same organisation for an explanation of swapnotes; John Ward of Dealogic on various matters and Lisa Clifton of Swiss Re for pointing out sources in the Sigma publications. The China British Council website includes a useful summary of Chinese banking.

In other cases, I have extracted figures from magazines like *The Banker, Euromoney*, the *Financial Times* and *Futures Industry*. In this connection also, I would like to mention the *GTNewsletter*.

The third edition of this book included the chapter on European Economic and Monetary Union for the first time. Whilst this has been extensively updated, I would like to acknowledge once again D.W. Urwin's excellent book, '*The Community of Europe. A History of European Integration since 1945* (Longman)' In a similar vein, in writing the material on hedge funds (Chapter 8), I found Robert A Jaeger's book, '*All About Hedge Funds*', (McGraw Hill), to be very useful. Finally, I drew heavily on the Swiss Re Sigma publication no5/2004, '*Exploiting the Growth Potential of Emerging Insurance Markets – China and India in the Spotlight*', for the insurance section in Chapter 16.

For this edition, I would like to thank my wife for carrying out the extensive and tedious keying necessary as well as coping with my hand writing. As with the first four editions, my thanks also go to Tina Shorter of Firm Focus for her excellent work in preparing the whole text for publication. Both she and my wife corrected my many inconsistencies, repetitions and lack of clarity. Those that remain are, of course, my responsibility.

Stephen Valdez

1 The Debt Merry-Go-Round

RAISON D'ÊTRE OF THE MARKETS

The beginning is always a good place to start. Let's go straight to the heart of the matter and ask the most fundamental question of all – what are the financial markets *for*? What is their purpose? What is the raison d'être?

The markets are all about the raising of capital and the matching of those who *want* capital (borrowers) with those who *have* it (lenders).

How do the borrowers find the lenders? Clearly, with difficulty but for the presence of intermediaries, such as banks. Banks take deposits from those who have money to save and bundle it up in various ways so that it can be lent to those who wish to borrow.

More complex transactions than a simple bank deposit require markets in which borrowers and their agents can meet lenders and their agents, and existing commitments to borrow or lend can be sold on to other people. Stock exchanges are a good example. Companies can raise money by selling shares to investors and existing shares can be freely bought and sold.

The money goes round and round, just like a carousel on a fairground (see Table 1.1).

Table 1.1 *The debt merry-go-round*

Lenders	Intermediaries	Markets	Borrowers
Individuals	Banks	Interbank	Individuals
Companies	Insurance companies	Stock Exchange	Companies
	Pension funds	Money market	Central government
	Mutual funds	Bond market	Municipalities
		Foreign exchange	Public corporations

Lenders

Let's have a look at some of those who might be lenders:

Individuals Individuals may have conscious savings in banks of various kinds. Individuals also may not think of themselves as conscious savers at all but, nevertheless, pay monthly premiums to insurance companies and contributions to pensions. Regarding pensions, there are different traditions. The US, UK, the

Netherlands, Switzerland and Japan have a strong tradition of pension funds. They invest the money paid into either private pension plans or employers' pension schemes. In France, the state takes care of most pensions and pays them out of current taxation, not out of a fund. In Germany, company pensions are important but the company decides on the investment, which may be in the company itself. Where pension funds exist, these funds of money, along with those of insurance companies, are key determinants of movements in the markets. They have to look ahead to long-term liabilities, and will assist the borrowers of capital by buying government bonds, corporate bonds, corporate equities and so on. The shortage of such funds in many of the newly emerging economies is a major reason for the slow growth of local securities markets there.

Companies We think of commercial companies as borrowers of capital. However, even if the company is a borrower, if some of the money is not needed for a short period of time, it will seek to make money by lending in the short-term markets called money markets (that is, transactions of up to one year in duration).

There are also companies whose cash flow is strong and who tend to be lenders rather than borrowers.

Borrowers

Who, then, are the borrowers of capital?

Individuals Individuals may have bank loans for domestic purchases or longer-term mortgages to fund house purchase.

Companies Companies need money short-term to fund cash flow. They need money longer-term for growth and expansion.

Governments Governments are typically voracious borrowers. Their expenditure exceeds their receipts from taxes and they borrow to make up the deficit. They may also borrow on behalf of municipalities, federal states, nationalised industries and public sector bodies generally. The total is usually called the 'Public Sector Borrowing Requirement' (PSBR). The cumulative total for all the borrowing since they started is called the 'National Debt'. The first surprise for many of us is that governments don't pay off the national debt, it just gets bigger. Of this, more in Chapter 3.

Municipalities and similar bodies Apart from the government borrowing on behalf of various local authorities, these bodies may borrow in their own name. This would cover municipalities like Barcelona, counties in the UK, federal states like Hesse in Germany.

Public corporations These might include nationalised industries, like SNCF in France or the German railways and post office authorities, or general public sector bodies like Crédit Local de France or the German Unity Fund.

Within an economy, many of the above will not be nationals but foreigners, with implications for the *foreign exchange* market.

Securities

When the money is lent, it may simply be a deposit with a bank. Most of the time, however, the borrower will issue a receipt for the money, a promise to pay back. These pieces of paper are, in the most general sense, what we call *securities*. There are, unfortunately for the beginner, masses of different names – Treasury bills, certificates of deposit, commercial paper, bills of exchange, bonds, convertibles, debentures, preference shares, eurobonds, floating rate notes and so on. At least we can console ourselves with the thought that they are essentially all the same – promises to pay back which show key information:

- ❏ HOW MUCH is owed
- ❏ WHEN it will be paid
- ❏ THE RATE OF INTEREST to reward the lender.

A major characteristic of the markets is that these securities are freely bought and sold. This makes life easier for the lender and helps the borrower to raise the money more easily.

For example, a young American wanting to save for old age spends $5000 on a 30 year government bond which has just been issued. After five years, he decides that this was not such a good idea and wants the money now. What does he do? He simply sells the bond to someone else. This is crucially important, as it means that he is more willing to put the money up in the first place, knowing that there is this escape clause. It also gives great velocity to the 'Debt Merry-Go-Round' as the same security is bought and sold many times.

Let's tackle the market jargon here. The first time the money is lent and changes hands, the first time the security is issued, is the *primary market*.

All the buying and selling that takes place thereafter we call the *secondary market*.

The secondary market is very significant as the flexibility it gives makes the primary market work better – it's the oil that helps the wheels to turn round.

Let's look at other terminology used (see Figure 1.1).

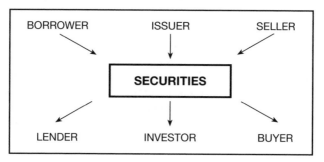

Figure 1.1   Market terminology

Suppose the government announces a new bond. We can say the government is *issuing* a new bond. We could just as easily say that the government is *selling* a new bond. We might see it as a sign of the government's need to *borrow* more money.

If you hear of the new bond, you may tell a friend that you've decided to *invest* in it. You might alternatively say you've decided to *buy* the new bond. You probably won't think of it that way, but you are the *lender* of money to a, no doubt ungrateful, government.

It may seem an obvious point, but all those terms might be used. Sometimes newcomers need to be reminded that whoever buys a security is directly or indirectly lending money unless it is equity.

RAISING CAPITAL

Let's look at an example. Suppose a commercial company needs $200m to finance building a new factory. We have just explained that the financial markets are all about the raising of money. What, then, are the choices?

Bank Loans

One obvious source of money when we need it is the *bank*. These days, with large sums of money, it may be a syndicate of banks to spread the risk. The banks are taking deposits lent to them and relending the money to the commercial company. It's their classic role as intermediary. In the international syndicated bank lending market, based in London, the money will not be lent at a fixed rate but at a variable rate according to market rates from time to time. This is called the *floating rate*. The banks may lend at a basic rate (such as the prime rate in the US or the interbank rate in Europe) plus a given margin such as ¾%. The bank will readjust the rate, say, every three months. The rate is fixed for three months but then changed for the next three months. Note that this creates *risk*. If rates fall, the lender loses income. If rates rise, the borrower pays more. (Note, however, that in many European domestic markets, the banks' tradition is to lend to corporates at a *fixed* rate.)

Bonds

Another choice would be to issue a *bond*. A bond is just a piece of paper stating the terms on which the money will be paid back. For example, it may be a 10 year bond, paying interest at 7% in two instalments per year. The word 'bond' implies that the rate of interest is fixed. If it's floating, then we have to find another name, such as *'floating rate note'*. The bond may be bought by a bank as another use for depositors' money, or it might be bought directly by an investor who sees the bond notice in the paper and instructs their agent to buy.

There is a strong obligation to meet the interest payments on the bond. If an interest payment is missed, the bond holders acquire certain rights and might even be able to put the company into liquidation.

Equity

A final choice would be to raise the money by selling shares in the company. Shares are called '*equity*'. If it's the first time the company has done this, we call it a '*new issue*'. If the company already has shareholders, it may approach them with the opportunity to buy more shares in the company, called a '*rights issue*'. This is because, under most but not all EU law, the existing shareholders must be approached first if any new shares are to be offered for cash. These rights are not protected as strongly in the US or in Germany.

The reward for the shareholders by way of income is the *dividend*. However, the income is usually poorer than that paid on a bond and the shareholders look to *capital gains* as well, believing that the share price will go up as time goes by.

Our three choices are shown in Figure 1.2 and the way the world's financial assets have moved between these is shown in Table 1.2 and the world's financial assets by market in Table 1.3.

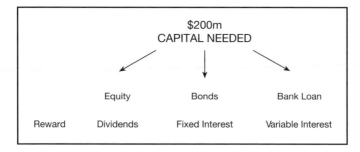

Figure 1.2 *Raising capital*

We must recognise that the equity choice is fundamentally different from the other two. The shareholder is part owner along with the other shareholders. There is, thus, no date for paying the money back (the shares may be sold on a stock exchange to someone else, but that's quite different). The shareholders accept risk – they could prosper if the firm prospers, or lose some or all of their money if the firm goes into liquidation. If the latter sad event happens, the shareholders are the last to receive a share of any money left. In addition, if the firm hits trouble, the dividend can be cut or even missed altogether.

In the case of bonds and bank loans, the money must eventually be paid back and there are strong legal obligations to meet the interest payments – they are *debt* not *equity*. Equity is the exception in the 'Debt Merry-Go-Round' in that it is not debt at all.

Table 1.2   *The world's financial assets, by asset class*

Asset class	2004 %	1980 %
Bank deposits	29	45
Equities	29	23
Private bonds	25	14
Public bonds	17	18
	100	100

Source: McKinsey Global Institute.

Table 1.3   *The world's financial assets, by market*

Market	2004 %
United States	35
Eurozone	24
Japan	15
United Kingdom	6
China	4
Other	16
	100

Source: McKinsey Global Institute.

Gearing

There's nothing wrong in principle with borrowed money. It enables the company to do more trading than it could on the shareholders' equity alone. The danger comes when too much money is borrowed, especially if boom times are followed (as they usually are) by recession. The firm may be unable to pay the interest out of its reduced profits, apart from the problem of repaying the principal sum itself.

Stock market analysts, therefore, look at firms' balance sheets and look at the ratio of long-term debt to equity. However, let's note here that when we say 'equity', we don't just mean the money raised by selling shares originally and by subsequent rights issues. The firm (we hope) will make profits. Out of the profits it will pay tax to the government and dividends to the shareholders. The remaining profit is retained for growth and expansion. This money also belongs to the shareholders. As a result, the phrase *shareholders' funds* is used for the total equity of the shareholders:

Original equity

+   Rights issues
+   Retained profit

=   Shareholders' funds

Analysts, then, look at the ratio between the long-term debt and the shareholders' funds. The relationship is called *gearing* or *leverage*.

The metaphor is from mechanics. A gear enables more work to be done with a given force. The lever is a similar idea. Remember Archimedes saying 'give me a fulcrum and I will lever the world'? The shareholders are doing more trading than they could with their money alone. How? By borrowing other people's money. The general idea behind gearing or leverage is to make a given sum of money go further. It can be summarised by the popular American expression 'more bang for your buck'! In this context, we do it by borrowing someone else's money. We shall also meet other contexts in this book.

The ratio between long-term debt and shareholders' funds is thus the *gearing ratio*. What ratio is safe? Frankly, this has become a matter of some controversy. Generally, people worry if the ratio reaches 100%, but that's only a crude guideline. For example, if the business is cyclical, analysts will worry more than if it's a steady business from one year to the next. They will also worry less if there are assets that can easily be realised, rather than assets which may not be easy to dispose of, especially during a recession (for example, property). In a low interest rate environment corporate gearing will tend to increase – the year 2005 saw some companies flush with cash and not borrowing much and others, wanting to take advantage of low interest rates, borrowing huge amounts especially for takeovers. At end 2005, the overall average gearing for the UK's top 100 companies was 33%.

Having looked at the three key choices for new capital – equity, bonds and bank loans – we should also be aware that, in Western financial markets generally, probably 50% of the money needed for growth and expansion comes from retained profits. 'Profit' can be a sensitive topic and, in some people's eyes, a pejorative term – for example, 'they are only in it for the profit'. However, profit provides not only rewards for the shareholders and taxes for the government, but funds for expansion which create further employment and a more secure environment for the employees.

We shall look at the concept of *international* markets in Chapter 6. Briefly, we are talking about equity raised across national boundaries; bonds issued in, say, London in dollars and sold to international investors; international banks getting together to syndicate a large loan. In addition to this would be capital raised in purely *domestic* markets. Equity, bonds and large syndicated loans usually refer to *long-term* capital. There is also the raising of *short-term* capital, for meeting cash flow needs rather than growth and expansion. Equity is not applicable here but there are various securities and types of bank loan which meet this need.

International figures can be misleading, as the emphasis may be quite different in *domestic* markets. Each country has its own traditions. The US is a big market for company bonds, as well as a large equity market. German companies, however, have a long tradition of close relationship with banks and use of bank finance. Equity finance is strong in the UK, with a higher proportion of companies publicly quoted than in most other European countries.

CONCLUSION

We have seen that the raison d'être of the financial markets is the raising of capital. Our examination of the choices for finding capital shows us the financial markets in action, and also the themes which we study in this book:

Banking In Chapters 2–5 we look at banking in all its aspects.

Money and Bond Markets In Chapter 6 we examine the domestic and international markets. We look at raising money short-term (money markets) and long-term (bond markets).

Equities Stock markets, brokers, market makers and institutions are explained in Chapter 7.

Enormous funds are being invested in the markets today by organisations called *Hedge Funds* and *Private Equity* – these are explained in Chapter 8.

Foreign Exchange The international character of the markets today and gradual deregulation create strong demand for foreign currencies. This is considered in Chapter 9.

Finance for Trade World trade is, of course, extremely important. The need for capital to back trade transactions and the need to control the risk pose special problems. These are discussed in Chapter 10.

EMU European Economic and Monetary Union started on January 1, 1999, as eleven countries moved to a single currency. This key development is discussed in Chapter 11.

Derivative Products Interest rates, currency rates, bond prices and share prices all go up and down, creating *risk*. There are financial products which are, paradoxically, used both to exploit risk and to control risk. These are called *derivative products* and are, possibly, the fastest growing sector of the financial markets today. This complex but fascinating subject is looked at in Chapters 12–14.

Insurance   The insurance market is one of the oldest world financial markets. Domestic and business risks create the need for insurance. The premiums paid in advance are a major factor in creating funds for lending to those who need capital, until such time as these funds are required to meet insurance claims. This is explained in Chapter 15.

The new tiger economies of *China* and *India* are examined in Chapter 16.

Key Trends   Finally, in Chapter 17, we analyse the key trends in the financial markets today.

SUMMARY

The purpose of the markets is to facilitate the raising of capital and match those who want capital (borrowers) with those who have it (lenders).

Typically, the borrower issues a receipt promising to pay the lender back – these are *securities* and may be freely bought and sold.

Money may be raised by a bank loan (commercial banking) or by the issue of a bond or equity (the capital markets). The first two represent debt. The relationship between debt and equity on a balance sheet is known as *gearing*.

There are domestic markets and international (cross-border) markets.

Banking

2   Banking Background

Money and the use of metal coins as money has a long history – going back at least ten centuries. Banking, certainly in today's sense, is rather more modern.

In many ways, the origins of capitalism as we see it today lie in the operations of Italian merchanting and banking groups in the 13th, 14th and 15th centuries. Italian states, like Lombardy and Florence, were dominant economic powers. The merchants had trading links across borders and used their cash resources for banking purposes.

The bankers sat at formal benches, often in the open air. The Italian for bench is '*banco*', giving us the modern word for bank. (If you happen to be in Prato, Italy, look in the Chapel of San Francisco for a fresco showing the money-changers' *banco*, or counter.) If the bank went into liquidation, the bench would be solemnly broken, giving us the *bancorupto* or bankrupt, as we say today. The early associations were partnerships, as shareholding companies did not begin until 1550. As a result, people might write to the '*Medici e compagni*', the 'Medici and their partners'. It gives us the modern word – the *company*. It is the Italians who claim the oldest bank in the world, Monte dei Paschi of Siena (1472).

For a long period, Florence was a major centre. As a result, many coins ended up with names based on Florence. The UK had a 'florin' until the coinage was decimalised in 1971; the former Dutch guilder had the abbreviation FL – florin; the Hungarian currency is the 'forint'. We also read that, in 1826, Schubert sold his D major piano sonata for '120 florins'. As a result of all this, at the EC Summit in Madrid in December 1996, John Major put forward the florin as the proposed name for Europe's single currency. The meeting finally decided on the rather more boring name, the euro.

Italian bankers had a long relationship with the British crown. The first bankers to lend money in London came from Lombardy and London still has 'Lombard Street' at the heart of the financial area. Bankers lent money to Edward I, Edward II and Edward III (naturally, to finance their various wars). Edward III, however, defaulted on the loan in 1345 and the proud families, the Bardi and the Peruzzi in Florence, crashed into liquidation as a consequence. Presumably this was the world's first (but not last!) international banking crisis.

Those bankers were very advanced for their time. They used bills of exchange (to be explained in Chapter 5), letters of credit, book entry for money instead of physically transporting it and double entry bookkeeping. The first textbook on double entry bookkeeping was published in 1494 by a Franciscan monk, Luca Pacioli. They experimented with marine insurance and evolved a body of mercantile law. The Bardi operated 30 branches in Italy and overseas and employed more than 350 people.

S. D. Chapman, in *The Rise of Merchant Banking* (Allen & Unwin, 1984) shows how the Medici bank helped an Italian firm in Venice sell goods to a firm in London using a bill of exchange. The Medici bank in London would collect the money and the bank would take care of the foreign exchange conversion and risk. The goods were invoiced at £97.18s.4d (in old pounds, shillings and pence). This was the equivalent of about 535 ducats. The Medici branch in Venice paid the local firm 500 ducats on the bill of exchange, making 7% on money they would not receive for 6 months, that is, about 14% p.a. The date? 20 July 1463.

The bill above was not 'discounted' in the modern sense, since this would imply charging interest on money and this was forbidden by the Roman Catholic Church as 'usury'. The bill represented a service to facilitate trade and change foreign money – it could not appear to involve the lending of money. On the deposit side, no formal interest could be paid for the same reason. Depositors received a share of profits paid at discretion. Thus the liabilities side of the balance sheet was headed, '*Discrezione*'. Islamic banking faces similar problems due to the Koran's rejection of the concept of interest as such. Today there are some 250 Islamic banks which follow the principle that the reward for deposits is not fixed but based on the profit from the use of the money (we return to this later in this chapter).

The one thing the Italians didn't invent was banknotes. For this, we look to goldsmiths in the UK. There, merchants would keep money for safe keeping in the Royal Mint. Charles I had many arguments with Parliament about money and solved one of them by marching down to the Royal Mint and stealing £130,000! Although the money was replaced later, confidence in the Royal Mint had gone. It was good news for goldsmiths who had secure vaults for gold and silver coins and began an era of goldsmiths as bankers for some 150 years. Coutts Bank, still going today, began in 1692 as a goldsmith bank. The goldsmiths found it convenient to give out receipts for a deposit of gold coins made out to 'the bearer' and to issue ten receipts for a deposit of ten coins. In this way, if the bearer owed someone else three gold coins, they could pass on three bearer receipts. Even better, if someone wanted to borrow five gold coins, the goldsmiths could lend them five of these nice pieces of paper and not give gold coins. We are now very much into modern banking traditions, except that today the notes aren't backed by gold or silver anyway! By the end of the 17th century, the goldsmiths' receipts had become banknotes in a formal sense, the first being issued by the Bank of Sweden in 1661.

Internationally, the emphasis in banking, which had been in Florence, moved to Genoa, as gold and silver were flooding in from the New World. Outside Italy, the Fugger family of Augsburg created a financial dynasty comparable to the Italians. They were originally wool merchants, but turned to precious metals and banking. They had gold, silver and copper mines in Hungary and Austria and became principal financiers to the Hapsburg empire in Germany, the Low Countries and Spain (see E. Green, *Banking, an Illustrated History*, Phaidon Press, 1989).

Later still, we have the rise of the two great rivals, the Dutch and British Empires and Amsterdam and London as rival financial centres. Amsterdam, for example, is Europe's oldest stock exchange.

We also see merchant banking (or investment banking) in the modern sense. Francis Baring was a textile merchant from Exeter and started Baring Brothers in 1762. In 1804, Nathan Mayer Rothschild opened up for banking business in London, after a brief spell in textiles in Manchester. In Holland, we had Mees & Hope (1702) and, later, Pierson, Heldring & Pierson – both still in business today as subsidiaries of the Fortis Group under the name Mees Pierson.

The merchant bankers had two key activities – financing trade, using bills of exchange and raising money for governments by selling bonds. Baring Brothers financed the huge reparations imposed on France after the Napoleonic wars with a large international bond issue. (As a consequence, the Duc de Richelieu dubbed them 'Europe's 6th super-power'!) In 1818, Rothschild's raised a large loan for Prussia, to be redeemed after 36 years. They arranged to pay dividends to bondholders in their local currency. The bonds were sold to merchants, private subscribers and the aristocracy. Prussia paid 7½% of which 5% was paid to bondholders and 2½% was used to create a 'sinking fund' to redeem the bond after 36 years (see Chapman, *The Rise of Merchant Banking*). The Dutch Bank Mees, together with Baring Bros, helped the American states finance the purchase of Louisiana from Napoleon in 1803. Later, corporate finance emerged as another investment banking business. In 1886, Baring Bros floated Guinness – police had to hold back the crowds!

In the second half of the 1700s and into the 1800s there was a large growth in Europe's population (from 180 million in 1800 to 450 million by 1914). This period also saw the growth of industrialisation and urbanisation. As a result, the spread of banking followed. While private banks continued to flourish in many cases, the gradual change in legislation to allow joint stock banks (that is, banks with shareholders) paved the way for the growth of larger commercial banks with many branches and a strong deposit-taking function.

In the US, the Bank of New York and the Bank of Boston (later First National Bank of Boston) opened in 1800. The water company, the Manhattan Company, became a bank around about the same time. (It became Chase Manhattan in 1955.) The 'City Bank' opened in 1812, becoming the National City Bank later and merging with First National Bank to form today's Citibank in 1955 (now Citigroup after further acquisitions).

In Europe, we see the Société Générale of Belgium formed in 1822; the Bayerische Hypotheken und Wechsel Bank in 1822; Creditanstalt in Austria in 1856; Crédit Suisse also in 1856; UBS in 1862; Crédit Lyonnais in 1863 and the Société Générale (France) in 1864 (by 1900 they had 200 and 350 branches respectively); Deutsche Bank in 1870 and Banca Commerciale Italiana in 1894.

In the UK, the Bank of England's monopoly of joint stock banking ended in 1826. There were 1700 bank branches in 1850, 3300 by 1875 and nearly 7000 by 1900. The Midland Bank opened in 1836 and the forerunners of National Westminster in 1833–36. Private banks, threatened by the greater resources of the new joint stock banks, were either bought out or merged. One such merger formed the Barclays we know today. One of the earliest of such private banks was Child & Co, at No. 1 Fleet Street since 1673 and nowadays part of the Royal Bank of Scotland. By 1884, the London Clearing House was clearing cheques worth £6 billion.

There is one interesting point about the UK. Although Rothschild's on the continent had a hand in setting up some of the commercial banks (Creditanstalt and Société Générale of France are examples), in the UK, the merchant banks ignored the new developments and stuck to that which they knew and did best (international bonds and trade finance). As a result, the British tradition has been one of looking at two types of bank – the 'merchant' bank on the one hand and the 'commercial' bank on the other (we shall examine the differences later in this chapter). It was only in the 1960s and later that the large commercial banks thought it necessary to open merchant bank subsidiaries or buy one (for example, Midland Bank buying Samuel Montagu).

On the continent of Europe, especially in Germany, Austria and Switzerland, the pattern became that of banks who did all types of banking – both 'merchant' and 'commercial'. This is the 'universal' bank tradition – banks like Deutsche Bank and UBS.

These developments take us into this century and the age of computers, communications, automated teller machines (ATMs), credit cards, bank mergers, electronic funds transfer at the point of sale (EFT-POS) and banking via the Internet or, even, mobile phones.

BANKING SUPERVISION

Let's start with the question: 'Who is in charge of the banks?' If you were in the Netherlands or Italy, you might reply, 'The Central Bank', and you would be correct. However, this is by no means always the case. Indeed, it is more common to find that the supervisory body is separate. The Bundesbank is not responsible legally for supervision – that is the task of the 'Federal Supervisory Authority' (BaFin) which, in April 2002, combined the supervisory roles of the three previously separate authorities for banking, insurance and securities. It does, of course, consult the Bundesbank and the latter collects detailed reports from all the country's banks. However, if any action is to be taken, it will be taken by BaFin.

There is a Banking Commission in France and Belgium and a Federal Banking Commission in Switzerland.

In Japan, the Financial Services Agency is in charge and, in the US, the picture is very mixed with differing roles played by the Federal Reserve, individual states, the Federal Deposit Insurance Corporation (FDIC), the Comptroller of the Currency and the Savings and Loan Associations reporting to the Federal Home Loan Bank System. For example, when Chicago's Continental Illinois Bank hit trouble in 1984, it was rescued by the FDIC and not the Federal Reserve. The US Congress has been promising to simplify this confusion for some time but has, so far, failed to do so.

In the UK, the Bank of England used to be the supervisory body, but in mid 1998, the Labour government transferred powers to the new Financial Services Authority (FSA).

In China, banking supervision is in the hands of the People's Bank of China, the central bank, and in India, too, the central bank, the Reserve Bank of India, is in charge.

Having decided who is in charge, what general rules will they lay down? Usually, the following:

- ❑ Conditions of entry
- ❑ Capital ratios
- ❑ Liquidity rules
- ❑ Large exposure rules
- ❑ Foreign exchange control
- ❑ Rights of inspection.

(The meaning of the more technical terms here will be explained within the banking chapters.)

TYPES OF BANK: DEFINITIONS

There are many different terms used, not all mutually exclusive. Let's examine the following:

- ❑ Central banks
- ❑ Commercial banks
- ❑ Merchant/Investment banks
- ❑ Savings banks
- ❑ Cooperative banks
- ❑ Mortgage banks
- ❑ Giro banks and National Savings banks
- ❑ Credit unions
- ❑ Islamic banks.

Central banks   Typically, an economy will have a central bank, like the Federal Reserve in the US or the Bundesbank in Germany. The role of the Central Bank will be examined in detail in Chapter 3.

Commercial banks   These are banks in the classic business of taking deposits and lending money. There are two further relevant terms here – *retail* banking and *wholesale* banking. Retail banking involves high street branches, dealing with the general public, shops and very small businesses. The use of cheques and plastic cards is normally of crucial importance; for example, 2090 million cheques were written in the UK in 2004 (as opposed to 3800 million in 1991). At the same time, some 5700 million card based transactions took place at point of sale, of which two thirds were debit cards. We are talking here of high volume but low value. Wholesale banking involves low volume and high value. It covers dealings with other banks, the central bank, corporates, pension funds and other investment institutions. Cheques and cards are not so important here, but electronic settlement and clearance is – systems like CHIPS (Clearing House Interbank Payments) in New York, CHAPS (Clearing House Automated Payments) in the UK, SIT (Système Interbancaire de Télécompensation) in France, EAF2 in Germany and TARGET for the euro. The dealings in the money markets which we describe in Chapter 6 are wholesale banking activities. Retail banking and other wholesale activities like corporate loans are discussed in Chapter 4. Foreign exchange may be retail (a member of the public going on holiday) or wholesale (a French corporate wants SFR10m to buy Swiss imports). Foreign exchange is discussed in Chapter 8.

A special subset of retail banking is *private* banking. This involves handling the needs of high net worth individuals – deposits, loans, fund management, investment advice and so on. Historically, it is a key Swiss speciality!

Merchant/Investment banks   *Merchant* bank is a classic UK term; *Investment* bank is the US equivalent and perhaps the more general and modern term. We shall use them interchangeably (but beware use of the term 'merchant banking' in the US, where it is applied to taking an active part with the bank's own capital in takeover/merger activities). If commercial banking is about lending money, merchant banking can be summarised as 'helping people to find the money'. For example, in Chapter 1 we examined three choices for raising capital – bank loan, bond issue or equity. Sometimes the choice is not necessarily clear. In September 1993, an article in London's *Evening Standard* criticised corporates for their fondness that year for rights issues, arguing that bonds would have been better value in the long run. Merchant or investment banks will give advice on this aspect. If the choice is bonds or equities, they will help the issuer to price them, will assist in selling them and, with other associates, *underwrite* the issue, that is, they will buy the securities if the investors do not.

There are other activities of merchant or investment banks and we will cover these in Chapter 5.

In many European countries (France, Germany, Italy, Austria, the Netherlands and Spain) there are banks that do not have outside shareholders but are 'mutually' owned in some way. These are the savings banks and cooperative banks.

Savings banks   What we have to distinguish here is the historical, traditional role of savings banks and their more modern role today. In the modern world they are looking more and more like ordinary commercial banks due to (a) growing mergers of previously autonomous savings banks, (b) deregulation, removing restrictions on their activities and giving them powers to act like commercial banks. In spite of

(a) and (b), what might still make them a little different is their ownership structure – usually they are 'mutuals', that is, owned by the members.

There are strong savings bank movements right across Europe with terms like:

❏ Sparkasse   Germany/Austria
❏ Cassa di Risparmio   Italy
❏ Caja de Ahorros   Spain
❏ Caisses d'Épargne   France/Belgium.

In the US, they are known as 'Savings and Loan Associations' or 'Thrifts' and in the UK (historically, but not today) – 'Trustee Savings Banks'.

There are about 500 savings banks in Germany with some 15 000 branches. As it is a federal republic, each federal state or county within a state guarantees the deposits and there is a central bank for the savings banks called the *Landesbank*. There is also an overall central authority to coordinate activities, the Dekabank, which is owned by the savings banks and the Landesbanks. It distributes products via the 15 000 branches of the savings banks who themselves account for 34% of bank deposits. Dekabank also operates wholesale banking and is the second largest fund manager in Germany.

Federal guarantees given to Landesbanks used to enable them to raise capital cheaply. Other German banks argued that this is unfair competition and the European Commission ended this in 2005.

Having some form of central bank for savings banks is not uncommon. In Austria it's the Girozentrale Vienna (later called GiroCredit Bank and now part of Bank Austria). In Finland, prior to its financial collapse in September 1991, it was the Skopbank. It was reorganised as the Savings Bank of Finland. Widespread mergers are taking place in Spain and Italy and even mergers with other banks. For example, in Italy the Cassa di Risparmio di Roma has merged with Banco di Roma and Banco di Santo Spirito to form a large bank called (curiously) Banca di Roma. In addition, the largest Italian savings bank, Cariplo, has merged with Banco Ambrovenuto and changed the name to Banca Intesa. A major force in Spain is the Catalan La Caixa, which has formed alliances with other savings banks. It has invested heavily in industry and its portfolio is worth €17 billion or 4% of Spain's stock market. It is, thus, a major 'back room player'. In total there are 46 regionally based cajas and they have 36% of the nation's banking income. In neither Spain nor Italy has deregulation of powers gone as far as in Germany.

In the UK, the movement was started in 1810 in order to accept small deposits (the minimum deposit for a normal bank was quite large). In 1817, the government passed a law that the banks must be run by trustees to protect the depositors, hence 'Trustee Savings Banks'. In 1976, they were deregulated and given normal banking powers. From a large number of distinct autonomous banks, the movement eventually came together as one bank, simply known as 'TSB Bank'. In 1986 the government sold shares to the general public and it lost its mutual status. Finally, in 1996, it was taken over by Lloyds Bank.

In France, too, the movement is coming together and sells and markets itself as 'Caisse Nationale des Caisses d'Épargne et de Prévoyance' (Cencep). This central body is France's third largest bank by Tier one capital (explained later) and coordinates the activities of 450 local savings banks who have 26 million customers. They have normal banking powers, and have expanded into *bancassurance* (see Chapter 4), lending to local authorities, leasing, venture capital, property investment and collective investment sales (UCITS). They account for some 20% of deposits in France and are allowed to run special tax exempt accounts (as is the National Savings Bank). As in Germany, the other banks are complaining that this is unfair competition.

In the US, deregulation of the Savings and Loan Associations in 1981 was a total disaster leading to a mixture of fraud and mismanagement. It created one of America's biggest banking crises.

In Japan, the mutual savings banks are called *sogo* banks and there are 70 of them. They take retail deposits and are important lenders to small businesses.

A list of Europe's top savings banks is shown in Table 2.1.

Table 2.1 *Top European savings banks, 2004*

Bank	Assets $bn
Groupe Caisse d'Épargne	740.8
Sparbanken Sverige	154.2
La Caixa (Barcelona)	154.1
Caja de Madrid	117.6
Caixa Geral de Depósitos	95.7
Hamburger Sparkasse	42.6
Stadtsparkasse KölnBonn	30.3
Caja de Mediterráneo	31.0

Source: *The Banker,* July 2005.

Cooperative banks   These are banks which are owned by the members and with maximum profit not necessarily the main objective – they may aim, for example, to give low cost loans to members.

Usually, the membership derives from a trade or profession. Much the most common is agriculture which gives us Crédit Agricole in France (in asset terms, France's biggest bank and the world's fifth biggest), the Rabobank in the Netherlands and the Norinchukin bank in Japan. In Table 2.2 we show the share of deposits in the EU accounted for by cooperatives. From this we see that they are significant in France, the Netherlands, Finland, Austria, Italy, Denmark and Germany.

Table 2.2 *Cooperative banks' share of deposits, end 2004 (except where noted)*

Country	%
France	50.2
Netherlands	39.0
Finland	32.3
Austria	32.0
Italy	29.1
Denmark (2000)	26.3
Germany	18.5
Hungary	10.1
Luxembourg	10.0
Poland	9.4
Ireland (2001)	7.0
Portugal (2001)	5.0
United Kingdom (2002)	2.0
Belgium	—
Sweden	—

Note: — Figures not available.
Source: European Association of Cooperative Banks.

The Crédit Agricole has 46 regional banks and is the largest high street banking group, handling some 30% of all mortgages. In 1996 it bought Banque Indosuez and, in 2003, the troubled Crédit Lyonnais. Crédit Agricole has a 28% share of deposits, having 22 million accounts and 9000 branches. In addition to this business in France, it has operations outside France which generate 34% of its turnover.

There are two other cooperative organisations in France – Crédit Mutuel (with a 15.8% share of deposits) and Banques Populaires (6.4% share).

Germany also has a strong cooperative tradition drawn from all sorts of trades and professions. There is, for example, the 'Chemists and Doctors' Bank' (Apotheker und Ärztebank). There are over 1300 cooperative banks with some 30 million customers. There exist regional cooperatives and a single central bank acting as a clearing house and using central funds wholesale and for international activities; this is the DV Bank. This has access to the customers of the cooperative banks and the investment books of the banks themselves. They are not obliged to use the DV Bank but 90% do. Cooperative banks take 18.5% of all deposits in Germany. The Rabobank in the Netherlands is the name for the central body which acts for local agricultural cooperative banks. It is the biggest bank in Holland in terms of Tier one capital. Rabobank has a AAA credit rating and acts for some 500 local cooperatives. It offers a wide range of banking facilities, is the market leader for mortgages and has more retail branches than any other bank and even operates retail branches in the USA and Australia. It also owns the Dutch insurer, Interpolis.

In Japan, there are cooperative banks in agricultural fishery and forestry. There is a Central Cooperative bank for Agriculture and Forestry called the Norinchukin Bank. There are also a large number of commercial credit cooperative banks.

The Agricultural Bank of China is the country's fourth largest in asset terms and there are 35 000 rural credit cooperatives and 1000 urban credit cooperatives offering finance to farmers.

India has 1872 urban cooperative banks and 106 919 rural cooperative credit institutions which lend to farmers and local small businesses.

In the UK, there is only one cooperative bank, called the Cooperative Bank. It works closely with the general retail cooperative movement and has normal banking facilities. However, its share of total UK bank deposits is about 2.0%.

Finland has many cooperative banks (just under 300) with their own central bank, the Okobank, which has joined with the Pohjola bank for insurance.

Mortgage banks   Some economies have a special sector dealing with mortgages and some do not.

The most obvious example of a special sector is the UK's *Building Societies*. Originally they were associations which came together to build houses and then disbanded. Gradually, they became permanent mutual organisations, collecting small high street savings and using the money to fund domestic mortgages. There were over 2000 in 1900, but only about 63 today in a movement dominated by the larger societies. They have 2000 branches, 15 million savers and 2.7 million borrowers. The Building Societies Act of 1986 deregulated them to the extent of allowing them to offer cheque accounts and unsecured loans as well as a variety of other services. However, the amount of such business that they can do is strictly limited. The Act also allowed them to become a public limited company if the members agreed. Abbey National took advantage of this and went public in 1989, becoming the UK's fifth biggest bank in asset terms. By 1995–96 the movement underwent considerable change. Lloyds Bank acquired the Cheltenham and Gloucester, Abbey National acquired National and Provincial and the merged Halifax/Leeds Societies, along with the Alliance and Leicester, the Woolwich and Northern Rock, all revealed plans to go public and become a bank. Others, like the Britannia, defended the 'mutual' principle and announced loyalty bonuses for their longer-term members. However, in late April 1999, one of the largest remaining mutual societies, the Bradford and Bingley, announced its intention to convert to a bank after a vote by its members. This has rekindled the debate and many believed that the remaining large mutuals would end up as banks. However, by mid 2006, the two largest – the Nationwide and the Britannia – were still mutuals.

Germany has 35 mortgage banks (Hypothekenbanken), often subsidiaries of other banks, and a few building societies (Bausparkassen). The largest mortgage bank is Eurohypo, owned by Commerzbank. The mortgage banks fund the mortgages with a special bond – the Pfandbriefe. The Netherlands has several mortgage banks which are subsidiaries of other banks (for example, Rabobank) or of insurance companies. Denmark has a small number of Mortgage Credit Associations which sell bonds on the Stock Exchange and hand the proceeds to the borrower whose property is security for the bond.

The specialists in mortgages in the US are the Savings and Loan Associations which were deregulated in 1981. Unlike the UK's 1986 Building Societies Act, however, prudent restrictions on new powers were not imposed and the movement hit serious trouble, as mentioned earlier.

Giro banks   Let's start by considering this word 'Giro'. It comes from the Greek '*Guros*', meaning a wheel or circle. The circle in finance is the passing round of payments between counterparties.

We find references to this term in early Italian banking. In the Middle Ages there were important trade fairs for the cloth industries of France and Flanders. Merchants would incur debts and any not settled could be carried forward to the next fair. Gradually, the merchants who were bankers began to offer a clearing system. One can imagine the circle of debt as – trader *A* owes *B* who owes *C* who owes *D* who also owes *A* (see Figure 2.1).

Figure 2.1   *The circle of debt*

The bankers set up a clearing system known as '*giro di partita*' – the giro of ledger entries. In 1619, the state of Venice set up a Banco del Giro to speed up payments to the state's creditors. The bank also issued interest bearing bonds to creditors and a secondary market gradually developed.

In the modern age, the word *giro* crops up in two connections. In the first case, it simply refers to money transfers by which an individual sends a giro slip to their bank instructing them to pay a sum of money to, say, the electricity or gas company. In Germany and Holland this is far more likely than sending a cheque directly to the company.

The second use is in the term *Giro bank* and the use of post offices to help those without a bank account pay their bills. The idea began in Austria in 1883. Those without bank accounts could pay a variety of bills at post offices and the money was then transferred to the payee. There is a Post Office Giro in Belgium and the UK set up a Girobank in 1968 which was sold to a building society in 1990. It is difficult to separate out postal giro from the general concept of a *postal bank*. This itself may be known instead as the *National Savings Bank*. In the UK, the Post Office Savings Bank, which was set up in 1861, became the National Savings Bank in 1969. The general idea is to encourage small savings rather than letting the bank engage in lending. France has a 'Caisse Nationale d'Épargne'; Ireland has a Post Office Savings Bank; in Finland we find the very important Postipankki, which handles much of the government's finances and Spain, too, has a Post Office Savings Bank. In the Netherlands, the Post Office Bank and the National Savings Bank merged to become Postbank, itself later merging with the NMB Bank and now known as ING Bank.

The Belgian Bankers' Association has claimed that the post offices' financial activities are subsidised and, in France, the opening of Banque Postale on 1 January 2006 met with furious opposition from the major banks. They are angry at its duopoly of a big savings account, Livret A, (26 million customers) which is tax free. Spain's Caja Postal has gone into leasing, asset management and property consulting. It has now been drawn together with other state-owned financial institutions into a single body called Argentaria and merged with the BBVA bank later.

Germany's Deutsche Post was owned by the government until early in 2005 when it was part privatised. The Kfw state bank, nevertheless, has one third of the shares. It is the country's biggest retail bank, operating through 9000 offices.

Japan's post office is the largest financial organisation in the world with assets of $4000 billion, 400 000 staff and 25 000 post offices. It delivers pensions, offers government-backed life insurance, and holds about one third of all government bonds in circulation. It has some $2900 billion in low yielding savings accounts and $600 billion in life insurance business. It offers cheap, easy finance to the government which many believe has led to wasteful spending. As a result, Prime Minister Koizumi announced plans in 2005 to privatise it and won a general election on this issue.

In both China and India, the government is unhappy about the inefficiencies of the post office movement. Savings are collected and handed over to the government with little attempt to sell other services or even loans to small businesses. China has now set up a formal Post Office Savings Bank and, in mid 2006, decided to turn it into China's fifth largest bank. It has no less than 800 million renminbi deposited with the government. India has 154 000 post offices, many in rural areas. The investment in technology has been poor but banks like ICICI and others are forming links with post offices to do money transfers and to sell other banks' products.

Credit unions The idea of credit unions goes back to 1849 in Germany when a local mayor formed a union to help people cope with debt and poverty. By the early 1900s, the idea had spread to Australia, Canada, New Zealand, Ireland, the UK and the US. The general idea is that a local credit union has some common bond – possibly membership of a church or place of work. The members save money and are allowed to borrow a sum of money, usually a multiple of the money saved. There may be tax privileges. For example, in the US, credit unions don't pay federal income tax. There are 15 000 credit unions in that country and 70 million members. The largest, Navy Federal, with assets of $10billion, is bigger than many regional banks. The commercial banks complain of unfair competition and are pursuing a case through the Supreme Court, claiming that the 'common bond' idea is being ignored in some cases. In the UK, there are 655 credit unions with 463 000 members, including British Airways and the London Taxi Drivers, and also community credit unions in deprived areas like Toxteth, Clerkenwell and Strathclyde. The number may reduce over time, as many unions are small and are struggling to comply with new regulation introduced by the FSA in 2002. The Association of British Credit Unions, therefore, expects a number of mergers in the coming years. In Ireland, 23% of the population are members. In Japan, there are some 460 credit associations. They also enjoy tax privileges.

Islamic banks   Over 250 institutions manage money in accordance with Islamic law or Sharia. Paying or receiving interest is not allowed but depositors are paid a share of profit on a range of permitted investments in companies (excluded are companies involved with gambling, liquor or tobacco). This is because, in the Koran, riba or interest is forbidden. Money must not earn interest as money but be put to use in trade (although, to be fair, a minority of Muslim experts interpret riba as usury or excessive interest).

The rise in Muslim consciousness since 9/11, and the massive flow of funds into the Gulf Cooperation Council region due to the high oil price, have led to an enormous increase in Islamic finance, both banking and bonds (which we discuss in Chapter 6). Some experts are even talking of an expansion rate of 40%–50% per annum.

The first Islamic bank is thought to be Mitshamr in Egypt in 1963. Today there are many Islamic banks and HSBC, Citigroup, UBS, Lloyds TSB, Barclays Capital, Deutsche Bank, BNP Paribas and Standard Chartered operate in this market.

Islamic banks are now into sale and leaseback to provide domestic mortgages and finance aircraft and equipment, for instance the $240 million funding of Pakistan's purchase of two Boeing 777s. For mortgages, the banks either buy property outright, renting it to the mortgage holder and hand over legal ownership when the contract ends (ijara) or resells the property to the customer at a fixed mark up price and is paid in monthly instalments (murabaha). Another version of murabaha is used for trade finance deals, like that offered in April 2006 for BXP, one of Australia's largest electronic retailers and valued at $A80 million ($55 million, £33 million). This was the first Islamic finance deal arranged for an Australian company.

Naturally, there is great interest in the near and far East. Singapore is promoting Islamic finance and Malaysia is probably the most proactive country in the world in promoting Islamic banking, which it believes will be 30% of their whole market by 2010. The Malaysian bank, CIMB, won the *Euromoney* magazine award for the best Islamic bank in Asia. Its chief executive officer, Badlisyah Abdul Ghani, said, 'We have seen a desire by a lot of Muslims to invest their wealth in Sharia-compliant activities, particularly after 9/11 and the Gulf War'.

In the UK, there is increasing interest. In June 2006, the Muslim Council of Britain organised a conference on Islamic finance and trade. This was addressed, amongst others, by the UK Chancellor, Gordon Brown. He announced his intention to make London a global centre for Islamic finance, said to be worth up to $400 billion (£240 billion) worldwide. He had already made a change in the April 2006 Finance Act to ease the murabaha technique for mortgages mentioned above. Since this involves the bank buying the property and then selling it to the customer, in theory stamp duty is to be paid twice. The Finance Act abolished the double stamp duty on such transactions and also resolved anomalies in the tax treatment of ijara rental and leasing transactions.

The Islamic Bank of Britain was formed in 2004 to cater for the UK's two million Muslims and is able to tap into funds of Islamic finance in the Gulf and the Far East. There is an internal Sharia auditor and a supervisory committee of Islamic experts. The rise in the popularity of Islamic finance has led to an increasing demand for such legal experts – there is now a bottleneck as enough cannot be found! If this was a modest beginning in 2004, we have now reached the point where, in June 2006, Lloyds TSB announced that they will roll out Sharia-compliant mortgages and current accounts in all 2000 branches. This is not only for Muslims but also non-Muslim ethical investors such as Quakers and other religious groups. Datamonitor, the research group, predicts that the Islamic mortgage business in the UK will reach £1.4 billion by 2009.

(Bonds issued under Sharia are discussed in Chapter 6.)

OTHER BANKING TERMINOLOGY

There are one or two other terms which, perhaps, should also be explained.

Clearing banks   This term is applied to the banks which are most involved in the system for clearing cheques. They will be the large domestic banks who are heavily into retail banking. Banks which offer cheque book facilities and have smaller volumes will arrange for one of the larger clearing banks to handle clearing of their cheques. Usually, each bank will clear its own cheques, that is, cheques drawn by a customer of the branch in favour of another customer of the same bank. Cheques drawn in favour of other banks are sent to a central clearing system where they can be gathered together and sent to each bank for posting to individual accounts.

The customer account number, bank branch code and cheque number are already encoded on the bottom line of the cheque. It only needs the amount to be encoded for the cheques to be sorted using electronic sorting machines.

Electronic clearing is becoming increasingly important for direct debits, standing orders, salary payments, supplier payments and high value payments made electronically by banks for corporate customers.

State or public banks   This term is used for banks owned by the state which are not central banks but carry out some public sector activity. State-owned Post Office or National Savings Banks are one example. Sometimes others are set up to lend to industry sectors or local authorities or provide finance for exports and imports. Germany has Kreditanstalt für Wiederaufbau, which was set up in 1948 to help finance reconstruction after the war and is now a general development bank for small to medium size companies. France has Crédit Local de France, which makes loans to local authorities, and Crédit Foncier, which finances house purchase and property development. Italy has Crediop which finances public utilities and makes other industrial loans. In Spain, a major change took place which resulted in the formation of one body from various state banks:

❏   Banco Exterior   the finance of foreign trade
❏   Banco Hipotecario   subsidised loans for social housing
❏   Banco de Crédito Agrícola   loans for agriculture and forestry
❏   Banco de Crédito Local   loans for local authorities
❏   Banco de Crédito Industrial   loans for industry
❏   Caja Postal de Ahorros   post office savings banks.

These were all united in 1991 as Corporación Bancaria de España which operates under the marketing name of 'Argentaria' and has since merged with the BBVA bank.

The position regarding state banks is changing somewhat as full or partial privatisation takes place (for example, Crédit Local de France and Argentaria).

Banks which have a role in lending to specialist industries are also known as *industrial banks*.

International banking   This involves a variety of activities such as deposits/loans to nationals in foreign currencies and to non-nationals in the domestic currency. It also covers cross-border operations, trade finance, foreign exchange, correspondent banking, international payments services, international finance with syndicated loans and/or Euromarket instruments, dealing in precious metals, international corporate advice and corporate risk management facilities on an international basis.

Clearly, the terms we have been using are not mutually self-exclusive – they overlap. International banking with a syndicated loan, for example, is commercial wholesale banking. International banking through a eurobond issue is investment banking and largely wholesale, but with sales at times aimed at *retail* investors.

A BANK'S BALANCE SHEET

Before proceeding any further into this chapter, we must look at a bank's balance sheet and the terminology which is used. Then we will be in a position to explain concepts like 'creation of credit', 'liquidity' and 'capital ratio'.

In this section and later, we use the terms 'assets' and 'liabilities'. A liability in accountancy does not have the meaning 'disadvantage' as it does in everyday English. It is money for which the entity concerned is *liable*, for example, if money is borrowed, the borrower is *liable* to repay it, hence it is a liability.

Looking at a bank, the *liabilities* show us where the money comes from. There are three key sources:

❏ Shareholders' equity plus additions from retained profit
❏ Deposits (the largest figure)
❏ Borrowings (for example, a bond issue).

The liabilities, thus, represent claims *against* the bank.

The first category is called 'shareholders' funds' and is the main source for a bank's capital. This is the part of the liabilities that can be relied upon because, being the owner's money, there is no date for paying it back. The bank has the indefinite use of the money. If times are hard, even the dividend may be passed. Deposits, on the other hand, can be withdrawn, a large part without notice, and borrowings have to be repaid and interest payments met.

Assets represent how this money has been used, for example:

❏ Notes, coin
❏ Money market funds
❏ Securities
❏ Lending (the largest figure)
❏ Fixed assets, for example, property.

The assets, thus, represent claims by the bank against others. Assets and liabilities will always balance.

Banks list assets in descending order of liquidity:

❏ Cash
❏ Balances at the central bank
❏ Money at call and short notice
❏ Bank and trade bills of exchange
❏ Treasury bills
❏ Securities
❏ Advances to customers
❏ Premises and equipment.

Its liabilities would be:

- ❑ Ordinary share capital
- ❑ Other share capital
- ❑ Reserves
- ❑ Retained profits
- ❑ Provisions against losses
- ❑ Bond issues
- ❑ Customers' deposits
- ❑ Other borrowing
- ❑ Trade creditors
- ❑ Tax.

The balance sheet is laid out with assets on the left and liabilities on the right (see Figure 2.2).

SUMMARY BALANCE SHEET, A. N. OTHER BANK As At 31/12/06

ASSETS	LIABILITIES
(that is, how liabilities have been used)	(that is, where the money comes from)
Cash	Shareholders' funds
Money market funds	Deposits
Other securities	Borrowings
Lending	

Figure 2.2   *Summary balance sheet*

The profit and loss account shows how a bank has traded during a particular *period*, such as 1 month, 3 months, or a year – for example: 'Profit and Loss Account for the year ended 31 December 2006'. Note that the balance sheet shows what the bank is worth at a particular *point* in time, for example: 'Balance Sheet as at 31 December 2006'.

Revenue is contrasted with costs and the resulting difference is the profit or loss. After paying dividends and tax, the remaining profit is transferred to the balance sheet and added to the shareholders' funds, thus *increasing capital*. Equally, a loss will *reduce capital*.

One of the assets listed above was 'Balances at the central bank'. Most central banks insist that banks within the country maintain certain reserves with it. Usually, these are substantial sums and help the central bank in its control of monetary policy and what is called the 'money supply'. We shall examine this in more detail in Chapter 3.

Even where the reserves are very tiny (for example, in the UK only 0.15% of eligible liabilities if sterling liabilities exceed £500 million), the main clearing banks have to maintain far higher working balances and *must not fall below these*. These balances are to cover things like the daily settlement for cheque clearing and the daily settlement for Treasury bill and bond purchases for themselves and clients for whom they are acting. There is also the total net payment by the bank's clients of taxes to the government. The government's balance at the central bank will rise – the individual bank's balance will fall.

THE CREATION OF CREDIT

As only a small proportion of deposits is drawn in cash, it follows that banks have considerable facilities to 'create credit'.

Imagine approaching a bank (not your own) to request flexible lending facilities up to $2000. The bank opens an account and sends you a cheque book. You wander down the high street writing cheques to the value of $2000. The recipients pay the cheques into their accounts and the amounts are credited to them three days later and debited to you. The bank has created $2000 of expenditure that did not exist one week earlier. The suppliers of the goods have $2000 in bank accounts – disposable money. Where did it come from? Not from you, because you didn't have any. It came from the bank that allowed you to overdraw to the value of $2000 – the bank has created money. Bank lending = spending, and excessive spending may mean unacceptable inflation and imports the nation can't afford.

Banks' credit creation has several implications:

1. A reminder that banking depends on confidence
2. Governments and central banks will want to control it in view of the implications for inflation and imports
3. Banks will need internal controls called 'liquidity ratios'
4. An external control enforced by bank supervisors called 'capital ratios' is required.

Banking Depends on Confidence

The system works because we have confidence in it and accept cheques in payment of debt. Where is the gold and silver behind this? Of course, there isn't any. Money is as much an entry on a computer disk as anything else. The economist, Frederic Benham, in his well-known text book *Manual of Political Economy*, points out that paper money could be seen as a 'gigantic confidence trick'. It works as long as people believe in it.

The Money Supply

Governments and central bankers will want to control credit and measure the 'money supply'. This figure is a measure of bank deposits as being the best guide to bank lending. The figure for deposits sounds like a motorway – M3 or M4, depending on the country. Another measure is M0 – notes and coin in circulation, plus banks' till money and balances with the central bank. Add to this the private sector's deposits at banks and you have the essential elements of M3 or M4. Control of inflation by controlling these monetary aggregates is part of what is meant by 'monetarism', the economic doctrines of the American economist, Milton Friedman. In the UK, the Conservative government of 1979 used them as a rather rigid instrument of government policy in the early 1980s. (Charles Goodhart, one time economic adviser to the Bank of England, has coined 'Goodhart's Law'. This says that 'when an economic indicator is used as an instrument of government policy, its behaviour then changes'!) Later governments have interpreted the figure more flexibly. The money growth in the mid 80s gave little warning of recessions in the US and the UK and monetary aggregates fell somewhat out of favour. The Bank of England in September 2005 announced that M0 would no longer be published from 2006, and the US Federal Reserve dropped the publication of M3 figures in April 2006, saying 'The role of M3 in the policy process has diminished greatly over time'. Even Milton Friedman admitted in June 2003 'The use of the quantity of money as a target has not been a success'. However, perhaps 'the maid is not dead but sleepeth'. References to the money supply increasingly feature in the speeches of Mervyn King, governor of the Bank of England, and the European Central Bank still studies monetary aggregates.

Interest rates remain the main economic tool in controlling monetary conditions, being raised to curb inflation or lowered to boost economic activity. The idea is that as interest rates are raised, mortgage payments go up and so does the cost of buying goods on credit. People therefore have less money to spend and the price of goods has to be lowered to attract buyers. Conversely, as we have seen at the start of the new millennium, when economies slow down they can be boosted by lowering interest rates. Mortgage payments come down, the cost of borrowing to buy goods on credit is reduced and, as people go out and spend more, this stimulates and sustains economic activity.

The central bank has a number of weapons – raising mandatory reserves which banks must deposit with it, raising interest rates and general 'open market operations', for example, selling more government paper than it needs to in order to drain credit and keep monetary conditions tight. It may also not be as quick as usual to help banks' liquidity when acting as 'lender of last resort' (see Chapter 3).

Liquidity Ratios

Bankers have internal controls based on 'liquidity ratios'. They know that it would be folly to take their deposits and lend 100% as three year personal loans. They have internal rules on what percentage of deposits should be held as cash, what percentage at call and short notice, what percentage as short-term securities (Treasury bills, bills of exchange) and so on. The controls may also be *external* and laid down by the central bank as they are in Spain, where they are called *coeficientes*. This is why banks list assets in *descending* order of liquidity, that is, the most liquid assets (cash) are first. Cash is particularly important as banks must keep a given percentage to meet cash withdrawals. In the case of the new bank accounts totalling $2000 which we discussed above, if cash withdrawals average 5%, then the bank must have $100 cash to back these accounts.

Capital Ratio

Capital ratio is the external control imposed by bank supervisors in the interests of prudence. It is a major issue in banking and we need to look at it in more detail.

CAPITAL RATIO

The Basic Concept

The basic concept has been around for hundreds of years. Bankers lend money and some people will default. Does this mean that the banks cannot repay depositors? The buffer, the money the bank can rely on, is its capital. Thus, there should be a prudent relationship between capital and lending – that is the capital ratio.

All this assumes that the bank has not made things worse by an excessive exposure to a few key borrowers. In 1984, for example, it was found that Johnson Matthey Bank in the UK had lent the equivalent of 115% of its own capital to just two borrowers. This loophole was plugged in the 1987 Banking Act. If exposure to one borrower exceeds 10% of capital, the Bank of England must be informed. Before exposure can exceed 25%, Bank of England permission must be obtained. Exposure to industry sectors (for example, textiles) and countries is also monitored. All central banks have 'large exposure' controls.

The older idea of relating capital to *lending* has to be extended to capital to *assets* in the modern age. However, all assets are not the same for this purpose – for example, what is the default risk with cash? Surely the answer is 'none'. Thus we end up with the concept of 'risked weighted assets'. A normal bank loan is, therefore, weighted 100%, that is, a loan of $500 000 counts as $500 000 for this purpose. However, cash is weighted at 0%, and a cash balance of $10 million thus becomes $0 for risk weighting purposes. Secured lending has a weight of 50% (see Table 2.3).

The capital ratio is thus determined by applying the ratio to the figure of risk weighted assets. If the agreed ratio were 10%, then, from the figures in Table 2.3, capital must be 10% × $1260m = $126m.

The Basel Committee

However, every central bank had different rules. The Group of 10 nations (see Chapter 3) together with Luxembourg, set up a 'Committee on Banking Regulations and Supervisory Practices' to draw up uniform rules. The Committee meets at Basel in Switzerland under the auspices of the Bank for International Settlements (BIS). It is thus typically (but not accurately) called the 'Basel' Committee or 'BIS' Committee. In 1988, after several years of discussion, the Committee announced agreement on uniform rules for capital ratio.

Table 2.3 *Risk weighting example*

Assets	Value $m	Risk weighting %	Risk weighted value $m
Cash	50	0	—
T. bills	100	10	10
Mortgages	500	50	250
Loans	1000	100	1000
Total	1650		1260

The first stumbling block was the definition of 'capital'. The Committee came to a compromise – the 'best' capital is called 'Tier 1' and must be at least half the necessary figure. It consists of:

❏ Shareholders' equity
❏ Retained profits
❏ *Non-cumulative* perpetual preference shares.

'Tier 2' capital is the remainder and would include:

❏ *Cumulative* perpetual preference shares
❏ Revaluation reserves
❏ Undisclosed reserves
❏ Subordinated term debt with maturity in excess of 5 years.

(For a discussion of preference shares, see Chapter 6. Subordinated debtors come after other debtors in the event of liquidation.)

The capital ratio itself is 8% and applied from 1 January 1993.

The risk weighting figures were agreed and we gave examples of some of these above. While unsecured loans are 100%, loans to or claims on OECD governments and sometimes other governments as well are weighted 0%. Thus loans to Saudi Arabia have not been given the full 100% weighting, but Kuwait, in raising a large syndicated loan for reconstruction of $5.5bn in Autumn 1991, was weighted 100%.

The risk weightings are not only applied to balance sheet items, but to *off-balance sheet* items that involve risk – loan guarantees, standby letters of credit, documentary letters of credit, derivative products such as options, futures, swaps and FRAs (all explained in later chapters).

The banks are very conscious of capital ratio rules and have tightened up the discipline regarding profit as a return on capital. If a transaction needs capital backing under the new rules, then the profit on the transaction must meet the bank's target for profit on capital employed. Some consultants call this 'RAROC' – 'risk adjusted return on capital'. While there is a capital requirement for off-balance sheet items, it is not as onerous as for on-balance sheet items and thus adds to the attraction of these transactions. For example, documentary letters of credit backed by documents giving title are weighted at 20%. A general standby letter of credit not related to a specific transaction is weighted 100%, but a standby letter of credit which is so related is weighted at 50%. As capital has a cost, the bank will ensure that the charges to the client cover the *cost of capital* as well as any other costs.

For their results for the year ending March 1996, Japanese banks finally recognised their true position regarding bad debts and began to write these off against profit. The three long-term credit banks, the seven trust banks and seven out of the top eleven city banks all declared a loss. As a result, some of the capital ratios were close to the minimum. Despite subsequent restructuring, mergers and a brief return to profit, by 2002 the four largest banks were again reporting substantial losses (totalling $32bn!) and reducing lending to maintain capital ratios. However, vigorous action to write off non-performing loans put the main Japanese banks in a much stronger position by the end of 2005.

In September 1998, the Basel Committee under its new chairman, William McDonough, President of the New York Federal Reserve Bank, held the first of a series of meetings to revise the original accord.

There was a general feeling that some of the rules were too crude. In March 1998, the Institute of International Finance, a Washington-based organisation representing commercial and investment banks, called on the Basel Committee to change the formula. For example, lending to banks in the Organisation of Economic Cooperation and Development (OECD) has a ratio of only 1.6%. Thus a loan to General Electric needs a capital ratio of 8% but one to a South Korean bank only 1.6%! Equally, a loan to a AAA rated company is treated the same as a loan to a company of much lower credit quality. In addition, where banks needed 8% capital backing for loans but internal models calculated the risk as far less, they were increasingly selling these loans to the market as securities with a lower weighting. (This is discussed later in this chapter and in Chapter 6.)

The use of credit ratings to make the risk calculation more scientific was discussed, but many European corporates do not have credit ratings. The use of statistical credit risk modelling was also discussed, but viewed with scepticism. A BIS committee report in April 1999, *Credit Risk Modelling*, confirmed that regulators were not yet ready to accept them.

In June 1999, the BIS Committee issued a new paper and suggested a ten month consultation period.

In spite of the absence of credit ratings in Europe, to which we have referred, the Committee came down heavily on the use of credit ratings to guide credit risk. Five 'buckets' were suggested, with sovereign governments in the AAA/AA category getting a zero weighting, A grade a 20% weighting and so on, down to 150% for grades of B- or less. Similar rules were drawn up for lending to banks and corporates. More sophisticated banks could use internal ratings as an interim measure, and supervisors could ask for more capital if they thought that banks were taking excessive risks. This has had an effect on pricing for bonds and syndicated loans.

With some reservations, the new proposals were generally welcomed.

All the above relates to *credit risk*. There is also *market risk* and *operational risk*. Market movements in the price of financial instruments may expose the banks to losses. The Capital Adequacy Directive (CAD) addressed this problem and applied from January 1996. In this case, however, use of banks' internal statistical models was accepted subject to monitoring by local central banks. These models are usually called *value at risk* (VAR) models. Operational risk recognises the risk of losses through failure or weaknesses in a bank's internal processes and systems. A good example of the latter is the collapse of Barings due to failure to control the activities of one trader. A new capital adequacy accord called Basel 11 was agreed in June 2004. It redefined credit risk and market risk but put new emphasis on operational risk – not easy to measure! In spite of much criticism from banks, the new accord was due to be implemented from January 2007. JP Morgan made an interesting comment that increasing the amount of capital to be held for high risks might tempt banks to offload these onto less regulated organizations, for example, hedge funds (see Chapter 8).

Finally, the CAD introduced the concept of Tier 3 capital – unsecured subordinated debt with a remaining maturity of more than two years.

Increasing Capital Ratio

If a bank does not have enough capital to meet the new requirements, what can it do? There are essentially only two possibilities:

(a) Find more capital
(b) Reduce assets.

(a) *Finding more capital* could involve a rights issue, reducing dividends (to increase retained profit), raising money through other forms of capital, for example, *non-cumulative* perpetual preference shares or perpetual variable rate notes. Tier 1 capital must, of course, be 4% and there is a limit to the value of certain Tier 2 items that can be used. Several German banks have issued their own type of cumulative preference share (*genusscheine*) to count as Tier 2 capital. National Westminster, NAB, Banco Santander, the Royal Bank of Scotland, Crédit Lyonnais and others have all issued perpetual variable rate notes to count as Tier 2 capital. In 2004, Barclays Bank issued non-cumulative perpetual preference shares to the value of €1billion to strengthen its capital.

(b) *Reducing assets* could involve selling off subsidiaries, selling off loans to other banks or converting assets into securities – *securitisation*.

   We shall meet the word 'securitisation' again in Chapter 6. In that context it means the change in emphasis in international banking markets from 1982, by which borrowers began to borrow on the capital markets by issuing bonds rather than by having a bank loan. The usage in our current context is similar, but here we take an existing loan off the balance sheet by converting it into securities. The best and most common example is selling off mortgage loans as mortgage bonds (pioneered by Salomon Bros – now part of Citigroup – in the US). Other examples include converting car loans into notes or bonds and converting credit card receivables into bonds (frequent issues by Citigroup). Another possibility is simply to bundle bank personal loans together and sell them as bonds or shorter-term notes, with the loans as the assets backing the security. The legalities are difficult, usually involving a special purpose vehicle or SPV to issue. Guarantees from insurance companies or other financial entities are involved and the idea is for the original lender to so weaken the link to the loan that it no longer counts for capital ratio purposes. The issuer usually continues to administer the loan, and will receive a fee for doing so. This is discussed further in Chapter 6.

CENTRAL BANK REPORTING

All banks operating within a country make detailed reports to the central bank as part of its supervisory role, even if any action to be taken will be carried out by a separate supervisory body.

Reports will be sent at varying frequencies – monthly, quarterly, 6 monthly, annually – and will cover the following items:

❑ Maturity of assets, that is, liquidity
❑ Large exposures
❑ Foreign exchange exposure

❏ Capital expenditure
❏ Assets/liabilities for overseas residents
❏ Assets/liabilities in foreign currencies
❏ Balance sheet
❏ Profit and loss.

Foreign banks operating in a country operate as either branches or as legal entities. If only operating as a branch, no reports on capital will be made as the capital is held by the parent company.

THE EU'S SECOND BANKING DIRECTIVE

This came into effect on 1 January 1993. The original intention of the European Community had been to achieve a full harmonisation of banking legislation throughout the EU. This has now been abandoned. Instead, under the Second Banking Directive, banks in the EU will continue to be authorised and regulated by their own national authority. This will be accepted as adequate for granting them freedom to operate throughout the Community. They will thus acquire a *European Banking Licence* or *Passport*. This will allow them to engage in investment as well as commercial banking, since 'universal banking' has always been the tradition in Europe. In countries where this has not been so, their banks will now be free to engage in activities throughout the Community that they may still be prevented from doing in their own country. (The specific Investment Services Directive is discussed in Chapter 11.)

Third country banks can operate within the EU if 'reciprocal treatment' is afforded in their country to EU member banks. At first this was taken to mean that they must be allowed to engage in the same activities as third country banks are permitted to do within the Community. This led to protest from America (where commercial and investment banks were traditionally separated). In response to this, reciprocity is now defined as equal 'national treatment' – that is, EU banks being treated the same as local banks in third countries. But, in individual cases, the Community may still insist on 'equal/comparable access'.

MAJOR WORLD BANKS

The UK *Banker* magazine for July 2005 published an analysis of the world's largest banks. Although 'large' was defined by holdings of Tier 1 capital, the asset figures were also disclosed.

We shall, therefore, first look at a 'Top 20' sequence of the world's biggest banks in *asset* terms (Table 2.4).

Table 2.4   *Top 20 world banks, by assets, 2004*

Ranking	Bank	Assets $bn
1	UBS	1533
2	Citigroup	1484
3	Mizuho Financial Group	1296
4	HSBC Holdings	1277
5	Crédit Agricole Groupe	1243
6	BNP Paribas	1233
7	JP Morgan Chase	1157
8	Deutsche Bank	1144
9	Royal Bank of Scotland	1119
10	Bank of America	1110
11	Barclays Bank	992
12	Mitsubishi Tokyo Financial Group	980
13	Crédit Suisse	963
14	Sumitomo Mitsui Financial Group	897
15	ING Bank	839
16	ABN Amro Bank	829
17	Société Générale	819
18	Santander Central Hispano	783
19	HBOS	760
20	Groupe Caisse d'Epargne	741

Source: *The Banker* (July 2005).

Looking at *nationality* in the Top 20 we find the following:

Country	Banks
France	4
UK	4
US	3
Japan	3
Switzerland	2
Netherlands	2
Germany	1
Spain	1

The Japanese provide three of the world's Top 20. In the 1992 table, however, they provided eleven out of the Top 20 (and eight out of the Top 10). The collapse of the stock exchange index, a serious fall in property values, a prolonged recession and high bank bad debts all caused a reduction in bank strength (the first four in the table by Tier 1 capital in 1992) and some withdrawal from world markets.However, it is fair to say that the position of the Japanese banks at the end of 2005 was much stronger. (The general position of international banking shares by nationality of bank is shown in Table 2.5.)

Citicorp was number 20 in 1992, with no other US bank in the table. Now the enlarged Citigroup is number two, the merged JP Morgan and Chase Manhattan at number seven and Bank of America at number ten.

Table 2.5 *International banking shares, by nationality of bank, end Q3 2005*

Nationality	%
Other European banks	22.0
Germany	19.9
Switzerland	12.0
France	11.3
UK	9.3
US	8.8
Japanese	8.7
Other banks	8.0
	100.0

Source: BIS Basel.

The other surprise, looking at Table 2.4, is to see the US only providing three banks out of the Top 20. We have to realise that banking is very fragmented in the US where there are no less than about 9000 banks! Unlike Europe, branch banking across the US was unknown. The McFadden Act of 1927 limited banking activities to within a single state; some local state legislation limits it to one branch in one *city* within the state! The Act, however, was repealed in 1994 by the US Interstate Banking and Banking Efficiency Act which permitted full interstate banking by 1997 unless local state laws prevent it. Many states did not wait for Congress but changed their laws and allowed reciprocal banking facilities with other states. The large number of mergers in the US (see Appendix 2 to this chapter) is fast changing the face of American banking. When we look at banks by Tier 1 capital (Table 2.6), we see the US with five banks as opposed to three by assets.

Finally, we can look at the original sequence of banks in *The Banker* magazine, that by *capital* (Table 2.6).

Table 2.6   *Top 20 world banks by capital, 2004*

Ranking	Bank	Tier 1 capital $m
1	Citigroup	74 415
2	JP Morgan Chase	68 621
3	HSBC Holdings	67 259
4	Bank of America	64 281
5	Crédit Agricole Groupe	63 422
6	Royal Bank of Scotland	43 828
7	Mitsubishi Tokyo Financial Group	39 932
8	Mizuho Financial Group	38 864
9	HBOS	36 587
10	BNP Paribas	35 685
11	Bank of China	34 851
12	Santander Central Hispano	33 259
13	Barclays Bank	32 179
14	Rabobank Group	30 810
15	Sumitomo Mitsui Financial Group	30 389
16	Wells Fargo	29 060
17	ING Bank	28 792
18	Wachovia Corporation	28 583
19	UBS	27 440
20	ABN Amro	26 993

Source: *The Banker* (July 2005).

The change of sequence to capital (it used to be assets) came about because of the so-called Basel Agreement in 1988. *The Banker* magazine decided that capital was the important thing for the future, and not assets.

There is an interesting change of sequence. Looking at nationality now, we see the following:

Country	Banks
US	5
UK	4
Japan	3
Netherlands	3
France	2
Switzerland	1
China	1
Spain	1

The spate of mergers which has occurred in the last few years is clearly reflected as American, Japanese and British banks dominate the Top 20 in terms of size of capital base. If you are wondering about Germany, Deutsche Bank just missed, coming in at 21.

SUMMARY

Supervision of banks may be carried out by the central bank (Netherlands) or other supervisory bodies (France, Germany, Japan, US, UK).

Central banks, commercial banks and investment banks are the main types of bank. There are also savings banks, cooperative banks and mortgage banks but, with increasing deregulation, the differences are generally weakening. Finally, there are credit unions. Islamic banking is managing money in accordance with Islamic law or Sharia.

On a bank's balance sheet, the *liabilities* are shareholders' equity, deposits and borrowings. The *assets* are cash, money market deposits, securities, loans and fixed assets like buildings.

The shareholders' equity (including retained profits) is at the heart of the bank's *capital*.

Bank regulators have set up a committee (usually called the Basel or BIS Committee) which lays down rules which suggest the capital required not only for the credit risk in bank lending but also the market risk of the financial instruments it holds and the operational risk inherent in a bank's activities.

In an era where money is no longer tied to gold or silver, the ease with which a bank can advance money is called *creation of credit*. It is limited by liquidity rules, capital ratio rules and central bank monetary policy.

The Second European Banking Directive allows banks in the EU to open branches anywhere in the EU under licence from their *home* central bank.

APPENDIX 1 – MAJOR BANKS ACROSS THE WORLD

AUSTRALIA	National Australia Bank ANZ Group Commonwealth Banking Group Westpac
AUSTRIA	Erste Bank Raiffeisen Zentralbank BAWAG – PSK
BELGIUM	Fortis Bank Dexia KBC
BRAZIL	Banco Itav Banco Bradesco Banco do Brasil
CANADA	Scotiabank Royal Bank of Canada Bank of Montreal Toronto Dominion Bank
CHINA	Bank of China China Construction Bank Industrial & Commercial Bank of China Agricultural Bank of China
DENMARK	Danske Bank Nykredit Group
FINLAND	OP Bank Group Sampo Group
FRANCE	Crédit Agricole BNP Paribas Caisse d'Epargne Société Général
GERMANY	Deutsche Bank Hypovereinsbank Commerzbank

GREECE	National Bank of Greece
	Alpha Bank
	Emporiki Bank
INDIA	State Bank of India
	ICICI Bank
	HDFC Bank
	Bank of Baroda
IRELAND	Allied Irish
	Bank of Ireland
	Anglo Irish Bank Group
IRAEL	Bank Hapoalim
	Bank Leumi
	Israel Discount Bank
ITALY	Banca Intesa
	UniCredito Italiano
	San Paolo
JAPAN	Mitsubishi Tokyo
	Mizuho
	Sumitomo Mitsui
LUXEMBOURG	Kredietbank
NETHERLANDS	ING Bank
	ABN Amro
	Rabobank
NORWAY	DnB Nor Group
PORTUGAL	Millenium bcp
	Banco Espirito Santo
	Banco BPI
RUSSIA	Sherbank
	Vneshtorgbank
	Gazprom Bank

SINGAPORE	DBS Bank
	United Overseas Bank
	Overseas China Bank
SOUTH AFRICA	Standard Bank
	ABSA
	Nedcor
SOUTH KOREA	Kookmin Bank
	Woori Bank
SPAIN	Santander Central Hispano
	BBVA Argentaria
	Banco Popular
SWEDEN	Nordea Group
	Svenska Handelsbanken
	Scandinaviska Enskilda
SWITZERLAND	UBS
	Crédit Suisse
TAIWAN	Bank of Taiwan
	Fubon Financial Holding
	Cathay United Bank
TURKEY	Turkiye Is Bankasi
	Yapi Kredi Bankasi
	Akbank
	TC Ziraat Bankasi
UNITED KINGDOM	HSBC Holdings
	Barclays
	HBOS
	RBS
UNITED STATES	Citigroup
	JP Morgan Chase
	Bank of America
	Wells Fargo

APPENDIX 2 – INTERNATIONAL AND DOMESTIC BANKING
COOPERATION AND MERGERS

(Some of the following are full-scale mergers; some are merely arrangements to
cooperate. They range over about fifteen years and illustrate the massive changes
that have taken place.)

1   Chemical Bank–Manufacturers Hanover to form Chemical Banking
     Corporation. Later merged with Chase Manhattan, using the Chase name.
     Chase acquired Robert Fleming. JP Morgan and Chase merged to form
     JP Morgan Chase, later buying Bank One following its merger with First
     Chicago

2   NCNB–C & S/Sovran to form NationsBank

3   NationsBank–Barnett Banks–Boatmen's Bancshares–Montgomery
     Securities

4   Bank of America–Security Pacific

5   Bank of America–NationsBank

6   Bank of America–Continental

7   Bank of America–Fleet Boston

8   Citibank–Salomon Smith Barney (Travelers Group), now Citigroup

9   Morgan Stanley–Dean Witter

10   Merrill Lynch–Smith New Court

11   Fleet Financial–Shawmut National

12   Fleet Financial–Bank Boston

13   First Bank Systems Inc–US Bancorp Deutsche Bank–Bankers Trust

14   Norwest–Wells Fargo, Wells Fargo–First Security (Wells Fargo)

15   Wells Fargo–First Interstate

16   First Union–First Fidelity

17   First Union–Core States Financial

18   Wachovia–South Trust of Atlanta

19   Crédit Lyonnais–BfG Bank

20   Crédit Agricole–Crédit Lyonnais

21   CCF/BHF Bank–Charterhouse

22 Crédit Local de France–Crédit Communale de Belgique–BACOB (now Dexia)

23 Deutsche Bank–Morgan Grenfell–Bankers Trust, now Deutsche Bank

24 Dresdner Bank–Kleinwort Benson

25 Bayerische Vereinsbank–Bayerische Hypobank becoming Hypovereinsbank

26 Austria–Österreichische Landerbank and Zentral Sparkasse to form Z-Landerbank (now Bank Austria)

27 Girozentrale–Österreichisches Credit Institut to form GiroCredit Bank

28 Bank Austria–majority holding in Bank GiroCredit

29 Bank Austria–Creditanstalt

30 Hypovereinsbank–Bank Austria

31 Unicredito–Hypovereinsbank

32 Kredietbank–CERA

33 ABN–AMRO Bank (acquired Hoare Govett later)

34 ABN–AMRO Bank–Antonvenuto

35 ING–Barings–Banque Bruxelles Lambert

36 Fortis–Générale de Banque

37 Cassa di Risparmio di Roma–Banco di Santo Spirito; then a merger with Banco di Roma to form Banca di Roma

38 Bergen Bank–Den Norske Creditbank

39 Den Danske Bank–Copenhagen Handelsbank–Provinsbanken to form the Danske Bank

40 Danske Bank–Northern Bank and National Irish Bank (from NAB, Australia)

41 Privatbanken–SDS–Andelsbanken to form UNI Bank, Danmark

42 Svenska Handelsbanken–Skanska Banken

43 Svenska Handelsbanken–Skopbank (Finland)

44 PK Banken–Nordbanken

45 Union Bank of Finland–Kansallis (now Merita Bank, later merged with Nordbanken)

46 Christiana Bank–Fokus–Postbanken

47   Banco de Bilbao–Banco de Vizcaya (BBVA)

48   LaCaixa–Barcelona Savings Bank

49   Banco Central–Banco Hispano Americano

50   Banco Exterior, Caja Postal and Instituto de Crédito Oficial form
     Corporación Bancaria de España (now trading as Argentaria)

51   BBVA–Argentaria

52   Banco Santander–60% of Banesto

53   Banco Santander–Banco Central Hispano Americano

54   Banco Santander Central Hispano–Abbey National

55   Cariplo–Banco Ambrovenuto (now Banca Intesa)

56   Crédit Suisse–Bank Leu

57   Crédit Suisse Group–Swiss Volksbank

58   Swiss Bank Corporation–Banc della Svizzera Italiana

59   Swiss Bank Corporation take over Union Bank of Switzerland and later
     Warburg Dillon Read – the group now called UBS

60   Mitsui–Taiyo Kobe merged into Sakura, Sakura–Sumitomo merged into
     Sumitomo Mitsui

61   Dai–Ichi Kangyo–Fuji–IBJ merged into Mizuho Financial Group

62   Sanwa–Asahi–Tokai to form UFJ

63   Mitsubishi Tokyo Group–UFJ

64   Bank of Tokyo–Mitsubishi

65   Hongkong and Shanghai Bank–Midland Bank

66   Lloyds Bank–TSB

67   Royal Bank of Scotland–NatWest

68   Royal Bank of Scotland–Citizens and Charter One

69   Halifax–Bank of Scotland (HBOS)

70   National Australia Bank–Yorkshire Bank

3 The Role of the Central Bank

HISTORY OF THE MAJOR CENTRAL BANKS

In the world, there are about 160 central banks employing 352 000 people. We shall begin by looking briefly at the historic background of seven major central banks – those of China, France, Germany, India, Japan, UK and US – and also at the formation of the newest – the European Central Bank.

China

The central bank was established in 1948 as the State Bank of the People's Republic of China. It began to function solely as a central bank in September 1983, upon approval by the state council. It is now known as the People's Bank of China. The Governor is Zhou Xiaochuan, appointed in January 2003 for no specific term.

France

The Bank of France was founded by Napoleon in 1800 to restore stability, especially in banknotes, after the turbulent years of the French Revolution. It was set up as a joint stock company. Napoleon himself was a shareholder and the top 200 shareholders elected the 'Regents', the bank's principal officers.

It was brought more firmly under government control in 1808 and this process was completed in 1836 with the appointment of bank councillors by the government. A monopoly over banknote issue was given in 1848. During the difficult financial years of 1929–30 it intervened to rescue Banque de l'Union Parisienne but allowed Banque Nationale de Crédit to go under. It was nationalised in 1945 and an Act of 1973 redefined its powers and organisation.

The Governor of the bank and two deputy Governors are appointed by executive order of the President of the Republic for six years. These three head the General Council which consists of ten people appointed for six years. The bank was not originally independent of the government but was given independence in 1993 anticipating the proposed European Central Bank. It has about 200 branches. The current governor is Christian Noyer. Many of its powers were passed to the European Central Bank when it was set up in 1999.

Germany

The forerunner of the German Bundesbank was the Reichsbank, founded in 1876 to 'regulate the amount of money in circulation, facilitate settlements of payments and ensure that available capital is utilised'. It was a private bank but control was in the hands of the Reichs Chancellor.

The terrible experience with inflation in the early 1920s led to a Banking Act of 1924 making the Reichsbank independent of the government.

Unfortunately, as Hitler acquired more power in the 1930s he was impatient with any idea of central bank independence; this was taken away in 1937 and the Bank nationalised in 1939.

After the Second World War, the old currency, the Reichsmark, was replaced by the deutschmark. A two-tier central banking system was set up. Each of the eleven Federal States had a Land Central Bank and between them they owned a central body, the Bank Deutsche Länder. It was responsible for note creation and policy coordination. In particular, it was independent of the government.

This system was abolished by the Act of July 1957 which set up the Deutsche Bundesbank – a unified central bank. The eleven Land Banks became part of it only as regional offices. They carry out the relevant regulations in their own area.

The Central Bank Council consisted of eleven representatives from the Federal States and a central directorate consisting of the President, Deputy President, and up to eight other people appointed by the President of the Republic and the Federal Government. The President is usually appointed for an eight year term. Unification would have added five more Länder representatives to the Council. It was, therefore, decided that from 1 November 1992, the 16 Länder would have nine representatives between them. There are about 150 branch offices run by the Länder.

It is independent of government instructions but must support the government's policy unless it conflicts with the primary task of controlling inflation. It has clashed with various governments but usually wins. The current President is Dr Axel Weber.

Like France, some traditional powers passed to the European Central Bank in 1999.

India

The Reserve Bank of India was set up in 1934 but nationalised in 1948. The governor is Dr Y.V. Reddy whose term is five years and who was appointed in September 2003.

Japan

A central bank, modelled on the Bank of England, was set up in 1882 and by 1889 had become the sole issuer of banknotes. The Governor and assistant Governor are appointed by the Cabinet for a five year term. Seven executive directors are appointed by the Ministry of Finance (MoF) on government recommendation. These nine form the Executive Board.

Technically, the bank is independent of the government. This was prejudiced to some extent by the fact that the MoF appointed so many members of the Executive Board. Also the MoF had the main responsibility for bank regulation and supervision. In April 1996, Mr Yasuo Matsushita, the Governor, urged a review of the central bank's legal status to grant it more independence. As a result, in 1998, as part of Japan's financial market reorganisation, the Ministry of Finance lost its power to order the central bank to delay interest rate rises, and banking supervision was passed to the new Financial Services Agency. The present Governor is Toshihiko Fukui.

The Zengin system for cheque clearing and electronic payments is run by the Tokyo Bankers Association.

UK

The world's first central bank is said to be the Swedish Riksbank in 1668. However, it was the formation of the Bank of England in 1694 that more clearly showed the potential for a state bank.

The bank was set up to help the government of William and Mary raise money for the wars against the French. Merchants of London and others raised £1.2m and the bank was granted a royal charter. It was the only joint stock bank allowed. From about 1715 onwards the bank was regularly raising money for the government by the sales of government bonds. By the 1826 Banking Act, joint stock banks other than the Bank of England were allowed, which led to a big increase in the numbers of banks. An Act of 1844 effectively gave the bank a monopoly of the note issue. Baring Bros hit trouble in 1890 (after unwise loans in S. America – yes, it's all happened before!) and the Bank of England rescued the bank, using a fund to which it and other banks subscribed.

The powers of the bank were exercised in fact rather than law and the bank was a private bank until 1946. In 1946 it was nationalised and banking legislation confirmed its powers in law in 1979 and 1987. In September 1984, it rescued the Johnson Matthey Bank, buying it for £1 and putting in its own managers to run it. Events during the First World War, rather than legislation, clearly established that the bank was an arm of the government and not independent. This finally changed in 1998.

The Bank of England Act of June 1998 set the statutory basis for the Bank's new Monetary Policy Committee and transfer of supervision to the Financial Services Authority.

The bank is run by a body quaintly called the 'Court'. It is headed by the Governor, two Deputy Governors and 16 non-executive directors. The Governor is appointed by the Prime Minister for a term of five years and is usually re-appointed. The current Governor is Mervyn King, formerly a deputy Governor.

US

In the US, the constitution of 1789 put management of the currency firmly in the hands of the Treasury and the Bank of the United States was formed in 1791. As such it pre-dates the setting up of central banks in France and Germany, although its record is not continuous. The bank was responsible for the issue of dollar bills and control of government debt.

Due to opposition, the bank's charter was not renewed in 1811 but it was started again in 1816. Bearing in mind that the US is a federal republic, doubt about the constitutional legality behind the formation of the bank led to a withdrawal of privileges in 1836 and concessions were transferred to individual state banks. As a result, the Bank of the United States went bankrupt in 1841. An Act of 1863 distinguished between banks which were licensed and regulated by the federal government – 'National' banks – and those licensed and regulated by individual states. (In some circumstances, a bank may choose to change regulators. Thus, in November 2004, JP Morgan Chase decided to be regulated by New York State no longer but chose national regulation. Having been allowed to have branches in other states since 1994, banks find state registration clumsy.) State banks generally gave up their note issues or converted into National banks. By 1880, there were 2000 National banks all issuing banknotes.

It was only in 1913 that the Federal Reserve System was set up with a single central bank controlling note issue and operating it through twelve Federal Reserve Districts. The Board of Governors was appointed by the President, as today. Having been appointed, the Board makes its own decisions on monetary policy without direction from the government, which it does through the Federal Open Market Committee. Ben Bernanke is the Chairman of the Federal Reserve, replacing the legendary Alan Greenspan (who had served 18 years) in January 2006.

Of the key central banks we discuss here, the Federal Reserve is the one whose authority as a central body is the least clear cut. As we noted earlier, the individual states can pass laws (and do); there is the role of the Federal Deposit Insurance Corporation (FDIC), as all deposits are insured up to $100 000; the Comptroller of the Currency supervises the national banks and the Federal Home Loan Bank System supervises the Savings and Loan Associations. Finally, credit unions are regulated by the National Credit Union Administrator. In October 2005, a detailed report was presented to the Senate Committee of Banking suggesting a simplification of regulation but received a lukewarm reception.

The European Central Bank

The European Central Bank (ECB) was created by the Maastricht Treaty of December 1991. It began operations on 1 June 1998, taking over from its predecessor, the European Monetary Institute. There is an Executive Board consisting of the President (Jean-Claude Trichet), the Vice-President and four other members, which will carry out policy by issuing instructions to the other central banks. The policy itself is determined by the Governing Council, consisting of the Executive Board plus the governors of the twelve central banks of the member countries. This is usually referred to as the 'European System of Central Banks' (ESCB). (Legally, the non-euro zone central banks are included but take no part in decisions on monetary policy.)

The prime objective of the ECB is price stability and the Maastricht Treaty says that it is also 'to support the EU's general economic policies'. Interest rate decisions are taken by the ECB by majority vote. The national central banks still conduct the bulk of money market operations and foreign exchange intervention but within policy set by the ECB. Bankers are as keen as anyone else to protect their jobs. In spite of the loss of powers by France to the ECB, the central bank still employs 15 600 staff as compared to 16 100 before 1999! The Bank of England, not in the euro zone, employs only 1908. To be fair, however, it is no longer responsible for bank supervision or the issue of government bonds.

CENTRAL BANK ACTIVITIES

We can summarise typical central bank activities as follows:

- ❑ Supervision of the banking system
- ❑ Advising the government on monetary policy
- ❑ Issue of banknotes
- ❑ Acting as banker to the other banks
- ❑ Acting as banker to the government
- ❑ Raising money for the government
- ❑ Controlling the nation's currency reserves
- ❑ Acting as 'lender of last resort'
- ❑ Liaison with international bodies.

Supervision of the Banking System

We saw in Chapter 2 that legally the central bank may not be responsible for banking supervision. There may be a separate supervisory body, like BaFin in Germany or the Financial Services Authority in the UK. Indeed, this is more often the case than not. Even in these cases, however, the practical day to day supervision and collection of information from the banks will be carried out by the central bank. The amount of information to be submitted (see Chapter 2) is considerable and may often involve several bank employees as a full time job.

Usually, the central bank will issue licences and may have to take decisions about rescues. In 1984, the Bank of England rescued the Johnson Matthey Bank. In the Autumn of 1991, the Bank of Finland had to step in and rescue the ailing Skopbank, the central bank of the savings banks. In March 1992, it was the Bank of Finland which announced a series of measures to bolster confidence in the bank sector, suffering due to the unprecedented recession. On the other hand, when Norway's banking sector was in trouble in 1991, it was the Bank Insurance Fund that set up a fund of state money to support the three major banks – Christiana, Norske Bank and Fokus Bank. In Sweden in 1992, the Ministry of Finance carried out rescues of Nordbanken and Forsta Sparbanken and later guaranteed all obligations of the Gota bank. When the Chicago bank, Continental Illinois, was in difficulty in 1984, it was the FDIC who moved in to help, not the Federal Reserve.

Special problems were created in the case of the infamous BCCI which collapsed in 1991. It was active in many countries but registered in Luxembourg, which may not have had the resources to monitor it properly. This problem is potentially more serious now as, in the EU, a 'single passport' policy applies. This says that an EU bank can set up a branch in any EU country with a licence from its *home* bank and not its *host* bank, although supervision will be carried out by the *host* central bank. However, following the BCCI collapse the G10 Banking Supervision Committee met at BIS in Basel and formed some new international rules. In particular, they say that a central bank may refuse a licence if it believes that a bank is not properly supervised by its home authority.

The Bank of England, stung by criticism over its role in the BCCI affair, pointed out that in the six years prior to 1992 it had quietly revoked 16 banking licences and obliged 35 banks to recapitalise, change management or merge. However, in mid 1998 its supervisory powers were passed to the new Financial Services Authority.

Monetary Policy

The decisions on monetary policy may be taken by the government if the central bank is not independent, or by the central bank itself if it is. In any case, the central bank will cooperate with the government on economic policy generally and will produce advice on monetary policy and economic matters, including all the statistics.

'Monetary policy' refers to interest rates and money supply which we discussed in Chapter 2. We noted that central banks can use various weapons to control money supply – interest rates, open market operations and changes in banks' reserves held interest free at the central bank. The central bank's role as 'lender of last resort' means that it can control interest rates. The mechanics are discussed in Chapter 6.

The independence of central banks has become a topical issue. In part, this is due to the EU setting up a single currency and central bank. Maastricht decided that it would be independent (even more independent and unaccountable than the mighty Bundesbank had been!). As a result, all eleven central banks of the constituent countries had to be independent too.

What is the argument about? It is whether the fight against inflation should be left to governments influenced by political motives and party political motives. On 11 September 1996, for example, the *London Evening Standard*, discussing a possible fall in interest rates, said, 'A party conference cut remains more rather than less likely'. The decision whether to cut interest rates was evidently thought to be influenced by the timing of a political party conference. The Bundesbank would have been horrified at any such possibility in its own market and, indeed, the new UK Labour government in May 1997 decided to give the Bank of England independence in setting interest rates within an inflation target set by government. However, there are, of course, *political* implications as high interest may mean low growth rates and high unemployment. As a result, although the Bundesbank's policies were admired by many, in August 1992, the head of the IG Metall trade union attacked the 'uncontrolled power' of the Bundesbank and said that it paid 'extensive and excessive' attention to inflation and ignored the need for economic growth and increasing employment.

Banknotes

The central bank controls the issue of banknotes and possibly, but not necessarily, coins also. Most payments these days do not involve cash but cheques, standing orders, direct debits, credit cards and so on. Nevertheless, cash is important as banks' cash holdings are a constraint on creation of credit, as we have seen.

Generally, we can say that, if the economy grows at 2%, the central bank will be willing to issue 2% more new banknotes to oil the wheels. On the other hand, less stable central banks may print banknotes to help the government. Usually, banknotes are backed not by gold but securities. The cost of printing is far less than the face value and the securities produce an income. This results in a special profit called *seignorage*. This special profit may go straight to the Treasury and not appear in the bank's books. The central bank will also replace used banknotes with new ones. There are local variations here. The British seem to dislike old banknotes much more than, say, the Germans. As a result, the Bundesbank replaces far fewer notes than the Bank of England.

Each year some 80 billion banknotes are printed by 186 currency issuing authorities in 124 countries. Some 51 have state printing works and 14 privately owned companies produce notes for the remaining 135.

Banker to the Other Banks

The central bank will act as banker to the other banks in the economy, as well as holding accounts with international bodies like the IMF and the World Bank. It is a common habit for the central bank to insist that the other banks hold non-interest bearing *reserves* with it in proportion to their deposits. Apart from helping the bank to make a profit, these serve as an instrument of control over money supply, as we saw in Chapter 2.

(For simplicity, we have talked of 'deposits'. In fact, the reserves are based on 'liabilities' in a more general sense. A bond due to be repaid by the bank is not a deposit but counts as a liability for purposes of reserve requirements.)

In any case, major banks will have to hold *working balances* for day to day settlement for various activities. Cheque clearing will end each day with a net sum of money owed by one bank to another or due to it. Dealings in government Treasury bills and bonds will be settled through the central bank accounts, and also tax payments. The total of a bank's clients' payments of tax will result in a fall in that bank's balance at the central bank and a rise in the government's balance.

The working balances which major domestic banks would need to keep at the Bundesbank, for example, are part of these reserves. The actual figures are averages of the balances held at the Bundesbank during the course of a particular month and the calculation is based on the daily average of the various types of liabilities held. The result is that, at the start of the month, the banks may hold reserves less than the required amount provided they catch up later, so that the overall average is the required figure. This leads to a lot of short-term lending and borrowing in the interbank market.

The whole system has now been reorganised for all twelve countries in Europe's Economic and Monetary Union. The ECB has imposed a minimum reserve requirement (similar to the Bundesbank but paying interest which the Bundesbank did not). Banks must deposit the equivalent of 2% of deposits with their central banks. National central banks will conduct open market operations to keep interest rates within a desired range. All this will be discussed in Chapter 6.

By contrast, the Bank of England abolished reserve requirements of this nature in 1979. The argument is that – as there are no exchange controls – sterling can be exchanged for foreign currencies and vice-versa without constraint. As London is a huge international banking centre, attempts to control money supply by sterling non-interest bearing reserves at the central bank would simply not be effective. The only reserve held is 0.15% of stipulated liabilities – not an instrument of monetary policy but a way of 'joining the UK bank club' and helping the Bank of England to make a profit! However, the main domestic banks must still maintain working balances at the Bank of England.

Banker to the Government

Normally, a central bank acts as the government's banker. It receives revenues for taxes or other income and pays out money for the government's expenditure. Usually, it will not lend to the government but will help the government to borrow money by the sales of its bills and bonds (see next section).

One exception here is Postipankki in Finland. Perhaps because it is owned by the government, it is this bank rather than the central bank which handles the government's money.

As citizens pay taxes, charges are made against their bank accounts and settled through their bank's own account at the central bank. The banks' balances fall and the government's rises. This is one reason why banks must keep working balances at the central bank. Of course, as tax rebates are made, the government's balance falls and the banks' balances rise.

As Treasury bills and bonds are paid for, money is passed to the government's account. As they are redeemed, money flows back to the banks' accounts. If the central bank discounts bills of exchange to help a commercial bank's liquidity, money moves into that bank's account. As the bill is presented for payment, money is credited to the central bank. As a result, there is a constant flow of money from the banks' accounts at the central bank to the government's accounts and vice-versa.

Raising Money for the Government

The government Treasury bill and bond markets are covered in detail in Chapter 6. While sometimes the Treasury or Ministry of Finance handles government issues, it is much more common for the central bank to control this and to settle payments through accounts that banks and financial institutions have with it. This is one of the reasons why these banks must keep working balances at the central bank.

We have seen that, in 1694, the Bank of England was formed specifically for the purpose of raising money for the government (although since 1998 responsibility has been passed to the Treasury's new Debt Management Office).

The cumulative sum of money owed by governments for all their borrowings is called the *national debt*. Over time, the debt grows and is not, in any real sense, ever 'paid off'. Does this matter?

The first point is that, for any individual, how serious debt is depends on their income. Governments are the same. Economists compare the national debt to the national income as a ratio to see if the situation is getting worse or better. For this purpose the figure for Gross Domestic Product (GDP) is used as equivalent to the national income.

In the US, due to heavy government borrowing in the 1980s, the ratio rose from 33% to over 50%, then started to fall in the 1990s as the government was in surplus and able to buy debt back. However, the economic slowdown of 2001–02 and the falling revenues from President Bush's tax cuts (designed to boost the economy) mean that the US is now back in deficit. The size of the deficit together with the trade deficit is causing international concern. In the UK, the figure, which was 100% at the end of the 1960s, has fallen to around 37%.

This relationship of national debt to GDP became an issue in the run up to a possible European single currency and economic union.

The meeting at Maastricht in Holland in December 1991 set out criteria which must be met before a nation could join in the single currency. (This will be examined in detail in Chapter 11.) One of the criteria was that the national debt/GDP ratio should not exceed 60%.

Inflation is also a key factor. As time goes by, inflation simply erodes the value of the debt. A national debt of $100bn in 1960 looks a quite different figure today. Debt servicing costs also play a role. Interest must be paid and this itself may limit further increases in debt. In Italy and Belgium, for example, debt servicing takes no less than 20% of all government tax receipts, and in India, 21%.

Finally, to whom is the money owed? Often the government bonds and bills are owned by financial institutions and individuals in the domestic market. There will be foreign holders but they will probably not account for more than, say, 20%. This is where the position of the emerging countries is so different – they largely owe the money to foreigners and it is denominated in a foreign currency (see Chapter 6).

Is there a level of national debt that is reasonable or safe? *The Economist* (27 February–4 March 1988) had an interesting article on this subject and this quotation provides a nice summary:

> *Neither economic theory nor history gives any clue as to what is the critical level of public debt ... The crucial factor is the willingness of investors to hold public debt. If they lose their appetite then, either interest rates must rise sharply or the government has to finance its deficit by printing more money and hence stoking up inflation.*

Controlling the Nation's Currency Reserves

Each nation has reserves of gold and foreign currencies held at the central bank. If the bank intervenes in the market to buy the domestic currency, it will do so using foreign currency reserves. If it intervenes to sell the local currency, it will acquire foreign currencies.

The foreign exchange markets are examined in Chapter 9. We shall see that the transactions in major currencies are considerable. The dealing in sterling, to take one example, is so great that the Bank of England alone can't control the exchange rate by its buying and selling. It can, however, influence the rate by careful timing and the knowledge by market operators that the central bank is acting in the market. Under the newer arrangements for European cooperation, several EU central banks may act together. Equally, major countries' central banks may act together as part of the arrangements of the 'Group of Seven' countries (G7, see below).

In the ERM crisis of September 1992, the Bank of France is thought to have spent about 40% of its reserves defending the franc – a sum perhaps as high as FFr150 billion.

Where a currency is not widely traded, the central bank will have a much better chance of controlling the rate. The central bank of Norway can control the rate for the kroner much more easily than the Bank of England can control that for the pound.

The reserves will usually include gold as well as foreign currencies but the position of gold has changed. The central banks in the European Union came to an arrangement for a controlled sale of gold in 1999. In September 2004, the arrangement was renewed, allowing the central banks to sell up to 500 metric tonnes a year. The Bank of England has sold most of its gold.

Acting as Lender of Last Resort

This does not only refer to the role of the bank as a periodic rescuer of banks in trouble. It refers to the fact that the central bank will help the other banks temporarily when they meet problems with their liquidity. As we have just seen, tax transactions and settlements for government securities are causing a continuous ebb and flow of money out of and into the accounts of the banks at the central bank. In all cases, they are obliged to keep minimum working balances and in most cases they must keep reserves at the central bank also, although these working balances may be part of the reserves.

The central bank smooths out the peaks and troughs by being prepared to assist the other banks with short-term help. Since the banks are ultimately dependent on the central bank, the rate of interest charged governs other interest rates. How the bank carries out this role is discussed in detail in Chapter 6.

Of course, sometimes a bank does need to be rescued. It is ironic that Baring Bros, which was placed in administration in February 1995, had been in trouble some 100 years earlier and had, on that occasion, been rescued by the Bank of England and other banks. Bad debts in Argentina were three times Baring's capital.

The precise role of the new ECB in rescuing banks in trouble is vague in the Maastricht Treaty. This is discussed later in Chapter 11.

Liaison with International Bodies

Central banks will liaise with other international financial bodies like the International Monetary Fund (IMF) and the International Bank for Reconstruction and Development, usually called the 'World Bank' (see Chapter 9). They also liaise with and take part in discussions at the BIS in Basel. This bank was set up in 1930. By 1929 it was evident that for Germany to pay the massive reparations imposed on it after the First World War was an impossibility and some new arrangement had to be made. The new plan which was devised was called the 'Young Plan' and part of it involved setting up the BIS which would help to transfer reparation payments and other international debts. Some 84% of the shares were held by 33 central banks and the rest by private shareholders. However, on 9 September 1996, the BIS announced that it was offering membership to nine other central banks, including those in areas like the Far East and Latin America, and these became members in June 1997. A total of 55 central banks are now members of the BIS.

Today, the BIS is used by some 90 central banks and can be regarded as 'the central bankers' central bank'. It handles the payments made between world banks, sponsors cooperation, handles initiatives on key topics and hosts monthly meetings of the world's bankers at its headquarters near Basel's railway station. It also holds 10% of the reserves of major world central banks.

There is far more cooperation on economic matters by the world's major powers than there was 20 years ago. Of key importance here are the periodic meetings of the seven most advanced economic nations, called the 'Group of Seven' or, simply, 'G7'. The seven are US, France, Germany, UK, Canada, Japan and Italy. These days Russia attends, making it G8. There is also a growing pressure to admit China and India.

G7 members meet periodically to discuss world economic and financial affairs. Central bankers play a key role in preparing for these meetings and briefing the politicians. The world's top powers had realised by early 1985 that the foreign exchange markets were so big that only concerted intervention by all the major central banks could have any effect. Worried about the dollar's inexorable rise, key central bankers led by Paul Volcker, the then Chairman of the US Federal Reserve, made a secret agreement. On Wednesday morning, 27 February 1985, they struck, selling dollars simultaneously. By the end of the day, the dollar had fallen from DM3.50 to DM3.30. In the process, the foreign exchange markets experienced what can only be called 'pandemonium'.

Later, in September 1985, the predecessor of G7 (G5) called a meeting at the Plaza Hotel in Washington (G5 is G7 minus Canada and Italy). Again the agreement was to force down the dollar, and again it worked. This first international agreement on currencies since Bretton Woods (see Chapter 9) is called the 'Plaza Agreement'. In later years there were other meetings (for example, the 'Louvre Accord' in February 1987). Usually, these were designed to push the dollar *up* and were not as successful.

A wider forum for international meetings is the so called 'Group of Ten' or 'G10'; this is G7 with the addition of Sweden, Belgium, Holland and Switzerland. The reader will not need to be a mathematical genius to see that this is eleven countries, not ten. It's all to do with Swiss neutrality: the Swiss are always there, but officially they aren't there. It's called 'G10' but actually there are eleven countries participating.

Sometimes the G10 members meet with Latin American and Far Eastern representatives on an *ad hoc* basis to form what is usually called G33 (for example to discuss the Far East crisis in 1997).

Another forum is called 'G24'. This consists of eight countries each from Asia, Africa and Latin America, and is used for liaison with the IMF and the World Bank.

THE POSITION OF CENTRAL BANKS TODAY

The last decade has seen a rise in the power and influence of central bankers. Years of high inflation have led to the view that politicians can no longer be trusted with monetary policy. One by one, central banks have become independent, culminating in the formation of the European Central Bank.

Inflation in advanced industrial countries was down to about 1.5% at the start of the millennium, its lowest rate since the 1950s. However, many governments are now concerned at the cost in growth and unemployment. Does low inflation necessarily mean low growth and high unemployment? Alan Greenspan, when Chairman of the US Federal Reserve, seems to have delivered good growth with low inflation despite the 2001–02 slowdown. Rising US interest rates in 2005 and the rise in oil prices, however, suggest that higher inflation may be on the horizon. The position is not as favourable in Europe, where high social costs and labour market rigidities have led to high unemployment (although not in the UK).

If a key role of the central bank is to combat inflation, this raises the question – how do we measure it? There is, for example, consumer inflation and industrial inflation. In particular, price indices do not usually include the prices of financial assets like shares. The collapse of these asset prices could also lead to economic and financial instability, as in Japan. In 1911, Irving Fisher, the economist, argued that a price index should include share and property prices. Joseph Carson, an economist at Deutsche Bank, New York, has constructed just such an index with shares in at 5%. Leading indices, such as the Dow, the Footsie and – most notably – NASDAQ, surged between 1996 and 1999 at a rate not seen since the late 1980s, and people talked of the 'new economy' and 'a new paradigm'. From the highs of end 1999, the Dow lost around 30% and the Footsie over 40% by 2003, with falls being triggered initially by the burst of the 'dot.com' bubble in Spring 2001, followed by the events of 11 September, and later by concerns over the validity of reported results in the wake of irregularities at Enron, Worldcom and other major corporations. While it is not the role of central banks to maintain stock market growth – and Greenspan warned of the excessive prices of many shares before they collapsed – the knock on economic effect of stock market instability is clearly of concern to central bank governors. Fortunately, from mid 2003 onwards, the stock markets began to recover.

Accountability is another current issue. For all their independence, the Bundesbank and the Federal Reserve are basically accountable to their governments, and the Federal Open Market Committee's minutes are models of openness. There is much concern, however, at the position of the ECB. The Maastricht Treaty prohibits it from taking orders from politicians, and members of the executive are appointed for eight-year, non-renewable terms. The President, Jean Paul Trichet, meets the European Parliament only once a year to explain policy. Outside of this, however, he has stated that no minutes of meetings will be issued. It may be more difficult for the ECB, therefore, to attract public support than the Fed or the Bundesbank.

Finally, what may seem a silly question – do we need a central bank? In 1900, only 18 countries had a central bank, compared to 160 today. Some economists still argue that private banks should issue their own banknotes in competition. This was the position before 1845 in Scotland, where notes were backed by gold but banks competed. Adam Smith admired the system.

But surely we need the role of the lender of last resort? Some argue that the near guarantee of a rescue encourages banks to behave imprudently – an issue called 'moral hazard'.

That wise man, Walter Bagehot, commented on moral hazard in his great work *Lombard St.* (1873):

> *If banks are bad they will certainly continue bad and will probably become worse if the government sustains and encourages them. The cardinal maxim is that any aid to a present bad bank is the surest mode of preventing the establishment of a future good bank.*

Like Adam Smith, Walter Bagehot also favoured the old Scottish system. However, he agreed that a proposal to do away with the Bank of England would be as futile as a proposal to do away with the monarchy. Now that the latter idea is no longer unthinkable in the UK, we may perhaps end up treating central banks with the same lack of reverence!

SUMMARY

The People's Bank of China was founded in 1948; the Bank of France was founded in 1800; the Bundesbank in 1957; the Reserve Bank of India was founded in 1934; the Bank of Japan in 1885; the Bank of England in 1694, the Federal Reserve in 1913 and the European Central Bank in 1998.

Worldwide, there are 160 central banks.

Central bank activities are:

Supervision of the banking system   Where it will play a key role even if legally there is a separate supervisory body.

Monetary policy   Controlling interest rates and the money supply. However, some central banks are independent in this respect and others are less so, but central banks all over the world have increasingly been given more independence with respect to monetary policy.

Printing of bank notes and minting of coins   This must be linked to the growth in the economy or inflation will follow.

Banker to the other banks   Domestic banks must leave sums of money with the central bank for various clearing and settlement systems. In some countries (for example, the euro area) the central bank imposes minimum *reserves* as part of monetary policy.

Banker to the government   In raising money for the government, the central bank controls the account into which the money is paid. As taxes are paid, the government balance increases and the commercial banks' balances fall. When the government spends money, the opposite happens.

Raising money for the government   This usually involves the sale of short-term Treasury bills and medium- to long-term government bonds. The cumulative sum of money owed for all borrowing not yet repaid is the national debt. It is usually shown as a percentage of Gross Domestic Product to see if the situation is worsening or getting better. Over time, however, inflation erodes the burden of the debt.

Controlling the nation's reserves   From time to time, central banks will buy or sell their country's currency to influence the rate. If they buy it, they will use the nation's reserves of gold and foreign currencies to do so.

Acting as lender of last resort   Sometimes this refers to the rescue of banks in trouble but, more generally, it is the willingness of the central bank to assist banks with liquidity problems. Usually, this means their inability to meet the necessary balance levels at the central bank (as a direct result of central bank policy!). The rate of interest involved in the transaction gives the central bank control over interest rates.

International liaison   This involves cooperation with bodies like the IMF, the World Bank and the BIS. It also involves supporting international meetings called G7 and G10. With the addition of Russia, G7 is now G8.

4 Commercial Banking

INTRODUCTION

Commercial banks are essentially banks which are in the classic banking business of accepting deposits and making loans. Banks like Barclays and Royal Bank of Scotland are commercial banks. Other banks, like Deutsche, UBS and Citigroup would say that they were 'universal' banks: that is, they cover all kinds of banking, including both commercial and investment banking. In the UK, if a commercial bank carries out investment banking, it will do so through a subsidiary, for example, Barclays Bank – Barclays Capital. In Germany and Switzerland (and to a lesser extent France, the Netherlands and Spain) they will do so within the same legal entity.

As we saw in Chapter 2, commercial banking may be *retail* or *wholesale*. Within their own country, the large commercial banks will carry out both retail and wholesale banking. Abroad, they will concentrate on the wholesale markets.

We shall cover retail banking in this chapter. We shall also explain some areas of wholesale banking, mainly the question of bank lending. Other aspects of wholesale banking will be treated in later chapters – money markets in Chapter 6, foreign exchange in Chapter 9 and finance for trade in Chapter 10.

RETAIL BANKING

Types of Service

Retail commercial banks offer an increasing range of services to their clients. Some relate to the handling of *money* – various forms of deposit accounts and loans. Others relate to *services* – advice, custody, purchase of stocks, shares, insurance and so on. Essentially, these are the two ways banks make their money: taking deposits, that is, borrowing money and lending it out at a profitable rate of interest on the one hand and providing useful services for which they can charge, on the other. The range of products is widening as the banks react to growing competition and falling profits. We hear more and more of the phrase, the 'financial supermarket'.

Retail banking tends to be dominated by a handful of domestic banks. According to figures from Merrill Lynch, the top four banks in the economy control 75% of banking assets in Holland and 60% in France. A Bank of England study found that the top five banks accounted for 75% of individual and small firm lending.

The one exception is the US where, due to the large number of banks (see Chapter 2), the ten biggest banks only account for 20% of deposits. In Germany savings banks and cooperative banks and in Italy, savings banks are strong competitors for deposits and, in the UK, the building societies.

Money Banking – Deposits

Current accounts   The principal kind of account offered by the retail bank is the current account, which is seen by the bank as a fundamental way of establishing a relationship with the customer and as a source of cheap money to sustain the various lending activities. The position regarding the charge to the client for providing the current account facility varies. In the present competitive environment, banks either maĸe charges but offset them with interest on credit balances or make no charges but have free use of the credit balances. French banks are not allowed in law to make charges, but many vary the amount of time to clear cheques, which can be as much as five days. In the UK and Spain, competition has led to payment of interest on credit balances for the first time. The current account carries with it the obligation to provide a range of payment services – cheques, Automated Teller Machines (ATMs), debit cards and so forth, the costs of which are quite high and consume some of the value of the low cost deposits.

Deposit accounts   These are various forms of interest-bearing accounts which usually do not allow cheques and often severely limit other withdrawal facilities. They may require a period of notice to be given before withdrawals, for example, seven days, one month or three months. The customer is paid interest on the understanding that the appropriate period of notice will be given before drawing out money. Alternatively, the money may be placed on deposit for a fixed term, similar to the above, whereupon it is repaid. Generally, the longer the customer is prepared to commit the funds, and/or the greater the amount, the greater will be the rate paid. The bank has the advantage that it can rely on notice or fixed term money much more than it can with current accounts, where the balances fluctuate.

Payments   Based upon the current account is a range of payment products which manifest themselves in paper or electronic form. Examples of the former are cheques and giro slip payments, while a growing number of electronic payments pass from business to business and business to individuals through computer to computer systems. Thus, in the UK, for example, more than 80% of the workforce receive their salaries by automated transfers from their employers' systems into their current accounts. Equally, Standing Orders and Direct Debits are very widely used to settle recurring payments. Intermixed with electronic payments passing through the current account will be paper-based transactions. People and companies can settle indebtedness by issuing cheques, which give rise to a charge on their account and a credit on the beneficiary's account. Alternatively, a bill may be paid by completing a giro form and sending the form to the beneficiary's bank so that money can be transferred to the creditor's account (very common in the Netherlands, Germany, Austria and Switzerland). Within the banking system, the transmission of payments between banks and the consequent financial settlement is called clearing, and this is discussed later.

Ever increasingly, payment activity is initiated by the use of plastic cards. Details of the account are embedded in a magnetic strip or a microchip, and these, when put together with value information generated at an ATM or at the point of sale, give rise to a current account transaction. There are 500 000 ATMs worldwide with 165,000 in the US and 140 000 in Europe. The UK has nearly 34 000 ATMs, and they are used for 70% of personal cash withdrawals. France, Germany and Italy also have large numbers of ATMs.

An alternative to the cheque for payment in a retail shop or similar outlet is the *debit* card, which will usually be also the ATM card of the customer. At the point of sale a machine, sometimes integrated with the till, creates what amounts to an electronic cheque from the information on the card and the amount of the transaction. This data is passed down a telephone line so that the appropriate charge can be made to the customer's account and a credit to the retailer's account. The customer will be called upon to identify themselves at the point of sale in one of two ways. They may put their signature on a paper slip for checking against a specimen on the back of the card by the retailer, or by entering their Personal Identification Number (PIN), as they would at an ATM.

If the customer wants to make a high value purchase, the retailer's machine will seek authorisation from the customer's bank before completing the purchase. Such is the sophistication of the network connecting retailers to the world's banking systems that this takes only a few seconds. In the UK, the growing use of debit cards means that, between 1991 and 2004, the volume of cheques used, which had been 3.8 billion, had fallen to 2.1 billion. In the same period, debit card purchases have increased from 0.3 billion to 3.8 billion.

There is a slight variation on the debit card idea in France and Germany where they have debit cards which charge transactions a month later. Unlike a credit card, however, this is charged to the current account and the holder is expected to have funds to meet the charge.

When a cheque is used, the same card may serve as a 'cheque guarantee card'. A retailer will accept a cheque up to a given maximum if the card is produced so that its specimen signature can be checked against that written on the cheque. The advantage to the retailer is that the bank guarantees to pay even if the transaction is fraudulent or the cardholder has insufficient funds. In the US, there is no such system and retailers are reluctant to accept cheques ('Don't you have a credit card?'). In France, also, there is no such system, but retailers are happier to accept cheques, as writing a cheque when there are no funds to support it is a criminal offence.

Some interesting figures from BIS on numbers of ATMs and point of sale terminals are shown in Table 4.1.

Four types of loan are common in the retail banking sector:

❏ Overdraft
❏ Personal loan
❏ Mortgage
❏ Credit card.

The *overdraft* is a popular method of borrowing in countries where it is permitted.

The account holder is allowed to overdraw up to a maximum sum for a given period of time – nominally, perhaps, 6 months, but in practice renewable. Interest is charged on a daily basis (and at a variable rate) on any overdrawn balance.

Table 4.1 *Number of ATMs, EFT-POS terminals and credit cards, end 2003*

Country	No. of ATMs per 1m inhabitants	No. of EFT-POS terminals per 1m inhabitants	No. of credit cards per 1000 inhabitants
Belgium	681	—	298
Canada	1394	30 351	1671
France	683	16 267	—
Germany	620	5733	393
Hong Kong	—	—	—
Italy	671	—	441
Japan	872	7503	1990
Netherlands	465	—	351
Singapore	371	—	835
Sweden	299	12 062	409
Switzerland	722	—	454
UK	783	14 508	1200
US	1275	64 938	4384

Source: BIS Statistics on Payment and Settlement Systems in Selected Countries (March 2005).

From the customer's point of view, the overdraft is informal and can be arranged quickly; it is flexible in that the amount 'lent' will vary and can be quite economical in that, when a monthly salary is paid in, the overdrawn balance will be reduced, or even eliminated, at least for a few days.

From the banks' point of view, the overdraft is also informal; the facility is reviewed at the stated time interval and, if necessary, it is repayable on demand – a condition of which many borrowers are happily ignorant!

The overdraft is common in the UK and Germany, not particularly common in France and simply not allowed as a facility in the US.

The *personal loan* is an agreement to borrow a specific amount over a specific period of time with a set sum repaid monthly. $1000 might be borrowed for two years. The rate of interest is fixed and charged on the whole amount. If the rate on the above loan was 10%, then 10% p.a. on $1000 for two years is $200. This results in 24 monthly repayments of $50. As some of the principal is being repaid every month, the bank is not owed $1000 for two years but, on the average, a much smaller sum. The result is that the 10% rate is purely nominal, the actual rate (sometimes termed the 'Annual Percentage Rate' or 'APR') will be nearly twice this.

Mortgages Although there may be specialised mortgage lenders, the commercial banks may offer mortgages too. The loan is secured on the property and such a loan will bear a much lower rate of interest than an unsecured overdraft or personal loan as the bank is less at risk. In some countries, banks and other mortgage lenders will not lend more than, say, 50% or 60% of the value of the property, but where they do, offering 90% or more, this can fuel a colossal rise in house prices, followed by a subsequent fall as recession strikes. A recent development in the UK has seen various implementations of the all-in-one account, which works like a hybrid between a current account and a mortgage. The accounts are actually or virtually merged to give the customer the benefit of fluctuations in their overdraft, say after pay day, with the lower interest rates of a mortgage.

Another way of lending money is by a *credit card* account. The major international brand names are Visa, MasterCard and JCB, the Japanese branding organisation. They are offered by banks, retailers and others. The plastic card, with coded information on a magnetic strip or microchip, is offered at the point of sale and the purchase is charged to the credit card account. The method is exactly the same as with a debit card. A statement is sent monthly with a given time to pay, usually two to three weeks. The consumer has the choice of paying the balance in full or paying only part and paying the rest later. It is very flexible in that the card holders can choose how much to borrow (within a pre-arranged limit) and how quickly to repay. Generally, the rate of interest is substantial when borrowing on a credit card account, but competitive pressures and desire for market share often cause the banks to offer very keen introductory or 'balance transfer' rates. Card holders can, of course, choose not to borrow at all but repay in full each month, with perhaps up to seven weeks elapsing between the purchase and the payment, at no cost to them. Most issuing banks seek to make an annual charge for the use of the card, but competitive pressures have, again, forced many to offer cards without fees. Recent years have seen a large increase in card issuers and types of card. Among the issuers are retailers, bodies like AT & T, General Motors, General Electric (US) and mutual funds. In the UK, some 1200 organisations – clubs, societies, unions and common interest groups of many kinds – have cards issued in their names. They contract the banks, or specialist organisations such as MBNA, to manage and operate the accounts, taking an introductory fee and a tiny percentage of the turnover through the accounts. Although not obvious to the card holder, the banks also charge the retailers a percentage of about 1% to 3% of the transaction value for providing the facilities by which the transactions are authorised, collected and cleared.

The familiar green American Express card and the Diners Club card are not credit cards in that they do not offer *credit*. The consumer is expected to pay the balance in full every month. They are usually called 'travel and entertainment' or charge cards.

In general, credit cards are now very widely used. Their acceptability internationally makes them a very useful way of solving foreign currency problems when travelling.

The one country where the use of credit cards was weak is Germany where, at the end of 1995, there were only 6 million credit card holders as opposed to, for example, 29 million in the UK. This was due to the opposition of the banks. However, things have changed somewhat although not dramatically. In mid 2005, there were 22 million credit cards out of a population of 67 million according to the German retailers' association, HDE, who estimate that, in Germany, only 5% of goods are bought with credit cards. Indeed, some prominent stores and supermarkets will not accept them. Germans, generally, are relatively conservative spenders. By contrast, the United States, with a population of 296 million has one billion credit cards.

The Electronic Purse

Another development using plastic cards which the banks are experimenting with is called 'the electronic purse'. This is based on a 'smart' card which stores information on a microchip. This includes a balance of 'cash' pre-loaded onto the card from an ATM or a suitably equipped telephone terminal. The idea is that the card may be used for a wide range of retail transactions, many of which would be too trivial for a credit card. The card is presented at point of sale and the value loaded in the card is decreased by the amount of the transaction. As with real cash, there is no paperwork. The retailer's equipment has in it a card to which the 'cash' flows and is accumulated. At closing time, the 'cash' can be paid in to the bank using an ATM or telephone terminal in the reverse of the loading procedure.

In the UK, National Westminster Bank and Midland Bank developed Mondex, an electronic purse which underwent trials in Swindon between 1995 and 1998. The idea was taken up by Midland's new owner HSBC with implementations in Hong Kong and the Far East, and by the Royal Bank of Canada and Canadian Imperial Bank of Commerce for trials in that country. Mondex, now majority owned by MasterCard, is franchised in 53 countries .

While there have been several trials of electronic purses in the US (including one for the Olympic Games in Atlanta), the most ambitious involved cooperation between Citicorp, Chase Manhattan, Visa and MasterCard. A trial was launched for New York's affluent Upper West Side late in 1996 and called off in November 1998.

In general, electronic purses are making slow progress. This is due to several factors: the cost of issue of the cards, the lack of compatible point of sale terminals, conflicting card encoding standards and a general lack of interest by the consumer. The first of these is being addressed by the issue of 'smart', that is, microchipfitted cards as a counter fraud measure for credit and debit cards; these will be readily capable of carrying an electronic purse application. At the same time, Visa, MasterCard and Europay are cooperating on agreeing global standards for chip cards. This will solve the encoding standard problem. However, the point of sale equipment problem will take longer to solve, as retailers are unwilling to make the very large expenditures necessary, but what is happening is that point of sale tills are now becoming more sophisticated and able to accept different types of card. The issue of consumer acceptance of the notion of electronic purses may remain; people are very conservative and the use of real cash is deeply embedded in culture all over the world.

The original Mondex concept has been replaced in some cases by a variety of pre-paid cards with less ambitious application. However, MasterCard in 2005 announced a 'cashplus' card targeting the 2.4 million people in the UK without a bank account which could be used to buy on-line and over the telephone. Belgium has a 'Proton' system like Mondex, and there are similar systems in the Netherlands and Luxembourg.

Other Services

There are a number of other services which are typically offered by banks.

Securities purchases   In some countries, like Germany and Switzerland, the 'universal' bank tradition has meant that the banks dominate stock markets and the commercial banking branches have been able to offer a full service to clients. Elsewhere, brokers have traditionally had a monopoly of stock exchange transactions and banks would act as an agent for their customers, passing the order to the broker. Today, this might still be the case but all over Europe deregulation has been the rule, starting with the UK's 'Big Bang' in October 1986. As a result, banks have been allowed either to own brokers or set up their own operations and offer their branch customers a securities service.

Securities custody   Often bonds and shares are in 'bearer' format and not registered. The share certificate will say that 'the bearer' owns, perhaps, 2000 shares in DaimlerChrysler. The problem is that, in the event of a burglary, the burglar is now 'the bearer'! Also, since there is no register, interest payments and dividends have to be claimed, voting rights followed up and so on. The banks will, therefore, often hold the certifications for safe-keeping, claim interest payments/dividends for clients, vote by proxy, notify them of AGMs, rights issues, scrip issues and other company events. Needless to say, a fee is charged for this service!

Mutual funds   These are pools of shares run by investment managers and giving the small shareholder a spread of risk. The banks often own these and part of the securities service might be the advice that the client would be better off in a mutual fund than owning shares directly. It would be no surprise to find that the fund recommended is one the bank owns! These are sold in France as SICAVs and FCPs, in the UK as Investment Trusts and Unit Trusts and as Mutual Funds in the

US. The idea has spread to Spain where 'Super Fondos' are now being offered by the banks. Following the European single market initiative, the term 'UCITS' may be encountered, and this is covered in Chapter 11.

Advice   The bank manager is available for advice. This may be about investments, trust funds for children, wills and similar issues. Indeed, the manager may end up as the executor for a will and trustee for funds left for children. This position as adviser puts the bank manager in an ideal position to sell the bank's products. This has caused much anguish in the UK due to the operation of the 1986 Financial Services Act. The ruling was that either the bank manager is an agent for the bank's products or an independent investment adviser. If the former, they must inform the client of this status and are not allowed to give wide ranging advice on a range of products. If an independent adviser, they must also make sure that the client is aware of this. If they recommend the bank's product it must be clear, beyond reasonable doubt, that this is best for the client or criminal prosecution may ensue. However, this was all changed in 2005 to something more complicated. There are now 'multi-tied agents' who can recommend products from a range of firms. Some independent advisers are becoming multi-tied agents but many banks are still selling their own products only.

Safe deposits   Banks provide safe deposit boxes to house jewellery, other valuable items and cash. When there is a break in and the boxes are forced open, those clients with large sums, of which the tax authorities are unaware, face a problem when making a claim!

Foreign exchange   Apart from the banks' wholesale foreign exchange operations, they will provide a service for their customers' holiday needs. This will involve supplying travellers' cheques and cash. They may also be involved in requests to transfer sums of money to accounts abroad. The rise of the credit and debit card, now very widely acceptable at point of sale and in ATMs has eroded this business along with the advent of the euro.

Insurance   Most banks are now offering insurance policies either through an association with an insurance company or through their own subsidiary. This is discussed more fully below when we look at key current issues in retail banking.

Delivery Channels

How shall the services of the bank – deposits, loans, payment products and all the other services – be delivered to the customer? Traditionally, there was only one answer: the branch office. Gradually, since the early 1990s, branches have been joined by telephone banking, PC banking and, more recently still, TV and mobile phone delivery.

Branch delivery   still dominates. In the UK, there were 11 000 bank branches at the end of 2004, down from 15 700 in 1990, with some of the reduction being caused by rationalisation from mergers and some from branch closure programmes. Branch numbers are down by over 50% in the Netherlands and 36% in Switzerland but with no great reduction in the US. However, many people now believe that the new channels are additional services rather than substitutes, with one major bank citing the fact that three out of four customers still regularly visited a branch. This all suggests that branches are here to stay, at least for the medium term. Branches are convenient for the customer and there is still a demand for face-to-face contact, particularly when discussing more complex financial matters. Branches give the bank high visibility on the streets and are a good base for attracting new customers, dealing with routine transactions and for selling more complex (and profitable) products. There has been a fairly rapid change in how the branches look to the customer. Traditionally, the customer was confined to a public space defined by the imposing barrier of the line of cashiers, behind their security screens. They had to go out of their way to ask to see someone who could open an account or deal with a more complicated transaction. This model of branch is rapidly being supplanted by one in which the space has been opened up and made more welcoming. After encountering some self-service machines – ATMs, deposit machines, statement and enquiry terminals – the customer sees before them desks with people variously described as 'personal bankers' or 'counsellors' awaiting an opportunity to engage them in helpful conversation. The cashiers are relegated to the back of the room. The purpose of all this is to encourage the customers to serve themselves for routine transactions and, as soon as they step beyond this, to expose them to sales opportunities. To make space for this more 'open' setting, something has had to be displaced. This is the clerical processing of payments and correspondence, which was formerly termed the 'back office' function. These activities are still required, but they have been moved out to other units who will, using higher capacity technology, take on the back office work of many branches.

The use of branches is still very much a current issue. Alliance and Leicester, for example, announced in mid 2004 that they intended to close one sixth of all their branches on the grounds that more and more customers are using the telephone and Internet. On the other hand, Abbey National (now part of Banco Santander Central Hispano) and RBS-National Westminster are putting more emphasis on branches, even making it a selling point in advertisements. Barclays, after several years of flat profits in retail banking, announced in 2005 through their then UK retail banking chief, Roger Davis, that they wanted customers to re-engage with their local branches, making the local manager and staff the kingpins again. There would be extensive refurbishment, more people and more branch based technology with the bank manager given greater autonomy. In all this they look to more effective cross selling of products like mortgages and insurance. Finally, when HBOS released their annual results in March 2006, they announced plans to spend £100 million on 50 new branches and noted that their share of new accounts had typically doubled in areas where the bank has a branch.

Some might say that this is not before time. The results of a survey by consultants, Booz Allen Hamilton, was published in March 2005. Over all Europe, the most friendly branches were in Switzerland and Germany, the least friendly in Spain and the UK. So far as product knowledge is concerned, the UK and Spain were also rated the worst. The survey covered 600 branches across Europe and found that 79% still prefer to buy products like basic bank deposits and savings accounts from a branch.

There were similar findings from the UK consultancy, Finalta. Banks have put more emphasis on selling but not very successfully. Another consultancy, Accenture, being in IT think that better use of IT is the answer (surprise!). In May 2005 they unveiled a demonstration of several new techniques based on IT – digital pens whose pen strokes can be transmitted to a computer, touch sensitive video walls and video cameras to monitor how queues form. Both RBS and Lloyds claim to have used IT to analyse and optimise the design of branches and set staffing levels.

As mentioned before, the number of bank branches has not fallen in the US; in fact many new branches have opened following the Riegle-Neal Act which repealed the McFaddeyn Act and allowed banks to open in other states. Many of these new branches look more like boutiques that the old cavernous banking halls of old.

Finally, one more criticism. Chris Skinner, founder of the consultancy Shaping Tomorrow, says that branches are mostly in the wrong place – consumer traffic has moved elsewhere. Relocate to major retail conurbations is his recommendation.

Telephone banking Most banks now offer, in parallel with the branches, a service using only the telephone as a means of communication. Staff in call centres offer a service for, perhaps, 24 hours per day. In October 2005, HSBC announced that business customers had logged on to their accounts 443 000 times in the previous 12 months between 11.00 p.m. and 6.00 a.m. The busiest period was 11.00 p.m. to midnight. Customers' routine enquiries can be satisfied and more complex services, for example bill paying, can be supported. Here, the names and bank account details for regular suppliers (gas, electricity, telephone and so on) are set up on file and, using special security passwords; a whole banking service can be initiated by the customer, using only the telephone. New accounts, loans and mortgages can be negotiated in the same way, with postal confirmation where necessary. Money can be drawn out by using plastic cards in the parent bank's ATMs. The bank has the advantage of not having the cost of a branch network, and will pay a higher than normal rate of interest on credit balances.

Examples of such systems are:

❏ Germany   Bank 24 (Deutsche Bank)
❏ UK   First Direct (HSBC)
❏ Spain   Open Bank (Banco Santander)
❏ France   Banque Direct (Paribas).

New entrants to banking, for example supermarkets and insurance companies, almost universally base their operations on telephone call centres.

Internet banking Since the middle to late 1990s there has been a growth in the use of the Internet by individuals to access their banks. Initially, special purpose application software and diallers had to be used to provide adequate security, but now the standard Internet browsers are perfectly satisfactory for home banking purposes. Banks have been divided in their approach to Internet banking. Some have set up separately branded operations, distanced from the parent bank, while others have merely added the Internet as a medium for contact, along with their telephone and branch channels. Examples of the separately branded operations are, in the UK, Smile (by Co-operative Bank), Cahoot (by Abbey National Bank) and IF (by HBOS Bank). Again, some new entrants have chosen this route, notably Egg, an Internet banking offshoot of the Prudential Assurance Company. A totally new Internet startup, First-e, was established in 1999, intended to be international, with an initial presence in the UK, Germany, Italy, France and Spain. It failed to be successful and had closed down by 2001. Egg, though heavily loss-making since its founding in 1998, finally broke into profit in the final quarter of 2001. It offers a wide range of deposit and loan accounts, credit cards, insurance and investment products as well as a 'shopping zone', where over 250 retailers have space on the Egg website to proffer their wares (which can, of course, be paid for using the Egg credit card or perhaps with an Egg personal loan!). However, it cannot have been too profitable as Prudential made several unsuccessful efforts to sell Egg but announced in October 2005 that it would keep it anyway and bought the 21% of Egg that it did not own.

France has an on-line banking facility which has its roots in a system called 'Videotex', developed much earlier than the Internet. This is commonplace because the government decided to give a boost to communication links by supplying free 'Minitel' terminals using the television set. One early use was to make telephone directory enquiries, but other information services were soon added. There are 5m Minitel subscribers. The banks supply software allowing balance reporting, enquiry of historical data and transfer of funds to creditors' accounts. More advanced software allows portfolio management and various financial calculations.

Clearing Systems

Clearing involves the transmission, exchange and settlement for payments between banks. There are clearing systems for both *paper* (for example, cheques) and *electronic* clearing. Usually, the central bank is involved to provide for interbank settlement and overall control of the process, but the extent of the involvement differs greatly from country to country.

In the US, the Federal Reserve runs 48 cheque clearing centres. There are also private clearing centres and arrangements made mutually between groups of banks. Some 30% of cheques are cleared internally by the banks on which they were drawn; 35% are cleared by private centres and mutual arrangements and 35% cleared by the Federal Reserve.

For salaries, standing orders, direct debits and supplier payments, data is encoded electronically and sent to an Automated Clearing House (ACH). For example, having processed salaries by computer and printed payslips for the employees, a corporate will send the data over to an ACH. Here, it will be sorted electronically and passed to the relevant employees' banks so that their salaries can be credited. There are 33 ACHs run by the Federal Reserve and a few are privately operated.

All Federal Reserve System Offices are linked for balance transfers between member banks by a system called Fedwire. The New York Clearing Houses Association runs CHIPS, an interbank funds transfer system in New York, and used for large international as opposed to domestic dollar payments.

In France, there are over 100 provincial clearing houses in towns where a branch of the Bank of France is located. If presented within the same catchment area as the bank on which it is drawn, the cheque will usually clear on the second working day after the presentation. Outside the catchment area, the bank will clear on the fifth working day after presentation.

Six banks have their own bilateral clearing arrangements.

Electronic clearing takes place through SIT (Système Interbancaire Télé-compensation). It is run by the Bank of France, which operates nine centres but policy is decided by the Bankers' Association.

In the UK, all clearing has been controlled since 1985 by a body called APACS. The Bank of England provides settlement between the banks resulting from the payment flows between them. APACS runs three main systems:

- ❏ General Cheque Clearing – Cheque and Credit Clearing Company Ltd
- ❏ CHAPS Clearing Company Ltd.
- ❏ BACS Payment Schemes Ltd (BPSL) (now BACSTEL-IP)

CHAPS is a same day interbank clearing system for high value electronic entries in sterling. In January 1999, CHAPS-Euro was added as a parallel system for euro-denominated payments.

BACS is for salaries, standing orders, direct debits and direct credits just like the ACHs in the US. It is by far the largest such operation in the world, handling some 4.6 billion items in 2004. At present this is three day clearing, but will be same day clearing by the end of 2007. BPSL manages the system and a company called Voca Ltd handles all the processing. From January 2006, a new system called BACSTEL-IP, an Internet-based system, replaced BACS – it is more reliable, more secure and faster.

Cross-border clearing is a subject attracting a lot of attention. In September 1990, the European Commission published a paper on cross-border cash and electronic payments. It acknowledged that the lack of a single compatible system would be a drawback in the age of the single market.

A group of European cooperative banks have set up a system called TIPA-NET (Transferts Interbancaires de Paiements Automatisés).

Giro clearing organisations in 14 countries have set up a cross-border transfer system called Eurogiro which started in November 1992. European savings banks have set up their own network called S. Interpay with links in ten countries.

Commerzbank, Société Générale, Credito Italiano and National Westminster have started their own cross-border transfer system called Relay.

Finally, it might be possible to link national ACH systems like CHAPS (UK), SIT (France), SIS (Switzerland), EAF (Germany), etc.

The plethora of independent and incompatible systems does not instil confidence for the future of an efficient system for cross-border payments, and there is already disappointment that, within Europe's new monetary union, cross-border payments in the euro are neither easier nor cheaper. The EU passed a regulation in July 2003 requiring banks to make the same charge for cross-border payments as domestic up to €12 500 in spite of the higher costs. The EU optimistically envisages a single, Europe-wide cross-border transfer system by 2010. Banks have set up a European Payments Council to decide how to do this.

Key Retail Banking Issues

Across all the Western financial markets, the commercial banks face a series of key challenges. They are:

1   Growing competition
2   Cost control
3   Sales of non-banking products
4   Use of Information Technology.

Growing competition   Banks face growing competition from:

❏   Other financial institutions
❏   Retailers
❏   Insurance companies
❏   In-house corporate facilities.

Growing deregulation has meant an increase in competition from *other financial institutions* previously precluded from offering a total banking service. This includes the Savings and Loan Associations in the US; building societies in the UK; savings banks generally; post office banks in some sectors; and mutual funds which also offer savings accounts. The competition for deposits has intensified and we see the banks in Spain and the UK offering interest on credit balances for the first time.

Banks and Savings and Loan Associations in the US are estimated to have 28% of the financial services market – half the figure of 20 years ago.

Retailers are increasingly active. In Germany, the huge mail order group, KarstadtQuelle, is offering a range of financial services, including credit cards. In Italy, Benetton are part of a major financial group, Euromobiliare. In Sweden, the furniture company, Ikea, offers current account facilities. In the UK, Marks and Spencer offer unsecured loans, mutual funds and life insurance. Key supermarkets, like Tesco and Sainsbury's, have offered bank accounts. However, no cheque book facilities are offered, thus avoiding one of the key expenses of retail banking. In the US Wal-Mart Financial Services is now offering money transfer services, money orders, pay cheque cashing and credit cards. It handles one million financial transactions per week. They are also hoping to get FDIC approval to set up a loan company to offer small loans to industrial workers and applying for permission to open a bank in Utah. This latter is strongly opposed by the banking community.

Insurance companies are competing vigorously for savings with schemes which link life assurance with a savings product. These often involve the use of mutual funds to improve the return on the fund. While this is not new, pressure has intensified in recent years. Some are forming banks. The Swedish Trygg Hansa launched a bank in mid-October 1995 and merged with Denmark's second largest bank in 1999. The UK's largest life assurance and investment group, the Prudential Corporation, launched its own bank (which transformed itself into Egg) with loss-making interest rates in late 1998, and within 6 months had 500 000 customers and £5bn in deposits – but losses of £175m! The plan was to sell these customers lots of other financial products. As the loss-leading interest rates were brought into line with the market (though still very competitive), Egg lost some of the 'hot' funds and customers, but it seems to have generated a self-sustaining business from a wide set of product offerings as time has gone by, and finally broke into profit in the last quarter of 2001.

In-house corporate 'banks' are now very common – Ford Motor Credit, Renault Crédit International, ICI Finance, Gemina (the Fiat financial services group), General Electric Financial Services and, in Germany, bank subsidiaries of VW, Audi, BMW and DaimlerChrysler to mention a few. While the largest effect here is usually on the banks' *wholesale* business, many are active in retail finance also. The General Electric subsidiary, for example, is into consumer loans and credit cards as well as leasing, real estate and corporate finance. It has annual revenues in excess of $30 billion and accounts for 40% of the earnings of its parent.

Cost control   Growing competition has made cost control even more important. Increasingly, the banks' annual reports are referring to their success (or lack of it) in cutting the cost/income ratio and increasing the return of capital on equity.

There is room for improvement. US banks' cost/income ratio averages 58%, but it is nearer 70% in France, Germany and Italy. Not surprisingly, return on equity in the US is 16% as against less than 10% in France, Germany and Italy. The UK comes out well with an average of about 25%.

In retail banking, a major cost is the branch network. What we have seen in recent years is rationalisation and branch automation. Rationalisation means dividing branches into those which only deal with corporates, full service branches (offering the complete range of products) and local sub-branches, which are largely points for paying in cash and withdrawing it. 'Branch automation' involves withdrawing paperwork to regional centres and making more of the branch a 'front office' for dealing with customers. Other issues relating to branches were dealt with earlier in this chapter.

The UK is still very wedded to expensive cheques and has not made as much progress with electronic banking as many countries. Things are changing, however, and the current projections of the UK clearing body APACS are shown in Figure 4.1. In addition, in December 2005, the UK banks announced that new systems will in due course cut the time for transfer of direct debits, standing orders and Internet payments to one day instead of three.

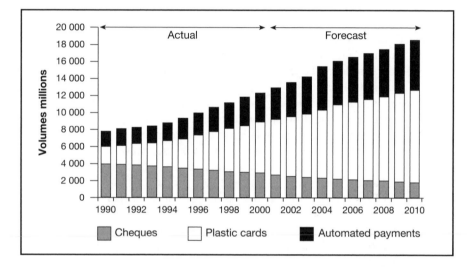

Source: Association for Payment Clearing Services, UK, July 1999.

Figure 4.1   *UK cheque, plastic card and automated transaction volumes, 1990–2010*

To help cut costs, there has been a growing trend of mergers or cooperation with other banks. The list in Appendix 2 to Chapter 2 shows the large number of mergers in recent years. Many of these are very large – Dai Ichi Kangyo, Fuji and IBJ; Bank of Tokyo and Mitsubishi; Swiss Bank Corporation and the Union Bank of Switzerland; Chemical Bank and Chase Manhattan, who later merged with JP Morgan; Bank America and Nationsbank; Citicorp and Travelers Group (100 million accounts worldwide!); Deutsche Bank and Bankers Trust; Banco Santander and BCH; BBVA and Argentaria; Bayerische Vereinsbank and Bayerische Hypo Bank. After a bitter battle with the Bank of Scotland, the Royal Bank of Scotland succeeded in the takeover of the UK's National Westminster Bank. Subsequently, the Bank of Scotland merged with the Halifax Bank, to make HBOS.

As an example of possible savings in costs, the mergers of Chemical, Manny Hanny and Chase resulted in savings of $2.5bn per annum.

Mergers do not, of course, necessarily go well. Wells Fargo, once a highly rated bank, bought First Interstate. Hit by service problems, many customers left and its share price fell heavily although it has now recovered.

In addition to those mergers, we are seeing increasing cooperation. Cooperative banks are arranging for cooperative banks in other countries to offer services to their customers when abroad. A group called 'Unico' links cooperatives in the Netherlands, France, Germany, Finland, Austria, Spain, Italy and Switzerland. Between them, they have 37 000 branches in these countries. In 1990, 15 European savings bank institutions jointly launched three mutual funds, covering money markets, bonds and equities.

Sales of non-banking products   Another way to reduce the costs of branches is to make them more productive by selling more services. Some of these are products like insurance or mutual funds which might not have been regarded as classic banking products at one time. Other activities include acquisition of travel agencies and estate agencies.

If banking is less profitable and costs are rising, then the banks must increase their selling and marketing skills and promote a wider range of offerings than in the past. Part of the aim of branch automation is to use terminals to give access to all the information needed on the full range of the bank's services. For example, TSB have installed computer terminals with coloured screens which give the details and advantages of all the bank products and will even produce an application form.

Banks now look at their customer base as being divided into social sectors, each with their own needs:

❑ Pre-teens – can we get them used to the bank's brand with piggy bank money boxes?
❑ Teenagers – high spending. Banks offer savings accounts, ATM cards and merchandise discounts.
❑ Young marrieds – no children yet, high joint incomes but a change to come as children arrive.
❑ High net worth – young professionals with high incomes – worth a special approach.
❑ Over 50s – children have now grown up, wives are back at work, houses paid for – but retirement looms!
❑ Retired people – often with high incomes from personal pension plans and savings. This group has special needs.

The above breakdown has preoccupied banks in many countries, resulting in the design of new bank accounts and mail order marketing which was previously associated with consumer products.

Backing up this effort are large customer databases on computer containing not just accounting information but background details to enable the bank to sell new services, either now or later. In retail banking, 'cross-selling' has become the key phrase of the moment.

One product of obvious relevance is insurance – life assurance, endowment policies, assurance products backing mortgages, householder policies, building policies, sickness cover and so on. We are seeing three major trends here. One is full mergers with insurance companies; another is closer cooperation in cross-selling each other's products; and a third is banks setting up full insurance subsidiaries.

In the Netherlands, the ING group merged with NMB-Postbank and later bought BBL and Baring Bros; Trygg Baltica has merged with Unidanmark and SE Banken; Halifax bought Clerical and Medical; Kredietbank/Cera merged with ABB Insurance.

Cooperation includes arrangements for cross-selling between the Swiss Bank Corporation and Zurich Insurance; Dresdner Bank and Allianz; Banco Popular and Allianz; BNP and the French insurer UAP; Banco Santander and Metropolitan Life.

Banks that have set up full insurance subsidiaries include Lloyds TSB, National Westminster, Deutsche, Barclays, Crédit Lyonnais, Banco Bilbao-Vizcaya, Monte dei Paschi di Siena and Crédit Agricole. Crédit Agricole's subsidiary, Predica, has moved into France's top three insurance companies since its formation in 1987.

Regarding the cooperative ventures, one element of doubt may be creeping in. The evidence suggests that the banks are much more successful at selling insurance products than the insurance companies are at selling banking services! These links between banks and insurance have led to much use of the French phrase 'Bancassurance' and the German phrase 'Allfinanz'. Some even suggest that 'Bancassurance' is on the decline, pointing to Citigroup selling of Travelers. On the other hand, HBOS interim results for 2005 noted 'Bancassurance up 17%'!

The growing effort to sell mutual funds, insurance, stocks, shares and other products has led to a rise in fee and commission income as opposed to interest. The desire to improve profits and control costs has also led to the banks increasingly charging fees for such things as arranging loans/overdrafts, an interview with the bank manager, sending an extra copy of a statement and so on.

Use of Information Technology   Modern banking is unthinkable without the use of Information Technology (IT). Without it, the numbers needing to be employed in banking would have made the expansion of the last 30 years quite impossible. Many of the developments we have discussed above have IT at their heart. Branch automation, new account databases, telephone and home banking, EFT-POS, automated electronic clearing – all are essential to the banks' new strategies and all involve a large investment. Looking at the emerging markets in Central and Eastern Europe and the former Soviet Union, an enormous expenditure on computers and communications infrastructures is required as an essential first step in setting up modern banking systems. As John Reed, Chairman of Citicorp, has put it, 'money is information on the move'.

One area with IT at its heart is, of course, the Internet. Early hopes (by some) for a massive migration to the Internet, with commensurate low costs, appear to be misplaced. It looks more likely that the Internet will take its place as an important delivery method alongside branches and call centres as part of a multi channel strategy for most banks. This would seem to give an advantage to the larger, established banks, who have the financial resources and spread of customers to justify the expenditure in the different systems.

A Booz Allen Hamilton survey of comparative transaction costs in the US has estimated the following figures:

> PC banking   13¢
> Telephone   26¢
> Branch $1.08

The UK building societies have produced similar estimates for the UK:

> Internet   8p
> Telephone   35p
> Branch   70p

Could the threat be exaggerated?   Internet banking will come and may be offered by non-banks (for example, computer and telecommunications companies), but progress is slow. For the present, retail banking still has stability and profitability. Other problems for commercial banks lie in the realm of *wholesale banking*, and that is our next topic.

WHOLESALE BANKING

Wholesale banking includes a bank's wholesale lending, which will be discussed now, and other activities which will be covered in later chapters: money markets, Chapter 6; foreign exchange, Chapter 8; trade finance, Chapter 9.

BANK LENDING

We can begin by breaking bank lending down into uncommitted facilities and committed facilities.

Uncommitted Facilities

Here there is little formal documentation and no network of various fees to be paid to the bank for setting up the facility. The bank agrees to lend money, usually on a short-term basis, but is not committed to renew the loan. The facilities are typically on a 'revolving' basis, that is, the client can repay the loan and then redraw money. There are three types:

Overdrafts   This is a great UK favourite with smaller firms. The client is allowed to overdraw up to a given maximum figure. Interest is charged daily on the overdrawn balance, most typically at bank base rates (not LIBOR, see below) plus a given margin. The arrangement may be for, say, six months. The bank is not bound to renew the agreement but may well do so. There is no formal arrangement for 'paying back' as there would be with a normal loan. In addition, the overdraft is legally repayable on demand (if necessary).

Lines of credit   Here the bank agrees to allow the client to borrow up to a maximum sum for periods such as a month, three months or six months. The rate of interest will be related to the interbank rate. The client can then repay and reborrow if required.

Bankers' acceptances   Here the bank agrees to accept bills of exchange up to a maximum figure – 'acceptance credits'. The bank accepts a bill and may also discount it, or the client may discount it with another bank. If the bill is, say, 1 month, the client is expected to repay but may do so by means of discounting another bill. If the bank discounts the bill, it may keep it on its books or itself sell it in the discount market. The best bills are bank or eligible bills. These bills:

(a) Are recognised as top quality by the central bank.
(b) Must represent a genuine trade transaction and one of a type not excluded, for example, property and insurance.

Eligible bills are eligible for sale to the central bank in its role of 'lender of last resort'. As a result, they are highly liquid.

There are thus bills signed by a bank *not* on the central bank list and these are 'ineligible bank bills'. There are also bills signed by the trader and, therefore, 'trade bills'. However, the trader may be more creditworthy than some banks on the central bank's list! Nevertheless, the central bank still won't rediscount them.

The above three types of facility are not committed. They are also usually 'self-liquidating'. For example, a bill matures in one month and is repaid. The loan is often to support the working capital required for debtors and/or stocks. A swimsuit manufacturer begins producing well before the season – stocks are built up and wages must be paid. As the swimsuits are sold, cash flows in and loans can be repaid.

Committed Facilities

The loan facilities here are typically for one year or more. The bank is committed to lend, there are formal loan agreements and a structure of fees. There are three main types and one special case – Project Finance.

Term loans   The term loan is typically up to five years but may be up to seven. The loan is amortised over the period, that is, the borrower pays back in stages, although there may be an initial 'grace' period. Sometimes the loan is payable in full at the end of the period – this is 'bullet' repayment. The interest is floating rate, linked to the interbank rate. The money borrowed cannot be relent when part is repaid.

Standby credit   Here, the loan can be drawn down in stages or tranches without losing the availability of the undrawn section. Once repaid, however, the money cannot be reborrowed. It tends to be much shorter-term than a term loan and may support other anticipated borrowings, for example, commercial paper. The standby credit may not even be drawn if the 'normal' borrowing method is successful.

The programme will be broken down into the total maximum commitment, the used amount and the unused. Thus, a $200m programme can be drawn down in tranches but repayments cannot be reborrowed. The banker's schedule as time goes by might be as shown in Table 4.2.

Table 4.2   *Drawing banker's commitment down in tranches*

		Total commitment $m	Used $m	Unused $m
1/1	Agreement	200	–	200
2/1	Borrows $75m	200	75	125
31/1	Borrows $25m	200	100	100
12/2	Repays $50m	200	100	100
1/5	Borrows $100m	200	200	–
1/7	Repays $100m	200	200	–
1/10	Repays $50m	200	200	–
1/1	Expiry	–	–	–

Note: Interest is floating rate linked to the interbank rate – LIBOR, EURIBOR, – or, in the US, 'Prime Rate'.

Revolving credit   Here, not only can the loan be drawn in tranches but, if repayments are made, the borrower can repay up to the limit: that is, the funds can be reused. Thus, the commitment is said to 'revolve' – the borrower can continue to request loans provided the committed total is not exceeded. The client gives the bank the appropriate notice and then reborrows within the terms of the agreement. If the amount were $200m, we can see the difference between this and the standby credit when we study a similar loan/repayment schedule in Table 4.3.

Generally these loans are unsecured. If bankers take security, it could well be one of the following: property, accounts receivable, plant/equipment, bonds/shares, bills of lading, inventories.

If the money is raised in the London market, the loans are floating rate 'linked to LIBOR' – but what is LIBOR (London Interbank Offered Rate)? To begin with, LIBOR fluctuates throughout the day. For purposes of loan agreements, LIBOR is that stated by the reference bank(s) at 11.00 a.m. If the loan is bilateral, it may simply be the lending bank's own LIBOR at 11.00 a.m. on the quarterly or six monthly day on which the loan is 'rolled over' at a new rate of interest. If it is a syndicated loan, three 'reference' banks may be nominated and LIBOR is the average of the three. It may also be quoted as the 'BBA', or colloquially the 'screen rate'. The British Bankers' Association list 16 reference banks for major currencies, such as dollar, euro and sterling. Reuters omits the four highest and four lowest of the 16 quoted rates and averages the remaining eight. Reuters disseminates this on its dealing screens at 11.00 a.m. each day – hence the reference to the 'screen' rate. LIBOR, of course may be sterling, dollar, yen, or any other currency. If the currency is the euro it is EUROLIBOR, not to be confused with EURIBOR, which is the interbank market in euros of the twelve countries of the monetary union.

Table 4.3 *Loan/repayment schedule*

		Total commitment $m	Used $m	Unused $m
1/1	Agreement	200	—	200
2/1	Borrows $75m	200	75	125
31/1	Borrows $25m	200	100	100
12/2	Repays $50m	200	50	150
1/5	Borrows $100m	200	150	50
1/7	Repays $100m	200	50	150
1/9	Borrows $75m	200	125	75
1/10	Repays $100m	200	25	175

Note: Interest is floating rate linked to the interbank rate.

A term often used in the loan documentation for standby and revolving credit is 'swingline facility'. Sometimes the borrower is due to repay investors in, say, dollars on a particular day and discovers late in the day that they cannot. Swingline is a guarantee of same day dollars in New York to meet this emergency need. (It may not be dollars, but dollars seem to be common.) One banker has described this as 'belt and braces' and reassuring to credit ratings organisations looking at an issuer's loan facilities.

As the bank commits to lend, whether the user draws it all or not and as there is a formal agreement, there are *fees* involved.

There will be a *front end* or *facility fee* for setting up the arrangement. There will also be a *commitment* fee. For example, a bank supports a three year standby credit facility for $50m which is never used. The bank has committed some of its loan capacity and used up capital under capital ratio rules. As a result, commitment fees are often charged on the undrawn amount. They are typically 50% of the lending margin. The *margin* is the spread over LIBOR charged on the drawn amount itself, for example, LIBOR + 50 basis points, or bp. (A basis point = $\frac{1}{100}$% or 0.01%.)

There are variations for commitment fees by which they may be charged on the whole facility or on the drawn amount *and* the undrawn amount (but at different rates). A recent loan to the Saudi European Petrochemicals Corporation referred to 25 basis points on drawn balances and 12.5 basis points on undrawn balances.

As we have seen in Chapter 3, the central bank may make all banks deposit some of their eligible liabilities with the bank and pays them no interest. As bankers relend their deposits, they regard this as a cost of lending and will seek to recoup this.

Project finance   This is simply a special case of a term loan. It is 'special' in that the projects are typically of much longer duration than the conventional term loan, and usually much more complex to structure. They are large-scale exploration or construction projects (for example, Eurotunnel, the bridge over the Bosphorus and similar projects) and require complex and time consuming loan arrangements. In particular, a guarantee from a government or parent body may not be available (the banks' recourse is to the flow of funds from the project, called 'limited recourse financing') in which case the banks will want to see a full set of revenue projections to ensure that debt repayments can be met. They may also wish to see firm contracts for the construction project itself and (if possible) firm contracts for the sale of the completed service.

Recent projects include a ten year $400m facility for Nesté Petroleum, a wholly owned subsidiary of a Finnish state-owned oil company; a $1.1 billion facility for oil exploration for BP Norway; $600 million for North Sea oil developments for Agip (UK), part of the Italian state-owned oil group, and the Teesside Power Station project – £795 million with the loan to continue until 2008.

In the case of Nesté, while there is no explicit guarantee, there is a tacit understanding that the parent will support the subsidiary. The Agip loan will be supported by the parent for two years but revert to limited recourse thereafter.

Teesside Power is a huge gas power station being constructed at Wilton, Teesside. Finance was first secured from 14 underwriters and then went out to syndication. The margin over LIBOR is 125 bp up to completion of the station, 112.5 bp after that up to eight years and 137 bp for the remaining years. However, these margins may be reduced, depending upon hitting performance targets. Semi-annual loan repayments began in April 1994. This is one of the largest and most involved limited recourse projects.

Syndicated Facilities

Syndicated loans arise because a bank does not wish to take on the whole amount of the loan. The task of syndication is also made easier by the fact that there are many banks that will be happy to take on some of the loan exposure at a second stage – banks that may not have a close relationship with major corporates or may not have the resources to compete at the primary stage.

Syndicated loans (sometimes involving as many as 100 banks) were common in the 1970s, when we saw 'petro-dollars' recycled in loans to sovereign borrowers and multinationals. This led to the LDC debt crisis, following Mexico's default in August 1982 (see Chapter 6). The volumes of large international syndicated loans fell somewhat for several years but recovered later. Many banks found that weakened balance sheets and capital ratio constraints made further loan expansion difficult. One result was the rise to popularity after 1982 of new types of syndicated facility – NIFs and RUFs.

NIFs and RUFs The 1980s became the era of the acronym – NIFs and RUFs, and later MOFs and many others. It was also a time of great competition, especially from Japanese banks. In 1986, the then chairman of Barclays accused the Japanese of 'dumping money', just as people had accused them of dumping goods in the 1920s and 1930s. NIF is 'Note Issuance Facility' and RUF is 'Revolving Underwriting Facility' (ask six bankers what the difference is and you will get six different answers!).

This was also a time in which we saw an increasing use of tender panels of banks, bidding competitively for loan business or bankers' acceptances. For example, a corporate which used bill finance frequently would periodically approach a tender panel to accept bills. This gave us yet another acronym – the RAFT, 'Revolving Acceptance Facility by Tender'.

NIFs and RUFs were facilities by which banks agreed to support note issues by corporates to raise money. The notes were usually called 'Euronotes' and were typically one, three and six months. In effect, they were a sort of short-term eurobond. On a revolving basis, the arranging bank would approach a tender panel to buy the client's notes. In the event that the notes could not be sold at or below a given lending rate, a further panel of underwriting banks stood by to lend the money. The facility was thus underwritten. It was, therefore, a mixture of commercial and investment banking techniques. Fees could be earned and US commercial banks could join in without contravening the 1933 Glass-Steagall Act. During the period 1982–86, NIFs, RUFs and Euronotes were all the rage.

Today, the formal one, three and six month Euronote has disappeared, its modern equivalent being either Eurocommercial paper or medium-term notes. (The Bank of England uses Euronotes as a generic term for short-term Euro paper, whether ECDs or ECP.)

MOFs From 1986–87, a more flexible facility – the MOF – appeared. This is 'Multiple Option Facility'. Instead of committing the underwriting banks to support one type of borrowing only (for example, Euronotes), the banks' commitment is to a range of possibilities. The 'multiple options' might be:

❏ Bank loan (multi-currency)
❏ Acceptances
❏ Commercial paper – domestic
❏ Eurocommercial paper.

On a revolving basis, the arranging bank would approach a tender panel of banks for prices for either a bank loan or banker's acceptance to meet the client's need for, say, $10m for three months. At the same time, the arranging bank would contact commercial paper dealers to check rates for the same deal. The bank would then report back to the client and use the most attractive option. However, if the best option was above a given borrowing rate, a panel of underwriting banks would agree either to lend the money or sign acceptances at the agreed figure. At first this seemed to be the sort of flexible facility that the market needed and MOFs were all the rage for several years. Later, problems emerged.

To begin with, bank supervisors saw this as a clear off-balance sheet risk and demanded capital cover. Suppose, for example, that the rate at which the underwriting panel would guarantee to lend was LIBOR + 50 bp. The supervisors argued that if the market demanded a higher figure, this might suggest that the client was less creditworthy. The underwriting panel was forced to lend to a client whose credit quality was declining. The Bank of England decided that 50% of the unused capacity must be treated as if the money had actually been lent, for capital ratio purposes. The Bundesbank took a less harsh view. Later, the rules were harmonised through the Basel agreement. The first disadvantage, therefore, was that the banks had to provide capital to back MOFs, although initially they hadn't.

The recession produced other problems. To begin with, the credit quality of many clients did indeed deteriorate, leaving the underwriting banks 'holding the baby'. Secondly, due to poor trading, many clients broke the loan covenants (see later). If covenants are broken, the whole agreement can be renegotiated but *all* the banks must agree the revised terms. Sometimes, one or two banks with the smallest commitment might not agree. In a famous incident in 1989, Laura Ashley was nearly pushed into liquidation in these circumstances.

Finally, the market became less competitive – a lenders' not a borrowers' market. In part, this was due to the departure of the Japanese. The stock market in Tokyo collapsed in January 1990 and property values fell. The Japanese drew in their horns. In 1989, they accounted for 37% of all international bank lending in foreign currencies (BIS figures). In 2005, the figure was 8.7%. The departure of the Japanese, capital ratio constraints and the recession now put the banks into the driving seat. They were no longer willing to be pushed into tender panels and unattractive deals. In London, margins over LIBOR widened as a consequence. Corporates, too, saw the problems. Beating down the banks to tight margins was one thing. Expecting them to be sympathetic when the going got rough was quite another. There was much talk of 'relationship banking' – of this more later. The OECD, in its *Financial Market Trends* for June 1992, commented on the change in the syndicated credit market and the fall in the number of syndicated facilities: 'uncertainties about the creditworthiness of many potential borrowers added to the caution of financial institutions engaged in a process of profit enhancement and asset quality consolidation'.

With the end of the recession in the West, banks were flush with cash again in 1995 and, although the MOF concept had largely disappeared, margins on loans fell again. Then, the 1997/98 global crises led to margins rising yet again! For example, PowerGen of the UK raised a £2.4bn five year loan in mid 1998 to purchase East Midlands Electricity at a rate of 50 bp over LIBOR. However, its previous syndicated loan had been at 22½ bp over LIBOR. Equally, the bid for Inter-Continental Hotels by Bass was funded by a $3bn syndicated loan at a range of margins over LIBOR (depending on the loan term). The range was 22½ bp to 27½ bp; its previous loan – a margin of 15 bp.

Recent years have seen a large rise in syndicated loans. According to figures from Dealogic, a data provider, the global syndicated loans rose 22.7% to $3207 billion (£1924 billion) in 2005. Many of them arose from refinancing of existing facilities.

To make things more flexible, the banks have organised a formal secondary market in which loan commitments may be sold off to other banks. Bank loans are frequently traded in the US, but until recently Europe was well behind. This particularly applies to what is called 'distressed debt'.

A 'Loan Market Association' was set up in London by seven banks in December 1996. It now has 54 banks as full members.

ICI's $8.5bn syndicated loan in 1997 was a watershed, as $1bn was traded within 6 months.

A code of conduct was issued for trading distressed debt in March 1999. This category includes, for example, EuroDisneyland and Eurotunnel. The risky loan has become just another product!

Syndicated loans are usually more flexible than bond issues. The money can be drawn down as needed, and arrangements may be made more quickly. The latter can be important in takeover bid situations.

Terminology The facilities we mentioned earlier – term loans, standby credits and revolving credits – are usually syndicated. This leads to a variety of terms being used:

1 *Arranger/Lead manager* Initially, the 'arranging bank' or 'lead manager' deals with the client and discusses the probable terms on which a loan can be arranged. They advise the borrower on the loan structure, maturity and covenants. The arranger will coordinate the participation of other lenders. It may be, however, that a 'book-runner' is appointed. Their job is to do the 'leg work' of putting a syndicate together. Once the syndicate is together, the book-runner's role is finished. One way or another, once initial discussions with the client are concluded, an invitation is issued to co-managers to participate.

2 *Co-managers* Along with the arranging bank, they agree to underwrite the loan so that the client is now guaranteed the funds. Each co-manager takes a share – for example, $200m.

3 *Participating banks* They now join the syndicate. A co-manager will invite, perhaps, four participating banks to take, say, $25m of the loan each.

4 *The agent* The role of the bank acting as the agent bank is critically important and a special fee is earned. The agency is an administrative role. The agent collects the loan from each participant and passes it to the borrower. Equally, the borrower payments as made are passed to the syndicate in agreed shares. The agent notifies the borrower of the new interest rate related to the interbank rate every three or six months as agreed. The agent is responsible for the documentation and will notify both borrower and lender of all information relevant to the loan agreement. There is no credit risk but there is still risk. If the agent makes a mistake that loses the syndicate members money, they will be responsible for making this good.

As in the case of a bilateral loan, there will be various fees:

1 *Facility or front end fee* For agreeing to the arrangement, there will be a front end or facility fee for all involved. This may be a flat fee or a percentage of the money. The arranging bank will also take an extra fee for their special role. This is called a *praecipium*.

2 *Underwriting fees* These are paid to the group of underwriting banks which took on the initial commitment prior to extending the syndicate. There is a definite risk. In the case of the management buyout of Magnet Joinery, for example, a small group of lead banks led by Bankers Trust found themselves alone as the potential syndicate members withdrew their support, sensing that the risk was unacceptable – very wisely as it happened!

3 *Agent's fee* This is paid to the agent bank for the role they play, which was described earlier.

4 *Commitment fee* This was mentioned before in the case of bilateral loans. It is a payment measured in basis points for the commitment to lend which needs to be backed by capital. As we have seen, it may be based on the whole loan, the drawn section, or the undrawn section (or a mixture). Usually the fee is on the undrawn section and typically 50% of the margin (see 5 below).

5 *Loan margin* This is the actual margin over the interbank rate charged for the borrowed money, for example, LIBOR + 50 bp. It may not be a constant figure but related to loan tranches taken by the syndicate.

While commitment fees are usually 50% of the margin, any variation is possible. For example, the German Thyssen Group arranged a $1.2 billion seven year revolving credit facility. There was a front end fee of eight basis points and the margin over LIBOR varies according to how much of the facility is used. For example, ten basis points if less than 33% of the loan but 20 basis points if more than 66% is used.

The NIFs, RUFs and MOFs were all forms of revolving credit. In general, the term loan, standby credit, revolving credit and project finance are likely to involve syndicates, unless they are of modest size.

The fierce competitive battles of the 1980s, however, led to much talk of 'relationship banking' and bilateral agreements.

Relationship banking   The inference here is that the corporate encourages a close relationship with a small number of banks and may negotiate bilaterally.

Bilateral agreements, however, can really only be used by corporates with skilled treasury departments with large resources, unless the number of banks is very small. The work done by the agency bank in policing the loan should not be underestimated. A thirty bank syndicate means, for the corporate, one line of communication – the agent bank, which does the rest. Thirty bilateral agreements mean thirty lines of communication – one with each bank.

The Loan Agreement

If the loan is syndicated, there will be one loan agreement and one set of terms but the amount owed to each borrower is a separate debt.

The loan agreement will typically have four sections:

1   *Introduction*   This will cover the amount of the loan and its purpose, conditions of drawdown and particulars of the participating banks.
2   *Facilities*   The loan may be drawn down in separate tranches with different terms on interest and repayment. The procedures for drawing down will be covered.
3   *Payment*   This covers the interest calculations, calculation of the interbank rate, repayment arrangements, fees, or any similar charges.
4   *Provisions*   To protect the bank there will be covenants, events of default, procedures if basic circumstances change.

The final documentation is sent to the agent bank prior to drawing the money. The agent must ensure that the documentation embodies that which was agreed.

Covenants   These are designed to protect the bank if the 'health' of the borrower changes. If covenants are breached, the banks' commitment will cease. The loan will have to be rescheduled. The usual covenants are:

❏   *Interest cover*   This is the relationship between profit (before tax and interest) and interest. This is to ensure that there is a comfortable margin over the loan interest. If there is not, how can the borrower repay the principal? Sometimes cash flow may be used instead of profit. After all, profit is not cash!
❏   *Net worth*   Suppose all assets were sold and liabilities paid, what is left? Normally, this should be the figure of share capital and reserves ± current

profit/loss, minus goodwill, tax and dividends to be paid. The agreement stipulates a minimum net worth.

❑ *Total borrowing*   This will be limited and must cover hire purchase, finance leases and 'puttable' capital instruments (see Chapter 6).

❑ *Gearing*   Long-term debt to capital as defined in net worth above – a maximum ratio will be stated.

❑ *Current ratio*   A minimum figure will be given for the ratio of current assets to current liabilities – a measure of liquidity.

Events of default   This is a list of circumstances in which the loan will be regarded as being in default, for example, insolvency, change of ownership or similar circumstances. A cross-default clause is important. This means that defaults on other loans or bonds will cause this loan to be in default also.

Negative pledge   Here the client undertakes not to offer security against a loan from any other party.

Assignment   One of the syndicate banks may assign part of its loan commitment to another bank. This cannot be done without the borrower's consent but the loan agreement usually says that 'such consent may not be unreasonably withheld'. However, there may be an initial delay in selling off any of the loan.

A *sub-participation* simply means that part of a syndicate bank's loan allotment will be lent to them by another bank and interest payments passed on to this bank. The loan agreement with the client is not affected.

With a *transfer* or *assignment*, the loan documentation changes, the borrower is aware of the change and the assignee is now legally the lender for this portion. Borrowers may worry here about not having a close relationship with the assignee if they hit trouble later.

Why sell part of the loan anyway? Capital ratio rules may make new lending difficult. A transfer would free part of the loan to be lent elsewhere, possibly more profitably. Alternatively, in order to improve capital ratio, the money may not be relent. If capital is no problem, the money may simply be released to take advantage of a more profitable opportunity. With a participation, we may be able to take, say, LIBOR + 22 bp from the client and pass on LIBOR + 20 bp, 'skimming' a little profit.

In the UK, sub-participation and assignment are subject to detailed regulations – BSD 1989/1, 'Loan Transfers and Documentation'.

Wholesale Banking Issues

The key problem for commercial banks is that corporate lending is increasingly unrewarding and becoming a shrinking market. Competition has forced loan charges down to levels which are scarcely profitable. The growth of international capital markets is such that bond and equity issues over the last ten years have increased their share at the expense of bank loans. The position has been exacerbated by the arrival of the euro. A single market for corporate bonds denominated in the euro for twelve countries has hastened the substitution of bond issues for corporate loans in mainland Europe, which has so far been a market where bank loans have traditionally been a more popular source of finance than bond issues.

One consequence of this has been a move to riskier but potentially more profitable loans. There are far more loans to either non-investment grade corporates or to hedge funds and private equity funds (see Chapter 8) which themselves are taking large risks. Indeed, a survey by Close Bros Corporate Finance in October 2005 accused the banks of encouraging private equity groups to take on too much debt! Corporate debt generally is increasing. Attracted by low interest rates, corporates are borrowing to buy back equity. Another consequence of this pressure on profit from lending is to take high quality but low margin loans off the balance sheet and sell them as securities – a process we explain in Chapter 6.

A final consequence is for commercial banks to seek salvation by buying investment banks – Deutsche Bank and Bankers Trust; Swiss Bank Corporation and Warburg/Dillon Read; ING and Barings. These moves have not always met with success. Both Barclays and National Westminster Bank in the UK lost a great deal of money through their investment banking subsidiaries, and made heavy cuts in their involvement. But Barclays narrowed their investment banking down to the debt markets with Barclays Capital. This has been extremely successful. Barclays results for 2005 showed Barclays Capital making 24.6% of total bank profit whilst retail earnings were relatively flat – an exception perhaps. Commercial banking and investment banking are cultures that are very different, and merging them causes severe problems. The belief seems to be that the bank should offer clients the full range of services, but do clients really care? Clients frequently use one bank for bond issues and another for corporate loans, and fail to see any particular disadvantage.

SUMMARY

Commercial banks are in the classic business of accepting deposits and making loans. The business is both retail (the general public, shops, very small businesses) and wholesale (other banks, corporates and institutions).

Retail banking covers current accounts, cheque facilities, savings accounts, credit cards and loan facilities like overdrafts, personal loans and mortgages. Increasingly, Internet developments are leading to the spread of home banking.

Clearing of payments may involve cheques or electronic payment systems. Cheques are expensive and banks are trying to reduce their use through Internet banking and the use of debit cards.

Key issues in retail banking today are the growing competition, control of costs, sales of non-banking products and the use of Information Technology. In particular, growing links between banks and insurance companies have led to the word *bancassurance*.

Wholesale banking covers bank lending to larger entities than those met in retail banking and activities described in other chapters – money markets, foreign exchange and finance for trade.

Loans may be uncommitted or committed.

Uncommitted facilities include overdrafts, lines of credit and bankers' acceptances.

Committed facilities include term loans, standby credit, revolving credit and project finance.

Syndicated loans are common for large value domestic and cross-border business. There are arranging banks, co-managers, participating banks and agent banks.

Various fees are involved – facility or front end fee, underwriting fees, agents fees and commitment fees. Finally, there is the loan margin.

The loan agreement covers the amount of the loan, its purpose, draw down facilities, interest calculations and provisions.

Among the provisions will be covenants. These are designed to protect the bank if the financial position of the borrower worsens. They include interest cover, net worth, total borrowing, gearing and current ratio.

Other provisions cover events of default. There will also be a negative pledge – the client undertakes not to offer security against a loan from another party.

A bank may assign or transfer part of the loan to another bank or it may be a less formal sub-participation.

Falling profit margins on corporate loans have led many commercial banks into riskier lending. Another reaction has been to spread the range of services by moving into investment banking.

5 Investment Banking

INTRODUCTION

We should, perhaps, recognise at the outset that 'commercial' and 'investment' banking do not exist in separate compartments. There are activities which overlap and are carried out by both types of bank, for example, accepting and discounting bills of exchange, foreign exchange and some aspects of trade finance. Nevertheless, there are certain activities which would be regarded as clear 'investment' banking (for example, underwriting share issues) and we shall discuss these in this chapter as well as those which involve a certain amount of overlap.

(The term 'merchant bank' has historically been the UK term for investment bank, but it has a far narrower meaning in the US.)

INVESTMENT BANKING

The range of activities of investment or merchant banks can be summarised as follows:

- ❏ Accepting
- ❏ Corporate finance
- ❏ Securities trading
- ❏ Investment management
- ❏ Loan arrangement
- ❏ Foreign exchange.

Accepting

Although commercial banks accept bills of exchange nowadays, it is a very historic activity for investment banks. Chapter 2 mentioned the Medici bankers helping a Venetian firm to trade with one in London using a bill of exchange in 1463. During the industrial revolution in the UK, enquiries were received from firms all over the world. The role of the British (and Dutch) merchant banks in backing this trade with bills of exchange was of crucial importance. Indeed, until December 1987, the club of top UK merchant banks was called 'The Accepting Houses Committee'.

While bills of exchange can be and are used in connection with inland business, their main use is for export/import business. An exporter sells goods for $100 000 to an importer. Their arrangement is that the goods will be paid for in three months, say, on 2 February 2007. The exporter makes out the bill of exchange and sends it to the importer to sign. Its effective message is shown in Figure 5.1.

November 2 2006

You owe me $100,000 for goods received. Please pay on 2 February 2007

Signed: A. N. Exporter

Yes, I agree.

Signed: A. N. Importer

Figure 5.1   *Skeleton bill of exchange*

As you may well imagine, the actual document is rather more formal than this! Nevertheless, it expresses the basic idea. Notice that the *exporter* makes out the bill, that is, *draws* the bill. (There are similar documents used in international trade called *promissory notes*. Here, the *importer* makes out the document and the exporter has less control over the wording.)

The importer now has three months to put the goods to work before paying. The exporter has an internationally acceptable form of debt. True, he has allowed the importer three months to pay (not necessary but very common), but his alternative choice might have been to send an invoice, optimistically headed by the words 'Payment Terms – 30 days', with no real assurance that the money will be paid on time.

What if the exporter cannot wait three months but needs the money earlier to fund cash flow? The exporter can visit their bank for a loan, armed with a heap of bills proving that cash is on the way. Alternatively, the exporter can sell the bill to a bank. The bank is being asked to put up the money now and to collect it from the importer in three months. As the bank is lending $100 000 for three months, they are not going to give the exporter all $100 000 but some lower sum reflecting risk and the cost of money – say, $97 000. The bill is sold at a discount and this process is thus called *discounting the bill*.

Let's look at the process in diagrammatic form (Figure 5.2).

The problem is that the bank may be unsure of the credit status of the trader and unwilling to discount the bill. As a result, the practice grew of asking the trader to find a merchant bank to sign the bill in their place. If, in the 19th century, the bill was signed by Baring Bros, Rothschild's or Bank Mees, the bank would have no hesitation in discounting the bill. Naturally, a fee was charged for this service, which is *accepting* the bill. (Whoever signs the bill, promising to pay, is accepting the bill. When people talk of 'acceptances', however, they usually refer to a bank's signature.) In effect, the bank is giving the bill its own credit status and not that of the trader. Hence its importance in the industrial revolution. (The large number of bills in existence in 1890 whose acceptor was Baring Bros led the Bank of England to rescue it that year after unwise investments in Latin America. In 1995, however, there was no second rescue!)

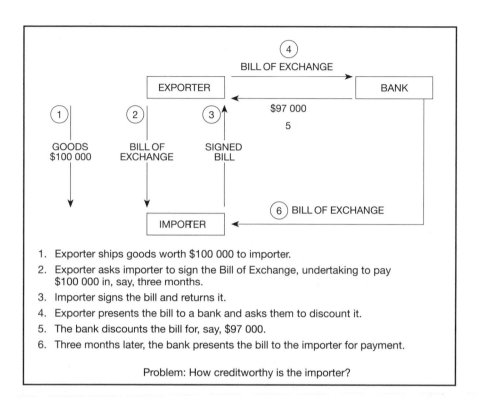

1. Exporter ships goods worth $100 000 to importer.
2. Exporter asks importer to sign the Bill of Exchange, undertaking to pay $100 000 in, say, three months.
3. Importer signs the bill and returns it.
4. Exporter presents the bill to a bank and asks them to discount it.
5. The bank discounts the bill for, say, $97 000.
6. Three months later, the bank presents the bill to the importer for payment.

Problem: How creditworthy is the importer?

Figure 5.2 *The Bill of Exchange: I*

We can find Josiah Wedgewood writing to an Italian customer in 1769,

My foreign correspondents name me a good house, generally in London, to accept my draft for the amount of the goods.

or Boulton and Watt in 1795,

We undertake no foreign orders without a guarantee being engineers not merchants.
(Quoted in Chapman, *The Rise of Merchant Banking*, Allen & Unwin, 1984)

Our previous diagram is now altered a little (see Figure 5.3).

Today, the whole procedure for trade finance is tied up by arrangements between the importer's bank and the exporter's bank. Usually, a documentary letter of credit is involved. We shall discuss this in Chapter 10.

1. Exporter ships goods worth $100 000 to importer.
2. Exporter asks a bank to 'accept' the bill, undertaking to pay $100 000 in three months.
3. The bank accepts the bill and returns it.
4. Exporter presents the bill to a bank and asks them to discount it.
5. The bank discounts the bill for $97 000.
6. Three months later, the bank presents the bill to the accepting bank for payment of $100 000. The latter will recoup this from the importer, or the importer's bank.

N.B.   A bill signed by a trader is a Trade Bill.
        A bill accepted by a bank recognised for this purpose by the Central Bank is a *Bank Bill* or *Eligible Bill*.
        The Central Bank will itself discount the bill as part of its 'lender of last resort' role.

Figure 5.3   *The Bill of Exchange: II*

So far, we have discussed the bill in the context of an explicit trade transaction. The market in bankers' acceptances has reached a new level of sophistication today, especially in the London market. Major firms of good credit quality will ask their bank (whether investment or commercial) to accept a bill promising to pay a given sum at a future period of time. The corporate now discounts the bill in the local discount market as a way of borrowing money for trade in general rather than for an explicit transaction. Indeed, in London, firms like Harrods or Marks and Spencer will do this even though they are not selling on credit at all but retailers receiving cash!

Commercial banks are very involved with accepting bills and this is one reason why the UK's 'Accepting Houses Committee' disbanded in 1987. The committee would not include either commercial banks or foreign banks. This was seen to be completely out of date. In any case, accepting had ceased to be a dominant role for UK merchant banks.

Bills of Exchange are used extensively in the UK, quite widely on the continent of Europe generally and very little in the US. They are generally used for exports to the Near and Far East, the Indian continent, Australia and New Zealand.

Corporate Finance

Corporate Finance is likely to be a department of major importance in any investment bank. This department will manage:

❏ New issues – equities/bonds
❏ Rights issues
❏ Mergers and acquisitions
❏ Research.

New issues   New issues of either shares or bonds will involve pricing the securities, selling them to investors, underwriting and general advice regarding the regulations that must be followed. Close liaison with firms of lawyers and accountants will be necessary and their fees will be substantial, as well as those of the bankers!

Underwriting is an undertaking to buy any securities that the investors cannot be persuaded to buy. Fees will be charged (of course) and the risk will be spread amongst other merchant banks and investment institutions. One of the most dramatic incidents in modern times occurred when the UK government was selling off its remaining shares in BP to the public. Unfortunately, the market crash of October 1987 occurred after the price was fixed but before the offer closed. The issue was a failure and the underwriters had to buy the shares at a substantial loss.

In the case of equities, the underwriters purchase the shares once it is clear that investors are not taking up their allocation. In the eurobond market, on the other hand, the syndicate of underwriting banks buys the bonds from the issuer and then attempts to sell them to investors.

Rights issues (discussed in Chapter 7)   These also need to be priced and under-written in case the market price falls below the offer price of the rights. Technically, BP was a rights issue as some shares were already quoted but new shares were being created. The government was allowing the public to buy these shares.

The many privatisations in the newly emerging free markets of Central and Eastern Europe, the former USSR, China and India have created work for US and European investment bankers. Their advice and help are being sought for circumstances which have little precedent. The biggest names tend to be those of the US houses – Merrill Lynch, Citigroup, Morgan Stanley, Goldman Sachs and JP Morgan.

Mergers and acquisitions   Firms planning a takeover will turn to investment banks for help and advice regarding price, timing, tactics and so on. Equally, the object of the takeover will turn to these bankers for help in fending off the predator. The fees involved can be substantial and in a large takeover there may be three investment bankers or more on each side. For example, when the Spanish

Telefónica's proposed takeover of O_2 was announced in November 2005, there was speculation that bankers' fees would total £50 million. Advising Telefónica were Citigroup, Goldman Sachs and RBS. Advisers for O_2 were Merrill Lynch and JP Morgan Cazenove.

Many takeover bids or mergers are cross-border – RMC/Cemex Mexico; Allied Domecq/Pernod; Banco Santander/Abbey National; UniCredito/HVB; Mittal Steel/Arcelor.

The top M&A houses in 2005 were Goldman Sachs, Morgan Stanley and JP Morgan (Table 5.1).

Table 5.1   *Top global M&A advisers, 2005*

Adviser	Deal value $bn
Goldman Sachs	848
Morgan Stanley	720
JP Morgan	679
Merrill Lynch	637
Citigroup	531
UBS	493
Lehman Bros	441
Deutsche Bank	371
Lazard	312

Source: Dealogic

In the US, the notorious 'junk bond' era (Chapter 6) saw small companies raising huge sums with bonds to buy much bigger companies. (In the film *Wall Street*, the speech made by Gordon Gecko to shareholders in his planned victim company was said to be based on an actual speech made by Ivan Boesky. He is reported to have coined the infamous phrase, 'greed is good'.)

The fees earned by Drexel Burnham Lambert for bond issues and takeover bids during this era made them quickly one of the highest earning firms on Wall Street (as long as it lasted).

Certain jargon has come to be associated with takeover battles. If a takeover seems inevitable, the merchant bank may find a rival bidder who is preferable to the original predator. This more acceptable bidder is the 'White Knight'. For example, in April 1999, Telecom Italia, facing a hostile bid from Olivetti, turned to Deutsche Telecom as their 'White Knight' (a tactic that did not, however, succeed).

Sometimes one or two people can be found who will take a substantial minority holding and block the takeover. These are the 'White Squires'. When Lloyds Bank tried to take over Standard Chartered in 1986, the bid was blocked by holdings taken (separately) by a few entrepreneurs in the Far East and Australia. As it happened, they did Lloyds a good turn as subsequent Standard Chartered problems would have severely weakened a bank with a high reputation for profitability.

Sometimes the 'White Squire' may become a 'Trojan Horse' (to mix our metaphors)! When Britannia Arrow faced a hostile bid in 1985, it found a White Squire in Robert Maxwell. Subsequently, he ousted the board and put in his own nominees.

Those who play computer games may be interested to hear of the Pac-man defence! Here you turn around and gobble up the monster who is chasing you! TotalFina, the Franco-Belgian group, launched a takeover bid for Elf Aquitaine, the French oil group in July 1999. Two weeks later, Elf Aquitaine made a counter-bid for TotalFina!

Sometimes, the bidder may be persuaded to withdraw by the company buying back the shares at a higher price. This is called 'greenmail' (in contrast to blackmail)! In 1986, Sir James Goldsmith, the Anglo-French entrepreneur, made an unpopular bid for the US tyre company, Goodyear Tyre & Rubber Co. In the end, after an acrimonious fight, the firm bought Goldsmith and partners out. He made $93m in the space of a few weeks. However, the incident did damage his reputation in the US, although he always denied the 'greenmail' charge.

A popular defence against hostile takeover bids in the US is the so-called 'poison pill'. This was invented by a top takeover lawyer, Martin Lipton, in 1980 and has been adopted by two thirds of companies in the Standard & Poor's 500 Index.

Once one shareholder's stake rises above a given percentage (usually 20%), the poison pill device is triggered. This allows the company to give all shareholders – apart from the 20% holder – the right to buy new shares at a large discount, often 50%. This makes the bid prohibitively expensive.

In November 2004, Liberty Media raised its voting stake in News International to 17%. The latter adopted a poison pill. If triggered, every shareholder except the bidder would be able to buy News International shares at half price, thus diluting the holding of the predator. A promise was made that this would be put to the shareholders for approval at the AGM in October 2005. In the event, Rupert Murdoch then announced that the poison pill would remain in place for a further two years after October 2005. The institutional shareholders were very angry and threatened legal action. In February 2006, the French government said that it was planning to allow French companies to use poison pills to frustrate a foreign bidder – not exactly in the spirit of the 'single market'!

M&A activity is buoyed by the continuing trend towards globalisation of industry and commerce and consolidation in specific industry sectors.

General advice   This is always needed by the treasury departments of major firms. They will meet their merchant bankers regularly to discuss the outlook for exchange rates, interest rates, risk management and generally to help them to clarify their policies. Sometimes the client may be a government or quasi-government authority – for example, the Saudi Arabian Monetary Authority (SAMA).

Research capability   This is clearly essential in the corporate finance department if the bank is to be able to give advice and play a major role in raising new capital. The firm may be innovative and invent new variations on standard techniques, for example, convertible capital bonds, perpetual variable rate notes, perpetual auction market preferred stock (AMPS) and similar instruments. Research may uncover potential victims for a takeover or give early identification of potential predators.

It is important to get a good reputation for research. Periodically, surveys are carried out of fund managers, asking them to nominate the best houses for research. One of these is the Thomson–Extel Survey, done each year in the UK. In the latest survey (2005), the top three houses were UBS Smith Barney, Citigroup and Merrill Lynch. Individual sector analysts are also surveyed, and they and their teams often become the object of poaching by other houses!

Securities Trading

In corporate finance we saw *primary* market activity – new issues and rights issues. Securities trading takes us into the *secondary* market dealing in the same equities and bonds.

The trading will take place in one of the modern dealing rooms with computer terminals and communications giving up to the minute prices and contact with other dealers and investors all over the world.

The dealings will cover domestic bonds and equities and international bonds and equities. International bonds are discussed in Chapter 6. International equities are those of companies outside the domestic market where the investment bank is situated.

The old tradition in many countries (France, Belgium, the UK, Spain, Italy) has been to reserve domestic bond and equities to stock exchange members, not allowed to be owned by banks. Change began with London's 'Big Bang' in October 1986 and spread to all the above markets. The result has been to allow banks access to these markets and break the previous monopolies. These banks are either pure investment banks as such, subsidiaries of commercial banks, or 'universal' banks (see Chapter 2).

Alongside these traders will be the experts in the so called 'derivative' products – options, futures, FRAs and so on. We shall discuss these in later chapters, but they enable traders and their clients either to take a view on future price movements with less capital than actually buying/selling the underlying instruments or to hedge their risk. If a commercial bank has an investment bank subsidiary, then the expertise in derivative products will be found in that subsidiary.

The traders in this department carry out a twofold role. They act on behalf of clients (some of whom may be in-house departments) and they take positions of their own – usually called 'proprietary trading'.

Investment Management

The investment funds which these managers are controlling may be the bank's own funds or they may be, in effect, 'looking after other people's money'. These may be:

❏ High net worth individuals
❏ Corporates
❏ Pension funds
❏ Mutual funds.

High net worth individuals   They may approach a commercial bank to handle all their affairs, including investments. In Chapter 2 we called this 'private banking'. They could also approach an investment bank to handle their spare funds (but a minimum sum will be stated). This type of business is also handled by stockbrokers but with lower minimum sums than an investment bank would require.

Corporates   They may either have good cash flow and wish to pay someone else to handle their investments or may build up a large 'war chest', ready for some takeover activity later and, temporarily, pay an investment bank to handle this.

The entity need not be a conventional corporate as such. An excellent example is the Saudi Arabian Monetary Authority (SAMA).

Pension funds   Where economies have pension funds (for example the US, the UK, the Netherlands, Switzerland and Japan), then they may feel that they lack the skill to manage the funds and pay others to do so. In these economies, pension funds will usually be the biggest clients of the investment management department.

Mutual funds   These are discussed in Chapter 7. They are collective investments in money market instruments, bonds or equities. The bank may run its own fund and advertise its attractions to small investors. In addition, it will manage mutual funds for others. Independent organisations provide regular statistics on fund performance and, if the manager has performed less well than comparable funds, they may find themselves being dismissed. This has led to charges of 'short-termism' in their investment decisions. However, as a director of one major fund commented to the author: 'The long run is the sum of the short runs. If we get them right, the long run will be right too.'

Typically, fund managers will charge a small percentage fee for handling the fund and the client will meet costs like broker's commission. Competition for the investment banks comes from firms of independent fund managers, who specialise totally in this business, or large pension funds who will look after the money of smaller funds as well as their own.

The role of fund managers as investment institutions who influence stock market activity will be discussed in Chapter 7.

Loan Arrangement

Where there are complex syndicated loans for special projects, we may often find that the arranger is an investment bank. The bank is using its special skills to decide on the terms of the loan and the cheapest way to find the money. It could involve using the 'swaps' market, for example, which we explain in Chapter 14. Often, several potential teams may be competing for these projects, for example, Eurotunnel, the new Hong Kong airport, the bridge over the Bosphorus. In the case of Teesside Power Station in the UK, a syndicate of banks put up the money but the loan arranger was the US investment bank, Goldman Sachs.

Outside of large, complex projects, investment bankers will help clients to raise finance for international trade. In this, there is an overlap with a major commercial bank activity. It may be a question of knowing sources of cheaper finance for exporter or importer (for example, a development bank) or even acting as an agent or middleman – an export house or confirming house. These activities are discussed under 'Finance for Trade' in Chapter 10.

Foreign Exchange

The foreign exchange markets are discussed in Chapter 9. Typically, we regard this as a commercial bank activity. However, investment banks that are permitted commercial bank functions will run a foreign exchange trading desk for their clients and their own proprietary trading and it may be an important source of profit. We make the above comment about being 'permitted commercial bank functions' because of the differing regulatory position in various countries, which we explain before the end of this chapter.

Typically, US and Japanese investment banks have had a modest foreign exchange section, but there are exceptions; Goldman Sachs, for example, have become a major player in foreign exchange dealing. UK merchant banks, fully licensed as banks, will often see foreign exchange dealing as a major activity and will, indeed, have a 'banking' department which will also offer deposit taking functions to clients.

Miscellaneous Activities

There are a range of miscellaneous activities which may be carried out by investment banks, possibly through separate legal subsidiaries. Commodity trading (including derivatives trading), for example, is quite common and one thinks here, for instance, of the links between the US Citigroup and Phibro and also of Goldman's who have a commodity dealing arm. Other activities include insurance broking, life assurance, leasing, factoring (see Chapter 10), property development and venture capital. This latter activity covers finance for new and growing companies which are not well enough established to attract money by equities, bonds or conventional bank loans. The venture capital company puts in a mixture of equity and loans and hopes to make large capital gains later when the firm obtains a flotation on the local Stock Exchange.

Many of these miscellaneous activities overlap with those of commercial banks – for example, leasing, factoring, venture capital and commodity dealing.

REGULATION

We have seen that many commercial banks have investment bank subsidiaries and that universal banks do all kinds of banking anyway. We have also seen that many activities overlap commercial and investment banking and that it is not always possible to draw a clear distinction. As a result, one might conclude that the distinction between the two types of banking is not really significant. However, the two terms are widely used to characterise a bank's activities and culture, and perhaps to compare or contrast it with another bank, or again, to comment on the merits and relevance or 'fit' of an acquisition. Moreover the two types of bank were until recently artificially separated by law in the two biggest markets of the world – the US and Japan!

When the Wall Street crash occurred in 1929, the US authorities concluded that, by engaging in stock market activities, commercial banks might be risking depositors' money. They decided to remove this risk by passing the Glass-Steagall Act of 1933 (named after the Chairmen of the relevant committees of the Senate and House of Representatives). This introduced a deposit protection scheme, gave the Federal Reserve Bank greater powers of supervision and separated commercial and investment banking. A commercial bank could take deposits but could not underwrite any securities. An investment bank could handle underwriting of securities but could not take deposits. As a result, we had US commercial banks on the one hand (Citibank, Chase Manhattan, Chemical, JP Morgan) and investment banks on the other (Salomon Bros, Goldman Sachs, Merrill Lynch). JP Morgan continued as a commercial bank but passed investment banking to Morgan Stanley, now a separate bank. In London, the already weak links with Morgan Grenfell were then broken.

The whole affair, however, may have been based on a misreading of the position. George Bentson, Professor of Finance at Emory University in Atlanta, has found that allegations that securities trading weakened banks had 'almost no basis in fact'.

As the Americans were in occupation of Japan after the Second World War, they passed the same restrictions into Article 65 of the Japanese Exchange and Securities Code. As a result, we had the commercial banks (Dai Ichi Kangyo, Mitsubishi, Sumitomo, Sakura) and, quite separate, the securities houses (Nomura, Daiwa and Nikko).

A similar law was passed in Italy in the early 1930s leaving Italy with just one major investment bank, Mediobanca (partly state-owned). In 1988, however, the law was repealed.

From 1987 onwards there were several abortive attempts to repeal Glass-Steagall, but although there were bitter disputes in Congress again in 1999 over a new banking bill, these were eventually resolved and Glass-Steagall was finally repealed in November 1999.

In Japan, in a similar way, there were various limited moves from 1993 onwards, but in June 1997, the Ministry of Finance announced plans for complete deregulation by the year 2001.

SUMMARY

Investment banking activities can be summarised as:

Accepting This is putting the bank's signature on a bill of exchange to give it a better credit quality. The bill of exchange is a promise to pay a trade debt. If the bank is one on the central bank's list for this purpose, the bill is a *bank* bill. Others are *trade* bills. The bill is frequently sold at a discount. Commercial banks will accept bills, too, but it is an historic investment bank activity.

Corporate finance This covers new issues of equities and bonds, rights issues, mergers and acquisitions and research.

Securities trading The trading includes money market instruments, equities, bonds and derivative products.

Investment management The funds managed are those of high net worth individuals, corporates, mutual funds and (especially) pension funds.

Loan arrangement While the bank may not lend the money, it may help to assemble a syndicate for large-scale financial products.

Foreign exchange The large foreign exchange dealers are commercial banks but investment banks will still need to run a foreign exchange section.

In the United States, investment and commercial banks were separated by the Glass-Steagall Act, but actions by the Federal Reserve weakened its provisions, and it has now been repealed.

The old Japanese restrictions of Article 65 of the Exchange and Securities Code regarding commercial banking, investment banking and insurance have been swept away.

Across Europe, banks which carry out both commercial and investment banking are called *universal* banks.

Securities Markets

6 The Money and Bond Markets

THE RATE OF INTEREST

So far, we have taken the rate of interest involved in borrowing and lending rather for granted. The time has come, however, to look at it more clearly.

The rate of interest is the price of money. We talk casually of *the* rate of interest but, of course, there is no single rate. There are rates appropriate for different borrowers and rates appropriate for different time periods. A middle-sized company making machine tools will expect to pay a higher rate than a government does. A government pays a different rate for borrowing for 3 months than for 10 years.

What affects the rate of interest? We have just touched on two key factors – *risk* and *maturity*.

Risk

Let's take the risk first. Quite simply, a lender will expect a greater reward for lending to the company making machine tools than for lending to a government. After all, the company may go into liquidation and default. We do not expect our government to default, although Mexico's government and those of other Latin American countries caused panic in international markets when they defaulted in the 1980s (more on that later!). Russia's default on its Treasury bills in August 1998 also had widespread repercussions.

So far as the governments of OECD countries are concerned, say, or the US government, the lowest rates of interest in their economies will apply to government transactions since they are regarded as the safest. The government rate thus becomes the benchmark for other rates. For example, an American corporate wishing to borrow for three months might be advised to expect to pay 'Treasuries plus 1%', that is, 1% more than the current rate for US government Treasury bills. It is more convenient to express it this way than as an absolute rate because rates vary in wholesale markets, even daily. For example, let's say three month Treasury bills pay 3⅞%. The rate for our US company is thus 4⅞%. However, tomorrow Treasury bills may be 3¾% and the corporate rate becomes 4¾%. As a result, we find it easier to express the rate as 'Treasuries plus 1%'. Of course, the corporate may become more secure as profits increase and the balance sheet improves. Their investment bankers may express the view that they now see their appropriate rate as 'Treasuries plus 90 bp'. What does this mean? A basis point is very common terminology and is useful for expressing small differences in rates. It is $\frac{1}{100}$ of 1%. Thus, 50 bp is equal to ½% and 100 bp is equal to 1%. The difference between any given rate and the benchmark US government rate will be called 'the spread over Treasuries'. In the above case, the corporate has found that its spread over US government Treasury bill rates has fallen from 1% to $\frac{9}{10}$%.

Maturity

Maturity is another important aspect, and it doesn't always make sense in practice. Economic theory tells us that lenders will want a higher rate of interest for lending money for five years than for three months. This relationship between the rate of interest and time is called the 'yield curve'. If rates for longer-term lending are higher than for shorter-term lending, we would expect the yield curve to look like that in Figure 6.1.

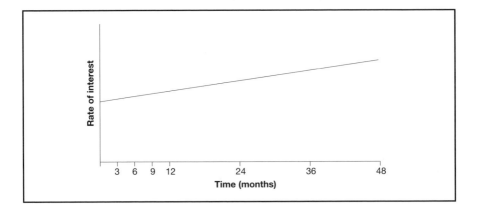

Figure 6.1   *The yield curve*

The yield curve is upward-sloping, or positive. Unfortunately, while this makes complete sense, it often doesn't work that way in real life at all. Sometimes short-term rates are higher than long-term ones and we talk of a 'negative' or downward-sloping yield curve. This may be due to government policy. They change short-term interest rates either to stimulate the economy or to slow it down. For example, from October 1989 to October 1990 in the UK, short-term rates were 15% while the government attempted to slow down a rate of inflation in excess of 10%. Investment in a ten year government bond, however, only returned about 11%. Conversely, in mid-1992, the US government was desperately trying to 'kick-start' the economy. Short-term rates were only a little over 3%, while the price of a 30 year government bond was such that it yielded about 7½%.

As interest rates increased in 2005 in both the US and the UK, the long-term yield became similar to short-term, and in early 2006 went lower. This led to a variety of explanations. There were those that saw it as a forecast of recession – high interest rates now to cool the economy; low later as the recession took hold. Some are strong believers in this, others more cynical. Milton Erzati, an economist at Lord Abbett, a UK fund manager, joked, 'The yield curve has predicted 12 of the last seven recessions!'. Some point to a growing confidence that central banks will keep inflation low and are thus reducing long-term uncertainty. A more likely explanation may be supply and demand. The US stopped issue of 30 year bonds in 2001 and only resumed in February 2006. On the demand side, in both the US and the UK, pension funds are looking for long-dated bonds to help solve the future pension crisis. There was a huge demand for the reintroduced US 30 year issue in February 2006. Let's also note that in Europe (not UK) and Japan, the yield curve is *upward-sloping*. Finally, Alan Greenspan said that he remained unworried about the inversion.

Expectations

Markets are also affected by *expectations*. Suppose everyone believes firmly that the general level of interest rates is due to *fall*. Lots of people will want to lend money for long periods and benefit from higher interest rates. Not many people want to borrow long-term – they would rather wait until rates fall. As a result, long-term rates start to fall in relation to short-term rates. Conversely, if rates are expected to *rise*, then everyone wants to lend short-term, hoping to gain from higher rates later. Borrowers prefer to borrow long-term and lock in to lower rates while they can. Long-term rates will now rise in order to attract funds to meet the demands of the borrowers.

Liquidity

Liquidity also affects the rate of interest – that is, how quickly can the lender get the money back? This is not quite the same as maturity. There may well be one rate for three month money and another for five year money but another consideration in the case of five year money is: can the lender change their mind and get the money back?

A savings bank will pay lower interest on a 'no notice' or 'sight' account than on a 'three months' notice' account. We have to pay (by way of a lower rate of interest) for the flexibility of being able to withdraw our money at any time.

In wholesale markets, if our lending of money is represented by a security, then one way of getting the money back prior to the normal repayment date is to sell the security to someone else.

Supply and Demand

Of course, we cannot ignore the whole question of supply and demand in different market sectors. For example, for over two years from 1988 to 1990, the UK government was in surplus and did not need to borrow by issuing bonds. The demand was still there, however, from UK and foreign pension funds, insurance companies and other investors. This contributed to a lowering of interest rates for government bonds. The supply/demand factor can be seen at its best perhaps when one looks at the yield curve for UK government bonds in April 1996 and May 1999 and their most curious 'kinks' (see Figure 6.2). They also show how yields vary from year to year.

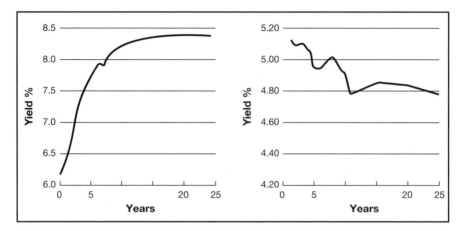

Figure 6.2   *UK gilts yield, 1996 and 1999*

Up to five years, there are plenty of lenders, for example banks and UK building societies. Over ten years, there are plenty of lenders – pension funds and insurance companies. From five to ten years there is a shortage and rates rise a little (if only 10 bp) to attract lenders.

In early 2006 in the UK, pension funds' desire for a certain income in the future led to a rush to buy the government's 50 year index-inked gilt. The *real* return (after inflation) fell at one point to only ½% – a clear supply and demand effect.

Inflation

Finally, whether a given rate of interest represents good value or not may depend on the rate of inflation. Economists talk of the *real* rate of interest, that is, the nominal rate of interest minus the rate of inflation.

In the UK in 1989/90, interest rates reached 15% while the government desperately tried to curb inflation, which had reached 11%. In 1992, the rate of interest had fallen to 10% but inflation had fallen to less than 4%. Thus, although nominal rates had fallen from 15% to 10%, the *real* rate had risen from 4% to over 6%. In late 2005, with nominal rates of 4.5% and inflation at 2½%, real rates were at a new low of 2½%.

YIELD

Yield is arguably the most important term in the financial markets. 'Yield' is the return to the investor expressed as an annual percentage. As the markets are all about raising capital, the yield is crucially important. Unfortunately, it's not as easy as it seems!

Suppose we have a bond issued in 1996 and maturing in 25 years – 2021. The bond pays a rate of interest of 10% once per year. What is the yield? At first, the answer seems obvious – 10%. 'If I buy the bond', you argue, 'I get 10% – where's the problem?' The problem is that your answer is only true if you paid the full price for the bond.

Par Values

Bonds have a 'par' or 'nominal' value. This is usually taken to be $1000, £100, €1000 and so on. This is the amount on which the rate of interest is based and the amount which will be repaid at maturity. You buy the 25 year 10% bond and pay the par value of $1000. Your yield is 10%. However, as secondary market trading begins, investors may pay either more or less than $1000 for the bond with a par value of $1000 – this affects the yield. The price of the bond is expressed as a percentage of the par value. For example, if the price is 90, then the price for $1000 par value is $900. In the UK, £100 is taken to be the par value. A price of 90 means that the price for £100 par value is £90.

Suppose the 25 year bond mentioned above is a UK government bond and you buy £5000 worth at issue: after all, government bonds are the safest, aren't they? Two years later, you need the money and decide to sell. Two years later, however, the level of interest rates has changed. The yield on long-dated government bonds is now 12½%. As you try to get full price for your 10% bond, no one is interested. Why should they pay you £100 to receive £10, when they could buy a new bond for £100 and get £12.50? They might pay you £80, because your bond pays £10 once per year and £10 for an investment of £80 is 12½%. Therefore, as interest rates went *up*, the price of your bond went *down*. The face rate of interest is 10% but by buying it more cheaply, the yield has increased to 12½% because £10 is 12½% of £80.

Let's say that you refuse to sell. Two years later, you have lost your job and life is grim. You must sell your bonds, come what may. However, by now things have changed again. The yield on long-dated government bonds is now only 8%. When you attempt to sell your 10% bond you will find no shortage of buyers willing to pay you more than par, because 10% is very attractive if current rates are 8%. As a result, as interest rates went *down*, the price of your bond went *up*. In theory, buyers might pay £125, because the income of £10 returns 8% which is the market rate. That is to say, £10 is 8% of £125.

Interest Yield

Just to cover more market jargon, the face rate of interest on the bond is called the *coupon* (for reasons which will be explained later). The calculation we made above when arriving at the yield was:

$$\frac{\text{Coupon}}{\text{Price}} = \text{Yield}$$

for example
$$\frac{\pounds 10}{\pounds 80} = 12.5\%$$

or
$$\frac{\pounds 10}{\pounds 125} = 8\%$$

This calculation of yield is called the interest yield (the terms *simple, flat, running* and *annual* yield are also used). It's not difficult, but not really helpful either.

Gross Redemption Yield

Let's go back to the illustration above of the effect of yields rising to 12½%. We suggested that someone might buy your bond for £80. We argued:

1   Buy the new 12½% bond for £100 – yield 12½%
2   Buy the existing 10% bond for £80 – yield 12½%.

Unfortunately, we've omitted one crucial factor – redemption, When the bond is redeemed, the government will pay £100. In case 1 above, there is no capital gain. In case 2, there's a capital gain of £20. As a result, the yield is more than 12½% if we throw this factor in. Equally, if anyone paid £125, they would face a loss of £25 at redemption. The market does its calculations on the assumption that the bond is kept until redemption.

We need, therefore, an all-embracing calculation that includes the interest yield and modifies it by any gain or loss at redemption. The resultant figure is the *gross redemption yield* (or *yield to maturity*). ('Gross' means ignoring tax. As we don't know the investor's tax status, we ignore consideration of any tax that might be due on the interest or on any capital gain.) The formula itself is quite complicated, as it's based on discounted cash flow. We are taking the future stream of revenue – interest and redemption – and calculating the yield that would equate this to today's bond price. Alternatively, we could feed into the formula a desired yield and calculate the price to be paid that would achieve that yield. That's why it's so important – it's how bond dealers calculate bond prices.

Suppose, however, that a bond pays 10% and the market yield is 12½%, but redemption is not in 2021 but two months away. Does this make any difference? Will the bond still only sell for about £80? Surely not – here is a piece of paper that, in two months, is worth £100. Why was the bond price so poor in our original example? It was because the bond offered 10% and the market wanted 12½% but, if there's only two months' interest payments left, this hardly matters. What matters is that redemption at £100 is quite near.

The result is that the nearer we get to redemption, the nearer the secondary market price moves to £100 and the less important interest rate changes are. Thus, long-dated bonds are highly sensitive to interest rate changes (interest rates *up*, bond prices *down* and vice-versa) but short dates are not.

Consider two 10% bonds. The ultimate reward for the buyer is the interest payments and the redemption value. Suppose one bond has 1 year to run and the other 20 years.

Case No.		Interest payments £	+	Redemption £	=	Reward £
1	1 year to go	10	+	100	=	110
2	20 years to go	200	+	100	=	300

In case 1, most of the reward is redemption, not affected by interest rate changes.

In case 2, most of the reward is interest payments. If these don't match the market yield, the effect on price will be very serious.

We could represent this diagrammatically, as shown in Figure 6.3.

Figure 6.3   *Volatility of long-dated bonds*

Let's verify this against some real prices. These are prices for UK government bonds in November 2005:

Bond				Price
1	Exchequer	8½%	2005	100.25
	Treasury	4½%	2007	100.20
2	Exchequer	8%	2021	140.25
	Treasury	4½%	2032	99.51

Notice that in case 1 we have two bonds, one paying 8½% and one 4½%. It might be thought that the 8½% would be much more expensive, when in fact the prices are nearly identical – they are both near redemption.

In case 2, one bond pays 8% and the other 4¼%, and this is fully reflected in the two prices. Here, redemption is 15–30 years away.

You will still find in US bond markets the use of fractions down to ¹⁄₃₂. Sensibly, Europe uses decimals. The smallest price movement, in one case ¹⁄₃₂ and the other 0.01, is called (curiously) a *tick*. Thus, a cry of 'Treasuries are up 5 ticks' in the US would mean ⁵⁄₃₂. A similar cry in Germany would mean 0.05.

You will gather from the above discussion that dealers holding an inventory of long-dated bonds are at risk to interest rate changes. They may seek to hedge this risk using a futures exchange, and we explain this later in Chapter 13. Equally, if you want to buy bonds as a short-term investment, it might be better to buy short-dated bonds, where the risk of market interest rate changes is less.

As an illustration of the dangers, you might like to read Michael Lewis's excellent *Liar's Poker* (Hodder & Stoughton, 1989). He tells the amusing story of how Merrill Lynch trader, Howie Rubin, lost $250m on long-dated bonds in 1987 in one fateful deal. (Well, it's amusing if you're not Howie Rubin!)

Accrued Interest

Unfortunately, there is one other factor to consider before we leave these somewhat technical questions. It is the question of the timing of the interest payments. Suppose the interest is paid twice per year on 16 January and 16 July. You buy a 10% bond in the secondary market on 16 January for £90. You have just missed the interest payment and will have to wait six months for the next one. Suppose that you have to sell after three months and that prices are unchanged. If you could only sell for £90, this would seem very unfair, as you've held the bond for three months and had no reward for your investment. Equally, the buyer would collect 5% although they had only held the bond for three months.

Naturally, it doesn't work like that. When you sell your bond you get the *accrued interest* to date. If you held £100 nominal value of the 10% bond for three months, you would get half the bi-annual interest, that is, £2.50. (The calculation is simply multiplying the half-yearly interest payments per £100 – £5 in this case – by the number of days the bond is held as a proportion of the days in the half year.) The accrued interest is almost always quoted separately (there are some exceptions in some markets, such as convertible bonds). The price without the accrued interest is the *clean price*. The price you see on a computer screen or in the financial newspapers is always the clean price. If you sell, you will receive the accrued interest in addition. If you buy, you will have to pay it. One reason for accounting for the accrued interest separately is that in many countries any gain in this area is subject to income tax. Gains on the clean price are capital gains.

There is a complication. There must be a cut off point, at which time everyone on the register of holders gets the interest. After this the bond is marked XD (ex dividend). Suppose the half-year payment is on 10 June. The bonds may go XD on 3 June. However, the interest accrues from 10 December to 10 June. Anyone selling on 3 June will get the half-year interest to 10 June although they did not own the bond in the last 7 days. Anyone buying the bond on 3 June will not accrue any interest until 10 June, even though they have invested their capital 7 days earlier. As a result, when bonds are sold in the XD period, the seller (who gains) *pays* the accrued interest to the buyer (who loses). This is the exception to the way accrued interest is treated.

CREDIT RATINGS

We have seen that the higher the creditworthiness of the borrower, the lower the rate of interest. Some markets (for example, the US) want the credit rating of the borrower officially assessed so as to guide them as to the risk and the appropriate rate of interest. There are several companies in the credit rating business but the two most important are Standard and Poor's (McGraw-Hill) and Moody's Investor Service (Dun and Bradstreet). For banks, there is a UK-based organisation called IBCA. This merged with the French Euronotation in October 1992. In 1997, they merged with the third biggest rating organisation in the US, Fitch Investor Services. Some see this as the first move to a pan-European body to rival Standard and Poor's and Moody's. The credit ratings business began in 1909 when John Moody issued his first-ever ratings of company debt – 200 American railway companies.

These organisations look at bond issues and commercial paper issues (to be covered later) and rate them according to the risk. To quote Standard and Poor's themselves, the ratings are based, in varying degrees, on the following considerations:

1 *Likelihood of default – capacity and willingness of the obligor as to the timely payment of interest and repayment of principal in accordance with the terms of the obligation*
2 *Nature and provisions of the obligation*
3 *Protection afforded to, and relative position of, the obligation in the event of bankruptcy, reorganisation, or other arrangement under the laws of bankruptcy and other laws affecting creditors' rights.*

A bond which is the best risk is rated AAA by Standard and Poor's and Aaa by Moody's. The full list for Standard and Poor's is:

AAA
AA
A
BBB
BB

B
CCC
CC
C
C1
D

A bond rated 'D' is either in default or expected to default.

As a further refinement, the grade may be modified by plus (+) or minus (–), for example, AA+ or AA. A bond may be issued as AAA but be reduced later to A if the position of the issuer deteriorates. This will increase their borrowing costs. Suppose the appropriate rate for an AAA bond is 10%. The rate for an A might be 10.75%.

Below the BBB rank there is a sort of invisible line. Bonds rated BBB and above are 'investment grade' – top quality if you like. Many investment funds will only invest if the grade is BBB or higher. Below BBB, to quote Standard and Poor's again:

Debt rated 'BB', 'B', 'CCC', 'CC' and 'C' is regarded as having predominantly speculative characteristics with respect to capacity to pay interest and repay principal. 'BB' indicates the least degree of speculation and 'C' the highest degree of speculation. While such debt will likely have some quality and protective characteristics, these are outweighed by large uncertainties or major risk exposures to adverse conditions.

'Junk bonds' are simply bonds which are not investment grade. This is quite a long story and we'll tackle it later.

Moody's have a similar system but use slightly different lettering.

The view of risk for a 3 month loan may be quite different from that for a 5 year loan. As a result, both organisations use a simpler system for the shorter-term commercial paper. For Standard and Poor's this is:

A1
A2
A3
B
C
D

Default could range from simply missing a payment to bankruptcy. A Moody's study in 2001 showed that over a 15 year period only 1.1% of bonds originally rated with the top grade went into default. For bonds rated CCC (Caa in the case of Moody's) or worse, the default rate was 41.1%. Unfortunately, the fall from grace of top companies in 2002 like Enron, WorldCom and Marconi has led to more defaults from highly rated bonds.

Clearly, non-investment grade will have to pay more than investment grade to compensate for the risk. The interest rate spread over investment grade debt was 300 basis points in 1997, but went much higher as we moved into the Russian-inspired crisis in 1998.

As an example of the way organisations can lose ratings, we have only to look at the banks. In 1990, there were eight banks (not owned by the state) whose bonds were rated AAA by both organisations – Rabobank, Deutsche, Morgan Guaranty, Barclays, Swiss Bank Corporation, Union Bank of Switzerland, Crédit Suisse and Industrial Bank of Japan. Due to commercial bad debts following recession, by mid-1992 the proud band of eight had shrunk to four – Rabobank, Deutsche, Morgan Guaranty and Union Bank of Switzerland and, then, by January 1997 had shrunk to one – Rabobank! (Rabo is still AAA with both these agencies.) In industry and commerce, previously 'blue chip' companies have also been downgraded, with both Corus and Cable & Wireless acquiring junk status in 2002. Finally, in 2005, the downgrades of both Ford and General Motors led to shock waves, especially in the derivatives markets.

Standard and Poor's and Moody's do not always move together. In 1992, for example, Moody's downgraded the Swiss Bank Corporation from AAA. Standard and Poor's did not follow suit until early 1995.

Credit ratings are used extensively in the domestic US market and the Euromarkets (to be explained later). It has not generally been a habit in Europe, but the default of Polly Peck's commercial paper issue in the UK led to an increasing use of ratings in this market. It is likely, in fact, that ratings will be used increasingly in Europe. Ratings are not only applied to corporate issues but also to government issues ('sovereign issues'). In June 1998, for example, Standard and Poor's downgraded Russian debt to B+, a clear sign of the trouble to come!

With the arrival of the Far East crisis in 1997, the rating agencies came in for considerable criticism for not anticipating the problems. The agencies were following the markets, not leading them. South Korea was AA– at January 1st but BBB– by December. The agencies had focused on external debt as a ratio of exports, underestimating the possibility of default. Short-term debt obligations turned out to be much higher than had been previously indicated. Moody's did issue a warning, however, in May 1996 about the gradual build up of short-term debt.

Credit rating agencies, of course, exercise considerable power. Moody's habit of publishing unsolicited ratings has led to criticism. Since this rating will be based on imperfect information, it leads to pressure on the company to pay for a full rating in the hope of getting a better one. (The bond issuers pay, not the investors.) In March 1996, Moody's found itself the subject of an investigation by the US Justice Department into a breach of anti-trust rules.

Discussing the question 'who controls the raters?', *The Economist* in an article on April 6 1996 concluded that:

In theory, the agencies have good reason to stick to the straight and narrow.
Even more than accountants and lawyers, they must trade on their reputations.
If bond investors lose faith in the integrity of the rating agencies' judgements,
they will no longer pay attention to their ratings ... companies and governments
will not pay their fees.

DOMESTIC MONEY MARKETS

We have previously mentioned that some markets are *domestic* (that is, transactions are in the local currency and under the control of the local central bank) and some are regarded as *international* (for example, a bond denominated in Japanese yen issued in London through a syndicate of international banks).

There are also *money* markets, which are short-term (that is, borrowing/lending of money for 1 year or less), and *bond* markets, which are markets handling medium- to long-term borrowing/lending.

In this chapter we deal with domestic markets first, covering the various instruments and practices of the money markets, and follow this with bonds.

Then we will look at the international markets, both short- and long-term.

When we look at domestic money markets, we find that there is no single marketplace here, like a stock exchange floor. All over the Western financial markets there are large numbers of people who spend their day buying and selling money in one form and another. Huge sums of money are borrowed or lent, sometimes simply 'overnight'.

Transactions involving the general public and small businesses, like shops, are called the *retail* market.

Transactions between the big players are typically called the *wholesale* market. The players are central banks, other banks, financial institutions, corporates and specialists, like money brokers.

Most of this chapter will be concerned with the wholesale markets.

Call Money

There is a market in money which is borrowed/lent for a very short period of time and is not represented by a marketable instrument or security. Bankers talk of 'call' money and the 'call money market'. Money is lent by one bank to another and may be called back at any time. There is also money lent overnight by one bank to another. 'Overnight' usually means 12.00 p.m. one day to 12.00 p.m. the next day. Sometimes the money may be lent with a right to have the money back with, say, three or seven days' notice. The result, on a bank's balance sheet, becomes 'money at call and short notice'. In most markets, the overnight rate is averaged and used for a variety of purposes. In Paris, for example, this was TMP (Taux Moyen Pondéré) prior to European Monetary Union. Now the rate for the twelve euro countries is

EONIA (Euro Overnight Indexed Average). For example, the French public entity, Crédit Immobilier de France, issued a two year bond where the interest rate is reset every night to EONIA. In London, the equivalent rate (confusingly) is EURONIA, that is the overnight indexed rate for dealings in the euro in London as opposed to the twelve countries. The rate for overnight dealings in London in sterling is SONIA.

The Interbank Market

Apart from the very short-term money mentioned before, there is generally a very strong interbank market in which the banks lend money one to another for periods ranging from several weeks to one year.

In our discussions on commercial banking, we concentrated on the idea of banks taking money from deposits and lending it to other people. The banks also top up their funds by borrowing from other banks which have spare liquidity. As this is the marginal cost to the banks for raising new money, their wholesale lending rates are based on the interbank lending rate.

The terms 'bid rate' and 'offer rate' are usually met in securities markets. The bid rate is the dealer's buying rate and the offer rate the dealer's selling rate. Obviously, the offer is higher than the bid, as the dealers will buy cheaper than they sell. The difference is called the 'spread'.

Curiously, when it comes to wholesale money, the deposit rate offered by a bank is called the bid rate and the lending rate is called the offer rate. Thus, the interbank rates in London are called LIBOR – London Interbank Offered Rate and LIBID – London Interbank Bid Rate. We find TIBOR in Tokyo, and EURIBOR for the twelve countries of the European Monetary Union. One exception is the US, where the interbank rate is called the 'Federal Funds Rate'.

We have already seen that interest rates vary with time and so the interbank rates for one month, three months, six months and 12 months will probably be different. The most common maturity used in the market is three months. If someone asks 'What's the £ LIBOR rate today?' they will be referring to three month LIBOR. Of course, the interbank market in London deals in dollars, yen, Swiss francs and other currencies and so, although LIBOR refers to London, it doesn't necessarily mean sterling. Again, these wholesale rates vary all the time and each bank's rate could be different. If we say £ LIBOR is $5\frac{1}{16}\%$ we mean the average of major banks in the market.

Let's look at rates quoted for three month money in currencies in London in November 2005 (Table 6.1).

As London is a huge international market, the rate we hear of most commonly is LIBOR. We have seen that as LIBOR is the marginal cost of new money, then the lending rate in wholesale markets may be quoted as 'LIBOR $+\frac{1}{4}$', 'LIBOR +35 basis points', 'LIBOR $+\frac{1}{2}$'. Equally, floating rate notes issued in London will have the rate reset periodically (typically every three or six months) as LIBOR plus a given margin. If the rate for a loan or floating rate note is reset every three months, but LIBOR is different at different times of the day, then we need to define this precisely. It is usually quoted as the average of the LIBOR rates given by nominated banks at 11.00 a.m. on the relevant day.

Table 6.1   *London Interbank Offered Rate (LIBOR) – three month – 3/11/2005*

$	4.28
€	2.26
£	4.59
¥	0.06

Source: *Financial Times.*

With the arrival of European Monetary Union, we now have the interbank market of the twelve countries in the euro and its reference rate EURIBOR, and we have the interbank market in London in the euro and its reference rate EURO LIBOR. As LIBOR has always been a major reference rate for bond issues, derivatives and other transactions the question arose – which one would win? The answer was EURIBOR. Even London's derivatives exchange LIFFE admitted defeat in February 1999 and changed its contracts to EURIBOR.

Money Market Securities

The markets we have described above – the call money market and the general interbank market – deal with wholesale borrowing and lending amongst banks and financial institutions. The transactions are not represented by any security that can be traded. We will now deal with money market transactions that do result in trading in securities.

Typical instruments are:

❏   Treasury bills
❏   Local authority/Public utility bills
❏   Certificates of deposit
❏   Commercial paper
❏   Bills of exchange.

Treasury Bills

Governments find that their income from taxes does not come in at a steady rate, nor is their expenditure at a steady rate. Apart from raising money with medium-to long-term government bills, it's convenient and useful to be able to borrow for shorter periods and balance their cash flow. The chosen instrument is the Treasury bill (UK, US); bon du trésor (France); Schatzwechsel (Germany, Austria); GKOs in Russia; or similar terms.

The bills may or may not be offered to the same organisations who buy government bonds. In the US, the bills for three or six months or one year are sold by auction weekly to the same primary dealers who buy federal notes and bonds. In the UK, the three and six month bills are sold every Friday by auction to banks. In France, anyone who has an account with the central bank can buy the three or six month or one year Treasury bill. They are sold weekly and money market dealers are usually called 'opérateurs principaux du marché' (OPMs). In Germany, the Bundesbank sells six month bills called 'Bubills' every quarter.

The payment of interest on an instrument which only lasts three months is not necessarily convenient. Most typically, money market instruments are sold *at a discount*. For example, suppose we are talking about a one year US Treasury bill, value $100, sold by auction. A dealer may bid $94. If accepted, they pay $94 and one year later receive $100 from the government. They discounted the $100 by 6% but now earn $6 for investing $94, which is 6.38%. Thus, the market refers to the *discount rate* and the resulting *yield*.

We have mentioned the term 'sale by auction' (or 'tender'). There are two kinds. In one, everyone pays the price they bid ('bid price auction'). In the other, everyone pays the same price (often called the 'striking price'). Anyone bidding at or above the striking price will receive an allocation, but not necessarily all they bid for.

Both types of auction are used in financial markets. For example, the Bank of England sells weekly Treasury bills by tender to the highest bidders – the bid price technique. Government bonds are also sold on a bid price basis, unless it is index-linked stock and then striking price is used.

Just to make matters worse, a German publication I have in front of me says that the money market instruments are sold by auction on a bid price basis, which it calls 'US style', calling a striking price auction a 'Dutch auction'. A French publication says that money market instruments are sold on a bid price basis which it calls a 'Dutch auction'. For what it matters, I think that the Germans are right. Let's avoid all mention of Dutch auctions and simply say that if everyone pays the price they bid, it is a 'bid price' auction, and if everyone pays the same price, it is a 'striking price' auction. Both methods are used. On balance, the bid price method seems to be the most common, although the Federal Reserve auctions are now using striking price.

Local Authority/Public Utility Bills

These may be offered by municipalities, geographic departments, federal states, or public bodies like railways, electricity, gas. There is a very strong market in public sector bills as well as bonds in France and Germany. There are issues by SNCF or Électricité de France, or by the railways and post offices in Germany (Bundesbahn and Bundespost), as well as by the individual federal states. The market in the UK for local authority/municipal bills is very weak but it is quite strong in the US.

Certificates of Deposit (CDs)

These are receipts issued by banks when soliciting wholesale deposits. The lenders may be other banks or corporates or investment institutions. The advantage to the *borrower* is that the money is lent for a specific period of time, for example, three months. The advantage to the *lender* is that, if they need the money back earlier, the certificate can be sold to someone else quite easily. There is a very strong CD market in the US and the European economies, with the exception of Germany.

There is usually an active and efficient market in certificates of deposit. As a result, yield rates will be a little less than those for 'sight' deposits, as we must pay for the advantage of liquidity.

Commercial Paper (CP)

So far, we have looked at short-term borrowing by governments, municipalities, public sector bodies and banks. There remains the question of corporates. Commercial companies can borrow in the wholesale markets and offer a security called 'commercial paper' (CP). It's just another promise to pay back. Central banks have to agree, as this is a deposit taking activity and must be controlled. There will be rules on which companies can or cannot borrow using CP. For example, in the UK companies must have a balance sheet capital of £25m and be publicly quoted on a stock exchange (although not necessarily in the UK). The minimum denomination is £100 000.

Commercial paper is an older market in the US (where it is a huge market with outstanding money owed over $1000 billion). It has hit Europe in the last 15 years. Germany was the last major market to allow CP issues, in January 1991. Before that it was not practical due to a securities tax and the need for prior notification to the Treasury. Outside of Europe, China started a CP market in late 2005. Let's have a look at some figures on domestic commercial paper markets in key centres (from the BIS) in Table 6.2.

CP issues are, of course, just another way of borrowing money and may provide an alternative to borrowing from the bank. In early 1990, the Bank of Spain was struggling to control the credit explosion and limiting banks' ability to lend. The result was a huge increase in CP ('pagares de empresa') issues, as companies borrowed by selling CP (in some cases to the same banks who couldn't lend them money!).

Deregulation applies here as in other markets. The French now allow non-French entities to issue domestic CP and Germany did so from August 1992. At the end of 1995, outstanding CP in Germany from foreign issuers was higher than that from domestic issuers.

How do the CP issuers find the lenders? They set up a programme (perhaps a five year programme) and announce a bank or banks as dealers. If the programme is $500m, then the issuer does not intend to raise $500m *now* (which would be the case if it were a bond issue) but will borrow money from time to time and repay it from time to time, up to the maximum figure. If they wish to borrow $50m for two months, they would notify the bank dealer(s), who ring round typical lenders (other corporates, banks and investment institutions) and tie up the deal, all for a small commission. The banks do not *guarantee* to find lenders but if lenders are scarce may buy the CP themselves as a matter of goodwill. The effect of borrowing from the lenders directly, instead of borrowing from the bank, means that the rate may be less than the interbank rate.

Table 6.2   *Domestic markets for commercial paper*

Market	Amount outstanding end 2004 $ billion
United States	1444.5
Japan	156.0
Canada	92.7
France	92.3
Spain	58.8
Ireland	50.1
Germany	35.6
Taiwan	24.6
Sweden	22.0
Austria	19.0
Portugal	14.9
Singapore	14.7
Belgium	13.7
Finland	7.9

Note: UK excluded as all CP issues in London are classified together, whether domestic or international

Source: BIS Basel.

Bills of Exchange

Another way in which a corporate might raise money short-term is by selling on a short-term trade debt (we met this in Chapter 5). The seller draws up a bill promising to pay for the goods supplied in, say, three months and asks the buyer to sign it. This is the bill of exchange. The seller of the goods can now sell this at a discount to the banks or general money market operators. We have seen that a bank's promise to pay may be better than a trader's and there is always a distinction between bills with the trader's signature (trade bills) and those with a bank's signature (bank or eligible bills). Bills may change hands several times in their short life. There are usually restrictions on the type of transaction that can be represented by a bill and so not all corporates can use bills of exchange. They are not especially popular in the US but widely used in Europe, especially in the UK. In France, the bill is 'lettre de change' and, in Germany, simply 'Wechsel'.

We have now already met several ways in which a corporate might raise money short-term – bank overdraft, a general uncommitted bank line of credit, a revolving credit programme, a CP issue or using bill of exchange finance.

CENTRAL BANK ROLE

A key role is played in domestic money markets by central banks. They have a function as 'lender of the last resort', which we met in Chapter 3. They are prepared to help the other banks (especially commercial banks) with their liquidity problems.

Why would banks meet liquidity problems? In the first place, the key commercial banks must maintain working balances at the central bank. Where central banks insist on special reserves being left (Chapter 3), there will be times when the reserves look comfortable and times when they don't. The reserves are usually based on average balances over a month. Until the end of the month, the banks are not sure what the figure will be. Those banks in surplus will lend to other banks; those in deficit will borrow from other banks. At times, all the banks may have problems. This happens when heavy tax payments are being made. The government's bank balance is going up; the banks' balances at the central bank are going down. The central bank will relend the money to keep everything on an even basis and to avoid wide fluctuations in money market rates. The rate set for the central bank's help gives it control over interest rates. When interest rates change, it is because the central bank changes the rate for its help to other banks.

There are two ways usually in which a central bank will help: direct assistance at special rates such as the *discount rate* or *lombard rate*; or by what is called *open market operations*.

What are these rates? The *discount rate* is the rate at which the bank will discount eligible bills of exchange (that is, top quality bills) for other banks. (The maturity of the bills must not exceed three months.) As this rate is below other rates, there is a quota for each bank, or life would be too easy. If we could discount a bill at $9\frac{1}{2}\%$ and then refinance ourselves at $8\frac{3}{4}\%$ at the central bank we would soon make a lot of money.

The *lombard rate* is an emergency lending rate against top quality securities (eligible bills, bills of exchange or government/federal bonds). Usually, as it is higher than money market rates, no limit to the quantity need be set. At times, however, limits have had to be set for temporary periods because the lombard rate was lower than money market rates.

Open market operations means that the central bank may be prepared to buy bills of exchange, Treasury bills or similar securities to help the banks' liquidity or to sell bills to help drain excess liquidity.

A popular method nowadays is the 'sale and repurchase agreement' (commonly called the *repo*). The central bank will buy nominated securities from the other banks for a stated period, for example, seven days, 14 days, 28 days. At the end of the period, the banks must be ready to buy them back at a rate which includes the rate of interest on the money. The banks sell the securities to the central bank but must repurchase later. This is a very common method all over Europe. In the UK, the more common method used to be that the Bank of England would simply buy eligible securities outright. Later, repos became much more common.

These operations exist not only to help commercial banks with their liquidity but can also be used to influence money supply and market conditions. The central banks may keep the banks short of liquidity to keep credit scarce and stiffen interest rates.

For example, when a repo falls due, there will normally be another repo to keep the banks funded but the second repo may be for a smaller sum than the first.

With the arrival of monetary union in Europe, the previously separate systems of the twelve countries have been unified into one system. Policy is laid down by the European Central Bank (ECB) but is operated on a decentralised basis by the member central banks. Its rates reset on 15 June 2006 were:

- ❏ fixed rate now: 2.75%
- ❏ marginal lending now: 3.75%
- ❏ deposit facility now: 1.75%.

The main refinancing operations are weekly tenders for funds with a two week maturity. There are also monthly tenders with a three month maturity. These tenders are essentially repos.

By way of contrast, the Bank of England used to operate on a daily basis using a mixture of repos and outright purchase of securities. (For those with long memories, and who seem to recall that the Bank did all of its refinancing operations through specialists called 'discount houses', this method has now been abandoned.) However, in May 2006, the whole system changed. From a small group of a dozen banks having to balance their books with the Bank every evening, in future some 40 or so banks and building societies – accounting for nearly all of the UK banking system's sterling balance sheet – will instead maintain a target balance with the Bank on average over the month between Monetary Policy Committee (MPC) meetings. To encourage this averaging, the Bank for the first time will pay interest, at the MPC's rate, on those bankers' balances.

At the start of the new system, these reserves were more than £20 billion. In addition, banks and building societies will be eligible to use standing facilities to place deposits with the Bank or borrow from it against high-quality collateral

– without limit but at a penalty rates of interest, which will place a corridor around the market rate. These measures should help to stabilise short-term interest rates; give the banking system more flexibility in managing liquidity; and make the sterling money markets more user friendly for non specialists.

The new system draws on the best elements from elsewhere, such as the US and the euro area, which tend to operate on a monthly basis rather than daily. The aim is to make the overnight rate more stable – it has tended to be more volatile than in other main currencies.

The decisions are made by the MPC, consisting of the Governor, two deputy Governors, two bank executives and four outsiders.

In the US, the Federal Reserve operates by influencing the overnight interbank federal funds rate and also the deposit rate for bank assistance. The rates are announced by the Federal Open Market Committee, consisting of the seven member board of governors and twelve members from regional Federal Reserve Banks.

DOMESTIC BOND MARKETS

Introduction

The term 'bond' applies to instruments which are medium- to longer-term. The term 'note' is also used in some markets. The US, for example, has two, five and ten year Treasury *notes* and a 30 year Treasury *bond*. In the UK, the same five year instrument would be called a bond.

Language here is a problem in that there is no consistency. The French, for example, call instruments up to five years (but prior to 1992, up to seven years) 'bons du trésor' and from seven years 'obligations du trésor'. The Spanish equally have 'bonos del estado' up to five years but after that they are 'obligaciones del estado'. On the other hand, the ten year issue in Italy is 'buoni del tesoro'.

Let's look at some general characteristics of bonds. As we saw in Chapter 1, they are simply receipts or promises to pay back money lent. We are not, here, talking of short-term money, however, but medium- to long-term borrowings – in excess of one year and possibly for 30 or more years.

The general features are:

- ❏ The name of the bond
- ❏ The nominal or par value in the currency of denomination
- ❏ The redemption value – usually the nominal value, but there are other possibilities (index linking, for example)
- ❏ The rate of interest expressed as a % of nominal value; this is called the 'coupon': the frequency of payment is stated
- ❏ The redemption date.

The rate of interest is called the coupon because 'bearer' bonds have no register of holders. The bond states that the issuer owes the 'bearer', whoever that may be. The bond therefore has attachments called 'coupons' so that the bearer may detach these as required and claim the interest. Even where bonds are registered and the interest can be posted to the holder's home, the market still refers to the 'coupon' or 'coupon rate'.

The coupon could be variable in cases where the rate of interest is changed periodically in line with market rates. As the word 'bond' implies a fixed rate of interest, instruments like this are usually called *floating rate notes*. If issued in London, the coupon may be defined as 'LIBOR +45 basis points' and reviewed six monthly.

Some stocks have no redemption date and are called *undated* or *perpetual*. If the holder needs the capital, they must sell the bond to someone else in the secondary market.

Typically, bonds are classified by remaining maturity. The scale may well be:

❑ *Shorts*   – life of up to five years
❑ *Mediums*   – life of five to 15 years
❑ *Longs*   – life of 15 years or over.

Notice that this is the *remaining* maturity. A 20 year bond is a 'long' at first but ten years later it's a 'medium' and six years later it's a 'short'.

At original issue, bonds may be sold as an open *offer for sale* or sold directly to a smaller number of professional investors and called a *private placing*.

In an offer for sale, a syndicate of banks with one bank as *lead manager* will buy the bonds en bloc from the issuer and resell them to investors. In this way, they underwrite the issue since, if the investors don't buy, the banks will be forced to keep them. Needless to say, they charge fees for this risk.

If the lead bank buys all the bonds and sells them to the syndicate, it's usually called the *bought deal*. The syndicate members may themselves then sell the bonds at varying prices. More commonly these days, the lead manager and syndicate buy the bonds simultaneously and agree to sell at the same price for a period – the *fixed price reoffering*. This is very common in the US and now in the so-called 'euromarkets'. Less frequently (apart from government bonds) there may not be a syndicate but the bonds are sold by competitive *auction*.

There are several types of bond according to the issuer:

❑ Government bonds
❑ Local authority/Public utility bonds
❑ Mortgage and other asset backed bonds
❑ Corporate bonds
❑ Foreign bonds
❑ Junk bonds.

Corporate bonds may also be:

❏ Debentures, or
❏ Convertibles.

and there is a hybrid type of instrument, the preference share or participation stock.

Government Bonds

Almost always, these seem to dominate the bond markets. Most modern governments are running a budget deficit and this leads to large-scale issues of bonds. Sometimes the secondary market is run on stock exchanges (France, Germany, UK) and sometimes outside stock exchanges (US).

As regards the types of bonds and method of issue, there are many variations:

❏ The bonds may be issued by the central bank (US, Germany, France) or by the Ministry of Finance (Netherlands, Japan), or general 'Debt Management Offices' (UK, Ireland, Sweden, Portugal, New Zealand).
❏ They may be sold on a regular day per month.
❏ The issue may be to specialist dealers (US, UK, France, Germany, Italy) or to a syndicate of banks in agreed proportions (Switzerland).
❏ Bonds may be 'bearer' status or registered. For example, in the UK, government bonds are registered and the registrar's department handles five million interest payments per year and one million changes of ownership. In Germany, the most important government bonds for the wholesale markets are bearer bonds. There are no certificates and buying/selling is entered on the computerised Bundeschuldenbuch.
❏ Some markets pay interest twice per year (US, UK, Italy, Japan), others only once per year (France, Germany, Netherlands, Spain, Belgium).
❏ US government bonds are priced in fractions (down to $\frac{1}{32}$). Elsewhere bonds are priced in decimals.

Let's look at some examples:

In the *US*, two year Treasury notes are sold every month, while five and ten year Treasury notes are sold every quarter. They are sold by auction, on regular dates, to some 40 primary dealers. The issues of 30 year bonds were stopped in November 2001 but resumed in 2006 after requests from the Bond Market Association. In general, markets have been keen to lock in relatively low interest rates.

In *France*, government bonds are called OATS (Obligations Assimilables du Trésor) and are sold on a regular monthly auction basis (on the first Thursday in each month). They are sold to primary dealers who have an obligation to support the auction. They must take up 3% of annual bond issuance and trade 3% of secondary market turnover. The primary dealers are called 'spécialistes en valeurs du trésor' (SVTs). However, at each auction the offerings are usually more of existing bonds rather than offering new ones each time. A point to note is that there are two and five year issues called Treasury bills rather than bonds. These are known as BTAN (Bons du Trésor à Intérêt Annuel). (Short-term Treasury bills are BTF – Bons du Trésor à Taux Fixe.) BTANs are sold on the third Thursday in each month.

In line with the trend towards longer dated bonds, the French Treasury issued a 50 year bond in February 2005.

In *Germany*, there were two and four year medium-term notes – Bundesschatz-anweisungen, but these maturities were lowered in mid-1996 to two years and referred to as 'Schätze'. There are also five year government bonds – Bundes-obligationen, and 10–30 year bonds – Bundesanleihen. The ten year issues are the popular ones (rather than of longer duration) and most are fixed rate, although there is the occasional Floating Rate Bond.

In Germany, there are bond issues from the Federal States (Länder), the railways and the post office. There are also issues from the German Unity Fund (Fonds Deutsche Einheit). All are issued for them by the Bundesbank.

The dealers in German bonds are known as the 'Federal Loan Bidding Group' and there are about 70 dealers.

Bundesobligationen are issued in series. A series is offered continuously for four–six weeks 'on tap'. They are aimed at retail buyers, as are the Treasury Financing Notes (Finanzierungschätze). At the end of the period, the unsold bonds are offered for sale by auction. The main retail bond for savers, however, is the Bundesschatz-briefe. These are sold continuously by all banks and financial institutions and are for six or seven years. The bonds can be sold back at par at any time but the longer the holder keeps them, the greater the rate of interest.

All *French* and *German* bonds are now issued in the new currency, the euro, and all outstanding bonds have also been converted to the euro.

In *Japan*, government bonds are sold by auction by the Ministry of Finance. Some 40% are sold to a bank syndicate in agreed proportions; 60% are sold by the auction method. Two, four, five, six and ten year bonds are sold monthly and 20 year bonds are sold quarterly. Interest payments are semi-annual. Government, municipal and public sector bonds are 60% of issuance and dominate the market. In December 2005, a goverment body controlling motorway development issued a 40 year bond – the longest maturity in the Japanese fixed income market.

In the *UK*, government bonds are called 'gilts' or 'gilt-edged', meaning a very secure investment (the term came into widespread use in the 1930s). The bonds are issued on regular dates and sold to 13 specialist dealers called 'gilt-edged market makers'. Bonds not taken up at an auction are bought by the Debt Management Office and sold whenever the dealers want them as 'tap stock'. Maturities range typically from 5 to 25 years but 50 year bonds have now been issued. There was particular interest in the issue in September 2005 of the world's first index-linked

50 year bond. It was not sold as usual by an auction but to a syndicate of investment banks; this allowed the issue to be increased if there was high demand. It was, in fact, increased from £1 billion to £1.25 billion. There was a large demand from pension funds and insurance companies, anxious to match long-dated liabilities with assets.

Gilts are divided into three main classes:

1   Dated
2   Undated
3   Index-linked.

New undated gilts are no longer issued but there are six still in existence. There is no redemption date. In bond markets, bonds with no redemption date may be called undated, perpetual or irredeemable. There is very little trading of undated gilts by the wholesale markets.

Index-linked gilts pay a rate of interest and a redemption value based on the change in the Retail Price Index in the same period. Other governments which offer index-linked bonds are Australia, Canada, Iceland, Israel, New Zealand, Sweden and, more recently, the US, France, Japan and Germany. China issued an index-linked bond in 1998. The UK index-linked sector is much the biggest of these, now 24% of all outstanding government bonds. Issue began in 1981. In May 1996, the US Treasury Secretary announced that they would issue index-linked Treasury notes and bonds for the first time, and began in January 1997. The French government followed suit with its first issue in September 1998.

(In 1973, the French government issued bonds – Giscard bonds – linked to the change in the price of gold between then and 1988. As the price of gold rose, this caused great embarrassment! The bond was used by Tom Wolfe in *The Bonfire of the Vanities*.)

Why do governments issue index-linked bonds anyway? There are three reasons:

❏   Risk averse investors, such as pension funds and retired people, like the idea.
❏   Monetary policy is more credible – the government has an incentive to keep inflation low.
❏   The yield helps the government and others to estimate market views on further inflation. The difference between the yield on index-linked stock and ordinary stock should equal the expected inflation rate.

The idea is not totally new. In 1780, the State of Massachusetts issued a bond where payment of interest and principal was linked to a commodity basket of corn, beef, wool and leather!

Spanish government bonds are called 'bonos del estado' with maturities of three and five years but the ten year maturity is called 'obligaciones del estado'. The central bank sells these on a regular date each month.

Italian government bonds are called BTP (Buoni del Tesoro Poliennali) if fixed rate. These are 2–10 years in maturity. However, there are floating rate bonds of similar maturity called CCT (Certificati Credito del Tesoro). Both are sold by the central bank to 20 primary dealers on fixed dates every month. There are also six year bonds which buyers can sell back after three years called CTO (Certificati del Tesoro con Opzione).

There seems to be a trend at the moment for some governments to issue longer-dated bonds than in the past. In early 1999, Japan and Greece issued their first 30 year bonds, and Switzerland issued a 50 year bond (the first for Switzerland since 1909!). In the whole eurozone area in 2005 there were far more issues of bonds with maturities of 15 years or more than in previous years.

As explained earlier in this chapter (see 'Treasury Bills'), some auctions of government stock are bid price and some striking price. A bid price auction might seem to be the obvious answer. The argument for striking price, however, is that it avoids the problem of the 'winner's curse', that is that some bidders may pay a higher price and end up with bonds that they can't sell. The belief is that striking price may encourage more bidders to participate. Either way, the evidence does not seem to be very strong. The US used to use bid prices, but now uses striking price; the UK, which used to use striking price, now uses bid price (except for index-linked). (An example of the result of a bid price auction is shown as Appendix 1 to this chapter.)

Most government bond markets allow dealing to begin a few days before the auction – the 'grey' or 'when issued' market. Institutions can buy from primary dealers at an agreed price which reduces the dealers' risk.

Local Authority/Public Sector Bonds

We have already mentioned issues in Germany by the railways, post offices, Federal states and the German Unity Fund. Public sector issues are also very common in France. There are the utilities like SNCF, Électricité de France and Gaz de France. There are also public sector bodies like Crédit Foncier (housing credits) and Crédit Local de France (local authority financing). Bonds may, of course, be issued by cities, like New York, or regions, like the Basque Country.

Local authority and public sector issues are very rare in the UK, although some long-dated bonds issued in the 1970s are still traded. Municipal bonds are a big market in the US.

Mortgage and Asset-Backed Bonds

In some markets, there is a big market in mortgage bonds. In the US, for example, it has been the custom for many years to bundle up mortgages and use them as the backing security for mortgage bonds. The mortgages may be guaranteed by bodies with names like Ginnie Mae, Fannie Mae and Sallie Mae. (They, naturally, stand for something much more formal and boring, for example, Government National Mortgage Association – GNMA and hence Ginnie Mae.) The US mortgage bond market is huge – over $1000bn outstanding.

In Germany, some 40 banks, including eight public mortgage banks, had the right to issue mortgage bonds called Pfandbriefe. That situation is changing, however, as from July 2005, any German bank could issue Pfandbriefe if they met the conditions laid down by the German regulator, BaFin. Banks also issue mortgage bonds in Denmark and Finland. These, however, are not the same as the US mortgage bonds. The latter involve taking the original mortgages off the balance sheet, placing them in a separate *special purpose vehicle* (SPV) and issuing bonds financed by the stream of principal and interest payments of the mortgages (see Figure 6.4). The German Pfandbriefe are simply a way for the banks to raise money to fund their mortgage loans (although they are, of course, a very secure investment).

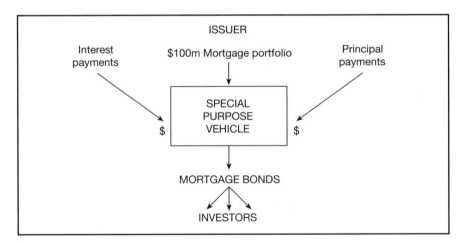

Figure 6.4   *Asset-backed security issue*

The technique involved in the US case is called *securitisation of assets* and we refer to *asset-backed securities* (ABS). You may also see reference to *collateralised mortgage obligations* (CMO) or *commercial mortgage-backed securities* (CMBS) While we have so far only mentioned the US, the technique is also used in Japan and Europe (and is growing).

Again, we have so far only referred to mortgages, but the technique can and has been used to take any stream of income payments (or income and principal payments) and use them to fund an ABS issue. (Why banks and others do this will be explained shortly.) The market is growing in ingenuity, as will be seen from the following list of income streams funding ABS issues:

❑	Auto loans	VW, General Motors and others
❑	Record royalties	David Bowie, Rod Stewart
❑	Telephone calls	Telemex, Mexico
❑	Future export revenues	Brazilian Iron Ore
❑	Football season tickets	Real Madrid, Lazio, Fiorentina
❑	Property rentals	British Land and others
❑	Rolling stock leases	Nomura in the UK
❑	Credit card receivables	Citibank, MBNA
❑	Bank corporate loans	National Westminster, Hypovereinsbank
❑	Non-performing loans	Banca di Roma
❑	Tax arrears	Portugal
❑	Life insurance premiums	Swiss Re.

Let's look at two examples.

The National Westminster Bank issue aroused tremendous interest. It was first used in November 1996 and again in 1997 under the acronym 'ROSE' (Repeat Offering Securitised Entity Funding). The first issue was to a value of $5 billion and represented as much as one third of NatWest's corporate loan book, being loans to some 300 large corporates in the UK, continental Europe and the US. They were issued as eleven classes of notes – various levels of seniority offering a range of risk/return ratios. The bank guarantees anonymity and continues to administer the original loans.

The British Land bond was issued in May 1999 and was based on the rental income of twelve properties in London's The Broadgate Centre. At £1.54 billion, it was the largest property securitisation in Europe so far. Like NatWest, the issue was made in several tranches of eurobonds varying between medium- and long-term.

To be feasible, all we need is a pool of homogeneous assets like mortgages, trade receivables, motor car loans and so on. The funds are pooled in the same SPV which has a 'firewall' between it and the original issuer. The payments are sometimes (but not always) guaranteed against default, and usually the bonds attract a high credit rating.

What, then, are the attractions of this technique for the issuer?

So far as banks are concerned, it is the ability to lighten the balance sheet and make better use of capital. Basel Committee capital ratio rules make it expensive to keep low profit items on the balance sheet. The money can, when released, be used for more profitable investments. For NatWest this was a major motive in the ROSE case. Low yielding loans were removed from its books without jeopardising client relationships. In the case of British Land, the money was used to pay back more expensive bank debt and get cheaper funding. The average cost of funds was said to have been reduced from 8.49% to 7.4%, saving at least £20m in 1999.

The example in the list above of 'tax arrears' refers to an issue by Portugal in April 2004 when bonds worth €1.7 billion ($2.0 billion) were sold backed by tax and social security arrears. Portugal had a budget deficit of over 6%, easily exceeding the eurozone limit of 3%. The bond was an attempt to accelerate cash flow. Unfortunately, by August, 2005 receipts were only 56% of the forecast figure and the bond was downgraded by Moody's and Fitch. As a result, further issues planned by Greece and Belgium were withdrawn.

Another example of how things can go wrong is the David Bowie record royalties. A slump in record sales led Moody's in May 2003 to put the bonds on negative watch.

Also in the list above is the securitisation of anticipated life insurance premiums by Swiss Re. These insurance bonds are likely to become more popular in the future. The Swiss Re issue in January 2005 followed issues by National Provident Institution, Barclays Life and Friends Provident.

Commercial mortgage-backed securities are a specific example of asset-backed securities (ABS) or collateralised mortgage obligations (CMO). Being based on commercial property they are at risk if property values fall. For example, hurricane Katrina materially affected some CMBS bonds.

Crédit Suisse estimates that the UK has 60% of the European market and Germany only 3%. Thus the potential in Germany is great, especially as there will have been many new issuers of Pfandbriefe with the change in regulations in mid 2005. In general, Germany has the highest total of bank loans in Europe (Crédit Suisse estimate €2300 billion ($2700 billion) with plenty of scope for securitisation. In addition, the Basel 11 rule will encourage banks to get low quality loans off the balance sheet.

Covered bonds is another term one may meet in the field of ABS. In an ABS transaction, the bond is issued by a special purpose vehicle (SPV) and is removed from the balance sheet of the issuer. With covered bonds, the assets remain on the balance sheet of the issuer and investors have recourse to the company in the event of bankruptcy. As the risk to the investor is reduced, the cost to the issuer is lower. The UK regulator, the Financial Services Authority, has ruled that 20% of a bank's or building society's assets may be covered by these bonds before additional capital is required. We have seen issues from Abbey National, Bradford and Bingley, Northern Rock and HBOS. Germany is a big market as Pfandbriefe are covered bonds with no SPV. Again, Basel 11 will make these products more attractive to the issuer.

Structured bonds or *structured finance* is another term applied to ABS issues which appear in a different form. What happens is that the assets which might form part of a normal ABS issue are pooled and transferred to an SPV as before. However, and this is the crucial difference, the asset pools are tranched according to credit risk – some low risk, some high risk. This is a more sophisticated way of handling the transfer of credit risk to the investor.

ABS in the US in 2005 passed $1000 billion (£600 billion) for the first time. Issues in 1985 were only $1.2 billion (£0.72 billion).

Corporate Bonds

There are, of course, bonds issued by corporates and there is a very strong market in the US. In Europe, as a generalisation, the corporate bond market is weaker, being overshadowed by the government and public sector bond market. In Germany there is, anyway, a big tradition of reliance on bank finance as opposed to either bonds or equities. Very large European corporates may, in any case, find it easier to issue the bond in London as a *eurobond* rather than as a domestic bond (see later in this chapter).

Corporate bonds can, however, be quite long-dated. In the UK, a property company (MEPC) issued a bond in 1988 that will redeem in 2032 – 44 years. Also, British Land did a 40 year issue in September 1995. Property companies look far ahead to long-term leases and commitments. Apart from these, we have seen 100 year bonds issued by bodies like Walt Disney, Coca Cola and IBM, although sometimes the issuer has an option to redeem the bond after 30 years. These bonds are so long-dated that they are almost equity, but the interest is tax deductible. IBM's 100 year bond only cost them 10 basis points more than their 30 year bond. Who among the investors looks so far ahead? The answer is pension funds and life assurance companies who have to meet long-term liabilities.

There are a number of variations on the theme:

Debentures are corporate bonds which are backed by security, for example, land and buildings. If the issuer goes into liquidation, these assets must be sold to pay the bondholders. Because they are more secure, however, the rate of interest is less. Some investment funds will only invest in corporate bonds which are debentures. Again, language is a problem. The definition given is the UK usage of the term. In the US and Canada, 'debenture' may be used to describe any bond. Just bear in mind that corporate bonds may be unsecured (the majority) or secured on specific assets. Whilst securing a bond gives a corporate cheaper finance, it's also inconvenient to tie up assets in this way. Lengthy and tedious legal procedures must be gone through before these assets can be disposed of and replaced by others. MEPC and British Land (mentioned above) have both unsecured bonds and debentures on the market. The unsecured bonds pay 1.1% more than the debentures in the case of MEPC and 70 basis points in the case of British Land.

A *convertible* is a bond which can be converted later, either into another type of bond (for example, convertible gilts) or into equity. The difference between the implied conversion price of the equity and the market price is called the 'premium'. For example, the bond may confer the right, after three years, to convert $100 of bond into 50 shares. The conversion price is $2 per share; if the market price is $1.60 at the time, then the initial premium is 25%. If the conversion price remains above the market price, then the bond will redeem in the normal way.

The attraction to the *investor* is the mix of risk and return – the steady income we associate with a bond with the possible capital gain we associate with a share.

For the *issuer*, the finance is cheaper as the interest rate will be less due to its attraction. What if investors wish to convert, where do the shares come from? The issuer creates *new* shares. Suppose the bond is $500 million. The issuer hopes that instead of having to find $500 million to redeem the bond, they will issue $500 million of new shares instead. True, the equity will be diluted but it probably won't be by a large margin. In Europe (but not as clearly in the US), shareholders must give approval for the issue of convertibles because, generally, any new shares issued for cash must be offered to the existing shareholders.

Sometimes convertibles hit unforeseen problems. The general fall in the Japanese stock market since 1990 meant that the market price of many shares was below the conversion price. With Japan seen as somewhat risky, refinancing these convertibles was expensive.

Sometimes the right to convert is into another company's shares (which the issuing company owns). For example, Deutsche Bank issued €1.5 billion in early 1999 to help fund its takeover of Bankers Trust. The bonds, however, are exchangeable into Allianz shares, which Deutsche owns. This is a way of Deutsche reducing its holding in Allianz without directly selling the shares and moving the price against it. The premium was 30%. Deutsche had previously done a convertible with the right to convert into shares of Daimler-Benz (as it then was), which the bank also owned. (The German banks are slowly reducing their shareholdings in large domestic corporates.) More recently, Société Générale issued a convertible bond in 2005 in which the conversion is into the shares of the Italian oil company, ENI.

An alternative to a convertible bond is to issue a bond in which the right to buy shares later at a certain price is contained in a separate *warrant*. This is more flexible than the convertible, in that the warrant can be used later to buy shares more cheaply while still keeping the bond. The warrants are often detached from the bonds and sold separately.

Sometimes, an entity which is not the company may issue warrants on the company's shares, for example, Citigroup offering warrants on Eurotunnel shares. This is often called the *covered warrants market* because Citigroup must cover the risk by owning the shares. If Eurotunnel issued a bond with warrants, it has the right to issue new shares if need be. Naturally, Citigroup do not have that right and must obtain the shares conventionally. Warrants may be (and frequently are) offered on a 'basket' of different shares. These covered warrants (very popular these days) are really simply part of the traded options market and priced accordingly (see Chapter 12).

Preference shares usually pay dividend as a fixed percentage rate. If there is any shortage of money, their dividends must be paid out before other dividends. In the event of liquidation, preference shareholders have priority over ordinary share-holders. They normally have no voting rights. If the dividend cannot be paid, it is legally owed to them. Hence they are 'cumulative' (normally). On the continent of Europe, these are typically called participation certificates or, in Germany and Switzerland, Genusscheine or Participationsscheine.

The Americans use the term 'preferred stock' and the French have several variations on this theme:

❑ Certificats d'investissement
❑ Titres participatifs – public sector only and the dividend may be partly fixed and partly linked to profit
❑ Actions à dividende prioritaire (ADP) – the dividend is the ordinary dividend plus a given percentage.

The general features of all the above are non-voting, preference in the event of liquidation and cumulative. They are hybrid instruments with some characteristics of a bond and some of an equity. Banks have done many issues to raise capital to count as Tier 1 Capital (National Westminster Bank, September 1991) or Tier 2. To count as Tier 1 they must be undated and non-cumulative. In April 1996, TB Finance did an issue of ¥100bn preference shares, convertible into common shares of Tokai Bank. As conversion at some point is mandatory, the issue counts as Tier 1 capital.

Hybrid Bonds

While preference shares were referred to above as a hybrid instrument, there are bonds called *hybrid bonds* which aim more specifically at having characteristics of bonds and equity. They are perpetual and deeply subordinated and may defer coupon payments (non-cumulative). Rating agencies tend to view them as quasi-equity and capital can thus be raised without putting credit ratings at risk. Early in 2005, Moody's clarified terms on which they could be treated as 70% equity. They are more expensive to the issuer but are treated as debt for accounting purposes and thus tax deductible. As a result of the Moody's decision, the market took off in the second half of 2005, with issues from Thomson, the Scandinavian energy group, Dong and Vattenfall and the German corporations, Bayer and Südzucker. The Bayer issue, as an example, paid 175 basis points more than the equivalent bund (the German government bond). One final point, if the issuer falls below investment grade, the bonds must be called at par.

As hybrid bonds seem to offer cheaper financing than alternative (equity or ordinary) bonds, they are becoming very popular. The *Financial Times* headline on 6 February 2006 was 'Scramble To Exploit Hybrid Financing'. Issues in the US in 2005 totalled $4 billion (£2.4 billion), but some observers forecast ten times this much in 2006.

Foreign Bonds

Foreign bonds are domestic issues by non-residents – 'bulldogs' in the UK, 'yankees' in the US, 'matadors' in Spain, 'samurai' in Tokyo and even 'kangaroo' bonds in Australia! In November 2005, the International Finance Corporation, the private sector finance arm of the World Bank, issued the first foreigner renminbi bond in Hong Kong – this is a 'panda' bond.

Notice that the bonds are domestic bonds in the local currency, it's only the *issuer* who is foreign. They should not be confused with *international* bonds (also called *eurobonds*), which are bonds issued outside their natural market.

Non-US firms seeking dollar funding, for example, have a choice. The bonds may be issued in London as 'eurobonds' or in the US as 'yankee' bonds. The investment community is different in both markets. While the ultimate investors in the US might have a slightly parochial attitude to European firms, the investment institutions themselves have sophisticated credit assessment teams. In the absence of formal credit ratings, they will make up their own minds. The eurobond market might be guided by credit ratings (or their absence) rather more slavishly. In any case, market conditions change from time to time. Sometimes it's easier to raise dollars in New York, sometimes in London.

Foreign bonds may be subject to a different tax regime or other restrictions. For example, 'yankees' can only be sold to qualified institutional buyers in the first 2 years.

Junk Bonds

This was a phenomenon which occurred in the US domestic markets in the 1970s and 1980s. We mentioned earlier in this chapter, under 'Credit Ratings', that bonds rated below BBB grade were essentially speculative. As a result, they offered a much higher rate of interest.

A clever researcher at Drexel Burnham Lambert, one Michael Milken, did a study of the behaviour of such bonds in the early 1970s. He proved that an investment in these bonds would return a better yield than investment grade bonds, even deducting the loss due to greater defaults. He was not the first to discover this – other academic studies had come to the same conclusion – but he was the first to do anything about it. At first, his firm dealt in underpriced bonds in this category in the secondary markets. They then began to look at the potential for new issues. At that time, the bonds of 90% of US corporates would, if issued, not be investment grade. Drexels (and Michael Milken) began to do primary issues too, arguing that the judgement of the rating agencies was too harsh.

Then the bonds were used to raise large sums of money for takeover bids. The market began to refer to them as 'junk bonds' (Drexels called them 'high yield bonds', a more respectable title!).

Junk bonds slowly became notorious because huge sums of money were raised with these bonds by entrepreneurs who bought companies much bigger than they were – the 'leveraged' takeover – for example, Nelson Peltz/National Can; Ronald Perelman/Revlon; Carl Icahn/TWA.

Each year at Beverly Hills, Drexels would hold a 'High Yield Bond Conference' at which the wheeler-dealers and the potential investors would sit at the feet of the 'junk bond king' Michael Milken and be entertained in lavish style. The rather less formal name for the conference was the 'Predators' Ball'. (The whole amazing story is told in Connie Bruch, *The Predators' Ball*, Simon & Schuster, 1988.)

Later, the US Securities and Exchange Commission decided that Drexels and Michael Milken had broken the law in various ways during the course of their activities. In addition, banks and other investors realised that they had gone too far, especially with the arrival of the recession. The bubble eventually burst. The firm of Drexel Burnham Lambert collapsed in early 1990 and the 'junk bond king' Michael Milken was jailed for 10 years for infringing various laws, although the sentence was reduced later.

Opinion is still divided between those who believe that Milken revitalised corporate America and those who think that his sentence wasn't nearly long enough!

For a long time there were no junk bond issues in London's eurobond market. In April 1997, however, a UK venture capital company, Doughty Hanson, issued a non-investment grade 10 year bond for DM157m to finance the takeover of a Swiss firm. Other issues followed. Foreseeing monetary union, interest rates in many European countries were falling and investors were anxious to find higher yields, albeit at higher risk. The Far East crisis in 1997 and the Russian default in 1998 dealt the market a severe blow as investors' liking for risk cooled dramatically! However, memories are short and, with the general recovery of the markets in 2004/05, investors were once more seeking higher interest payments for higher risk. In March 2005, Standard and Poor's did a report on the decline in ratings. In the 1980s, 32 industrial companies in the US were rated AAA. This was down to six by the time of the report. In 1980, two thirds of Standard and Poor's corporate ratings were investment grade but now two thirds were non-investment grade. This has not stopped sales of securities issued by these companies due to investors' current appetite for risk. According to Moody's Investor Services, 91.3% of international bonds in London were investment grade in 1997, but only 69.1% in 2005.

Islamic Bonds

In Chapter 2, we mentioned Islamic banking techniques to conform with Islamic law or Sharia. There are also Islamic bonds issued on a similar principle and known as *sukuks*. For example, to fund its proposed takeover of P&O Ports, DP World, from Dubai, issued the biggest sukuk to date – $3.5 billion (£2.1 billion) with a duration of two years. To conform with Islamic law, no interest payments will be made. The bond was to be repaid in two years with conversion rights for part of the value into DP World shares. In May 2006, Moody's calculated that total global issuance was now $41 billion (£25 billion) from almost nothing five years ago.

Malaysia is the largest Islamic bond market in the world and, by June 2006, 75% of issues were Islamic-compliant.

INTERNATIONAL MARKETS

Background: Eurocurrencies

Some markets are called *international* markets or, misleadingly, *Euromarkets*.

We are talking here of dealing outside the natural market of the transaction. For example, December 1996 saw the second biggest privatisation of all time – Deutsche Telekom (the Japanese NTT being the biggest). Shares were offered in tranches to Germany, UK, the rest of Europe, the Americas and Asia.

In late 1991, Kuwait raised a huge dollar loan, $5.5bn, from a syndicate of banks in London to repair the damage caused during the Gulf War. It's an 'international loan'.

Bonds are frequently raised in London by syndicates of banks of all nationalities and in dollars, yen, euros and other major currencies. We call them 'eurobonds' or, more correctly, 'international bonds'. For example, SNCF (the French railways) may decide to issue a bond in London and in dollars, instead of in Paris and in French francs.

How did all this begin? Its origins lie in the period after the Second World War. Russia and so-called 'Iron Curtain' countries which held dollars were worried that the US authorities might seize them for political reasons. The Russians owned a bank in France, Banque Commercial pour l'Europe du Nord, and concentrated their holdings there. This bank lent the dollars to other non-US banks in Europe. Some say that the term Eurodollars was used because the telex code of the bank was Eurobank. Others believe that it was a natural name for dollar dealings outside the US.

In the post-war years there were plenty of dollars in the hands of non-Americans. American spending in Europe through the Marshall Plan was one source. The year 1957 saw the Treaty of Rome and the arrival in Europe of American multinational firms – earning dollars and spending them. A European firm might earn, say, $20 million for sales to US firms. The dollars were credited to its account with, perhaps, Banque Nationale de Paris. These were now Eurodollars and could be lent to other entities in Europe. They were dollars outside the control of the US authorities. For years, for example, there was a strict control on interest rates called 'Regulation Q'. It put an upper level on interest rates offered to depositors. If our mythical European firm above chose not to convert the dollars into francs but lend them to BNP on deposit, BNP's interest rate was not constrained by Regulation Q – hence an increase in dealings in dollars held by non-US residents.

(The *Oxford English Dictionary* in 1972 suggested that the first recorded reference to the phrase 'Eurodollar' was in the financial review of *The Times,* 24 October 1960.)

In July 1963, President Kennedy decided to tax 'yankee bonds'. Remember yankees? They are dollar bonds issued in the US by non-residents. The perception was that perhaps these bonds could be issued in Europe, finding the investors amongst those non-US residents who held dollar balances. In 1963, Warburgs lead managed a bond issue in London worth $15 million for the Italian motorway authority, Autostrade – generally believed to be the first eurobond – a dollar bond issued in Europe and not the US. London, with its non-protectionist policies and its long traditions, became the natural market for this new business. To quote Al Alletzhauser in his interesting history *The House of Nomura* (Bloomsbury, 1990):

> *Almost overnight the world's financial centre shifted to London. The big four Japanese stockbrokers wasted no time in setting up offices there. If they could not sell Japanese stock to the Americans, they would sell them to the Europeans. Over the years, it proved to be one of the most profitable moves Japan's brokers ever made abroad.*

In 1950, there were 140 foreign banks in London; by 1973 the number had risen to 340 and today there over 500. It was a vital shot in the arm for the London financial market which had suffered from the post-war decline of the UK as a major economic power.

We said earlier that the term 'euro-' is misleading. For example, dealings might take place in Tokyo, relending dollars held by Asian organisations. The terms 'euromarkets' and 'eurobonds' are well established, however, although 'international markets' is a more correct term for dealings in a currency outside its natural domestic market (and, thus, outside the *control* of its domestic market). There is now a further confusion between a eurobond and a bond denominated in the euro! Eurocurrencies is a wider term, reminding us that the currency might not be dollars but yen, euros, drachma and so on.

For reasons we shall see below, eurocurrency dealings grew enormously from an estimated $1 billion in 1959 to an estimated $12 trillion (£7.2 trillion) in 2005 (Thomson Financial figures). The irony is that while these markets grew as a result of restrictions in the US, they did not disappear when the restrictions were later abolished.

The Syndicated Loan Market

In 1973–74 came events that led to a large increase in dollars held by non-US residents – the OPEC countries' oil price increases. Oil, which was $3 per barrel in October 1973, was $10.5 per barrel by January 1974. This led to a huge rise in dollar balances held by OPEC countries and a huge reduction in the dollar balances of many sovereign states. The services of international banks were required to recycle these dollars from those with the surpluses to those in deficit, many of whom were underdeveloped countries – largely in Africa and South America.

The original use of the eurodollars was for the short-term interbank market. Then we saw syndicates of banks getting together to lend the dollar balances as part of, say, a seven year loan to Mexico. As the source was dependent on what might be short-term balances, the loans were all at floating rate, so that rates could be adjusted according to the new LIBOR rates in London. The banks might argue (as we look back on this period) that they were encouraged to lend by the world's financial and political authorities, worried about a bottleneck in the world's financial system.

To share the risk, the banks spread each loan across a syndicate of banks, perhaps with as many as 100 banks in a syndicate. Notices of these loans would appear in the London *Financial Times* and other relevant publications – 'as a matter of record only'. What was the notice for then? It was an advertisement for the banks concerned – a *tombstone* notice, in the jargon of the trade (some say because financial notices in the last century were placed next to those for births and deaths!).

Whether the banks were encouraged to lend or not, they did so and on a large scale – plenty of dollars, plenty of borrowers and nice rates of interest. To be fair, they must have looked at some borrowers, for example, Mexico or Nigeria and thought 'How can we go wrong, when they have this precious commodity, oil?'

The biggest lender was Citibank, whose chairman, Walter Wriston, encouraged the others with the famous words 'Sovereign borrowers do not go bust.' He meant that governments come and go but countries would always survive and they had assets which could, if necessary, be seized.

The International Debt Crisis

Walter Wriston couldn't have been more wrong. For a time, indeed, 'all went merry as a marriage bell' as the poet Byron says. However, his next line is: 'But hush! hark! a deep sound strikes like a rising knell!'

The deep sound in this case was the voice of the Mexican finance minister telling an audience of bankers in New York, on 20 August 1982, that repayment of principal on bank loans was to be deferred for three months. Brazil, Argentina and others quickly followed suit.

Falling oil prices, falling commodity prices generally and a large rise in dollar interest rates (remember, the loans are floating rate) had done the damage. Mexico followed its announcement by imposing total exchange controls and nationalising all the banks.

To understand the banks' reaction to this, we must realise that the three largest South American debtor nations owed commercial banks $150 billion, and that Mexican debt alone accounted for 44% of the capital of the nine largest US banks. The very survival of some of the world's largest banks was in question, and that meant that the whole international financial system was in jeopardy.

The banks met in fear and panic at the IMF in Toronto in September 1982. A wit described the meeting as 'rearranging the deckchairs on the Titanic'. The key figures – Jacques de Larosière, IMF managing director, Paul Volcker, Chairman of the Federal Reserve Board, Gordon Richardson, Governor of the Bank of England and Fritz Leutwiler, Chairman of BIS – mapped out a strategy. The essence was to buy time – to ask the debtors to implement economic policies to reduce the deficits that had led to the initial problems and to ask the banks to give the new policies time to work. The loans were to be rescheduled and repayments of interest deferred.

In a sense, it was a cat and mouse game. J.M. Keynes once said, 'if you owe the bank £1000 you may be in trouble; if it's £1 million, maybe the bank's in trouble.'

The banks were as much at risk as the debtors. Cut them off from new supplies of money and they can no longer buy Western goods. Drive them into the ground with austere economic programmes and you may provoke a coup d'état and a communist government. America hardly wants a communist government in Mexico, on its doorstep.

Things were not easy. In 1985, the IMF suspended loans to Brazil and Argentina as economic targets were missed. Peru announced a limit on debt repayments. In December, oil halved in price from $30 per barrel to $15 – Mexico's situation worsened.

Everyone called it the 'LDC debt crisis' (LDC, Less Developed Countries). 1987 was a crisis year, as Brazil suspended interest payments and spent all year arguing with the banks.

Up to 1987, banks had had bad debt reserves of only about 5%. Walter Wriston's successor at Citibank, John Reed, decided in May 1987 to grasp the nettle and increased the bad debt charge against profit to $3bn (30%), plunging them into loss. Other banks followed suit. Of the UK's big four banks, Midland and Lloyds, the two smallest, had the largest exposures and declared in 1987 their first losses of the century. This was followed by their second losses of the century in 1989, as all the banks added to these bad debt reserves, which now ranged in total from 40% at Citibank to 100% in the case of JP Morgan's medium- to long-term LDC debt.

The LDC debt crisis was sad news for the ordinary citizens of these countries. It would be nice to think that the money (about $300 billion in total) had been spent strengthening the infrastructure of the countries but a great deal was wasted on grandiose prestige projects. Even worse, much has found its way into bank accounts abroad. Meanwhile, at home, the poorer citizen took the consequences – *sunt lacrimae rerum*.

Several attempts to solve the LDC problem have been tried:

❏ Banks sold LDC debt at a large discount to other banks, simply spreading the risk.
❏ Debt for equity swaps – some LDC debt was exchanged (at a discount) for equity in the country concerned. For example, the American Express Bank swapped $100m of its Mexican debt at a discount for equity in Mexican hotels. In a bizarre incident, some Brazilian debt was used to buy a Brazilian centre forward for Eindhoven, the Dutch football team! Other Brazilian debt was purchased at a discount and invested to protect rainforests.
❏ In 1985, US Treasury secretary, James Baker, unveiled the 'Baker Plan' – economic reform to promote growth in LDC countries combined with increased lending by commercial banks.

❏ In 1989, the new US Treasury secretary, Nicholas Brady, launched the 'Brady Plan'. Building on experience gained with the Baker Plan, this envisaged encouraging the creditor banks to allow debt reduction. For example, LDC debt would be exchanged at a heavy discount for 30 year LDC government bonds backed by 30 year zero-coupon US Treasury bonds, thus guaranteeing eventual repayment of principal. Alternatively, banks prepared to lend new money would be rewarded by no write down on the existing debt.

The first case was Mexico in 1989–90. Of the creditor banks, 90% swapped $42bn of debts for bonds on terms implying a discount of 35%. Some 10% of the banks lent new money. Later, 'Brady Plan' type deals were struck with the Philippines, Uruguay, Venezuela, Costa Rica, Peru, Brazil and Argentina. These bonds, which are still traded in secondary markets, are known as Brady Bonds. With the recovery of the Latin American economies generally, many of the governments are buying back their Brady Bonds, At peak, the IMF estimate the total was $156 billlion (£93.6 billion). Whey the buy-backs are finished, JP Morgan estimate that there will be only $10 billion (£6 billion) outstanding.

Later, Latin America reappeared in the world's financial markets and new capital inflows increased rapidly. Unfortunately, history repeated itself. Excessive bank lending led to further crises in 1997 and 1998.

Whatever the eventual outcome, for the banks concerned the LDC crisis was a disaster. Standard and Poor's and Moody's didn't like what they saw and reduced credit ratings. Not only did this mean that the cost of new money for the banks went up, but often their best customers had a better credit rating than they did. In 1982, banks like Chase, Bank America and Manufacturers Hanover were all of AAA status. By 1990, they were hanging on to single A if they were lucky. Manny Hanny was BBB – almost a junk bond! Yet in June 1986, Marks and Spencer, the famous UK retailer, issued a $150m eurobond rated AAA by both the main organisations. Why should M and S borrow from Lloyds or Midland Bank in 1986? Its credit rating was better than either.

Capital, too, was hit by bad debt reserves and the changed situation. Due to capital ratio constraints, banks found it difficult to expand their lending but still needed to earn money. In Chapter 4, we saw how new techniques were tried – the NIFs, RUFs and RAFTs followed by the MOF. Unfortunately, however, many corporates could avoid the banks by borrowing from other lenders, using the securities market. For example, top quality borrowers could raise money by selling commercial paper to lenders, with the bank role limited to taking a commission. The classic role of the bank is that of intermediary. It takes money from depositors and lends it to borrowers. Cutting out the bank, borrowers meeting lenders directly is often called *disintermediation*. Another term is *securitisation*, that is borrowers borrow by selling a security to lenders rather than borrowing from the bank. The biggest illustration of this process of either disintermediation or securitisation was the rise in the issue of eurobonds from 1982 onwards.

We mentioned that due to the huge oil price increases in 1973, the banks were encouraged to recycle this money. It is interesting that, following large oil price increases in 2004/05, the same question is beginning to be asked.

The Eurobond Market

From 1982, we see a fall in the size of the international syndicated loan market and a rise in the issue of eurobonds. Banks which could not expand their lending due to capital ratio constraints could make some money by underwriting bond issues. Borrowers found that the holders of eurocurrencies, which provided a short-term deposit market, could now be persuaded to buy bonds denominated in the same currencies and create a longer-term market. As before, London became the major market for these bond issues.

Typical terms for eurobonds were in the range of 3–25 years (the longest so far – 50 years – was issued by British Gas in 1994). A syndicate of banks with a *lead manager* underwrote the issue, sold the bonds to investors and ran secondary markets.

Settlement between the professionals (in the secondary market) is three working days: that is, buy the bond on Monday, pay on Thursday; buy the bond Tuesday, pay on Friday and so on. There are two settlement and clearing organisations – Cedel and Euroclear. The first is owned by Deutsche Börse AG and the second by banks, the first is in Luxembourg and the second in Brussels. What they do is to ensure that bonds are transferred to the ownership of the buyer and that money is taken from the buyer's account to pay for them. Using another technique, which always seems curious to an outsider, they can arrange to lend bonds to sellers who have sold bonds they don't actually own. The sellers can use these bonds to settle the deal and buy them later in the market in order to return them to the lender. This is *stock lending* and is very common in bond markets everywhere. The lender earns a small fee for their trouble and it makes life easier for the seller.

There is an International Primary Markets Association (IPMA) and an International Securities Markets Association (ISMA) to coordinate issues in the secondary market.

The techniques for selling these bonds are investment banking techniques, as opposed to the commercial banking techniques used for syndicated loans. The rise in eurobond market activities after 1982 led to a big increase internationally in investment banking at the expense of commercial banking.

The *borrowers* in this market are governments, quasi-governments (for example, the EU), international financial organisations (for example, the World Bank), banks and large corporates.

The *lenders* are retail investors (that is well-off private individuals), banks and investment institutions.

The interest on the bond is paid gross and, therefore, the onus is on the retail investor to declare this to the local tax authority. On the other hand, the bonds are *bearer* bonds (that is, no one knows who owns them). While it is, of course, wrong to think evil of people it is, unhappily, seldom incorrect. As a result, there is a strong incentive for the retail buyer to indulge in sheer tax evasion and enhance the yield on the bond by not paying any tax. The cliché in the market for the retail buyer is the 'Belgian dentist'. The idea is that they cross the border into Luxembourg (where the paying bank often is), present the coupons and pay the money into a local bank account. (Luxembourg banks have a great tradition of secrecy, like the Swiss.) The European Union is determined to put an end to this and has implemented a Savings Directive. The aim is to reduce tax evasion by people living in one EU country who earn savings income in another. Some countries have agreed to exchange information and others (Austria, Belgium, Luxembourg and Switzerland) to impose a withholding tax of 15% which will gradually increase to 35% by 2011. The directive applies to bank deposits, corporate and government bonds and some investment funds but not dividends or pension income.

In Luxembourg, however, certain types of SICAV funds (mutual funds) are exempt as they are not widely offered to individual investors but to institutional investors or private clients. As a result, by October 2005, there was a huge flow of money into Luxembourg funds launched by Swiss banks. Were people moving money to escape the Directive's net? (Probably.)

For professional investors, who will not indulge in tax evasion, there is still a *cash flow* advantage because the interest is paid gross. By the time they come to year end and the auditors agree the tax figures with the authorities, it may be 18 months before the tax is actually paid.

As a result of the tax situation, eurobonds may offer a yield that seems less than general market rates.

An early variation on the theme was the *floating rate note* (FRN). This pays a variable and not a fixed rate of interest. This appeals to financial institutions, which *lend* at floating rate and therefore find it easier to *borrow* at floating rate. If rates fall, their income falls, but so do their costs. Assets and liabilities are nicely matched.

Let's look at some eurobond issues to get the flavour of the market, both for types of issue and types of currency (see Table 6.3).

You may wonder why some of these issuers want a particular currency and why, for example, a financial institution like the UK's Abbey National was borrowing at fixed rate. The curious answer is that perhaps they don't want the currency at all, nor does the Abbey National want a fixed rate commitment. It's all to do with the world of *swaps*, which we discuss fully in Chapter 14. The investment bankers advise you in which currency in the prevailing market conditions it will be easier to raise the money. They then swap it for the currency you really want. They advise you whether a fixed rate bond or FRN will be best received by the market, and then swap the interest rate obligation with you.

Let's take the Abbey National case. First we have the *currency swap*:

Abbey National   *Swap Bank*

Swiss franc

£

They arrange at the same time to swap back at maturity so that the Abbey National can redeem the bond.

Then we have an interest rate swap for the interest element:

Abbey National   *Swap Bank*

Floating £ rate

4.875% Swiss franc

The swap bank passes the Abbey National a stream of money in Swiss francs to pay the interest. The Abbey National passes them a stream of money in sterling at floating rate. The obligations of the Abbey National to the bond holders are unaltered.

Notice that in the above case, we have not only swapped a fixed commitment for a floating one but the floating is in sterling and the fixed is in Swiss francs, that is we have arrived at the CIRCUS (Combined Interest Rate and Currency Swap).

Table 6.3   *A selection of eurobond issuers*

Issuer	Currency
Abbey National (now Santander Group)	Swiss franc
Vietnam	US dollars
Shell International Finance	US dollars
Nestlé	Australian dollars
Province of Quebec	New Zealand dollars
Kfw	Icelandic krona
Kfw	Mexican peso
EIB	Turkish lira
G E Capital	pounds sterling
BBVA	pounds sterling
Air Products	euro
Fortis Bank	euro
Eurohypo	Swiss franc
Leaseplan Finance NV	Slovenian tolar

The result is that issuers raise money where it is easiest and cheapest to do so and then the investment banks swap it into the arrangement they really want.

In November 2005, the Italian telecoms company, Wind, raised $50 million in ten year bonds and swapped the proceeds into euros, saving 40 basis points over borrowing in euros in the first place.

Our real discussion on swaps is in Chapter 13 but it's impossible not to mention them here, as it is estimated that 70% of eurobond issues are swapped one way or another.

The market is very innovative and ingenious. It was noted at an early stage that some professional investors were stripping off all the coupons separately, leaving behind a bond paying no interest. Perhaps they wanted a capital gain rather than income from a tax point of view. As a result, the market invented the *zero coupon bond* in the primary market.

If the bond pays no interest, why buy it? The answer is that the investor buys it at a substantial discount. Suppose market yields for five year bonds are 10%. An investor could buy a 10% bond at par. Alternatively, they could buy a zero coupon bond for $62.09 for each $100 nominal. They invest $62.09 and in five years receive $100 – also a yield of 10%.

For example, British Gas offered a 30 year zero coupon bond in dollars. The bonds were sold at $8.77 for each $100 nominal value.

From a tax point of view, it may suit the investor to receive capital gain and not income. In Japan and Italy, for example, the increase in the bond price is taxed as a capital gain, not as income (but this is not the case in the UK). In addition, if the bond is in a foreign currency, the exchange rate risk is limited to the principal not the coupons. These bonds are also even more sensitive to interest rate changes than a normal bond. This might suit a speculator who was convinced that interest rates would fall. Remember – interest rates *down*, bond prices *up*.

Take a conventional ten year bond paying 10%. The market yield falls to 9% and the price goes up to $106.4 (a rise of 6.4%). Suppose an investor had bought a ten year zero coupon bond instead. A price of $38.55 per $100 nominal would give a yield of 10%. However, when yields fall to 9%, the price goes up to $42.24 (a rise of 9.6%). This is due to the *gearing* effect. In taking a position on a ten year bond for $38.55 instead of $100, the investor has increased their exposure to the market. This is another aspect of the term 'gearing', which we met in Chapter 1.

Of course, if bond yields go up and not down, then the loss on the zero coupon bond is even greater. (The unfortunate Merrill Lynch dealer mentioned under 'Gross Redemption Yield' earlier was not only holding zero coupon bonds but had made them zero coupon by selling the coupons separately!)

In early 1992, the perception was that yields in European bond markets (especially in Spain, Portugal and Italy) would slowly fall to those on DM bonds. As a result, there were several zero coupon issues to take advantage of later price increases as interest rates fell.

Coupon Stripping

We mentioned earlier that it is not uncommon for innovative investment banks to take an ordinary bond and remove the coupons, making it a zero coupon bond. This is called 'stripping' the bond and is very common with US Treasury issues (see Figure 6.5).

	Normal bond	*Stripped bond coupons*					*Principal*	*Total*
		1	*2*	*3*	*4*	*5*		
Payment now	100	9.09	8.26	7.51	6.83	6.21	62.1	100
Receipt:								
Year 1	10	10						10
Year 2	10		10					10
Year 3	10			10				10
Year 4	10				10			10
Year 5	10					10		10
Year 5	100						100	100
TOTAL	150	10	10	10	10	10	100	150

Figure 6.5   *Coupon stripping*

For example, take a $100m five year 10% bond and assume that the market yield is 10%, the bond selling for 100.0. The interest payments are stripped to form five zero coupon bonds of $10m each, maturing one per year in years 1–5. The principal of $100m is itself now a zero coupon bond. Someone needing $10m in three years can buy the three year zero coupon bond for $7.51m in three years. This enables investment institutions to match future assets and liabilities more closely.

The first US government bond was stripped in 1982. Strips began in Canada in 1987, in France in 1991, in the UK and Germany in 1997 and in Italy and Spain in 1998. Almost all markets have stripped bonds now.

Other Variations

There are many, many variations on the theme in the eurobond market – far too many to cover them all here. Let's just look at a few to get some idea of the possibilities:

Callable/Puttable bonds   If *callable*, the issuer can redeem the bond at a stated earlier date if they choose to. The investor is compensated for this disadvantage by a higher coupon. If *puttable*, the investor can sell the bond back at a stated earlier date. The investor has an advantage now and pays for it by receiving a lower coupon. The UK government's huge $4 billion FRN issued in 1986 was *both* callable *and* puttable.

Convertibles   Corporate bonds which can be converted into equity are common, as in domestic markets. However, conversion could be from fixed into floating or floating into fixed.

Warrants   Again, as an alternative to a convertible, separate warrants entitling the investor to buy equity later may be attached. When the Nikkei index in Japan rose strongly up to 1990, Japanese convertibles and bonds with warrants were so popular they accounted for 20% of the market. When the bubble burst as the Nikkei fell, eurobond issues in 1990 fell as a result.

Dual currency   These are bonds which pay interest in one currency but redeem in another.

Rising/Falling coupon   A 10 year bond might be 3% for the first five years and 10% for the last five (or some other variation).

Both the above variations were combined in one with an issue by Banca Nazionale del Lavoro. The issue was in yen with 60% of the redemption in yen and 40% in dollars at a fixed rate of ¥163. In addition, the coupon was 4.7% for the first five years and 7.5% thereafter!

Collars   In mid-1992, several banks, led by Kidder Peabody, issued FRNs with both a lower and upper limit to the interest paid. This idea had been used in 1985 and called 'mini-max'. The revival was due to the unprecedentedly low US interest rates in mid-1992. A *floor* giving a lower limit was attractive, even if there was a maximum upper level to the interest paid.

Reverse FRNs   As the interest rates go *up*, the interest on the FRN goes *down* and vice-versa. In December 1997, the World Bank issued a complex 12 year reverse floater in lira. For the first 4 years, rates were fixed on a falling scale, 12% down to 7%. For the next 7 years, the rate was calculated by a formula: $15.5\% - 2 \times \text{LIBOR}$. Thus, as LIBOR goes up, rates fall. This expressed the view that Italian rates would fall due to the arrival of the euro. As a further variation of the FRN theme, Aegon, the Dutch insurance company, did a 12 year issue in 1992 which was an FRN for the first two years and fixed 8¼ for the remaining ten!

Global bonds   Pioneered by the World Bank in 1989, global bonds are designed to be sold in the eurobond market and the US at the same time, thus increasing liquidity for the bond. The two markets have different conventions – eurobonds are bearer, pay interest gross and annually; US bonds are registered, and pay interest net semi-annually. However, the eurobond issues are registered with the Securities and Exchange Commission (SEC) in the US and can be sold to all classes of US investors. Eurobonds cannot be sold into the US initially unless registered under SEC rule 144a, when they can only be sold to qualified institutional investors anyway. In September 2005, Brazil issued a ten year global bond denominated in its own currency, the real.

Dragon bonds A dragon bond is similar to a eurobond but is listed in Asia (typically Singapore or Hong Kong), aimed at investors in the region and launched in the East Asian time zone. The first issue was made by the Asian Development Bank at the end of 1991. With the growing importance of China, dragon bond issues have become very frequent.

The market is very competitive and each investment bank is seeking ways to score over its rivals with some new innovation. The cliché here is the rocket scientist – the highly numerate trader who invents more and more complex instruments.

Medium-Term Notes (MTNs)

These became very popular in the period 1991–92, and have remained popular since. They are very flexible programmes. Within the same programme and legal documentation, the issuer can issue bonds in various quantities, maturities and currencies and either fixed or floating. MTNs were designed in part to meet investor-driven transactions. In other words, an investor might request, say, $10m more of a previously issued bond and the issuer will release more to meet this demand. The issuer can thus issue a new bond, more of an existing bond, or create a bond to a specification suggested by the investor. The structure is particularly useful for issuing small tranches of notes/bonds. Indeed, one investment banker has suggested that issues down to as little as $500,000 are now practical.

For the borrower, the MTN allows them to by-pass the costly and time-consuming documentation associated with issuing a stand-alone bond. The market can then be tapped at very short notice, compared with a delay of several days for a stand-alone offering. They can thus react quickly to a given opportunity.

Amongst those who launched programmes are IBM International, Abbey National, the European Bank for Reconstruction and Development, GMAC Europe (the finance arm of General Motors), Monte dei Paschi di Siena, Finnish Export Credit and GE Capital, the market's most frequent issuer.

Sometimes the programmes are underwritten, like bond issues, sometimes not.

The Money Markets

We have been looking at syndicated loans and eurobonds. Short-term transactions in eurocurrencies which are not simply deposits/loans but are represented by securities result in *Eurocertificates of deposit* (ECDs) and *Eurocommercial paper* (ECP). The generic term for these short-term transactions is usually *Euronotes*. The *committed* loan facilities which we mentioned in Chapter 4, like NIFs/RUFs and MOFs, have largely died.

The strong interbank market in London in the eurocurrencies gives rise to references to Eurodollar LIBOR, Euroyen LIBOR and similar expressions for other currencies.

Repos

Earlier in this chapter, we mentioned that a central bank may use a 'repo' to help out other banks in its role as lender of last resort. A repo is a sale and repurchase agreement. Party *A* may sell stock to *B* and receive a collateral payment. At a later point in time (which may be fixed or variable), Party *A* must buy the stock back and return the collateral plus interest to Party *B* (see Figure 6.6).

Figure 6.6 *The repo*

The repo technique is used very widely outside its use by central banks. Any dealer may find that they have a short position in stock, that is they have sold stock but not yet purchased it. As an alternative to buying the stock, the dealer can get hold of the stock on a temporary basis using the repo technique. The stock is used to settle the deal and purchased later for its return in the second leg of the repo. Why bother? Maybe the dealer found some difficulty in buying the stock at an attractive price. Perhaps the dealer believed that stock would be cheaper in a few days' time. Sometimes the dealer has actually bought and sold stock but the buy side of the deal fails settlement, and it is the settlement department that uses the repo to fulfil the bank's obligation to deliver. This, of course, gives the market more flexibility and encourages liquidity. For this reason, the technique is often referred to as 'stock lending and borrowing'. (The classic repo is not quite the same as stock borrowing and lending, but let's not get too complicated!)

Often the repo is used for the opposite reason – that is not to get hold of the stock but to get hold of the collateral. A dealer must fund their position. If the bonds which have been purchased are not needed at once, they can be sold via the repo to obtain the cash to fund the purchase. As the borrowing is secured, it will be at a cheaper rate than unsecured borrowing. The repo here is simply a technique for borrowing money.

The repo thus suits everyone. The bond dealer can use it either to run a short position or to borrow money at the best rates. An institution which chooses to lend stock earns a small percentage to enhance yield on the portfolio and the deal is secure as collateral has been received.

Repos are widely used in the US Treasury markets; the Bank of England allowed repos in UK gilts in 1996 and the market began properly in Japan in April 1996 after new regulations solved problems with the previous rather weak repo technique (collateral surrender could not be enforced).

Participants and Top Traders

As we have seen, these are large wholesale markets and the transactions involve:

❏ Governments
❏ Municipalities
❏ Public sector bodies
❏ International financial institutions
❏ Commercial banks
❏ Investment banks
❏ Investment institutions:
    1 Pension funds
    2 Insurance companies
    3 Mutual funds
❏ Large corporates.

There are also brokers who act as intermediaries, displaying anonymously on computer the best prices in the market and putting principals in touch with one another for a small commission (as little as two bp).

The top traders for international debt issuance are shown as Table 6.4.

The Euromarkets are the most important financial development of the last 30 years. They have created a vast pool of international money seeking investment in the best place it can, with no especial loyalty to any particular market.

It seems appropriate to close this chapter with a quotation from Citicorp's Chairman from 1970 to 1984, Walter Wriston (quoted in Adrian Hamilton, *The Financial Revolution*, Penguin, 1986):

The information standard has replaced the gold standard as the basis of world finance. In place of systems, like the gold standard, based on government established rules, communications now enable and ensure that money moves anywhere around the globe in answer to the latest information or disinformation. Governments can no longer get away with debasing the coinage or controlling the flow of capital. There now exists a new order, a global marketplace for ideas, money, goods and services that knows no national boundaries.

SUMMARY

The rate of interest is the price of money. It varies with risk, maturity and liquidity. There is, finally, supply and demand.

Bonds have a par or nominal value. They may sell at below or above par value and the resulting return to the investor is *yield*. If we ignore the profit or loss at redemption, it is interest yield. If we do not, it is gross redemption yield. As interest rates go up, bond prices go down and vice-versa. This volatility is most marked for long-dated bonds. If the bond is sold before going ex dividend, the buyer pays *accrued interest*.

Credit ratings (such as AAA or BB) are assigned to bonds to guide investors as to the risk and, hence, the necessary yield.

Money markets cover transactions whose maturity is one year or less. They include:

Money at call and short notice   Liquid funds lent for very short periods.

Interbank market   The rate at which one bank will lend money to another is the offer rate for money, hence London Interbank Offered Rate (LIBOR) or Tokyo Interbank Offered Rate (TIBOR).

Treasury bills, local authority and public sector bills   These represent the short-term borrowing of these entities, say, three, six and 12 months.

Certificates of deposit   Short-term borrowings by banks.

Commercial paper   Short-term borrowing of corporates, very big in the US.

Bills of exchange   Discussed in Chapter 5.

Central banks control short-term interest rates using key rates such as lombard rate, discount rate, repo rate and similar terms.

Bonds are transactions in excess of one year. The face rate of interest is called the coupon and they may be short-, medium- or long-dated. They may be sold through an offer for sale or a private placing.

Government and public sector bonds are usually the most important. Frequently, they are sold at monthly auctions on set dates to specialist dealers.

Mortgage and other asset-backed bonds use the flows of interest and capital to back bond issues – these are *asset-backed securities* (ABS). Other terms used are *collateralised mortgage obligations* (CMO), *commercial mortgage-backed securities* (CMBS), *covered bonds* and *structured bonds*.

Debentures (in the UK) are corporate bonds secured on assets.

Convertibles   are bonds that may be converted to another bond or equity. The right to buy equity later at a set price may be contained in an attached *warrant*.

Preference shares   usually pay the dividend as a fixed rate of interest. They are preferred to other shareholders for dividends and in the event of liquidation and are non-voting.

Hybrid bonds   have the characteristics of both bonds and equity being perpetual, deeply subordinated and non-cumulative. They are growing fast in popularity.

Foreign bonds   are those issued in the domestic market by non-residents.

Junk bonds   are bonds below investment grade, offering high yields.

Islamic bonds   are issued to conform with Islamic law and do not pay interest in the conventional way. They are known as sukuks.

International or *Euromarkets*   refers to primary market activity (loans, bonds or money market instruments) outside the domestic market of that currency, for example, a dollar loan raised in London or a dollar bond issued in Singapore. London is the major centre for these activities.

Coupon stripping   refers to detaching the coupons from a bond and selling the principal and the coupons all separately. They are all now *zero-coupon bonds*.

Medium-term notes   are flexible programmes for issuing paper in any currency, any maturity, any quantity and fixed or floating.

Repos   stands for sale and repurchase agreements. These are used either to borrow bonds for short positions or finance long positions.

APPENDIX 1 – ANNOUNCEMENT OF RESULT OF A UK BID PRICE AUCTION FOR GOVERNMENT BONDS

United Kingdom
Debt
Management
Office

DMO-TAS041/404

Eastcheap Court
11 Philpot Lane
London EC3M 8UD

Tel. 020 7862 6500
Fax. 020 7862 6509

46/05

27 September 2005

PRESS NOTICE

RESULT OF THE SALE BY AUCTION OF £2,750 MILLION OF 4 3/4% TREASURY STOCK 2020

The United Kingdom Debt Management Office ("DMO") announces that the auction of £2,750 million of 4 3/4% Treasury Stock 2020 has been allotted in full.

(Note: all prices in this notice are quoted in pounds and pence)

1   All bids which have been accepted at the lowest accepted price have been allotted approximately 78.0% of the amount bid for.

Competitive bids made at prices above the lowest accepted price have been allotted in full. Competitive bids made at prices below the lowest accepted price have been rejected.

2   The range of bids accepted was as follows:

	Price	Yield
Highest Accepted	£104.61	4.32%
Non-competitive allotment price (i.e. the rounded average accepted price)	£104.59	4.32%
Lowest Accepted	£104.57	4.32%
Tail in basis points		0*

3   The total amounts allotted and bids received were as follows:

Amount allotted to competitive bids		£2,471.300 million
Amount allotted to non-competitive bids		
	Gilt-edged market makers	£275.200 million
	Others	£3.500 million
Total		£2,750.000 million
Total bids received		£5,194.674 million
Times covered		1.89 times

4   Cheques may be presented for payment. Refund cheques, where appropriate, will be sent as soon as possible by post. Stock allotted to members of CREST will be credited to their accounts by member-to-member deliveries on the relevant settlement date if they so requested.

*Tail is calculated as the yield at the lowest accepted price less the yield at the average accepted price (using unrounded yields). This figure is then multiplied by 100 to convert it into basis points.

Notes: A non-competitive bid is one in which no bid price is entered and is allocated at the rounded average price of the auction.
CRND – Commissioners for the Reduction of the National Debt.

APPENDIX 2 – CHANGES TO THE UK GILTS MARKET OVER THE LAST 10 YEARS

- ❏ Control of the gilts market transferred from the Bank of England to the Debt Management Office, April 1998.
- ❏ Cedel/Euroclear option for settlement.
- ❏ XD period reduced from 35 days to 7.
- ❏ Coupon stripping allowed late 1997.
- ❏ Dates for regular auctions announced in advance.
- ❏ Each quarter the gilts to be sold in the next 3 months are announced.
- ❏ In general, there will be fewer tap issues.
- ❏ Priced in decimals (not 32nds) from November 1998.
- ❏ Gilts repos no longer confined only to the gilt-edged market makers (1996).
- ❏ Bank of England daily assistance to include gilts repos as well as bills of exchange and Treasury bills (1996).
- ❏ Institutions to pay income tax on capital gains as well as income (1996).
- ❏ Payments to institutions made gross (1996) – tax to be paid 3 months later.
- ❏ All gilts eligible for bearer status for recognised foreign buyers, not just selected issues (1996).
- ❏ Half-yearly interest calculations to be based on precise number of days in the half-year (1998).
- ❏ Settlement of gilts transferred from the Bank of England's Central Gilts Office to CREST CO (the UK equities settlement body) in May 1999.

7 Stock Exchanges

HISTORY OF ASSOCIATIONS FOR TRADING

The early associations for trading were either sole owners or partnerships. The first modern shareholding enterprise is generally recognised as the proposal by Sebastian Cabot, the British explorer, to set up an enterprise to find a North East trade route to China and the Orient.

In 1553, 250 merchants put up £25 each to equip three ships for the voyage. They thus shared the cost and any eventual profit. Two ships foundered but one reached the port of Archangel and the crew were taken to the court of the so-called Ivan the Terrible. Trade was started between England and Russia and the company's short name was the 'Muscovy Company'. As the shares were held jointly, they were 'joint stock companies'. The famous East India Company was formed in 1600 and was dominant in trading up to about 1850. Of these early trading companies, several are still in existence, the most famous being the Hudson's Bay Company (1668). With the importance of the Dutch Empire, we also see the formation of the United East India Company of the Netherlands in 1602 and the Dutch West India Company in 1621.

Trading began in the shares of these companies. Amsterdam opened a stock exchange in 1611, Europe's oldest. The Austrian Bourse opened in Vienna in 1771, largely to trade government bonds to finance war. By the end of the 19th century it had 2500 equities listed and was one of Europe's most important financial centres. In London, brokers and jobbers (as they were called) met in coffee houses (see Dickens, *Little Dorritt*, Chapter 24: '*Mr Affery went about to other counting-houses and to wharves and docks, and to the Custom House and to Garraway's Coffee House and the Jerusalem Coffee House.*'). To regulate the market, New Jonathan's Coffee House was converted into the 'Stock Exchange' in 1773. Curiously, there seems to be some doubt about the formal start of securities trading in New York. A newspaper called *The Diary*, indicated in an issue of March 1792 that dealers in stock met each noon at 22 Wall Street (so called because of the building of a wall to keep livestock in and Indians out by early Dutch traders who founded New York). Most trading was in government bonds and bank shares. Inspired by the success of an organisation set up by brokers in Philadelphia, a 'New York Stock Exchange and Board' was set up in 1817 (quoted in F.L. Eames and Thomas G. Hall, *The New York Stock Exchange,* 5th edition, John Wiley, 1987). In 1850, the US actually had 250 stock exchanges, However, by 1900, New York was totally dominant due to the introduction of the telegraph and ticker-tape.

In France, we can trace an early shareholding company, the 'Société des Moulins du Bazacle' in Toulouse with 96 lots or shares which could be bought and sold. Quite logically, this became the local electricity company in the 19th century and was quoted on the Toulouse Stock Exchange until 1946. This was, of course, an earlier example than the Muscovy Company but more of an isolated instance. A form of stock exchange, a 'Bourse', appears in Lyons in 1540 with dealers called, in a decree of 1639, 'agents de change'. A bourse was established in Paris in 1724 but does not seem to have been particularly active. With the revolution, agents de change were abolished in 1791 and the exchange closed in 1793. Under Napoleon, the bourse was officially opened again in 1801 with the agents de change given a monopoly of trading but not allowed the privilege of limited liability.

THE ROLE OF A STOCK EXCHANGE

We should perhaps begin by considering the role of a stock exchange. It provides the regulation of company listings, a price formation mechanism, the supervision of trading, authorisation of members, settlement of transactions and publication of trade data and prices.

However, sometimes listing rules are made by government-sponsored bodies, like the Securities and Exchange Commission in the US. Separate settlement and custody bodies may be taking over this role, as in the UK where CREST Co Ltd (now merged with the London Clearing House, part of Euroclear) has taken over settlement from the London Stock Exchange. Some people are questioning the future role of a stock exchange as computerised matching systems outside exchanges are capturing business (like Posit and INET (formerly Island) in the US and Virt-X in London), or trades are handled by broker/dealers like Instinet. With the arrival of the Internet and growth of on-line trading, could Microsoft be the exchange of the future?

STOCKS AND SHARES

We refer to 'stocks and shares' as though there is a clear difference. Strictly speaking, shares are equities in companies, paying (typically) a variable dividend. Stocks are instruments where the payment is by way of interest, such as bonds and similar instruments. Unfortunately, while 'shares' is only used to refer to shares in companies, 'stocks' is a much vaguer term in everyday parlance. In the US, shares are 'common stock' and the shareholders are the stockholders. In the UK, the term 'stocks' is frequently used to mean either shares or bonds, and we shall follow this practice.

Generally, however, exchanges always split turnover between the fixed interest element and equities. Whilst most transactions in number are usually equities, the bond values are high because of the importance here of the professional investors with high value deals. In the UK, for instance, the average domestic equity deal is about £50 000 and the average government bond deal about £3m. In general, bonds are about 55% of turnover in London, 75% in Spain, Europe's exchange with the most bond trading, 22% in Germany but in New York, however, almost all turnover is in equities as few bonds are traded on the exchange.

Figures for the world's largest exchanges are shown in Table 7.1. The initials NASDAQ stand for 'National Association of Securities Dealers' Automated Quotations'. They have never had an exchange as such and deal on computer screens. The shares are, therefore, technically 'over the counter' (OTC) but the companies are much larger than one usually finds with OTC trading and include many technology stocks such as Microsoft, Intel and Apple.

Table 7.1   *International stock market comparisons, turnover, market capitalisation and number of companies listed, end 2004*

Exchange	Equity turnover £bn	Domestic equity market value £bn	Number of companies listed Domestic	Foreign
New York	11 618	12 707	1834	459
NASDAQ	8767	3533	2889	340
London	5169	2865	2486	351
Tokyo	3218	3557	2276	30
Euronext [1]	2472	2441	1000	334
Germany	1541	1194	660	159
Italy	969	790	269	9
Switzerland	791	826	282	127
Taiwan	719	441	697	5
TSX [2]	651	1177	3572	32
Hong Kong	439	861	1086	10

Notes: [1] Brussels, Amsterdam, Portugal, Paris, [2] Canada
Source: World Federation of Stock Exchanges, *Annual Report and Statistics*, March 2005.

Looking at Table 7.1, one can see that there is no simple answer to the question: which are the world's biggest stock exchanges? What does 'biggest' mean? It could be market value, total turnover or just equity turnover.

The market value is the number of shares in existence multiplied by the share price. It's also called 'capitalisation' (but beware – it's nothing to do with capital on the balance sheet). Share prices go up and down and the capitalisation is only that at the moment when the calculation is done. That's part of the problem. Had one taken Tokyo at the end of 1989, before their market crashed, Tokyo would have appeared as the world's biggest exchange.

Of the London equity turnover figure of $5169 billion, the claimed foreign equity content is $2290 billion, the highest in the world, and more than the foreign turnover of New York, NASDAQ, and Tokyo combined! This again highlights the international character of the London markets.

Taking capitalisation at the end of 2004 our sequence is:

❑ New York
❑ Tokyo
❑ NASDAQ
❑ London
❑ Euronext
❑ Germany.

Taking turnover, the next question is whether we take equities only or total turnover including bonds. If we do the latter, it may not seem fair for exchanges where bonds are traded outside the exchange.

If we take *equity turnover* only, however, our top six become:

❑ New York
❑ NASDAQ
❑ London
❑ Tokyo
❑ Euronext
❑ Germany.

We have included NASDAQ, although this is not an exchange and OTC dealings have not been included in other exchanges' figures.

From the above you will see that the question, 'which are the world's biggest stock exchanges?' elicits a somewhat complicated response! The very statistics are themselves controversial. Some exchanges insist that trades handled by local brokers are recorded locally for regulatory reasons even if the trade is actually passed to a foreign exchange. For this reason, London's claim for its foreign equity share has been attacked by many as an exaggeration.

INTERNATIONAL EQUITY

In the 1980s and 1990s, it became common for multinational companies to seek a listing on several foreign stock exchanges. This may have been to attract a wider investor market or because the local exchange is a little small for the ambitions of the company (for example, Stockholm and Electrolux). The result has been a large expansion in primary market issues and secondary market trading in non-domestic equities.

For example, although German accounting rules are not as tight as those in the United States, Daimler-Benz listed in New York and accepted the implications for greater transparency. The French insurance group, Axa, became the first French financial services company to secure a US stock exchange listing in mid-1996. There are still problems, however, as SEC rules require approval for rights issues. Ericsson had to wait three months, during which its share price fell 56%. New legislation following the scandals of Enron and others have also brought in new restrictions. Michael Oxley, Chairman of the House of Representatives Financial Services Committee and Senator Paul Sarbanes brought in the Sarbanes-Oxley legislation (SOX). This makes managers fully responsible for maintaining 'adequate internal control structures and procedures for financial reporting'. It also lays down new rules for audit and accounting and has established a Public Company Oversight Accounting Board. New criminal penalties await transgressors.

SOX is very controversial, not least because of its huge cost (a bonanza for firms of accountants for the same reason!). As a result, some firms have withdrawn their listing in the US, for example, the Rank Group. However, this is not as easy as it sounds. The firm must prove that they have less than 300 US shareholders – difficult when so many shares are held in nominee accounts. There are 113 British firms with listings in the US. BP calculate that the cost of confirming to SOX is about £67 million.

Will it work? Again, doubts have been expressed in some quarters but perhaps a better prevention may be the jail sentences handed out to various fraudsters – Bernie Ebbers (WorldCom), 25 years; John Rigas (Adelphi), 15 years; Dennis Kozlowski (Tyco), 8–25 years.

Large new equities are now offered on an international basis and there have been many involving national telephone companies. The second biggest privatisation of all time was Deutsche Telekom, offered to markets all over the world at the end of 1996. The offering was split as follows:

- ❏ Germany 462 million shares
- ❏ Americas 98 million shares
- ❏ UK 57 million shares
- ❏ Rest of Europe 38 million shares
- ❏ Rest of World 34 million shares.

A further slice was offered in June 1999, again on a worldwide basis, leading Deutsche Telekom to claim that they have more shareholders outside their domestic market than any other company.

One key factor here is that US mutual funds and pension funds have gradually become less parochial and are investing more abroad.

INDICES

Share indices are usually based on market capitalisation. If the index is of, say, the top 50 companies, then 'top' means biggest by market capitalisation. Sometimes, the index is described as 'weighted'. This simply means that a 1% change in the price of the largest company in the index will have more impact than a 1% change in the price of the smallest. Since the share price is always changing, it follows that the 'top' shares are not always the same. There is provision for removing some shares and adding others, say, every quarter. There are rules on this designed to prevent firms moving in and out as they go from 99 to 101 in the index and back.

In the modern age, the desire to use an index for purposes of options and futures transactions (see Chapters 12 and 13) has led to the creation of several new indices, which are recalculated every minute of the day.

Strictly speaking, we should distinguish between *averages* and *indices*, although the terms are used as if they were the same. In 1884, for example, Charles Dow (publisher of the *Wall Street Journal*) began publishing share *averages* beginning with an average of eleven railway stocks. The modern Dow Jones industrial average began in 1896 with twelve shares, and was increased to the present 30 in 1928.

As an average, the Dow simply averages the share prices and (but for stock splits, which we explain later) would divide the total of all 30 prices by 30. If, however, a stock split causes a price to fall from $100 to $50, this must be taken into account. The method used is called 'constant divisor'. The Dow used to be calculated hourly but is now done every minute.

In London, the Financial Times Ordinary Share Index began in 1935. Its average is even more complicated. The 30 share prices are multiplied together and a thirtieth root of the answer taken.

Modern indices are based on taking the number of shares and multiplying by the price. This gives proper weight to the companies worth the largest capitalisation. In 1957, for example, Standard and Poor's introduced the S&P 500. In 1983, the Chicago Board Options Exchange began trading options on its 100 share index, changing its name to the S&P 100 in July of that year. Both these indices are based on market capitalisation.

Also based on market capitalisation was the New York Stock Exchange index, introduced in 1966 and now consisting of some 1500 stocks. The American Stock Exchange introduced its American Stock Exchange Index in 1973. It is another capitalisation index and is based on about 800 stocks. One interesting and unusual feature is the inclusion of dividends as additions to the index. Thus, the index measures a *total* return (as does the German DAX – see later).

As a competitor to the Dow Jones index, the American Stock Exchange introduced its 'Major Market Index' (MMI) of 20 top stocks in 1980. Its composition and calculation make it similar to the Dow Jones and it has a 90% correlation.

Other important US indices are: the NASDAQ Composite Index (1984); the

NASDAQ Industrial Index (1984); the NASDAQ 100 (1985); the Philadelphia Stock Exchange Value Line (1700 stocks – 1985).

In Japan, the main index is the Nikkei Dow 225, an index of 225 shares. It is, however, based on average prices, not capitalisation. As a result, a Nikkei 300 was introduced in 1984. There is another index based on capitalisation, the Tokyo Stock Exchange Price Index (TOPIX), an index of all shares listed in the first section of the TSE.

In London, the need for a more satisfactory measure than the 30 ordinary share index led to the Financial Times Stock Exchange 100 Index in January 1984. This is the FTSE index and, thus, known locally as the 'Footsie'. It is also based on capitalisation, but only using the 'free float' shares – that is, those freely available for sale and not held by founders or similar entities (this adjustment made in June 2001). It is calculated every fifteen seconds from 8.30 a.m. to 4.30 p.m. (with a pre-index level calculated from 8.00 a.m.). The index began at the level of 1000. It represents 77% of the capitalisation of the whole market.

In October 1992, it was decided to broaden the indices and two new ones were added. The FTSE 250 is the 250 shares after the FTSE 100 and the FTSE Actuaries 350 is the addition of the FTSE 100 and 250. It is calculated every minute and includes figures for market sectors. An older, larger index is the Financial Times Actuaries Indices, started in 1962 and widened to include over 800 stocks in December 1992. It covers 97% of the market's capitalisation.

In France, the CAC 40 was started in 1987. It is based on capitalisation and is calculated every 30 seconds. It is 60% of the capitalisation of the whole bourse but the top seven stocks account for 43% of the CAC 40. One interesting point is that the CAC 40 is chosen to represent *all* major market sectors. The FTSE 100 is the top 100 regardless of sector. The older index in Paris is the SBF 240 which is based on opening prices and only calculated once per day. In September 1993 this was replaced by the SBF 250 index which is calculated every minute and integrates dividends as well. At the same time, a new index – the SBF 120 – was introduced. This is based on the 40 shares in the CAC 40 and 80 others. It is calculated every minute. In May 1995, an additional index of middle capitalisation stocks – the MIDCAC – was launched.

The older German indices are the FAZ 100 (from the business newspaper *Frankfurter Allgemeine Zeitung*) and the Commerzbank index of 60 shares on the Dusseldorf exchange. Both these were started in the 1950s and are calculated once per day. The popular new index, however, is the DAX (Deutscher Aktienindex) index of 30 shares introduced in December 1987. This is not only a modern index, calculated continuously, but includes dividends and thus calculates a total return. This makes it especially attractive for some 'swap' transactions of a kind we shall discuss in Chapter 14. It represents 80% of stock market capitalisation and covers all the country's exchanges. The next 70 shares provide the MDAX.

We mentioned above that some indices will attempt to apportion sectors (for example, CAC 40) and some will take all sectors if their market capitalisation warrants it (for example, FTSE 100) With the oil increases of 2004 and 2005, the FTSE 100 was becoming seriously unbalanced. Shell's decision in 2004 to transfer its primary listing to London increased its FTSE 100 weighting by 8%. By end 2005, oil and gas accounted for 20% of the index and mining (like Rio Tinto Zinc) another 5%. Banks account for about 23% so that oil, gas, mining and banks were almost 50% of the index.

In the US, the pattern is different with a large base of IT and industrial stocks such as Microsoft and General Electric. The Paris CAC40 is more varied, including retailers, contractors, civil engineering, media companies and fashion and beauty (LVMH, Oréal). Of the DAX 30 shares, 18 are manufacturers with some big financial organisations like the banks and Allianz.

Other prominent indices are:

Amsterdam	AEX
Bombay	B&C Sens
Brussels	Bel 20
China	Shanghai A
	Shanghai B
	Hong Kong Hang Seng
India	Mumbai SENSEX 30
Madrid	Madrid SE
	IBEX 35
Milan	S&P MIB
	MIDEX
Zurich	SMI

With the growth of international equities in investor portfolios, we also have the use of international indices. There are *world* indices, such as the Morgan Stanley World Index, that run by Citigroup and Russell and the *Financial Times* Actuaries World Indices. There is also the S&P Global 200 and the FT Global 500.

For *Europe*, there is the FTSE Eurotrack 100 (not including UK shares) and the FTSE Eurotrack 200 (including the UK) – both from the London Stock Exchange, the FTSE 300, a cooperation between Amsterdam and London, the STOXX series of European shares, a cooperation between the Dow Jones company and the French, German and Swiss exchanges, the S&P Euro indices and MSCI Euro indices (Morgan Stanley).

One problem for Europe is, what exactly is meant by Europe? There is the Europe of the twelve countries forming the monetary union but excluding an important market in the UK, the European Union of 25 countries but excluding an important market in Switzerland, and some wider geographical definitions. All this leads to a proliferation of European indices! As if we didn't have enough, in June 1999, FTSE International launched a new index based on the 29 largest and most heavily traded stocks in the eurozone, like Siemens, Royal Dutch Petroleum and Carrefour. The index is called E Stars and is aimed at the growing body of retail investors.

The indices mentioned above may actually be traded as *exchange traded funds* (ETF). These are listed securities that mimic the behaviour of stock market indices or other benchmarks – for example, the Dow Jones, the S&P 500, the FTSE 100 or any other popular index. ETFs can be bought and sold on a continuous basis and are traded between investors on a stock exchange. They are very popular in the US but interest elsewhere is growing. Morgan Stanley estimated that, at end 2005, there were 453 ETFs globally, controlling about $417 billion (£250 billion) of assets. In October 2005, the London Stock Exchange launched 14 new ETF funds to add to the 15 already traded. Using these funds, investors can make large changes to their asset allocation at relatively low cost.

Financial Research Corporation, the Boston data company, forecasts US growth in EFTs to continue at 32% p.a. and says they are 'Low cost, tax efficient and easy to understand'.

WHO OWNS SHARES?

Small Investors vs Institutions

The pattern of ownership varies in different world markets. In the US, there is still a strong tradition of equity ownership by private investors who own 50%. In Germany, the figure is 17% and in France 31%. The UK, after a rise because of the many privatisations, is now down to 14.1%. On the other hand, foreign investors probably own about 33% of UK share values.

Private share ownership is usually contrasted with that of the 'institutions', by which we mean pension funds, insurance funds and mutual funds. In some markets, private pension funds look after the pensions of individuals whether collected by their firms or contributed individually. Life assurance companies collect premiums for years in order to provide a payout at death. General insurance companies also invest premiums paid in advance but face greater uncertainty with regard to payouts. Storms, hurricanes or oil disasters like the Exxon Valdez lead to unexpectedly large payouts. Mutual funds are explained below.

Sometimes people compare market capitalisation as a percentage of GDP. Figures for leading centres are:

- ❏ London   160%
- ❏ New York   120%
- ❏ Tokyo   55%
- ❏ Paris   50%
- ❏ Frankfurt   39%

Pension Funds: Funding vs Unfunding

How active the equity market is will usually depend on the activity of the institutions and, especially, pension funds. The precise effect may depend on the asset allocation policy of the pension fund as between equities and bonds.

This brings us to the fundamental question: how are pensions funded? The first point is whether pensions are largely provided by private funds or the state. The second is whether there *is* a fund or whether the pensions are paid out of current taxation and contributions.

Where money contributed by private individuals is invested in funds to provide pensions, the biggest markets are the US, UK, Netherlands, Japan and Switzerland.

Figures for the size of assets are in Table 7.2 and provided by UBS Asset Management. In some of these cases, the funds are handled by the state.

In Germany, the employees' pension contributions are handled by the company and held in a *book reserve* in the accounts of the company. The amounts are available for the general purposes of the company and the payments are made from corporate funds. It's interesting that events which caused horror in the UK – Robert Maxwell having access to the pension funds – are the routine in Germany. There are some invested funds but the total is relatively modest, as can be seen from Table 7.2.

Table 7.2 *Pension funds, size of assets and percentage of GDP, various dates*

Country	Pension fund assets	Percentage of GDP	Old age dependency rate 2005	Old age dependency rate Projected 2010
	$bn	*%*	*%*	*%*
Australia [1]	513	80	25	36
Japan [2]	2735	59	38	56
Netherlands [3]	708	124	27	38
Sweden [4]	276	80	35	48
Switzerland [4]	426	120	28	36
UK [5]	1511	71	32	39
US [4]	7541	65	25	34

Notes: Assets at: [1] end 03, [2] March 04, [3] September 04, [4] end 04, [5] end 03
Old age dependency rate = population over 65 as a percentage of working population.

Source: UBS Asset Management, *International Pension Fund Indicators 2005.*

In Sweden, pension provision is largely by the state, but the money is invested and the system can be regarded as funded. In France, on the other hand, whilst the state also handles most pension payments through the Caisse de Retraite, they are not funded but paid for out of current taxation. Private pension provision is largely confined to schemes for senior executives.

This 'unfunding' is likely to change due to demographic factors. Right across Europe (and Japan), populations are ageing. With six or seven employees funding each pensioner the older systems may have been satisfactory. The future is likely to see two or three workers for every pensioner. Figure 7.1 shows the incidence of ageing populations.

Source: UN.

Figure 7.1   *Ageing populations, % of population aged 65 and over*

The World Bank estimates that, by the year 2030, the number of people over 60 will triple to 1.4 billion. A British think tank, Federal Trust, published a report, *The Pensions Time Bomb in Europe*. It calculated a dependency ratio, that is the ratio of people aged 65 and over to the 15 to 64 age group. Over the twelve countries of the EU (prior to 1995), this ratio is expected to increase from 21% in 1990 to 43% in 2040 and 48% in Italy and the Netherlands (see Table 7.3). The Netherlands, at least, have funded pensions; Italy does not. In Germany, by 2030, pension contributions could be 30% of gross income with one worker for every pensioner. China is in an even worse position. The 'one child' policy means that the flow of young people to replace those retiring will not be enough. By 2040, today's young workers will be retired and there could be one hundred million people aged over 80 (the second largest population figure outside of India). At present, funded or unfunded pensions are not remotely big enough to cope with this.

Table 7.3   *Age dependence ratio, persons over 65 as a % of persons aged 15–64*

Country	1990	2040
Belgium	21.9	41.5
Denmark	22.2	43.4
France	21.9	39.2
Germany	23.7	47.1
Greece	20.5	41.7
Ireland	18.4	27.2
Italy	20.4	48.4
Luxembourg	20.4	41.2
Netherlands	17.4	48.5
Portugal	16.4	38.9
Spain	17.0	41.7
UK	23.5	39.1
All EU	21.4	42.8

Source: Federal Trust Report, *The Pensions Time Bomb in Europe.*

Countries are slow to make progress on this issue. How can we persuade people to pay tax now to fund today's pensioners and put aside extra money for their own retirement at the same time? The French have increased the number of years private sector personnel must work for a full pension from 37.5 to 40. An attempt to do the same for the public sector met with strikes and was withdrawn! This is in spite of the fact that by 2040 France is expected to have 70 people over 60 for every 100 aged between 20 and 59, double the current level. The UK government announced plans to increase the retirement age for public sector workers from 60 to 65 but also backed down in the face of trade union opposition. The Germans passed a law in 1992 making it less worthwhile to retire before 65. All this, however, is really only tinkering with the problem, although the announcement by Deutsche Bank, in April

1996, that it would set up its own funded pension scheme was seen as significant.

In Japan, pension funds are big but past protectionist rules have curtailed competition and performance has been poor. However, deregulation from April 1996 opened the markets to foreign investment advisers on a wide scale.

The coming of the European single market should have resulted in abolition of many restrictions on pension fund investment. For example, Italian funds cannot hold more than 20% in private company equities; Portuguese and Danish funds cannot invest in other countries' securities; German funds cannot hold more than 5% in foreign bonds; and, in Belgium, 15% of the fund must be held in domestic government bonds.

Work was done on a European Commission pensions directive which sought to abolish these restrictions or at least modify them. After fierce argument, however, it was withdrawn in 1995.

Brussels is still working on proposals for a directive to liberalise the EU pension fund market. They aim to lift investment restrictions and allow greater competition. Unfortunately, the directive will not tackle the thorny issue of tax at all. Attempts to change taxation require a unanimous vote.

In Britain, Tesco's and a number of other leading companies have decided not to offer guaranteed salary-related pensions to employees, as the cost of doing so becomes prohibitive, and recent accounting rules require this cost to be disclosed as a contingent liability. This is exacerbating the general concerns over pension provision noted earlier in this chapter.

Equity Investment

The effect of pension fund activity depends, of course, on the attitude to asset allocation. The key choice is between equities and bonds with a further subdivision between domestic and international. Boots, the British retailer, announced in autumn 2001 that it would in future be investing exclusively in bonds and switched funds out of equities. Property is a popular investment in some markets and, clearly, there will also be liquid funds on deposit and invested in money market instruments, like certificates of deposit.

Table 7.4 shows the asset allocation in the four major countries where pensions are funded.

With pension funds usually the major operators in stock exchanges, their importance for the equity and bond markets can readily be seen. In the last edition, we commented on the then 'cult of equity'. Comparing 1989 with 1998, the US's percentage in equities is up from 39 to 62, Japan's from 29 to 67 and the Netherlands' from 14 to 46. The UK always had a high percentage in equities, partly due to its poor performance on inflation. The general belief is that equities will give better protection than bonds – that is, firms will put their prices up and make more money in nominal if not real terms. However, the equity market's prolonged decline in 2001/02, together with lower inflation and the problems of some pension funds, has led to a change in attitude. In the UK, legislation has been passed forcing pension funds to be more cautious in matching future liabilities with assets. The UK's 71% in equities in 2000 was down to 67% in 2004 (and still falling) while the bond total of 21% in 2000 was up to 24% by 2004 (and still rising). A more recent survey, from Mercer Investment Consulting in May 2006, calculates the UK's holding in equities as 62%. Japan's 57% in equities in 2000 was down to 45% by 2004 – again, poor equity prices plus very low inflation have led to a change of emphasis. A huge 11% in cash suggests some uncertainty!

Table 7.4   *Asset allocation – major pension markets*

Country	Domestic equities %	International equities %	Domestic bonds %	International bonds %	Cash %	Real estate %	Other %
Australia[1]	31	22	17	5	6	12	7
Japan[2]	29	16	26	11	11	1	6
Netherlands[1]	7	40	7	32	4	4	6
Sweden[3]	21	16	29	26	2	6	0
Switzerland[3]	13	14	34	10	8	16	5
UK[3]	39	28	23	1	2	7	0
US[4]	47	13	33	1	1	2	3

Notes: Figures at: [1] September 04, [2] March 04, [3] End 04, [4] September 04.
Source: UBS Asset Management – *International Pension Fund Indicators, 2005.*

Many have noted that the move to bonds, while bringing more certainty is, ironically, likely to lead to poorer performance. They believe that in the end equities will recover, driven by technology, productivity and world trade.

The figures also show the rise in global trading. The international content of funds between 1989 and 2004 as a percentage is up in the US from 2 to 14, in Japan from 14 to 27 and in the Netherlands from 10 to 72 – very striking changes, and accounting for the current high level of cross-border trading.

Mutual Funds

If a small investor has, say, $3000 to spend on equities, there are two choices. The money can be spent on just one or two companies' shares or spread widely over ten companies' shares. In the first case, the risk is great if one company performs badly. In the second case, with $300 spent on each share, the dealing costs are discouragingly high. The answer may be to put the money into *mutual funds*. These are collective investments, run by fund managers. They may be investments in money market instruments, equities or bonds. Indeed, nowadays, there are funds whose investments are in financial futures (see Chapter 13).

In the case of equities, the fund will invest in a wide range of equities; the $3000 is thus spread over a range of shares but without excessive risk. The fund is run by skilled managers and fees must be paid. There are two kinds of fund.

The open-ended fund (Unit Trusts in the UK)   Here the fund raises, say, $50m and spends it on a wide range of shares. Simplifying, the fund is divided into 50m units at $1 each. Later investors can buy units from the managers or sell them back to the managers. If investors with $5m to spend *buy* units, the managers buy more shares and the fund is now $55m. If investors with holdings worth $10m now *sell* the units back to the managers, shares will have to be sold to raise the money and the fund is now only $45m. Hence, we have the term 'open-ended fund'. As the shares grow in value, so do the units and this is how investors make their money. In practice, there are fees to pay and also the basic costs. Units thus have a bid/offer price like an ordinary share.

The closed-ended fund (Investment Trusts in the UK)   Here the fund is a shareholding company, much like any other. It raises $50m and, instead of being in engineering or groceries, invests the money in a portfolio of equities. If, later, investors with $5m to spend want to join in, they buy the shares of the fund on the open market *from someone else who sells them*: that is, the fund doesn't get the money but remains at $50m – hence, 'closed-ended fund'. The idea is that if, in three years, the shares double in value, so should the market share of the fund itself. The investors can now sell and take their profit this way. The extent to which the share price may not double but remain at a discount to the asset value per share attracts a lot of attention from analysts and needs to be studied by potential investors. This is because the share price of the closed-ended fund will reflect supply and demand as well as the underlying asset value.

These mutual funds are well established in the US, UK, the Netherlands, France, Germany, Italy and Spain. In France, they are very popular, partly due to tax concessions. The open-ended fund is the SICAV (Société d'Investissement à Capital Variable) and the closed-ended fund, the FCP (Fonds Communs de Placement). As well as equity funds, SICAVs and FCPs for money market instruments are very popular.

As one might expect, the concentration in the UK is on equity investments and in Germany, bonds. Mutual funds were allowed in Italy in 1983 but the equity funds lost popularity after the October 1987 crash. Today, some 55% of the money is invested in Treasury bills.

The US is a huge market for mutual fund investment. By the end of 1998, $4.5 trillion was invested in some 5800 mutual funds and 45% of US households were fund holders. The country's biggest fund group is Fidelity with over $300bn of assets under management. This alone is more than the total UK market! Investment is about 50% equities and 50% bonds and fixed interest. Europe has some $1.5bn in these funds, and the equity content is 30% and growing. The continually rising US stock market has resulted in a phenomenal increase in US mutual funds. The above figure of $4.5 trillion compares with total banking assets of $4.7 trillion.

The defined contribution retirement programmes being introduced and planned will increase mutual fund activity.

UCITS is a term which has arrived due to an EC directive in October 1989. These are 'Undertakings for Collective Investment in Transferable Securities'. The directive sets minimum standards for open-ended funds (not closed-ended). For example, no more than 10% of the investment can be in one security. Investment in commodities, property and money market instruments is excluded. The UCITS managers can take a fund which has domestic authorisation and offer it anywhere within the EU. It must be recognised by regulators in the country where the fund is to be marketed. However, while the marketing regulations are those which are in use locally, investor compensation is from the home country of the fund.

Amendments to the UCITS Directive were ratified in February 2002 and were due to be adopted by February 2007. The new UCITS III allows greater flexibility, including some use of derivatives.

Luxembourg has become a popular centre for UCITS to be sold across Europe. This is because the dividends can be paid gross. A UK UCITS, for example, will deduct tax on dividends at source. While foreigners can reclaim tax, French and German investors, for example, will be reluctant to fill in the forms of the UK Inland Revenue!

Active vs Passive Management

It is beyond the scope of an introductory book of this nature to explain the various theories which exist on asset allocation and pricing of securities. One issue, however, should be mentioned and that is the question of active vs passive management of the funds. Active management can be summarised as 'picking winners', that is, active selection of specific securities with frequent reorganisation of the portfolio. This is often driven by sophisticated computer models and called 'programme trading'. (The same term, however, is used to cover stock index arbitrage and dynamic portfolio insurance strategies.) Passive management, on the other hand, makes an investment in all the stocks in a well known index, such as the S&P 100, and leaves the fund to perform as the S&P 100. The argument for this is that statistics show that less than 50% of funds beat the index anyway and also that 'index tracking' (as it is called) incurs fewer dealing costs. The subject is, naturally, controversial. It appears that in the US, some 50% of pension funds are indexed and in the UK, perhaps 15%–20%.

The first tracker fund was launched by Wells Fargo in 1973, but the idea did not catch on until the mid-1980s. Some 53% of US public sector pension funds are based on tracking. The UK pension performance measurement company, CAPS, pointed out that while the UK's FTSE 100 index rose some 14% in 1998, the median performance of active funds was only 10.4% – the biggest difference in ten years.

Only 21% of the active funds beat the FTSE 100. The UK's National Association of Pension Funds estimates that 39% of private UK pension funds and 49% of public funds use tracking for at least part of their portfolio. On the question of costs, active funds are usually charging fees of some 50 basis points, as opposed to five to ten basis points for tracker funds.

As one might expect, the idea of active vs passive is not completely black and white. Many so-called 'passive' funds are also using quantitative models to add a little to their performance and are not purely tracking.

The activity of the tracker funds is now distorting some of the indices following the mergers of large companies – Vodafone/AirTouch, BP/Amoco, Astra/Zeneca.

When a company drops out of the index, the tracker funds immediately sell it; when one joins the index they immediately buy it. When the Dutch insurance group, Aegon, joined the MSCI pan-European index in early 1999, its price jumped 10% in one day; when Shell left the S&P 500 in June 2002 the opposite occurred.

Custodians

One term we should perhaps mention in this context is that of the *custodian*. Acting for pension funds, mutual funds and the like, the custodian actually looks after the securities, carries out settlement, handles stock lending (if the fund rules permit) and notifies the fund of corporate actions such as rights issues, dividend notification, AGMs and so on. They will also collect and remit dividends and reclaim withholding taxes.

These days this is very big business and dominated by large global custodians like Bank of New York, JP Morgan Chase, State Street, Deutsche Bank, Citigroup, Mellon Trust and Northern Trust. To do this world-wide they either have their own offices or use *sub-custodians*.

DEALING SYSTEMS

Systems in stock exchanges for buying and selling stock usually follow one of three patterns:

- ❏ Order-driven systems
- ❏ Quote-driven systems
- ❏ A mixture of the two.

Order-Driven Systems

Most systems on the continent of Europe are order-driven. That is to say, an intermediary (usually a broker) matches buy and sell orders at a given price. The broker takes no risk in that shares will not be bought or sold unless there is a counterparty with the equivalent deal on the other side. The broker makes a living by charging commission. The systems in France, Germany, Belgium, Italy. Spain and Switzerland are of this type.

The older type of system saw activity on a physical floor with the broker for a given share surrounded by others calling out buy and sell orders. The broker then matched the orders and declared an official price, which might last until the next session. Today, computer systems are usually used, at least for the major shares. A popular system in Europe is the one taken from the Toronto Exchange, called CATS (Computer Assisted Trading System). Sometimes it is given a different name locally, such as CAC in Paris (Cotation Assistée en Continu).

The French have rewritten the system as Nouveau Système de Cotation (NSC) or SuperCAC and sold it back to Toronto. It is also used in São Paulo, Brussels, Lisbon and Warsaw.

Let's take Paris as our example. Orders may be keyed into the system directly, fed to member firms, or fed to the CAC system from member firms.

Orders are entered with a price limit, for example, a buyer is prepared to buy 500 shares up to a limit of €154 or a seller will sell 400 shares but at a price no lower than €151. Some enter an order to be filled at the 'market price'. From 9.00 a.m. to 10.00 a.m., these orders are fed into the system. At 10.00 a.m. the market opens. The computer then calculates the opening price at which the largest number of bids and offers can be matched (see Table 7.5).

Table 7.5   *Opening prices*

Stock XYZ			
Buyers		*Sellers*	
Quantity	*Price limits*	*Price limits*	*Quantity*
500	Market price	Market price	400
200	156	150	250
250	155	151	400
500	154	152	500
750	153	153	600
1000	152	154	1250
3000	151	155	1700

Source: Paris Bourse.

In this example, the market reaches equilibrium at €153 with 1700 shares at the offer rate (that is, 200 + 250 + 500 + 750 – all these are prepared to pay at least €153) and 1750 shares at the bid rate (that is, 250 + 400 + 500 + 600 – all these are prepared to accept €153).

All the orders at the market price are now filled in so far as it is possible. Unfilled orders at the market price are carried forward with €153 as the limit price.

From 10.00 a.m. to 5.00 p.m., trading takes place on a continuous basis and the arrival of a new order will trigger a match if matching orders exist on the centralised book. An in-depth display of data on a given security is given at the same time.

London's SETS (Stock Exchange Electronic Trading System) is used for FTSE 100 stocks, stocks in the Eurotop 30 index and stocks with traded options on LIFFE. It was introduced in October 1997 and is an order matching system like the French NSC. Orders can be placed at a limit price or simply 'at best'. Further options allow the user to decide if a part-match is acceptable and whether any unmatched order is to remain on the order book. The information shown on a screen once continuous order input takes place is shown as Figure 7.2. On the left, we can see that the best 'buy' price for Barclays is £21.98 and the best 'sell' is £22.00. Total buy orders are 896 and total sell orders are 19 846. Stock exchange members, however, can still do deals outside SETS, reporting them through the system. This is why some prices reported are AT (automatic trading) and some are not.

The white strip (yellow in real life) contains the similar information as Level 1 plus four extra values (numbered 1,2,7,8)

Lower left window shows those wanting to buy shares

Lower right window shows those wanting to sell shares

Definitions
NMS = Normal market size
ISIN = Registration number for stock
MQP = Mandatory quote period (i.e. 8.00 a.m. – 4.30 p.m.)
OBT = Order book trading
GBX = Great British £
Cum Vol = Total number of shares traded today
Pub.Limit = Publication Limit
Trades = Number of trades actioned today
SET1 = FTSE 100; SET2 = FTSE 250 ; SET3 = FTSE 350
LAT = Last automatic trade
Mid = Calculated mid price
VWAP = Volume weighted average price (Total volume of shares traded
divided by the total number of shares that have been traded)

Key
1   Total number of shares available at best price at bid
2   Number of orders in order book at the current best price at bid (i.e. how
    many 'best buyers')
3   Total number of shares awaiting 'buy' transaction
4   Number of orders (bid or offer) placed/queued at current time
5   Green for share volume
6   Share price. Note that the most recent Order is displayed in the user-selected
    'down' colour, the second most-recent Order is displayed in the user-selected
    'up' colour, and the third most recent Order is displayed in green.
7   Total number of shares available at best price at offer
8   Number of orders in order book at the current best price at offer (i.e. how
    many 'best sellers')
9   Total number of shares available at offer

Source: Proquote.
Figure 7.2   SETS *screen*

Very large orders present a problem. They may wait quite a long time until they
can be matched and their very presence will tend either to raise or lower the price.
Block trades between institutions can be matched by brokers if there is a matching
price but stamp duty (amongst other things) prevents a *market maker* in Paris (*teneur
du marché*) either buying a large block (not knowing to whom they will sell them)
or selling a large block they will now have to buy. The liquidity in trading for large
orders attracts business to London from Paris, Frankfurt, Milan, Brussels and Madrid
because London's traders are used to taking risks, previously the only system used
involved *market making*, which will be discussed shortly.
    In Germany, on the official market there are official price fixers (Amtliche

Kursmakler), on the second market there are independent brokers (Freimakler). The whole system is dominated by the banks handling their own and client orders. As a result of conflicts of interest, there have been three rival computer systems – the banks with IBIS, the Kursmakler with MATIS and the Freimakler with MIDAS. However, IBIS eventually became the sole system for top shares and was itself replaced by Xetra in December 1997. The Vienna exchange will also use Xetra.

In Japan, there are eight stock exchanges: Tokyo, Osaka and six others. The Tokyo exchange trades the shares of about 1800 companies and accounts for 70% of Japan's trading, with Osaka doing 18%. (Osaka, on the other hand, is very strong in derivatives.) Investors place their orders with stock exchange members. Specialists – *saitori* – match orders through an open outcry system. The details are circulated on computer screens.

Quote-Driven Systems

In quote-driven systems there is someone called a *market maker*. They quote continuously bid and offer prices at which they will buy or sell shares. The difference is the *spread*, that is their profit margin.

As a result, they will buy shares at the bid price, not knowing to whom these shares will be sold. They also agree from time to time to sell *short*, that is, to sell stock that they don't actually own but will now have to go out and buy. This clearly involves risk and needs capital (not to mention strong nerves!).

The systems, therefore, tend to be driven by the quotations. The prices, especially first thing in the morning, do not necessarily reflect the prices at which deals have taken place, as the market makers can change the quotations whenever they wish. Usually these prices are firm for a given quantity of shares and may be shown thus:

Share XYZ	Bid	Offer	Bid quantity	Offer quantity
	100	102	50	50

Seen on a computer screen in the UK, this would indicate that the market maker will buy shares at say £1.00 or sell them at £1.02 for any quantity up to 50 000 shares. For higher quantities, brokers will then negotiate on behalf of clients.

The main quotation driven systems are NASDAQ (in the US) and London's SEAQ (Stock Exchange Automated Quotations), which was heavily modelled on NASDAQ. Although the top 100 shares in London are traded on the SETS previously discussed, other shares are still handled by SEAQ, which was used for all shares until October 1997. Where there are such systems, there are now two types of trader – the *broker* and the *market maker*.

The broker approaches market makers on behalf of clients and buys shares from them for the clients or sells the clients' shares to them. They make a living by charging a commission and do not take risk. In London, a broker may match buy/sell orders from a client provided the price is better than that available from a market maker. This is a slight complication and leads to the term *broker dealer*. Generally, however, the role of the broker is that of an agent, especially for smaller clients.

Large clients, like the investment institutions, don't have to use a broker but may approach a market maker directly. If they do use a broker, it will be on a *quid pro quo* basis – that is, the broker in return for the business will make available equity research reports free of charge. As a result, providing top quality equity research is essential to attract business.

The market is very competitive and there may be 15–20 market makers competing in a particular share with the prices freely available to all. This ability to take risk is useful for large deals as the market maker will buy and sell and keep liquidity going. Very large deals hit problems with order-driven systems. On the other hand, market makers are reluctant to handle small company shares in which there is little trading. The spreads are very wide and this further discourages trading!

To combat this, the London Stock Exchange launched a new system in October 1992 called SEATS – Stock Exchange Alternative Trading System. This is a hybrid system, similar to those in New York which we discuss below. A single market maker is appointed for illiquid stocks and will be obliged to make continuous two way prices. At the same time investors will be able to post buy and sell orders at limit prices. When market makers trade they must fulfil orders that are posted first if they are at the same price or better than a proposed trade. In addition, any orders to be matched in brokers' offices must first be offered to the official market maker who may trade at a better price on their own account or by matching the posted orders.

The NASDAQ and SEAQ systems are very similar. Let's examine the SEAQ type of display for a major share, such as Babcock International, in Figure 7.3.

Definitions
NMS = Normal market size
ISIN = Registration number for stock
MQP = Mandatory quote period (i.e. 8.00 a.m. – 4.30 p.m.)
OBT = Order book trading
GBX = Great British £
Cum Vol = Total number of shares traded today
Trades = No of trades actioned today
VWAP = Volume weighted average price (Total volume of shares traded divided by the total number of shares that have been traded)

Key
1   Market maker's identification at the best price at bid
2   Number of quotes at the current best price at bid
3   Blue (cyan) – Market maker's ID
4   Yellow – Bid spread

5   Yellow – Number of shares at bid/offer (see below)
6   Grey –Time the order was placed
7   Arrow and colour indicates direction of last price change for market maker (red for down, cyan for up)
8   Number of quotes at the current best price at offer
9   Market makers identification at the best price at offer

Source: Proquote.
Figure 7.3   *SEAQ screen*

Normal market size is the minimum quantity of shares for which a firm quotation is given. (Smaller market makers can register as 'reduced size market makers' and post half this figure.) We can see that for Babcock International, there are 11 market makers competing for the business. The main display shows the market makers' initials, the bid/offer price and the bid/offer quantity. For example, on left towards the bottom we see that CSFB are quoting a price of 100p bid and 104p offered for quantities of 15 000 shares bid and offered.

We don't even need to search for the best prices as the panel halfway up shows us the best bid and offer, 101–104. These are called the 'touch prices'. The spread at the touch is usually measured and a record kept as an indication of the market's efficiency. Above these figures are shown the cumulative volume of shares traded so far and the latest price and trading history. All prices must be entered within 3 minutes of the conclusion of the deal.

Note that the trading itself is not automated. If the broker wishes to deal, the arrangement is concluded on the telephone. Only the SETS is automated.

Hybrid Systems

Hybrid systems, with both order-driven and quote-driven characteristics, are found in New York and Amsterdam.

In New York, each share is allocated to a *specialist*. The specialist acts as a broker, executing orders for other brokers on a commission basis. However, they may act for their own account (like a market maker) by buying from the public when there are no other buyers and selling to the public when there are no other sellers, all at or near the price of the last transaction. In other words, they match buyers and sellers when there are plenty of them but will keep the market going, by buying on their own account, when there is a shortage. There are about 60 specialists on the New York exchange and the system dates from before the First World War.

In a given stock, a specialist may have buyers at $45¼ and sellers at $45½ – these are the best prices, that is, highest bid and lowest offer. A broker approaches and is quoted '$45¼/$45½'. The broker's client wants to buy 100 shares. He tries '$45⅜' in case anyone in the crowd surrounding the specialist wishes to match this. If this fails, he raises the bid to $45½ and the specialist calls out 'sold' and gives the broker the name of the first order on his book at that price.

At the start of the day, the specialist is faced with many orders – some at the closing market price, some at limit prices. His duty is to set a price as near as possible to the close (to maintain an orderly market) and yet also match as many orders as possible. Sometimes the system works well in a crisis, sometimes not. On Monday, 26 September 1955, following President Eisenhower's heart attack the previous day, there was frenzied trading. Specialists, holding stocks worth $50m, bought almost another $50m to help stabilise the market. However, on 'Black Monday', 19 October 1987, the specialists were overwhelmed and for hours there was no trading in two key stocks, IBM and General Motors. In London, the market makers kept going but there were frequent accusations of not answering the telephone!

There is an important automatic electronic order execution service in New York, DOT (Designated Order Turnaround), which was introduced in 1976 to transmit to the trading posts orders of up to a given maximum size and to send back confirmation of completed orders. In 1984, this was replaced by SuperDOT, able to handle bigger volumes. This itself was integrated with OARS (Opening Order Automated Report Service) which collected and stored the opening orders each day. The system pairs buy and sell orders and specialists can quickly see imbalances and determine the day's opening prices.

An order matching system called Direct Plus has been introduced. This matches orders directly and accounts for some 10% of all trades in New York.

In Amsterdam, the market is split between retail and wholesale. Retail orders go via the 'hoekman' who may match orders or take a position like a market maker. Wholesale orders go through an order matching system called AIDA. Banks and brokers can also advertise their desire to buy and sell via a system called ASSET.

Although the London SETS is essentially order matching, in practice it is more of a hybrid system. Users are not obliged to enter orders via the system. London's culture for years has been one of market making. As a result, many institutions still telephone stock exchange members and ask if they want to buy or sell and take the risk. Sometimes the dealer will accept a large order at a protected price but attempt to better it by feeding it through the system in smaller batches or offering it to other institutions. These very large orders are called *worked principal orders* and publication details are delayed. Since currently less than half the orders are going via order matching for automatic execution, we can describe the SETS system as a kind of hybrid with characteristics of both order-driven and quotation-driven systems. A new system, SETS MM, specifically incorporates market maker quotes into the system.

A rival system to SETS MM is Plus, operated by Plus Markets, owners of the OFEX market, described later in this chapter under 'Second Markets', The system operates for the 160 OFEX companies and, by June 2006, another 670 small and mid cap companies. They claim that research from Cass Business School and Imperial College London shows that the Plus system offers better prices and greater market depth than SETS MM.

All the above systems may be suspended at moments of crisis (like 9/11 in New York) when trading becomes frantic. In London this is called a *fast market*. When bombs went off in London on 7 July 2005, the LSE declared 'fast market' for a period.

Inter Dealer Brokers

In some markets (for example, London), transactions between market dealers are facilitated by *inter dealer brokers* (IDBs). Their function is like brokers in money markets or foreign exchange. They publish (on computer screens) large potential deals at bid and offer prices, but anonymously. Another dealer may see the quotation and decide to make a trade. The transaction is carried out by the broker and the two counterparties never learn of each other's identity. The dealer who identifies a trade and indicates a willingness to conclude it, pays the commission and is called (curiously) the 'aggressor'. Anonymous order matching systems have not impacted the market as much as many people thought. Inter dealer broking exists for equities, bonds, foreign exchange and derivatives. The world's biggest is ICAP who employ 2900 and claim 28% of the world market. Next is Collins Stewart Tullett, only a little behind. Tradition, a Franco-Swiss group, have perhaps some 12% of the market. These groups have taken over old names like Prebon Yamane, Garban and Exco.

Stock Borrowing and Lending

A dealer may sell shares or bonds they don't have, going 'short'. An alternative to buying the stock prior to settlement is to borrow it from institutions who will lend stock for a commission and pass over money (or other securities) as collateral. Typically, the stock is paid for and the money returned when the dealer actually buys the stock and returns it. This facility greatly assists the liquidity of the market.

On the other hand, dealers have to fund their 'long' positions. One way to fund them is to lend stock not needed and take the money to help fund other positions.

Thus stock lending may be done by institutions merely to enhance income, or may be done by dealers as a means of financing their position.

To complicate matters, although everyone calls it stock *lending*, in fact, the stock is *sold*, albeit on a temporary basis. In other words, the whole arrangement is the sale and repurchase agreement, or *repo*, which we met in Chapter 6. There it was a means of banks funding their liquidity by selling stock (temporarily) to the central bank.

This market is particularly large for bonds, although there is some lending of equities.

The language, as usual, is used loosely. Generally 'stock lending' is used where dealers want to cover short positions and is driven by borrower demand. 'Repo' is used where the transaction is to meet funding needs. The legal agreements for stock lending and repos are, however, different.

As we will see in Chapter 8, hedge funds use stock borrowing extensively to cover their short positions.

Bought Deals/Block Trades

Occasionally, very large share deals are executed called *bought deals* or *block trades*. The investment bank involved buys the shares using its own capital and hopes to sell them to investors at a profit. It can be very lucrative but also involves great risk.

It is usually a competitive process. In December 1995, for example, NM Rothschild held an auction for the sale of the UK government's remaining stake in BP. SBC Warburg won the business by offering £5.08 per share and later sold them for £5.13m making about £5m. The sales total was £500m.

In March 1999, the German energy group, Veba, sold its 10.2% stake in Cable and Wireless – the biggest block trade in the European stock markets. Some 246 million shares were placed by ABN Amro at £7.35, raising £1.8bn, a discount of 11.5% to the latest stock price. ABN Amro was believed to have paid £7.24 for the stake, leaving a profit of £26m, about 1.5%. In February 2004, UBS sold a block of 21.2 million shares in Astra Zeneca on behalf of Investor, the Swedish investment company. The block was sold for £550 million in thirty minutes at a discount to the market price of 1.51%.

It doesn't always go well, of course. *The Banker* magazine, in May 2005, reported losses on two block trades of €35 million for Citigroup and €40 million for Goldman Sachs.

Share Buy-Backs

An interesting issue is that of companies buying back their own shares. This is very common in the UK and the US. In 2002, GlaxoSmithKline bought back the first of two instalments of £42bn of its shares. The idea is to cancel the shares so that profit and dividend per remaining share are then enhanced. In France, however, it is common to buy shares back as a defensive move, either to support price or prevent a takeover. Under a new law passed in 1998, the AGM has powers to authorise a buy-back of up to 10% in the next 18 months. Once bought, the shares may be cancelled (subject to EGM approval) or allocated to employees.

Critics point out that if a company is unable to employ surplus capital profitably, this is a sad reflection on the business vision of the company's management and does not augur well for the company's prospects. Consequently, a share buy-back may actually result in a fall in the share price (this happened in the case of GlaxoSmithKline and has also happened to Reuters).

Share buy-backs were illegal in Germany until a new law of March 1998 permitting companies to buy back up to 10% of their shares in an 18 month period. The BHF-Bank took advantage of this to buy back 3.4% of its shares.

In Japan, share repurchases have not been as common and have traditionally been frowned upon as a way of manipulating share prices. In any case, no more than 3% could be bought back. With economic recovery, many companies believe that their capital will be better spent on research and development. In spite of this, Toyota Motors bought back 1.2% of its shares, Komatsu 2% and Asahi Breweries 1.9%. Then, at the end of 1997, a new law increased the possible buy-back percentage to 10%. With the huge oil price increase in 2004/05, both BP and Shell launched substantial buy-back programmes.

We said above that the idea of the company buying back its own shares is to cancel them to enhance profit and dividend per remaining share. The company, however, may not necessarily be obliged to cancel the shares, depending on local legislation. In the UK, for example, cancellation was mandatory until a law in 2003 allowed the company to continue to hold the shares as treasury stock. Why would the company do this? Treasury stock allows the shares to be reissued later, either for a rights issue or even as part of a takeover bid. BP holds 7% of its own shares and UBS 10%. Typically, 10% is a maximum limit.

SETTLEMENT

Settlement is the basic question of paying money and receiving stock or receiving money and delivering the stock. If the stock cannot be delivered without money being credited to pay for it, this is called 'Delivery Versus Payment' (DVP) and is the ideal. It is a recommendation of a G30 report on settlement.

Sometimes settlement systems are 'rolling settlement', for example, rolling 5 working day settlement. This means that a deal on Tuesday must be settled on the next Tuesday, a deal on Wednesday must be settled on the next Wednesday and so on. This is called 'T+5', that is, 'Trade Date +5'. The G30 report recommends rolling settlement systems and 'T+3' if possible. The US is T+3, Germany T+2 and France T+3 under their 'RELIT' system (Règlement Livraison de Titres).

The alternative is the system of an 'account period'. For example, Paris has its Règlement Mensuel, which can still be used to settle if requested. The 'month' is the 5 last working days of the month plus the next month up to 5 working days from the end. All deals within this month are settled on the last trading day of the month. There is, however, also a cash market (marché au comptant). This is used for less actively traded stocks, all the second market, OTC and all bonds.

In New York, the Depository Trust Corporation (DTC) holds large blocks of stocks registered in its name for safe custody. Between the New York Stock Exchange and the DTC is the National Securities Clearing Corporation, which acts as a clearing function for the exchange and passes the transfers to the DTC. Net money due to or from a broker is settled daily by a single payment.

The UK had a fortnightly account system. Settlement day was a week on Monday, following the end of the two weekly account ending on the Friday. All member firms' deals were then settled as one net figure. Its successor abolished the use of share certificates, but only for professionals, and implemented T+2 rolling settlement. The private investor is still able to use share certificates if they wish. The system is called CREST and is run by a new company – CREST Co – with the Stock Exchange as one shareholder amongst many. It started operation in the second half of 1996. (Later, CREST merged with the London Clearing House part of Euroclear.) Where paper certificates no longer exist and transfer of ownership is on computer register only, this is called *dematerialisation*. The French *RELIT* system is of this type.

Italy dropped its monthly settlement system and moved to T+5 rolling settlement in February 1996.

In general the trend is towards new rolling settlement systems and dematerialisation.

NEW ISSUES

Handling issues of shares of new companies coming to the market is very much the essence of a stock exchange.

We should, perhaps, begin by asking – why do companies go public anyway?

There is a variety of reasons.

In the first place, the company may be seeking new capital for an expansion plan.

This may be a more attractive way of getting the money than, say, bank loans or trying to attract more private shareholders. (If a company feels it is not yet ready to go public, but is looking for more capital, it may seek as a new shareholder a bank which specialises in this, and is usually referred to as a *venture capital* company.) In later years, if the company needs more capital, it can go back to the shareholders with a *rights issue* (which we discuss shortly).

Secondly, going public produces a price for the shares and a market. Without this, if one of the original private shareholders wishes to sell out and retire, there may be a problem. What price do we put on the shares? Who can afford to buy them? In addition, giving staff the right to buy shares through one of a variety of share purchase schemes provides a valuable incentive. It is also cheap for the company. To sell shares to the staff, the company usually creates new shares. The number is so small that any dilution of the share price is not noticeable.

Finally, in a takeover situation, the company can now offer new shares in its own company instead of cash to the victim company's shareholders. This can be very useful and is also very common. If the victim shareholders would prefer cash, institutions can be found to buy the shares, usually referred to as a *vendor placing*.

In general, there are two systems – the public offer for sale and the placing, or private placement.

In the case of a *public offer for sale* (an *initial public offering* or *IPO* in the US) the offer receives wide publicity and investors are invited to submit applications for the shares. If oversubscribed, some form of rationing or allocation must take place.

Usually, a detailed prospectus giving details of the firm's history and accounts must be produced. The issue is brought to market by a bank or stockbroker. They will advise on the pricing of the issue, will attempt to persuade the market of its merits and arrange *underwriting*. This means that, in so far as the investing public does not buy the shares, the group of underwriters undertake to purchase them. For this they receive a fee, perhaps 1½% to 2% of the value underwritten. The risk is spread widely and investment institutions will often participate, hoping to keep the fee and sleep well at night. 'Black Monday' in 1987 occurred in the middle of the UK government's privatisation of further shares in British Petroleum. The underwriters had to purchase the shares at the offer price and incur a considerable loss. Sometimes, if the market is seen to be weak, a planned issue is withdrawn.

In the *placing*, the broker concerned contacts investment clients with the details of the offer and sells the shares without any public offering. The number of shareholders for a given sum raised is usually set at a minimum by local stock exchange rules.

The placing is much easier and cheaper from the administrative point of view and also saves underwriting fees. Other things being equal, firms may prefer a placing. However, there are usually local stock exchange rules on this subject. For example, in the UK, if the sum of money raised was more than £3m, a placing was not allowed. In 1986, this limit was raised to £15m and in 1991 more complex rules were introduced. These envisaged the possibility of a new issue which was part placing and part offer for sale, a 100% placing being ruled out if the amount raised exceeded £50m. In 1992, there were several new issues which were 50% offer for sale and 50% placing. However, from 1 January 1996, these rules were abolished and there is now no limitation on the amount that can be raised by a placing.

Sometimes we hear of an unquoted company taking over a 'shell' company. This is a company with few assets, profits in decline or non-existent and a low share price. The takeover company usually imposes its own name. It's a way of getting a listing without going through all the procedures of an official new issue.

Another possibility is for a company to be admitted to the list of shares which are being traded on an exchange by an *introduction*. This is typically a firm quoted on a foreign stock exchange which seeks an admission to the list of firms traded on a domestic exchange. Normally, no new money is being raised at that time. This became very common in the 1980s as part of the 'international equity' idea which we discussed earlier in this chapter. The Japanese firm Toshiba, for example, is listed on nine European stock exchanges. Daiwa began to trade on seven European stock exchanges simultaneously in April 1990. Volkswagen was listed on all four Spanish stock exchanges in June 1990 and Volkswagen and Bayer Chemicals became the first foreign companies to be listed on the Milan Stock Exchange in the same year. Daimler-Benz became the first German company to list on the New York Stock Exchange in 1993. The National Bank of Greece listed on the New York Stock Exchange in mid-1999. However, as mentioned earlier in this chapter, the Sarbanes-Oxley legislation is now something of a deterrent to listing in the US. Indeed, some US companies are considering having their IPO in London instead.

Foreign shares listed in the US would have a disadvantage if quoted and dealt in their own currency. There are also higher costs for investors in buying foreign shares and worries (in some cases) about receiving share certificates. As a result, many foreign companies' shares trade in the US as American Depositary Receipts (ADRs). The receipt for one or more of a foreign company's shares is held by a trustee (often Morgan Guaranty Trust) and the receipt is traded rather than the shares themselves. For example, a BP ADR is worth twelve ordinary shares. The US investor avoids the inconvenience of collecting dividends and converting them to dollars. The sponsor bank takes care of this. The first ADR was issued in 1927 for the British–American Tobacco Company. There are some 2000 ADR programmes in existence.

A more general theme is Global Depositary Receipt (GDR) which refers to using the same technique as ADRs for listing shares on exchanges outside the US. The first of these was issued in 1990 and they have proved very useful for emerging markets. For example, at November 2005, there were 144 companies which traded as GDRs in London. Among those in 2005 were Sistema (Russia's largest float up to that point), Investcom (Lebanon) and Kumho Types (Korea).

There is also now the European Depository Receipt, launched by the Paris Bourse and Citibank in 1998, for issues in euros and cleared through the Paris Sicovam.

RIGHTS ISSUES

Later, a firm may decide to offer the existing shareholders the right to buy some new shares in proportion to the shares they already hold. This is why they are typically called 'rights issues'. Across most of Europe, the law requires that existing share-holders have pre-emptive rights to any new shares issued for cash. (New shares may not necessarily be issued for cash – they may be issued in order to fund a takeover bid by offering them to the shareholders of the company to be taken over.)

In the US, shareholders' rights to new shares are not so firmly established. The whole question of these pre-emptive rights is controversial. Periodically, articles appear arguing that firms should be able to issue a block of new shares by auction without offering them first to the existing shareholders.

Although pre-emptive rights are common across Europe, one exception is Germany. In March 1998, Mannesman, the industrial conglomerate, issued new shares to the value of DM3bn without offering them to existing shareholders. In March 1999, Deutsche Bank was raising money to fund its takeover of Bankers Trust. It raised DM4bn by means of a rights issue to existing shareholders but also sold a further DM2bn of new shares worldwide on a non-rights basis.

Of course, the shareholders may be approached to waive their rights. When Midland Bank sold 14.9% of its shares by way of new shares to the Hong Kong and Shanghai Bank in 1987, they approached the existing shareholders for their permission.

The new shares will be offered at a discount to the existing shares, for example, an offer of one new share at $90 may be made for every three existing shares whose market price is $110. The discount is more apparent than real. The firm is regarded as having diluted the value of the issue by this offer of extra shares at a discount. An averaging or pro-rating now takes place as follows:

			$
3 existing shares	@ $110	=	330
1 new share	@ $90	=	90
Therefore each block of four shares		=	420
So 1 new share		=	105

When the shares are declared *ex-rights* (XR), the price will be $105 if the market price remains at $110. 'XR' means that anyone buying the shares does not enjoy the rights to the new shares. It now seems that the shareholder will not gain from taking up the rights in any explicit sense but will lose if they do not. They may have 100 shares at $110 per share and soon will have 100 shares at $105 per share!

They may not have the money to buy the new shares. Some shareholders sell some of their existing shares to buy new ones or the rights may be sold to someone else for a quoted premium. In the above case, the premium would be $15. The purchaser of the rights will pay the shareholder $15 and later pay the company $90, paying $105. The shareholder has shares at present for which each set of three are valued at $330 and will soon be valued at $315 – however, they sold the rights for $15.

The market price does not obligingly remain stable while the shareholders make up their minds. The premium for buying the rights thus goes up and down. What is particularly serious is if the rights price ends up above the market price. Suppose the market price in the case above falls to $80. How many people will wish to buy shares at $90 if the existing shares can be purchased for $80? This reminds us that a rights issue must be underwritten just like a new issue.

In 1991, in the UK, British Aerospace announced a rights issue at £3.80 at a time when the market price was £5.00. The announcement of poor profit prospects, however, saw the market price plunge to £3.60 as the market lost faith in British Aerospace. The underwriters took up 95% of the offering.

Rights issues are examined carefully by the market. The new money needs to be used wisely if profit per share and dividend per share are not to suffer. Sometimes, the rights issue is seen as positive and well received, sometimes as negative, the sign of a firm in trouble and the share price suffers.

SCRIP ISSUES AND SPLITS

Sometimes firms offer shareholders free shares in proportion to the shares they own. For example, they may be offered one free share for every share owned. This is the *scrip* issue. Alternatively, the shares are *split*. For example, every share, 'par' or 'nominal' value $1, is replaced by two shares, 'par' or 'nominal' value 50¢.

In each case, the market value of the share will fall to half of the previous figure. The idea is that markets recognise a broad range of trading prices for shares. With growing profits and dividends over the years, the share price increases. Sometimes, the market feels that the new price is inconvenient and deters small shareholders from buying. The theory is that shareholders are happier with 100 shares at $50 than ten shares at $500. If this doesn't seem logical it is because it is, in fact, quite illogical – it's pure investor psychology.

For example, the UK market likes share prices in a range, say of £1–£10. Above this level, companies frequently do scrips or splits to bring the price down to a 'better' trading price, one which is thought to lead to a more widespread holding and more liquidity. Thus, in the autumn of 1998, the Logica share price was £20. They did a 4 for 1 scrip issue to bring the price down to £4.

In the US, the same idea prevails, but at much higher share price levels. On the Continent of Europe, too, shares trade typically at far higher prices than in the UK. When Paribas was privatised, for example, 3.8m applied for the shares and received just four each – but the price each was about FFr450. Switzerland is a place where, traditionally, the shares of the banks, pharmaceutical companies and Nestlé have traded at a price equivalent to several thousand dollars. However, the law, which required a minimum legal value of SFr100 per share, was altered to lower this to SFr10 per share. In May 1992, Nestlé took advantage of this to replace each share, legal value SFr100, by 10, with legal value of SFr10 each. The effect was to lower the price each from SFr9600 to SFr960. Other large Swiss companies have followed suit. In Spain, the bank Argentaria split its nominal value of Pta 250 to Pta 125 to halve the share price.

In the US, they get less comfortable when share prices exceed $100. Fast growing shares end up doing many splits. In January 1999, Intel announced its 12th split when the share price hit $137. In the US, buying in multiples of 100 attracts cheaper commission – the split makes this easier. In the same week, IBM and Microsoft also did splits.

We have seen from the above that shares typically have a 'par' or legal value which may not bear any relationship to the market price – IBM at $1¼, for example, or AT&T at $1. There is no minimum for the legal value either in the US or the UK. In Germany, however, there was a minimum legal value of DM50, but this was lowered to DM5, which may have been part of a move to a lower average price. A low par or legal value enables the company to issue more shares when it is first formed and gives it greater flexibility later.

The scrip issue does not change the par value but gives, say, one additional share free. This doubles the par value on the balance sheet and the money is taken from reserves. A split does not alter the *total* par value owned as, say, one share at $75 is replaced by three at $25 – the total par value on the balance sheet is unchanged, but the par value of each share is. Thus Barclays' 4 for 1 split in 2002 reduced the par value of each share from £1 to 25p.

Finally, let's note that a *reverse split* or *consolidation* is possible. Here, say, five existing shares are replaced by one new one whose par value is five times as high. This is for situations where the share price is so low that it suggests a firm in serious trouble. Again, it's simply psychology. For example, in June 1992, the British advertising group Saatchi and Saatchi carried out a 1 for 10 consolidation when the share price touched a low of 15p each.

SCRIP DIVIDENDS

A common practice in many markets is to offer a choice of cash dividends or more shares – the scrip dividend. From the firm's point of view, it saves cash as it's easier to create new shares than pay dividends. From the investor's point of view, if dividends are not needed as income, it's a way of getting new shares without paying share tax or broker's commission.

SECOND MARKETS

It is quite common to have a 'second market' for shares that do not fulfil all the requirements for a full official listing. Both France and Belgium have 'second markets'; the UK has the 'Alternative Investment Market' (AIM); Germany has the 'Geregelter Markt' and a third market, the 'Freiverkehr'; Amsterdam has its 'parallel' market.

In addition to this, there may be an active 'Over the Counter Market'. Paris has its 'Hors Cote', the US the huge NASDAQ market; and the UK a market called 'OFEX' with about 160 companies, including the Arsenal and Glasgow Rangers football clubs. There are four market makers and it has a quote-driven system, Plus, which we mentioned earlier in the chapter.

Usually, the key requirements that the second or third market firm may not fulfil are the number of years' trading record and the percentage of shares in outside hands. The general European rule, under the 'Mutual Recognition of Listing Particulars', is that 3 years' trading is needed for a full listing and for recognition of a firm already listed on another EU exchange.

In both Paris and London, for the official list, 25% of shares must be in outside hands. The rule for the Paris Second Market is that only 10% need be in outside hands. There were 1383 firms at end 2005 on the AIM in London and the top 50 are now handled by SETS MM as well as by Plus.

During the period 1998–99, new markets in France, Germany, Belgium and Holland formed an alliance called 'Euro.NM'. The markets are Nouveau Marché (France), Neuer Markt (Germany), Euro.NM (Belgium) and NMAX (Holland). They have common members, common data feeds and the shares trade and are monitored on a single workstation (but not on a common system). The Italian Nuovo Mercato joined in the Spring of 1999 and by mid-year there were 250 firms trading, with a total capitalisation of €59bn. This was providing severe competition for other secondary markets, such as the UK's AIM. The alliance suffered a setback, however, when the Germans announced, in September 2002, that the Neuer Markt would close in 2003.

A consortium of US and European banks formed a new pan-European market called EASDAQ, modelled on the US NASDAQ market. The aim was to attract high growth companies. Here, 20% of the shares must be in outside hands. It began in late 1996, but by mid-1999 had only 43 companies listed with a total capitalisation of €21bn. In 2001, it was taken over by NASDAQ.

ANALYSTS' RATIOS

When a firm makes an initial public offering of its shares, how does it decide what price to ask for the shares? A simple answer seems to be 'divide the value of the company by the number of the shares'. The problem is that the value of the company is the share price!

Sometimes people suggest 'asset values' as a possible guide. However, on 1 October 1987 companies' share prices were a great deal higher than at 31 October 1987, after the market crash, and yet the assets were the same. In any case, some firms are quite valuable but have few assets. 'People' companies like computer software houses or stockbrokers are like this.

The fact is that price is simply what the market will pay. We must, therefore, look at what the market does pay for similar companies. Their share prices will all be different, which doesn't immediately help. There are two rewards for buying a share – dividends and an increase in the share price. Both of these depend on *profits*, so what we need to do is see how the price per share of comparable companies compares to the profit per share. We might find an overall relationship of, say, 10. That is, if the profit is $4 per share, the share price is typically $40. If our profit per share is $3, this suggests a price of $30. Let's make it $28 and persuade everyone that it's a bargain!

This relationship of share price to profit is the *P/E* – the price/earnings ratio and the most famous ratio of them all. We've seen one of its key uses, to help us set a price initially. Each time new profits are announced, a new P/E is calculated and the share may seem cheap or dear now compared to its peers in the market sector.

Sometimes analysts look at the P/E for the whole stock market, and compare this with historic values to see if the market is overpriced or not.

Sometimes it is not easy to find the market sector. When the composer, Andrew Lloyd Webber, went public as the 'Really Useful Group', it was difficult to find anything comparable! In that case, what took place was the *offer for sale by tender*. Investors put in their various bids and the share allocation is decided accordingly. In that case, it was a 'striking price' tender, that is, everyone paid the same price.

As dividends are part of the reward for holding shares, the market looks at dividend income as a percentage of the share price. To avoid complications, the dividend is grossed up if it is normally paid net, for example:

$$\frac{\text{Gross dividend}}{\text{Share price}} = \frac{\$2.5}{\$50} = 5\%$$

This ratio is the *gross dividend yield* or, simply, the *yield*. It will be compared with the yield on other shares and with the yield on bonds in particular. Analysts talk of the *yield ratio* – the ratio between the yield on government bonds and the yields on shares. As shares may have capital gain, the yield is usually less than that on medium maturity bonds (although this has not always been the case). Typical P/E ratios and yields for key exchanges in November 2005 are shown in Table 7.6.

Looking at the dividend paid, we may want to see how comfortable the firm was when paying the dividend out of profit. Was all the profit used? How much profit is retained for growth?

We compare the profit per share with the *net* dividend per share, for example:

$$\frac{\text{Profit per share}}{\text{Net dividend}} = \frac{\$5}{\$2} = 2.5$$

Table 7.6 *P/E ratios and yields, November 2005*

Exchange	Index	Yield	P/E
US	S&P Ind	2.5	18.8
Germany	DAX 30	2.3	13.1
UK	FTSE 100	3.6	13.7
France	CAC 40	2.8	14.2
Japan	TOPIX	1.0	19.5

Source: Financial Times.

This ratio is the *cover*. If the profit is small but the firm feels it must maintain the dividend, the net dividend paid may exceed the profit per share. We say the dividend is *uncovered*. Clearly, it is being financed out of the reserves (that is, previous years' profits) and the firm's capital is being weakened.

At a time of recession, there is fierce argument about the extent to which firms should try to maintain dividends even if they are not justified by profits. Pension funds or insurance companies who need income to meet commitments are concerned when dividends are cut or not paid. Trustees of some investment funds will not allow investment in any firm which has passed a dividend in a given previous time period.

Finally, analysts look at *earnings per share* and use this as a record of the firm's performance. Problems arise when accounting conventions may allow (legitimate) massaging of the profit figure. Should extraordinary items for unprecedented events (for example, acquisition costs) be charged against profit for this purpose? More recently, analysts have focused on a new measure – earnings before interest, tax, depreciation and amortisation (EBITDA) which gives a useful guide to cash flow.

For the EU, trying to impose common national standards is a veritable minefield. However, a new standard for public companies, the International Accounting Standards Board (IACB), came into force on 1 January 2005. The European Union has adopted it and it affects some 7000 companies. It involves new treatment of R&D, goodwill, stock options and off-balance sheet vehicles. The idea is to make inter-firm comparisons easier.

Due to political pressure, some of the requirements to mark derivatives at their current market price have been removed. There is also the problem of reconciliation with US companies' standards. The whole issue is very controversial and will lead to more volatility in the companies' results in view of the general emphasis on marking all prices to current market value. This is just one of many controversial issues in this area and of course mis-stated profits at WorldCom, the hiding of debt at Enron and other recent accounting scandals have shaken investors' confidence and contributed in 2002 to a decline in world stock markets.

US STOCK MARKET – THE NEW PARADIGM AND THE BURST OF THE DOT.COM BUBBLE

The performance of the United States economy up to and beyond the millennium seemed to have broken all normal economic rules. The stock market also experienced a period of unprecedented expansion.

For three years the US GDP grew at 4% per annum with no sign of inflationary pressures. Consumer price inflation at the end of 1998 was 1.7%, the lowest for 20 years, and unemployment, at 4.2%, the lowest for 30 years. At this point (according to normal rules) labour shortages should have appeared and competition for labour have forced wages and inflation up. Instead of declining productivity as poorer quality labour is employed, productivity in the years 1997 and 1998 doubled.

People referred to this as the 'new paradigm' – an era in which the old rules no longer applied. They pointed to declining commodity prices, cheaper imports due to the strong dollar, high productivity due to technology and an intensification of global competition making companies reluctant to increase prices for fear of losing market share.

The Dow Jones responded in kind, rising two and a half times in the three years 1996 to 1998, and continuing to rise in 1999 – the only small blip coming with the Russian crisis in August 1998. The number of US households in mutual funds rose from 10m to 40m. At one point Alan Greenspan, the chairman of the Federal Reserve, issued warnings about 'irrational exuberance', but then seemed to content himself with pointing out that share prices implied confidence in a very strong growth in corporate profits.

Would the old rules reassert themselves in the end? Those who wanted to spoil the party pointed out that the stock market rose threefold between 1925 and 1929 and everyone talked of 'a new era'. The market then fell 89% from its peak to a low point in 1932.

With the burst of the dot.com bubble in 2001 and accounting scandals in 2002, the markets fell around 40%, and the Dow having peaked at over 12 000 fell below 8000 in 2002. The FTSE 100 peaked at 6930 in December 1999, fell to a low of 4122 in September 2001, recovering somewhat in 2002, but Iraq war uncertainty led to a new low of 3281 in March 2003. Since then, the market has recovered steadily moving to 5618 at end 2005. The Dow, too, recovered from its own low levels, moving over 10 500 at end 2005. UK, US and other world markets surged much further in the early months of 2006, but suffered a fall in May and June. At the time of writing, analysts are unsure if this is a temporary setback or not.

EU RULES

Investment Services Directive

At the end of June 1992, EU finance ministers reached agreement on the final shape of the Investment Services Directive (ISD). This extends the 'single passport' idea seen in the Second Banking Directive. Stockbrokers in one country have the right to deal in the shares of any other EU country, without having to set up a local office or buy a local stockbroker.

The ISD took effect from 1 January 1996. From this date, firms have been able to operate in any EU member state provided they are regulated in one of them. This operation is subject to local rules on conduct of business.

In addition, all exchanges and futures and options markets can trade throughout the EU. The effect of all this is to increase competition between the Union's stock exchanges and derivatives exchanges. Thus, from 1 January 1996, NatWest Markets began trading on the Swedish stock exchange but from their office in London. There was no longer any need to pay a local Swedish broker. Equally, the German DTB, the derivatives exchange, opened an access point in London for local members to do business directly with Frankfurt.

Markets in Financial Instruments Directive

The Markets in Financial Instruments Directive (MIFID) is due to be implemented by Spring 2007, although at the time of writing full details are not yet finalised. It is designed to let banks and investment groups authorised in their home market to offer services across the EU without further accreditation and brings in new rules on transparency of trading which will affect all OTC trading. The general aim is to open up Europe's financial markets by making it easier to trade cross-border. It requires extensive changes to computer systems and compliance. Banks and investment groups are groaning under the weight of new regulation – Basel 11, Sarbanes-Oxley and now, MIFID.

Capital Adequacy Directive

Alongside the ISD is the Capital Adequacy Directive (CAD). This has also provoked fierce debate. Where there is a universal bank tradition, like Germany, the banks were happy to cover the investment banking activity under commercial bank capital ratio rules. US and UK operators, however, not owned by banks, were strongly opposed to this. The rules require dealers to have a minimum amount of capital to back their transactions but taking into account the precise nature of the risk and allowing for hedging of transactions.

From 1 January 1996, the European CAD came into operation. Investment banks must allocate capital to cover the risks of losses through changes in market prices.

The BIS ratios, as we have seen, only covered default risks for lending. Large banks were covering this risk anyway but have had to cover the costs of rewriting IT systems to follow the new rules and monitor exposures constantly. Since most countries had local rules to cover capital adequacy, the effect has not been too serious in terms of banks having to provide extra capital.

Mergers and Acquisitions

The EU agreed a Merger Regulation in 1989. This defined circumstances in which a merger would have a 'European dimension' and come under the rules of the EU, and when a merger would be decided by national bodies. In one case, in particular, the Commission vetoed the takeover of De Havilland, the Canadian aircraft maker, by Aérospatiale of France and Alenia from Italy (to the fury of all concerned). On the other hand, objections to the Nestlé takeover of Perrier had little effect and Nestlé and BSN of France now control 75% of the French mineral water market. In the UK, Airtours abandoned its bid for First Choice in June 1999, following objections from the regulatory authorities in Brussels.

The EU has abandoned the idea of a detailed takeover bid directive in favour of one which outlines principles with which local legislation must comply – for example, equal treatment of all shareholders. However, the problem was stalled for 13 years, despite a clear need for general principles to be adopted. In France, BNP made a bid for Société Générale and Paribas. The last two can (and did) deal in BNP shares but BNP cannot deal in theirs. Gucci, facing a hostile bid from LVMH, sold 40% of new shares to an ally, François Pinault. This was only possible due to lax takeover rules in Amsterdam, where Gucci is listed. One current compromise floats the idea of 'joint jurisdiction', where a company is listed in one country but registered in another (like Gucci).

In 2002, a new takeover code was agreed by EU lawmakers. It curbs companies' use of poison pill (see Chapter 5) takeover defences and requires bidders and targets to treat all shareholders equally. Also, predators will be required to make a formal bid once their stake reaches a certain threshold. EU nations should by now have implemented the rules but some, as usual, have not.

However, in early 2006 various countries, especially France, were finding loopholes in the code to allow them to permit poison pills to frustrate foreign takeover bids.

By July 2005, the European Commission was still investigating possible barriers to M&A in the financial sector – legal, tax, economic, attitudes and the need for a supervisor's approval. There was much anger at actions by the Bank of Italy to frustrate a takeover of Banco Nationale del Lavoro by Spain's BBVA Bank and also a takeover of Bank Antonvenuta by the Dutch ABN Amro. Even the Italian authorities criticised Bank of Italy actions in the latter case and the takeover went through.

The Commission was toying with the idea of a pan-European supervisor but was not clear if it would be better to somehow link local supervisors.

CHALLENGES TO TRADITIONAL STOCK EXCHANGES

As we have already mentioned, stock exchanges do not necessarily have a monopoly of trading. Rival order matching systems are common and assisted by the growth of electronic networks. Traditional brokers face competition from brokers like Charles Schwab who offer cheaper Internet trading.

In the UK, Tradepoint opened up in 1995 in competition with the London Stock Exchange. Initially, it was a failure and ran up losses of £30m. However, in a rescue package in May 1999, new partners took a 55% stake and revitalised it by putting their own trades through it. These new partners included Instinet, Morgan Stanley, Dean Witter, JP Morgan and Warburg Dillon Read. In addition, Tradepoint became the first foreign exchange to receive clearance to operate in the US from the SEC. In 2001, it was bought by the SWX Swiss Exchange (formerly the Zurich Stock Exchange) and renamed Virt-X as a cross-border trading system for blue chips. It is still based in London.

In the US, Electronic Communications Networks (ECNs) act as mini-exchanges. They include Instinet, E*Trade, Charles Schwab, Datek, Island and Posit (now operating in the UK). E*Trade took over Telebanc on 1 June 1999 in a move to add value with advice and research. Even worse for the traditional exchanges, the SEC is considering recognising ECNs as official exchanges.

Some brokers have now set up links with them – Goldman Sachs, Lehman Bros and Bear Stearns. Eyebrows were raised in June 1999 when Merrill Lynch revealed plans to enter discount on-line broking using the Internet in direct competition with Charles Schwab. Merrill's Internet service offers a fee of $29.95 per transaction, far less than its normal commissions, but still in excess of other on-line discount brokers. The Internet is becoming a major factor now. It is estimated that 61% of trades with Charles Schwab go through the Internet. In the UK, Barclays Stockbrokers have launched an on-line Internet service, and the Swedish bank, SEB, has a very successful Internet operation and claims that 20% of its customers use it. Charles Schwab already operates in the UK and E*Trade plans to do so.

One reaction of stock exchanges has been to offer more flexibility with evening sessions. NASDAQ announced plans in May 1999 for evening trading on the NASDAQ 100 stocks only. The New York Stock Exchange is considering the same move. However, staffing costs will be a problem as overheads go up for limited revenue.

In order to have greater flexibility for raising capital, the London Stock Exchange went public in June 2000 and NASDAQ did so in early 2003. The CME was the first major US market to float when it went public in December 2002 with a market capitalisation of about $1bn. Finally, the New York Stock Exchange went public in 2006.

Other moves to cut costs include mergers with derivatives exchanges and mergers with other stock exchanges.

The key stock exchange and derivatives exchange have merged in the following markets: Germany, France, the Netherlands, Sweden, Austria, Switzerland and Hong Kong. In the US, NASDAQ has merged with the American Stock Exchange and acquired the Instinet electronic exchange, but the big news was the announcement by the New York Stock Exchange in late 2005 that it was to acquire the electronic exchange Archipelago, and offer both floor and electronic trading systems.

In Scandinavia, Sweden and Denmark announced a common system, Norex, and expect to include Norway and Finland. The new Stockholm system, SAX-2000, will be used, and trading, regulations, clearing and settlement will all be unified.

The big talking point in Europe, however, was a planned pan-European exchange spurred on by EMU. The first move was the announcement in mid-1998 that the London and Frankfurt exchanges planned to merge. Paris was understandably upset and began to talk of a rival merger with other European exchanges. Nevertheless, a meeting took place in December 1998 attended by the exchanges from London, Frankfurt, Paris, Brussels, Madrid, Milan, Zurich and Amsterdam. At a further meeting in May 1999, the six other exchanges signed a memorandum of understanding with London and Frankfurt. The long-term objectives included a single electronic trading platform, common trading regulations, and common access and trading hours. London and Frankfurt had already announced common trading hours and one or two minor trading details. All German company trades are now handled in Frankfurt, and UK company trades in London.

There were, however, severe problems to be overcome. Which trading system to use – London or Frankfurt? Which settlement system? (CREST, London's system, formed an alliance with the Deutsche Börse Clearing in May 1999.) Which indices will be used? How will ownership of the exchange be structured? Will the latter be based on turnover or capitalisation? Germany's share based on capitalisation, for example, would be about 15% but 20% based on turnover. So severe are these problems that the partners, in September 1999, announced an alliance rather than a new unified exchange, giving access to all exchanges on one screen with anonymous trading and a central counterparty. In 2001, plans for a merger between Frankfurt and London were abandoned and, in 2002, the LSE announced that it was purchasing a 76% stake in OM, the Swedish exchange (and previously an unsuccessful bidder for the LSE).

While they deliberated, the competition was not standing still. Euronext was created in September 2000 as an amalgamation of stock exchanges in Amsterdam, Brussels and Paris, and with the goal of becoming a fully integrated, cross-border, European market for equities, bonds, derivatives and commodities. One major step towards this goal was the acquisition of LIFFE, London's derivatives exchange, in January 2002. Later Lisbon joined as well. The SWX Swiss Exchange and the Deutsche Börse formed Eurex to offer derivatives trading.

In 2005 and early 2006, the market was swept by offers or proposed offers for the LSE by Deutsche Börse, Euronext, the Australian, Macquarie, and NASDAQ. The UK competition authorities were worried about the threat to competition if an exchange also controlled settlement. What the EU wants (and many users) is pan-European clearing and settlements. At the time, nothing came of any of these moves but in May 2006, NASDAQ started to build up a holding in LSE shares which eventually became 25%. This leaves NASDAQ in a position to frustrate any other bidder without yet having made a formal bid itself.

At much the same time, the New York Stock Exchange offered a 'merger of equals' to Euronext (the union of the exchanges in Amsterdam, Brussels, Paris and Portugal as well as LIFFE). In early June 2006, Euronext announced that its board was recommending the offer to shareholders. The new exchange will be called NYSE Euronext, will have its headquarters in the US and will have a combined market capitalisation of about €15 billion ($17.5 billion, £10.5 billion). The Italian exchange, Borsa Italiana, have expressed interest in joining.

There may be political problems looming. Euronext is dominated by the French and their government is not happy about the US link. They would prefer a merger with Deutsche Börse, who may yet launch a hostile bid and try to frustrate the NYSE. At the time of writing, none of this has been finally resolved.

SUMMARY

Strictly speaking, stocks are fixed interest securities and shares are equities.

Share indices are usually based on market capitalisation and calculated every minute.

In most economies, the major shareholders are investment institutions (pension funds, insurance companies and mutual funds) rather than private shareholders. The world's ageing populations will lead to a growth in funded pensions.

Mixed pools of shares are popular investments. They may be *closed-ended* (for example, UK investment trusts) or *open-ended* (for example, US mutual funds).

Order-driven dealing systems are those where orders of buyers and sellers are matched. Quote-driven systems are those where *market makers* quote firm bid and offer prices. Hybrid systems, like New York, involve elements of both types.

Dealers with *long* positions can lend stock to get collateral to fund their position and those with *short* positions can borrow stock (offering collateral) to match their sales. This is *stock borrowing and lending*. Very large deals are *bought deals* or *block trades*.

Sometimes firms buy their own shares back in order to cancel them and enhance dividends and earnings per share.

Settlement systems are usually *rolling settlement*, although settlement of all deals in a given trading period still exists (for example, France).

With new issues, shares may be a *public offer for sale* (or *initial public offering*). The alternative is the *private placing*, although sometimes a mixture of both is used.

An offer of more shares to existing shareholders is a *rights issue*.

A *scrip* issue offers shareholders free shares and a *split* divides the par value of the existing shares. The objective in both cases is to lower the price to improve liquidity. A *consolidation* replaces a number of existing shares by one new one to enhance the price. A *scrip dividend* is an offer of shares instead of cash dividends (optional).

As well as the normal market for shares, there may be a secondary market for newer companies who do not meet the requirements for a full listing. There may also be dealing outside the exchange – *over the counter* (OTC).

When a firm goes public, we look at the relationship between the price of similar shares and the profit per share to guide us as to the correct offer price of the new share. This is the *price/earnings ratio* (P/E). We also look at the likely dividend as a percentage of the share price to calculate the *gross dividend yield*. To check if the latter is achieved by giving away all the profit, we compare the profit per share to the net dividend to calculate the *cover ratio*. Finally, analysts look at the *earnings per share*.

From 1 January 1996, the EU *Investment Services Directive* took effect. This enables member firms to trade across all 15 markets.

Also taking effect from 1 January 1996 was the EU's *Capital Adequacy Directive*, which links capital to market risk.

In the US, the New York Stock Exchange has acquired Archipelago, the electronic exchange, and NASDAQ has merged with the American Stock Exchange and acquired Instinet, the electronic exchange.

In Europe, the exchanges in Paris, Amsterdam, Brussels and Lisbon have formed Euronext and bought London's LIFFE derivatives exchange. The German and Swiss exchanges have formed a merged derivatives exchange – Eurex.

In general, the future for traditional exchanges is under threat from Internet trading and the growth of *electronic communications networks* (ECNs).

Finally, NASDAQ has acquired a 25% holding in the LSE, and the NYSE has announced an agreed merger with Euronext. However, the Deutsche Börse may reply with a hostile bid.

8 Hedge Funds and Private Equity

INTRODUCTION

In the last edition of this book (March 2003), the only mention of hedge funds came with a reference to the dramatic collapse of Long Term Capital Management in August 1998. Private equity only came into the picture with specific deals, like the takeover of RJR Nabisco by Kohlberg Kravis Roberts (KKR) in the late 1980s for $25 billion and immortalised in the book *Barbarians at the Gate*. Nowadays, we can't open the financial press without seeing reference to both hedge funds and private equity companies and activities on a very large scale.

Since hedge funds are largely unregulated and private equity companies are somewhat secretive about their activities, the size of their interventions in the market depends on estimates. The IMF, for example, estimated that hedge funds had grown from 6200 funds in 1999 and investments of $480 billion to 9000 funds and investments of $1000 billion by end 2004. HedgeFund Intelligence, the publishers of *Eurohedge*, the industry bible on these markets, estimated in March 2006 that hedge funds' assets under management exceeded $1500 billion (£900 billion) managed by 8000 hedge funds worldwide. The US is the biggest market, accounting for $850 billion (£510 billion); Europe's figure is $300 billion (£180 billion) and Asia's is $115 billion (£69 billion). London is Europe's major centre. A research group, Private Equity Intelligence, estimated that private equity companies raised $262 billion (£157 billion) by end 2005 – 58% in the US, 31% in the UK and 11% in Asia. Private equity companies employ 2.7 million people in the UK, 18% of the private sector workforce.

These are very considerable figures and it is time for an initial look at what these organisations do. A more detailed look will come later.

Hedge Funds

A hedge fund is an actively managed investment fund that seeks an attractive absolute return, that is, a return whether markets go up or down. This contrasts with the investors in an index tracker, for example, who will only gain if the index goes up. To achieve this absolute return, hedge funds use a wide variety of investment strategies, many of them quite complicated. They are not designed for the retail investor but either high net worth individuals or investment institutions. Unlike mutual funds, they will typically be limited partnerships. The funds themselves may be small – $100 million to $1 billion but a hedge fund company may run many funds, each differentiated by their particular strategy. They think of themselves as small and nimble. Since their interest is an absolute return, they are not interested in relative returns, unlike a conventional fund manager. The latter will claim victory if a given index grows by 7%, but they have achieved 9% – this is definitely not the world of hedge funds. Although we shall discuss detailed strategies later, one common way of achieving this is short selling, that is, selling securities the fund does not own. This is achieved by borrowing the securities, something we met earlier in Chapter 6. They will also borrow a lot of the capital, hence frequent references to a word we also met earlier – leverage. If the security falls in price, the hedge fund can now buy it and close the deal at a profit. (While this is a common hedge fund technique, it is not unique to hedge funds – the proprietary trading desks of investment banks have done this for years.) A list of the largest funds appears in Table 8.1.

Table 8.1　　*World's largest hedge fund managers*

Fund		Assets managed $bn
D E Shaw	US	19.3
Bridgewater Associates	US	18.7
Goldman Sachs Asset	US	15.3
Man Investments Management	London	14.2
Farallon Capital Management	US	13.8
Barclays Global Investors	US	12.5
Caxton Associates	US	12.3
Citadel Investment Group	US	12.3
Maverick Capital	US	12.1
Och Ziff Capital Management Group	US	12.0

Sources:　　Bloomberg, Hedge Fund Research, 30 September 2005.

What are the origins of hedge funds? Generally, one refers here to Alfred Winslow Jones in the US who formed a partnership, AW Jones & Co, in 1949. They took both long and short positions in the shares of similar companies in the same sector, thus 'hedging' the portfolio. If their preferred firm did well, they made money. If its shares fell due to a fall in the sector, the shares sold short made money. This is the origin of the word 'hedge' in hedge funds, which puzzles people since they are well aware that hedge funds take very speculative positions. Jones raised $100 000 from friends and borrowed more money to leverage the position, producing extra profit. His aim was to charge a management fee of 2% and offer a 20% share of profits. Although, as the years went by, he would not be the only one doing this. *Fortune* magazine stumbled on this in 1966 and a score of imitations started up. Even the prudent Warren Buffet started a hedge fund in the 1950s and produced a

24% annualised return. He used the profits to buy Berkshire Hathaway in 1966 and dissolved the hedge fund in 1969. George Soros is another well known name. He left a Wall St brokerage in 1974 to go independent and form his Quantum fund.

Private Equity

Private equity is a mixture of venture capital for early stage companies and management buyouts – a public company is taken private for a few years and then either sold to a private buyer or floated on the stock exchange again. The European Private Equity and Venture Capital Association estimate that in 2004 venture capital accounted for 28% of the investments and buyouts 72%. Venture capital has always existed, but the emphasis these days is on buyout deals, usually heavily leveraged. The largest public equity groups are shown in Table 8.2

Table 8.2 *Top 10 private equity groups by spending on investment banking fees*

	Group	Fees $m
1	Apax Partners	267
2	Texas Pacific Group	255
3	Kohlberg Kravis Group	242
4	Blackstone	234
5	Permira	223
6	PAI Partners	219
7	Warburg Princus	214
8	Thomas H Lee Partners	205
9	CVC Capital Returns	204
10	Goldman Sachs Capital	194

Source: Dealogic.

Buyouts occur for many reasons. Perhaps a company is in difficulties and wishes to sell a subsidiary. Alternatively, it may have made a major acquisition but does not want to hold on to some of the non-core assets. Sometimes, the original owners of the business may want to retire or sell their stake. Private equity firms like to have the existing management team on board as they know the business well, and may offer them a 20% stake to keep them committed and give them an incentive to improve the business. The nature of the private equity is such that the timescale is much longer than the normal hedge fund deal – probably a return is sought in three to five years. This affects the investors in private equity firms as liquidity is thus constrained. While we normally talk of a 'management buyout', there is sometimes a management *buy in*. For example, when Legal and General Ventures bought nine hospitals from BUPA, a UK private healthcare provider, they brought in new managers to run them. Usually, private equity deals involve large sums of money and it is rare to see deals of less than $100 million but common to see deals in excess of $1 billion. To summarise, private equity firms seek to make good returns by buying public companies or neglected subsidiaries at good prices and turning them into more attractive businesses. Usually, debt forms a large part of the purchase price, at least twice the capital put in by the private equity firm.

Like hedge funds, this activity is not particularly new. We saw this in the UK from Slater Walker in the 1970s and Hanson in the 1980s. In both cases a downturn in the markets brought this to an abrupt halt. As markets began to recover from the recession of 2000–02, we began to see a strong resurgence of both hedge fund and private equity activity. They have been assisted by low inflation, low interest rates, the market's increased appetite for risk and a huge amount of liquidity available. How dangerous it all is and how far it is a threat to the stability of the financial world is something to which we shall return later.

HEDGE FUNDS

Hedge funds must not be confused with ordinary fund managers. Apart from the objective of absolute return not relative, which we have mentioned, they have a freedom most funds don't enjoy. Mutual funds (unit trusts) have limitations on borrowing, short selling and use of derivatives. Investment trusts may borrow but have the other two limitations. Pension funds, too, usually have limits although, curiously, they are now making investments in hedge funds as we shall see later. Another problem for mutual funds and investment trusts is that they must provide daily liquidity for their investors – this would be a big handicap for hedge funds who operate on a monthly or quarterly cycle and sometimes less often. Finally, the hedge fund managers will have a major personal investment in the firm which the ordinary fund manager does not. Hedge funds have a small base of much more sophisticated investors.

We cannot understand hedge funds without looking at their strategies which we shall do next. As a simplification, however, we can say that they carry out the typical operations of the proprietary trading of an investment bank but often using a much greater range and with less restraint on volatility of earnings. For example, it is believed that the proprietary trading of Salomon Bros became much more restrained when it was taken over by Citigroup – the latter were not as keen on volatility of earnings. Finally, hedge funds have (so far) been free of the regulation and control under which investment banks operate.

Leverage and Short Selling

Before looking at the strategies in detail, we shall remind ourselves of two tools which are important here.

Leverage we will meet in Chapter 12 on traded options – it's the ability to carry out a deal with a small amount only of the investor's capital. One way is to put forward a premium or margin. Another is to borrow all or most of the money. The effect in both cases is the same – a given percentage change in the price of the security produces a bigger percentage profit or loss for the investor. For example, suppose an investor buys $100 000 shares in IBM. Then $20 000 of the investor's own capital is used and $80 000 is borrowed. After three months, the IBM share price goes up 20% and the shares are now worth $120 000. The investor sells the shares and pays back to the lender the original $80 000 plus, lets say. $2000 interest. Deducting from $120 000, we now have a profit of $38 000, a 90% profit on the original $20 000. Note that the share price only went up 20% but has given the investor 90% – this is the essential attraction of leverage. The problem is risk. Suppose the IBM price falls 20% and the shares are now worth $80 000. If the shares are now sold and the lender paid back $82 000, the investor has lost all the capital of $20 000 and an extra $2000 in addition. This is a loss of 110%, although the share price only fell 20%. Leverage may bring huge percentage profits but risks high percentage losses and even the whole of the original capital. Nevertheless, in view of its attraction, leverage is used very frequently in hedge fund transactions and also private equity – hence the term 'leveraged buyout'. (In the above cases dealing costs have been ignored in the interest of simplicity.)

Short selling is a way of making money out of a price fall as we have already mentioned. The first step is to sell a security we don't own. Let's say the $100 000 of IBM shares. Since we will be expected to deliver them in the required timescale, the next step is to borrow the stock from one of the many lenders and use this borrowing to deliver the shares. The lender requires collateral to the value of the shares and a little more (see repos and stock borrowing and lending in Chapters 6 and 7). This could be cash or securities. The cash could be borrowed if necessary but, in any case, this will only be for a short period as we will receive the payment for the shares of $100 000. If we have left securities as collateral, the money can now earn interest. Let us say that later the shares fall 20% to $80 000. We can now buy the shares with the money received from the sale and repay the stock to the lender who will return the collateral. Forgetting the interest and dealers' costs, we bought shares for $80 000 we had sold for $100 000 – a gross profit of $20 000. It will be evident that if the price of the shares goes up, the short seller faces a losing position. For hedge funds who are seeking absolute returns, short selling is an essential weapon and often used to provide the 'hedge' part of the transaction. Short selling may have to follow rules of the exchanges which limit it, for example, the New York Stock Exchange. Sometimes it is banned outright, as in Japan.

Strategies

There are many hedge fund strategies and one research organisation, Hedge Fund Research, tracks results by 39 strategies. We, however, will concentrate on five main headings within which there may be sub-headings for more specific strategies:

- ❏ Equity hedge funds
- ❏ Global asset managers
- ❏ Relative value arbitrage
- ❏ Event-driven investing
- ❏ Short sellers.

In January 1996, Evaluation Associates Capital Markets Incorporated launched the EACM 100 as an index benchmark for alternative investment strategies. A hundred private hedge funds were chosen to represent the above five broad strategies. The index is rebalanced each year.

Equity hedge funds   These are equity managers who will sell short and use leverage. They will analyse individual companies and individual shares. Some may specialise in geographic sectors, others in either large capitalised companies, or small capitalised. We may find that some managers are 'long' biased with perhaps 50% of long positions, others are 'short' biased with the opposite. Some will be looking for good long-term growth, others at shares which look cheap in view of their potential. A manager may take the view that a sector is now overvalued, for example technology stocks prior to the burst of the dotcom bubble. Timing, however, is crucial and many hedge funds got out too early – the sector kept rising. Some managers will take a shareholding in a company whose shares have underperformed with a view to taking aggressive action, ousting managers or forcing other changes. This happened to Time Warner late in 2005 as three hedge funds led by Carl Icahn started to 'rock the boat'. Lehman Bros commented in September 2005 that hedge funds probably held 25% of the shares of Germany's blue chips believing them to be undervalued.

In July 2005, the *Financial Times* noted an increase in long only funds. The only difference now between this and a normal fund manager is the former's greater freedom to use leverage and derivatives.

Global asset managers   While the equity hedge managers will focus on specific stocks, the global asset managers take a broader view. They will look at stocks, bonds, currencies and physical commodities from a global point of view. If they believe that the UK is a better prospect than, say, Italy, they will be long of UK and short of Italy – probably using stock indices and not individual stocks. They may be referred to as *macro* investors because they look at broad themes as opposed to *micro* investors looking at individual stocks. As with conventional managers and analysts there are those who use *technical analysis*. The fundamentals look at inflation, interest rates, GDP figures, unemployment figures, P/E rates and so on.

The technical analysts or *systemic* managers identify trends using basic techniques or complex algorithms.

Relative value arbitrage concentrates on the relative value of individual shares, bonds, currencies and so on. They will put in place extensive hedges. They concentrate on the difference in performance of two given securities in a homogenous universe. For example, if they believe that, say, BP will do better than another firm in the oil sector, the manager goes long on BP and short on the other firm. So long as the relative gain of BP over the other firm gets bigger, they will gain whatever happens to the price. This also applies to bonds in the same way. For example, many investment funds are not allowed to hold non-investment grade bonds. When a bond falls below investment grade, this forced selling may cause an exaggerated fall in price. Hedge funds buy the bonds cheaply but short bonds of similar issuers in case the whole market falls (another example of the 'hedge' in hedge funds).

A common strategy within the relative value arbitrage is to take positions with convertibles. As we saw in Chapter 6, a convertible bond gives the holder the right but not the obligation to convert into the underlying equity. It is, therefore, a special form of options which we meet in Chapter 12. In view of the attraction of a possible conversion later, the interest paid is less than the normal rate for that organisation. Suppose the right to convert is at a price of $9 per share and the market price is $7. If the share price goes up to $8, the convertible has a better chance of future profit and the price will go up. On the other hand, if the share price goes down to $6, the possible conversion looks less likely and the price of the convertible will go down. The hedge fund manager will buy the convertibles if there is a belief that in the end a profitable conversion will be possible. However, as a hedge against the share price falling (and the convertible falling), the manager will short the shares. If the share price keeps changing, as is likely, the amount of hedge needs to be changed. The relationship is complex. To try and keep this simple, suppose the conversion price is $9 and the share price is $2. The share price changes to $2.30. The likelihood of profitable conversion has hardly altered, it is still remote and therefore the convertible price will not change. The amount of shares shorted to form a hedge need not be altered. Suppose, however, the share price is $11 and changes to $11.30, the profit has increased by 30¢ and, other things being equal, the convertible will increase by 30¢ and the amount of the hedge needs to increase. Thus the amount of shares shorted to provide a hedge needs continually to be altered as the share price changes. (Technically, this is known as *dynamic delta hedging* but let's not worry about that.)

Other factors to be taken into account are the interest earned on the convertible and interest on money received from the short sale. There are, of course, other risks than that of the share price falling. If market interest rates rise, the convertible will fall in price. If the credit status of the company itself falls, so will the convertible price in view of the greater risk of default.

Nevertheless, hedge funds have become huge buyers of convertibles on first issue – good news for the company. They also then short the shares – bad news for the company!

Event-driven investing   looks at special situations and seeks to exploit them. A special case of this is 'distressed' debt which we shall come to shortly.

One strategy relates to takeover bids. The victim's price usually does not rise to the offer price due to uncertainties – will the offer be withdrawn? Will there be a referral to the competition authorities? Often, in an all share offer, the bidder's price goes down due to the costs of takeover and delay in producing the profits. The hedge fund will buy the victim's shares and short the bidder. The worst case is if the deal does get referred or does indeed collapse. In the UK, in the autumn of 2005, HMV (owning one bookshop chain) made a bid for Otakars, another one. Everyone expected the deal to go through but to general surprise, due to fierce lobbying by authors, the deal was referred to the competition authorities. A more spectacular case occurred in the US in October 2000 when General Electric bid for Honeywell. Honeywell's price moved up from $35 to $52 – the US authorities approved the deal. Then came the bombshell – the European regulators blocked the deal (to the fury of the Americans) and the Honeywell price fell back again.

Periodically, there are changes in indices like the FTSE 100, which are based on capitalisation, as the capitalisation of underlying shares changes. Index trackers must sell the shares of any firms which fall out of the index and buy those of new entrants, but they cannot do this until the news is confirmed. Hedge funds will move in earlier and go long on the shares expected to join and short those expected to leave. Of course, once again, there is risk as a late share price may mean that a 'leaver' stays or a 'joiner' fails to join. Another point which applies to a lot of these strategies is that once all the hedge funds start to do it, there is very little profit left.

A major activity under event-driven investing is *'distressed debt'*. This relates to shares and bonds in companies that go into bankruptcy. An analysis of the real value may lead to profit in buying these shares/bonds, especially if there is a capital reorganisation. For example, when Delphi, the US spare parts supplier, filed for bankruptcy, a hedge fund, Appaloosa, bought a 9.3% stake. A capital reorganisation may take a long time. Rather than wait for the outcome, trade and bank creditors may sell their debt to a hedge fund. Hedge funds may buy the high yield bonds which, in the end, may be exchanged for a combination of debt and equity in the reorganised company. Mutual funds and pension funds may need the money and will be prepared to sell defaulted bonds. Again, there is risk – interest rates generally may go up or a change in the economy may worsen the defaulter's position.

Short sellers   There is very little to be said here. These are specialist funds which are looking exclusively for overvalued assets – whether bonds, shares, currencies or commodities. At the start of 2006, for example, the price of gold reached new highs which many experts found illogical. Any hedge fund sharing this view might well be a short seller.

In all the above strategies, extensive use will be made of derivatives (covered in Chapters 12, 13 and 14). Some funds will even concentrate on this exclusively. Amongst other things they offer a form of leverage, in that positions can be taken on premiums and margins without having to invest the full capital. As credit risk is one of the hedge fund's problems, they are frequent users of credit derivatives, described in Chapter 14. Indeed, Fitch, the ratings organisation, estimate that hedge funds account for 30% of the trading volumes in credit derivatives.

Range of Hedge Funds

The range of hedge funds is considerable. They range from large organisations like Man who operate a large range of funds and small niche operators which concentrate on one strategy. For example, Clarksons, one of the world's biggest ship brokers, has launched a hedge fund investing solely in shipping securities and derivatives, especially freight derivatives. The Man group, on the other hand, lists no less than 120 funds in the appropriate page in the *Financial Times*.

Some Examples of Hedge Fund Activity

In May 2005, DaimlerChrysler said that 15% of their shares were owned by hedge funds.

Two UK-based hedge funds, Toscafund and Lansdowne Partners, bought aggressively into Commerzbank, about whose future there were endless rumours.

In August 2005, Saint-Gobain, the French group, first bid for British Plaster Board at £7.32 a share – hedge funds bought 15% of the shares sensing a later much higher bid – they were right! In the autumn of 2005, Dubai-based DP World made a bid for the UK's P&O port and ferry operator at £4.43 a share. Although there were murmurs of interest from Singapore's state-owned PSA, the market was a little surprised to see it launch a firm bid on 10 January 2006 at £4.70 a share. Among buyers of P&O was a hedge fund, DE Shaw, who bought 450 000 shares at £4.59, anticipating a bid battle from two state-owned institutions with plenty of cash. At close of business on 11 January, the price was already over £4.90.

Research by Goldman Sachs at the end of 2005 suggested that as much as 20% of the huge oil price increase that year was as a result of hedge fund buying.

All the hedges put in place which we have discussed depend on one thing – liquidity. That is, that they can get out when they want to. If they want to sell, there will be buyers. If they want to buy, there will be sellers. The classic case of Long Term Capital Management (LTCM) illustrates the pitfalls. In 1998, they were long of Russian government bonds, denominated in dollars. If dollar interest rates went up, the chance of default would be greater but other dollar bonds would fall in value. Thus, shorting US Treasury bonds seemed a logical hedge. Unfortunately for LTCM, in August 1998, the Russian government defaulted. There began a panic-stricken rush to buy Treasury bonds. As LTCM had gone short on the bonds, to unwind was to buy them – but so was everyone else! No-one wanted to sell and LTCM was caught in a vice. In addition to the losses on the Russian bonds came the losses on the Treasury bonds. To make matters worse, LTCM was leveraged to a huge degree; they had borrowed $125 billion on a capital of $2.3 billion, wildly excessive by any standards. The Federal Reserve Board saw a threat to market stability. They persuaded the major Wall Street firms that were involved to act together. The creditors seized the whole LTCM portfolio and organised a gradual unwinding of positions. Those who were not involved may have derived some pleasure from the irony that on the LTCM board were two academics who had been awarded Nobel Prizes for their contribution to risk theory!

When General Motors were dramatically downgraded to non-investment status in the spring of 2005, many hedge funds bought the bonds and sold the stock in a classic move. However, the stock suddenly rose as Kirk Kerkorian, an existing shareholder, moved to buy more – sending the share price up and spoiling the hedge.

The Deutsche Börse made a bid for the London Stock Exchange in early 2005. Many shareholders thought that this was a bad move and one of them, the London-based Children's Investment Fund (a hedge fund), was active in forcing the resignation of both the chairman and chief executive of Deutsche Börse. (This caused great disgust in Germany, and led them to announce, in January 2006, a proposed change in the law to tighten the disclosure level for holdings in shares down from the current level of 5% to 3%.)

Energis is the UK's third biggest fixed line telecoms operator. It was taken over by a consortium of banks in 2002 after it became insolvent following heavy losses. In August 2005, came a bid from Cable and Wireless. A group of hedge funds controlling a large part of Energis' junior debt tried to block the deal, holding out for a higher price. The group of nine hedge funds claiming to control 25% of junior debt were co-ordinated by Close Bros. For the deal to go through, 75% acceptance was needed. In the end they were unable to block the deal and Cable and Wireless took over Energis in due course.

In another case, hedge funds achieved success and unexpected praise. US hedge funds, holders of shares in a French retirement home operator, Medidep, arranged a takeover by a similar operator, Suren, at a price 15% higher than that obtaining over the previous six months. Colette Neuville of Adam, the country's leading small shareholders' group, said that the hedge funds should be praised for once!

Some market watchers say that hedge funds probably account for one third of the turnover of New York and London stock exchanges and perhaps 30% of all foreign exchange trading. As a result, they provide huge business for the brokerage sections of investment banks. Research from Morgan Stanley estimated that the prime brokerage operations of investment banks generated revenues of more than $5 billion in 2005, an increase of 28% on 2004 – much of this is attributed to the growing importance of hedge fund business. The big names in the investment banks are Goldman Sachs, Morgan Stanley, Bear Stearns, Citigroup, Crédit Suisse, Deutsche Bank, Merrill Lynch and UBS. The funds going into hedge funds from their own investors have been slowing down, leading them to more complex and illiquid instruments to get better returns.

There are, of course, more commissions to be earned than from a conventional fund manager due to hedge funds going long and short and using derivatives. The leverage also means that their lending will create further fees from the bank. In an article in the *Sunday Telegraph* on 4 December 2005, the head of one of Europe's largest conventional fund management operations said that he had become a second class citizen in the City. He instanced two funds, each starting with $1 billion invested. One is a conventional fund, the other a hedge fund. He showed that the hedge fund will create 16 commission opportunities compared with two from the conventional fund. In addition, there will be fees and interest on the loan. He estimated that between 30% and 40% of large investments banks' income comes from hedge funds compared with almost nothing 10 years before.

Investors

Who then are the investors in hedge funds? Originally they were confined to high net worth individuals but today the various institutions are big investors – insurance companies, pension funds, banks, endowments and foundations.

In an attempt to bring the entry price lower, a US mutual fund, Rydex Investments, launched a fund in September 2005 to give investors access to hedge fund-like strategies for a minimum investment of only $2500. The problem is that fees are higher than for mutual funds and hedge funds cannot offer the liquidity that private investors expect. More realistically, individuals need assets of $1 million to $5 million to consider investing in hedge funds. However, there is one possible exit for retail investors who do not have the liquidity they would like – a forum for secondary trading has started on the Internet. Hedgebay lists more than 600 hedge funds and offers secondary market trading.

Another way for small investors to spread risk is to buy into a 'fund of funds'. As the name implies, this is a hedge fund that invests in a wide variety of funds to spread the risk. Unfortunately, there are now two lots of fees to be paid.

Regarding the prominence of institutional investors, there are various estimates. Tremont Capital, a US research firm, estimates that institutions account for well over 50% of new inflows into hedge funds. Greenwich Associates, another research organisation, found that 32% of all European institutions invested in these funds in 2004. A study by Russell Investment Group estimated that by 2007, institutional investors would have 25% of their money in 'alternative investments', which means hedge funds, private equity and real estate. US funds already have more than 20%, European funds just under 20% and Japanese funds 14%. Finally, Kinetic, an investment management consultancy, surveyed 70 hedge funds who confirmed that the profile of investors is moving heavily towards institutional investors. David Butler, founding member of Kinetic, commented (December 2005): 'The era of high net worth investors is fading as institutions become the main investors.'

A slightly curious development in 2006 was the decision by some hedge funds to list themselves on the stock market. One of their characteristics had been the ability to operate with as little scrutiny as possible. Nevertheless, Close Brothers raised £145 million ($240 million) through an AIM flotation of Close AllBlue in

May 2006. The private Swiss bank EFG is planning to raise $500 million (£300 million) some time before the end of 2006, and Goldman Sachs hope to raise £400 million ($660 million) through a fund of hedge funds vehicle, Goldman Sachs Dynamic Opportunities.

One big attraction for investors is liquidity. We mentioned above that hedge funds cannot offer the liquidity that private investors expect. For shares, however, there is always a quoted price and investors can get in or out easily.

Returns

How profitable are hedge funds? The increase in the number of funds and the rush of investors would suggest high returns. Certainly most funds are aiming to produce a return of 20%, but how many do? Frankly, the evidence is mixed and even contradictory.

GLG, for example, is a London-based hedge fund and one of Europe's biggest. It claims that two thirds of its funds had double digit returns in 2005 and several in excess of 20%. They have $11.2 billion under management. What would be interesting, of course, is what happened to the remaining one third. By contrast, the Man group, one of the world's biggest, admitted that clients lost $2.2 million invested with the company in the first six months of 2004. Industry estimates suggest that 2005 was not, in general, a good year for hedge funds, with returns in a range of 4% to 8%. Bearing in mind the high risk and loss of interest on the money, not very exciting. Hedge funds are, in principle, looking for mispriced assets. As there are more and more hedge funds, how many mispriced assets can there be?

In July 2005, Eleonore Dachicourt, hedge fund advisor in Crédit Suisse private banking, commented: 'There have been so many new hedge funds recently and so much money pouring in, that the dispersion of returns between the good quality manager and the average managers has never been so pronounced.' In fact, three academic studies carried out in the US in the three years 2003–05 claimed that 1208 hedge funds studied lagged the stock market on average by 14% although a few did very well. Actually, it's quite difficult to believe this in view of the huge increase in hedge funds over this period and the increase in the money pouring in.

The Cass Business School did a report in February 2006 which concluded that only 17.7% of hedge funds outperform and that the performance of successful hedge funds deteriorates over time. Hedge fund returns were compared with a replicated portfolio that traded S&P 500, T Bond and Eurodollar futures. Deducting fees, the majority of hedge funds would have underperformed this simpler, cheaper alternative. The survey did not included 2005, which was not a good year for most hedge fund categories.

Then a Barclay's Capital report in March 2006 said that hedge fund figures for returns were exaggerated by as much as 6%. They pointed out that many surveys ignore funds that have already closed and failed. In addition, some funds do not report figures, especially when they have performed poorly.

What does seem clear is that the future must be more difficult than the past with so many funds chasing the same objectives. This explains why many are turning their attention to emerging markets which have shown high returns overall in the last three years and where it may be easier to find mispriced assets.

Regulation

Generally, hedge funds have been described as 'unregulated funds'. However, this is now changing. The US Securities and Exchange Commission (SEC) ruled that from February 2006 any fund with holdings in excess of $25 million must post results through them for all to see. In the UK, the Financial Services Authority (FSA), having spent more than 12 months analysing the sector, has set up a hedge fund supervisory scheme and has identified 25 hedge funds which it will watch carefully. The International Organisation of Securities Commissions is carrying out its own review. As the market is global, the FSA has also suggested that the world's watchdogs should work together to avoid driving funds to less regulated markets. It also wants to look not only at the hedge funds but banks that finance them with large loans.

Finally, the Managed Funds Association, a hedge fund industry association, has published a 'Sound Practices Guide'. In view of registration with the SEC, it calls for greater internal controls, faster processing of trades, better disclosure to investors and more accurate valuations.

Is all this regulation necessary? Do hedge funds really represent a threat to the world's financial markets? Have we forgotten LTCM too quickly?

There are certainly plenty of warnings. Gary Duncan, in an article in the *Sunday Times* of 25 October 2004 spoke of 'Hedge funds – operations that may now pose a threat greater than Saddam Hussein and his elusive weapons of mass destruction'. In its annual report published in May 2005, the BIS was worried about the exposure of banks. It felt that they were at risk by not knowing what hedge funds were doing. It argued that the hedge fund activity was not really a diversification of risk, although Alan Greenspan has argued that they provide a mechanism to absorb shocks. At a Goldman Sachs conference in September 2005, Jochen Sanio, head of Germany's regulator BaFin, said that it was only a matter of time before there was another LTCM –'I am as scared as hell'. Not surprisingly, his audience, including top hedge funds, did not agree! Warren Buffet, the so-called 'sage of Omaha', makes a typical comment, 'when you combine ignorance with leverage, you get some pretty interesting results'. Perhaps the most startling warning of all came from the European Central Bank in June of 2006. It warned that hedge funds have created a 'major risk' to global stability for which thee are no obvious remedies. This followed a call in May 2006 by Germany's Bundesbank for an international system of 'self-regulation plus' which would include public grading of hedge funds by rating agencies and a code of conduct. However, almost at once, no less an authority than Ben Bernanke, the US Federal Reserve Chairman, expressed scepticism about these proposals and urged caution about regulators taking an overly heavy hand.

Although London's FSA is now studying the top 25 funds closely, the chief executive, John Tiner, makes some measured comments. He claims that (contrary to the BIS view quoted above) they 'diversify markets', and is relaxed about leverage which is 'something that should not spook us too much'. In the end it is difficult to avoid the view of such a veteran as Alan Greenspan, who was chairman of the US Federal reserve from August 1987 to 31 January 2006. He argues strongly that hedge funds play an important role in fostering deeper and more liquid capital markets worldwide. It is also true that, so far, there have been few scandals and few bankruptcies in an industry of 8000 funds and sitting on $1 trillion of assets. However, if interest rates go up further and we see a market downturn…

PRIVATE EQUITY

As we have seen in the introduction to this chapter, private equity is not in the same business as hedge funds, although both have incurred the same criticism over the amount of leverage involved.

To recap: private equity firms make good returns by buying public companies or neglected subsidiaries at good prices and turning them into more attractive businesses. They will gear up with debt that a public company would not want to risk (the private equity purchases will normally be turned into non-quoted companies). Although debt may be high, one advantage is that interest payments are tax deductible. It is, however, essential to have good, reliable, cash flows. The private equity firms get involved in the business, will bring in their own expertise and give the existing managers big incentives to improve the business. They will seek to cut costs, squeeze suppliers and sell unwanted assets. In addition, they may sell and lease back property. As we shall see later, there are certainly many cases where they have made considerable improvements. In rarer cases, they may buy a stake in a private company that simply looks undervalued and wait until it goes public later (see the example of Quinetic later). As private companies they will escape some obligations of public companies – scrutiny of share price, rules on appointments to the board and, of course, financial disclosure. They will look to fees of 1–2% and take 20% of profits as 'carried interest'.

The private equity companies will take their profit in a variety of ways. One is to refloat the company. Another possibility is to sell the company to someone else in the same business. Another popular way of getting an early return is refinancing. Once some improvements are clear, the private equity company goes back to the banks and borrows more money, paying itself a substantial dividend from the proceeds. This was particularly common in 2005, and Standard and Poor's reported in October 2005 that private equity firms had taken out more capital in Europe in the nine months up to September than they had put in – a figure of €11.4 billion compared with €5 billion in the whole of 2004. Sometimes the results of refinancing are spectacular. In December 2003, a group of private equity firms – Texas Pacific, CVC and Merrill Lynch Global Private Equity bought the UK department store, Debenhams, for £1.7 billion, of which £600 million was their own capital. In two refinancings in 2004 and 2005, they reconstructed the balance sheet with new borrowings and paid themselves back £1.3 billion – twice their original capital, in about 18 months. They hoped to refloat Debenhams before the end of 2006 if all went well.

Obviously, things do not always go well. Sometimes debt has to be sold as 'distressed debt' to hedge funds. There are two US funds which specialise in this – Apollo Management and Cerberus.

One other development in 2005 is that trade buyers seem to be less willing to be pushed aside when opportunities present themselves. When it became clear that Amena, the Spanish telecoms operator, was for sale, France Telecom battled two strong private equity consortiums and won.

The whole private equity industry has become very widespread and influential. In the UK, very well known firms are now owned by private equity groups – Debenhams, the AA, Saga, Odeon and UCI Cinemas, KwikFit and National Car Parks. KPMG's private equity group, which tracks UK buyouts with a value exceeding £10 million, calculated that 162 buyouts were completed in 2005 totalling £24.0 billion, a 27% increase by value on 2004. They put down the buoyancy of the business to private equity firms themselves having record amounts to invest following successful fund raising, aided by the liquidity of debt markets.

Investors

Who, then, are the investors who are putting money into private equity? These include institutions, like insurance companies, pension funds desperate for higher yield, subsidiaries of investment banks and, in the US, endowments like Yale. For private investors, the inability to withdraw money quickly is a major disadvantage together with the minimum funds involved. The best way for them is through private equity investment trusts, a private equity fund of funds and venture capital trusts.

In June 2006, the European Venture Capital Association released an interesting analysis of investors in the European private equity industry. Pension funds overtook banks as the main source of capital in 2005, accounting for 24.8% with banks following with 17.6%; funds of funds contributed 13.1%; insurance companies 11.1% with private investors just 6.0% (although many will have money in funds of funds).

Examples

In this section we give examples of some private equity deals. Failures will be mentioned as well as successes.

Debenhams was mentioned earlier as an example of refinancing. The turnround, however, is impressive. The buyout took place in December 2003. Before the buyout, Debenhams had a profit of £153.6 million on a turnover of £1.7 billion. For the year to September 2005, the profit was £212.3 million on a turnover of £2.0 billion.

Very large deals in 2005 included Wind Telecoms, €12.1 billion, and SunGard, $11.3 billion. Three private equity groups bought New Jersey-based Hertz car rental business for $15 billion, the highest since the RJR Nabisco deal in 1989. (However, as we go to press, rival private equity groups are bidding around $33 billion for HCA, the American hospital chain. If this succeeds, it would pass the $31.3 billion buyout of RJR Nabisco, although not in real terms.) Earlier, SunGard data systems was purchased by seven private equity groups for $11.3 billion. In terms of finance, some of the money was found by an asset-based bond (see Chapter 6), the assets being future rentals. In November 2005, five private equity groups, including Kohlberg Kravis Roberts, announced a bid for TDC, Denmark's leading telecommunications group. The bid was worth $12 billion, Europe's largest ever. The offer was recommended by TDC's board but the bid hit a snag in early January 2006 when ATP, a Danish pension fund holding 5.5% of TDC shares, the biggest shareholder, said that it would not accept the offer. The offer was conditional on receiving a 90% acceptance rate. Somehow, TDC succeeded in lowering the acceptance rate to 85% and got 88.2% acceptance in the end.

CVC Capital Partners bought KwikFit from Ford for £300 million and later sold it for £800 million. They also bought Halfords from Boots and doubled the value in three years.

Energy proved to be a fruitful area for private equity firms when the market boomed in 2005. Some had picked up energy firms when prices were low. Triana Energy Holdings, an affiliate of Merrill Lynch, bought Columbia Natural Resources for $330 million in 2003 and sold it late in 2005 for a figure in excess of $2.2 billion. A group including KKR, Texas Pacific and Blackstone bought Texas Genco in 2004 for $900 million and sold it late in 2005 to NGR for $5.8 billion.

Finally, the UK government found itself in an embarrassing situation in early 2006. The Defence Ministry's advanced research laboratory, Quinetiq, was partially privatised in 2003. The US Carlyle Group took the opportunity to invest £42.4 million and acquired 31.1% of shares. The government decided on a full flotation late in 2005 and, in early 2006, it looked as though it would be valued at £1.1 billion, making Carlyle's stake worth £340 million, eight times as much as it had paid and forgetting a payment to them of £28.5 million in 2004. In June 2006, it actually floated at £1.3 billion. Not easy to accept for a Labour government!

Private equity firms operate right across the globe. This is even hitting China, in spite of the general resistance to foreign ownership. Carlyle Group took over Xngong group, the construction machinery maker, taking an 85% holding from the state owner. China, however, says that it wants to encourage its own private enterprise and venture capital funds.

Naturally, it is not all sweetness and light. There are also the deals that did not do well.

Cinven bought Dunlop Slazenger in 2001 and in the end lost all the £70 million equity it had put in.

Carlyle Group owned a German vehicle component maker, Edocha, and carried out a recapitalisation to enable it to withdraw €80 million of its €185 million equity stake. Unfortunately, Edocha then experienced a serious downturn.

In 2005, there was a well publicised strike at Gate Gourmet, supplier of catering to British Airways and others, doing great damage to BA in particular. It had been bought by Texas Pacific Group and earlier in the year had stopped payments on its SFr 760 million debt. A squeeze by Texas Pacific followed and resulted in industrial unrest and much opprobrium for the owners.

Among private equity-owned firms that collapsed are Gateway Supermarkets, Le Meridien Hotels, Allsports, Furnitureland, Unwins (wines/spirits retailer)and MVC (music retailer.) In many cases, the burden of debt has proved to be the problem. It remains to be seen whether Malcolm Glazier will come to regret his hubris in buying Manchester United Football Club and incurring huge debts just as the club may be going into a relative decline.

Leverage

The question of heavy borrowings has been mentioned several times. Is leverage a threat, is it really excessive? Debt is usually measured as a multiple of earnings (strictly earnings before tax, interest, depreciation and amortisation – a figure aimed at showing the cash flow of the company and usually abbreviated as EBITDA). A consortium bought Rexel, a subsidiary of Pinault-Printemps-Redoute for €3.7 billion – debt was 7 times EBITDA. This was 2004, when Standard and Poor's found that over 60% of deals were based on debt multiples in excess of 5. Close Bros Corporate Finance estimated in October 2005 that multiples averaged 5.6 compared with 4.2 in 2002. Blackstone and Lion Capital bought Cadbury Schweppes' European beverage arm for €1.85 billion in late 2005 on a multiple of 7.

Fitch, the ratings agency, issued a warning in August 2005 that there were unprecedented amounts of capital being raised by buyout groups with leveraged recapitalisations in Europe. Buyout groups had paid themselves $10 billion in the first half of 2005 leaving companies vulnerable to rate changes or a downturn. However, Close Bros Corporate Finance in its review of the market in October accused the *banks* of encouraging private equity groups to take on excessive debt levels. Some 90% of mid-market groups surveyed said that they took less debt than was offered by the banks. A JP Morgan report issued at the same time also claimed that it was the leverage of commercial banks that was too high.

In Chapter 14, we explain the world of credit derivatives where those faced with debtors buy insurance against default and pay a premium measured in basis points. Naturally, the higher the risk, the higher the premium. As soon as a bid for VNU, the Dutch media group, was launched and terms were known, the credit derivative premiums for VNU widened considerably. The same thing happened once the bid for TDC was launched.

Finally, a spirited defence of the current levels of leverage was launched by George Roberts, founder of the famous Kohlberg Kravis Roberts in January 2006. He dismissed the idea that private equity groups were recklessly applying too much debt to the businesses they were buying: 'We are not being reckless with our investments.' Whilst one has to respect the opinion of such a successful market practitioner, one also recalls the words of Mandy Rice-Davis – 'Well, he would, wouldn't he.'

Hedge Funds and Private Equity Coming Closer

There is now growing evidence of firms with a foot in both camps. Many private equity funds have set up hedge funds, especially in the US, for example Blackstone. They are attempting to raise $10 billion to set up hedge funds. The first will be distressed debt, the second long/short equity and then multi-strategy. In the UK, the Active Group has set up both a hedge fund and a private equity group.

This does raise questions of conflicts of interest and insider trading. The advantage of the alliance is that both groups can share information about market trends and attract investors looking at either vehicle. The disadvantage is the scope for insider trading. The private equity groups acquire intimate knowledge of the firms in which they have invested. Most of these will not be public companies, but what of those that are or are near to being floated? If hedge funds trade shares based on information passed on to them by their associates they would be in breach of US regulations.

Sometimes the titans clash. In 2000, a powerful consortium of hedge funds challenged private equity groups KKR, TPG Hillman and Friedman when both made a bid for Texas Genco mentioned earlier. Many will argue that hedge funds do not have the experience in running a company to do this – another argument for an alliance. The word on everybody's lips these days is 'convergence'.

Profits on Private Equity

Everyone knows that there are deals which are spectacularly profitable and we have seen some – but what about average profitability, taking losses into account? George Roberts, of KKR, says that they continue to anticipate beating the S&P index by 5% to 7%, but, of course, this is one of the biggest and most successful firms.

An academic study from the University of Chicago Graduate School of Business and the Sloan School of Management at MIT did a survey of 700 private equity funds and found that returns, net of fees, from 1980 to 2001 were a little less than those on the S&P 500 Index. The academics even warn of suspected under-reporting by the worst performing funds. The reporting was based on completed transactions, where cash was paid to investors from liquidated funds, and not valuations of unsold investments. The study also concludes that funds raised in boom years (like 2005) tend to perform poorly. It is clear that returns between different funds vary considerably. It is also true that we tend to hear of the successes and not the failures.

Is private equity somehow a superior form of ownership? Has it, as John Lovering (a key player) claims, 'added freedom to Britain's commercial scene because it has introduced a parallel universe to traditionally owned and managed firms'?

Surely, overall, only a small number of firms can be relatively inefficient and subject to a dramatic turnround. Is public ownership such a disadvantage – the quarterly reports, dividends and transparency also provide a discipline. Can one believe that the private equity companies understand debt better than public companies? The claim is that they can borrow much more than a public company and that public companies are thus at a disadvantage – but what does theory say here? The Modigliani and Miller research in 1958 on the cost of capital concluded that a company's enterprise value is not increased by borrowing other than by way of a minor tax advantage.

The disadvantages for private equity are the lack of liquidity for its investors, the need to pay a premium to obtain control and the fact that sometimes there are no obvious industrial synergies. As we have seen, most research concludes that returns overall are no better than the S&P 500 in spite of the risks. The best, of course, do very well and employ talented people but the average may not be impressive. Like the conclusion at the end of the hedge funds section, everyone is assuming that interest rates will not go up further or that we will avoid a serious downturn.

There are predictions that it will all end in tears, rejected by others who are pointing to a new paradigm, as people said of the equity market before the dotcom bubble burst. As one unnamed City fund manager said, 'The people riding the boom always say that it's different this time but it never is.'

SUMMARY

A *hedge fund* is an actively managed investment that seeks an attractive *absolute* return, that is, a return whether the market goes up or down. To achieve this, a wide variety of strategies are used, especially *short selling* of securities – the selling of borrowed assets in the hope of buying them back at a lower price.

Private equity is a mixture of venture capital for early stage companies and management buyouts. The company that is bought out may be refloated on the stock market later to achieve a profit or sold to a trade buyer.

Both activities seek to enhance profits by heavy borrowing, known as *leverage*.

Hedge funds use a wide variety of strategies, many of them very complicated. They are similar to those used by the proprietary trading desks of investment bankers, but with much greater freedom for risk and leverage since the funds are not regulated in the way that investment bankers are. As a result, it is claimed that they often account for 30% of trading of bonds, equities, foreign exchange and credit derivatives (Chapter 13).

The US Securities and Exchange Commission ruled that, from February 2006, any fund with holdings in excess of $25 million must post results through them. The UK's Financial Services Authority has identified 25 hedge funds which it will watch carefully under a new hedge fund supervisory scheme. Other than this, hedge funds are regarded as an industry that is largely unregulated.

Investors in hedge funds were originally high net worth individuals but now the various institutions are big investors – insurance companies, pension funds, banks, endowments and foundations.

The investment institutions are also heavy investors in private equity companies. They have a disadvantage for private investors due to the inability to withdraw money quickly, as these companies will be prepared to wait three to five years for a return. There are, nevertheless, private equity investment trusts, private equity funds of funds and venture capital trusts. Private equity companies are so called because they are usually private companies as this gives them greater freedom of action.

The high leverage used by private equity groups has drawn attention – up to as much as seven times profit before tax, interest, depreciation and amortisation.

Both hedge funds and private equity groups have attracted investment in view of the large profits apparently being achieved with returns of the order of 20% p.a. being claimed. However, no academic studies have been able to verify high *average* profits over the whole range of activity. While there are, without doubt, spectacular successes, there are also many failures. In 2004 in the US, 1000 new hedge funds were formed and about 1000 closed down.

Foreign Exchange and International Trade

9 Foreign Exchange

INTRODUCTION

The Market

Foreign exchange dealing rooms at times of peak activity resemble bedlam. Shirt-sleeved dealers look at computer screens, talk into several phones at once and yell to colleagues. They talk in the space of minutes to key centres – London, New York, Paris, Zurich, Frankfurt. The phrases are terse and mysterious – 'What's cable?'; '50/60'; 'Mine!'; 'Yours!'; 'Cable 70/80 – give five, take three'; 'tomnext'.

The foreign exchange market is international, open 24 hours a day, adjusts prices constantly and deals in huge sums. 'Five' always means 5m whether of dollars, yen or sterling. 'Yards' is a billion. Central bankers have now fallen into a pattern of doing a full survey of the size of the market every three years. The year 1986 showed a total world market which traded over $300 billion every *day*. The 2004 survey showed a figure of $1.9 trillion – a huge increase. London is the biggest centre in the world, trading $753 billion daily, with New York at $461 billion and Tokyo $199 billion. In a study released in June 2006, ClientKnowledge, a UK research consultancy, estimated that, by 2010, the daily figure would reach $3.0 trillion.

Buyers and Sellers

Who is buying and selling all this foreign exchange? One's first thought is of importers and exporters. BIS calculate the daily value of imports and exports. The latter are $\frac{1}{32}$ of the value of daily foreign exchange dealing! What drives the market these days is huge capital transactions. Looking at buyers/sellers of foreign currencies we see:

❑ Importers/exporters
❑ Tourists
❑ Government spending (for example, for troops abroad)
❑ Speculators
❑ Banks and institutions.

We've mentioned importers/exporters and the role of tourism and government spending is easy to understand and not crucial.

As exchange controls have been abandoned by major centres, pension fund managers, investment fund managers and insurance companies can invest in foreign equities and bonds. They then need the foreign currencies to pay for them.

Investors with spare funds will move money around freely. Convinced that Spain,

Italy and the UK offered high interest rates together with low exchange rate risk due to the Exchange Rate Mechanism (ERM), they put their funds into these currencies. The head of research at Mitsubishi Bank in London, for example, estimated that free funds of some £40/£50 billion flowed into the UK during 1985–92 attracted by high interest rates. As the ERM all but collapsed in the dramatic days of September 1992, the funds flowed out of the high yielding currencies as exchange rate risk became a reality once more. Amongst these investors could be corporate treasurers at multinationals trying to protect their overall position. Those with heavy dollar earnings might worry if the dollar weakened and move spare funds into euros. We saw huge currency outflows again in 1997 as Far East countries, like South Korea, hit trouble.

The banks not only deal on behalf of their customers but do proprietary deals of their own. They will 'take a position': that is, what anyone else would call 'speculate'. If dollars seem to be falling they will sell dollars and expect to buy them back more cheaply 30 minutes later. In September 1992, as the lira fell below its official floor in the ERM, dealers would buy knowing that the central banks would have to support the lira. As it rose to its official floor of L765.4 to the deutschmark, they would sell it again at a guaranteed profit. As they all sold, the lira would fall again and the process would restart.

During this period of turbulence, banks selling sterling and lira (which both eventually left the ERM) made tens of millions of dollars profit. One dealer at Bank of America who casually revealed his huge profits to a television reporter was later said to have been disciplined!

For the 2004 survey, the BIS reported a 36% increase in volumes at constant exchange rates compared to 2001. The increase was put down to increased usage by asset managers, commodity traders and especially hedge funds (see Chapter 8). Deals between the banks themselves were 53% of the market, deals with other financial institutions were 33% (up by 5% from 2001) and deals with non-financial customers (for example, treasurers) were 14%.

Bank Profits

Foreign exchange profits are important for the major banks. The US comptroller of the currency calculates that foreign exchange dealing accounts for half the profits made by the big commercial banks.

The risks have grown, too. Big corporate customers have become more sophisticated, some with their own dealing rooms; new capital ratio rules have increased the cost of foreign exchange exposures; counterparty risk has become a major worry; dollar volatility in recent years has become more unpredictable. As a result, the business is increasingly concentrated in a handful of major banks. In the US, 75% of foreign exchange market transactions were conducted by only 11 banks, and, in the UK, 75% by 16 banks. Top traders according to *Euromoney* magazine are shown in table 9.1.

WHAT DETERMINES EXCHANGE RATES?

Amongst economists, the most popular theory for explaining exchange rates is that of *purchasing power parity* (PPP). At its simplest, if a given basket of goods is priced at £10 in the UK and $20 in the US, this suggests the exchange rate should be £1 = $2. If the exchange rate is actually £1 = $1, then the Americans can buy a basket of goods in the UK at half the price it costs them at home and dollar imports will rise heavily, causing the dollar to weaken. As time goes by, one factor causing US goods to become either more or less expensive than British goods is inflation. If UK inflation is higher than the US, then they may sell less goods to the US, but if the sterling/dollar exchange rate moves in the dollar's favour, the cost to the Americans is the same.

At least, that's the theory. Like most economic theories, it raises serious problems in practice. To begin with, what should go in the basket of goods, since nations' purchasing habits are different? Again, many of the prices in the basket will be for goods and services not traded internationally anyway. It also assumes that the price is not distorted by tax differences (VAT or Sales Tax) and that there are no artificial barriers to trade, such as tariffs.

(The *Economist* has some fun periodically with its McDonald PPP: it compares the price of a hamburger in key world capitals and arrives at an exchange rate which it compares with the real one! It started as a bit of fun, but has inspired several serious studies – for example, 'Purchasing Power Parity Theory and the Big Mac', Federal Reserve Bank of St Louis, January 1996.)

Table 9.1   *Top 10 traders by % share of foreign exchange market*

Rank	Bank	% share
1	Deutschebank	16.7
2	UBS	12.4
3	Citigroup	7.5
4	HSBC	6.3
5	Barclays	5.8
6	Merrill Lynch	5.7
7	JP Morgan	5.3
8	Goldman Sachs	4.4
9	ABN Amro	4.1

Source: *Euromoney* (June 2005).

If inflation in one country is consistently higher than in another, then the expectation is that the exchange rate will deteriorate in the country with the higher inflation. How do we persuade foreigners to hold this currency? Answer – by offering them higher interest rates than they can get at home. The higher interest rates compensate for the anticipated higher inflation rate. Thus interest rates enter the equation along with inflation and balance of payments figures.

The relationship between inflation and the exchange rate was nicely shown by Samuel Brittan of the *Financial Times* in an article in the issue of 9 October 1992 (using original figures from Datastream). Brittan plotted the declining purchasing power of the pound against the declining deutschmark/sterling exchange rate from 1964 to 1992. The correlation was striking. Underlying this is the fact that beginning with £1 in 1950, we needed £17 to buy the same goods in 1992. Beginning with DM1 in 1950, we only needed DM3.5 in 1992 to buy the same goods. The German consciousness of the risks of inflation reflects the horrifying experiences following the First World War. In 1918, a loaf was 63 pfennigs and in November 1923, 200 billion deutschmarks!

The balance of payments is the difference between what a country buys and what it sells. It buys and sells physical goods and services. There are also the financial items called 'invisibles'. A French investment bank holds US government bonds and earns interest on these bonds. A German firm pays Lloyd's of London premiums for insurance. The balance between all the above items is the *current account*. Then there is the holding of assets – foreign securities, factories, land and so on, called the *capital account*. The balance of payments is said to always balance because any deficit on current account will be offset by a surplus on the capital account. Unfortunately, the figures don't always balance and so we have 'balancing items' to account for errors and transactions which cannot be traced. Sometimes, the balancing items are huge, reducing confidence in the figures.

If a country has a consistent deficit on the current account, the inference is that the country is not competitive and the expectation is that the exchange rate will weaken in the future.

Since trade sales/purchases only account for a small amount of foreign exchange daily dealing as opposed to capital movements, attention has switched away from PPP to the question of investments. Investors are looking for high real interest rates, that is, the return after taking account of inflation and currency risk. The theory is that investors will shift assets from one country to another according to the relative prices of international assets, expectations of inflation, expectations of exchange rate stability or volatility and actual exchange rates. This is the *portfolio balance model*.

In a way this is more attractive than PPP if we look at the sheer volatility of exchange rates. In January 1991, for example, the dollar had weakened dramatically – it was virtually $2 = £1. Within weeks, however, the dollar strengthened to $1.70 = £1. Had the price of a basket of goods changed in this period? Surely not.

The problem with all these theories is when artificial systems, like the ERM, interfere with market forces. For example, in October 1990, the UK joined the ERM with a target rate of DM2.95 = £1. Although UK inflation rates fell over the next two years and German rates increased, the UK had on average higher inflation in the period and lower productivity in manufacturing. In the middle of a severe recession, it was running an extraordinary deficit on current account suggesting structural problems and severe difficulties to come as the economy came out of recession. In addition, UK interest rates were barely higher than Germany in September 1992. While inflation then, on a like for like basis, was much the same as Germany's, investors' *expectations* were different. They were far more confident that Germany would get inflation lower than they were that the UK would stop it rising further. They also had greater confidence in the Bundesbank holding interest rates high (unpopular politically but the Bundesbank is independent) than in the Bank of England (not independent at that time) keeping interest rates high in the middle of a severe recession.

In spite of this, sterling moved over the 23 months within its ± 6% band compared to the deutschmark. However, sentiment that the pound was overvalued and would have to devalue grew stronger. Financial institutions and corporates holding pounds sold them. Speculators joined in. Finally, the leak that the Bundesbank thought that sterling should seek a new parity was all that was needed for the dam to burst. On Wednesday, 17 September, the UK government withdrew sterling from the ERM and saw the rate fall in two weeks from a level of about DM2.80 to DM2.50 causing the experts to produce their favourite quotation, 'you can't buck the market'. The Italian lira had a similar experience. This was followed by further turbulence in July 1993, when currencies like the French franc were attacked, leading to a fundamental change in ERM rules.

Finally, what we can't ignore in looking at exchange rate determinants is the sheer psychology of the markets – the 'herd' instinct, for example, which causes dealers to act in concert and for the market to frequently 'overshoot' when new data is released. Paul de Grauwe and Danny Decupere of the Catholic University of Leuven in Belgium produced a study of 'Psychological Barriers in the Market' in 1992. They found, for instance, that traders tended to avoid certain exchange rates, especially those ending in round numbers!

Perhaps because of psychology, there are forecasters of movements called *chartists* who plot historic price data and look for patterns and trends such as 'heads and shoulders', 'double bottoms/tops', 'broadening top' and so on. This is also called *'technical analysis'*. They talk of upper (resistance) levels and lower (support) levels. If a level is broken, the chartists believe that the break will be decisive. Those who look at the underlying economic factors – interest rates, inflation, productivity, balance of payments – are the *fundamentalists*. The same two approaches are used in equity and bond markets. The chartists and fundamentalists often clash in battle, like Guelphs and Ghibellines in mediaeval Italy or Catholics and Protestants. In fact, all banks use a blend of both techniques.

BRETTON WOODS

In the post-war period up to the early 1970s, currencies did not fluctuate as they do today but operated on a fixed basis. The system was set up at a conference in Bretton Woods (New Hampshire, US) in 1944. The conference was attended by world finance ministers and major economists, like J.M. Keynes, from 44 countries. It was called to discuss the international financial arrangements that would apply after the Second World War. In particular, it set up:

❏ A system of exchange rate stability
❏ The International Monetary Fund
❏ The World Bank.

Exchange Rate Stability

Exchange rate stability was achieved by members adopting an external or *par value* for their currency, expressed in terms either of gold or of the US dollar. America had no choice but to adopt a par value for the dollar expressed in gold; the dollar was convertible to gold on demand at $35 per oz but all other members pegged to the dollar. This Bretton Woods system was, therefore, termed the *Gold Exchange Standard*, with the dollar being linked directly to gold and other currencies indirectly linked to gold via the dollar. Having adopted a par value, the central banks of member countries had to routinely intervene in the foreign exchange markets to keep their exchange rate against the dollar within 1% on either side of the par value: selling their currency (and buying the dollar) when it threatened to rise above 1%; doing the opposite when it fell 1% below the par value. The central banks' efforts to keep their currency at the agreed rate could be supported by the International Monetary Fund (IMF) – hence its relevance to these arrangements.

International Monetary Fund

The decision to set up the IMF was taken at the Bretton Woods Conference in 1944 but the Fund did not come into operation until 1946. Its headquarters are in Washington, DC. The prime object in setting up the Fund was to prevent any return to the restrictive international trade environment and erratic exchange rate fluctuations of the inter-war period. The Fund's main task was to preside over a system of fixed exchange rates. Ancillary to this, it provided borrowing facilities for its members, these also allowing trade deficit nations to embark upon more gradual corrective policies that would be less disruptive for trading partners.

When a member country had a balance of payments deficit, it borrowed from the IMF to finance it, as well as to obtain supplies of foreign currency with which to buy up its weak currency in the foreign exchange markets, in order to prevent it falling more than 1% below its par value. Thus, in this way the *borrowing facilities* function was ancillary to the stable exchange rate goal. When members exhausted their borrowing entitlement, they had perforce to adopt a new, and lower, par value. *Devaluation* (and revaluation) was possible but had to be carried out in discussion with the IMF, the latter having to be satisfied that a state of 'fundamental disequilibrium' in the member country's balance of payments did exist. Thus, although under the Bretton Woods system exchange rates were fixed, they were not immutably fixed.

For example, the UK, having sold every foreign asset to pay for the war, was in a weak position.

After the war it adopted (possibly foolishly) an exchange rate of $4 = £1. In 1949, however, it devalued to $2.80 = £1. Devaluation is always difficult. Governments cannot announce devaluations in advance as everyone will immediately sell their currency. As a result, they always deny any intention to devalue in the strongest terms. Then, they suddenly devalue. The result is that protestations about a determination not to devalue may, in the end, simply be disbelieved. When enough people disbelieve it, devaluation is inevitable due to the massive selling of the currency. The chaos in the ERM in September 1992 illustrates these forces at work.

Member countries had to pay a subscription to the IMF, related originally to their pre-war value of trade. This subscription had originally (but no longer) to be one quarter in gold, with the remainder in the member's own currency. In this way the IMF acquired a vast pool of gold and members' currencies, giving it resources to lend. *Borrowing entitlements* were basically 125% of subscription, although the needs of small-subscription countries, as well as the oil price rise of the 1970s, called for additional categories of borrowing facilities to be brought into being. IMF loans are conditional upon the borrowing country agreeing to adopt certain corrective economic policies, generally of an unpopular, restrictive nature.

In the late 1960s, there had been concern that *international liquidity* (the means of payment for international trade) would not keep pace with the volume growth in trade, thus exerting a deflationary pressure. A new function for the IMF was therefore brought into being, that of creating man-made international liquidity in the form of *Special Drawing Rights* (SDRs). These were credits created in the books of the IMF and allocated to members to pay for their balance of payments deficits (surplus countries accumulating SDRs). SDRs were first issued in 1971 but thereafter, with the fear now being one of inflation rather than deflation, further subsequent issues of SDRs have been limited. The value of an SDR is calculated daily, based on an average of the exchange rates of the world's major currencies. As Switzerland did not join the IMF formally until 1992, Swiss francs were not used.

The World Bank

The main operating company is the *International Bank for Reconstruction and Development* (IBRD). The IBRD began operations in 1945 and was initially concerned with the 'reconstruction' of war-devastated Europe. Nowadays, it is primarily concerned with helping less developed countries (LDCs) to develop their economies. It makes loans for up to 20 years at rates of interest slightly below the commercial level, with repayment being guaranteed by the government of the borrowing country. The majority of these loans are for specific projects in the areas of agriculture, energy and transport. Recently, more generalised 'programme' and 'structural adjustment' loans have also been extended to aid less developed economies. The IBRD obtains its funds from members (the same 100 or so countries that are members of the IMF) as well as by the issuance of international bonds. The IBRD is a major borrower in the eurobond market. Under the umbrella title of the World Bank are two other institutions.

The *International Finance Corporation* (IFC) was set up in 1956 as a multilateral investment bank to provide risk capital (without government guarantee) to private sector enterprises in LDCs, as well as being a catalyst in encouraging loans from other sources. In the latter respect, the IFC is also concerned to stimulate multinational corporations' direct investment in LDCs, this being further encouraged by the Multilateral Investment Guarantee Agency to provide insurance against non-commercial risks.

The *International Development Association* (IDA) (1960) is the soft-loan arm of the World Bank. It gives interest-free loans for up to 50 years to the poorest of the developing countries. The IDA's resources come from donations from the rich members of the World Bank, with the US usually contributing not less than 25% of funds.

FLOATING RATES

By August 1972, there were huge pressures on the dollar, partly due to the cost of the Vietnam War. In August, the US authorities abandoned any guaranteed convertibility of the dollar into gold. An international meeting took place in Washington and attempted to hold the fixed exchange rate system together but the effort failed. The European Common Market was concerned that freely floating rates would upset the operation of the Common Agricultural Policy (CAP) and set up an arrangement known as the *snake*, designed to keep currencies within a band of $\pm 2\frac{1}{4}\%$. The oil price rises of the 1970s put the arrangements under pressure and membership gradually dwindled.

The arrival of floating rates meant that central banks didn't have to intervene to the same extent and didn't need the IMF to help with intervention. However, nations still needed to finance their balance of payments deficits. The fact that these were often less developed countries with large international debts and seeking World Bank assistance has led some observers to comment on a confusion between the roles of the IMF and the World Bank and indeed, a certain amount of rivalry. We discuss this further in Chapter 16.

In this period of floating exchange rates, the dollar has proved to be a very volatile currency. Foreign trade as a proportion of GDP is much less for the US than for many countries and they seem to be able to live with wild fluctuations that would cause havoc elsewhere. It has implications for world trade that may cause international central banks to wish to intervene, and we shall examine this later in the chapter.

Sterling has not exactly been a stable currency either. Table 9.2 is an extract of dollar/sterling rates over the years 1972–2005.

Table 9.2 *Sterling/Dollar exchange rates, 1972–2005*

	Year	Sterling/Dollar rate $	
	1972	2.50	(year of floating)
	1977	1.75	
	1980	2.32	
Jan	1985	1.03	
Late	1985	1.40	
Jan	1991	1.98	
Mar	1991	1.70	
Aug	1992	1.98	
Jun	1993	1.55	
Jun	1999	1.60	
Jun	2002	1.52	
Nov	2005	1.72	

Our previous comments about the effect on an exchange rate of one country's higher inflation and lower productivity are dramatically illustrated by looking at the list of sterling/deutschmark exchange rates shown in Table 9.3 up until EMU in 1999 and its equivalent rate since.

We can see the efforts of the UK government in the 1980s to reduce inflation and increase productivity culminating in accepting the ERM 'straitjacket' in October 1990.

EUROPEAN ECONOMIC AND MONETARY UNION

Moves to European Economic and Monetary Union led to changes which had an important impact on foreign exchange markets – the introduction of the Exchange

Rate Mechanism in 1979 and the adoption of a single currency for eleven countries, the euro, in January 1999.

These moves are so significant that they have a special chapter of their own (Chapter 11).

Table 9.3 *Sterling/Deutschmark exchange rates, 1960–2002*

	Year	Sterling/Deutschmark rate DM	
	1960	11.71	
	1980	4.23	
Feb	1987	2.85	
July	1989	2.76	
Oct	1990	2.95	(ERM target)
Sep	1992	2.51	(Sterling leaves ERM)
Apr	1996	2.27	
Dec	1998	2.80	
Sep	2002	3.13	(equivalent – introduction of the euro)

FOREIGN EXCHANGE RISK FOR CORPORATES

Types of Risk

Companies which compete in an international marketplace are at risk to changes in foreign exchange rates. These risks are of three types:

1. Transaction risk
2. Translation risk
3. Economic risk.

Transaction risk   This is the most obvious and common risk. A Swiss importer needs to pay for dollar imports in six months which are ordered today. If the Swiss franc weakens against the dollar, the imports will cost more. A Swiss exporter has sold goods to someone in the US to be paid for in dollars. By the time the goods are shipped and paid for, say in nine months, the Swiss franc may have strengthened against the dollar, making the dollar earnings worth less money.

Most corporates will decide to reduce this risk by the technique called hedging. Our concentration in this chapter will be on this type of risk.

Translation risk   A French firm has overseas subsidiaries reporting profits in Swiss francs. It also owns land and property in Switzerland. If the Swiss franc weakens against the euro, the profits are worth less in euros when included in the annual report. The value of the land and property may be unchanged but, translated in euros, the assets seem to have lost value.

Should these exposures be hedged? This is a subject of huge controversy. Not hedging may distort asset values and earnings per share. On the other hand, hedging means spending real money to protect accountancy figures. In any case, sophisticated investors will take the exposure into account. Knowing that our French firm has a heavy exposure to Switzerland, they will adjust their view of the firm's prospects. If, however, the risk has already been hedged away, their view will be incorrect. It may be complicated by the fact that the French firm makes extensive purchases in Swiss francs, thus giving a natural offset of risk.

We can sum this up with the totally opposite views of two firms in not dissimilar businesses.

SmithKline Beecham, the former UK-listed pharmaceuticals group, made 90% of its profits outside the UK. The treasurer (in the *Financial Times,* 27 November 1991) argued in favour of producing less volatile earnings by hedging: 'stable and predictable earnings are more valuable to investors'.

The UK chemicals and pharmaceutical group, ICI, made 55% of its earnings overseas but did not hedge. Their treasurer (1991 *Financial Times* article) argued: 'Translation exposures do not have any immediate cash flow consequences yet any hedging activity will involve cash expenditure.'

Economic risk   This is by no means as obvious as the other two. Suppose a Dutch firm is selling goods into the US and its main competitor is a British firm. If sterling weakens against the dollar, the Dutch firm has lost competitive advantage. The UK left the ERM in September 1992. Sterling fell 15% against the deutschmark in a matter of weeks but the Dutch guilder did not. Obviously this is serious for the Dutch firm but it may not be easy to hedge such a risk. It does need to be considered as part of marketing and competitive strategy.

Transaction Risk – Forward Rates

Let's take a German computer software company which imports computers from the US, paid for in dollars. It resells them with its added-value services – software, installation and so on. A contract has just been signed with a German customer and two computers ordered from the US in order to fulfil the contract. In its own accounts, the German firm would use euros. The rate for the euro/dollar could fluctuate. The computers cost $100 000 and the exchange rate is $1 = €1.10. The cost is, therefore, €110 000. By the time the computers arrive and the German firm is due to pay for them (say, in three months' time), the dollar may have strengthened and the exchange rate changed to $1 = €1.25. The cost in euros is now €125 000. If the German firm costed the computers at €110 000 when making the sale, then €15 000 has just been lost from its profit. How can it prevent this happening?

This is, of course, the standard problem facing all importers and exporters. Importers pay later but don't know what the exchange rate will be. Exporters earn foreign currencies at a later date but equally don't know how rates will move.

One simple solution for the importer is to buy the dollars today at $1 = €1.10. The dollars are not needed for three months, so the $100 000 is put on deposit to earn interest. In three months' time, they are taken out of deposit and used to pay for the machine.

In principle, there's nothing wrong with this solution apart from the assumption that the importer has the €110 000 now to do this as opposed to having to find it in three months when, perhaps, his own customer has paid. However, there is another solution which is so common that this is probably the one that would be used. The importer buys the dollars from the bank *three months forward* – the *forward* deal.

The bank is requested to provide $100 000 in three months in exchange for euros. Today's rate (called *spot*) is €1.10. The bank may quote, say, €1.1055 for the three month deal. The importer now has certainty. The rate could depreciate later to €1.25 but the purchase of dollars will be made at €1.1055. It's a little bit worse than the spot rate but it has bought peace of mind.

The question is, how did the bank decide that €1.1055 was the correct rate? Does the bank have analysts studying key exchange rate trends and making a forecast? Do they have, in a discreet corner of the dealing room, a gypsy and crystal ball?

The bank is, of course, now at risk instead of the importer. If they do nothing, then in three months they face buying dollars at, say, a rate of €1.25 and only getting €1.1055 from their customer. Before, we suggested that the firm could buy the dollars today and put them on deposit. The bank can do the same. It can buy the dollars today at €1.10 and simply lend them in the interbank market for three months until their client needs them. The question is – what is the cost to the bank?

The consequence of their action is that money which had been in euros and earning interest (or borrowed – the argument is much the same) is now in dollars and earning interest. But suppose dollar rates for three months' money are 3% p.a. and euro rates are 5% p.a.? The bank has lost 2% p.a. (that is, ½% in three months) through being in dollars. It is what economists call the 'opportunity cost'. It has lost the opportunity to earn interest on euros and the cost is ½%. This will be charged to the client as a worsening of the spot rate from €1.10 to €1.1055. Thus forward rates arise *from the difference in interest rates in the two currencies concerned.*

We can try this argument from another angle. A rich American, with $1 million on deposit in the US earning 3%, sees that euro interest rates are 5% and moves into euros for one year to earn an easy extra 2%. The snag, of course, is that, if euros depreciate by, say, 5% against the dollar, then the original $1 million will later only be worth $950,000 and this loss has wiped out the interest rate gain. To prevent this, the American arranges to sell the euros (and buy back the dollars) one year *forward*. If the charge for this is any less than 2%, then our American has a locked in profit and no risk. This will apply to dozens of other Americans with spare funds. The result is that billions of dollars will flow into euros until the laws of supply and demand put up the cost of the forward rate by 2% and make the whole exercise no longer worthwhile. The activity of trying to make a risk-free profit by exploiting price discrepancies is known as 'arbitrage', but of course supply and demand eliminate the possibility very quickly – if indeed it arises in the first place.

As dollar interest rates are less than euro interest rates, we say the dollar is at a *premium* (and the euro at a *discount*). Notice, however, the effect of this on an *exporter* in Germany. This firm will, say, earn $100 000 in three months and ask the bank to quote a forward rate for buying the dollars from them and providing euros instead. What steps can the bank now take to avoid risk? As it's a little more complicated than our previous example, let's lay out the steps the bank can take:

Today	1	Borrow $100 000 for three months
	2	Buy €110 000 with the dollars at today's rate of €1.10
	3	Put the €110 000 on deposit for three months.

3 months later	1	The €110 000 comes off deposit and is sold to the bank's client for dollars
	2	The client gives the bank the $100 000 earned from exports
	3	The dollar loan is repaid with the $100 000.

The effect of this is that the bank has paid 3% p.a. interest on the dollars and earned 5% p.a. interest on the euros for three months (that is, gained ½%). The bank has now made money from the interest rate difference and the forward rate is *more favourable* than the spot rate.

(In all these examples, the question of bid/offer spreads has been ignored in the interests of simplicity.)

Where the dollar is at a *premium* to the euro this means that:

❑ For the *importer* the forward rate is *less* favourable
❑ For the *exporter* the forward rate is *more* favourable.

The importer may not be quite sure when they will pay for the dollars and ask for a forward purchase of dollars, for example, 'between 1 and 28 February'. This is a *forward dated option contract* and not to be confused with 'options' as such. (In today's market there is, in fact, nothing like this difference between US and euro rates, as you may be aware. For purposes of illustration, however, it is usually easier to pick figures which the beginner can easily understand.)

Transaction Risk – Options

Let's go back to the case of our German importer. The $100 000 needed for imports are bought forward at a rate of €1.1055. However, in three months, the rate is actually €1.05 and has improved from the euro point of view. The $100 000 could be bought spot for only €105 000. However, they can't be bought spot as the importer has already committed to buy forward at €1.1055. This illustrates a most important point about forward purchases:

> *The forward purchase protects against a deterioration in the rate but the forward buyer cannot now gain should the rate improve.*

The importer will probably not worry about this, being happy to have protected the profit in the computer deal. Others may not take this view and argue as follows:

> *Today's spot rate is €1.10. I want protection if the rate worsens in three months to €1.25 – I still want to buy dollars at €1.10. On the other hand, if the rate improves to €1.05, I want to forget the above protection and buy spot at €1.05.*

In other words, there are those who wish to have their cake and also eat it. The markets, being advanced and ingenious, provide a means by which this can be done called *options*.

Options can become quite complicated when considered in detail. Happily, the principle is very easy. The importer does not commit to buy the dollars forward at €1.10 but pays for an *option* to do so. If, later, the rate has worsened, the importer takes up the option at €1.10. If, however, the rate has improved to, say, €1.05, the importer abandons what was only an option and buys dollars spot at the better rate.

This is clearly more flexible and advantageous than buying forward and naturally costs more (or who would buy forward?). The cost is called the *premium* and usually paid in advance. We can, therefore, say of options:

> *The option purchase protects against a deterioration in the rate but the option buyer can still benefit from an improvement in the rate. There is a cost – the premium.*

Where would the importer (or exporter) go to buy this option? There are two possibilities:

❑ Deal through a Traded Options Exchange, or
❑ Deal through a bank – called OTC ('over the counter') .

There are very few currency options contracts available in Europe on trading exchanges. This is largely due to the strength of the OTC market there. The biggest currency option deals are handled in the US at either the Chicago Mercantile Exchange (CME), also called the International Monetary Market (IMM), or the Philadelphia Stock Exchange (PHLX).

The characteristics of an exchange are that there are standard contract sizes and standard expiry months. If we take our German importer, he could go to either the CME or PHLX for dollar/euro options and would find the terms shown in Table 9.4.

Table 9.4 *Dollar/euro options terms*

US EXCHANGE	$/E	OPTIONS
Exchange	*Contract size (euros)*	*Contract months*
CME	125 000	Jan/Mar/Apr/Jun Jul/Sep/Oct/Dec and spot month
PHLX	62 500	Mar/Jun/Sep/Dec plus 2 near months

The first problem for the importer is that €110 000 need to be covered and the contract size is €125 000 (or 2 × €62 500). The next problem may be that the expiry in three months is 18 February and neither exchange handles this expiry date.

The advantage of the standard contracts is that, being standard, there is plenty of competition for the business. In particular, the contracts can be sold back later, called '*trading the option*'.

Finally, the exchange protects contracts from default by the use of a body called a 'Clearing House', and we shall explain this further in Chapter 12.

Going to the bank, the terms can be tailored to the needs of the option buyer, for example, €110 000, expiring 18 February. The bank may also offer a number of variations on the deal (see below). However, the options cannot normally be traded and, if the bank is BCCI and crashes into liquidation, the contract is not guaranteed. In currencies the OTC market with the banks is huge. Perhaps this is because the bank may be helping the importer/exporter with general finance for trade anyway and it seems natural to ask them to handle the options business. In addition, the banks may construct attractive variations on the options theme, some of which have proved very popular. Here are three examples.

Breakforward This was invented by Midland Bank. Here the client is offered a forward rate (at a rate not quite as good as the normal forward) but, at a pre-determined rate, the contract can be unwound, leaving the client to benefit from a future favourable rate.

For example, a British firm needs to import dollar goods and buy dollars in three months. The forward rate is £1 = $1.89. The firm wants downside protection but feels that it is just as likely that sterling will improve.

The bank offers a 'floor' rate of $1.88 and a 'break' rate of $1.91. The effect is that, up to a rate of $1.91, the client will buy dollars at $1.88. Above $1.91, the client is freed from this obligation and can buy dollars at the spot rate less 3¢ (that is, the difference between the 'floor' and the 'break' rate which the bank is cleverly using to buy an option!).

Thus:

❑ Future spot rate $1.80, client buys at $1.88
❑ Future spot rate $1.91, client buys at $1.88
❑ Future spot rate $1.98, client buys at $1.95.

The firm thus gets almost complete downside protection but can benefit from a forward rate to a large extent. This leads naturally to participating forward.

Participating forward   Again, a 'floor' rate is agreed as is a participation level in future favourable rates. Let us say that the normal forward rate is $1.89, the 'floor' is $1.86 and the agreed participation in improvement above $1.86 is 80%. If the spot rate later is worse than $1.86, the client buys dollars at $1.86. If the rate is, say, $1.96, the client rate is based on 80% of this improvement. The spot rate is 10 points better than $1.86 so the client can have a rate 8 points better, that is $1.94.

Thus:

❑ Future spot rate $1.80, client buys at $1.86
❑ Future spot rate $1.91, client buys at $1.90
❑ Future spot rate $1.96, client buys at $1.94.

Again, the client has substantial downside protection but can also benefit to a large extent from an improvement in the rate. The client can discuss the desired participation level with the bank – the higher the level, the lower the floor rate!

Cylinder or Collar   This technique is identical to the 'collar' technique used in interest rate futures.

Again, a UK importer needs to buy dollars in three months. Let us say that today's spot rate is $1.90. The importer can come to an arrangement with the bank that the future dollars will be bought within a range of, say, $1.85–$1.95. (As a result, the technique is also called 'range forward'.)

❑ If the future spot rate is worse than $1.85, client buys at $1.85
❑ If the future spot rate is better than $1.95, client buys at $1.95
❑ If the future spot rate is between $1.85 and $1.95, client buys at that rate.

The client now gets some downside protection and also some upside gain. Depending on the rates chosen, the cost may be small or even none at all.

How does the bank achieve the above end objectives for the client? The answer lies in very ingenious use of option techniques.

The whole question of option trading is treated in detail in Chapter 12.

FOREIGN EXCHANGE DEALING

Quotations

The foreign exchange dealer is surrounded by computer terminals giving exchange rates quoted by banks all over the world. The main information providers are Reuters and a system originally owned by 13 big foreign exchange banks called EBS, but now owned by the UK broker, Icap. The rates quoted are 'indicative' only. For a firm rate the dealer must telephone and ask for a quotation for a given currency pair. The dealer merely asks for a quote and does not say if this is a sale or purchase.

The market has its own curious jargon for exchange rates, for example:

Cable	Dollar/Sterling
Swissy	Dollar/Swiss franc
Stocky	Dollar/Swedish Kroner (from Stockholm)
Copey	Dollar/Danish Kroner (from Copenhagen).

In London, even Cockney rhyming slang is used. The Japanese yen rate is the 'Bill and Ben'!

As elsewhere in financial markets, rates are given as 'bid and offer', that is, buying/selling. For example, asked for a 'Swissy' quote, the reply might be SFr1.4250/SFr1.4260 or more likely '50/60' as the dealers are following rates every second of the day. If in any doubt, the enquirer will ask, 'What's the big figure?' and the reply is, '1.42'.

This means that the fellow dealer will *buy* dollars at SFr1.4250 or *sell* dollars at SFr1.4260. The 10 bp in the rate is the profit margin or 'spread'.

We can see this by following it through slowly. Suppose the dealer begins with SFr1.4250 and buys $1. Now the dealer owns $1 (they would say, 'is *long* of dollars'). On a second enquiry, the dealer sells the dollar at the selling rate of SFr1.4260. Now the dealer, having started out with SFr1.4250, has ended with SFr1.4260 after buying and selling dollars.

If this all seems terribly obvious, we apologise. The problem is that foreign exchange can be very confusing for the newcomer. For example, two currencies are involved, not one (as when buying bonds or equities in the domestic currency). Thus, if the dealer buys dollars at SFr1.4250, that is also the rate at which he *sells* Swiss francs. If the dealer sells dollars at SFr1.4260, that is also the rate at which he *buys* Swiss francs. So bid/offer is buy/sell for dollars. For Swiss francs it is best viewed as sell/buy.

It gets more confusing if we consider sterling. Here the convention is to quote a rate of *dollars for the pound sterling*, for example, the rate is given as $1.70. Everywhere else, we give a rate for each currency against the dollar. Asked to quote for 'cable' (sterling/dollar), the dealer quotes '60/70' or, in full, $1.7360/$1.7370. This time the buy/sell rate is in terms of *sterling*, that is, the dealer buys sterling at $1.7360 and sells it at $1.7370. In dollars, it's the sell/buy rate.

The result of this way of quoting sterling can be seen when we consider an importer who wishes to buy dollars. One importer is in Switzerland and the other in the UK. The quotes are (mid-point rates):

Dollar/Swiss franc   SFr1.50
Dollar/Sterling $1.73

Later, the rates change to SFr1.55 and $1.78 respectively. For the Swiss, the increase gives a *worse* rate as they must give up SFr1.55 to buy $1 instead of SFr1.50. For the UK importer, the increase has given a *better* rate. For each £1 they obtain $1.78 instead of $1.73. (Notice that, for an exporter, the results would be exactly the opposite.)

Foreign exchange rates can be very confusing for the newcomer, unless these basic points are borne in mind from the outset:

The market is oriented to the dollar. The dealers quotes are normally given as an amount of the currency to the dollar and the bid/offer is buy/sell from a dollar point of view.
Sterling is the exception, typically quoted as an amount of dollars for the pound sterling. From the dollar point of view, the bid/offer is now sell/buy.

Cross-Rates

When a Swiss firm telephones their bank to buy Canadian dollars, the bank will buy US dollars with the Swiss francs and with the US dollars buy Canadian dollars. The market is wedded to the dollar and finds organisation easier and simpler if dealers go in and out of the dollar, even if some 'double counting' is involved. To attempt to deal directly between any pair of currencies would be too complex. The BIS survey of the London market (the world's biggest), in April 2004, found that over 89% of deals involved the dollar. The dollar is the world's reserve currency. 66% of the world's foreign exchange reserves are in dollars (25% in euros, 4% in yen and 3% in sterling). A reserve currency needs a home economy with a large share of global trade and finance. It must also be a currency in which people have confidence.

An exchange rate between two currencies, neither of them the dollar, is a *cross-rate*. If a dealer goes directly from Swiss francs to sterling, it would be called a direct cross-rate deal or *cross*. Due to the anticipated arrival of the euro, crosses between European countries became more popular. With the replacement of twelve currencies by the euro, the figure has fallen.

Foreign Exchange Swaps

When we discussed the problem of the mythical German importer, we suggested that the bank, requested to *sell* dollars to its client in three months, might buy the dollars today and put them on deposit. For a client wanting the bank to *buy* dollars in three months, the procedure was more complex but involved borrowing dollars for three months, buying euros and putting them on deposit.

Whilst both techniques are quite feasible, they tie up balance sheet assets and liabilities. They impact on the banks' credit limits, involve counterparty risk and use up capital under capital ratio rules.

As a result, the problem is usually solved instead by the *foreign exchange swap*. Before going any further, these swaps have nothing to do with the swaps market for interest rate and currency swaps. The use of the same term can cause confusion. Many foreign exchange dealers simple call them 'forward' deals because that's how they handle forward requirements.

The swap is *one* transaction which combines *two* deals, one spot and one forward. In the first deal a bank buys a currency spot and in the second simultaneously sells it forward for delivery at a later date. The bank will, therefore, return to the original position at the future date. Thus, bank *A* may have £10 million and enters into a swap with bank *B* for dollars:

1   Bank *A* sells £10 million *spot* for, say, $20 million to Bank *B*
2   Bank *A* sells the $20 million *forward* for £10 million in three months.

At the moment, then, bank *A* has $20 million. In three months, bank *A* will exchange the $20 million for £10 million, returning to the original position.

Thus, the foreign exchange swap is a combined spot and forward deal.

When a bank commits to sell a customer a currency at a future date, there may be others wanting to buy the currency for the same date. However, while some deals will offset in this fashion, in most cases the dealer won't be so fortunate. If they have sold $2 million for delivery on 20 March, they may find that they are due to buy $2 million for £s on 30 March – leaving an exposure 'gap'. Alternatively, they are due to buy $s for £s on 20 March, but only $1 million, leaving the dealer 'short' of $1 million for 20 March delivery.

One way of handling the problem is to buy $2 million today and put it on deposit until 20 March. This may mean having to borrow the £s to do it. This involves finding suitable lenders and borrowers and ties up lines of credit with other banks.

Instead it will be easier to buy $2 million spot. The $s, however, are not required until 20 March, so the dealer now enters the *swap*:

1   The dealer sells the $2 million spot for £s, returning back to a £ position
2   At the same time, the dealer sells the £s forward for $2 million to be delivered on 20 March.

The counterparty to the swap that had £s originally is now sitting on $s until 20 March. If $ interest rates are lower than the £ the swap rate will reflect the difference in interest rates. Thus if UK interest rates were 6% higher than the US, then a six month forward deal would involve a *premium* of 3% (ignoring yield curve variations). If spot were, say, $1.80, then the six month forward premium would be about 5.40¢. The spot rate might thus be quoted as $1.8000/$1.8010 with a forward margin or spread of, say, 5.40¢/5.30¢ (or quoted as basis points, 540/530). As the $ is at a premium, these rates will be *subtracted* from the spot rates (if at a discount, the rates would be added to the spot rates).

Thus, an *importer* wanting to buy $s for £s in six months will be quoted as follows:

Spot	$ 1.8000
Premium	540 –
Forward rate	$1.7460

An *exporter* wanting to sell $s for £s in six months will be quoted as follows:

Spot	$ 1.8010
Premium	530 –
Forward rate	$ 1.7480

The *importer* has a *worse* rate than spot as they only get $1.7460 for £1 rather than $1.80.

The *exporter* has a *better* rate than spot as they only give up $1.7480 to obtain £1 rather than $1.8010.

Thus the swap handles the request from a customer for a forward deal. It would also handle a situation where the dealer was 'long' in spot $s (and thus at risk) but 'short' of the same quantity for delivery in three months. He sells the $s spot for £s (and is no longer 'long' of spot $s) and sells the £s back for the $s in three months.

(Those who have very quick minds will see that, while the dealer is no longer at risk to changes in currency rates, they may be at risk to changes in interest rates. The cost of the swap is based on an interest rate difference between dollar/sterling of 6% p.a. But what if this changes to 4% p.a. or 7%? There is, indeed, a potential problem here but the solutions are outside the scope of an introductory book of this nature! Suffice it to say that there is a risk – market risk – which could result in losses if not hedged, and which will be taken into account by the risk management policies and practices of the bank as well as by regulators in setting capital ratios.)

Often swap deals are very short-term. Many are for delivery spot (two days) but will be reversed the following day, called 'spotnext'. Others are for delivery the next day and reversed the following day, called 'tomnext'. It all adds to the horrible jargon of the markets!

The foreign exchange swap is different from the forward transaction we met earlier in the chapter. The BIS survey of 2004 analysed the market over spot, forward and swaps. Average daily dealings in billions of dollars were:

Spot	621
Forwards	208
Swaps	944

(The difference between the total of these three and the total of $1.9 billion daily mentioned earlier is due to 'gaps in reporting'.)

Brokers

In these markets, extensive use is made of brokers. A dealer who is long on dollars and anxious to sell may not wish to reveal their position to others. The desire to sell, say, $50m for sterling at a given rate can be passed to a broker who will disseminate this information anonymously using computer screens or voice boxes. Another dealer, who finds this rate acceptable, may close the deal via the broker. The broker takes no risk. The clients settle directly and the broker takes a small commission.

A broker may quote 'Cable 70/80 – give five, take three'. Cable is sterling/dollar and the broker has a client who will buy £3m at, say, $1.7370 and sell £5m at $1.7380.

The new Reuters system, Dealing 2000/2, was released in mid-1992. This enables the computer system itself to match deals automatically and anonymously and was followed by an even more powerful system – Reuters 3000. Fearful of Reuters acquiring a potential monopoly position, eleven banks funded a rival development via Quotron called EBS which was released in 1993. A third, similar, system was MINEX which was developed by Telerate and KDD of Japan.

By April 1995, there was very little doubt that the new electronic broking systems were having an impact. The EBS group bought out MINEX, which resulted in just two competitors. It is clear that conventional brokers were losing business. The Bank of England 1995 survey showed, as we have said, that 35% of business was placed via brokers but, of this, 5% was already handled by electronic broking. The 1998 survey showed that only 27% of business was placed via brokers, with 16% going to voice brokers and 11% to electronic broking. Voice brokers thus had 30% of the business in 1995 but only 16% in 1998. One unusual side effect was the fact that small banks began to use the broking systems, to some extent, instead of placing orders with larger banks. This electronic broking was at first only used for spot markets. However, in July 1999, the US company, Bloomberg, announced that it would join with the London-based voice broker, Tullett & Tokyo, to launch an electronic broking system for the forward market as well before the end of 1999.

FX All is a system started in 2000 and is integrated with 57 large foreign exchange banks and deals with 700 institutions. It offers spot and forward and dealt with $4.9 trillion of transactions in 2004. It must not be assumed that voice broking is dead. It is probably about 5% of the spot market and in excess of 10% for forwards and swaps. Prominent are ICP, Collins Stewart Tullett and Cantor Fitzgerald. Icap and Cantor's launched integrated voice and electronic trading systems in 2006. Then, in April 2006, Icap bought EBS and became the world's largest inter-dealer broker.

The duopoly enjoyed by Reuters and EBS will be challenged before the end of 2006 by a new inter-dealer trading platform launched by LavaFX, owned by Citicorp.

Settlement

Getting paid is, naturally, crucially important. Doing the deal on the telephone is called 'front office'. Getting paid, reconciling accounts and so on is 'back office'.

In some systems, the dealer writes the details of the deal on a slip of paper. These are later encoded into the computerised back office system. In other cases, the dealer enters the deal into the computer system used for front office which prints a deal slip and holds the data electronically for transfer to the back office system.

A domestic bank thinks of its account with a foreign bank in the foreign currency as its 'nostro' account. For example, BNP Paribas thinks of its dollar account with Citibank in New York as its 'nostro' or *our* account with you. Equally, it regards Citibank's account with itself, BNP Paribas in euros as the 'vostro' or 'loro' account, that is, '*your* account with us'. This all goes back to those clever Italian bankers years ago.

The department dealing with settlement and reconciliation is thus the 'nostro department'. Agreeing our calculation of the value of the foreign currency account with the foreign bank's statement for the same account is 'nostro reconciliation', an important but tedious chore for which computer systems are used to speed up the process.

Banks today are most concerned about counterparty risk (even before BCCI!). For example, all spot deals are settled in two working days. What if we settle the foreign currency deal but the counterparty doesn't? The bankers call this Herstatt risk, following the failure, on 26 June 1974, of ID Herstatt, a German bank, to settle the dollar side of its transactions (six hours behind) although the deutschmarks had been paid to it. This risk has led to the use of techniques called *netting*. The influential bank 'think tank', G30, produced an important report on settlement. Amongst other things, it recommended netting arrangements to reduce risk.

The first system of bilateral netting in London was FX Net and involved 16 banks. It will serve to illustrate the principle.

Netting no longer requires the exchange of two payments for each pair of currencies dealt with. The two parties make or receive one net payment for each currency deal for each settlement date.

For example, suppose counterparty *A* and counterparty *B* enter into the four transactions for the same settlement date, as shown in Figure 9.1.

In the conventional way, each counterparty would process eight transactions each, paying away four and receiving four.

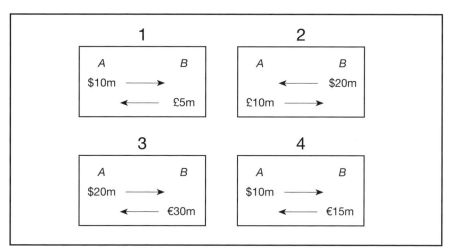

Figure 9.1 *Netting by counterparties*

In the FX Net system, running accounts were maintained for each currency and settlement date and at settlement each counterparty would process three *net* deals, one for each currency. The running accounts would appear as shown in Figure 9.2.

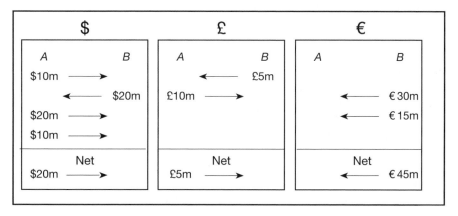

Figure 9.2 *Running accounts*

Settlement of the net amounts occurs as each settlement date is reached.

Using conventional settlement methods, if we take the $ account, *A* will pay *B*

$40m and *B* will pay *A* $20m. Taking the £ account, *A* will pay *B* £10m and *B* will pay *A* £5m. Suppose *A* defaults and does not settle? *B* will lose $40m and £10m. Under the netting, *B* would lose $20m and £5m. In other words, a key reason for net settlement is to reduce substantially the underlying risk of foreign exchange dealing.

If bilateral netting has advantages, then multilateral netting has even more.

A multilateral netting system called Echo began operations in London in 1995, as did a similar system called Multinet in the US. Then, in March 1996, came the announcement that 20 major banks, 'the group of 20', were setting up a global clearing system to handle foreign exchange settlement which would operate in real-time. This was an instantaneous settlement system in which payment by one bank is immediately offset by payment by another, eliminating Herstatt risk. With this announcement, Echo and Multinet merged, and later merged with the new system, called CLS Services. This became operational in September 2002, having completed trials in July 2002. This now has 71 banks as shareholders, deals in 15 currencies and offers swaps as well as spot transactions.

ARBITRAGE

'Arbitrage' is a term that was first used in the foreign exchange markets. In the days when communications were not as good as today, one might find a disparity in rates quoted for the same pair of currencies. Perhaps the offer price for dollar/sterling in Paris is less than the bid price for dollar/sterling in London or any similar disparity in rates quoted by various banks. A currency could be bought in Paris and resold in London for an easy profit.

In general, arbitrage is taking advantage of any pricing anomaly. More arbitrage opportunities and more sophisticated arbitrage opportunities than ever before are being spotted due to the use of computers, often linked to constant feeds of live prices and using 'expert systems' techniques. At the same time, the paradox is that a dealer has to be quicker than ever to take advantage of an arbitrage opportunity, because everyone else is using computers too!

For example, a dealer may spot that another dealer's forward rate does *not* eliminate the difference in interest rates. As a result, perhaps the low interest rate currency is borrowed, sold for the high interest rate currency and this put on deposit for, say, six months. At the same time, to avoid currency risk, the low interest rate currency is bought back forward in six months' time so that the original loan can be repaid. The forward rate cost, however, is less than the interest rate difference leaving a risk-free profit. This is called *covered interest rate arbitrage*.

Arbitrage can be found in any market these days, not just foreign exchange. As it is essentially risk-free, it's good business if you can find it. All the banks employ arbitrage specialists who look for these opportunities, especially in the derivative products marketplace. The argument in its favour is that it keeps pricing efficient. In spite of this, arbitrage between equities and futures markets *(stock index arbitrage)* rouses great suspicions and is a subject of considerable controversy.

(One of the earliest records of telegraphic links was that between Rothschild's of London and Behrens of Hamburg in 1843 to exchange prices of securities, currencies and bills of exchange. Rich arbitrage opportunities for those quick off the mark!)

CENTRAL BANK SURVEYS

At the start of this chapter, we explained that global central banks carried out a simultaneous survey of their markets in 1986, 1989, 1992, 1995, 1998, 2001 and 2004.

Recent results in the major centres can be seen in Table 9.5.

The first point to note is the huge size of the figures. London trades 753 billion dollars' worth of business each day and every day! The BIS, in Basel, collects all the figures and eliminates double counting (a deal done in London with a New York bank will be reported in both centres). The total figure in 1986 was just in excess of $300 billion daily but by 2004 the figure was $1.9 trillion.

Table 9.5 *Central bank foreign exchange surveys – daily foreign exchange dealing*

Centre	2001		2004	
	Amount $bn	Share %	Amount $bn	Share %
UK	504	31.2	753	31.3
US	254	15.7	461	19.2
Japan	147	9.1	199	8.3
Singapore	101	6.2	125	5.2
Germany	88	5.5	118	4.9
Hong Kong	67	4.1	102	4.2
Australia	52	3.2	81	3.4
Switzerland	71	4.4	79	3.3

Source: BIS Triennial Central Bank Survey, March 2005.
(Adjusted for local and cross-border double counting.)

Trading in the individual currencies of the twelve euro member countries against the dollar accounted for 37% of total volume in 1998; dollar/euro trading now accounts for 28%. The Appendix to this chapter gives the breakdown of trading by currency pair. Note that the dollar is the main traded currency, featuring in 89% of dealing, followed by the euro (37%), yen (20%) and then sterling (17%).

Tokyo is an interesting case. We saw in Chapter 4, on Commercial Banking, that the Japanese have withdrawn a little from the international markets. Cross-border capital flows have slowed down. Trust banks in Japan, major players at one time, have been hit by the decline in trust fund investment. The fall in the Nikkei index after January 1990 and the collapse of property values has hit the market generally. Bank mergers have reduced the number of players and the BIS capital ratio rules in 1993 made the banks more cautious although the Japanese system now seems to be improving strongly.

One problem for central banks, intervening from time to time to support their currencies, is that the forces that can be marshalled against them are much bigger. If we look at the ERM crisis as it unfolded in August/September 1992, we see the Bank of England sitting on reserves of gold and foreign currencies of about $44bn. The trading in deals involving sterling, including cross-rate, amounted to some $79bn every single day. Even with the assistance of the Bundesbank, the resistance was simply swept away.

What we saw at one time is concerted action by major central banks acting in tandem and usually agreed at G7 meetings.

It all began at the beginning of 1985. The rise of the dollar was making US exports uncompetitive and the pound/dollar rate was nearing parity. After a series of secret telephone calls, the world's major central banks hit the dollar simultaneously on Wednesday morning, 27 February. There was near pandemonium on the foreign exchange markets and within an hour the dollar had fallen 6% against the mark, from DM3.50 to DM3.30.

Intervention came again in September that year. The Group of Five (G5) major economies (later to expand to G7 and include Canada and Italy) met at the Plaza Hotel, New York on 22 September. A statement was issued that the dollar was overvalued, but although that seemed to be words only, it did the trick. On Monday 23 September, the dollar fell 3.5% without the central banks spending anything. The dollar/mark rate was then DM2.70. Later, the central banks did intervene to reinforce their wishes and, by November, the dollar/mark was DM2.50. This has become known as the 'Plaza Agreement' and was, perhaps, the first international agreement on currencies since Bretton Woods.

If the Plaza Agreement seemed to mark a new milestone, this has not really proved to be the case. The central bankers met again at the Louvre in Paris (February 1987) and this time declared the dollar undervalued. It also announced a resolve to hold major world interest rates within narrow bands. This became known as the 'Louvre Accord'. However, this and several concerted attempts later to boost the dollar were not nearly as successful as attempts earlier to halt its runaway success. Nevertheless, the US and Japan moved to support the yen in June 1998 and, for a time, moved the rate from ¥143 to the dollar to ¥136.8; by 2002 it was trading in the ¥120 – ¥125 range. Generally, these concerted central bank moves have become much less common over the last decade.

WHY LONDON?

The figures shown in the last section reveal London not only as the biggest foreign exchange market in the world, but by a considerable margin, as it accounts for 31.3% of world foreign exchange dealings. In view of the decline of the UK as an economic power and the weakness of the pound as a major currency, one may well ask why it is the major foreign exchange market.

There are, perhaps, four factors:

❏ *Time-zone*   London is well placed here. It can talk to Tokyo for an hour in the morning; the Middle East at about 11.30 a.m.; New York/Chicago at 1.30 p.m. and Los Angeles/San Francisco at 4.30 p.m. New York and Tokyo are in non-overlapping time zones.
❏ *Tradition*   London has a historical and traditional role as a major financial centre. There are over 500 foreign banks trading there and it has the infra-structure needed – accountants, lawyers, speciality printers.
❏ *Euromarkets*   The Euromarkets have large implications for foreign exchange. London's traditional role and its lack of protectionism led to the Euromarket business emanating from London and the huge population of foreign banks to which we have just referred.
❏ *English language*   English is the major language in international finance. The use of English as a first or second language is actually growing. This certainly helps London to score over Paris or Frankfurt. Indeed, the French insistence (at the highest official level) on the use of French militates against their desire to promote Paris further as an international centre.

SUMMARY

The foreign exchange market is huge, trading $1.9 trillion a day in 2004 with London the biggest market.

The demand for foreign exchange arises from trade, tourism, government spending, international security trading and speculation.

Interbank business in London is 53% of the market by value and the top ten banks dominate. Foreign exchange dealing accounts for half the profits of the big US commercial banks.

One economic theory for explaining exchange rates is *purchasing power parity* (PPP). Pricing the same basket of goods in two countries should result in the exchange rate. If a country consistently has higher inflation than another, its currency will tend to weaken compared with that of the country with lower inflation. The high inflation country will have to offer higher interest rates to persuade non-nationals to hold its currency. The theory that investors will shift assets according to factors like these is the *portfolio balance model*.

The post-war period of fixed exchange rates was agreed at a meeting at Bretton Woods in 1944. This also set up the IMF and the World Bank.

Foreign exchange risk for corporates has three elements – *transaction* risk, *translation* risk and *economic* risk.

Spot rates are today's exchange rates with settlement in 2 days. *Forward* rates are fixed rates for a transaction at a later date. They are determined by the difference in interest rates in the two currencies concerned. Worldwide, 60% of deals by value are forward and 40% spot.

The forward rate, being fixed, protects against the currency moving to the buyer's/seller's disadvantage, but they cannot benefit if it moves in their favour. This can be achieved by *currency options*. Options can be dealt on an exchange or over the counter (OTC).

Foreign exchange quotations are shown as a bid/offer rate. The dollar lies at the heart of foreign exchange dealing, as most transactions involve moving in and out of the dollar. Sterling and currencies which were linked to sterling quote so many dollars to the domestic currency. Other currencies quote a quantity of that currency to the dollar. A rate between two currencies, neither of them the dollar, is called a *cross-rate*.

The purchase of a currency spot accompanied by its simultaneous sale forward is the foreign exchange *swap*.

Brokers are active and link buyers and sellers on an anonymous basis. Electronic broking systems like Reuters 3000 and EBS are now being used.

A bank's foreign currency holdings with banks abroad are its *nostro* accounts. The foreign banks' balances with it in the domestic currency are *vostro* accounts. Multilateral netting is now used to reduce settlement risk. The system is CLS Services which has 71 banks as shareholders.

Arbitrage is taking advantage of an anomaly in rates to make risk-free profit.

Central banks carry out a foreign exchange survey every three years (2004 was the last occasion) with the results coordinated by the BIS.

APPENDIX

Table 9.A1   *Foreign exchange turnover by currency pairs, daily averages*
in April 2001 and 2004 in billions of USD

Currency pair	2001		2004	
	Amount	*Share* %	*Amount*	*Share* %
US$/€	354	30	501	28
US$/Yen	231	20	296	17
US$/£	125	11	245	14
US$/SwFr	57	5	78	4
US$/CAN$	50	4	71	4
US$/AUS$	47	4	90	5
US$/Other	195	17	292	16
€/Yen	30	3	51	3
€/£	24	2	43	2
€/SwFr	12	1	26	1
€/Other	21	2	39	2
Other currency pairs	26	2	39	2
All currency pairs	1173	100	1773	100

Source: BIS Triennial Central Bank Survey, March 2005.
          (Adjusted for local and cross-border double counting.)

10 Trade Finance

GENERAL PROBLEMS

One important aspect of global markets is, of course, international trade. If we consider the various problems which will arise in the export/import business, there are many ways in which banks can provide assistance:

1 *Payment services*   The basic question of money transfers
2 *Collection of debts*   The heart of the matter – how to ensure that we get paid
3 *Extension of credit*   This involves ensuring that we get paid and the question of extending credit using, say, the bill of exchange
4 *Finance*   This may be for the exporter to fund completion of the contract or for the importer to help pay for goods
5 *Foreign exchange*   Sales/purchases of foreign currency spot, forward and by way of options, which are discussed in Chapter 8
6 *Trading guarantees*   This covers many questions – quality of goods already paid for (importer), failure of chosen supplier to perform on award of a tender (importer), insurance against political risk, sudden withdrawal of export licences (exporter)
7 *Miscellaneous*   This involves market intelligence, letters of introduction, correspondent banking facilities and similar services.

PAYMENT SERVICES

There are various ways in which the banks may arrange to remit funds:

❏ *Mail transfer* (MT) – instruction by letter
❏ *Telegraphic transfer* (TT)
❏ *SWIFT* – the Society for Worldwide Interbank Financial Telecommunication, is the bank-owned cooperative supplying secure messaging services and interface software to 7800 financial institutions in 202 countries. SWIFT helps its customers reduce costs, improve automation and manage risk. In addition to its 2292 member banks, SWIFT users include brokers, investment managers, securities deposit and clearing organisations and stock exchanges.
❏ *International money transfer* (IMT) or *Express* IMT – modern terms for the mail transfer and telegraphic transfer
❏ *International money order* (IMO) – A UK bank, for example, may issue a cheque drawn on their New York office

❑ *Bank draft* – This will be drawn on a bank's home account or on their nostro account at a correspondent bank.

The last two documents are usually sent by the customer and not their bank.

SWIFT reported its network traffic grew 11% in 2004 to 2.3 billion messages, compared with, say, 812 million in 1997. On an average basis SWIFT is handling more than 9 million messages per day.

Securities traffic grew 9% in 2004. The securities sector represents 32% of SWIFT's total message volume. Securities messages are the second largest category of messages used by SWIFT's customers.

There are four message categories for which the share of business at end of 2004 is shown in Table 10.1.

Table 10.1 *SWIFT message categories and share of business, 2004*

Market	Traffic (millions)	Share %
Payments	1355	58.9
Securities	737	32.1
Treasury	148	6.4
Trade services	47	2.0
System	12	0.6

Source: SWIFT.

COLLECTION OF DEBTS

There are methods which may not involve extension of credit:

❑ *Advance payment* This seems ideal but there are still problems. Suppose the advance payment is not received? What if the order is cancelled *prior* to sending the payment? Time must be allowed to clear the cheque/draft anyway. From the *importer's* point of view, the goods may not be shipped, or the wrong goods may be shipped, or the shipping documents may be wrong.

❑ *Payment on shipment* The exporter emails notice of shipment and awaits payment. The exporter could find themselves having shipped goods and yet the payment does not arrive. The bill of lading may give the importer title to the goods. From the *importer's* point of view, the goods may be found to be faulty or the wrong goods.

❏ *Open account trading* We despatch the goods and send an invoice marked 'payment within 7 days' (for example). Full of risk but quite suitable for circumstances where a valuable trading relationship has been set up and trust exists. This is very common in the US.

EXTENSION OF CREDIT

We now consider methods which involve extension of credit or cash on delivery but where we ask for a bank's help in collecting the money and guaranteeing arrangements to a certain extent.

Bill of Exchange

This is drawn by the exporter on the importer, with the latter agreeing to pay on demand or at a determinable future time the value of the goods to a specified person or bearer of the bill. This is explained fully in Chapter 5.

❏ *Sight bill or demand draft* Immediate payment upon presentation of the bill and documents, with no required acceptance of the bill by the importer, as part of a documentary credit.
❏ *Usance, tenor or term bill* Payable in a number of days or months, usually 'accepted' by a bank, the exporter then sells to a bill broker who holds to maturity or trades.
❏ *Documentary bill* With documents (bill of lading, invoice, insurance cover and similar documents) attached.
❏ *Clean bill* Without documents.

Documentary Letter of Credit

A bill of exchange is drawn by the exporter. A documentary letter of credit is opened by the *importer*.

There is an international code of practice for documentary credits set out in the International Chamber of Commerce's *Uniform Customs & Practices for Documentary Credits*.

(The International Chamber of Commerce was set up in 1919 to define the rules and norms by which trade is carried out. Sixty national commissions make up its federal structure.)

The importer opens a documentary credit with his bank (*issuing bank*). This arranges for the issuing bank, upon instructions from the importer, to:

(a) make payment to the exporter (the *beneficiary*); or
(b) pay on or accept a bill of exchange drawn by the exporter; or

(c) authorise another bank (probably its correspondent bank in the exporter's country) to be the *advising bank*, which makes payment to the exporter or accepts his bill of exchange (thus becoming a 'documentary acceptance credit'). The advising bank may also be asked to be the *confirming bank*, to add its guarantee that the exporter will get paid if the issuing bank does not. (However, some countries, for example Iran, prohibit banks from opening credits on terms that require an advising bank to add its confirmation.)

All the above have to be backed by *stipulated documents*. These documents include:

❑ *Transport documents*   Usually by sea under a *bill of lading*, which gives evidence that the goods have been dispatched, purport to be of the type and quality ordered and be properly transported. A copy of the bill of lading is the buyer's claim to possession of the goods when they arrive.

With container traffic these days there may be a *forwarder's bill of lading* – not necessarily a document of title.

If by air there is an *air waybill*, not however a document of title, merely acknowledgement of acceptance for delivery.

If by road or rail there is a *carrier's receipt* or *railway receipt* and this is also not a document of title.

❑ *Commercial invoice*   Specifying quality, quantity and unit and total price.

❑ *Insurance documents*

❑ *SAD document*   Simplified customs form for the EU.

❑ *Other documents*   Certificate of origin; certificate of quality; health certificate; veterinary certificate; weight note.

There are potential problems with documents – documents missing, incorrectly completed or showing an invoice value different from that on the documentary letter of credit. The bank's staff check these and should see, for example, 'freight paid' on the bill of lading and insurance certificate if goods are sent CIF (including cost, insurance and freight). Incorrect documents can cause delays at the port on landing and incur costs such as local storage.

Types of Documentary Credit

❑ *Confirmed credit* – when the advising bank also guarantees payment.

❑ *Revocable/Irrevocable credit* – *revocable* may be amended/cancelled by the issuing bank if the importer is not satisfied. This is obviously not usually acceptable to the exporter but may be suitable for selling to overseas subsidiaries where letters of credit must be used by local regulation. *Irrevocable* can only be amended/cancelled with agreement of the confirming bank and the beneficiary.

❑ *Sight credit, term or acceptance credit*
Sight – the exporter draws a demand draft (bill) and presents it to the correspondent bank for payment.
Term/acceptance – the exporter draws a draft for a period of time (30, 60, 90 days) on the issuing or confirming bank.

❑ *Negotiation credit* – the confirming bank is instructed by the advising bank (if they are not one and the same) to negotiate the bill which is drawn on the advising bank. *Or* the bill may be drawn on the confirming bank who will accept it, making it a bank bill and therefore 'discountable'.

❑ *Standby credit* – to fall back upon if payment has not been made to the beneficiary by the other arranged methods.

❑ *Deferred payment credit* – payment made later.

Typically, in the Western world, all questions of import licences, exchange controls, insurance and documentation have been settled prior to issuing the letter of credit.

From the point of view of the *exporter* there are these advantages:

❑ Assurance of a payment or acceptance on shipping the goods.
❑ If an acceptance, then it will be a banker's acceptance and at best discount rates. Who pays the discount is a matter for negotiation!
❑ Generally, the reassurance of a bank (or banks) rather than just the importer's promises.

The *importer*, too, has advantages:

❑ No money will be paid until the goods are shipped and the required documents lodged.
❑ There may be time to pay, if a bill of exchange is involved. Again, acceptance will not be made until the goods are shipped.
❑ All formalities are complete before authorising the letter of credit.

There is, finally, the question of the relationship of the *bank* and the *bank's client* wanting to issue a letter of credit. The request to the bank for a letter of credit must be signed by someone in authority as it incurs obligations for the client (the 'accountee'). Links with the bank in this day and age may be *electronic*. The whole trade deal must conform with local import regulations and EU rules if the client is a member of that community.

From the *bank's* point of view, this is a contingent liability and affects existing credit agreements and limits. It is also an off-balance sheet transaction which needs capital under BIS capital ratio rules. The bank will probably charge the client a deposit and needs authority to debit expenses and charges. If a bill of lading is not used, the bank may require the goods to be at the disposal of the bank or consigned to the bank.

If the bank is the *advising* bank, it is responsible for seeing that the proposed credit is authentic.

Documentary Collection

The exporter ships the goods and presents the documents through a bank. The bank may be requested either to collect the payment in return for the documents or to see that a bill of exchange is accepted in return for handing over the documents.

The bank, however, is only using its 'best efforts' to collect the money or acceptance. The importer may still refuse the documents. If the goods have been shipped and the documents are *not* documents of title, the importer might even be able to collect the goods anyway. We may request the collecting bank to protect our interest in the event of default. If the importer doesn't pay or refuses the transaction, the goods (having been despatched) may have to be stored locally.

Effect of 1997 Asian Crisis

Prior to the Asian crisis in mid-1997 (see Chapter 15), much international trade had moved to an open account basis or was transacted through payment on documentary collection. The demand for confirmed letters of credit naturally increased after the crisis. Although this is more expensive for the exporter, it provided more secure cover for sales to countries like South Korea, Thailand and Malaysia. The bank issuing the confirmation would look at it on a case-by-case basis.

FINANCE FOR THE EXPORTER

The exporter may need finance while waiting to be paid other than that provided by, say, discounting the bill of exchange. Two possibilities are forfaiting and factoring.

Forfaiting This is traditionally associated with longer-term high value capital goods and construction projects. In the UK, London Forfaiting has a high concentration of deals in excess of £50 million in value. However, others have also done a lot of 60 day business with £250 000 probably a minimum figure.

A bill of exchange or promissory note is bought 'à forfait', meaning *without recourse* to the exporter: that is, the purchaser forfaits all recourse to other parties. They look to the importer's bank to sign the bill or promissory note to guarantee payment and the bill/note will be unconditional. They can then sell the note/bill in an active secondary market. The major currencies are dollars, Swiss francs and deutschmarks.

For the exporter, forfaiting has the advantage that the finance is without recourse and has no effect on credit limits with their bank or any other. It is useful where export credit guarantees (or private insurance) are not available and, where it is available, avoids cash flow problems while waiting for a claim to be met. However, the forfaiter needs to be satisfied about client, country and political risk and the discount may be expensive. Also, they may not finance 100% of the value.

Factoring   Factoring companies purchase trade debts of clients and usually pay 80% of the full value of debts due to be paid in less than six months. Normally, this is used for continuous rather than *ad hoc* business. The remaining 20% is passed to the client after all the debt has been collected. The factor runs the sales ledger and collects the money. Factoring can be with or without recourse. The latter can be very convenient, especially for export business, but is, naturally, more expensive. Frequently 'open account' terms are used. As well as a charge for providing finance, there is also a service fee for running the sales ledger and collecting the debt. This service fee varies from ½% to 2%. A variation on the theme is *invoice discounting*, in which the factor provides finance against invoices as before but the client runs the sales ledger and collects the debt. In the UK, invoice discounting is 85% of the market and factoring 15%. This is because it is cheaper, companies like to keep control of the sales ledger and it is more confidential.

The overseas agent of a factor will investigate credit status so that a quick report can be made to the factor, and the agent will usually underwrite the debt and deal with any queries locally. Factors may have their own offices abroad or be part of a network of independent factoring organisations. The largest such network is Factors Chain International (FCI), founded in 1968. It has 150 members in 50 countries and factoring/invoice discount business of €760 billion in 2004. In the UK, the Factors and Discounters Association reported that 40 000 businesses used the services of 38 full members and 8 group members in 2004. At the end of the second quarter in 2005, turnover for the year to date was £70.9 billion of which domestic invoice discounting was £59.0 billion. Factoring companies are often subsidiaries of banks – for example, in the UK, Barclays Sales Financing, HSBC Invoice Finance and Lloyds TSB Commercial Finance. The exporter has the advantages of dealing with a bank subsidiary, funding working capital on normal finance terms, not having to run the sales ledger and collect the debt and (in the case of non-recourse) peace of mind.

As stated, factoring is only provided for short-term debts and continuous sales of consumer items. In principle, it is similar to an overdraft.

While most factoring is *domestic*, international factoring is on the increase. The biggest markets using international factoring are the Netherlands, Germany, Italy, the UK, France, Belgium and the US.

Other finance   The exporter may require more general financial help than that merely required to bridge the gap while waiting to be paid – finance to produce capital goods, for example, that may take up to a year to deliver. Most large banks have departments which specialise in export finance and have 'packaged' schemes available. Sometimes some form of government aid or support may be available and the most important of these is insurance from a government export credit guarantee body (discussed later). If it is a large international project, then the term used may be 'project finance' with a syndicate of banks involved, and recourse is available only to the stream of funds from the project. The exporter, in some cases, may be interested in the question of aid to the *importer* to help purchase the goods. In a small number of cases, where factors are involved, the factor's overseas agent may get involved with providing finance to the importer also. On many occasions, however, a key component will be official sources of finance.

There are programmes from donors such as the World Bank, the EU and the African Development Bank. It is estimated that more than one third of sub-Saharan African imports are aid-financed. Assistance is focused on countries implementing the economic reform programmes of the IMF and the World Bank. The paperwork and bureaucracy are formidable but payments are guaranteed and there is no currency risk.

In other cases, banks provide 'buyer credits' in conjunction with export credit guarantee insurance.

FOREIGN EXCHANGE

This subject was dealt with in Chapter 9.

TRADING GUARANTEES

The question of guarantees has been mentioned and the concerns of both exporters (political and currency risk) and importers (faulty goods or general non-performance of contracts). There is a series of schemes for trading guarantees other than export credit guarantees. These refer to guarantees backed by banks.

Bid or tender bond   This is required to support an exporter's offer to supply goods or a contractor's offer to carry out a service.

The bond safeguards a buyer against loss if the tender is awarded but the seller fails to proceed by signing the contract or submitting a performance bond.

A bid bond is guaranteed by the seller's bank and is usually 2%–5% of the value of the contract.

Performance bond   When the seller's bid is accepted, the bid bond is replaced by a performance bond, usually 10% of the value of the contract.

It is issued by the seller's bank, guaranteeing that he will supply goods (to the standard required by the buyer) or perform a service. If the buyer does not accept that goods are up to standard then they can claim under the performance bond.

Advance payment guarantee   The buyer pays the seller an agreed percentage of the contract price as an advance payment, which can be claimed back if goods/ services provided are not satisfactory.

Retention monies guarantees / progress payment bonds   Part of the contract price (usually 5%) can be held back by the buyer for a certain period to give time to assure themselves that the goods or services supplied are satisfactory, or stage payments may be made on a similar basis.

These may be conditional or unconditional – for example, conditional on the seller admitting the fault or having won an arbitration proceeding or legal case. The bank must have a counterindemnity with their client, authorising debit of the said sum if money is paid under the guarantee. 'Unconditional' means that the bank will pay up simply on the signed statement by the buyer that the seller has failed in their obligation.

The bank guarantee may have to be paid *even if the bank's client goes into liquidation.*

Export credit guarantees Government departments often provide exporters with facilities for insuring their shipments of goods against default by foreign importers and most other risks, except for normal marine insurance. Premiums are charged but the service is generally provided on a non-profit making basis. Such government departments do not themselves extend export finance but in providing insurance against risk encourage the banks to do so.

There are, however, also private insurers that will quote premiums for trade risk; for example, in the UK, Trade Indemnity. The UK's Export Credit Guarantee Department was founded in 1919. There is a distinction drawn between short-term projects, up to two years, and longer-term risks. The short-term end was located in Cardiff and called the Insurance Services Group (ISG). However, the government sold this in December 1991 to the Dutch insurer NCM. The new name is 'NCM Credit Insurance'. NCM also took control of the short-term export insurance in Sweden following the collapse of Svenska Credit.

The insurance protection is against non-payment, insolvency, withdrawal of import licences, problems due to foreign government decree and war and earthquake. Cover is typically up to 90%. The element of risk can be noted when we see from a report in 2003 that the UK's ECGD had run up debts of £9 billion, dating back three decades, much of it to poor countries. It was estimated that only £2 billion was recoverable.

Given export credit guarantees, the banks are obviously happier to provide export finance and may arrange and administer the policy as part of the deal.

Other export credit guarantee organisations are:

❏ Euler Hermes	Germany	(private sector)
❏ NCM	Holland	(private sector)
❏ COFACE	France	(state majority holding)
❏ SACE	Italy	(state majority holding).

An example of international cooperation here is seen in the case of the financing of the two A340 and three A320 Airbus passenger jets for China Eastern Airlines. Export credit finance of $363 million has been organised by BNP Paribas with the assistance of the US Export-Import Bank, ECGD (UK), Coface (France) and Euler Hermes (Germany).

The biggest names in international trade finance are ABN Amro, Citigroup and Deutsche Bank.

MISCELLANEOUS SERVICES

Export houses   These are market experts who know about shipping, insurance, quotas, licences, exchange terms and local conditions. They may:

❏   Handle all the paperwork and even promote sales abroad but the exporter is still the principal although the export house carries the risk
❏   Act for an overseas buyer – find a supplier, arrange shipment and insurance and confirm the contract on the buyer's behalf
❏   Act as an agent and buy goods and resell them but only against firm orders.

Confirming houses   Similar to export houses but will place an order for a buyer as a *principal* and will pay the exporter when the goods are despatched. May arrange credit for the buyer.

International credit unions   Finance houses and some banks have entered into reciprocal arrangements to arrange local finance to help an importer to import goods from a fellow member. An exporter, for example, may be asked by the importer of capital goods for instalment terms of payment. The bank may be able to arrange this through the partner in the credit union in the foreign company. The local bank/finance house will investigate and arrange finance – typically for machinery and capital goods generally. Examples are European Credit Union, Amstel Club, Export Finance International.

Barter/Countertrade   These arrangements are common where currencies are not convertible or subject to any restrictions preventing normal issue of export licences. Barter is a simple exchange of goods; countertrade is a wider term including things like counterpurchase and buy-back. Under these arrangements, exporters may agree to buy back goods from the importing companies, for example, the exporter of textile machinery must agree to buy back textiles. Alternatively, the exporter agrees to buy back goods in a more general way to a given percentage value of the exports.

For many years, Russia dealt with Finland on the basis that Russian oil purchased by Finland accumulated credits that could only be used to buy Russian goods. Other examples: car imports into Tunisia (Peugeot, VW) were only permitted on the basis that spare parts were purchased from Tunisian companies to a value of 50% of the cost of the car; Balfour Beatty in the UK won a contract for £2 million in Malaysia on the basis that Balfour Beatty had to find buyers for tin, palm oil and rubber goods.

Barter and countertrade have now become a very big international business, with specialist companies like ICON International and Attwood Richards. For example, Keebler, a US biscuit company, was left with $1 million of unusable packaging. Attwood Richards asked Keebler UK to fill the packaging with biscuits worth $14 milion for sale in markets where Keebler had no presence – Russia, Ukraine and the Baltic States. Keebler was paid in trade credits, eventually exchanged for packaging and shipping services. Attwood Richards also arrange barter for surplus seasonal goods – swimwear, beach umbrellas and golf clubs. Trade credits have also been used to buy office furniture, computers, cleaning services, hotel rooms and airline seats.

General Banks also provide a host of other services in connection with export/import business – market intelligence, credit status enquiries, letters of introduction, correspondent banking, translation, legal and accountancy facilities.

SUMMARY

Banks facilitate international trade with cross-border payment systems. The *SWIFT* system is the most important.

Simply sending an invoice to the importer and awaiting payment is *open account trading*.

Credit may be extended by the use of a *bill of exchange* which may be a *sight*, *tenor*, *documentary* or *clean* bill.

A promise by the importer's bank either to pay for the goods or to sign a bill of exchange on despatch is a *documentary letter of credit*, which may be *revocable* or *irrevocable*. The importer's bank is the *issuing* bank in this connection and the exporter's bank is the *advising* bank.

The exporter is the *beneficiary*. If the exporter's bank agrees to pay for the goods, even if the importer or the importer's bank doesn't, it is a *confirmed* letter of credit.

With *documentary collection*, the exporter's bank attempts to obtain payment by offering the shipping documents to the importer's bank.

Finance for export might be based on *forfaiting* or *factoring*. There may also be official help from development banks. Export credit guarantees, offered by governments or the private sector, insure against non-payment. The banks offer other guarantees such as *bid* or *tender bonds*, *performance bonds*, *advance payment guarantees* and *progress payment bonds*.

Miscellaneous services offered by banks include acting as *export* and *confirming houses* and assisting with *barter* and *countertrade*.

11 European Economic and Monetary Union

INTRODUCTION

The world is increasingly becoming one vast global market – general deregulation, the collapse of artificial barriers to trade, modern electronic communications – all have contributed to this state of affairs.

A supreme example of globalisation is surely Europe's Economic and Monetary Union (EMU). Twelve sovereign states, with a total population of 312 million, have accepted a single currency and central bank. The phrase 'cross-border' has become less significant as the EMU area moves (with limitations) to become simply one market. In many ways, it is the most dramatic political and economic development of our time. Hence this separate chapter, looking at this phenomenon in more detail.

We shall begin by examining the history of the European Union generally and look at its institutions, moving on from there to consider the history of previous monetary unions and the history of EMU and its new institutions in particular.

We shall then discuss the objectives of EMU. Why create it in the first place? What advantages should it bring? What are the problems? During this, we consider the effect of EMU (actual and anticipated) on the securities markets in their various aspects.

One country in Europe not yet a member is, of course, the United Kingdom, where the arguments still go on although the support for joining the euro seems to be weakening.

Finally, we look at the general arguments for and against the UK joining (while trying not to upset anybody!).

HISTORY OF THE EUROPEAN UNION

Early History

Most of us believe that the impetus towards European Union came in the post-war years after 1945. While this is generally true, the concept has a long history. Several people have thought of the idea of drawing Europe together by military conquest, from the Romans through Charlemagne to Napoleon. The general idea then was to maintain peace and provide defence against enemies.

Peace was certainly what the UK Quaker, William Penn, had in mind when he argued in 1693 for a European parliament and an end to the nation state. Jeremy Bentham also argued for a European assembly and Jean-Jacques Rousseau wanted a European federation.

In 1814, Henri Saint-Simon actually produced a detailed scheme with a European monarch, government and parliament. He invented the phrase 'A United States of Europe', a phrase used later in the century by Victor Hugo at the Paris peace conference of 1849.

All these people, of course, were only on the fringes of political power and had little practical influence on what happened.

More important was the setting up in 1923 of a 'Pan-European Union' by an Austrian aristocrat called Richard Coudenhove-Kalergi. He argued for a European federation and, importantly, attracted as members several young politicians who later were able to wield considerable influence. Among these were Konrad Adenauer, Georges Pompidou and Carlos Sforza.

One key objective (as today) was to compete better in the world's economic markets. Interestingly, the UK was never regarded as a potential participant. No practical results were achieved, although the idea had general support.

1945

After 1945, things changed. Europe had been devastated by the third major war in less than 100 years. There was a widespread feeling that the nation state had no future. There was an awareness of Europe's weakened state economically, the dominance of the United States and fear of Russia and communism.

In 1948, the Organisation for European Economic Co-operation (OEEC) was formed to oversee the distribution of US aid. It had a Council of Ministers, with each state having one voice, and decisions needed a unanimous vote. After the widespread devaluations of 1949, the OEEC set up a European Payments Union in 1950 to act as a sort of central bank for intra-European trade and payments.

The OEEC was not a foundation stone. It had no political implications and limited economic power. It was still, however, a major exercise in Europeans working together. In 1960, it became the wider Organisation for Economic Co-operation and Development (OECD) which we have today, with membership from the US and Canada and, in 1964, Japan.

The Council of Europe

In 1947, an International Committee of the Movements for European Integration was formed and held a Congress of Europe in the Hague in May 1948. Several hundred delegates attended from 16 states. Delegates wanted a European assembly and a European court. A European movement was formed to carry on the debate and put pressure on politicians.

After the UK's unique position in the war, many looked to them for leadership here, but did not get it. The Attlee government was preoccupied with its own problems in implementing a socialist economy.

The idea of a European assembly was, however, supported by many pro-Europe politicians, notably Paul-Henri Spaak of Belgium, and Robert Schuman, France's foreign minister.

In May 1949, representatives of the states agreed to set up a Council of Europe in Strasbourg to achieve ' a greater unity between its members for the purpose of safeguarding and realising the ideals and principles which are their common heritage and facilitating their economic and social progress'.

The Council of Europe met in August 1949, with a Committee of Ministers, meeting twice per year, and a Consultative Assembly. Paul-Henri Spaak was the first president.

No positive move towards European integration took place, and often the Committee of Ministers and the Assembly were at loggerheads. Nevertheless, the Council did useful work on human rights and founded the European Court of Justice in 1959. It also worked on co-ordinating policies in transport, civil aviation and agriculture. Again, Europeans were trying to work together.

The European Coal and Steel Community

In May 1950, Robert Schuman, the French foreign minister, produced the 'Schuman Plan', proposing a pooling of coal and steel resources. They were to be pooled and administered by a new supranational authority in conjunction with the various states involved. Tariff barriers would be eliminated gradually.

It is most important, however, to see the political motivation here. There was a recognition that stability and security in Western Europe rested on France and Germany coming together. Indeed, the initial proposal was for a Franco-German coal and steel pool with others invited to join (incidentally, the Council of Europe had made a similar recommendation earlier). It was also seen as the first step to political integration.

A specific plan was drafted by Jean Monnet, head of the French Planning Commission.

The Treaty of Paris, setting up the European Coal and Steel Community (ECSC), was signed in April 1951 and ratification by local parliaments took a further year. Members were France and West Germany with Italy, the Netherlands, Belgium and Luxembourg – the Common Market's original 'six'. Although the Attlee government in the UK lost the 1951 election, the new government under Churchill (a supposed European) was no more enthusiastic about the ECSC than they were, to the disappointment of many dedicated Europeans.

People committed to a form of common future for Europe were now in positions of power – Schuman and Monnet in France, Adenauer in Germany, de Gasperi in Italy, Spaak in Belgium and Beck in Luxembourg.

It is very common for people in the UK to talk of a 'hidden agenda' behind EMU, namely some form of political federation. Certainly some UK pro-Europeans have played this aspect down, but the agenda has always been in the open. The founders of the ECSC wanted to foster economic expansion, growth in employment and a rising standard of living, it is true. They were, however, very clear about political motives – a check on Germany to reduce the risk of war and, ultimately, a form of political federation. Schuman's declaration said openly 'Europe must be organised on a federal basis' and also said that this was 'a first step in the federation of Europe'. That is not to say that people in the mass were in favour of this move but, like today, were led towards it by political leaders dedicated to the idea.

Jean Monnet was the first president of the ECSC. There was a Common Assembly of 78 members, a Council of Ministers and the new High Authority, whose supranational powers had caused a long debate before parliaments ratified the treaty. The first meeting of the High Authority was in 1952.

'All Roads Lead to Rome'

The ECSC was not a total success but did much useful work on trade discrimination and restrictive practices. Although nothing political was achieved, it had started a process of European decision making on matters of vital interest.

However, whatever aspirations some politicians may have had, Europe was not yet ready to make any dramatic move towards political union. A treaty was actually signed in May 1952 for a European Defence Community, but defeated in the French Assembly in August 1954 – France was alarmed at any idea of re-arming Germany.

The ECSC move led to discussions within the OEEC and the Council of Europe on co-operation in other sectors such as transport, agriculture, health, postal services and communications. Gradually, however, the 'six' felt that a number of separate organisations was not the way forward, but rather a single body to oversee integration of the economies.

The idea of some form of common market gathered strength by the mid-1950s, and the foreign ministers of the six met at Messina in Italy in the middle of 1955 to launch 'a fresh advance towards the building of Europe'. They agreed to set up a committee under Paul-Henri Spaak to report back on concrete proposals. The Spaak report was discussed at the ECSC Common Assembly in March 1956 and approved by foreign ministers of the six in May. The Spaak Committee then drafted two treaties – one for a European Economic Community (EEC) and one for a European Atomic Energy Authority. The six made it clear that other countries, especially the UK, could join. In March 1957, the two treaties were signed in Rome. The atomic energy initiative became known as 'Euratom' and was largely a failure. The same could not be said of the EEC!

The European Economic Community

By December 1957, the Treaty of Rome had been ratified by the six states, and the first meeting of the Assembly took place in Strasbourg in March 1958. The first elected president was Robert Schuman. Support had come from France, who saw in it export potential for its agriculture, and Germany, who saw the export potential for its industrial goods.

The treaty ran to 248 articles, supplemented by four annexes, thirteen protocols, four conventions and nine declarations. It emphasised that the problems of one member state would be the problems of all. The treaty was to remain in force for an unlimited period and could not be revoked.

The main objectives were expressed in economic terms – setting up a common market, ending price fixing, dumping, unfair subsidies and ensuring free competition. Behind it all lay the political motives. The treaty's preamble spoke of 'the foundations of an even closer union among Europe's peoples'. Walter Hallstein, the first president of the European Commission, said 'We are not integrating economies, we are integrating policies.' In 1964, Paul-Henri Spaak reminded the Council of Europe: 'Those who drew up the Rome Treaty ... did not think of it as essentially economic; they thought of it as a stage on the way to political union.' So much for the 'hidden agenda'.

Membership of the EEC meant a commitment to the free movement of capital and labour, a common investment policy and co-ordination of social welfare policies. Three funds were set up, a European Social Fund, a European Investment Bank and a European Development Fund.

The general institutions of the EEC are discussed in the next major section.

In 1965, the Commission absorbed the equivalent bodies in the ECSC and Euratom.

Progress continued over the next ten to eleven years in moving to a common market. A customs union was declared operational in 1968, with a single external customs duty and the abolition of all internal tariffs. That year also saw the commencement of the Common Agricultural Policy.

The 1960s generally saw the greatest tensions over the future direction of the Community. These concerned the extension of the EEC to other members and the question of the powers of the Commission.

Wider Membership

The year 1961 saw Ireland, Denmark and the UK formally applying for membership of the EEC, followed by negotiations with Norway. However, the 1960s also saw a French government headed by Charles de Gaulle, who vetoed the UK's application in 1963 and again in 1967. What particularly incensed France's partners was that de Gaulle's 1963 veto was announced at a press conference and without prior consultation with the other governments.

A summit at the Hague in 1969 agreed on the principles for enlargement, and discussions re-opened with Ireland, Denmark, the UK and Norway. Treaties were signed in 1972 but a referendum in Norway rejected the idea, leaving the other three to join in 1973. The 'six' were now nine at last. Greece joined in 1981, and Spain and Portugal in 1986. The nine were now twelve. Sweden, Austria and Finland joined in January 1985, giving us fifteen, and then ten countries joined in June 2004 to give us the twenty-five we have today, with a total population of some 450 million.

The de Gaulle Stalemate

Apart from arguments with de Gaulle about accession of other members, a more serious dispute took place with France in the mid-1960s about the whole question of EEC powers as opposed to those of the members. Margaret Thatcher was not the first to question the powers of the Commission. They were also questioned by an equally dominant personality – de Gaulle.

In 1965, the European Commission, under Walter Hallstein, proposed that the EEC should have its own independent source of revenue and budget (instead of direct contributions from national treasuries). It was also proposed that the European Parliament should have more powers, especially over control of the budget. The third proposal concerned the setting up of a more formal agricultural policy. De Gaulle wanted the agricultural policy but not the first two. He was against them because they would increase the supranational characteristics of the EEC.

The community then faced its biggest crisis so far. De Gaulle attacked the powers of the Commission as taking away the powers of national governments. A federal Europe did not appeal to him any more than to Margaret Thatcher! To make things worse, the Treaty of Rome had envisaged a switch to majority voting for most cases after January 1966. De Gaulle was totally opposed to this. The French simply boycotted the Council of Ministers for seven months. However, this also meant no progress on the agricultural policy which France wanted. A compromise had to be found.

In Luxembourg, in January 1966, the six agreed that a state could continue to exercise a veto if it felt that its own vital interests were at stake. As a result, majority voting was *de jure* but not necessarily *de facto*. The Commission, in turn, agreed that it would consult more closely with the Council of Ministers and inform governments at all stages of any new initiatives.

The Hague Conference of 1969 was much more positive. It agreed proposals for the financing of the Common Agricultural Policy (CAP) – itself finally agreed in 1968 – and also the budgetary powers of the European Parliament. The latter had been discussing plans for direct elections and these began in 1979.

The Hague Conference also agreed on the principle of monetary union, to be reached by 1980. We discuss this more fully in the history of EMU in a later section.

The European Council

Periodically, heads of government had met to discuss issues affecting the EEC. The meetings of heads of state were institutionalised in 1974 by calling it the 'European Council'. This was a body which could resolve disputes, set new objectives and decide on future progress. It was outside the Treaty of Rome and not, therefore, subject to, for example, the European Court.

The whole question of the future for a more political union for the EEC was on the agenda in the late seventies and early eighties. This included the vexed question of majority voting. The European Council meeting of June 1983 ended with a rather extraordinary 'Solemn Declaration on European Union'. The Council saw itself as responsible for a general political impetus to the construction of Europe. There was fine rhetoric but not too much action.

However, the European Council meeting in Milan in June 1984 decided to set up an intergovernmental conference to discuss the future for the EEC and the question of majority voting. Their proposals, put to the European Council in December 1984, became the Single European Act.

The Single European Act

The Single European Act (SEA) set the target of a genuinely single internal market by the end of 1992. It aimed to sweep away all the obstacles that still remained to achieving a genuine single competitive market. In addition, it referred to new forms of decision making and legislative processes within the EEC, extending its scope to cover foreign policy and some matters of defence.

The economic aim of a single market, however, involved questions like tax, law, accountancy, national standards and social welfare as well as the question of frontiers themselves. In other words, we were back to politics.

On the question of the veto, it was agreed that this applied to the introduction of new members and the general *principles* of new policies.

The actual *implementation* of the policies in detail would be subject to qualified majority voting, in practice 54 out of 76 votes then available at the Council. This was a very significant change, and one accepted by the arch-anti-European, Margaret Thatcher.

The reforms for the European Parliament did not go as far as many people would have liked. Where the Council of Ministers had decided on a proposal by qualified majority, the Parliament could amend or reject the proposal. The Council of Ministers could then only override this by *unanimous* vote – a significant change, not totally appreciated at the time.

Finally, the SEA asserted that member states should formulate a European foreign policy and should work more closely together on defence issues.

After certain delays, the SEA was finally ratified by all parliaments by 1987.

European Free Trade Area

As an alternative to full membership of the EEC, the UK had raised the question of forming a free trade area within the Community, during the late 1950s. When this failed, the UK joined with Austria, Denmark, Norway, Portugal, Sweden and Switzerland in forming the European Free Trade Area (EFTA). Its aim was to work for the reduction and eventual elimination of tariffs on most industrial goods between the members. Special provisions were made for fisheries and agriculture. EFTA was launched in May 1960. It was not nearly as ambitious as the EEC, simply, as the name implied, a free trade area.

With the projected arrival of the single market, post-1992, many EFTA members were worried about its future. Austria, in particular, had decided to join the EEC anyway. As a result, they opened discussions with the EEC (by now simply called European Community – EC) about a European Economic Area (EEA). The two sides reached agreement in October 1991. Essentially, the EEA was a large free trade area with no internal tariffs but no common external tariffs. The EFTA states, for example, did not necessarily have to accept the Common Agricultural Policy (by then, of course, Denmark, Portugal and the UK were members of the EC anyway, but Iceland had also joined EFTA). The EEA came into force in 1993, but in rather unreal circumstances. Switzerland rejected the idea in a referendum in December 1992, and all the states except Iceland had either applied for full membership of the EC or were very near to doing so.

The Maastricht, Amsterdam and Nice Treaties

The most important decisions taken at Maastricht in December 1991 concerned monetary union, and for that reason are covered under that heading later in this chapter. However, once again, many people failed to notice that the treaty was in two parts – economic and monetary union and *political* union. We shall cover the latter aspects now.

The political section of the Maastricht Treaty decided on the following points:

❏ An inter-governmental foreign and security policy
❏ A concept of 'European citizenship'
❏ A central role for the principle of 'subsidiarity'
❏ A new 'social chapter' (the UK opted out)
❏ An increase in the powers of the European Parliament – co-decision authority with the Council of Ministers on certain subjects
❏ An intergovernment framework for justice and home affairs.

There is nothing too dramatic, but political nevertheless, and the European Community became the European Union (EU).

Some of the perceived shortcomings of the Maastricht Treaty were redeemed by the Amsterdam Treaty, signed in 1997. Unlike Maastricht, the Amsterdam Treaty was solely concerned with political issues. The key points were:

❏ Safeguarding human rights, with penalties for states in breach
❏ Providing for the establishment of 'an area of freedom, security and justice in the EU'
❏ Gradually, bringing asylum, visas, immigration and external border control under common rules
❏ Allowing the UK and Ireland to opt out of the above two provisions

❑ Allowing the European Parliament co-decision policy within the Council over a wider range of issues than Maastricht
❑ Giving the Commission president greater powers in selecting commissioners
❑ Making promotion of high employment an EU goal
❑ Providing for a 'high representative' to put a name and face to EU foreign policy.

The Amsterdam Treaty came into effect in March 1999.

The Nice Treaty of December 2000 again did not involve EMU as such but was held largely to resolve issues caused by the prospective admission (at that stage thought to be from 2004 onwards) of twelve new members – Bulgaria, Cyprus, Czech Republic, Estonia, Hungary, Latvia, Lithuania, Malta, Poland, Romania, Slovakia and Slovenia. The key points were:

❑ Expansion of qualified majority voting while retaining vetoes in key areas
❑ Reallocation of votes to a total of 342, allowing for the new members
❑ A Charter of Human Rights
❑ A European Rapid Reaction Force
❑ An increase in European Parliament members to 738 when all new members had joined
❑ Changes in the composition of the European Commission.

However, all these splendid ideas suffered a setback when Ireland rejected the Nice Treaty in a referendum in June 2001! In spite of this, it was decided in December 2001 that ten of the twelve new applicants could still be ready for membership in 2004, Romania and Bulgaria being the exceptions. A date for the latter of 2007 is still a possibility. These ten will add 75m people to the EU's existing population of 375m. Romania and Bulgaria would add another 30m. Ireland voted again on 19 October 2002, and this time passed the Nice Treaty by 63% to 37%. The key question asked had been altered to reassure the Irish on neutrality in view of the Rapid Reaction Force. Once again, the reaction of the EU when faced with a setback was to move the goalposts!

Admission of the ten new members in 2004 was formally confirmed at the Copenhagen Summit in mid-December 2002. Much of the time of the meeting was taken up by the subject of Turkey, which was pressing hard for an early date to discuss its admission. Some countries (UK, Italy) were sympathetic, but others were not (France, Germany). In the end, October 2005 was set as the date to begin consideration of Turkey's entry, although the actual entry date is unlikely to be before 2010. In addition, a last-minute attempt to resolve the Greco/Turkish division of Cyprus failed and, the new entrant is 'Greek' Cyprus and not the whole island.

In theory, citizens from any of these countries can work anywhere in the Union. In practice, fears of cheap immigrant labour caused most countries to postpone the free movement of labour until 2009 (Britain being an honourable exception along with Ireland and Sweden). Then, in May 2006, Finland, Greece, Portugal and Spain also allowed free movement of labour, leaving major economies like France and Germany still holding back. In addition, the potential increased cost to the CAP is such that payments to the new entrants will be phased in over ten years. Originally, the CAP was to be reorganised, resulting in lower payments to countries like France and Germany. However, these same countries have forced a delay in any such move.

Before we look at more recent developments in the EU, we shall look at the institutions of the EU, a history of previous monetary unions and then the development of Economic and Monetary Union itself. Finally, we shall bring ourselves up to date with the key current issues.

THE INSTITUTIONS OF THE EUROPEAN UNION

The European Council

In a sense, this is not really an institution of the EU. From the early days, frequent 'summit' meetings of heads of government were called to resolve key issues of principle. At a summit in Paris in September 1974, it was decided to regularise these meetings under the name 'European Council' (not to be confused with the Council of Europe!). It consists of the heads of government with the President of the Commission entitled to attend. A decision to meet three times a year was amended to twice a year in 1985; the presidency of the meeting to rotate over the various countries of the EU every six months. It does not, of course, appear in the Treaty of Rome.

The Council of Ministers

This is the main political body of the union representing the elected governments of the 15 countries. They make the main strategic decisions, leaving the Commission to draw up the necessary directives. On some issues, each country has a veto.

The European Commission

This is, in effect, the civil service of the EU. They are the permanent officials. The President of the Commission (currently José Manuel Barroso) is picked by the Council of Ministers. The President, in turn, decides on the 19 individual Commissioners, with the usual horse trading to ensure that each country gets it fair share. The choice of Commissioners needs to be approved by the Parliament. The Commission prepares recommendations on broad macroeconomic guidelines and monitors member states' performance.

The European Parliament

This is, of course, an elected body. Until recently its powers were limited, leading to complaints about the undemocratic nature of the EU generally. However, its powers have been strengthened by both the Maastricht Treaty (1991) and the Amsterdam Treaty (1997). Although a formal vote of censure failed, its criticisms of the Commissioners for a mixture of incompetence and fraud led to the resignation of all of them, including the President, Jacques Santer, in March 1999. This dramatic move was seen as a 'sea change' so far as the Parliament is concerned. (Not quite as dramatic as was then thought as the incompetence and fraud don't seem to have diminished!)

The powers of the Parliament are summarised below:

❏ The Maastricht Treaty gave the Parliament co-decision with the Council of Ministers in 15 areas. The Amsterdam Treaty increased this to 38 areas. The exceptions are tax, agriculture and EMU itself. In the 38 areas, the Parliament can amend drafts of the Commission, can reject them by majority vote or work with the Council on a compromise.
❏ It has the power to amend the draft budget prepared by the Commission, and also approve (or not) the Commission's handling of the budget.
❏ It has the right to approve or veto the appointment of the Commission's president and the Commissioners themselves. It can also pass a motion of censure on the Commissioners.
❏ It has the right to ratify any foreign treaties.

Ecofin

This body replaces the former EU Monetary Committee. It is the prime forum for macroeconomic policy and is responsible for broad economic guidelines. The finance ministers of all 15 states meet monthly. An agenda for the meetings is prepared by finance ministers, member central bank representatives and two members of the Commission. This body is called the Economic and Financial Committee. Where matters arise which concern the twelve members of EMU only, a smaller version of Ecofin consists of the twelve finance ministers, and currently goes by the popular name of 'Euro-X'. It is a political hot potato. The UK is against it and the French are strongly in favour (surprise, surprise!).

The European Central Bank

(Although the setting up of the European Central Bank is clearly part of the move to economic and monetary union, we discuss it here, together with the other key institutions of the EU generally. On paper at least, the European System of Central Banks includes the non-members of EMU, as we shall see.)

There are technically no less than three terms here. There is the *European Central*

Bank (ECB), which with the 25 *National Central Banks* (NCBs) form what is called the *European System of Central Banks* (ECSB). Note that this includes countries which are not part of EMU. They do not, however, take part in the decision making regarding the single monetary policy for the euro area and the implementation of such decisions. The governing council of the ECB, however, to avoid confusion has introduced a fourth term – the *Eurosystem* – for the ECB and the 25 NCBs. Unfortunately, it has, perhaps, created further confusion, as even the technical press do not seem to be aware of this distinction.

There are two decision-making bodies:

❏ *The Governing Council*   This is the supreme decision-making body, and consists of the ECB and the twelve NCBs, that is, the Eurosystem. The Council adopts guidelines and makes decisions to ensure performance of the tasks entrusted to the Eurosystem. It also formulates the monetary policy of the EU – monetary objectives, interest rates and reserves.

❏ *The Executive Board*   This consists of the President, Vice-President and four other members. They are appointed by the governments of the twelve member states on a recommendation from the European Council, after consultation with the Parliament and the Governing Council (in the first instance, the European Monetary Institute, the forerunner of the Eurosystem). The main responsibilities of the board are to prepare the meetings of the Governing Council, to implement the monetary policy that the Council has laid down and generally to be responsible for the ECB.

The President and Vice-President serve for a minimum of five years and the other four for eight years, non-renewable. (To prevent all eight terminating at once, in the first instance there is a staggered system.) The first six appointments were:

❏ President – Wim Duisenberg (Netherlands)
❏ Vice-President – Christian Moyer (France)
❏ Otmar Issing (Germany)
❏ Tomasso Padoa Schioppa (Italy)
❏ Eugenio Domingo Solas (Spain)
❏ Sirrka Hamalainen (Finland).

The members in May 2006 were:

❏ President – Jean Claude Trichet (France)
❏ Vice President – Lucas D. Papademos (Greece)
❏ Jürgen Stark (Germany)
❏ José Manuel González-Páramo (Spain)
❏ Lorenzo Bini Smaghi (Italy)
❏ Gertrude Tumpel-Gugerell (Austria).

Jean Claude Trichet took over on 1 November 2003.

The basic tasks to be carried out by the Eurosystem are:

❑   To define and implement monetary policy
❑   To conduct foreign exchange operations
❑   To manage the official foreign reserves
❑   To promote the smooth operation of member systems.

The Maastricht Treaty stipulates that the ECB's main goal is 'price stability'. It also directs the ECB 'to support the general economic policies of the Community' but 'without prejudice to the objective of price stability'. The bank itself decides what price stability means.

The ECB has already decided that monetary policy will be based on a maximum inflation figure of 2% and a mixture of economic indicators including money supply. Inflation is based on a new harmonised index of consumer prices (HICP). It uses a narrower range of goods and services than most national indices and (for the technically minded) is based on a geometric mean rather than an arithmetic mean, to reduce the impact of sharp movements in a small number of prices. (In the case of the UK, the HICP usually produces a figure about 1% less than the local retail price index, although the HICP has now been adopted as well as the retail price index.)

All banks in member countries will deposit reserves with their central bank equivalent to 2% of their eligible liabilities. Gold is some 15% of the total reserves of gold and foreign currencies held at the ECB. Each central bank surrenders a percentage of its gold and foreign currency reserves to be held at the ECB. This percentage is based on a formula taking account of relative GDP and population. Whether gold should be held at all is a matter of some controversy these days. The world's central banks have been selling off gold for several years.

The total system is a decentralised one, as discussed in Chapter 6. The ECB sets three interest rates – a fixed rate tender or repo rate, a marginal lending rate and a rate at which deposits with central banks are paid. (Initially, these rates were 4.5%, 3% and 2% respectively and on 15 June 2006 were 3.75%, 2,75% and 1.75%.) The fixed rate tenders are carried out by the twelve central banks, who will also carry out any foreign exchange transactions called for by the ECB.

The monetary system is similar to that of the Bundesbank, showing the influence of Germany on the final decisions and the need to get the German public to agree to diminution of the power of the mighty Bundesbank. As Jacques Delors once said, 'Not all Germans believe in God, but they all believe in the Bundesbank.'

Nevertheless, various aspects of the Eurosystem have attracted criticism.

To begin with, this is the most independent and unaccountable central bank the world has ever seen. In the US, the Federal Reserve chairman has to appear before Congress every three months and knows that politicians could, if they wished, change the law. Equally, the Federal Open Market Committee publish minutes of their deliberations. In Germany, the law regarding the Bundesbank could be changed by a simple majority in parliament.

All this is totally absent for euroland, although the ECB must submit to questions from the European Parliament and publish annual and quarterly reports. The Maastricht Treaty explicitly forbids the ECB and its decision-making bodies to 'seek or take instructions from Community institutions or bodies, from any government of a member state or from any other body'. Any revision of the Treaty would require unanimity from all 25 states.

The system is also decentralised. The ECB lays down the crucial interest rates, but repos are carried out by the twelve central banks, who will also carry out any forex intervention.

Managing the currency has been divided from banking supervision. In any case, in only two of the twelve states is supervision in the hands of the central bank. In terms of voting, the twelve central banks have twelve votes as opposed to the six of the executive board. Could this lead to tensions later?

The ECB also does not have any role as the rescuer of a major insolvent bank. Multilateral supervision is, in any case, a tough challenge (witness BCCI). If there is a crisis, is it solvency or liquidity? Suppose there was a cross-border merger – say BNP and Barclays, and the bank is in trouble – who bails it out?

The French, in particular, are worried about the lack of control of the ECB, and urged the creation of some form of supervising economic committee. This view did not find support. The bank started out confidently enough. It published a full monthly report and it also resisted attempts by Oskar Lafontaine, the former German finance minister, to bounce it into premature interest rate cuts to stimulate higher employment – it won, he lost. Nevertheless, Paul de Grauwe, Professor of Economics at the University of Leuven, has concluded that the design of the ECB is flawed and will need to be changed. 'Failure to do so', he says in the *Financial Times* of 12 November, 1998, 'will jeopardise the whole European project of economic and monetary union'. Certainly, with Europe experiencing high levels of unemployment, the bank's refusal to cut rates, even increasing them at the end of 2005, has caused widespread concern.

Perhaps we have to bear in mind Milton Friedman's comment on central banks. He suggested that they had two principal objectives: avoiding accountability on the one hand and achieving public prestige on the other!

The European Court of Justice

This was set up to interpret the Treaty of Rome and ensure that the original EEC institutions and member states were fulfilling their obligations under the Treaty. Originally, the Court was set up with six judges, one from each state, and a seventh selected by the Council of Ministers.

The Court gradually built up a body of case law. It repeatedly upheld the superiority of Community law over national law in an increasing number of sectors.

HISTORY OF PREVIOUS MONETARY UNIONS

We have many examples of previous monetary unions, especially in the last century. They are of different types and arise for diverse reasons.

Political Empires

The most obvious example is the existence of some form of political empire such as the Roman Empire, the British Empire, the Austro-Hungarian Empire and the Soviet Union. It is noticeable that when parts break away from the empire, the monetary union collapses. The newly independent parts want their own currency for three reasons: (a) sovereignty and political symbolism, (b) the ability to influence economic activity by altering interest rates and the exchange rate and (c) insulation from direct foreign influence on the currency.

Political Unification

Another example is unions which arise from political unification. These are the ones which usually survive – Germany, Italy and the United States, where the Federal Reserve was finally established in 1913.

Voluntary Unions

There are also voluntary monetary unions, perhaps with more limited political ambitions. The Latin Monetary Union (1865–1926) was formed by France, Italy, Belgium, Greece and Switzerland. However, each state retained its own currency, tying it to the other states at a fixed exchange rate. Britain seriously considered joining the union in 1869 under Gladstone's government, but drew back in the end. Interestingly, the coins used had one side in common, the other being used for a national symbol (just like the current euro). The absence, however, of a central bank led to abuses in Greece and Italy, with excessive issue of banknotes. The French found themselves coping with 50 types of coin which were all legal tender. The excessive flexibility in the system led to its collapse in 1926.

A similar union was the Scandinavian Currency Union, 1873–1920, formed by Norway, Denmark and Sweden. It benefited from a more stable political and economic environment. Volatility of exchange rates, following suspension of the gold standard in 1914, led to the collapse of the union in 1920.

Smaller Unions

Paul de Grauwe of the Catholic University of Leuven has claimed that 'Not a single monetary union in the past came about because of a recognition of economic benefits of the union. In all cases, the integration was driven by political objectives.' This is perhaps too sweeping a statement. The political motives of the Latin Monetary

Union were fairly weak, although the union was not a tight one, as we have seen.

Small unions of a kind have been formed with economics to the foreground. This applies to the Belgium–Luxembourg Union (1923) and the West African CFA franc zone, formed by former French colonies. These are, of course, relatively small countries, but the unions survive.

Looking at the large unions which have survived – Germany, Italy and the United States – a strong political union is clearly a key element, and many believe that this must also be the case in the end for EMU. Indeed, Roger Bootle, MD of Capital Economics, in an article in the *Sunday Telegraph* in May 2005, argued forcefully that many people thought that the single currency would lead to a political union whereas the problem is that Economic and Monetary Union won't work without political union. He comments that no-one wants to face up to this reality, the cart has been put before the horse.

HISTORY OF STEPS TO EMU

The Werner Report

As early as 1962, the European Commission had started discussing proposals for a single currency as a way of binding the original six countries together. Little progress was made, however, until 1969, when Willy Brandt revived these original plans. The theme was taken up in the Werner Report of 1970, which proposed a move to a single currency by 1980. The report was approved by European heads of state in 1971, but the collapse of the Bretton Woods system in 1971/72 stopped developments in their tracks. The 'snake' was set up in 1972 to align the European currencies to the deutschmark, with an allowed fluctuation of ± 2¼%. The snake did not work well, especially with the oil price explosion at the end of 1973. The UK joined in May 1972 and left six months later. France and Italy joined, but left twice. The next move was the European Monetary System (EMS).

European Monetary System

This was set up in March 1979 and had three elements:

- ❏ The Exchange Rate Mechanism (ERM)
- ❏ The European Currency Unit (ECU)
- ❏ The European Monetary Cooperation Fund.

The ERM was the successor to the snake. This time, two bands of fluctuation were allowed – the narrow band of ± 2¼% and the wide band of ± 6%. Target rates for each currency against the others were established (the 'parity grid') and periodic realignments were allowed for. If rates moved near to their limit, the central bank concerned was expected to defend the currency by buying it and, perhaps, also raising interest rates. Currencies could be borrowed from other central banks to enable it to do this. By 1992, of the twelve countries of the EU, Greece was not a member, the UK, Spain and Portugal were members at the wide band and the other eight were members at the narrow band.

The ECU was calculated from a weighted basket of all European currencies (not just those in the ERM). It produced a common unit of accountancy and was used for all EU statistics, some currency dealings, some cross-border public sector invoicing within Europe and as a denomination for some Treasury bills and bonds (government and corporate). Clearly, the idea was that this laid the basis for a genuine future currency. If all countries in the ERM could move in time to the narrow band on a stable basis, this would make the transition to a single currency easier.

The European Monetary Cooperation Fund was actually set up following the Werner Report, but was effectively dormant until the EMS. Each country in the EU deposited 20% of their gold and foreign currency reserves and received ECUs in exchange. The funds were held at the BIS in Basel. This was the *official* ECU as opposed to the *private* ECU, as used for Treasury bills and bonds. This central fund was only to be used for transactions between EMS central banks and named monetary institutions. Central banks obliged to intervene in the markets because of ERM rules could draw on an unlimited credit within the system. Apart from this, it had little practical use during the life of the system.

Changes to the ERM

In September 1992, the growing belief that a realignment was due and that sterling and the lira were overvalued led to great turbulence. The UK and Italy left the ERM, while devaluations of the peseta, escudo and punt followed. Further turbulence returned in July 1993, with attacks on the French franc and other currencies. In early August, a decision was taken to widen the bands to ± 15% (except for the deutschmark/guilder, which remained at ± 2¼%). These were black days for the ideal of monetary union.

The Delors Plan

The ultimate aim for Europe was Economic and Monetary Union (EMU). A blueprint was drawn up in 1989 by central banks chaired by Jacques Delors, President of the European Commission, and thus called the 'Delors Plan'. This set up three stages towards EMU:

- ❏ All members in the ERM; no exchange controls; achievement of a single market in financial services
- ❏ Setting up the European System of Central Banks (ESCB)
- ❏ Locked exchange rates; monetary policy controlled by ESCB; eventually, a single currency.

The Maastricht Treaty

This blueprint was broadly endorsed by the Madrid EC Summit in mid-1989, and mid-1990 was set as the starting date for Stage 1. The matter was further discussed at the intergovernmental conference which began in December 1990, and prepared for a treaty to be drawn up at Maastricht in December 1991. The Maastricht summit laid down a timetable for European Monetary Union as follows:

❏ End 1996, a decision on a possible EMU in 1997 if a minimum of seven nations could meet the convergence conditions (described later).
❏ By 1999, there would be EMU in any case if two nations were able to meet the convergence conditions.
❏ A European Central Bank to be set up six months prior to EMU, but a body called the 'European Monetary Institute' (EMI) to coordinate policies prior to setting up the Central Bank, and to be set up in 1994.
❏ Special protocols allowed the UK to opt out of a final move to a single currency, and Denmark to hold a referendum in June 1992.
❏ The convergence conditions were:
  (a) Inflation rate within 1½% of the best three nations
  (b) Long-term interest rates within 2% of the average of the lowest three nations
  (c) Currency within the 2¼% ERM band, and no devaluation in the previous two years
  (d) Budget deficit to GDP ratio not exceeding 3% and national debt not exceeding 60% of GDP.

The Danish referendum in June 1992 rejected the Maastricht Treaty by a narrow majority. Nevertheless, the other states decided to continue with the process of having the Treaty accepted by their parliaments. A French referendum in September 1992 narrowly voted in favour and the German parliament passed it in December, although this was challenged by the German Constitutional Court. Finally, after concessions, Denmark accepted Maastricht in a new referendum in May 1993.

The new European Monetary Institute (EMI) started operations in January 1994, located in Frankfurt. Sweden, Finland and Austria joined the Community on 1 January 1995, and Austria joined the ERM. Later, Finland joined, Italy rejoined in November 1996, and Greece joined in early 1998.

The EMI laid down firmer plans for monetary union in November 1995:

1 January 1999	Start of monetary union, with locked exchange rates
1 January 2002	Introduction of new notes and coins
1 July 2002	The new currency to be legal tender.

The December Madrid meeting decided to call the new currency the 'euro' (not the 'ecu'). The rates to be locked on 1 January 1999, were decided at a meeting in May 1998, which also decided which countries would join the monetary union.

EMU Begins

The countries joining should have met the Maastricht conditions described above. Embarrassingly, Belgium and Italy, key candidates, had a national debt/GDP ratio well in excess of 100%. The budget deficit/GDP ratio of 3% was based on 1997 figures. Many countries used what could only be called 'creative accounting' to come below the 3% level. Such was the strong political will to have EMU, however, that these problems were ignored, and the system began as planned in January 1999 with eleven members – Austria, Belgium, Finland, France, Germany, Ireland, Italy, Luxembourg, Netherlands, Portugal and Spain. This left Greece, Sweden, the UK and Denmark outside. Later, Greece joined EMU making the eleven into twelve.

The permanently fixed rates for the euro against euro area currencies are shown in Table 11.1.

Table 11.1 *Euro rates against euro area currencies*

Country	Currency	€	Country	Currency	€
Austria	Sch	13.7603	Ireland	I£	0.787564
Belgium/Lux	BFr/LFr	40.3399	Italy	L	1936.27
Finland	FM	5.94573	Netherlands	Fl	2.20371
France	FFr	6.55957	Portugal	Es	200.482
Germany	DM	1.95583	Spain	Pta	166.386

As the rate for, say, the French franc and the euro, and also the Italian lira and the euro, are fixed, it follows that one multiplication gives us a fixed franc/lira rate, and so on.

No notes and coins were due until January 2002, but the euro was used for domestic bonds and eurobonds, as well as interbank transactions. It was also used for cheques or credit cards or any transaction where notes and coins are not used. Control of interest rates and monetary policy were in the hands of the new European Central Bank, which we described earlier.

Maastricht laid down a target budget deficit/GDP ratio of 3%, but said nothing about variations once EMU had started. This is covered by the so-called 'Stability and Growth Pact'. The position of the ERM now that EMU has started is 'ERM II'. We discuss both these subjects now.

The Stability and Growth Pact

Further changes to the European Union were discussed at Amsterdam in June 1997, leading to a new treaty which became law in May 1999. Whilst at Amsterdam, heads of government discussed the question of control over excessive budget deficits once EMU had started. They agreed on a common code of fiscal conduct to uphold discipline in the management of government finances. Budgets are normally to be kept close to either a balance or small surplus. This should ensure that even in recession the maximum deficit/GDP ratio can be kept to 3%. Sound government finances are regarded as an indispensable requisite for macroeconomic stability. This common code is known as the 'Stability and Growth Pact'.

Technically, all countries in the EU are part of this pact, not just the twelve of EMU. All countries submit their forward budgetary plans to the Ecofin Council. This should enable early warning to be given of any slippage. Deficits in excess of 3% are only permitted in exceptional circumstances, such as a fall in GDP in excess of 2%.

The problem of sanctions for those who break the rules caused much argument, with the Germans wanting much tougher action than most other countries. It was decided that the Ecofin Council will formulate recommendations for correction, and measures must be taken within four months. The decision is taken by qualified majority, and the Ecofin Council could impose sanctions – a non-interest bearing deposit which might be converted later into a fine if effective action is not taken.

In April 1999, we saw the ECB issue a sharp warning that many governments risked breaking the budget limits agreed, and that safety margins were not sufficient.

Following this warning, we saw the pact in action in May 1999. Italy, whose forecast deficit was 2.0%, asked permission to raise this to 2.4%. Weak growth and high unemployment had led to this position. GDP was due to grow 1.5% in 1999. The Ecofin Council agreed to Italy's request, and many saw this as an ominous sign for the future. The euro then fell sharply on the forex markets.

Worse was to follow. Ironically, Germany, which had been so keen on tough action, found itself facing a formal warning for breaking the pact in February 2000. With the usual EU compromise, Germany said it would 'endeavour' to balance its budget by 2004. Otmar Issing, chief economist of the ECB, said, 'if all other European states want the same treatment in future, the early warning system is useless'.

Then, in June 2002, Ecofin finance ministers criticised France for not balancing the budget. However, French finance minister, François Mer, refused to say that the country would be in balance by 2004, although they had promised to do so at the Barcelona Summit in March. Pressed again at the Seville Summit in June 2002, France agreed (reluctantly) to bring its budget 'close to balance' by 2004. Then, later in June 2002, Portugal admitted that its budget deficit as a percentage of GDP would probably be 3.9%, well above the so-called limit of 3%. In September 2002, the European Commission put off the deadline for members to balance their books to 2006 once it became clear that Germany, too, would breach the 3% limit. Jacques

Chirac was reported as telling his finance minister to 'ignore the Stability Pact'; in October, Romano Prodi, the President of the Commission, described the Stability Pact as 'stupid' because the decisions made were too rigid.

That was the position when the last edition of this book was published early in 2003. If anything, the position regarding the pact has become worse since then. We discuss this under 'current issues' at the end of this section on the setting up of European and Monetary Union in 1999.

ERM II

On 1 September, 1998, the Governing Council and the Executive Board of the Eurosystem of Central Banks agreed on a text for the successor to the ERM. The Maastricht Treaty had had a condition that countries joining EMU had to have had a two year period in the ERM at the narrow band. The replacement of the narrow band by ± 15% had led to a dispute. Most governments believe that this is still a prior requirement. This view is opposed by the UK, which argues that it has been overtaken by events. As departing from the ERM was part of a grave financial crisis in the UK, no government wants to be the one to suggest rejoining!

Nevertheless, what is called 'ERM II' has now been defined. The main change is that participating countries agree to maintain their currencies within a band of an agreed rate against the euro. The twelve central banks will intervene, if necessary, to support a currency, and loans are available to the participating countries from the ECB. These loans can only be drawn after first drawing on the country's own reserves. The loans are repayable in three months and subject to a ceiling on cumulative borrowings.

The bad news for the UK was that Denmark and Greece accepted the new rules and joined ERM II. Denmark's krona is being held within a 2¼% band and Greece's drachma was held within a ± 15% band prior to joining EMU fully.

Key speeches by two ECB executive board members in March 2002, aimed at prospective new EU members, again stressed that a minimum period of at least two years in ERM II was a precondition for joining EMU. Later, when ten new members joined the EC, six of them joined ERM II.

Next Members?

Waiting in the wings to join the EU in 2004, and some time later EMU, were Cyprus, the Czech Republic, Estonia, Hungary, Latvia, Lithuania, Malta, Poland, Slovakia and Slovenia.

To join the EU itself, countries must meet all the rules and obligations of membership. The document recording these runs to 80 000 pages – banking laws, competition policy, state aid, veterinary inspection standards and so on. They also need efficiency in public administration to enforce the rules.

EMU Statistics

Some interesting statistics are shown in Table 11.2.

We can see that while the euro area is a very large trading block, it is still some way behind the United States, if bigger than Japan. The US has a bigger share of world GDP and a smaller public sector.

We see the euro area as having higher unemployment (8.3% as against 4.9%).

European companies (and Japanese) have tended to turn to bank loans for finance, as opposed to the US, where the capital markets are clearly much bigger.

Within the euro area itself, the market is dominated by Germany, France and Italy, who account for 72% of the total GDP. Germany alone accounts for 32%.

Table 11.2   *Key characteristics of the euro area*

Characteristic	Reporting period	Unit	Euro area	EU	United States	Japan
Population	2004	m	312.0	460.0	294.0	128.0
GDP (PPP)	2004	€ trillion	7.7	10.3	10.2	3.3
Unemployment	2005	%	8.3	8.5	4.9	4.6
Central expenditure	2004	% of GDP	47.7	47.3	32.3	38.7*
Deficit (−)	2004	% of GDP	2.7−	2.6−	4.7−	7.7−*
Debt securities outstanding	2004	€ trillion	9.4	12.4	16.5	6.6
Stock market capitalisation	2004	€ trillion	4.0	6.6	10.9	2.7

Notes: PPP = Purchasing Power Parity; * = 2003 figures
Source: *ECB Statistics Pocket Book,* January 2006.

Payment Systems

The official interbank payments system for the euro is TARGET (Trans-European Automated Real Time Gross Settlement Express Transfer). After some controversy, access to TARGET is open to national central banks and participants in Real Time Gross Settlement (RTGS) systems in non-euro area member states. These non-euro central banks must deposit a sum of money with the Eurosystem by 8.00 a.m. each day (for example, three billion for the Bank of England). This is to ensure the availability of intraday liquidity.

In addition to TARGET, there is a euro clearing system available through the Paris-based European Banking Association (EBA). It is, however, not RTGS but end of day netting (and thus cheaper).

There are also the individual national systems for clearing of these high value euro-based payments – EIL-2V and EAF2 in Germany, TBF in France and CHAPS-Euro in the UK.

EMU – The Benefits

Having looked at the history and all the facts and figures, we are still left with the basic question 'why?'. What are the objectives of EMU? What advantages should accrue?

We will put the arguments for EMU here and then the counter arguments in the next section. The specific position in the United Kingdom will then be considered.

After this, under the heading 'Current Issues', we will examine all the developments from 2003 to 2005 in the EC and the EMU to see to what extent the hopes for both have been fulfilled. We will end by looking at a provocative question, already being aired: 'could the euro fail?'.

These issues split naturally into *economic* issues and *political* issues. Let us begin with economics.

One key argument is that the use of a single currency in twelve countries with a population of 312 million will lead to more transparency of prices, and make it much more difficult to sell goods at a higher price in the Netherlands than, say, Italy.

Many studies have drawn attention to the disparity in motor car prices. Pre-tax differentials exceed 20%. A Bayerishe Landesbank study has shown that consumer prices in Austria and Finland are about 11% higher than those in Germany, France, Belgium and Portugal. On the other hand, prices in the Netherlands, Italy and Ireland are 8% lower than in those countries, and prices in Spain 11% lower.

A KPMG survey on pricing policy in March 1999 claimed that there was great scope for more uniformity of prices. Price variations in 31 standard consumer goods dwarfed any that could be explained by sales taxes and duties.

If these views are correct, then greater price competition will lead to lower prices and more trade. With no worries about currency movements, it will be easier for manufacturers to move production to cheaper areas. There may be pressure in high cost countries for lower taxation and more flexible labour markets.

All the above are part of a wider argument that a single currency will make the euro area more of a genuine single market.

A more obvious example of the benefit of the introduction of a single currency is the saving to importers and exporters of buying/selling foreign currency. We saw in our foreign exchange chapter (Chapter 9) that there are spreads to be paid on spot and forward deals, and perhaps premiums if options are chosen. Not only is useful money now saved, but it is easier to look at the euro area as a single area. In particular, it streamlines European Treasury operations. Cash can be managed on a pan-European basis, saving currency and interest rate spreads and leading to greater efficiency.

Another area of cost saving for corporates is a reduction in the cost of capital. We know from the statistics that Europe has relied far more on bank finance than the US, which uses capital markets much more. In Germany, for instance, 40% of bond issues are public sector bonds. If Pfandbriefe (used for loans to local authorities) are included, the figure is nearer 70%. Prior to the introduction of the euro, fund managers and investors all over Europe were constrained by foreign exchange risk (and sometimes regulations) when it came to cross-border purchases of securities. These constraints have now gone. If the euro area produces more of a single market in bonds and equities, then raising finance should be cheaper, to the benefit of the companies concerned.

There is a common view that pension fund managers and others would stop looking at countries and look at market sector instead. However, we need to be cautious here. A study by the University of Liège, in Belgium, found that only four market sectors had high correlation across Europe – oils, pharmaceuticals, financials and consumer brands.

Of course, for fund managers there is still a basic question – what is Europe? There is the Europe of the twelve, the Europe of the 25 and then Europe including Switzerland. Here is a country with two of Europe's biggest drug stocks (Novartis, Roche), two huge banks (Crédit Suisse and UBS), two of the world's biggest insurers (Swiss Re and Zurich Financial Services) and the world's biggest food company (Nestlé) – and it isn't even in the EU!

Interestingly, as well as bonds and equities, the syndicated loan market has also expanded in the euro area. We are seeing major acquisitions funded in the first place by a syndicated loan (for speed and confidentiality). Later it may be replaced by a bond issue.

Judged strictly as an economic venture, EMU will be a success if, over the coming years, we see countries benefiting from growing trade and investment, declining unemployment and low inflation.

In the *Financial Times* of 14 June, 1999, Graham Bishop of Salomon Smith Barney was quoted as saying: 'companies all over Europe are merging and restructuring, and this is largely due to the effects of the single currency'.

All the above are *economic* benefits, but what of the *political* angle?

There are two key points here. One is the view that EMU will never work without tighter political union, whether we like it or not. The other is that political union is not merely necessary for EMU, but desirable in its own right.

On the first point, the argument is that there can never be a free market and full competition if the same goods can be at different prices in different countries purely due to value added tax.

Equally, how can there be full and fair cross-border competition between companies if some pay more tax than others? Payment of tax, in turn, depends on the definition of profit, which, to be fair, needs common accountancy principles. Finally, surely a company can be registered in 'Europe' rather than in one of the countries of the twelve?

Common taxes, common fiscal and monetary policy, common accountancy standards, common law – all this is very close to a political union.

Those who agree with the founders, like Schuman, Monnet, Spaak and so on, argue that political union is desirable if war is to be avoided and a single European entity is to bring justice and peace.

The Counterarguments

Having looked at the benefits of EMU and its political implications, there are naturally those whose views are different.

Perhaps the most common counterargument relates to the 'one size fits all' implication of the ECB, with its single interest rate and exchange rate. The fact that countries are at different phases in the economic cycle means that some may need high interest rates at the same time that others need lower ones. We had a perfect example of this as EMU started. Italy and Germany were growing GDP at 1.5%, while Spain and Portugal were growing at 3% and Ireland at a massive 7%. Irish interest rates prior to EMU were 6% and then fell to 2½% on entry with a later rise to 3%. Inflation took off and soon reached 7%, with little the Irish government could do about it.

One response to this would be to change fiscal policy. However, this is limited by the Stability and Growth Pact. If a country is in recession, but interest rates are going up in EMU because others are in a boom, it could normally stimulate the economy by lower taxes and high government spending – but it no longer has the right to do this except within defined limits.

Those in recession when interest rates are high may find that unemployment rises to socially unacceptable levels.

One result of all this is that the Stability and Growth Pact is coming under immense strain, as we have already reported.

Another argument is that the promised convergence within EMU is not happening and is unlikely to happen. There are differing rates of interest, inflation, unemployment and growth.

If one state is in recession and one experiencing strong growth, one response is for labour to move from one to the other. Economists claim that a monetary union needs high labour mobility. After all, the US is a monetary union. Texas may be suffering where New England is prospering. This is where the euro area faces severe problems. The US has high labour mobility, the euro area very poor mobility. In Germany, even to move from one federal state to another is a major decision. There is a fundamental and dangerous weakness here.

Another problem from 'one size fits all' is that different states react differently to changes in interest rates and exchange rates. In Ireland, for example, 80% of people own their homes, and variable rate mortgages are the most common. An interest rate increase has much more effect on consumers than in, say, Germany.

Looking at exchange rate changes, exports outside the euro area are 14% of the German economy but 24% in Belgium and Finland and 44% in Ireland.

To the above can be added what some people see as the weaknesses of the ECB and the Eurosystem, to which we referred earlier – its lack of accountability or any kind of control; the division of managing the currency from supervision; the possible struggle between the Executive Board and the Central Bank governors who could outvote them; the absence of a role for a 'lender of last resort' in the event of a crisis.

One of the key benefits which is claimed for EMU is the transparency of prices, which will lead to growing competition, higher efficiency and lower prices. Critics, however, point to the effect of varying VAT rates and, in particular, transport costs. Goods made in Spain which have higher transport costs will certainly not sell for the same price in Finland as they do in, say, Spain and Portugal.

There are great hopes for the euro area as a powerful, efficient, single market competing with the US and Japan. Many, however, point to severe weaknesses in Europe which are not currently being tackled.

One is high labour costs due to social security costs borne by employers. A Morgan Stanley Dean Witter study estimates social costs at 28% of hourly compensation in the US, and 45% in Germany. The hourly compensation in manufacturing in the euro area they estimate at 12% higher than the US. Another study shows Europe well behind the US in the use of IT, Western Europe spending 2.26% of GDP on IT as opposed to 4.08% in the US; white collar workers in the US having 103 personal computers per 100 workers as opposed to 52 in Western Europe.

Labour laws are much more inflexible in Europe than the US. In the latter, it is much easier to restructure and lay workers off. One's first humane reaction may be to see this as a bad thing, until it is realised that the alternative may be for everyone to lose their jobs as the firm is put out of business by global competition. It is much harder to sack people in the euro area than in the US, and yet the euro area has unemployment at 8.3% of the labour force, and the US 4.9%. In addition, as we saw from Table 11.2, government expenditure in the euro area is 47.7% of GDP and only 32.3% in the US. High government expenditure means high taxes.

On the question of growing efficiency in capital markets due to the single currency, there is little doubt that this will take place, and that it has already started.

Even here, there are some reservations. The cross-border government bond markets are no longer affected by forex risk, but there is still the question of liquidity. Finland, for example, has a far better debt/GDP ratio than Belgium, and a better credit rating, but the spread of its bonds over Germany's are the same as Belgium. This is simply due to lack of liquidity as Finland issues fewer bonds. It's a reminder that there's more to bond prices than foreign exchange and credit rating.

In the equity markets, the proposed 'pan-European' stock exchange based in London and Frankfurt faced the massive problems outlined in Chapter 7 regarding trading systems, indices and regulation, and the plan was abandoned.

Many of the problems above will be worsened by enlargement. Presumably most of these countries hope that, having joined the EU, they will qualify in time for EMU; and perhaps the missing three will also join. The euro area of twelve countries is one thing, the euro area of, say, 25 might be another. If 'one size fits all' is a problem for the twelve countries, it will surely be much worse when we embrace Central and Eastern Europe and the Baltic States.

One assumes that the weaknesses in the single market, especially in finance, which we discussed earlier, will finally be resolved, but it does seem to be taking a long time.

In retail banking, there is a different mentality from wholesale. 'Savings regulations and fiscal laws continue to be efficient barriers to multinational retail banking activity', says Daniel Bouton, Chairman of Société Générale.

Let us finish this particular discussion by looking at the words of that much-maligned thinker, Niccolò Machiavelli, in his work *The Prince*. Referring to the introduction of something entirely new, he comments:

> ... *there is nothing more difficult to take in hand, more perilous to conduct, or more uncertain in its success than to take the lead in the introduction of a new order of things. The reason is that the innovator has for enemies all those who have done well under the old conditions, and lukewarm defenders in those who only may do well in the new. This coolness arises partly from fear of the opponents who have the laws on their side, and partly from the incredulity of men, who do not readily believe in new things until they have had a long experience of them. Thus it happens that whenever those who are hostile have the opportunity to attack they do it like partisans; whilst the others defend lukewarmly, in such wise that the prince is endangered along with them.*

The UK Position

The major EU economy absent from EMU is, of course, the United Kingdom. We shall finish by looking briefly at the arguments raging for and against.

The general arguments for joining EMU can be summarised as:

- ❏ Stability of the exchange rate.
- ❏ Lower foreign investment in the UK if outside. In recent years, 40% of foreign direct investment in Europe has come to the UK.
- ❏ The UK will progressively have far less influence on monetary and economic policy in Europe if outside. Frankfurt will gain, the City of London will lose. The ECB is already in Frankfurt, the LIFFE exchange has lost business to EUREX and EURIBOR is used as the reference rate, not EUROLIBOR.
- ❏ There will be savings on foreign exchange transactions.
- ❏ The UK is too small an economy to stay outside – it would gradually lose business and influence.
- ❏ As a matter of philosophy, the UK should join in this exciting historic venture and take its full place in Europe.

❏ The fear of federalism and political integration is exaggerated because in practice it will never happen.

Against this, the arguments range as follows:

❏ Stability of the exchange rate will only apply in the euro area. The UK will still have instability against the dollar, the yen and the Swiss franc.
❏ Decisions on foreign investment are not only influenced by currency risk – the UK has low labour costs, flexible labour laws and lower taxes than most of the euro area.
❏ The UK's GDP would only be 14% of the GDP of the euro area if it joined, and that is the extent of our probable influence – one seventh. Most currency transactions in London are not sterling anyway. LIFFE has already captured most of the derivatives business in short-term euro interest rates. London has 31% of world forex trading and Frankfurt only 5%. London trades 70% of the international bond market and has a far bigger OTC derivatives market than the rest of the euro area. London has a pool of skilled labour, lower social taxes, the infrastructure of accountants and lawyers and the use of English as a language.
❏ Savings on foreign exchange transactions are useful but probably only ½% of GDP.
❏ The UK is small, but big enough to survive outside – look at Switzerland. 'One size fits all' would be a major problem with a business cycle out of line with France and Germany and the highest ratio of outstanding variable rate mortgage debt to GDP in Europe.
❏ The great new historic venture is not likely to succeed.
❏ EMU needs political integration to work properly.

Officially, the government's policy on EMU is that the United Kingdom will join 'when the time is right'. The decision as to whether the time is right or not will be taken after a periodic examination of five tests:

1   Convergence of business cycles with those of the EMU countries over a sustained period
2   The flexibility of the economy's adjustment to economic shocks
3   Investment – would EMU create better conditions for inward investment into the UK?
4   Impact on financial services
5   Promotion of higher growth, stability and a lasting increase in employment.

This fifth test is largely a summary and conclusion of the previous four.

The typical British attitude (rightly or wrongly) is summarised in the following quotation:

> *We see nothing but good and hope in a richer, freer, more contented European commonality. But we have our own dream and our own task. We are with Europe, but not of it. We are linked, but not compromised. We are interested and associated, but not absorbed.*

This was written by Winston Churchill in an American periodical in 1930. In spite of the huge decline in British influence and power since then, it's probably still a fair summary of the attitude of many in the UK today.

CURRENT ISSUES

The European Constitution

The European leaders decided at a meeting in Brussels in October 2001 to produce a constitution and set up a convention of 20 national and European parliamentarians under Valéry Giscard d'Estaing, the former French President. The mandate was to bring Europe closer to its people which, in hindsight, seems somewhat ironic. Reference was made to the United States constitution. However, the US constitution is 20 pages. Europe's, when it emerged, was 300!

One of the reasons for the constitution was the enlargement to 25 members. It provided for more democratic voting and an end to the rotating presidency. The real reason was a move to political deepening of the union by those whose ideal was ultimate political union.

After the usual fierce arguments, the constitution was finally drafted and agreed at a summit in Ireland in June 2004. An opinion poll in France at the time showed that 66% would back the constitution.

The main features of the constitution were as follows:

1   The European Council President was to be elected for a 2½ year term to replace the six month rotating system.
2   The European Council to meet quarterly. Voting to be by consensus unless otherwise provided for.
3   The Council of Ministers would be chaired for 18 months under overall control of the new president.
4   A new Minister for Foreign Affairs to be appointed by a qualified majority of member states.
5   The power of oversight by the European Parliament to be increased to 80 policy areas and the Parliament to vote on approving the Commission President and team. Generally to enact legislation with the Council of Ministers.

6 The EU to be a legal body with the right to sign international treaties.
7 A complicated system of qualified majority voting to apply based on numbers of members and percentage of EU population.
8 The Charter of Fundamental Rights not to override national laws on sensitive issues such as employment legislation.

One result of the constitution was the loss of veto in 43 new areas (no veto on immigration policy), increased powers for the Parliament and a new President of Europe able to frame pan-European foreign policy.

Those wanting political union did not win everything but did get a European Foreign Minister, a legal personality for the Union and a formal statement of the supremacy of European law. However, foreign and taxation policy was still to be subject to a veto.

The constitution needed to be ratified by the various governments. Most decided not to have a referendum but the French and Dutch did, in July 2005, which led to the biggest shock to the EU since the walkout by de Gaulle in 1965. The vote in France was only 45% in favour and only 38% in Holland. Bearing in mind that these two were part of the 'original six', this was extremely significant and a major setback for those in favour of 'ever closer union'.

Prior to the vote, Spain had voted in favour in a referendum and, shortly after the vote, the Grand Duchy of Luxembourg also voted 'yes'. Eleven countries had voted in favour without holding a referendum. As a result of the French and Dutch vote, all the other countries postponed ratification and the general mood was that the constitution was dead. This did not stop a few flat earth believers claiming victory in that 13 in favour out of 25 was a majority.

What happened? It appears that the French and Dutch voted on the European Union as a whole and not just the constitution. The French were alarmed at the idea of what is usually called 'Anglo-Saxon liberalism' – a reference to the attitudes in the US and the UK. What is puzzling is that some voted against because they saw the constitution as promoting this liberalism and others voted in favour because they saw it as a bulwark against liberalism. The Dutch were alarmed at their growth rate of only 0.8% and their acceptance of fiscal discipline ignored by major partners like France, Germany and Italy. They wanted lower interest rates to stimulate the economy but could not have them due to the single EMU interest rate.

A euro summit followed the referendum defeats. What was needed was a thorough examination of the reasons for the discontent within the EU and the steps to be taken to promote higher growth, productivity and lower unemployment.

The report of the European Commission in October 2004 had forecast growth of only 1.9% for the EU. The Lisbon agenda of 2000 called for a drive to make Europe the 'most competitive and dynamic knowledge-based economy in the world' by 2010. This was clearly not happening and almost a sick joke in view of the total lack of any progress at all.

President Chirac distracted attention from the real issues by attacking the UK's rebate, negotiated by Margaret Thatcher in 1984. The UK chaired the meetings for the last 6 months of 2005 and replied by a major attack on the CAP – 40% of the total budget for only 5% of members. This attack found little support and debates on the future of Europe were replaced with acrimonious arguments about the rebate and Europe's budget for 2007.

Following the French and Dutch rejection, three summits took place, the last of these in December 2005. The budget for 2007/13 was agreed with the CAP estimated at 43% and measures to improve competitiveness at only 8.5%. The original German/French accord in 2002 fixed the CAP until 2013 and this was left unchanged. A great opportunity to discuss first principles was missed.

The EU had completely ignored the changed world with fierce competition from China, India and other emerging markets. Rigidities in labour markets, union power, higher taxes and social costs and over-generous unemployment benefits in the worst performing states had left Europe with low growth, high unemployment and vulnerability to the new global economy.

The French and others were alarmed at the idea of US/UK labour market freedom and willingness to let uncompetitive companies fold. Their instincts were not only to protect their industries from foreign competitors, but their labour force from cheaper or more skilled labour from the new members of the EC. The UK had welcomed the Poles and gained from their arrival in the UK but, as one German official pointed out, the Polish border is 1800 km from London, only 80 km from Berlin. On the other hand, lower wages might help to save some companies that would otherwise fail facing low wage economies on the other side of the world.

Some saw a 'third way' in what was called the 'Nordic Model' – a high investment in universities and R&D; a flexible labour market with active policies designed to bring young people, women and the elderly into the workforce. Only Finland and Sweden spend more than 3% of GDP on R&D, some spend less that 1% (UK 2%).

Guy Verhofstadt, the Belgian Prime Minister, published a book in December 2005, *The United States of Europe*. He claimed that the constitution was dead and gave up on the 25 as a vehicle for further integration. He saw the 12 member eurozone as the most coherent framework for the future. However, would this new core wreck the wider EU?

Nicolas Sarkozy, the French minister, suggested a renegotiation of the constitution to reduce reforms to an essential core of rules and a charter of rights. The rest would be a set of detailed regulations on the single market and outside the formal constitution. He has also argued that Europe should be led by a group of six countries – France, Germany, the UK, Italy, Spain and Poland. This is a somewhat curious idea and hardly likely to be welcomed by other members of the EU. Finally, the Brussels Summit, in June 2006, decided that the EU should try and decide by the end of 2008 which parts of the constitution could be salvaged.

Some light on the above may be thrown by looking at various more specific issues within the EC and EMU.

The Stability and Growth Pact

Earlier in this chapter, we saw that the above pact had begun to hit trouble in the period 2000/02. Things did not improve later.

In November 2003, at a meeting in Brussels, the EU finance ministers ordered Germany and France to cut their deficits to below 3% or face a fine of 0.5% of GDP. However, it was decided by a majority to ignore this. The new ECB President, Jean Claude Trichet, was alarmed and said, 'Non-disciplined financial policies ... could lead to inflationary pressures'.

At a meeting at Lake Como in September 2004, the European Commission put forward proposals to reform the pact which were received with politeness rather than enthusiasm. Much later, timetables for correcting excessive deficits were suggested and governments were simply encouraged to repay debt in boom times. One clear problem is that fiscal policy remains the province of individual governments, but monetary policy that of the ECB. Government debt is over 100% of GDP in Belgium, Italy and Greece and the annual deficit over 3% in six countries. Worse was to come.

In October, the new Greek government announced a revision to its statistics showing markedly higher deficits than originally reported. The 2004 deficit was expected to be 5.3%. In April 2005, the new Portuguese government said that their deficit was at least 5% and not 3%. Interesting how a change of government leads to new openness as the previous government can be blamed! In between these two events, more concessions were made. Jean-Claude Juncher, then President of the EU, suggested that states would be allowed to negotiate temporary exemptions from the pact – Germany for reunification costs, France for spending on defence and Italy for investment in infrastructures. The move was opposed by Austria's Finance Minister, Karl-Heinze Grasser, as 'a huge joke'. Standard and Poor's did not see the funny side and downgraded Italy and Greece to AA- and the outlook for Portugal was cut from 'stable' to 'negative'.

Previously, Gordon Brown, the UK's Chancellor of the Exchequer, had inflamed colleagues by a superior 'holier than thou' attitude. These colleagues must have derived a smug satisfaction in September 2005 when the EU Monetary Commission pointed out that the UK had broken the 3% level for two years and that the rate for 2005/06 was likely to be 3.25%. Such satisfaction was further increased when the Commission declared in January 2006 that the UK was on track to break the 3% level for four years running. Although the UK is not in the eurozone, all EU members are expected to obey the pact, although non-eurozone members cannot be fined. As no-one is being fined, anyway, this difference is now academic.

By September 2005, 12 out of the 25 countries were in breach of the rules and the Greek deficit was at a new high of 6.6%. Italy went to the polls in 2006 and France will do so in 2007 – neither wanting to impose unpopular measures prior to the election. National self-interest was back and members were not showing any political commitment to the EU.

The European Central Bank then made a potentially significant move. Showing serious concern at the degeneration of fiscal discipline, it warned that it will not accept the government bonds of any country whose credit ratings slip too far. In its provision of financial liquidity, it will not accept bonds whose rating is below A–. In its weekly repos it advances cash on a short-term basis against the collateral of government bonds, so the loss of this facility would be very serious. That same week, Portugal had to increase the yield on a new bond to give it a better spread over German government bonds. Italy, Greece and Portugal are all rated AA–.

At the end of the last edition, the section on this topic ended with the words 'Is the Stability and Growth Pact dead?'. Frankly, the answer seems to be 'yes' but both the ratings agencies and the ECB are providing a new restraint.

Convergence

The whole point of the EU and EMU is that it should lead to the free movement of capital, goods and services and thus gradually arrive at convergence across Europe. Deutsche Bank published a paper in August 2004 in which it claimed 'We do not see that eurozone economies have converged', pointing out that, since 2001, the difference between member states' GDP has actually increased. Its pessimistic conclusion was that 'Economic instability in the euro era is likely to be higher and trend growth lower that it would have been without monetary union.' In this subsection we will examine various ways in which convergence is or is not happening.

Protectionism   We should be seeing cross-border mergers if convergence is happening. There are, to be fair, some structural problems here. In Germany, most banks are publicly or mutually owned – the cooperatives and savings banks are of great importance, probably 50% of the market. Takeovers are virtually impossible. France is similar with its own cooperatives and savings banks. However, in terms of non-banking companies, France (to the fury of the European Commission) went further in August 2005 and listed strategic sectors in which takeovers would be banned on security grounds – nuclear activities, certain pharmaceutical laboratories, cryptology, private arms manufacturers, biotechnology, computer security, defence and casinos (money laundering). Earlier in the year, a possible bid for Danone by Pepisco was greeted with outrage. Later, Mittal Steel bid for Arcelor in which the French have interests. Again, a French government spokesman spoke out angrily against the bid. Nevertheless, St Gobain bid for the UK BPB, France Telecom took over Spain's Amena while Siemens was prevented from taking over Alstom.

In Italy, a bid for Banca Antonvenuta by ABN Amro was frustrated by a counterbid by Banco Populare Italiana (BPI) who, with allies, removed the board of Antonvenuta. BBVA bid for Banca Nationale del Lavoro (BNL) but a counterbid was launched by the much smaller Unipol. In both cases, the Central Bank Governor, Antonio Fazi, showed blatant and probably illegal favouritism. A later court decision ruled that the removal of the board at Antonvenuta was invalid and magistrates impounded the shares of BPI, whose chief executive was later arrested. Antonio Fazi was appointed for life but, after mounting pressure, resigned in December 2005. A new governor, Mario Draghi, was appointed but, with a change in the law, given a 6 year term not an appointment for life. The way seemed clear for the bids by ABN Amro and BBVA to proceed, except that a dramatic bid by Banque Nationale de Paris Paribas for BNL in early February 2006 seemed certain to succeed as BBVA appeared to give up its fight. Incidentally, Italian banking is the most expensive in the eurozone for the retail customers.

The Italian bank, UniCredit, took over the German HVB in 2005. As each owned a bank in Poland, UniCredit proposed to merge them. The Polish government refused to give permission and defied the Commissions's disapproval. In the end, what can Brussels do? A legal challenge in the European Court of Justice can be mounted but this takes years.

Early in 2006, things got much worse. Eon, Germany's power group, launched a bid for Spain's Endesa, although a merger between Endesa and Spain's Gas Natural had already been agreed. The Spanish authorities were furious and said that they would block the deal. Italy's ENEL was looking to make a bid for France's Suez group. The French government stepped in to promote a merger between Suez and the state-owned Gaz de France, which would then be privatised. This angered both Italian and French trade unions.

Then France announced that it would give companies the right to use poison pills to frustrate hostile takeover bids from foreign companies, taking advantage of loopholes in the EU Takeover Directive.

Not much convergence in the M&A area then.

Capital markets   In theory, cross-border trading of equities, bonds and investment funds should be easier. So far as bonds are concerned, some progress seems to have been made. Late in 2005, the European Fund and Asset Management Association (EFAMA) said that improvements had been made in the areas of tax treatment, reporting and registrations. A joint report from EFAMA and the professional services firm, PCW, suggested that barriers to a single market in funds were coming down. A previous report in 2001 had listed 20 barriers but now many of these had gone. Tax rates were equalising and double taxation waning. Biggest problems were in Germany, Austria and Denmark.

Regarding general dealing costs, Charles McCreevy, EU's Internal Market and Services Commissioner, wants to cut cross-border dealing costs for all securities. He feels that trading and post trading should be split, which the London Investment Banks Association has long been urging. Trading costs in the US are ⅙ to ⅛ of cross-border costs in Europe. On the question of cross-border clearing and settlement costs, Pierre Francote, Chief Executive Officer for Euroclear said (in a letter to the *Financial Times* in September 2005) that the capital markets in Europe were still much more a juxtaposition of 25 separate markets than an integrated, regional market.

Retail sphere   The European Commission would like to see a unified retail market, allowing people to shop around a number of states for mortgages and insurance policies. The problem in insurance is one of after sales service as well as cultural and language barriers. There are also lots of other local rules such as cooling off periods, consumer rights, compensation and so on. Even the European Consumers Association has lost heart, telling a meeting on this subject, 'Let's drop the dream of a perfectly integrated retail market, it's not going to happen.'

Prices What of prices? The introduction of the euro saw hope that competition would start to equalise prices. A Dresdner Kleinwort Wasserstein report in late 2004 found that prices were still as divergent as in 2001. The average difference in prices across six selected cities was 14.6%. Regarding the costs of banking, a study by ING and Capgemini in mid-2005 found huge variations in the price of core banking services, ranging from an average of €252 a year in Italy to €34 in the Netherlands. Another study, by Mercer Oliver Wyman, compared the average price of keeping a current account in various European countries: €133 in Italy, €94 in France, €86 in Spain and €68 in Germany. However, 50% of Italians share a bank account and British and Dutch banks make more money than Italian on extra services, such as mortgages and consumer loans.

Regulators It would, of course, be easier if, at least, the eurozone had one regulator instead of 12. By mid-2005, a series of so called 'Lamfalussy' committees had been set up for securities (CESR), insurance and pensions (CEIOPS) and banking (CEBS). The idea was to promote regulatory convergence. Also, a Committee of European Services Regulators has been set up to promote more and better cooperation. The idea is to present a single front for discussion with outside regulators like the US SEC on matters like market abuse, retail investment funds, clearing and settlement, accounting standards and company prospectus contents. However, Charles McCreevy, Commissioner for the Internal Market and Services, has said, 'Politically speaking, for the foreseeable future, there is not going to be a single European regulator. It won't be agreed to by the member states.' Attempts are concentrating on more cooperation and clarification of rules.

The European company At last, some progress has been made here. The idea is that groups operating in several states will be able to merge and operate on the basis of a single set of rules and a unified management and reporting system instead of a complex web of subsidiaries subject to different laws. This has been argued about for 30 years, but legislation finally entered into force in October 2004. It is to be known as Societas Europaea (SE). Among the companies that have already made the switch are Sweden's Nordbanken, the Finnish electronics firm Elcoteq and Germany's giant insurer, Allianz. Elcoteq employs 19 000 people in 15 countries. It cannot change their domicile without dissolving itself and incurring a tax charge. It will be able to merge subsidiaries, creating cost savings and efficiencies. Allianz made its decision in September 2005. The management board will have directors of six different nationalities. It wants to buy out minority shareholders in RAS, its Italian subsidiary, and SE provides an easier way to do a cross-border merger. Allianz hopes to save several millions of euros as a result. They no longer have to have subsidiary companies in each European country where they operate. Others considering the move are Suez, SAP and DaimlerChrysler.

One final point – an SE must conform to the rules of the country of domicile for tax, insolvency rules, auditing and accounting.

The four freedoms   From all the above it can be seen that the position on convergence is not at all encouraging and – for the EU/EMU enthusiast – depressing. Katinka Barysch, chief economist at the London-based Centre for European Reform, said in January 2006 that protectionism is on the rise since the ten new states were brought in. There is now a wide gulf between high and low wage economies. She asked whether the EU today would reaffirm its support for the four freedoms that are enshrined in the Treaty of Rome – capital, goods, services and people. 'If we were to write a new treaty today, would we be able to get these clauses accepted? I'm not sure.'

The European Commission is valiantly combating protectionism and trying to improve convergence through a series of new directives. We will look at these after considering the current position of new and prospective members, a summary of banking trends since EMU and the position of London's financial market.

New and Prospective Members

Ten new countries joined the EU in 2004, but will they join the eurozone? Before doing so, prospective members must join the ERM II system for two years. Six new members have done so – Cyprus, Estonia, Latvia, Lithuania, Malta and Slovenia. Slovakia has started talks but the Czech Republic and Hungary have delayed a decision until, perhaps, 2009. To qualify for the eurozone, apart from two years in ERM II, they must have inflation within 1.5% of the best three EMU members and a budget deficit less than 3%. Slovenia will be the first and will join the eurozone in 2007. It had been anticipated that Lithuania would also be admitted, but it was turned down on the grounds that inflation was within 1.6% of the best three and not 1.5%. Naturally this decision was greeted with anger, and not just by Lithuania. There was resentment at one rule for the big coountries – ignoring the breaking of the Stability and Growth Pact – and tighter rules for the small. Indeed, at the Brussels meeting in June 2006, five new members joined forces to criticise the blocking of Lithuania's bid to join the eurozone – the Czech Republic, Hungary, Lithuania, Poland and Slovakia. Their view, however, was not accepted by the bigger powers. All the Baltic states joined ERM II and looked likely to be early eurozone members, but have slipped a little. Hungary, with inflation of 7%, looks a long way from membership.

Possible new members for the EU as a whole include Albania, Bosnia, Belarus, Bulgaria, Croatia, Georgia, Herzegovina, Moldova, Montenegro, Romania, Serbia, Turkey and Ukraine. The fact that they are on the list does not mean that membership is imminent, although Bulgaria/Romania may not be far away. Another problem is that the Treaty of Nice does not provide for any enlargement beyond 27 countries – there is no system for allocating voting rights or numbers in parliament. So, after Bulgaria and Romania, what then? France, Germany and Austria have little enthusiasm for more members until the whole constitution question is resolved. One possibility is a looser membership category under 'European Neighbourhood Policy'. This gives access to the single market plus financial and technical aid in return for reforms bringing them nearer to EU political and economic models. Apart from the above countries, it might apply to some countries of North Africa, the Mediterranean, Eastern Europe and the Southern Caucasus.

The most important (and most vexed) question is that of Turkey. After much argument, talks began in October 2005. One of the main arguments for not inviting countries to join is that of human rights, which has applied here. In addition, some countries fear an influx of low-paid workers and some are against the admission of an Islamic state into so called 'Christian' Europe. Successfully integrated, however, it would show Islam to be compatible with Western democracy, would aid settlement in Cyprus and would extend the EU into the Southern Caucasus and help to stabilise oil and gas pipeline routes from the Caspian. On the other hand, rejection could move Turkey nearer to fundamentalist Islam. The outlook is not good due to hostility from France, Austria and Denmark in particular.

To end on a more positive note, a detailed study by Joaquim Almunia, EU Monetary Affairs Commissioner, published in May 2006, concluded that the 'big bang' enlargement from 15 to 25 countries had been a clear cut economic success. It had boosted growth and increased trade. The incomes of the ten new members had risen from 44% of the average for the old EU to 50%. Poland and the Czech Republic, in particular, had increased exports to the old EU considerably. Equally, the West European countries had increased trade to the East and still enjoyed big trade surpluses. The commission also repeated its claims that the Western migration by workers from the new member states had been beneficial to those countries that kept their borders open – the UK, Ireland and Sweden. That not everyone believes this can be seen from the fact that, by June 2006, only seven countries of the previous 15 members had opened their borders to the new members.

Banking Trends

In a special supplement to the *Banker* magazine in July 2005, Eden Riche, an MD within the Royal Bank of Scotland, outlined some key trends in banking since the formation of the eurozone.

Using some figures from Dealogic, he pointed to changes in the bond market in the EMU area. Sovereign and supranational issues, which had been 25% of all issues in 1995, were down to 8% by end 2004, with issues involving special purpose vehicles as much as 15%. Total bond issues which were $439 billion in 1995 had risen to $2023 billion in 2004.

The banks were increasingly taking a role as intermediaries instead of principals and thus commercial and investment banking were merging. Other figures from Dealogic revealed that the top ten underwriters in 1995 included only three commercial banks, but the top ten in 2004 had seven.

Finally, Riche saw the rise of what he calls 'commoditisation' – a range of standard products competing on price and distribution capability.

London's Financial Market

As we saw earlier, one argument for the UK joining the eurozone was the possibility of a threat to the dominance of London's financial market and competition from Frankfurt. As we saw, EUROLIBOR has lost out as a reference rate to EURIBOR. Apart from this though, London seems to have tightened its position since 1999 for a variety of reasons:

1   9/11 has increased mutual suspicions. The Middle East buyers fear asset seizures and are directing deals in US assets through intermediaries in London.
2   Sarbanes-Oxley has put a huge competitive burden on the NYSE and NASDAQ. Delisting is expensive and difficult. Figures from Dealogic show that, in 1999/2000, IPOs in the US raised $80 billion, ten times that raised in London, but in 2005 the US figure was only $6 billion against London's $10.3 billion.
3   London's freer labour laws have made it a more attractive location than many European centres.
4   London's domination of the world's foreign exchange markets continues, with 31.3% in the latest BIS survey as opposed to Frankfurt's 4.9%, and it continues as the main centre for Eurobond dealings. In general, big banks have shifted wholesale staff to London. BNP Paribas, for instance, has far more staff in London than Paris.

European Commission Directives

As we commented earlier, the European Commission continues its efforts to make the EU and EMU more of a reality with various directives.

The Markets in Financial Instruments known as 'MIFID', is one of the most important. It is supposed to be implemented by the spring of 2007 but may be delayed to allow time for further consultation. Its purpose is to open up Europe's financial markets by improving transparency and making it easier to trade cross-border. This will let banks and investment groups authorised in their home market offer financial services across the EU without further accreditation. It will require massive changes to computer systems and compliance systems. It deals with a host of issues – investment advice, equity market transparency, conflicts of interest, best execution, compliance, consumer protection and record keeping. Along with Basel II and new accountancy standards, the banks to which this applies face considerable development costs. Bob Fuller, head of IT at Dresdner Kleinwort Wasserstein says MIFID 'is the biggest piece of financial services legislation ever passed in the world'. The most significant change is that investment firms will no longer be required to route orders exclusively through stock exchanges. This could prove a threat to stock exchanges and one that has not so far aroused particular attention.

The *Single Euro Payments Area* (SEPA)　This is a plan to make small value payments through the EU from a single bank account and a single universal system. It will cover direct debits and credit transfers. At present, moving money across borders is ludicrously expensive – all national systems are separate from cross-border. This would, for example, make the sale of products like life insurance much easier. Charles McCreevy, the European Internal Market and Services Commissioner, believes that savings to users will be in a range of €50 billion to €100 billion per year. Naturally, the banks who charge the high prices will lose revenue and have to pay an estimated cost of €8 billion to develop the system. The rules are being finalised by the main EU banks under the auspices of a body called the European Payments Council, consisting of 60 banks. They are preparing a new legal framework and hope to introduce this in 2008.

EU Services Directive　This addresses the breaking down of national barriers for service providers and was agreed in May 2006. It will allow total recognition of the qualifications of professions – accountants, plumbers, electricians, caterers, consultants – who find it impossible to offer their services abroad. Services are said to be two thirds of Europe's jobs and economic activity. The service provider was to be subject only to home country regulation. Commission President, José Manuel Barroso, put detailed proposals forward for discussion in 2006 and said, 'We believe a properly functioning services market, together with SME (small and medium enterprises) reforms, are the most important drivers for the creation of jobs in Europe.' However, France, with its usual protective instincts, strongly opposed the move, as did European trade unions generally, and the idea that the service provider will be subject only to home country regulation was heavily modified after rejection by the European Parliament. One useful improvement is that service providers will no longer need to set up an office in each country in which they operate.

When the French rejected the constitution in May 2005, one reason was discontent with what they saw as the EU's increasingly 'liberal' policies, and worry about scrapping restrictions on cross-border services was a big factor. The fact that a compromise was reached at all was seen by many as a return to the 'European spirit'. It may not be what many had hoped for, but at least there will be fewer obstacles to doing cross-border business.

Savings Tax　In mid-2005 a Savings Tax Directive was passed. EU states and others either share information with others about non-resident savings in their country or will impose a withholding tax, initially 15% (Austria, Belgium, Luxembourg and Switzerland). Surprisingly, some tax havens like the Cayman Islands, British Virgin Islands, Jersey, Guernsey and the Isle of Man have adopted the directive. It applies to bank deposits, corporate and government bonds and some investment funds, but not pensions or dividend incomes.

Patents   There has been a year of total deadlock over the creation of a low cost EU-wide patent. The absence of such a patent is a major complaint of business leaders. The cost of registering patents across the EU has been estimated at between €37 500 and €57 000. To register a US patent is the equivalent of €10 000.

Pensions   An EU Pensions Directive has already been passed. Each state is free to define what it expects of an occupational pension – the product itself, therefore, is not covered by the directive but the provider is. It is not a detailed directive but concentrates on qualitative concepts rather than quantitative. There is a general obligation on member states to cooperate with each other as supervisors and to define pension product requirements clearly. The EU is trying to put occupational pensions in an EU context while respecting local standards. It applies the 'EU passport' idea – one single licence to operate throughout the EU under home state control. Whether it will have much impact remains to be seen since the provisions are very general. The directive was passed in mid-2003 and countries should have implemented it in local law by end 2005. In fact, by the end of 2005, less than half the EU states had done so.

The last sentence reminds us that the EU Commission can pass directives (unless challenged by the parliament) but they do need to be passed by 25 local parliaments and this is often a problem. An EU report in July 2005 showed that Italy was the worst country for implementation. It has failed to implement 66 directives. Worst performers, apart from Italy, are the Czech Republic, Greece, Luxembourg and Portugal. Generally, directives on biotechnical inventions and mutual recognition of professions had not been implemented for several years.

COULD THE EURO FAIL?

The poor progress towards the achievement of the 'four freedoms' that we saw above, together with the disappointing economic performance of the eurozone, has led some people to think the unthinkable – could the euro fail? We seem now to be hearing some people moving from thinking it to articulating it.

How does a country stop using the euro and go back to its own currency? This was examined by Anatole Kaletsky in the *Financial Times* in August 2005. While Mr Kaletsky is by no means a fan of EMU, the article was quite dispassionate. The legal angle is of key importance – can Italy recreate the lira legally? Hal Scott of the Harvard Law School and Charles Proctor of London law firm Nabarro Nathanson produced a chapter on this topic for a legal bible on international law – *Mann on the Legal Aspect of Money*. Both agree that Italy would have the legal right to recreate its own currency. The government would be entitled to rewrite Italian financial contracts, including government bonds, into new lira. Holders of Italy's €1.5 trillion public debt would face severe losses, possibly threatening the solvency of many banks.

Presumably not many investors think this a practical possibility, since the yield on Italian government bonds over Germany is still only 21 basis points (although this has widened from only 6). Many banks have picked up risk-free profits from buying Italian government bonds and going short of their German equivalent.

In December 2005, Standard and Poor's seemed to offer a different view. It looked at two uncompetitive economies – Italy and Greece – and supposed an exit from the euro on the last day of 2006. The new lira and drachma would have a devaluation of 27% and 49% respectively against the euro. Competitiveness would be regained but S&P assume that government debt must legally be repaid in euros. Public debt would jump to levels that would cause a fall in credit ratings. Neither government could service these debts without considerable strain. Whether it would be legal or not to change the public debt to a new currency doesn't alter the fact that it would provoke a huge crisis.

Anatole Kaletsky had earlier reported that, at the meeting at Lake Como of various EU political and financial leaders in September 2004, he noted a change. He saw, for the first time since the launching of the euro in 1999, 'the single currency's long term survival being seriously questioned'. The concerns lurked beneath the surface rather than being openly expressed. There has been much open speculation in Italy on this question and in a *Der Stern* opinion poll in Germany, 56% of Germans wanted the deutschmark back.

In January 2006, a former EU External Market Commissioner from 1999–2004, Frits Bolkenstein, a Dutchman, made a speech to Dutch business leaders in London. He predicted that the euro would face a huge test in ten years – a massive growth of people hitting pensionable age in Europe. Italy is especially unprepared for the jump in pension claims. Governments would have to borrow more, increasing the budget deficit and leading to more inflation and higher interest rates. He concluded, 'In my view, the long-term chances of survival of the euro should be seriously questioned.'

Having said all that, arch-critic Anatole Kaletsky admitted that at the Davos conference in January 2006, European leaders seemed to have a new confidence. They had had a better 2005 economically than most people (including himself) had predicted. The 'social market model' beloved of France and others had survived the so-called Anglo-Saxon threat. One answer may be that European companies have been restructuring their businesses to meet the new threats, making them more innovative and efficient. Certainly, stock markets had had a good year and profits were up. A second answer may lie in the continuing boom in the US and China causing a demand for Europe's exports, especially Germany's. A further reason for good performance lies in retail spending caused by the house price boom. This has been important for countries like France, Italy and Spain whose export performance was weak. Mr Kaletsky points out that a house price slowdown and reduced growth in the US and China could lead to a different result for 2006. The US and China could be hit by higher interest rates (in the US) and the lagged effect of high oil prices.

SUMMARY

The origins of the European Union as it is today lie in the *European Coal and Steel Community* in 1952, a pooling of coal and steel resources in Belgium, France, Italy, Luxembourg, the Netherlands and West Germany. These six countries signed the *Treaty of Rome* in 1957 and began the concept of a common market and the *European Economic Community*. Its early institutions included the *Council of Ministers*, the *European Commission*, the *European Parliament* and the *European Court of Justice*. The motives were economic and political.

Enlargement of membership came later with the addition of Denmark, Ireland and the UK in 1973, Greece in 1981, Spain and Portugal in 1986 and Austria, Finland and Sweden in 1995.

In 1974, the periodic meeting of heads of state became the *European Council*. Today it meets twice per year, with the presidency rotating six monthly between the various states.

The *Single European Act* of 1987 (which came into force in January 1993) aimed to eliminate all final barriers to trade within Europe, and to establish a genuinely efficient and competitive single market.

The European Economic Community (EEC) had already been shortened to *European Community* (EC). With the Single European Act it became the *European Union* (EU).

Later, in mid-2004, ten new countries joined the EU – Cyprus, the Czech Republic, Estonia, Hungary, Latvia, Lithuania, Malta, Poland, Slovakia and Slovenia. However, free movement of labour from these countries was postponed to 2009 other than to Ireland, Finland, Greece, Portugal, Spain, Sweden and the UK.

The first moves to a single currency and monetary union were suggested in the *Werner Report* of 1970, proposing a single currency by 1980. Upheaval in the 1970s (the collapse of Bretton Woods and oil price inflation) prevented any progress.

The next move was the *European Monetary System* in 1979. This set up the use of the ECU as a common unit of accountancy, and also the *Exchange Rate Mechanism* (ERM) tying currencies to bands around a target rate against other currencies. The bands were $\pm 2\frac{1}{4}\%$ or $\pm 6\%$. By the end of 1990, eleven of Europe's twelve countries were members.

Attacks on currencies in the ERM in 1992 and 1993 led to a revision of the band to $\pm 15\%$ (except for the guilder/deutschemark rate, remaining at $\pm 2\frac{1}{4}\%$).

In 1989, a report by Jacques Delors, the Commission president, set out steps towards economic and monetary union. A treaty at *Maastricht* laid down convergence conditions, the setting up of a *European Monetary Institute* (EMI) in 1994 to precede the *European Central Bank* and the possibility of *Economic and Monetary Union* (EMU) beginning in 1999. It was later decided to call the new currency the 'euro'.

Following detailed plans laid down by the EMI, economic and monetary union began on 1 January 1999.

Initially, the euro was used for interbank and other wholesale purposes, with notes and coins following on 1 January, 2002. In the meantime, the relevant currencies were locked together in fixed exchange rates.

Eleven countries joined the new system – Austria, Belgium, Finland, France, Ireland, Italy, Germany, Luxembourg, the Netherlands, Portugal and Spain. Denmark, Greece, Sweden and the United Kingdom remained outside. (Greece joined later and so EMU now covers twelve countries.)

The European Central Bank (ECB) began operations in June 1998. It has six executive members who form the Executive Board. They meet with the twelve governors of the member states to form the Governing Council. This grouping of the ECB together with the twelve governors is usually called the *European System of Central Banks* (ESCB). However, the ECB has pointed out that legally this includes the governors of the non-EMU states, even though they play no part. It prefers to use the name *Eurosystem*.

To prevent excessive budget deficits, there is a *Stability and Growth Pact*, which limits budget deficits to a maximum of 3% in relation to GDP although this has so far proved to be ineffective as half of the countries in the eurozone have exceeded the limit.

Those countries wishing to join EMU are expected to have spent two years in the successor to the ERM, known as *ERM II*.

The EMU area has a population of 312 million people, as against 294 million in the United States, and it accounts for 16.2% of world GDP, as against the US which accounts for 21.9%.

The new interbank payment and settlement system for the euro is *TARGET*.

The objective of EMU is to produce a range of benefits – price transparency leading to more competition; a logical completion of the move towards a single competitive market; a saving in foreign currency transactions; a reduction of the cost of capital through more efficient capital markets – bonds, equities and derivatives. In addition, there is the desire for more political integration to make EMU work better and to produce a stronger and more peaceful Europe.

Critics, however, point to the problems of a 'one size fits all' policy in interest rates and currencies; the strains in fiscal policy that will emerge; the lack of labour mobility; some weaknesses in the structure of the ECB; the fact that full price transparency will not exist due to VAT and transport costs and weakness in Europe due to high social costs, inflexible labour markets and a large public sector. These problems will be worsened by enlargement of the euro area.

The major EU country not in EMU is the United Kingdom.

Those in the UK who wish to join want to continue to encourage foreign investment in the UK; to enjoy lower forex costs; to have greater stability of the currency; and believe that the UK outside would lose influence and the City of London lose ground to Frankfurt.

Others believe that the threat to foreign investment is exaggerated; that the lower forex costs are modest compared to the total picture; that there will still be currency instability against the dollar, yen and Swiss franc and that the London dominance in financial markets will not be affected. Finally, they believe the UK will suffer from the 'one size fits all' policy and fear greater political integration.

Later, the EU governments drew up a constitution which was published in 2004. The rejection of this in referendums in France and Holland created a major crisis which has not yet been resolved.

It is now possible to set up a company which will trade across the whole EU as a single entity, the *Societas Europaea (SE)*.

The great hopes of the EC and EMU for four freedoms – of capital, goods, labour and services, have not yet been fulfilled.

The European Commission has pressed on with a series of directives to help rectify this – the Market in Financial Instruments (MIFID), the Single European Payments Area (SEPA) and the Services Directive are the most important.

There has been some talk of the possibility of a country abandoning the euro and returning to its old currency. There are serious legal obstacles and such a country would face a financial crisis.

Derivative Products

12 Traded Options

13 Financial Futures

14 Other Derivative Products

12 Traded Options

Probably the fastest growing sector of the financial markets today is that of what are called *derivative products*. They are so called because they derive from another product. The buying of $1 million for sterling is the product. The option to buy $1 million for sterling later at a price we agree today is the derived product. Borrowing $1 million at floating rate for five years is the product. A bank offering (for a fee) to compensate the borrower should rates rise above a given level in the next five years is the derived product – and so on.

In currency rates, interest rates, bonds, equities and equity indices there is volatility. Where there is volatility, there are those who believe they know what the next price movement is and back their judgement with money. We call them *speculators*. There are those who will lose money from a given price movement and seek to protect themselves from this. We call them *hedgers*. Both will use the derivative markets for this purpose. The interesting paradox is that one is using them to take risks and the other to reduce risks. Finally, there are those who perceive pricing anomalies and seek to exploit this. They are the *arbitrageurs*.

Thus, the three types of professional users of derivative products are:

- ❏ Speculators
- ❏ Hedgers
- ❏ Arbitrageurs.

Additionally, derivatives are being increasingly packaged with retail banking products to provide, for example, fixed rate mortgages or guaranteed investment funds.

Speculators are easy enough to understand but, before we look at hedgers and arbitrageurs, it will be as well to explain one of the derivative products first.

The two key products are *options* and *futures*. If readers can obtain a good working knowledge of these products, they are well placed to understand others (FRAs, swaps, caps) since they are simply variations on the options and futures themes.

This chapter will discuss options, Chapter 13 covers futures and Chapter 14 the remaining derivative products.

One last point. In Chapter 9, we mentioned that currency options could be purchased on a trading exchange or OTC, that is, direct with a bank or trader. While this was mentioned in the context of currency options, it is generally true that there are exchanges for traded options and financial futures but that these products can also be purchased OTC.

The advantage of a trading exchange is that there is plenty of trading liquidity, there are competing traders to ensure good prices, and there is the implicit protection against default provided by a body called the *clearing house*. The disadvantage is that the products are standardised and may not suit the user's exact requirements. To take an example that we've already met, the cable contract on the Chicago Mercantile Exchange is based on multiples of £62 500. This means that if the amount required to be bought or sold for dollars is £75 000, then the product offered is not an exact fit.

The big advantage of OTC dealing is its flexibility. The product offered to the users can be tailored to their exact needs. On an exchange, however, it may be possible to 'trade' the product later – that is, sell it back to the exchange. Sometimes OTC products cannot be traded or, if they can, the user is very much in the hands of the seller for a price. This market is often accused of a lack of liquidity when it comes to trading even standardised products at a later stage. Finally, the user must consider the risk of default. If the seller is Deutsche Bank or UBS, we can be quite happy, but the US house Drexel Burnham Lambert crashed in February 1990 and defaulted on any OTC products outstanding. On the other hand, when Baring Bros defaulted on their obligations at the Singapore Monetary Exchange (SIMEX), no counterparties lost any money due to the operation of the clearing house.

In an effort to counteract the flexibility of OTC, some exchanges have introduced more flexible contacts themselves. In 1995, the Philadelphia Exchange introduced the possibility of tailored exercise prices and expiry dates. Similar moves have followed from other exchanges.

Let us turn now to the subject of options.

TRADED OPTIONS: EQUITIES

Calls and Puts

Traded options are standardised options which grant the buyer the right (but not the obligation) to buy or sell financial instruments at standard prices and dates in the future. A premium is charged for this right, and is usually paid when the option is bought.

Let us take a simple example. Suppose we look at a hypothetical UK company, XYZ Ltd, and the share price is £1.86. We may be optimistic and believe that the price may well rise to, say, £2.10 in the next three months. The option to *buy* a given quantity of XYZ Ltd shares at £1.86 in the next three months is very attractive. If we are right and the price goes to £2.10, we can use the option to buy the given quantity of shares at £1.86 and sell them again in the conventional way at £2.10. If we are wrong and the price falls or remains constant, we don't have to do anything as it was only an option, not an obligation. This is clearly a privileged position, and we must pay for it. The price we pay is the *premium* for the option. This right to *buy* a financial product later is the *call* option. We buy a call when we wish to gain from an increase in price later.

We may, alternatively, be pessimistic about XYZ Ltd and believe that the price of £1.86 will probably fall to £1.60 in the next three months. The option to *sell* a given quantity of XYZ Ltd shares at £1.86 in the next three months is very attractive. If we are correct, we can buy them later for £1.60 and use the option to sell them at £1.86. If we are wrong and the price rises or remains constant, we don't have to do anything as it was only an option, not an obligation. Again, we pay a premium for this privilege. The right to *sell* a financial product later is the *put* option. We buy a put when we wish to gain from a fall in price later.

Let's look at some figures. Suppose the call or put contract is for 1000 shares and that the premium in each case is 10p per share. We'll look at the call and the put in turn.

Call option We have the right to buy 1000 XYZ Ltd shares within the next 3 months at £1.86 and pay a premium of 10p per share (= £100) up front.

XYZ Ltd share price later:

£1.60?   ◄——————— £1.86 ———————►   £2.10?

Suppose the price falls to £1.60 and we have come to the end of the three months. The right to buy at £1.86 is of no value as we can buy them at the market price of £1.60. The option will expire. There is no action to take – we just abandon our option. Our loss is the premium of £100 (which we've already paid). Notice that whatever happens, we *can't lose more than the premium*.

Suppose the price rises later to £2.10? Now, we can contact our broker, advise them that we are exercising our option to buy 1000 shares at £1.86 and ask them to sell them in the usual way for £2.10 (no further capital needs to be paid). We have made 1000 × (£2.10 - £1.86) = 1000 × 24p = £240. We paid a premium of £100 so the net gain is £140 or 140% (for convenience, dealing costs have been ignored).

The share price rose 24p from £1.86, a rise of about 13%. This rise of 13% generated us a profit of 140%. This effect is called *gearing*, which we met in Chapter 1 (the Americans call it *leverage*). In general, it's making a given sum of money go further. It's well summed up in the American expression 'more bang for your buck'! In Chapter 1, we looked at balance sheet gearing – making money go further by borrowing other people's money. This is another example. If we had bought 1000 XYZ Ltd shares, we would have paid £1860. We backed our view on £1860 of shares with just £100 premium. In addition (at least in theory) the remaining £1760 can be in the bank earning interest. The result, as in the above case, is that a small change in the price of the underlying asset (13%) may lead to a large percentage profit gain (140%). However, gearing cuts both ways. A small fall in price of just, say, 4% could result in 100% loss of our premium! Nevertheless, gearing is a big attraction in derivative products.

Put option We now have paid for the right to sell 1000 XYZ Ltd shares within the next three months at £1.86 and pay a premium of 10p per share (= £100) up front.

XYZ Ltd share price later:

£1.60?   £1.86   £2.10?

At this point the reader might wonder how we can buy the right to sell shares that we don't even own. We shall find that not only is this not a problem, it is part of the beauty of the put option!

Suppose the price rises to £2.10 and we have come to the end of the option period. We have the right to sell 1000 shares at £1.86. If we had the shares (which we don't), we could sell them on the market for £2.10. Our right is of no value and will expire, losing the premium of £100.

Suppose the price falls later to £1.60. We have the right to sell 1000 shares at £1.86 but don't actually own any. What we do, of course, is buy 1000 shares in the conventional way at £1.60 and use the option to sell them at £1.86, making 26p per share or a net 16p after deducting our cost of 10p per share. Our profit is £160 or 160% although the change in share price was only about 14%.

Option Writers

Who, in the first instance, sells us the XYZ Ltd shares at £1.86 when the market price is £2.10? Who, in the second instance, buys our shares from us at £1.86 when the market price is £1.60? The answer is the person who sold us the option in the first place, called the *writer* of the option. They took our premium and believed that it was a good price for the risk.

There are, thus, four possibilities in the option game. One can buy calls or puts and one can write calls or puts. The risk profile is quite different for buyers and writers:

	Maximum loss	*Maximum gain*
Buyers of options	The premium	Unlimited
Writers of options	Unlimited	The premium

Because the writers of options face unlimited risk, they pay a deposit, called *margin*, to the clearing house. When the deal is opened they pay *initial margin*. If the price moves against them they must pay more margin – *variation margin* – to cover their losses. If they go into liquidation, the deal is honoured by the clearing house.

Trading Options

In the above cases, we either abandoned our option or exercised it. On a trading exchange, there is the further choice of *trading the option*.

Let's illustrate this, and some of the real life complications, by looking at the prices that might be quoted for XYZ Ltd shares at any one time on London's Euronext.liffe exchange. The exchange deals in the shares of about 87 UK companies and also offers options on the main share index, the FTSE 100 (to be explained later) as well as many other contracts.

The position is more complicated than in our previous example:

❏ There is a choice of share prices at which calls/puts can be bought/written. They are called *exercise* or *strike* prices. There is a choice of dates for expiry of the contract. Three dates are offered to a maximum of nine months ahead.
❏ Options must be dealt in set multiples or standard contract sizes (typically 1000 shares on Euronext.liffe, but varying by exchange).
❏ Options can be traded – that is, sold back to the market for a later premium.
❏ Having bought an option, it can be exercised at any time prior to the expiry date. This is called an *American* option. (It's nothing to do with America! Most options on European exchanges are American options.)

Let's first look at the matrix of choice and assume that we came to the market on 27 March and looked at options for XYZ Ltd (Table 12.1).

Table 12.1 XYZ Ltd, *call options, 27 March*

Market price	Exercise price	Exercise expiry dates		
		April	July	October
	180			
186	200			
	220			

Notice that we have standardised exercise prices of £1.80, £2.00 and £2.20 (in reality there might be several more, but these would tend to be the most liquid). None of them is the market price (£1.86) except by coincidence. We have a further choice of expiry in April, July or October – a maximum of seven months. Had we come to the market on 1 February, we would still have seen April, July and October and hence, our maximum time horizon of nine months.

There are thus nine choices and for each there is a quoted premium in pence per share. Suppose the premiums for all three exercise prices were the same? Naturally, we would pick the exercise price of £1.80 since we all like to be able to buy at the cheapest price. It will be no surprise to find that the premium for £1.80 is more expensive than that for £2.00 and much more expensive than that for £2.20. Again, suppose the premiums for all the three expiry dates were the same? Naturally, we would pick October to give XYZ Ltd the maximum time to go up in price. For the same reason, the writer of the option (who is not stupid!) wants a higher premium for October than April.

Let's look now at the full list of prices in Table 12.2.

On 27 March, the right to buy XYZ Ltd shares at £1.80 before an expiry in April costs 16p per share. For the minimum contract of 1000 shares this is £160. On 27 March, the right to buy XYZ Ltd shares at £2.00 before an expiry in October costs 21p per share. For the minimum contract, this is £210. Notice the gearing. To *buy* 1000 XYZ Ltd shares today would cost £1860.

Table 12.2   XYZ Ltd, *call options, 27 March*

Market price	Exercise price	April	July calls	October
	180	16	24	32
186	200	7	14	21
	220	3	7	12

Which of these nine options do we choose? There is no magic answer. It depends how strongly you feel XYZ Ltd is undervalued, how soon you think the price will rise, and how risk averse you are.

You could choose £1.80, already cheaper than the stock market price and October expiry, giving the largest time for XYZ Ltd to go up in price. It looks attractive but at £320 per 1000 shares is the most expensive.

At the other extreme, you could choose £2.20 and expiry in April. This is 34p dearer than the stock market price and there are perhaps only 4 weeks to the expiry date. It doesn't look attractive but it's cheap at £30 per 1000 shares.

Intrinsic Value and Time Value

The £1.80 option is already 6p cheaper than the market price of £1.86. We can argue, therefore, that the premium must be at least 6p. Suppose the premium was 4p. You would buy as many options as you could possibly afford and immediately exercise, buying the shares for £1.80 and selling for £1.86. An obvious profit of 6p for a cost of 4p. No chance! The market has a piece of jargon for this 6p – it's called *intrinsic value*. This occurs when the call exercise price is cheaper than the market price or a put exercise price is dearer than the market price.

The option premium for the April expiry is 16p. We know that it must be at least 6p and can see that 10p has been added to cover the possibility of XYZ Ltd going up in price prior to expiry. We call this the *time value* in the option. The exercise price of £2 is dearer than the market price and it has no intrinsic value (we don't use negative intrinsic value).

Breaking the premium down like this, into intrinsic value and time value, let's look at the £1.80 calls for April, July and October and the £2.00 calls for the same expiry dates in Table 12.3.

Table 12.3   *£1.80 and £2.00 calls for April, July and October*

Exercise price	Expiry	Intrinsic value		Time value		Premium
180	April	6	+	10	=	16
	July	6	+	18	=	24
	October	6	+	26	=	32
200	April	0	+	7	=	7
	July	0	+	14	=	14
	October	0	+	21	=	21

We can see how time value goes up steadily for later expiry dates.

Calculation of the Premium

Where does this time value come from? How are the premiums calculated?

Usually, in human activity, if we want to forecast the future, we start with the past: as T.S. Eliot tells us, 'In my beginning, is my end.' We look at the previous behaviour of the share price, say over the last 6 months, and project this forward using statistical techniques and laws of probability. These may suggest that there is a given probability that the XYZ Ltd share price in October will be within a given range. We look at the exercise price, the current market price, one or two other factors we don't need to go into, and the statistical calculations use the past behaviour to produce a theoretical or *fair value* for the premium. There may then be a question of whether the option writer believes that future price behaviour will be different, and also sheer demand and supply. If there are more option buyers than sellers, premiums will rise, and vice-versa. Experts will compare the market premiums with the fair value premiums and decide if the premiums look cheap or expensive.

These statistical techniques were developed in May 1973 when Fischer Black and Myron Scholes wrote a paper on the pricing of options in the *Journal of Political Economy*. The Black-Scholes formula, with one or two possible modifications, is still widely used to calculate premiums. Black and Scholes were professors at the

University of Chicago and the timing was apt as the Chicago Board Options Exchange had started trading options in April 1973. A few years later, more professors appeared – Messrs Cox, Ross and Rubenstein. (They were also assisted by Professor Robert Merton. In October 1997, Scholes and Merton received the Nobel Prize for their work. Black was not included as the prize is never awarded posthumously and, unfortunately, Black died the previous year.) They produced a similar formula (one based on a binomial progression for those who understand such things). Other areas of probability theory are also used, for example, Monte Carlo simulation. David Gershon, chief executive of SuperDerivatives, promotes alternative formulae for foreign exchange and interest rate options. In late 2005, he made these available on the Internet so that investors could check quoted prices from dealers. The experts argue about the merits of one formula as opposed to another; for the lay person, the results are very similar. (For more technical information, consult the companion website mentioned at the beginning of the book.)

In looking at the past behaviour of two shares, one may be much more volatile than another although the average price may be similar in each case. The more volatile share may produce higher or lower share prices later than the less volatile one and thus the premium will be higher. Look at Figure 12.1.

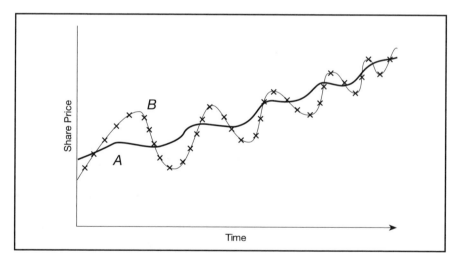

Figure 12.1   *Price behaviour of two shares, A and B*

For the writer of the option, share *B* is clearly more dangerous and risky than share *A,* even though the average price over time is much the same. Without knowing anything about statistics, we can accept that the option premiums quoted for share *B* will be higher than for share *A*. Those who understand statistics will be aware that this volatility is the standard deviation and a key element in the pricing formula. Experts will analyse market premiums to see the *implied volatility*. They will then decide if they agree with this figure, bearing in mind that future volatility may not be the same as past or *historic volatility*. These are advanced considerations that need not concern us in an introductory text. Be aware, however, that 'volatility' is a big word in the options game. Indeed, in September 2005, the Eurex exchange launched contracts that were based on the implied volatility in the equity index contracts in the German, Swiss and pan-European markets. This enables traders to trade volatility itself.

Volatility is usually quoted as a percentage figure, for example, 20%. This would mean that, over 1 year, there is a 68% chance in laws of probability that a share price will be either 20% higher or lower than the starting price.

Suppose a share price is £1.00 and the volatility is 20%. The premium for a 1 year call option, the right to buy the share at £1.00 within the next year, would be 9.9p per share. If the volatility were 40%, the premium would be 17.1p.

(The above assumes 10% interest rates and 5% dividend yield, factors that are also taken into account.)

The Russian crisis of August 1998 is an example of how the volatilities of financial instruments can change. The Hong Kong and Shanghai Banking Corporation (HSBC) estimated the volatility of the UK's FTSE 100 index in July 1998 at 20%. Two months later, following the Russian crisis, it was 40%. Its range in 1995/96 was just 12% to 15%. In 2002, after two years of dramatic daily movements and large annual falls, the market was estimating volatility of the FTSE 100 at 25%–30%. As option premiums go up as volatility rises, this means that just as people are looking for protection because the situation has become more uncertain, protection costs a lot more!

Exercise or Trade?

Going back to the XYZ Ltd prices on 27 March, let's assume that we bought a call option with exercise price £1.80 and expiry in July. Let's also assume that it's the minimum of one contract, that is, 1000 shares. The premium is quoted as 24 and so we will pay £240 plus broker's commission and a small charge for the costs of the clearing house.

(The premiums are actually quoted with a bid/offer spread so that 24 may be a mid-point representing a quote of 23/25. We will ignore this in the interests of simplicity.)

Let's move on now to 6 June in the same year. We can look at the current call option premiums in Table 12.4.

We see that the April month has gone and been replaced by January, the next month in the series. We also note that the share price has gone up 20p and the £1.80/July call premium is now quoted as 36.

If we are new to options, this might puzzle us. We could argue that, as the share price has gone up 20p, the right to buy at £1.80 must be 20p more valuable. If the old premium was 24, it should now be 44. To understand what is happening to the premium we must break it down into intrinsic value and time value and compare the positions on 27 March and 6 June. We can see this in Table 12.5.

Table 12.4 *XYZ Ltd call options, 6 June*

Market price	Exercise price	July	October	January
	180	36	44	52
206	200	18	28	38
	220	6	13	24

Table 12.5 *Breaking down premium into intrinsic and time value*

Premium date	Market price	Intrinsic value		Time value		Premium
27 March	186	6	+	18	=	24
6 June	206	26	+	10	=	36

We can see that intrinsic value has gone up by 20 but time value down by 8, giving a net increase of 12. The time value is down simply because, at 6 June, there is less time left to expiry. If we need more time value for more time, as we saw earlier, then we need less time value for less time.

It is most important to grasp this. It means that there is an element in the premium, the time value, *which is steadily going down*, regardless of what is happening to the share price. There is an element, intrinsic value, which may be going *up* or *down* – that depends on the share price movement. Since we may *trade* the option, that is, receive the quoted premium, we must understand its behaviour.

Suppose we decide to take profit at this point, We have two choices – *exercise* the option or *trade* it. Let's examine each in turn.

If we exercise the option, we buy 1000 shares at £1.80 and sell them at the market price of £2.06, making 26p per share, ignoring dealing costs. As the option cost is 24p per share, our profit is 2p.

If we trade the option, we sell it back for 36p, today's quoted premium. As the option cost is 24p per share, our profit is 12p.

In the first case we make £20 and in the second, £120. Why was trading more profitable? When we exercise we buy at the exercise price (£1.80) and sell at the market price (£2.06). We have a term for this gap – intrinsic value. When we exercise we receive the intrinsic value, in this case 26p. When we trade, we receive the premium, that is, intrinsic value *plus* time value. The premium is 36 because 10p of time value was added to the intrinsic value. In other words, we are gaining from the protection built into the premium by the option writer. In fact, when we trade the option we *are* an option writer! However, as we previously bought the same option, we are not left with any outstanding position in the market. It follows that, at expiry, there is no time value and exercising the option or trading it will produce the same result. There is one final point regarding the time value. We have noted that it declines as time passes. However, this decline accelerates as we approach expiry. An option buyer may defer taking profit for several weeks, allowing the share price to rise even further. It may well be, however, that the time value declines faster than the intrinsic value rises and the total premium falls in value. This will be particularly true with a few weeks of expiry.

Other Terminology

We have noted the term 'intrinsic value' which is used when a call option exercise price is below the market price or a put option exercise price is above it. The option is also described here as *in the money*. If the exercise price is the same as the market price, we say the option is *at the money*. If the call exercise price is dearer than the market or the put exercise price cheaper we say the option is *out of the money*. Please note, however, that the use of standard exercise prices means that it is only rarely that one is the same as the market price. As a result, it is very common to call the at-the-money option the one which is *nearest* to the market price.

We described these LIFFE options earlier as *American* options, that is, they can be exercised at any time prior to the expiry date. The alternative is the *European* option which can only be exercised at expiry. We will give an example of this shortly. Typically, options on trading exchanges are American options but European options are quite common in the OTC market. Both options can be *traded* at any time on trading exchanges.

Options on Indices

Having looked at options on individual shares, we can now consider options on a whole share index, for example, S&P 100, FTSE 100, CAC 40, AEX and so on.

In principle, we can see that the idea has advantages. Now we can back a view on the whole market, not an individual share. Alternatively, we may be a market maker or fund manager owning all the top shares. The index might be a good way of hedging market risk. The practice of index options may be puzzling at first. One can readily envisage exercising an option and buying XYZ Ltd shares. What if we exercise the index option and buy the FTSE 100 index or the CAC40? What exactly do we receive?

The contracts are *cash settled*. Since there isn't anything to deliver, the contract is settled by paying cash. The index must be regarded as a price. If a call option on the FTSE 100 index is bought at an exercise level of 6000, then money will be made if the level rises to 6100 because 'the price' is higher. If the option buyer exercises, buying at 6000 and selling at 6100, then 100 points have been gained. To turn this into money, we settle at £10 per point per contract. For one contract, the gain is $100 \times £10 = £1000$. For ten contracts, it would be £10 000, and so on. The premium paid would have to be deducted in the usual way to arrive at the net profit. Alternatively, the option could be traded in the way described earlier.

A fund manager with a holding of £30 million in shares might be nervous of a fall in the market but not nervous enough to actually sell the shares. If an assumption is made that their holding of shares will behave in a similar way to the FTSE 100 (the correlation will be measured), then the manager could buy put options on the index contract. If the market falls, the puts will win some money to help compensate for the fall in the value of the portfolio.

How many contracts should the manager buy? Let us say that the index is at a level of 6000. If the contract is settled at £10 per point per contract, then the whole index is $6000 \times £10 = £60\ 000$. As this is one contract, the total number of contracts needed to cover a portfolio of £30 million is:

$$\frac{£30m}{£60\ 000} = 500$$

The manager buys 500 put options on the index at an exercise level of 6000 and pays the premium, say, £500 per contract or $500 \times £500 = £250\ 000$ in total.

(The premiums are also quoted as *index points*. In this case 50 index points. At £10 per point, this gives us a premium of £500.)

If the index falls 10% to 5400, the value of the portfolio of £30 million is reduced by £3 million. However, the manager could exercise the put option, that is, selling at a level of 6000 and buying at a level of 5400, making 600 points. Bearing in mind that the manager bought 500 contracts and that they are settled at £10 per point, the gross gain is:

$$600 \text{ points} \times £10 \times 500 \text{ contracts} = £3 \text{ million}.$$

From this we deduct the premium of £250 000 giving a net gain of £2.75 million (ignoring dealing costs). This is a substantial compensation for the fall in the value of the portfolio of £3 million. This is a classic *hedge*.

If the index rises 10% to 6600, the put option will expire worthless with the loss of the premium of £250 000. On the other hand, the value of the portfolio is now £33 million not £30 million, to help offset this loss. In particular, the manager is pleased that the portfolio was not liquidated due to nervousness about the market.

This is how options on an index are traded everywhere. At Euronext.liffe many index options are traded as well as the FTSE 100 – AEX, CAC40, BEL20 and others. The CAC40, for example, is offered in two contracts, one priced at €1 per point and the other €10 per point.

The Chicago Board Options Exchange trades the S&P 100 at $100 per point (American). The Chicago Mercantile Exchange trades the S&P 500 at $250 per point and a mini S&P at $50 per point (both European and American).

In the US, the main markets for equity options are the Chicago Board Options Exchange, the New York Stock Exchange, the American Stock Exchange and the Philadelphia Stock Exchange.

In Europe, the main original markets for equity options are shown in Table 12.6.

Table 12.6   *Main European markets for equity options (originally)*

Exchange	Country
Deutsche Termin Börse (DTB)	Germany (1990)
European Options Exchange (EOE)	Netherlands (1978)
London Traded Options Market (LTOM)	UK (1978)
Marché des Options Negociables de Paris (MONEP)	France (1987)
Swiss Options and Futures Exchange (SOFFEX)	Switzerland (1988)

From 1998 onwards the above picture changed dramatically. Earlier, LTOM had merged with the futures exchange LIFFE. Then, in 1998, the German and Swiss exchanges merged to form Eurex and gradually offered derivatives (futures as well as options) over a range of products – indices, like the DAX, MDAX, SMI and an index of top European stocks called Eurostoxx. This was invented by Dow Jones and covers certain market sectors as well. German treasury notes and longer-dated bonds are offered as well as interest rates – one month EONIA and three month Euribor. They have their own clearing company, Eurex Clearing.

In 2000, the exchanges in Amsterdam, Paris and Brussels merged to form Euronext, later adding Lisbon. The three stock exchanges in Paris, Amsterdam and Brussels took over their local derivatives markets (the MONEP mentioned in Table 12.6 merged with the futures market, the MATIF, and became part of the Paris Bourse). In London, the LIFFE was taken over by Euronext. It was renamed Euronext.liffe and all the derivative offerings were brought together under this name. The full range is shown under Table 13.1 in the next chapter. A single electronic trading platform called Connect was used for all these products. Later, the Euronext Clearing Company, Clearnet, merged with the London Clearing House. As a result of all this, there is now rivalry as contracts like one month EONIA, three month Euribor and some German government issues can be traded on Eurex and Euronext.liffe.

It should, perhaps, be mentioned that the Spanish exchange, MEFF, is still independent and trades options and futures on the IBEX 35 index of key Spanish shares and government bonds.

Outside Europe and the US, important exchanges exist in Tokyo, Osaka, Singapore, Hong Kong and Sydney. The Singapore Exchange (SIMEX), which started in 1984, has done particularly well and has become the dominant player in the Far East.

TRADED OPTIONS: OTHER OPTIONS

Currencies

In this chapter so far, we have covered options on equities and equity indices. In Chapter 8, we discussed options on currencies and ways in which importers and exporters could hedge risk.

Having looked at the mechanics of options, let's return to the 'breakforward' option which we explained in Chapter 8. We showed that a buyer of dollars for sterling in 3 months might be offered a floor rate of $1.88 and a break rate of $1.91. If the spot rate in 3 months was less than $1.88, the importer will buy dollars at $1.88. If the spot rate later was better than $1.91, the importer could buy dollars at the spot rate less 3¢. Thus, if spot later were $1.98, the importer could buy dollars at $1.95 and thus benefit from an improvement in the rate while still getting substantial protection from any worsening. There is no cost to the importer.

The bank has bought a sterling put option at $1.91.

If the spot rate later is, say, $1.85 the bank exercises the option to buy dollars at $1.91 and sells them to the client at $1.88, making 3¢.

If the spot rate later is, say $1.98 the option is abandoned. The bank buys the dollars spot at $1.98 and sells them to the client at $1.95, again making 3¢.

The 3¢ cover the option premium and a profit margin. The client is happy with the blend of risk protection and profit participation and the bank makes a profit. A simple example of some of the clever ways in which options can be used.

Bonds

Options are also available on bonds. Many of the major exchanges trading equity options will also trade bonds. Those on Euronext.liffe, for example, are shown in Table 13.1.

These bond contracts work in a similar way to the options on shares we described earlier. They can be used to speculate or hedge risk.

For example, the option on the German government bond on the Eurex offers standard exercise price levels, such as 108.5, 109, 109.5, 110, 110.5, 111. The contract size is €100,000 and the premiums are expressed as a percentage of the bond's nominal value to two decimal places. Thus, the March call at 110 exercise price may have a premium quoted as 3.25. In money terms, this is 3.25% of €100,000 = €3250. Each full 1% is €1000. If the bond price is 112, we can see that an exercise price of 110 has 2% of intrinsic value since it is the right to buy the bond at less than the market price. If the bond price rose to 114, the call buyer could make a profit of 4% = €4000 *less* the cost of the premium. If there is some time left to expiry, the call option buyer may trade the option and make even more profit. If the market price is 114, the right to buy at 110 has 4.00 intrinsic value plus an element of time value. Since the contract size is €100 000 a bond dealer wishing to hedge a portfolio of €10 million, will need to deal in 100 contracts.

(The above explanation has been simplified. At this point, we have ignored the complication that the bond is called *notional* and that the option is an option to have the futures contract. This is explained in Chapter 13.)

Interest Rates

The equity, currency and bond options covered above can *go to delivery*. That is, we can use the option to actually purchase or sell the relevant equities, currencies or bonds.

We also met index options, which cannot go to delivery as there is no real underlying product. These are called *cash settled*. Interest rate options are of this kind. We cannot use the contract to borrow or lend money at a given rate of interest. Just as the index option was settled on the basis of a value per point of index change, so the interest rate option is settled on the basis of a value per 0.01% change in interest rates.

For example, the Chicago Mercantile Exchange trades 3 month Eurodollar interest rates. The contract size is $1 million. Thus, with an underlying sum at risk of $20 million, the options user would be dealing in 20 contracts. Each 0.01% of interest rate change will gain or lose $25 per contract. The option user buys a call or a put on a given level of interest rates and pays a premium. If rates change to the profit of the option user by 0.50%, the gain is 50 × $25 = $1250 per contract.

In the case of index options, the price per point is arbitrary. It is picked to produce a sensible contract size. In the case of the interest rate contract above, the $25 per 0.01% is not arbitrary but follows logically from the contract size of $1 million. If the whole contract, that is 100%, has a value of $1 million, then 0.01% has a value of $100. However, this is a three monthly contract, so the value is a quarter of this, that is, $25.

So far, the procedure for trading interest rates has seemed quite straightforward. The level of interest rate for 3 month Eurodollars is regarded as a price, like any other, and we either buy cheaper than we sell or face buying dearer than we sell, in which case the option is abandoned. Each 0.01% of gain on the price level wins $25 for each contract traded. We can either use the contract to speculate or hedge interest rate risk.

There is, unfortunately, a complication. This relates to the pricing of the contract. We might expect to see prices like 3.50%, 5.00% or 8.00%. What the market actually does is subtract the desired rate of interest from 100 to arrive at the price level of the contract. Thus an interest rate of 4.00% trades as 96.00 and one of 8.00% trades as 92.00.

Let's look at the effect of this pricing:

Interest rate	*Contract price*		
10.00%	100 – 10%	=	90.00
9.00%	100 – 9%	=	91.00
11.00%	100 – 11%	=	89.00

Notice that as the interest rate goes *down* from 10% to 9%, the contract price goes *up* from 90.00 to 91.00. As the interest rate goes *up* from 10% to 11%, the contract price goes *down* from 90.00 to 89.00.

We met this reverse relationship before when we discussed long-dated bonds – interest rates down, bond prices up; interest rates up, bond prices down. The Chicago markets did start trading interest rates in the obvious way (in 1975). After a few weeks, however, the traders preferred to trade the contracts in the way we have just described. It suited bond dealers who were hedging risk and it suited the psychology of traders. After all, as a generalisation, higher interest rates are seen as bad news – equity and bond prices fall. It seemed logical that with higher interest rates, the contract price fell.

This means that the call/put logic we learned earlier must be reversed in the case of interest rate contracts. If you wish to gain from higher interest rates buy *put* options – the contract price will fall. If you wish to gain from lower interest rates, buy *call* options – the contract price will rise. Other than that, it's easy really!

Let's take an example. Suppose a US corporate has a $20 million loan from the bank at floating rate and reviewed every three months. The rate is linked to Eurodollar LIBOR. Let us also suppose that the dates for the CME three monthly contracts coincide with the bank's rollover of the loan. The bank has just fixed the rate for three months based on Eurodollar LIBOR of 3.75%. The corporate believes that rates are due to rise and seeks a hedge using the CME contract.

As the contract size is $1 million and the loan is $20 million, they deal in 20 contracts. As they wish to gain if interest rates go up, they buy 20 *put* options for the next expiry at a level of 3.75%, that is, a contract price level of 100 - 3.75 = 96.25. The premium is quoted as 0.30 and also must be interpreted at $25 per 0.01 per contract, the way the contract is settled. Thus 0.30 = $750 per contract and the corporate bought 20 contracts, paying 20 × $750 = $15 000.

Assume that at the expiry of the contract the Eurodollar LIBOR rate is 4.75%. The bank notifies the client that the interest charge is 1% higher on the $20 million loan for three months – an increase of $50 000.

At the CME, the contract price is 100 – 4.75% = 95.25. The corporate bought 20 put options at 96.25, that is, the right to sell at 96.25. The contract is exercised by selling at 96.25 and buying at 95.25, a profit of 1% for each of 20 contracts. Since 0.01% = $25 the gain is:

$$100 \times \$25 \times 20 \text{ contracts} = \$50\,000$$

Deducting the premium of $15 000, the corporate has $35 000 to help meet the bank's extra interest charge of $50 000.

Suppose interest rates had fallen to 2.75%? The CME contract is not profitable and will be abandoned for the loss of the premium of $15 000. However, the bank notifies the corporate of a reduced interest charge for three months of $50 000. The corporate has bought protection from higher rates but can still gain if they fall.

This is the essential character of options to which we referred in Chapter 8 on foreign exchange. It is worth repeating.

The option purchase protects against a deterioration in the rate but the option buyer can still benefit from an improvement in the rate. There is a cost – the premium.

(Again, the complication that the CME contract is an option to have the future has been ignored.)

OPTION STRATEGIES

The experts in the option market will not content themselves with one position, such as buying a call at a particular exercise price and expiry but will combine several positions in order to carry out complex strategies.

For example, in the case of XYZ Ltd in equity options above, we might buy both a call *and* a put on the exercise price of £1.80 for July expiry. If the share price rises we win, if it falls we also win. Well, in principle at least. The problem is that two premiums have been paid. The call premium is 24 and the put might be 18, that is, 42 in total. Having paid 42 for a £1.80 call, the price must go up to £2.22 (£1.80 + 42) to break even and that ignores dealing costs. Having paid 42 for a £1.80 put, the price must fall to £1.38 (£1.80 – 42) to break even. In other words, this is a strategy for a very volatile situation. A sharp share movement is expected, either up or down. It might be that there is a takeover bid struggle. The bid will either fail and the victim's share price fall sharply or the bidder will come back with a higher offer and the opposite will happen.

The most dangerous situation for the buyer is if the price remains stable at £1.86. The call option will be worth 6p and the put will expire worthless. The loss is 42 – 6 = 36: for a single 1000 share contract, £360 lost out of the premium of £420. (This has ignored *trading* the option prior to expiry in order to cut the loss and take advantage of remaining time value in the premium.)

This is quite a well known strategy called the *straddle*. The straddle buyer expects a volatile situation; the straddle writer thinks they are wrong.

Another strategy might be to buy the July £1.80 calls and write the July £2.20 calls. The premium for the July £1.80 calls is 24p and for the July £2.20 calls, 7p. If the share price goes over £2.20 later, we have bought a call and also sold one at this level and so no further gain can be made, the purchase and sale will cancel out. However, we have offset the 24p premium for the £1.80 call by receiving the premium of 7p when we wrote the £2.20 call. Our net cost for a 1000 share contract is 24 – 7 = 17p per share or £170 instead of £240 had we simply bought the £1.80 call alone. We have reduced our possible loss from £240 per contract to £170 per contract and brought the break even point down from £1.80 + 24 to £1.80 + 17. What we gave up to achieve this was any profit above a later share price of £2.20.

This strategy is called the *bull spread*. We give up some of our unlimited profit potential in order to cut cost and risk. It has become so popular that the Chicago market offers this embedded in the option product. If we are pessimistic about XYZ Ltd, we do the opposite and buy the £1.80 put but write the £1.40 put – a *bear spread*.

There is no end to the permutations and variations on this theme. There are books on option strategies which will list a figure in excess of 50 possible strategies. Often they take their name from the shape of the graph showing the potential profit and loss from future changes in the market price, for example, the forked lightning, Mexican hat, Mae West, condor, butterfly and many others.

Look at all the variables there are to play with:

❏ Number of contracts
❏ Calls/puts
❏ Buy/write
❏ Exercise prices
❏ Expiry dates.

Apart from trading strategies like these, there are may other variations on the options theme. There is no place in an introductory text like this to mention them all, but we can cover a few just to give the reader an idea of the sheer ingenuity and imagination involved!

Some markets trade *share ratios*, that is to say not the share's absolute price and its movement but how it compares with others. For example, the Australian Stock Exchange offers contracts on leading shares (such as ANZ Bank, Broken Hill, News Corporation) based on the ratio of their price movement compared with the All Ordinaries Index.

Spread trading is similar, and is based on the difference between two prices. Other spreads are *calendar spreads*, the difference between the option premiums for different expiry dates – for example, March and June. We may believe that the difference between the premiums will either get bigger or smaller, and trade accordingly.

There is also a class of options on the OTC market called *exotic options;* for instance *barrier options* which are very popular at the moment. The idea in this case is to cheapen the option premium by attaching some condition. Typically, the option may only be valid if the market price reaches a certain level or barrier (the 'knock in').

Suppose that today's price of a given share is £1.00. We may wish to sell shortly but are prepared to bear a loss down to 90p. We could buy a put option at 90p. A variation is to buy a put option at £1.00 which is only valid if the share price hits 90p – the 'knock in'.

Alternatively, we could buy a put option at £1.00 but agree the option is cancelled if the price ever hits £1.05.

If the price hits £1.05, we may accept cancellation of the option on the basis that prices are going up not down, and accept the risk for a cheaper premium – the 'knock out'. The risk is that having hit £1.05, the price falls later to less than £1.00.

Usually, the option is knocked in or out if the barrier level is reached at any time prior to expiry, and usually the options are European style. A refinement might be that the barrier price only relates to the closing price each day, not the price at any time during the day.

There are also, within the exotics list, *compound options* – that is options to have … another option! At this point, the brain begins to hurt, so let's leave it at that. You get the message. There are many exotics, and teams at banks regularly launch new variations: lookback options, digital options, binary options, up and unders, down and outs, ladder options, rainbow options and so on! Sometimes these endure and become relatively mainstream (like the lookback), sometimes they fade away. The Asian option, (where the strike price is the average over the option period) is now traded on the London Metal Exchange.

Computers are an essential tool to carry out the necessary calculations, produce the profit/loss graphs and control the total exposure contained in a trader's book of option deals.

Unfortunately, the activities of Nick Leeson, the Baring's derivatives trader who is alleged to have lost £860m and bankrupted the bank, have led many people to believe that derivatives trading is all about gambling.

It would be quite wrong to regard it all as simply sophisticated gambling. Risk management is a key topic today and options make their contribution. The description in Chapter 9 shows the ingenious use of options by banks to provide situations which are attractive to importers and exporters and which yield the banks a profit as well. Another possible tool is the *future* transaction, and that's the one which will be covered in Chapter 13.

SUMMARY

The users of derivative products are *speculators*, *hedgers* and *arbitrageurs*. The key products are *options* and *futures*. All the others (like FRAs and swaps) are simply variations on the same theme.

An option gives the buyer the right, but not the obligation, to buy or sell financial instruments or commodities at an agreed price and at an agreed future date or time period.

Options can be purchased on a trading exchange or over the counter. The exchange has the advantage of the protection of the *clearing house*, but the OTC market will more easily tailor a product to suit the user's needs.

Options to buy a given product at a later date are *calls*. Options to sell are *puts*. There are *buyers* of options and *writers* (sellers).

The price of the option is the *premium*, the price of the product at which the option buyer can exercise is the *exercise* or *strike price*. Options can also be *traded*.

The option buyer cannot lose more than the premium, the option writer cannot gain more than the premium.

To protect against default, the clearing house asks option writers for *initial margin* and, each day, *variation margin*.

If the option to buy or sell is at a price more favourable than the market price, the option is said to have *intrinsic value*. The balance of the premium is *time value*, which will fall as the expiry date approaches.

Trading the option will be more profitable than exercising if the option has time value.

A small percentage change in the price of the underlying asset leads to a large percentage change in the premium. This is *gearing*.

The premium is based on the past performance of the share price. The more volatile the performance, the higher the premium.

Options at a price more favourable than the market price are said to be *in the money*. If the price is less favourable than the market, they are *out of the money* and if the price is the same as the market they are *at the money*.

There are options on equities, equity indices, bonds, currencies, interest rates and commodities.

Combining option positions leads to options strategies such as a *straddle, bull spread* or *butterfly*.

Other non-standardised options are referred to as *exotic options*, for example, barrier options, lookback options, digital options, and so on.

The market in Europe for options and futures has seen an upheaval in Europe's exchanges such that these products are now handled by just two bodies – Eurex and Euronext.liffe.

13 Financial Futures

Background

Transactions very similar to options and futures contracts today have existed in commodity markets for hundreds of years. There was an astounding Dutch tulip bulb mania in the 17th century. As tulips became more and more fashionable, people bought tulips several months in advance of the harvest. As the price went up, the contracts at the old prices were more valuable and could be sold to other people without waiting to take delivery at harvest time. In the end, the government had to step in when more tulips had been bought than were actually in the ground and several people made large losses.

(For details of this and other amazing financial speculations, see *Extraordinary Popular Delusions and the Madness of Crowds* by Charles Mackay, Harmony Books.)

Commodity prices fluctuate and where there are fluctuations, we find speculators and hedgers. The harvest may be good or bad and the product is only available once per year anyway. It would be natural to buy or sell ahead of the harvest. As prices went up or down, some of these contracts became more valuable and could be sold on to other people.

Metals are not crops but prices do fluctuate and it takes some time to receive a consignment from overseas. The London Metal Exchange's three month contract came into use after the Suez Canal was opened and metals like copper and zinc could be shipped in three months.

The largest commodity markets in the world settled down in Chicago at the Mercantile Exchange and the Board of Trade. It was here too, that the modern futures contracts were developed. The Board of Trade opened in 1848 and the Mercantile Exchange in 1874.

Before looking at the mechanism of futures as opposed to options, let's look again at the hedging technique.

Hedgers vs Speculators

A hedger is at risk if a given potential price movement happens. Hedgers seek to create a profit from this price movement in another market so as to create a gain in partial compensation for the loss.

A sugar dealer may have sold sugar short for future delivery. That is, the dealer hasn't yet bought the sugar to meet these contracts. If the price of sugar goes up before the purchase is made, a loss will occur.

Let's look at the hedge diagrammatically in Figure 13.1.

PHYSICAL MARKET   **HEDGE MARKET**

$ x- $ y+

PRICE INCREASE

[P]   [P]

PRICE DECREASE

$ x+ $ y-

Figure 13.1   *Structure of a hedge*

If a given rise in the price of sugar will lose $x in physical trading, the sugar dealer could buy call options on sugar contracts at the Chicago Coffee, Sugar and Cocoa Exchange. This will create a profit of $y to, at least, offset the loss of $x in physical trading.

If the price of sugar falls, the dealer will have lost money on the call option but will be delighted because, having sold sugar short, even more profit is made on physical sugar trading. This explains why some traders with large losses may walk off the floor of the futures or options exchange and seem to be smiling. They must be hedgers. The price movement they feared hasn't happened. Speculators, of course, will have genuinely lost money.

This is a simple but most important principle, often misunderstood. It's worth repeating:

> *If hedgers lose money in the hedge market, they must make money in the market being hedged because the price movement they feared has not happened.*

We will find that futures, unlike options, involve unlimited risk. For the reason just explained, hedgers can accept this risk. Indeed, the bigger the loss on the futures hedge, the bigger the offsetting gain in the physical market.

There is another important principle – who is on the other side of the hedge? It may be another hedger but one whose position is the opposite – someone who will lose money if the price of sugar goes *down,* not up. This means that whatever happens to the price, both will get the hedge they are looking for. The broker will make a living, the exchange will make a profit and everybody goes home happy.

In financial markets, people are too quick to claim that it must be what they call a 'zero-sum game' – that is, what someone wins, someone else must lose. This is sometimes the case, but by no means always. There are usually plenty of opposite hedgers.

Those with loans at floating rate are hoping interest rates will go *down*. Those with investments at floating rate are hoping interest rates will go *up*.

It all seems too good to be true, and it is. The problem is that there won't be the same value of opposite positions except by a miracle. The hedger wants to do a deal and no one wants to say 'yes' or, at least, not at a reasonable price. That's where speculators come in. They provide the trading liquidity, so that trade hedgers can reduce the risk and do the deals they want. Usually, they are called *locals*, a term from the Chicago markets, where more than half the membership is locals. Even the conservative London Metal Exchange, where no one can be a member unless they physically trade metals, agree in their literature that speculators play an essential role in providing liquidity. It's a new light on a term that most people regard as being totally pejorative.

Commodity Futures

A futures transaction provides an alternative to an option as a way of hedging risk. Its characteristics are different. A futures contract is a commitment to buy or sell a given quantity of an underlying product by a given date in the future at a price agreed now.

Let's note that a futures transaction is a *commitment*, not an option. If the price moves the wrong way, the option buyer can abandon the contract. As this is a privilege, a premium is paid. A futures contract cannot be abandoned in this way. Since no privilege is involved, no premium need be paid. For the same reason, a futures contract is riskier.

Options had calls, puts, buyers and sellers. Futures contracts only have buyers and sellers. To that extent, they are simpler.

Our sugar trader, worried about the price of sugar going up, could take a futures position in white sugar on the above-mentioned Chicago Exchange (or the exchange in London, now part of Euronext.liffe).

Let us say that the trader commits to buy 100 tonnes of sugar by the next expiry date at $250 per tonne.

It is clear that if the price of sugar goes up to $280 a tonne, a contract that can buy at $250 a tonne has value and can create profit. That is not difficult to grasp but what people do find hard to understand is that the above trader hasn't the slightest intention of buying any sugar!

What happens then if sugar rises to $280 a tonne? The trader *closes the position* with the opposite contract – the trader commits to *sell* 100 tonnes of sugar by the next expiry date at $280 per tonne. The contracts are not settled in sugar but on the price difference of $30 a tonne, that is, our trader has gained $100 \times \$30 = \$3000$. This is to offset the trading loss which will result from having sold sugar short and being obliged to buy physical sugar at a higher price.

People tend to ask at this point – but what happens to the sugar? They have a vision of someone at expiry date trying to handle all the sugar that no one seems to want.

Let's realise that no one can contract to buy sugar unless someone contracts to sell. Equally, no one can contract to sell unless someone contracts to buy. If everyone closes their position with the opposite contract later (as we described above) there isn't anybody left at expiry, nor can there be.

If the sugar trader did not close the position, they would indeed buy 100 tonnes of sugar at $250 a tonne. But if they did remain open at expiry as a buyer, there must also be a seller with an open position. If there are three buyers left, there will be three sellers and so on.

The sugar is only the means to the end – the hedge or speculation. Either way, with the occasional exception, cash settlement is quite acceptable.

The fact that the contract *can* go to delivery, however, is crucially important. It means that the price of sugar in the futures exchange must relate to the real price of sugar. If it was cheaper, traders would use the futures exchange to buy it and sell it at profit in the cash market – arbitrage.

The contract is not an option, and we see the difference if we assume that sugar were to fall in price to $220 a tonne. If this were an option, the contract would now be abandoned – there is no point in buying sugar at $250 in order to sell it at $220. As a futures contract, the trader is committed to buy at $250 a tonne. The position is closed out by later entering the opposite contract to sell 100 tonnes of sugar at $220 a tonne, losing $3000.

This loss is not a problem. As the price of sugar has fallen, the short position in the physical sugar market is even more profitable as sugar can be purchased much more cheaply than it was sold. As we observed earlier, for the hedger a loss in the hedge market must mean a gain in the market being hedged.

Notice the symmetry in the futures contract – a rise in price of $30 a tonne gained $3000, a fall in price of $30 a tonne lost $3000. Options are not symmetrical because, when the price moves the wrong way, the contract is abandoned.

Finally, we now have two terms – *forward* and *futures* – which ought to mean the same, but don't.

- ❏ *Forward* is buying or selling for actual delivery at a future date at a price agreed now.
- ❏ *Futures* is similar to forward, but usually there is no intention to take or make delivery; later, the position will be closed with the opposite contract and settled in cash.

Forward is for those who want the physical commodity, futures for those who are speculating or hedging and happy with cash settlement.

Thus, we need futures exchanges where everyone realises what the end objective is. There will be formal contract sizes, fixed delivery dates and the guarantee offered by the clearing house. The latter will take margin (deposits) from *both* parties as both are at risk. All contracts are legally with the clearing house. *Initial margin* is paid with the first contract. If the contract moves into loss, extra margin, called *variation margin*, is debited on a daily basis but if the contract moves into profit, variation margin is credited. The major players will have what is, in effect, a bank account with the clearing house. The locals will arrange to clear with someone who is a full clearing member.

Financial Futures

If options and futures are essentially driven by price volatility, the only surprise is that it took so long to be applied to financial contracts. Looking at interest rates, currency rates, equity prices, equity index levels and bond prices, there is huge volatility and also huge risk for many of the parties involved.

There are four main types of financial contract – bonds, interest rates, currencies and equity indices, as well as commodities and even a weather future! As we will see, options are typically options to have the futures contract. The contracts are listed in Table 13.1. (Among the contracts are 'swapnotes'. Swaps will be discussed in the next chapter.)

Many options are options to have the futures contract. This doesn't make any difference if the buyer is trading the option but any exercise is into the futures contract. A key difference between this and a direct option is that, in the case of the direct option, having used (say) a call option to purchase the product, it can be sold at the market price. The seller of the option would have to purchase the product. If it is an option to have the futures, the buyer finds themself the buyer of the futures contract (a 'long futures' position). This can be left to go to delivery. The seller of the option is now the seller of the futures contract (a 'short futures' position). However, if they don't wish to physically sell the products they have time to close their position by buying the contract and letting someone else go to delivery. In the case of a direct option, they would have no choice. Most option contracts on futures exchanges are options to have the future.

From the last remarks, the reader will realise that in some cases, the contracts can go to delivery if the position is not closed out. The gilts contract size is £100 000. A buyer of 20 contracts can let the position go to delivery and buy £2 million of gilts at the agreed price. All the bond contracts except the Japanese Government bond can go to delivery in this way. Prices will be kept in line with cash market prices or arbitrage will take place.

The FTSE 100 can't go to delivery (as there isn't anything to deliver) and the interest rate contracts can't go to delivery either, they can't be used to borrow money at an agreed rate of interest. This raises two interesting points. Since the contract can't go to delivery, what happens if a buyer *doesn't* close the position with the opposite sale? For the same reason, how do we know the price will relate to that of the underlying product in the cash market?

Table 13.1   *Euronext.liffe contracts, November 2005*

Contract type – individual contracts

Bonds
  Long Gilts; 2 year German Treasury Notes (Schatz); 10 year German
  Government Bonds (Bunds); Japanese Government Bond (JGB).

Interest Rates
  1 month IONIA; 3 month Euribor; Eurodollar; Sterling; Swiss Franc; TIBOR;
  1 year mid curve options on 3 month Euribor, Eurodollar and Sterling.

Equities
  Equity Indices – AEX; BEL 20; CAC 40; FTSE 100; FTSE Eurofirst 80,
  100 and 300; Eurotop 100; FTSE 100 flex options; FTSE 250;
  MSCI Euroindex; MSCI Pan-European; PSI 20.
  Individual share options on 250 companies.
  Options on European and US tracker funds.

Swapnotes
  2, 5 and 10 year Euro and Dollar.

Currencies
  Euro/$ and $/Euro.

In addition, there are a number of commodity contracts.

Note: The above contracts are sometimes options, sometimes futures and sometimes
both.

Source: Euronext.liffe.

Any buyer or seller who doesn't close the position is automatically closed by the clearing house as the contract can't go to delivery. If the buyer or seller is letting the contract go to delivery, they don't need to take any action as the position will be closed for them.

The problem of correlation with the market price is solved by the convention that the expiry price is always the market price. The expiry price of the FTSE 100 is called the Exchange Delivery Settlement Price (EDSP). At 10.10 a.m. on the expiry day an auction takes place for each share in the index and this leads to the EDSP which is declared at 10.30. The old method of simply averaging the prices in this 20 minute period was abandoned in November 2004 for technical reasons. The expiry price of the short sterling interest rate contract is the average of the sterling LIBOR rate of 16 named banks at 11.00 a.m. on the expiry day, the highest and lowest four values being excluded.

Index Futures

In Chapter 12, we discussed options on share indices – S&P 100, FTSE 100, CAC40 and similar indices. Futures contracts are also available and make a good starting point, as we've already met options on the indices.

The futures contract is a commitment and there is no premium to pay, only margin to the clearing house.

An insurance company investment manager may be planning to sell £24 million of shares in three weeks to meet claims for storm damage. The manager does not wish to sell at the moment as market conditions are poor. The worry about waiting, however, is that the market may fall in the next three weeks and the same quantity of shares raise less than £24 million.

The answer may be a full hedge using the futures contract on the FTSE 100 contract. This is a way of locking in to today's index level without actually selling the shares.

The first question is – how many contracts? Cash settlement is based on £10 per point. If the index is 6000 then the whole index is valued at 6000 × £10 = £60 000. Since the value of shares to be hedged is £24m, then the number of contracts is:

$$\frac{£24m}{£60\ 000} = 400$$

The fund manager sells 400 contracts for the next expiry period. The first complication is that although the stock exchange index is 6000, the figure in the trading pit may be, say, 6020 (reflecting supply and demand, market expectations and certain technical factors). So our manager has 400 contracts to 'sell' the index at 6020.

Three weeks later the market is down 10% at 5400. The manager sells the shares at this level. For the same quantity of shares that might have been sold three weeks earlier, £21.6 million is received not £24 million, a loss of £2.4 million.

The position in the exchange is now closed. If the contract in the pit is being traded at a level of, say, 5430, the position is closed by buying 400 contracts at 5430. The gain is:

Sell contracts at	6020	
Buy contracts at	5430	
Gain per contract	590	points

The contract is cash settled at £10 per point, a gain of £10 × 590 = £5900. For 400 contracts, the total gain is 400 × £5900 = £2.36 million. Thus, waiting three weeks lost £2.4 million on the share sale but the contract gained £2.36 million.

An initial margin was paid of £2000 per contract and thus £2000 × 400 contracts

= £800 000. However, as this was only a deposit to cover possible loss, this sum is returned. In addition, one can usually negotiate interest on initial margin.

There will be brokers' costs to pay and a fee to the clearing house. These might be about £4 per contract or a total of £4 × 400 = £1600 in this case.

If the index rose in the three week period, the contract cannot be abandoned, as in the case of options. If the index rose 10% to 6600, the futures position is now loss making. If the pit level is 6610, the position is now closed by buying 400 contracts at 6610. It is the opposite of the previous case:

Sell contracts at	6020	
Buy contracts at	6610	
Loss per contract	590	points

The total loss is:

£10 per contract × 590 points × 400 contracts = £2.36m

We commented before on the essential symmetry of the futures contract. A fall in the index traded of 590 points gains £2.36 million but a rise of 590 points loses £2.36 million. Unlike options, the futures contract faces potentially unlimited loss. However, we are not talking here of a speculator but a hedger. When the investment manager sells the shares, the market is up 10% and the shares are sold for £26.4 million not £24 million. The gain of £2.4 million offsets the loss of £2.36 million on the futures contract. This is the point we made earlier in the chapter. For a hedger, a loss on the futures means a gain in the physical market being hedged.

Note one important point. Although the manager was protected against loss arising from a market fall, no profit can be made from a rise in the market.

Let's spell out this essential element in futures, as opposed to options:

Futures give the user protection from an adverse price movement but they cannot benefit from a favourable movement. Risk is unlimited but there is no premium to pay.

The manager could give up some of the protection to allow room for a gain should the market rise. Instead of selling 400 contracts, 200 could have been sold.

The effect would be that a loss of £2.4 million due to a 10% market fall would be offset by a futures gain of only £1.18 million. However, it follows that a gain of £2.4 million due to a 10% market rise would be offset by a futures loss of only £1.18 million.

The manager has a range of choices varying from not hedging a position at all right up to an attempted 100% hedge.

One final point. In the above case, there is an implicit assumption that the manager's mix of shares will behave in the same way as the market, that if the market fell

10% so would the mix of shares the manager is selling. It's not an unreasonable assumption but it won't be left to chance. Using computer techniques the manager measures the correlation between the volatility of the shares in the portfolio and the volatility of the FTSE 100 – it's called the *beta factor*. If the shares move in the same way as the index, the beta is 1.0. If the shares move by 90% of an index movement, the beta is 0.9. If the shares move by 110% of an index movement, the beta is 1.1. The number of contracts traded will be adjusted by the beta factor. (Just for the record, the *alpha* factor refers to the individual behaviour of a share, for example how BP's performance might differ from that of Shell.)

Bond Futures

In principle, bond futures are not difficult. The US Treasury bond contract in Chicago, for example, is based on an underlying value of $100 000. The smallest price movement, or tick, is ½₂. If the contract is £100 000, then 1% = $1000 and ½₂ = $31.25. If ten contracts are sold at a level 10 ticks higher than they were bought then there is a gain of:

$$10 \text{ ticks} \times \$31.25 \times 10 \text{ contracts} = \$3125$$

The contract need not be closed out but left to go to delivery. Certain days are *delivery days*. In the case of the Treasury bond contract and gilts, it's any business day in the delivery month. In the case of the German government 'Bund' contract, it's the tenth calendar day of the delivery month (if a working day). The decision as to which day is delivery day is made by the *seller*.

The principle, then, is not difficult but the practice is more complicated. Most bond futures contracts are based on a *notional* bond – that is, one that doesn't exist. Newcomers will find the idea of trading in a bond that doesn't exist very strange but the market takes it in its stride. The exchange makes available a list of bonds which can be delivered. The Treasury bond is a 6% coupon bond as the unit of trading. Delivery can be made from a list of actual bonds with 15 years left to maturity. If one of these is an 8% bond, an 8% bond is inherently more attractive than a 6% bond and has a better price. The exchange makes available a *conversion factor* which calculates the sales value which must be used for delivery purposes. If the contract is for a 6% bond with $100 000 nominal value, then an 8% bond can deliver $100 000 nominal to meet the contract specification but receive a higher price. There will be one bond in the list which is cheapest to deliver. The price in the trading pit will be based on this *cheapest to deliver* bond – if not, arbitrage between this and the cash market will take place. For example, someone will buy the underlying bonds, sell the futures contract at the current price level and actually deliver the bonds at a profit.

As a result, the list of bonds available for delivery is significant and the exchange will make changes from time to time. The German Bund contract traded on Eurex, for example, has become the most traded contract in Europe. The underlying basket of deliverable bonds is relatively small compared with these huge volumes. Although far less than 5% of bonds go to delivery, the market is nervous of this position and a possible 'squeeze' if a high percentage went to delivery. The bond contract is based on a notional coupon of 6%. There are suggestions that it should be lowered to 4% and the list of deliverable bonds raised. These worries are not theoretical. If several dealers don't close out a position but ask for delivery, they may find that one or two other dealers are holding large stocks of the cheapest to deliver bond and may operate what is called a 'squeeze'. The counterparties now asked to make delivery are 'held to ransom' in effect. There were problems in the US in June 2005 with the 10 year Treasury Note futures when there was a huge increase in trading volumes.

Interest Rates

The interest rate contracts create valuable opportunities for those at risk from interest rate changes to hedge that risk. The Euronext.liffe contracts offer short sterling, euro, eurodollar, euroswiss franc and euroyen interest rates.. Rival euro interest rate contracts are offered at the other exchanges (MEFF, Eurex and so on), but Euronext.liffe's three month euro interest rate contract is the biggest in Europe.

Interest rate contracts are cash settled – they cannot go to delivery. At expiry, any open positions are closed by the clearing house at the expiry price, which is always the market price. As we said in Chapter 11, the pricing of the contract is based on subtracting the implied rate of interest so that, for example, 10.00% is traded as 90.00.

The normal rule with futures is that the contract is bought in the first instance if a gain is to be made from a price increase. If a gain is to be made from a price fall, the contract is sold in the first instance. If a hedge is involved, then buying the contract is the *long hedge* and selling the contract is the *short hedge*.

Once again, interest rate contracts reverse the logic. To gain from a price increase, we *sell* the contract (because, if the price goes up, the contract level will fall). To gain from a price decrease, we *buy* the contract (because if the price goes down, the contract level will go up).

In Chapter 12, we used the example of a corporate with a $20 million loan at floating rate related to Eurodollar LIBOR and reviewed every three months. To hedge interest rate risk, put option contracts were bought. The effect was that, when interest rates went up, the $50 000 extra bank bill was offset by a gain of $35 000 on the option contract. When interest rates went down, the $50 000 fall in the bank bill was only offset by the loss of the premium at $15 000. The option buyer still benefited.

Let's look at a futures hedge in the same circumstances. To keep it simple, we will assume that the interest rate level traded in the pit is the same as current real interest rates (since this was the assumption with the interest rate contract, we need to be consistent).

As the loan is $20 million and the contract size on CME is $1 million, then the corporate needs to deal in 20 contracts. As they wish to gain from an interest rate rise, they sell 20 contracts for the next expiry at a level of 3.75%, that is, a contract price level of $100 - 3.75 = 96.25$. No premium is paid but the initial margin is $500 per contract, so $20 \times \$500 = \$10\ 000$ is paid to the clearing house.

As before, we assume that at the expiry of the contract, the Eurodollar LIBOR rate is 4.75%. The bank notifies the client that the interest charge is 1% higher on the $20m loan for three months – an increase of $50 000.

At CME, the contract price is $100 - 4.75\% = 95.25$. The corporate's position is closed by buying 20 contracts at 95.25. The position is:

Sell 20 contracts	@ 96.25
Buy 20 contracts	@ 95.25
Gain per contract	1.00

Each 0.01% is settled at $25 so the gain is:

$$100 \times \$25 \times 20 \text{ contracts} = \$50\ 000$$

There is no premium to deduct, so the bank's extra $50 000 interest is met by the gain of $50 000 on the CME contract (in the best of all possible worlds). As there was no premium to deduct, the futures contract has so far worked out better.

But what happens if interest rates fall to 2.75%? The bank notifies the corporate of a reduced interest rate charge for 3 months of $50 000.

At CME, the contract price is $100 - 2.75\% = 97.25$. The position is closed by buying 20 contracts at 97.25. The position is:

Sell 20 contracts	@ 96.25
Buy 20 contracts	@ 97.25
Loss per contract	1.00

The loss is:

$$100 \times \$25 \times 20 \text{ contracts} = \$50\ 000$$

This is, of course, the symmetry in futures. A rise in interest rates of 1% gains $50 000, a fall in interest rates of 1% loses $50 000. The result is that the corporate does not gain from the fall in interest rates as the reduced interest rate bill is offset by the loss on the futures contract. Here options gained, as the contract was abandoned when the interest rate fell for the loss of the premium, allowing the corporate a net gain from the interest rate reduction.

Currency Futures

We commented in Chapter 8 on foreign exchange on the strength of the OTC market in currency futures. Currency options and futures closed in London in 1990. Very few are now traded in Europe.

The trading of the futures follows the lines we have explained in this chapter. The CME euro contract, for example, is based on €125 000 as the contract size and is quoted at an exchange rate of dollars per euro. A tick is 0.01¢ and is valued at $12.50. A contract can be bought at a dollar/euro exchange rate of $1.0384 and sold at $1.0484 – a gain of 100 ticks or $1250 per contract traded. Contracts can be left to go to delivery if required.

Some Problems of Futures Exchanges

In general, corporates are not enthusiastic about use of futures exchanges. The contracts are standard sizes, so a small corporate with a loan of $800 000 finds the interest rate contract size of $1m inconvenient. The expiry dates of the contract are unlikely to coincide with real life needs. Margin calls upset cash flow calculations and no interest is paid on variation margin in credit. For interest rate and currency contracts, the banks offer an attractive range of OTC products, some of which we will meet in Chapter 13.

For banks themselves, however, the exchanges have one key advantage – the security of the clearing house. At a time when counterparty risk is a major worry, this is increasingly a key benefit.

For fund managers, too, the index contracts provide secure, liquid trading and the chance to carry out asset allocation smoothly. Suppose a fund has £100 million in assets. A decision may be taken to decrease exposure to equities by 2% and increase exposure to gilts by 2%. With one phone call, the fund manager can sell FTSE 100 index contracts to the value of £2 million and buy gilts contracts to the same value. Over time and at leisure, the manager can progressively sell the equities, buy the gilts and close the futures position.

Open Outcry or Computers?

A major talking point at present is whether traders will continue to buy and sell in trading pits on a floor or whether the market will move to computerised order matching.

The large US markets are based on *open outcry* trading but the last European exchange to open on an open outcry basis was the Paris MATIF in 1986. The argument for open outcry is that it's the quickest way to trade high value standardised contracts. With computerised trading, however, the expensive floor is no longer needed and a firm audit trail is produced making fraud more difficult. (In 1989, 47 traders were indicted for fraud in Chicago following an undercover investigation by the FBI.)

The signalling in the pits usually follows the Chicago practice. There are three variables:

❏ Number of contracts
❏ Buy or sell?
❏ Price.

As in foreign exchange, only the last two digits of price will be quoted. If the interest rate contract level is 92.55, the price will be '55'. If the trader is buying, the hand begins away from the face and moves back to the forehead. The price is shouted with the hand away from the face and the number of contracts at the forehead. A buyer of 10 contracts at 92.55 will yell:

'55 for 10'

If the trader is selling, the hand begins at the forehead and moves away, shouting the number of contracts first and the price second:

'10 @ 55'

If there are no takers, the price may have to be moved up to 56 or 57 until a counterparty yells 'sold!'. The two traders fill in dealing slips, the trades are matched by computer and matched trades are sent electronically to the clearing house.

The Chicago pits are very busy with frenzied shouting and pushing. The classic story is of the trader who died but couldn't fall over because the pit was too busy. Later, other traders who had lost on deals, filled in slips and put them in his pocket, leaving it to his insurer to pay up!

Computer systems are more boring, being based on order matching electronically. There is a CME/Reuters system called GLOBEX. This is being used when the exchanges are closed, enabling them to continue trading and cross time zones with Europe and Japan. The CBOT already operates an evening session and the floor at the PHLX is open 18 hours per day.

London's LIFFE exchange (before it was taken over by Euronext) introduced an electronic trading system, Connect, and its success was such that the trading floor closed in early 2000. As was mentioned in the last chapter, Connect is now Euronext's trading platform for all derivatives.

In 2003, CBOT decided to use Connect and introduced it in January 2004 at the same time as announcing joint clearing with the CME to help meet competition in the US from Eurex. Some 90% of the trading in US Treasury futures is now electronic. By contrast, 90% of trading in agricultural products is open outcry at CBOT but electronic trading was being introduced in 2006. At the CME, most futures trading has moved to the GLOBEX system. Options are more difficult but volumes are growing.

Outside of financial contracts, the International Petroleum Exchange (IPE) in London trades the Brent oil futures, the industry's benchmark. They went from open outcry to electronic trading in May 2005. The US rival, the New York Mercantile

Exchange (NYMEX) opened an office in London in May 2005 in direct competition and using open outcry hoping to attract disgruntled traders at IPE who were unhappy with the move to electronic trading. Up to the end of 2005, volumes were poor. NYMEX is the world's largest energy and metal futures exchange, with 134 years of pit trading – but it, too, offered electronic trading in 2006. Its rival, the Intercontinental Futures Exchange (ICE) had already done so in 2005. Finally, one of the world's oldest exchanges, the London Metal Exchange, went electronic in 2005.

Another factor affecting exchanges is the increase in decisions to go public. The CME listed in late 2002, CBOT in October 2005. NYMEX is likely to be next. IPE is owned by the Intercontinental Exchange, Atlanta, who are themselves considering a flotation.

Contract Volumes

The volumes in the major exchanges in 2005 are shown in Table 13.2.

Table 13.2   *Global derivative trading, January–September 2005, million contracts*

	Exchange	Total
1	Korea Exchange	1897
2	Eurex	938
3	Chicago Mercantile Exchange (CME)	793
4	Euronext	583
5	Chicago Board of Trade (CBOT)	523
6	Chicago Board Options Exchange (CBOE)	334
7	International Securities Exchange, New York	319
8	Bovespa, Brazil	209
9	New York Merchantile Exchange	153

Source: Futures Industry Association.

Please note that these figures from *Futures Industry* magazine do not include options on individual indices. If they had, EUREX would be shown as the second biggest exchange after CBOT, with CBOE fourth and LIFFE fifth. The CBOE is the world's biggest exchange for options, trading options on 850 companies and 35 different equity indices. It took over the options business of the New York Stock Exchange in 1997.

('Millions of contracts' as a guide to size can, of course, be misleading, since it depends on the size of contract. The biggest percentage rise in option trading volume in 1998 occurred on the Paris MONEP, but it also coincided with a fall in contract size for individual stock options from 100 shares to 10. It also explains the very high volumes for Korea and Brazil.)

SUMMARY

Futures trading began with crops which were only available once per year and whose price fluctuated.

Buyers and sellers might seek to reduce the risk of an adverse price movement by a *hedge*.

A futures contract is an agreement to buy or sell a product at a set price at a later date. Unlike options, however, it is a commitment. Speculators, therefore, are exposed to unlimited risk but hedgers can offset losses with profits on their physical positions.

Usually, futures contracts do not go to delivery. An opening contract to buy is closed by a later contract to sell; an opening contract to sell is closed by a later contract to buy. The position is cash settled. In contracts like equity indices and interest rates, delivery is not possible anyway.

A *forward* deal is one where the intention is to go to delivery.

A *futures* deal is one which is likely to be closed with the opposite and lead to cash settlement. They are traded on futures exchanges with set contract sizes, set expiry dates and the protection of the clearing house.

Futures exist on the same range of products as options although futures on equities are rare.

Many options contracts on futures exchanges are *options to have the future*.

Some exchanges use a trading floor and *open outcry*. Others use systems of order matching by computer. Order matching is now increasing at the expense of open outcry.

14 Other Derivative Products

INTRODUCTION

All the derivative products which we shall describe in this chapter are essentially options and futures in another guise. They are not, however, traded on exchanges but are OTC products. In addition, as interest rates, the price of money, lie at the heart of the financial markets, the original products were all about *interest rate risk*. In recent years, however, *credit risk* has become more important and led to new products called *credit derivatives;* these are described later in the chapter.

FORWARD RATE AGREEMENTS (FRAs)

To begin with, we must consider the term 'forward/forward'. This is an arrangement between two counterparties to borrow or lend an agreed sum of money at an agreed rate for an agreed period which will not begin until a future date. For example, *A* will lend *B* $1m at 5% for six months commencing in six months, called '6 against 12' or simply '6 × 12'.

It may be that a corporate needs a bank loan of $1m in six months and is worried about rates going up. They ask the bank to quote a rate of interest now for lending money in six months for six months. This is rather like an importer asking a bank to quote a rate for buying dollars against euros in six months. In foreign exchange, we argued that the bank could avoid risk by buying the dollars today and putting them on deposit for six months until needed by the client.

In the interest rate market, if asked to quote forward/forward, the bank could equally borrow money at today's rates and put it on deposit until needed by the client. In the above case, the bank will borrow money for 12 months, deposit it for the first six months and then lend it to the client for the remaining six months. The rate quoted will depend on:

- ❏ The bank's cost of borrowing and return from lending
- ❏ The yield curve: if positive, the bank borrowing for longer periods costs more than borrowing for short periods
- ❏ The reinvestment of the interest it earns on the money in the first six months.

This is how such deals were actually handled until the 1980s, when other techniques were developed. The banks are not keen now to quote these forward rates since the borrowing/lending uses up the bank's line of credit with other banks and also the line of credit with its own customers.

The *forward rate agreement* (FRA) is the bank's answer to the request for the forward/forward deal.

The FRA is not about borrowing money, but about a future level of interest rates. The future level is compared to an agreed level and the agreement is settled on the difference between the two rates. The future level in the London market will be based on the LIBOR rate – in this case, Eurodollar LIBOR.

For example, the corporate arranges with a bank that the 'target rate' of interest for six months ahead is 5% on a notional principal of $1 million. If, in six months, interest rates are 5%, then nothing happens. If rates are 4%, the corporate pays the bank 1% of $1 million (but will have lower borrowing costs elsewhere). If rates are 6%, however, the bank pays the corporate 1% of $1 million to help offset their extra borrowing costs (see Figure 14.1).

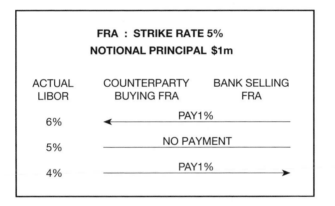

Figure 14.1 *Accounting for differences*

This is 'accounting for differences', and has the advantage of less credit risk. The bank, for example, is not borrowing or lending $1 million, only accounting for the difference in rates from a target of 5%.

The corporate has fixed its rate for borrowing in six months in an indirect way. If rates go up, the corporate pays more for the money but is compensated for the extra cost by the FRA. If rates go down, the corporate will not benefit because the lower borrowing costs are offset by a payment under the FRA.

This line of explanation may well sound familiar. It's the same effect that was achieved by the interest rate futures transaction in Chapter 13. In selling the futures at 3.75%, the corporate was agreeing to settle on the difference between 3.75% and market rates at expiry. When rates were 4.75%, the corporate received 1% on the underlying contract value of $20 million. When rates were 2.75%, the corporate paid the futures exchange 1% on the underlying $20 million. The FRA is really an OTC future being arranged with a bank and not a futures exchange. It has the advantage of flexibility on both dates and amounts of money.

Typical FRA periods are '3 against 6' and '6 against 12'. This is because floating rates on loans and FRNs are revised at three month or six month intervals. A bank with a gap in its asset/liability management can thus close the exposure with an FRA. There will be a corporate market with corporates talking to their commercial banks for deals down to, say, $1 million or £1 million and a professional market, the banks between themselves, for typical sums from 50 million to 100 million and in sterling, yen, Swiss francs and euros.

How does the bank make a profit? The FRA is a product, like any other product, and sold with a bid/offer spread. Just as a market maker will buy shares and hope to sell them at a better rate, so the bank expects to buy FRAs at one rate and sell them at another. It will base the price for future interest rates on the deposit market yield curve or the prices of futures exchange contracts. Suppose that a '3 against 6' dollar FRA is quoted at 5.54/5.50. A bank will sell an FRA based on 5.54% but buy one based on 5.50%. If the rate at the three month date is 6%, the bank pays 46 basis points on the FRA it sold but receives 50 basis points on the one it bought. If rates are 5%, the bank receives 54 basis points on the FRA it sold but pays only 50 basis points on the one it bought (see Figure 14.2). Four basis points may not seem much for the administrative cost and the risk (*and* capital ratio for the risk) and it isn't. The market is very competitive and banks need to be totally efficient to make any money. As a result, the trader may choose not to offset the FRA with one in the opposite direction but believe they will receive more money than they will pay. This does, of course, now involve interest rate risk and risk limits must be set.

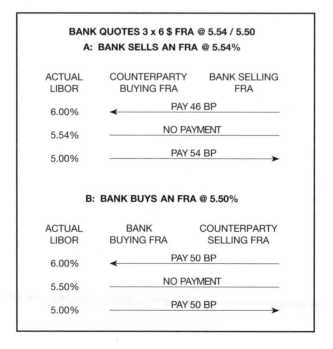

Figure 14.2   *How the bank makes a profit from an FRA*

(One technical point. With an FRA which is, say, in three months for three months, then the payment is made in *advance* of the second three month period. As a result, only the net present value is actually paid.)

It may be that an FRA buyer is unsure of the direction of interest rates. The FRA will protect against a rise in rates but no benefit will arise if rates fall. If this is unacceptable, the answer here is to pay for an *option* to have an FRA. If rates rise, the option to have the FRA is exercised. If rates fall, the option is abandoned. (Simple, really!)

The FRA solves the problem of an interest rate risk for one future time, but what about risk over, say, five years? For this we turn to *swaps*.

SWAPS

Comparative Advantage

Interest rate swaps exploit what could be described as arbitrage opportunities, and in doing so create a market in which others can hedge or speculate on the movement of interest rates.

It begins with the 19th century economist, David Ricardo, and his 'Theory of Comparative Advantage'. Ricardo argued that two countries could benefit from international trade even where one made all products more productively than the second.

Let's take two countries, *ABC* and *XYZ*, and two products, *A* and *B*. The product rates per hour for *A* and *B* in both countries are shown in Figure 14.3.

	ABC		*XYZ*	
Product *A*	100	Product *A*	50
Product *B*	100	Product *B*	70

Figure 14.3 *International trade – comparative advantage*

Ricardo argued that country *ABC* should concentrate on producing product *A* and country *XYZ* concentrate on product *B* and then trade. This is because, while country *ABC* is superior in both *A* and *B*, it has a great *comparative advantage* in *A*. Country *ABC*, thus, produces all product *A* and exports the surplus to country *XYZ*. The latter produces all product *B* and exports the surplus to country *ABC*. Both countries gain as *ABC* exploits to the full its comparative advantage in producing product *A*. This will become clearer from a study of the corresponding examples from the financial markets (see Figure 14.4 and the accompanying explanation).

We translate this now to borrowing rates instead. The two products become fixed rate finance and floating rate finance. The two countries become two companies, *ABC* and *XYZ*. Investors' perception of risk is not the same in the fixed interest rate market as it is in the floating rate market. Thus, company *ABC* may be able to borrow more cheaply than *XYZ* at either fixed or floating rate but the difference is not the same – that is, there is a comparative advantage to be exploited.

Company *ABC* can raise fixed rate finance at 7% or floating at LIBOR (really wants floating rate funds).

Company *XYZ* has to pay 10% for fixed rate borrowing and LIBOR + 1% for floating rate funds (really prefers fixed rate financing).

ABC can borrow cheaper than *XYZ* in both fixed and floating rate markets but has greater comparative advantage in fixed.

Therefore:

ABC raises fixed at 7% but agrees to pay LIBOR to *XYZ*. *XYZ* borrows floating rate funds at LIBOR + 1% but agrees to pay 8% to *ABC* (Figure 14.4).

Figure 14.4 *Using the swap technique*

Thus:

ABC pays 7% fixed but receives 8% from *XYZ*. It pays LIBOR to *XYZ* but in effect is paying LIBOR −1%, less than if it borrowed at floating rate at LIBOR.

XYZ pays LIBOR + 1% but receives only LIBOR from *ABC*, thus costing *XYZ* 1%. It pays 8% to *ABC*, in effect paying 9% – but this is less than if it borrowed fixed at 10%. (This is another example of a technique that is not a 'zero-sum game'.)

ABC and *XYZ* are each saving 1% on their cost of borrowing by using the swap technique. This swap opportunity occurs because floating rate lenders do not distinguish between the credit standing of borrowers to the same degree as fixed rate lenders. We might imagine that if one borrower has AAA credit rating and one BBB, then the difference between the rates of borrowing, whether fixed or floating, would be the same. In fact, this is not the case. If lesser rated credits want to borrow at fixed rate instead of floating, then the rate is not quite as attractive.

Interest Rate Swaps

In our example above, the difference in rates was a considerable exaggeration on a real life situation. This was in order to simplify a concept that always seems complex to newcomers. The principle is the same even if the real life difference is only a matter of a few basis points.

There are, therefore, two aspects to an interest rate swap. One is simply that one party agrees to pay a fixed rate on a notional principal sum of money for a period of time and the other agrees to pay floating rate. In our FRA example (Figure 14.2) a counterparty bought an FRA at 5.54% from a bank. In effect they agreed to pay a fixed rate (5.54%) and receive a floating rate (LIBOR) from the bank. Thus the swap and the FRA are logically the same. Unlike an FRA, which was only for one future time period, a swap is for several time periods ahead, for example, six monthly rate comparisons for, say, five years.

The other element is a possible profit arising from the comparative advantage concept which we just described. Even without any 'profit' element, one party with a floating rate commitment may feel happier swapping into a fixed rate commitment.

The elements in the swap are:

❏ The fixed rate
❏ The variable rate
❏ The settlement periods
❏ The total maturity
❏ The underlying notional principal.

For example, the parties may agree that one pays 5.5% and the other pays Eurodollar LIBOR on a notional underlying principal of $50 million. The swap is to last five years and the settlement periods are six monthly. That is, every six months 5.5% is compared with Eurodollar LIBOR and a net sum of money is paid over. If the difference was 1%, then 1% of $50 million for six months is the sum to be paid over – $250 000. The money, however, is not in fact paid over until the end of the six monthly period, not at the beginning. That is because interest payments are paid in arrears. A bank, for example, sets the rate on an actual loan for six months at 5.5% but the interest is paid at the end of six months, not the beginning.

Making a Market in Swaps

How do these companies, *ABC* and *XYZ*, find each other? Obviously, with difficulty. So there is a role for banks to bring the parties together and take a piece of the action. In Figure 14.4, the bank could take 8% from *XYZ* and only pass on 7¾% to *ABC*. It could take LIBOR from *ABC* and only pass on LIBOR – ¼% to *XYZ*. *ABC* and *XYZ* will still profit from the deal but the bank now has ½% for its trouble.

The market began in 1982 and as it grew banks became prepared to carry out a swap just for one counterparty, pending finding another counterparty later. This is called a *warehouse* swap. The bank is prepared to 'warehouse' the swap until a counterparty can be found, in the meantime taking hedging action as we will explain later. It is called an 'unmatched swap'.

The swap, therefore, has simply become another product which the banks market with the usual bid/offer rates.

The bank may quote, for example, 5.80/5.75 for a five year dollar swap (Figure 14.5).

Figure 14.5   *Bank swap quotation*

If the bank stands in the middle between two counterparties (the matched swap), then the bank has no interest rate risk and a locked in five basis points profit. If LIBOR goes up, the bank pays more to counterparty *XYZ* but receives it from *ABC*. If rates fall, the bank receives less from *ABC* but pays less to *XYZ*. *XYZ* pays 5.80% to the bank and the bank pays 5.75% to *ABC*, keeping five basis points (Figure 14.6).

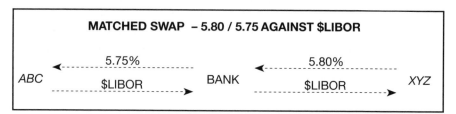

Figure 14.6   *Using matched swap*

The bank may have no interest rate risk but it does have counterparty risk. What if *ABC* or *XYZ* goes into liquidation and the bank is left with an unmatched swap? Under today's rules from regulators, capital must be provided for this risk.

In providing a market in swaps the banks are exposed to risk until they can find someone who wants to do a swap in the opposite direction. In the meantime they can adopt hedging strategies:

❏ If the bank is at risk to a *fall in interest rates* (because it has lent floating and borrowed fixed), then it will buy fixed interest securities, whose price will rise when interest rates fall.

❏ If the bank is at risk should *interest rates rise* (because it has borrowed floating and lent fixed), then it can hedge in the *futures* market by selling an interest rate future, giving the right to borrow at prevailing rates of interest. When interest rates rise this right becomes valuable and the bank will make a profit on the futures contract.

(Notice the language used above. The bank receiving LIBOR and paying 5.75% can be said to have *lent floating and borrowed fixed* (and vice-versa).) Other language used is a reference to the 'payer' and the 'receiver'. This always refers to the fixed rate element.

Actual market rates tend to fall between the rates quoted for an AAA borrower and a single A borrower for borrowing for given periods of time. If $s, they are usually expressed as a given number of basis points over US Treasury bond rates for the fixed element. If £s, they are usually expressed as a given number of basis points over the gilts rate. The variable rate is Euro or domestic LIBOR.

Users of Swaps

Assuming that a five year dollar swap rate is quoted as 5.80/5.75, who are the users of these swaps? We find that the market talks of *liability swaps* and *asset swaps*.

❏   Liability swaps are simply swaps for borrowers of money.
❏   Asset swaps are simply swaps for lenders of money.

The treasurer has a bank loan based on $LIBOR (see Figure 14.7). Worried that rates will rise, he does a swap, changing the floating rate bank loan into fixed rate by this indirect route.

We can also envisage a situation in which a treasurer with a fixed rate loan could receive 5.75% and pay LIBOR, turning the fixed rate loan into floating rate. A further variation is possible. If the loan is, say, $100 million, the treasurer can do the swap for only $50 million – leaving half the money at fixed rate and half at floating (quite common).

Using the swap technique, a eurobond issuer may not only change the fixed rate basis into floating but create a profit margin of ten basis points due to the general comparative advantage concept (see Figure 14.8).

What the issuer may well do is equalise the fixed rate payment and receipt and use the profit margin to cut the LIBOR rate (see Figure 14.9).

The issuer agrees to receive 5.65% instead of 5.75% and to pay LIBOR – 10 instead of just LIBOR. What we say is that the issuer has achieved 'sub-LIBOR funding'.

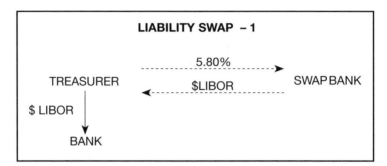

Figure 14.7 *Swap to change floating rate bank loan into fixed rate*

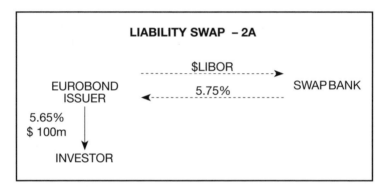

Figure 14.8 *Swap to change fixed rate bond into floating rate*

Figure 14.9 *Equalising the fixed rate payment and receipt*

The investor is receiving floating rate income based on $LIBOR (either from a loan or FRN). Believing that rates will fall, the issuer swaps into a fixed rate return. We say that the investor has changed the FRN into a 'synthetic' fixed rate bond (see Figure 14.10).

Figure 14.10   *'Synthetic' fixed rate bond*

Banks often buy fixed rate bonds from lesser rated corporates (that is, higher interest rates) to use for an asset swap to create floating rate income well above LIBOR (see Figure 14.11).

Figure 14.11   *Bank profit from an asset swap*

In Figure 14.11, the bank receives 6.25% from a bond but only pays 5.75% on the fixed leg of the swap. It also receives LIBOR and thus a total receipt of LIBOR + 50. It will probably 'package' the deal and pass it on to a fund looking for good floating rate income, the bank taking some profit while doing so.

Swaps and Futures

Swaps are really a strip of futures or FRA contracts lasting over several years. They are, of course, OTC with all the flexibility that that involves. When the corporate sold an interest rate future at 3.75%, we saw that the effect was the same as the

FRA based on 3.75%. In the same way, selling an interest rate future at 3.75% is choosing to borrow fixed and lend floating (the alternative language we used for swaps). It's a swap (or FRA) for a single time period only. Equally, the buyer of an interest rate future is choosing to borrow floating and lend fixed – the other side of the swap.

Because the language and terminology used in FRAs and swaps is different from that used for futures, newcomers think of them as essentially different products when they are really all variations on the same product. They therefore have the essential characteristic of futures – that a hedger can gain protection from an adverse rate movement but will not benefit from a favourable one.

Futures are for three month time periods ahead (although we could book all eight quarterly contracts for the next two years – called a 'strip' of futures). FRAs are for one time period ahead but not necessarily three months and, again, a strip of FRAs could be purchased or sold. For periods of two years or more, swaps are more attractive. Most swaps are in the range 2–10 years. However, the former UK Halifax Building Society issued a 25 year bond which was said to have been swapped into floating rate for 25 years!

Other Swaps

A swap buyer may want a swap but only wish to commence in, say, six months' time. This becomes the *forward swap*.

In six months' time, the forward swap buyer's view of interest rates may turn out to be incorrect. The buyer is, however, committed to the swap. Another possibility, therefore, is to pay a premium for an option to have the swap later (just like the option to have an FRA). This is called by a curious piece of jargon – the *swaption*.

It may be that the notional principal in the swap is not constant but on a 'reducing' basis. For example, a swap based on a notional principal of $10 million for five years but the amount of the principal is reduced each year. This could apply when the swap backs a loan of which some of the principal is constantly being repaid or a bond for which a sinking fund is being accumulated to redeem the bond. This is called an *amortising swap*.

The notional principal at risk might also vary but up and down rather than on a declining basis. This is the *roller coaster swap*.

There are swaps in which both parties pay floating rate, but on a different basis. For example, one pays Eurodollar LIBOR and the other pays three month US Treasury bill rates. This is the *basis swap*.

Swapnotes and the Swaps Yield Curve

The list of contracts traded at Euronext.liffe (Table 13.1 in Chapter 13) included swapnotes. This is potentially confusing in that the contract is actually a bond futures contract and not a swaps contract as such. The bond is a notional bond with a coupon of 6% p.a. and a payment of principal on final maturity (we met the idea of a notional bond in Chapter 13). You will remember that the net present value of a bond is arrived at by discounting all the future cash flows at the yield curve interest rates. The swapnote contract is similar in that the settlement price is derived in the same way but uses a different yield curve – the one known as the *swaps yield curve*. The normal yield curve is based on government borrowing rates which is fine if you are using the futures to cover the risk on government bonds. What about corporate bonds? The swaps yield curve is based on the appropriate interest rates for top quality non-government borrowers. Since swaps involve credit risk, the swaps yield curve is studied to ascertain the appropriate interest rates for a swaps contract. For those whose risk is in corporate bonds or mortgage bonds (like pfandbriefe) the swapnote is more appropriate for bond futures than using the conventional government bonds contracts.

Other users might be swaps traders hedging risk due to possible future changes in the swaps yield curve. The swapnote could also be used to track the spread of these corporate rates over government rates. For example, in a recession, one would expect this spread to increase.

Of course, many corporates are not top quality anyway – indeed, there are many non-investment grade issuers these days. When they issue a bond, the language used is 'issued at x basis points above the swaps yield curve'.

CURRENCY SWAPS

The swaps market began with currency swaps. It may be that a US-based issuer wants Swiss francs but is not well known to Swiss franc investors. A Swiss corporate or public body, well known in Switzerland, may want dollars but is not well known to dollar investors. The US issuer will have to pay a premium to raise Swiss francs and the Swiss issuer will have to pay a premium to raise dollars. The answer is for the US issuer to raise dollars, the Swiss issuer to raise Swiss francs and then swap the proceeds. This is the classic *currency swap*.

The first major case was in 1981, with the World Bank wanting a further Swiss franc issue and faced with paying a premium to persuade Swiss franc investors to hold even more World Bank paper. IBM wanted a dollar issue but faced the same problem. Salomon Bros arranged a swap. The World Bank raised the money in dollars and IBM raised the money in Swiss francs. Dollar investors were pleased to hold World Bank paper and Swiss franc investors were pleased to hold IBM paper. The two entities swapped the proceeds. On redemption (in 1986), they arranged to swap back at the same exchange rate.

In the meantime, IBM sent dollar interest payments to the World Bank who sent Swiss franc interest payments to IBM.

Again, as the market grew, banks took on unmatched deals and made a market in currency swaps. Sometimes, though, the bank can be lucky and match two investors coming to the market at the same time.

In September 1996, the European Investment Bank (EIB) and the Tennessee Valley Authority (TVA) came to the market at the same time. The EIB wanted 10 year deutschmarks and the TVA wanted 10 year dollars. However, the EIB could borrow in dollars 7 basis points less than TVA, but only 4 basis points less in deutschmarks. As a result, the EIB borrowed $1 billion, the TVA borrowed DM1.5 billion and they swapped the proceeds. It was a classic case of exploiting comparative advantage. In swapping directly, both parties also saved bid/offer spreads and reduced transaction costs.

CAPS, FLOORS AND COLLARS

Introduction

Sometimes, the user in this market may require protection in one direction only. For example, a corporate may seek protection from interest rates rising but seek to benefit should they fall. An investor, receiving money at floating rate, may seek protection from rates falling but seek to benefit should they rise.

This end objective can be achieved by interest rate options on trading exchanges. If the rate moves the wrong way for our market position, the option is exercised and compensation obtained. If the rate moves the right way for our borrowing/lending position, the option is abandoned and we benefit from better rates.

Exchanges, however, have drawbacks, as we have seen. The OTC market has responded with two flexible products to meet the above situations for borrowers and investors – the *cap* and the *floor*.

Caps

The interest rate cap sets a maximum level on a short-term rate interest rate. Buyers are compensated if the interest rate goes above a certain level (the strike level).

For example, the arrangement may be based on three months LIBOR and have a term of three years. The strike level is 5%, the revision of the rate is quarterly and the notional principal is $10 million. Thus, if LIBOR is 6% in three months, the seller pays the buyer 1% of $10 million for three months – say, $25 000 (see Figure 14.12).

If rates are 5% or less, nothing happens and the cap buyer can benefit from lower borrowing rates. The fee is, of course, the option premium. The OTC cap can not only offer the precise dates we require but it is a continuous arrangement, like a swap, and not just for one time period ahead.

There are the usual variations on the theme that we associate with options. If the buyer is prepared to accept some interest rate risk, the strike rate in the above example could be chosen as 6%. This is 'out of the money' in options terms and the premium will be cheaper.

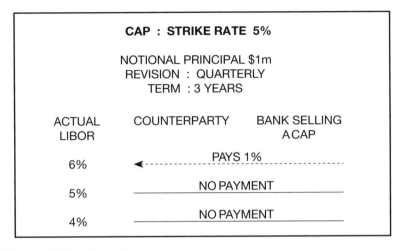

Figure 14.12   *Using the cap*

Floors

The interest rate floor is simply the opposite product. An investor, receiving income at floating rate, may buy a floor. This sets a minimum level to a rate of interest. The buyer is compensated if the market goes below this level (see Figure 14.13).

The terms could be exactly as described for the cap, but on the basis that payment is made if rates fall *below* the strike rate.

It may be that the user is fairly sure about interest rates for one year, but not thereafter. The cap or floor can be arranged to commence in one year's time – the *forward* cap or floor.

```
          FLOOR : STRIKE RATE 5%

             NOTIONAL PRINCIPAL $1m
             REVISION : QUARTERLY
               TERM : 3 YEARS

  ACTUAL        COUNTERPARTY      BANK SELLING
  LIBOR                            A FLOOR

                   NO PAYMENT
    6%        _____

                   NO PAYMENT
    5%        _____

                     PAYS 1%
    4%        ◄---------------------------
```

Figure 14.13   *Using the floor*

Collars

We will have seen from the above that the cap buyer pays a premium and receives payment if rates rise above a given level.

The floor seller receives a premium, but must make payment if rates fall below a given level.

Imagine simultaneously buying a cap at 6% and selling a floor at 4%.

The effect of this is shown in Figure 14.14.

The net effect is to lock into a band of rates – the *collar* – for the next three years.

If rates are between 6% and 4%, we borrow at the market rate. If rates rise above 6% we are protected. If they fall below 4%, we don't benefit. The effect of paying a premium and receiving one is that the cost is reduced. Rates can be chosen at which the two premiums are the same – the *no cost collar*.

This is an attractive device and very popular at the moment. All our other devices have turned around a given rate of interest. Here we select a band instead.

We have actually met this product before. It was in Chapter 8 on foreign exchange, and it was the 'cylinder' or 'collar' or 'range forward'. The future buyer of dollars will never have a worse rate than $1.85 per £ but never have a better rate than $1.95. It's just the same logic applied in a different market.

Caps, floors and collars are a series of interest rate options over a period of time. At present, 2–5 years is the most popular range.

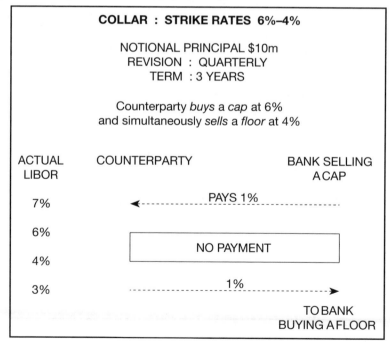

Figure 14.14   Using the collar

CREDIT DERIVATIVES

We have become familiar with market risk, such as interest rates, currency rates, equity and bond prices – but what about *credit* risk? We have seen huge losses from the original LDC crisis in the 1970s and the more recent Far East and Russian crises. The original Basel agreement included credit risk and there is more emphasis in Basel 11. In addition to this, there is the more general risk to commercial lenders when borrowers can't pay and to investors when bonds default.

In the last five years, a market to lay off risk has exploded. This is the market for *credit derivatives* – a market that scarcely existed in 2000. We have mentioned banks selling off loan books to others to reduce risk and clear the balance sheet. What has happened with credit derivatives is the possibility of simply selling the risk itself and keeping the loan or bonds.

The basic product is the *credit default swap* (CDS). A buyer holding $10 million worth of a five year bond may ask someone else to take on the risk of default in return for a premium. The premium is paid for five years and, if the bond has not defaulted, the seller of the CDS keeps the premiums and has nothing to pay. If the bond defaults, the buyer of the CDS, the bond holder, hands over the bond in return for its face value. The premium or spread is usually quoted as basis points. It will relate to the spread of the issuer's bond's yield over the government or risk free rate. If the spread is 70 basis points, the investor holding $10 million of the five year bond will pay $70 000 p.a. for five years to the seller of the CDS – see Figure 14.15.

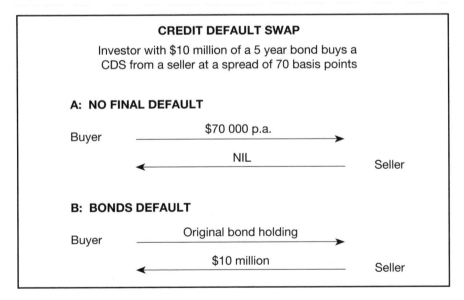

Figure 14.15 *Credit default swap*

Let us say that the risk-free rate is 5% and an investor has a bond paying 5.7% at issue. The spread of 0.7% is the risk element in the bond. The investor is paid 0.7% to take the risk of default. Why not sell this risk to someone else? That is exactly what the CDS does. It might be that the spread in the market is only 0.6%. In that case, the investor now has a risk-free return on the bond of 4.1%. However, this will not last long as arbitrageurs will move in to take advantage and the spreads will soon equalise. The spread on a triple A bond is likely to be about 20 basis points, but non-investment grade bonds could be several hundred basis points. When TDC, the Danish telecommunications group, was taken over by a group of private equity companies with huge leverage, the market was quoting the premium as 253 basis points. Thus, to insure against default on €10 million of bonds, would cost €253 000 p.a.

This is, of course, no different from an individual paying an insurance company $400 p.a. to cover the risk of damage to their car. Indeed, many of the sellers of CDS are insurance companies. What makes it different is that, as you might have guessed, the market complicates it considerably.

For instance, just as a seller of bond futures may not own the bonds, so a buyer of a CDS may not own the bonds either but be taking a speculative position. Of course, if there is a default, we could have the embarrassment that there are more bonds traded on CDS contracts than actually exist. This was the case with US motor parts supplier, Delphi, who filed for bankruptcy on 8 October 2005. The market got together and found a way of cash settlement. An auction determined the price of Delphi bonds, say 30¢ in the dollar. The CDS seller now pays 70¢ in the dollar as settlement. The buyer has 70¢ in the dollar, plus the estimated value of the bond of 30¢ in the dollar, and is compensated for the risk without selling the bonds.

The next complication comes with the creation of default indices – Dow Jones IG index in the US and iTraxx indices in Europe. They track the credit profile of, say, 125 companies in the investment grade index and 100 in the case of a high yield index. They are thus a proxy for the credit of the corporate bond market at that grade. The compilers usually reset the index every six months. Some firms may move from one index to another if their fundamental credit rating changes. A default of one name in the index triggers a partial settlement. It works like a single CDS but for only a fraction of the notional value, for example 1% if there are 100 names in the basket.

The market is not just about the credit on bonds. Banks, in particular, may wish to sell off some risk to improve their capital ratio. In Chapter 6, we covered structured bonds when a whole portfolio of bonds was split into tranches according to risk. This is very common in the credit default market. The first tranche carries the highest risk of default and is called the *equity tranche*. The bank usually keeps this. The second tranche is called the *mezzanine tranche* and is a little less risky. Finally, we come to the least risky *senior debt tranche*. As an example, Citigroup in December 2005 took emerging market credits worth €500 million and split them into 100 equally weighted entities. The senior debt tranche was rated triple A and paid 35 basis points over EURIBOR; the BB tranche in dollars paid, by contrast, 425 basis points over EURIBOR; Citigroup kept the riskiest equity tranche which represented 6.5% of the portfolio.

The above was structured from bank loans. It could have been structured from bonds or existing credit default swaps. The income is distributed to tranche holders according to risk. We are in the world of the *synthetic collateralised debt obligation.*

Who is buying and selling these risks? Obviously there are banks and also insurance companies. In addition, there are hedge funds and pension funds. Hedge funds are active players – some have estimated that they may account for 70% of the volume of trading. They move fast and may be in and out of a deal before it can be confirmed on paper. They also often assign the deal to other participants, adding a third party to the deal. All this, and the huge increase in the market, has led to a worry about back office procedures and possible legal problems if there was a crisis. This is not helped by the fact that the market is not transparent, leading many to call for new regulation.

Gerald Corrigan (former President of the New York Federal Reserve) set up a Market Practice Group and, in the last quarter of 2005, and persuaded the 14 key players in the US to adopt new procedures. They agreed to cut backlogs, provide more information, adopt new procedures for third party assignments, increase cash settlements and permit easier cancellation of offsets (where two deals effectively cancel each other out).

To assist this, software systems were released – T-Zero Market Access and TradeWeb. These systems aim to send trade electronically to risk management systems, back office and the Depository Trust and Clearing Corporation. They usually tackle the indices first as this is easier – elsewhere there is a mass of bespoke deals which make automation more difficult.

As we mentioned above, the plethora of deals being done leads to deals between traders which cancel each other out. The trade, therefore, needs a netting system, exactly like foreign exchange in Chapter 9. TriOptima, a financial technology company, now runs just such a netting service. It collects trade data from dealers and identifies offsetting transactions that can be terminated, leaving dealers with a net exposure to trading partners. Big dealers still buy and sell the bulk of credit derivatives.

Figures for the size of the market are produced by the International Swaps and Derivatives Association (ISDA). There is a notional value of contracts and a true market value. So in the case of Figure 14.15, the notional value is $10 million but the trade value $5 \times \$70\,000 = \$350\,000$. At end 2005, the ISDA produced a trade figure of $17\,300 billion for the whole market, an increase of 50% in the first half of the year and a further 39% in the second. A survey carried out of 23 derivative traders found that the average increase in the use of CDS trades in 2005 rose to 80%. In Europe, as opposed to the US, some claim that usage of CDS trades trebled in 2005 (with hedge funds large users). Either way, the figures are huge for a market which scarcely existed five years ago. Some 50% of the market is in the UK and the other half in the US.

The usual question can be asked – how risky is all this? No less an authority than Alan Greenspan, former President of the Federal Reserve, seems relaxed about it, commenting that a wide spread of risk was a good thing. On the other hand, Warren Buffet, the 'sage of Omaha', describes credit derivatives as 'time bombs'. In the UK, John Tiner, the chief executive of the FSA, says, 'Credit derivatives bring speculators and hedgers into the market and that means they bring information into the market. I think this makes markets more transparent and that must be good for all players.' The sudden move of General Motors and Ford from investment to non-investment grade caused major tremors in the market and the BIS itself expressed concern. However, the market survived without major bankruptcies, although possibly only by the skin of its teeth.

THE MARKET IN DERIVATIVE INSTRUMENTS

The BIS has carried out periodic surveys of the volume and value of derivatives contracts traded both on exchanges and on the much larger OTC market and now carries the updated figures in its quarterly reviews.

The figures in Tables 14.1 and 14.2 illustrate the growth between 2002 and 2005. If we go back to 1985, the growth is even more spectacular. Our OTC total at June 2005 is $270 100 billion notional value of outstanding contracts, the 1985 figure was $47 412 billion. The total figure for trading on organised exchanges at September 2005 is $58 281 billion notional value of outstanding contracts, the 1985 figure was $9187 billion. If we look at interest rate options on traded exchanges, 1985's figure of $2742 billion notional value of outstanding contracts has grown to $32 795 billion. Baring's and other scandals led some commentators at the time to suggest that the derivatives bubble of the early 90s had burst – or at least that the growth era was over. This is clearly not so. Please note that the figures do not include credit derivatives which are, in part, just a special form of insurance.

This growth in the market and the growth in sheer complexity have led the BIS and others to draw attention to the dangers of controlling the risks, and deficiencies in systems for controlling these risks.

To the usual counterparty and position risks we have to add legal risk and tax risk. The UK sterling swaps market was thrown into confusion by a decision that local authority swaps were illegal. Conflicting tax treatment in Australia and the US led to Westpac paying out an extra $80 million in tax to the US authorities and cutting its dividend.

The outstanding example of the risk in derivative transactions was the collapse in early 1995 of the UK's oldest merchant bank, Baring Bros, alleged to be due to the activities of one trader, Nick Leeson. The bank's controls were woefully inadequate and management allowed one trader's activities to ruin the bank at a cost of £860 million. At Kidder Peabody, in the US, one trader, Joseph Jett, is alleged to have concealed losses of $350 million over a period of 2 years. The rogue trader at Daiwa in New York (who lost a similar sum to Nick Leeson) had apparently been concealing his mounting losses for eleven years! Mr Hamanaka at Sumitomo used derivatives allegedly to corner the world copper market, culminating in losses of around $2.4 billion!

Table 14.1   *Notional amounts outstanding of OTC derivatives by risk category and instrument in billions of dollars*

Instrument	June 2005	Dec 2002
Foreign exchange		
Outright forwards and forex swaps	24 267	15 422
Options	6809	3226
Interest rate contracts		
FRAs and swaps	77 322	87 912
Options	27 071	13 746
Equity-linked contracts		
Forwards and swaps	176	364
Options	527	1561
Commodities	1694	923
Other *	27 793	18 328
Grand total	270 100	141 865

Note: * Other covers estimated positions on non-regular reporting institutions.
Source: BIS, December 2005.

Corporates, too, have incurred losses – Allied Lyons, Codelco, Metallgesellschaft, Procter and Gamble and Gibsons Greetings Cards were well publicised examples. The last two sued Bankers Trust and both settled out of court.

Perhaps we should not get this out of perspective. The banks lost enormous sums due to the LDC debt crisis, and also incurred large losses due to the global crises in the Far East and Russia. The bail out of Crédit Lyonnais, privatised in 1999, is estimated to have cost the French government somewhere between the equivalent of £10 billion to £19 billion (nobody seems quite sure!). The banks are owed £8000 million by Eurotunnel and haven't a hope of getting back more than half. This makes Baring's £860 million loss seem less significant! These losses were incurred in bank lending, which we've had for the last 600 years. There aren't too many weighty reports on the risk in bank lending and yet reports on derivative risk have been written not only by the BIS but by the IMF, Bank of England, General Accounting Office (US), Federal Reserve and the G30 group of bankers.

Table 14.2   *Derivative instruments traded on organised exchanges, by instrument (notional principal in billions of US dollars)*

Instrument	Sept 2005	June 2002
Foreign exchange futures	110	48
Foreign exchange options	63	30
Interest rate futures	19 860	9415
Interest rate options	32 795	12 477
Equity index futures	727	365
Equity index options	4726	1750
Grand Total	58 281	24 085

Source: BIS, December 2005.

It's unfortunate that the intellectual effort required to gain an understanding of these products leads some people to dismiss it all as 'gambling'.

Suppose we have two corporates facing significant interest rate risk over the next three years. One buys certainty by doing an interest rate swap and electing to pay fixed. The other does nothing.

Who is gambling? Surely, it is the corporate that does nothing and leaves itself open to whatever volatility of interest rates comes along.

The paradox about these products is that the ability to use them to lay off risk means that bankers can take more risk. Insofar as they can take more risk, the more they can offer end users ingenious products which they find beneficial.

As the markets grow, there are more opportunities for laying off a growing variety of risks in an ever more efficient way. As a result, more and more end user products are being released which they find attractive.

This is the beneficial aspect of these markets. Of course, there are the gamblers (speculators) and the markets couldn't exist without them, but to dismiss it all as gambling is to make a serious mistake.

We are seeing this in the consumer markets, where individuals can now have fixed rate mortgages for up to 20 years, capped mortgages and an increasing range of exotic variations. These allow the individual to budget with peace of mind.

Equally, investment products have been launched with a variety of guarantees, typically using options, to ensure that an individual is protected against a market downturn. This, again, allows the person in the street to know that their long-term savings are not exposed to undue risk.

SUMMARY

Forward rate agreements (FRAs) are a way of fixing a rate of interest for a date in the future and for a given period of time (*forward/forward*).

The buyer is compensated by the seller if market rates on the given date exceed the given *strike rate*. The buyer, however, must compensate the seller if market rates fall below the strike rate.

Borrowers seeking protection will *buy* FRAs, investors will *sell* them. Banks make a profit through the use of a bid/offer spread.

Essentially, the FRA is the equivalent of the exchange-traded interest rate futures contract in the OTC market.

The FRA is for one forward period only. *Swaps* are agreements for many forward periods (for example, one per year for the next 10 years). Again, the market rate of interest (usually LIBOR) is compared with a given strike rate leading to a compensatory payment from one party to the other.

The buyer in the case of the FRA is usually called the *payer* in the swap (that is, the payer of the fixed rate). The seller in the FRA is usually called the *receiver* in a swap (that is, the receiver of the fixed rate).

The above are *interest rate swaps*; there are also *currency swaps*.

Profit may arise for both parties from the application of the theory of *comparative advantage*. Banks will make a profit through the bid/offer spread.

Swaps for those borrowing money are *liability swaps*; swaps for investors are *asset swaps*.

Swaps are essentially a series of FRAs. A swap starting at a future date is a *forward swap*; an option to have a swap is a *swaption* and a swap of two floating rates is a *basis swap*.

A borrower can be protected from an interest rate rise but still benefit from a fall using an interest rate *cap*; an investor can benefit from an interest rate rise but still be protected from a rise using an interest rate *floor*.

The combination of a cap and floor leads to a range of interest rates for future transactions called a *collar*.

Caps, floors and collars are variations on *options*.

Central banks carried out a survey of the OTC derivatives market in June 1998. Its initial estimate of the notional value outstanding was $71.5 trillion, but the replacement cost was estimated at just $2.58 trillion. The BIS estimate for the notional value outstanding of exchange traded contracts in mid-2002 was $24.1 trillion.

Interest rate derivatives accounted for much the largest category for both OTC and exchange-traded derivatives.

Credit default swaps (CDS) are an arrangement by which the risk of default on a bond issue, or a basket of bond issues, is sold for a given premium. This is part of the market for *credit derivatives* generally, which is the fastest growing sector of the market today.

Insurance

15 Insurance

15 Insurance

BACKGROUND TO THE INSURANCE MARKETS

History

> *But ships are but boards, sailors but men: there be land rats and water rats,*
> *water-thieves and land-thieves, I mean pirates: and then there is the peril of*
> *waters, winds and rocks.*
> (*The Merchant of Venice,* Act I, Scene III)

Shylock is quite right and Antonio is soon to discover that an insurance premium is cheaper than a pound of flesh any day! While the history of insurance is lost in the mists of time, our modern history surely begins with marine insurance.

Ship owners would meet with rich merchants who would agree to jointly pay for any losses for a share of the premiums. A contract was drawn up and merchants added their name at the bottom. As they wrote underneath the text, they were *underwriters*. Apart from this, a group of ship owners might agree to raise a levy on all members and share losses between them. This principle continues today with the so-called 'P&I' club (see below).

Meetings in London for business took place in coffee houses. In 1688 we have the first mention of Edward Lloyd's coffee house in Tower Street. They moved to Lombard Street in 1691. Then, as now, information was power and, in 1734, they began a publication, *Lloyd's List*, which gave shipping information and also some financial data. It is still published today.

The insurance world in those days was as full of scandals as the world of stocks and shares. Just as the Stock Exchange was set up to bring respectability and rules so, in 1769, one Thomas Fielding set up a new organisation meeting in Pope's Head Alley and, in 1771, drew up a document setting up a ruling committee. A move to the Royal Exchange building in 1774 was followed in 1781 by the first constitution of Lloyd's. These were the early origins of the famous Lloyd's of London, of which more later.

Even earlier than Edward Lloyd's coffee house, the Fire Office Company was set up in 1680. The Amicable followed in 1706 and the London Assurance and the Royal Exchange Assurance in 1720.

The basic idea of insurance is the *sharing of risk*. Experience may suggest that, of an insurance population of buildings, 2% will have a fire in a given year. Dividing the anticipated claims by the numbers seeking insurance gives us the *premium* to be paid. Those who haven't had a fire have contributed to a pool to pay for those who have, while buying protection in case they were the unfortunate ones.

The Insurance Market

The biggest markets in the world by total premium income are the US, Japan, the UK, France and Germany. Premiums in the US in 2005 were $1143 billion, Japan $476 billion, UK $300 billion, France $222 billion and Germany $197 billion. The premiums for Western Europe as a whole totalled $1241 billion, of which the UK, France and Germany contributed 58%.

There are clear differences between life and non-life business. Over the whole world, total life premiums were $1973 billion and non-life $1452 billion. Non-life business is 62% of the market in the US, 40% in Europe, but only 20% in Japan. Taking life business only, Europe is the biggest market in the world, followed by the US.

Another way of looking at it is by market penetration, that is, as a percentage of GDP. Here, countries like South Korea, Taiwan and South Africa come out well. Of the industrialised countries, the largest by this measure are the UK, Switzerland, Japan and Ireland. The potential in the fast growing countries of China and India can be seen by the low penetration – only about 3% in each case. (Figures from Swiss Re *Sigma* publication July 2006.)

The main characteristic of the UK insurance companies is the international flavour of the business. This is discussed under the heading 'The London Market' later in this chapter.

Table 15.1   *World's largest insurance companies*

Company		Premiums 2004 $bn
AIG	USA	66.8
Met Life	USA	58.7
Axa	France	58.4
Allianz	Germany	56.2
ING	Netherlands	49.9
Generali	Italy	49.9
Nippon Life	Japan	45.5
Aegon	Benelux	42.0
Aviva	UK	37.6
Great Western Life	Canada	34.0

Sources: Swiss Re *Sigma* publication No. 1/2006

Assurance/Insurance

Assurance is the cover for events which are certain. Since death comes to us all, life insurance (strictly speaking, 'death insurance'!) is providing cover for an event which is certain, only the timing being open to doubt. The study of the relevant statistics and laws of probability by a profession called *actuaries* leads to an accurate estimate as to how many of an insured population will die in a given year. As a result, it would be very unlikely that the claims would exceed the premiums. In other words, the company expects to make an *underwriting* profit. In addition, premiums are paid in advance and will be invested prior to any money being paid out. The second source of profit is thus the return on the investments. Ironically, interest rate risk will be more than mortality risk! Finally, people take out a life policy and perhaps do not change this for the whole of their life. As a result, the business is stable and can invest for the long-term. The nature of this business is such that it is natural for them also to invest funds to provide pensions in the longer-term. We, thus, talk of the 'life and pensions business'.

The industry has been ingenious in working out variations on the theme of a simple life policy. One variation is *term assurance*. The life cover is for a given number of years such as 10 years. As death is no longer certain, the policy is cheaper. We can have heavier protection for a vulnerable period (a young family) than later.

Endowment policies add the element of investment. Life cover is provided up to the age of, say, 50 and if death has not taken place a sum of money is guaranteed. Often the 'life' element is only 10% of the premiums or even less.

Living assurance is a new type that has become popular in the US. This policy will pay out on the diagnosis of serious diseases such as cancer, heart disease, and so on.

Life policies can be with or without *profits*. The with-profits policy declares bonuses annually (*reversionary*) and at termination.

A variation on this theme, which has become popular in many countries (US/Canada/UK/France), is to link the policy to mutual fund performance (*unit-linked*), as the fund is usually divided into units (see Chapter 7).

Insurance is providing cover for events which may or may not happen: for example, theft, fire, accident, storms, and so on. Judging the probability of these events is much more difficult than judging the incidence of death and frequently claims exceed premiums – an underwriting loss. In recessions, for example, the incidence of arson mysteriously increases!

At times, too, premiums are driven down to uneconomic levels due to fierce competition. The industry is cyclical. It is not difficult to start up in insurance and, when profits are good, firms are attracted in until the extra competition produces losses. Firms then depart until profits rise again and the whole cycle starts once more. The 1980s and early 1990s were a very bad period for insurance, exacerbated by an extraordinary series of disasters – hurricanes, the Exxon Valdez spillage, and so on. Heavy losses were made, but then things settled down a little. Profits rose once again, new entrants came in and there was overcapacity in the industry, premiums fell and things were difficult, leading to a new spate of mergers. The events of 11 September 2001 changed things again. Premiums increased considerably and we moved to a new phase in the cycle. Equally, the losses of 2005 due to the tsunami and hurricanes like Katrina have sent premiums up again.

The possibility of underwriting loss means that a good profit from the investment of the premiums is essential since this may be the only profit there is. To make matters worse, premiums are specifically renewed annually and the insured party may look around and decide to switch to another company, leading to less certainty regarding future income.

The investment policy of the insurance company, therefore, has to pay much more attention to liquidity than the investment policy of companies in life and pensions.

As a result of the two sides of the business – assurance and insurance – we find companies which do assurance only, insurance only and companies which are in both markets, called *composites*.

As well as public companies with shareholders, it is very common to find companies which are not public companies but are owned jointly by the policy holders. These are called *mutuals* and this is very common across all the Western markets, especially for life companies.

Regulation

The importance of insurance, and the fact that it is often bought by members of the general public, means that it is an industry which is closely regulated. The collapse of the Vehicle and General Company in the UK in 1971, for example, left 800 000 motorists uninsured overnight!

In the US, regulations are made by both the central government and the states themselves. In the UK, regulation is from the Financial Services Authority, in France from the Direction des Assurances and in Germany from a body called the BAV. In Japan, insurance is now controlled by the Financial Supervisory Agency, set up in 1998.

Where countries have regulatory bodies, their objectives are similar – namely to promote efficient, orderly and fair markets and to help consumers achieve a fair deal. These objectives are aimed at providing confidence in the market to encourage the concept of individual responsibility for one's family and future.

Regulations may cover general supervision, licensing, solvency ratios, accountancy practices and annual returns. They will also cover the question of compulsory insurance, such as third party motor insurance, public liability and so on.

Solvency ratio is similar to the concept of capital ratio in banking (see Chapter 2). In banking it was, in essence, a prudent relationship between capital and lending. In insurance, it is a prudent relationship between capital (shareholders' equity plus reserves) and premiums. Money spent buying *reinsurance* from others can usually be deducted from the premiums (up to a maximum figure), thus allowing the insurer to take more business. The rules are complicated and alternative calculations are often possible. Each country tends to have different rules but the EU single market regulations are imposing common minimum standards. Liquidity is important and the regulations may demand that part of the capital must be held as a *minimum guarantee fund*. In the US, if claims arise from risks written in London, they must be covered by a letter of credit.

Distribution

The question of the distribution channel for selling personal insurance is very important. Essentially, insurance is a 'distress purchase'; few people have life insurance or pension provision as top of desired purchases. Similarly, motor and house insurance in more advanced countries is mandated by government or lenders. Thus there is an old adage that 'insurance is sold and not bought'. This results in distribution being extremely important in this market. It has led to insurers linking with banks to use them as a channel for selling policies (see Chapter 4) and banks buying or starting insurance companies.

Typical distribution channels are:

❏ Tied agents
❏ Direct sales staff
❏ Independent financial advisers (IFA)
❏ Part-time agents
❏ Brokers
❏ Telephone-based.

Tied agents are usually self-employed and sell only the policies of one company – Allianz, for example, has 43 000. They are also very common in France, where there are about 80 000.

A direct sales force is often employed, especially in assurance. In Japan, much of insurance is sold by a unique sales force of 'insurance ladies'.

Independent financial advisers will make recommendations from a range of products. They may charge a fee for their advice or simply take a commission on the policy offered from the company concerned. In the latter case, the possibility of bias towards high commission policies may lead to the 'independence' of IFAs being questioned. The UK has struggled with this problem in recent years and regulations forced IFAs to register with a 'Self-Regulatory Organisation' (SRO) and declare their commission on the recommended policy. Another rule called 'polarisation' ruled out combining the roles of IFA and tied agent in any way. For example, a bank manager might act as agent for the bank's mutual funds but act as adviser in other matters. This is not permitted. A seller of mutual funds and life policies must inform the prospective buyer in writing whether their status is that of IFA or tied agent. However, the Financial Services Authority has been looking at the possibility of altering the rules on polarisation, and from 2004 the strict division between independent advisers and tied agents was abolished. Firms are able to continue to describe themselves as tied agents provided that they offer the customer the option of paying a fee for the advice they give. Advisers are required to disclose a menu of charges and fees prior to a sale.

Part-time agents are usually solicitors and estate agents who will handle personal assurance and insurance on a casual basis and take commission. However, from 1 January 2006, all selling insurance as a sideline in the UK must register with the Financial Services Authority – this complies with the EU's Insurance Mediation Directive. If they do not register, they are not covered by the financial services compensation scheme.

Brokers are very common in the US, the UK and the Netherlands and occupy a strong position in Latin America and South East Asia. The large brokers typically serve corporate clients with complex and large exposures. They help clients determine their exposures, structure their insurance programmes, and negotiate rates, terms and conditions. In addition, they provide multiple services along the insurance value chain, for example, with consulting arms for pensions and employee benefits. Smaller brokers handle personal lines and small commercial risks. Much of it, like motor and household, is not particularly lucrative. For the broker it is the contact from which they hope to sell more profitable life and pensions business. This phenomenon is termed 'cross-selling' and is becoming increasingly important to company profitability.

Corporations with large commercial and industrial risk rely on the expertise of insurance brokers to provide adequately priced coverage and risk management services. Terrorism, rising medical costs and increased litigation (for example, concerning asbestos) have made life much more difficult.

The industry is highly concentrated. Marsh and McLennon and Aon account for over 50% of the industry's brokerage levels. The world's top brokers can be seen in Table 15.2. For the UK, Jardine Lloyd Thompson is the biggest broker.

Commercial business remains strong, but personal business is in decline as people are going directly to the insurer or using the Internet to find the best price. The banks have also moved into insurance, as we saw in Chapter 4. In London, for example, 80% of large commercial business is still broker-based but the percentage of personal lines business is less than 30%, compared to 70% in 1990 (figures from Swiss Re *Sigma* publication No. 2/2004).

There is also a type of distribution called *industrial*, branch or IB. This involves calling door to door to collect premiums in cash over the lifetime the policy remains in force. The term was used in the 19th century as it was regarded as insurance for people employed in the factories. In the UK, the Prudential was famous for its industrial sales force, giving rise to a cliché, 'the man from the Pru'.

Today this business is hardly sold, as most people now have bank accounts from which to pay premiums. However, in-force policies will continue until 2040 in the

UK. As the collection is high, insurers are encouraging these policies to be 'paid up' – a term whereby the insurer pays the outstanding premiums, as they are cheaper than the cost of collection, and the policy holder receives the maturity payment as if the policy had gone full term The percentage cost of premiums collected was much higher than for other types of business. It suited some policy holders who manage their lives on a week-to-week cash basis! For others, sadly, loneliness is a factor. There will be someone to talk to each week even if it's only the person from the insurance company. Many companies have abandoned this type of business. The UK Prudential gave up taking new policies from January 1995, at which time it employed 8000 people visiting 1.6 million homes. It finally abandoned this business in 2001.

Table 15.2   *The world's leading insurance brokers*

Company
Marsh & McLennan
Aon
Willis Group
Arthur J Gallagher
Acordia
HLF Group
Jardine Lloyd Thompson
Alexander Forbes
Hilb, Rogal and Hamilton
Brown & Brown

Sources: Swiss Re *Sigma* publication No. 2/2004.

Lastly, mention should be made of the fact that company pension schemes (where they exist) usually provide life assurance cover automatically wrapped within the pension arrangement.

Telephone-based, as a way of cutting costs, is becoming very common. In the UK, this was pioneered by Direct Line, a subsidiary of the Royal Bank of Scotland, which now has three million motor policies, the largest private sector insurer in this market. They have now set up Línea Directa in Spain using Bankinter and similar bodies in Italy, Germany and Japan. Other insurance companies such as Axa and Zurich have followed suit as well as others in the UK.

Self-Insurance

As insurance is essentially a spreading of risk, the rising premiums in some market sectors have led to a growth in *self-insurance*. For example, municipal authorities with their common interests might form their own pool of premiums, especially for public and employers' liability.

For a single entity, a large multinational company, for example, self-insurance might simply involve putting aside an amount of money each year into a fund to build up a sum to meet given insurance risks. This could apply if the company felt that it was a much better risk than the general insured population of firms for a given risk and was paying excessive premiums as a result. It also saves on insurance commission and expenses.

Sometimes several large multinationals in the same industry will join together. Thus, Astra Zeneca, GSK and others have set up 'Pharmaceutical Insurance Ltd' in Bermuda to cover claims for property damage and business interruption. Oil and gas companies and international telecommunications firms have taken similar action.

Brokers have seen an opportunity here and have set up consultancy arms. They can advise clients on setting up self-insurance vehicles and even help establish them.

In marine insurance, an association of ship owners will organise mutual aid for risks not covered under a marine hull policy. Each member will contribute to a pool to cover losses up to a given sum. Above this sum, reinsurance will be used (see below). These associations are known as *Protection and Indemnity Associations* or P&I clubs. There are 39 in the London market.

Captives   Another type of self-insurance exists where large companies set up an in-house insurance 'captive' to assess the risks across the business and place insurance policies directly with providers. This essentially cuts out the middle man. This has been increasingly common with the growth in multinational businesses with property estates around the world, while tens of thousands of employed staff make it worthwhile to manage insurance risk internally.

REINSURANCE

Definitions

Reinsurance is the form of insurance by which an insurance company can transfer to another company all or part of its liability for claims of a given type. This reduces the risk that excessive claims could seriously weaken the company.

The company transferring the risk is the *reinsured* and is also known as the *ceding* company. The company accepting the risk is the *reinsurer*.

The reinsurer may themselves pass on some of the risk to another company – this is a *retrocession* contract.

The reinsured company now has protection against excessive claims or a large accumulation of claims and can write more business than if it was standing 100% of the loss.

The amount of business it can take is limited by the solvency margin. The reinsured company can deduct premiums due to reinsurers when calculating this (although EU regulations restrict this to 50%).

Generally, reinsurance is divided into *proportional* and *non-proportional*. Top reinsurers are shown in Table 15.3.

Table 15.3 Top reinsurers by net premiums written, 2004

Company
Swiss Re / GE
Munich Re
Berkshire Hathaway Re
Hanover Re
Lloyd's
Allianz Re
Everest Re
XL Re
Partner Re

Source: S&P *Global Reinsurance Highlights*, 2005.

Proportional and Non-Proportional Reinsurance

Proportional   The reinsurer takes an agreed share of the risks ceded in return for the same share of the premiums less a *reinsurance commission*. This latter is to offset commission paid to intermediaries and also the expenses incurred.

Quota share reinsurance   Here the reinsurer takes an agreed proportion of all insurances of a given type written by the ceding company.

Surplus reinsurance   This occurs where the original insurer cedes the whole contract to a treaty where the original insurer bears some risk and the reinsurers the rest. Occasional risks, not covered by the treaty, may be reinsured on a *facultative* basis.

Non-proportional   The reinsurers contribute to losses in excess of a given figure in return for a premium. This may be *excess of loss* or *excess of loss ratio*.

Excess of loss   Here the reinsurers agree to pay any loss in excess of a given figure up to a maximum stated amount. This may be on a *per risk* basis (that is specific to, say, a ship or building) or on an *event basis* (for example, a hurricane, and often called *catastrophe* cover). It is typically written in layers according to the risk of a 'hit'.

Excess of loss ratio   Here the excess of claims over an agreed loss ratio is reinsured. The loss ratio is the ratio of claims to premiums. For example, a reinsurer might cover 90% of losses above a loss ratio of 75% to a maximum of 110%. Suppose the premium income was $10m. A 75% loss ratio would arise for claims of $7.5m. A 110% loss ratio arises with claims of $11m. The difference is $3.5m. A reinsured might agree to cover 90% of this figure, leaving the reinsurer to bear some of the loss (an important principle).

Financial Reinsurance

This has three key features:

❑   A ceiling on the liability for the reinsurer
❑   A recognition of the time value of money
❑   A sharing of profits through premium rebates.

The first policies were the *time and distance* policies of Lloyd's syndicates in the 1970s. The reinsurer undertook to meet a number of future claim payments. The reinsured undertook to pay a premium equal to the net present value (that is, the discounted value) of the above payments. The reinsurer, in a tax haven, would make a profit by reinvesting the premium at a higher rate of interest than that used in the discounting calculation.

The reinsured was left with no responsibility for the correct investment of the premium and might still benefit from a rate of return it could not achieve by itself. There was no transfer of risk and the arrangement was purely financial.

Today's financial reinsurance contracts do involve a transfer of risk, for example, timing risk, that is, that claims payments may be made earlier than expected. They might also agree to cover a sum higher than that implied by the premium (*finite risk*).

Financial insurance contracts can be:

❑   *Retrospective* – the schedule of future payments is guaranteed in respect of business already written
❑   *Prospective* – providing cover for future losses on business currently being written
❑   *Loss portfolio transfer* – a transfer of liability for losses from policies already written up to a maximum figure.

The Reinsurance Market

Lloyd's (to be discussed below) covers reinsurance, as do many insurance companies. Reinsurance is, however, a specialist international business rather dominated by specialist companies like Swiss Re and Munich Re, the world's two biggest. The German and Swiss firms are helped by being allowed to build up catastrophe reserves which can be offset against tax. In the US, high general catastrophe reserves are allowed – the tax position is much more favourable than in the UK.

As in most financial markets, consolidation has taken place. The US General Re, the world's third biggest, took a majority holding in Cologne Re, but was itself acquired by Berkshire Hathaway in 1998. Swiss Re bought Life Re (US) and Munich Re bought American Re. Then, in 2005, Swiss Re acquired GE Reinsurance and became the world's biggest – see Table 15.3 for the top names.

Reinsurance brokers also operate internationally and play a very important role in non-proportional reinsurance and also in handling unusual risks. Reinsurance broking is especially strong in the UK. The biggest in the US are Towers, Perrin and John B Collins and in the UK, Benfield and BMS.

Financial reinsurance is a growing area and Zurich Insurance is probably the largest specialist. Its subsidiary is Centre Re and it has bought the Pinnacle company in Bermuda, which has underwritten many reinsurance policies for Lloyd's. Bermuda is the centre for financial reinsurance due to its tax-free status.

The banks have also become involved in financial reinsurance and Bankers Trust have set up a subsidiary to handle this in Jersey (Channel Islands). JP Morgan and Marsh & McLennan have set up a joint venture catastrophe insurer based in Bermuda.

The excess of loss market was particularly badly hit by a string of disasters in the 1980s and early 1990s. This includes Hurricanes Gilbert, Hugo and Andrew; the Philips Petroleum explosion; the Piper Alpha oil rig disaster; the San Francisco earthquake; the Los Angeles riots; the Exxon Valdez oil spill; and the storms in Southern England in October 1987 and January 1990.

This spate of catastrophes even led the Chicago Board to set up futures and options for 'catastrophe insurance' and then catastrophe bonds. They are issues backed by a pool of insurance policies and designed to spread the risk. They offer a high yield and the possibility of a loss of some or all capital. An interesting example is the issue by Tokyo Fire and Marine of $100 million 10 year bonds in November 1997. They are based on the risk of losses if Tokyo is struck by an earthquake. Swiss Re estimate that the value of catastrophe bonds has risen from $700 million to $5 billion today.

The US derivatives exchanges have also seen the rise of 'weather derivatives'. Swiss Re estimate that these have a notional value in excess of $5 billion. Chicago Mercantile Exchange contracts cover 29 cities worldwide. There are some very specific risks – for example, the number of days' frost at Amsterdam airport.

The above deals bring giant insurers into competition with investment bankers. Swiss Re and others have set up capital market divisions and investment bankers, like Goldman Sachs, have set up insurance arms.

The years 2004 and 2005 saw further disasters like the South East Asian tsunami and the US hurricanes, like Katrina. As a result, the demand for catastrophe insurance has grown enormously and reinsurance prices have gone up. As capital must be held to counterbalance risk, by mid-2006, some reinsurers were having to seek more outside capital. *Retrocession* – the reinsurance that reinsurers buy, has also risen. The UK reinsurance broker, Benfields, estimate that the whole season will cost the global market $80 billion (£48 billion) of which reinsurers will pay $30 billion (£18 billion).

THE LONDON MARKET

What people refer to as 'The London Market' consists of:

❑ Lloyd's
❑ The International Underwriting Association (IUA).

The IUA was itself formed in 1998 from a merger of the marine insurance body, The Institute of London Underwriters, and the corresponding organisation for non-marine insurance, The London Insurance and Reinsurance Association. The IUA has 117 members.

The London market enjoys a unique status in the insurance industry as the most important trading centre for risks from all over the world. It is a concentration of the biggest providers of insurance in one place, with brokers (160) as agents, the insurance companies (some 200) and Lloyd's syndicates as providers. Some 40% of aviation premiums world-wide and 60% of premiums for offshore oil and gas rigs are collected here. Apart from the Lloyd's brokers and IUA insurers, there are 39 P&I clubs specialising in the insurance of ships and cargo (for P&I see under Self-Insurance).

There is increasing cooperation between Lloyd's and the IUA to strengthen the appeal of the London market. There is a common standard slip and common terms, the 'General Underwriting Agreement' (GUA). In addition, there is now a common service company. Lloyd's own Policy Signing Office has merged with Xchanging and the equivalent IUA body to form 'Insure'.

Lloyd's has always been particularly strong in international marine insurance and the time has come to consider this important body.

LLOYD'S

Organisation

Lloyd's of London is a special case and merits special treatment. The Corporation of Lloyd's (formed in the 1771 reorganisation) does not itself insure anyone. The council of Lloyd's lays down the regulations for members' financial status, provides premises and general central support services. The insurance itself is provided by individual members called *names*.

There are at present about 1625 names and they used to risk their personal wealth in providing insurance underwriting as they had unlimited liability. The theory is that, with unlimited liability, people will behave more prudently. The problem is, that with 1625 names and only 62 professional underwriters actually doing the work, controlling their actions is difficult. Much of the debate in Lloyd's over the last 20 years has turned on the question of giving the names more control, especially when it is borne in mind that in 1988 there were over 30 000 names! Most people will have read of individuals in Lloyd's having all their personal wealth destroyed (it even featured in a hugely praised play on Broadway and London's West End – *Amy's View*). This was because Lloyd's lost £8bn between 1988 and 1992 and, in these circumstances, unlimited liability became a personal disaster. Why did the names take such a risk? It was because, historically, it had been very profitable with generous tax concessions … or, if you want to be harsh, because of greed. New names nowadays do have limited liability – they cannot lose more than the capital they put up.

The actual underwriting is carried out by professional underwriters organised into 62 *syndicates* (in 1980, there were 437). Each syndicate is run by a *managing agency*, of which there are 45. As is often the case, they are dominated by the biggest (Ace, Limit, Amlin, Wellington) and the top 10 manage 50% of the capacity.

Originally the syndicate ran for a year and was then reorganised. The accounts for that year were published three years later. For example, the accounts for 1997 were published in 2000. This allowed time for claims to be made and settled. Even then, there may still be potential further claims, so these were reinsured so that the books could be closed – *reinsurance to close*. More recently, Lloyd's has made a move to one year accounting and we discuss this later.

Each name is looked after by a member's *agent* and they advise the members on the rules, risks and which syndicates to join. There are 20 agents.

Lloyd's will use brokers but only those who are the *Lloyd's brokers* (some 160). They have to be able to distribute premiums to several syndicates and collect payment of claims from several syndicates. There are also some direct sales, especially for motor insurance.

To facilitate dealings between underwriters and brokers, there is a central service provider, *Inssure*. This not only handles the distribution of money for premiums and claims but will also prepare the wordings of policies and check them.

The names must have personal disposable wealth of £350 000. They will deposit 40% of their maximum premium capacity. If the capacity is £1 million, they will deposit £400 000. At this level, the risk will probably be spread over some 10–15 syndicates.

The big attraction for the aristocracy and wealthy sports and pop stars has always been the threefold opportunity for income:

- ❏ The investment revenue from the deposit
- ❏ The investment income from the premiums
- ❏ The share of underwriting profit.

In addition, the attitude of the tax authorities in previous years was not as strict as it is today.

In June 2005, CBS Private Capital, a members' agent, launched a fund to give the public access for a minimum of £50 000. The government has also approved in principle a new vehicle for private investors – a limited liability partnership. This was expected to be available some time in 2006. Members will be able to offset losses for tax purposes and maintain control of underwriting decisions. Profits will be treated as earned income and thus can be used for pension contributions.

The names contribute 2% of premiums to a central fund for the protection of the insured and can themselves insure against excessive claims (although this has become more difficult and costly in recent years).

Lloyd's is run from the £160m Richard Rogers building which was opened in 1986. At the heart is the *room*. This is the area where underwriters sit on uncomfortable desks called 'boxes' and are visited by brokers seeking cover for particular risks. A broker gets agreement from a prominent underwriter (the 'lead underwriter') first – this is a *line* which is expressed as a percentage of the total risk. They then visit other underwriters (who will probably follow this example from one of their eminent colleagues) until they have enough 'lines' to cover the policy. Sometimes they may cover more than the required total to spread the risk further – say to 125%. In this case, each underwriter is scaled back ('signed down'). So, an original 5% would be scaled down to 4%. However, an original percentage is never 'scaled up' and there may be no change if there is an initial agreement for a 'line to stand'.

In the room is the famous Lutine Bell. This was salvaged by Lloyd's from *HMS Lutine* during the Napoleonic wars. In the days when communications were not as good as today, one ring was bad news (a delayed ship was lost) and two rings was good news (the delayed ship had arrived safely in harbour). It is now rung on ceremonial occasions only. The bell was rung when the Queen opened the building in 1986. In view of the many scandals which surrounded Lloyd's at the time, one wit asked whether it would be one ring or two! It was also rung on 4 September 1998, when the Department of Trade and Industry approved the market's recovery plan – the Equitas vehicle (see below).

Lloyd's is run by the Lloyd's Council of 18 members – active names, non-active names, corporate members, the chairman and chief executive and six others nominated from outside. There used to be a regulatory board and a market board, but these were replaced by the new franchise board in 2003.

Lloyds has appointed Richard Ward, formerly of the International Petroleum Exchange, as chief executive to succeed Nick Prettejohn; the chairman is Lord Levene of Portsoken.

Lloyd's is a major centre for world reinsurance, of key importance for aviation insurance and marine insurance, and has pioneered policies for new risks such as AIDS and computer fraud. It has also always specialised in unusual risks such as multiple births, a famous film star's legs (Betty Grable, many years ago) and the world's largest cigar! Its reputation in the US was enormously enhanced by its prompt settlement following the 1906 San Francisco earthquake, in contrast to many other insurers.

Early Problems

From the late 1960s onwards, the operation of Lloyd's began to attract increasing criticism. The accounting information was weak (and prevented names from realising the true facts); managing agencies shared profits but not losses; some syndicates were exceeding premium limits; periodically huge losses arose; and finally, the ownership of managing agencies by brokers led to conflicts of interest.

Most of these problems were addressed by the Lloyd's Act of Parliament, passed in mid-1982 and becoming law in January 1983.

Before it even became law, Lloyd's was hit by massive scandals involving illegal transfers of money to offshore companies abroad. These transfers resulted in heavy losses, most of which had to be met by a special fund set up at Lloyd's. They led to a further change in which the outside members of the Lloyd's Council (nominated by the Bank of England) and nominations of the non-working names were to be in a majority. This was implemented in 1987.

Commercial Problems

The problems that hit Lloyd's in the late 1980s and early 1990s were commercial problems, partly due to poor underwriting rather than fraud.

The names had, of course, unlimited liability and began to find themselves facing huge losses, in many cases involving personal ruin.

This was particularly true in the excess of loss market (LMX). Here one syndicate reinsures the losses of another or of a company outside the Lloyd's market. At first, syndicates specialising in excess of loss were very profitable and attracted new and undercapitalised names. The old minimum wealth level of £100 000 had been kept at this figure for far too long and was only raised to £250 000 in 1990 (and today is £350 000). Gooda Walker syndicate 290 went from underwriting capacity of £6.2m in 1982 to £69.4m in 1989. As the string of catastrophes occurred, to which we have already referred, names faced huge losses. Accusations began to be made that 'insiders' only put money into the safest syndicates and that some agents packed innocent names onto weak syndicates as cannon fodder. The insiders put their money into safe syndicates, known as 'baby' or 'preferred' syndicates. In particular, there had been excessive passing on of reinsurance risks from one syndicate to another.

Members of the Oakley Vaughan syndicates brought a unique court case against the Corporation of Lloyd's itself, claiming that it had failed in its duty to protect the names. In June 1992, the High Court came to a decision. It was decided that Lloyd's had a duty to regulate the market and act fairly, but no specific duty of care to the names.

Another problem was caused by huge payments for compensation as a result of litigation arising in the US. The cases concerned pollution and asbestosis. In some cases, the law was even changed with retrospective effect. The uncertainties this created led to a large number of years' accounts being left 'open' – a highly undesirable state of affairs. Normally, the accounts were closed after 3 years by 'reinsurance to close'. If the value of potential claims is so uncertain that they cannot be reinsured, the accounts are left open. The names then faced unlimited future claims on their resources.

The Rowland Report   David Rowland, Chairman of Sedgwicks, was asked to head a task force and produce a report on how Lloyd's could be a safer place for the names and respond to the latest difficulties.

Rowland made his report in January 1992. After allowing time for discussion of its revolutionary proposals, he then produced a firm business plan in April 1993.

The key elements of the Rowland proposals were:

1   Corporate members with limited liability to be admitted in 1994.
2   The formation of a new reinsurance company called Equitas, to which all the claims for earlier losses not yet settled would be transferred; this would enable a cap to be placed on names' losses.
3   A system like unit trusts to be set up to allow names to put money into a 'pool' of multiple syndicates.
4   The size of the Council to be reduced to make it more effective.

We must remember that the essence of Lloyd's had always been that of private members with unlimited liability. The admission of corporates with limited liability was a revolutionary change. Many new corporates were set up to trade at Lloyd's, usually via a quoted investment trust, spreading investment over a range of syndicates. Some larger investment trusts have bought underwriters and some underwriters have bought capacity on their own syndicates. For example, one of the largest corporate capital providers, Angerstein, has merged with one of the largest managing agencies, Murray Lawrence. Today, limited liability members provide 89% of the capacity at Lloyd's. (As well as corporates, individual names can change to a form of limited liability.) Outsiders also bought in to Lloyd's – General Re bought managing agency D.P. Mann, and Bermuda-based Ace has bought Charman Underwriting.

The second part of the above plan was the proposal to concentrate all old business into one new company and cap names' losses. All losses not settled up to 1992 were to be transferred to Equitas, but the names had to agree. The offer was put to 34 000 names who were affected. It was approved by 90% of the names by 30 August 1996, when the offer went unconditional. The DTI then gave the go-ahead for the Equitas plan and on 4 September David Rowland, now Lloyd's chairman, rang the Lutine bell – not twice, but three times! Clearly, the hope was that the nightmare was over, although Equitas is not a guaranteed solution and was forced to increase its resrves by £128 million ($213 million) in 2005 to cover asbestos-related claims.

The plan put a cap on names' losses prior to 1993 and enabled an out-of-court settlement of claims. In addition, a new 'auction' system enabled names to sell places on syndicates to others. These schemes, together with a pooling system for syndicates which operates like a unit trust, finally paved the way for the new Lloyd's into the 21st century.

In April 2006, Lloyd's reported a loss for 2005 of some £103 million ($170 million) due to the hurricanes in the US. This was the first loss since 2001 and followed good profits in 2002–04. Ironically, there was great pride in the 2004 profit after the worst year ever for catastrophe losses. Obviously, no-one imagined that 2005 would be even worse. However, the impact on the central fund was expected to be minimal. Lloyds expected to increase its capacity in 2006 to £14.7 billion ($24.5 billion) as opposed to £13.7 billion ($22.8 billion) in 2005.

In January 2002, the 'Chairman's Strategy Group' (CSG), acting on behalf of the Council with consultants Bain and Co., put forward some far-reaching reform proposals. The CSG was set up with a specific objective, which was to determine 'the future vision and strategy for Lloyd's which will maximise the wealth of capital providers to Lloyd's over the next ten years'. The key proposals were:

❏ Lloyd's to move to a formal franchise structure, with Lloyd's as franchiser and managing agents as franchisees, under a new relationship defined in a set of 'Franchise Principles'.
❏ The existing regulatory and market boards to be replaced by a new franchise board.
❏ Full annual accounting on the basis of the EU's new International Accounting Standard to be implemented from January 2005.
❏ A new mechanism for third party capital called the 'Single Reinsurance Syndicate' to be created.
❏ No new names to be admitted to the market from 1 January 2003.
❏ Existing names with limited liability to cease trading as such from 1 January 2005.

Lloyd's held an extraordinary AGM on 13 September 2002, and the CSG proposals were passed by an 80% majority. Although opposed by many names, the votes were weighted by underwriting capacity, which counted against them.

In November 2002, Lloyd's unveiled membership of its new franchise board, which started work in the beginning of 2003. It was led by Lloyd's new chairman, Lord Levene. This new franchise board has tough powers to scrutinise the business plans of the market's underwriting syndicates as well as managing agents. Syndicates can be forced to put up more capital and to accept strict guidelines on the insurance portfolio. Nick Prettejohn, the then chief executive, took the unusual step of naming syndicates who had drawn on the central fund, ultimately used to pay compensation when a syndicate can't pay.

In late 2005, Lloyd's announced yet another strategic plan – 'Building the Optimal

Platform'. This time, the 3 year plan is a radical overhaul to tackle the increasing competition from rival centres, such as Bermuda. According to Benfields, the reinsurance broker, some $7.4 billion (£4.4 billion) of new capital was raised in late 2005 by nine new Bermudan companies, but no new vehicles chose Lloyd's. Indeed, two of Lloyd's biggest insurers, Hiscox and Amlin, have set up new operations in Bermuda. Hedge funds also like Bermuda as it is tax-friendly and it is easy to get in and out.

Referring to the plan, Lord Levene, the Lloyd's chairman, said, 'We operate in a fiercely competitive market and we cannot afford to stand still.' Key objectives are:

❏ A review of how capital is raised each year
❏ To make it easier for businesses across the globe to access Lloyd's policies
❏ To match the capital required from each insurer to their performance instead of to a set figure
❏ The setting of clear performance standards and an increase in efficiency in day-to-day dealings
❏ A wider representation for Lloyd's in the world's most important insurance market.

In spite of current problems, Lloyd's still has unique strengths:

❏ Underwriting skills – exotic risks that normal insurers will not touch
❏ Security – premium trust funds of £21.8 billion ($36.3 billion), capital requirements of members – £9.6 billion ($16 billion), member's assets not held at Lloyd's but declared of £220 million ($366 million) and, finally, the central fund of £556 million ($926 million).
❏ Global reach – Lloyd's is licensed to do business in 60 countries.

THE MARKET TODAY

General

The third edition of this book (2000) laid much emphasis on the spate of *takeovers*, *mergers* and *alliances* that had taken place in the previous three years. This activity seems to have settled down. The equity market decline between 2000 and 2002 led to a slowdown. Life insurance was hit by capital losses, especially in Europe. This led to a slowdown in mergers and acquisitions activity. One interesting move in the period since 2002 is the sale by Citigroup of Travelers Property and Casualty Unit to St Paul, finalised in April 2004, and the announced sale of Travelers Life and Annuity to Metropolitan Life. The Nordic region's biggest insurer, Old Mutual, merged with the UK's Scandia early in 2006 and Axa agreed to buy Winterthur from Crédit Suisse. A significant move in the world of reinsurance was the acquisition of GE Reinsurance by Swiss Re in 2005, which now becomes the world's biggest reinsurer with total premiums of $32 billion (£19 billion), passing their rival, Munich Re, which has total premiums of $28.9 billion (£17.3 billion).

Financial engineering This has increasingly become more important. One area is that of credit derivatives, where many insurers have entered this market. This is a way of insuring against, for example, bond issues defaulting. This is explained in Chapter 14. Insurance companies have also learned how to reduce the cost of capital by issuing bonds secured against a stream of premiums – asset-backed securities (see Chapter 6). At the end of 2005, for example, we saw Axa issue a €200 million ($242 million, £145 million) bond backed by its motor insurance portfolio. At much the same time, Swiss Re issued its second asset-backed bond to the value of $370 million (£252 million). Jacques Algrain, Chief Executive of Swiss Re, has noted that, whereas underwriters and actuaries had dominated the industry, financial engineering had become essential to future success – 'The industry is going through a major transformation and awakening. There is increasing use of the capital markets wherever possible.'

Emerging markets Meanwhile, emerging countries are beginning on the route to new prosperity. Brazil, Russia, India and China, the so called BRIC countries, have become significant world-wide economies in recent years. India and China, for example, qualified as two of the top ten world-wide economies in 2005. With this prosperity comes the desire for luxury goods, savings and investments. Thus many of the world's largest insurers have begun operations in these emerging countries. Prudential of the UK has been one of the more aggressive, with 2005 income from Asia at 34% of the total. This was less than 2% ten years earlier.

Regulation The growth in regulation has continued in recent years as market confidence has suffered. In Shakespeare's *Othello*, Cassio cries, '*O. I have lost my reputation! I have the immortal part of myself, and what remains is bestial.*' He knew that image is everything and is extremely difficult to recover.

Against this background, there have been regulatory moves for more transparency in insurance with Spitzer and Sarbanes-Oxley (SOX) regulation and – on a global basis – Basel II and IAS (International Accounting Standard) aimed at ensuring capital reserves are adequate to cover all types of risk in financial markets including insurance.

Non-Life

The sharp escalation in judicial awards and the introduction of stricter legal standards in several jurisdictions, including the US, have led to a new emphasis on what is known as *liability insurance.* This comprises the following – commercial general liability, product liability, professional indemnity, directors' liability, product recall, personal liability and motor liability. Commercial firms have had to pay far greater attention to this type of insurance, with the rise in strength of the consumer lobby everywhere and potentially ruinous court awards. At the same time, it represents an opportunity for the insurance industry. It is also picking up in many of the emerging economies.

Life and Pensions

Across most of the Western world, life and pensions business has become a significant political issue. State pensions schemes mostly operate on a 'pay as you go' basis, where today's payroll deductions fund today's pensioners. This was fine until the demographic changes slowed population growth. In the UK, for example, in the 1950s there were nine working people for every pensioner. Today the ratio is three to one and declining. Furthermore, life expectancy has increased dramatically. These two factors together create a massive burden for future generations. Without fundamental reforms, most Western countries face ruin.

The way out of the problem, however, also has political ramifications. States have only a limited number of choices: increase tax, extend the retirement age or make some kind of saving compulsory. The latter has been introduced in Australia, for example. In Europe the problem is at its most acute in Germany. French and Italian state pensions are very generous, some at 70% of final salary.

Clearly, going to the polls on a ticket of increased taxation or forced savings will be unpopular. Thus the problem continues to be deferred, only exacerbating it. On the good news side, this should eventually result in opportunities for life and pensions providers.

There are, nevertheless, some particular problems in the UK. New regulations have insisted on a more precise match between future assets and liabilities. It is difficult to be precise about the future value of equities and this has led many insurance and pension funds to move out of equities and into bonds. This has sent bond prices up and yields down, making matching assets less effective and leading to more purchases of bonds – which lowers yields ... it's a self-perpetuating problem. Gross yield on UK gilts, which was 4.5% at the beginning of 2005, had fallen to 3.7% at the end. The real yield on index-linked 50 year gilts (a popular choice) had fallen to 0.5% or less. Many with-profit funds promise a minimum annual growth of 4% – now a considerable challenge. One can, perhaps, be forgiven for thinking that a mass exodus from equities in favour of these low yielding assets is an act of collective folly.

EU REGULATION

While some progress has been made with EU directives on general insurance, progress with life assurance has been very slow. However, in June 1992, two key directives were finally passed – the Third Non-Life Insurance Directive and the

Third Life Assurance Directive. These became law on 1 July 1994. From this date, insurers need only be authorised once, in their own country. This is the same 'single passport' idea that will apply in banking. However, marketing and selling practices will still be regulated by the country in which the insurance is sold. For example, cold calling is banned in Denmark and Germany.

There will still, of course, be problems with foreign insurers, especially at the retail level – language, distance, law and local support. Will policy holders wish to pursue a case in a foreign court? Following a European Court decision in 1992, it was ruled that a German, living in Belgium, could not claim tax relief from the Belgian government on insurance policies he was buying in Germany. For this and other reasons, the chairman of Allianz said in October 1995 that the single market in insurance was a 'myth'! What was needed first was harmonisation of legal, tax and social security systems.

The Bureau Européen des Unions des Consommateurs produced a report on comparative premiums in the life market. Using 100 as the cheapest cover, they produced the following figures:

Ireland	100
UK	102
Germany	118
France	151
Portugal	345

There is clearly scope for more competition!

SUMMARY

The biggest insurance markets in the world are in the US, followed by Japan, UK, France and Germany.

Assurance is cover for events which are certain (death). *Insurance* is cover for events which may or may not happen (accident, fire, catastrophe).

Offering insurance protection is *underwriting*.

Some companies do assurance only, some insurance only, and some (called *composites*) do both.

The equivalent of capital ratio in banking is *solvency ratio*.

The distribution of the insurance product is a key issue with the possibility of agents, direct sales staff, independent financial advisers, part-time agents, brokers and telephone selling.

Sometimes a large multinational or a group with similar interests will cover their own insurance – *self-insurance*.

Reinsurance occurs when the underwriter spreads the risk with other insurers or specialist reinsurers. There are various terms used such as *proportional, non-proportional, quota, share, surplus* and *excess of loss*.

A reinsurer may offer to reinvest premiums to provide future cover. This is *financial reinsurance.*

There are reinsurance companies, reinsurance brokers and a large reinsurance market at Lloyd's of London.

The so-called *London market* consists of *Lloyd's* and the *International Underwriting Association of London* (IUA).

Lloyd's of London is an organisation of individual members called *names* who offer insurance. They used to have unlimited liability which led to heavy losses and this has now been changed. The actual underwriting is carried out through *syndicates* and syndicates are run by *managing agencies*. Names are advised by *members' agents.*

Syndicates accounts may be terminated by *reinsurance to close.*

Lloyd's uses *Lloyds's brokers* and a central service provider, *Inssure.*

Lloyd's has faced increasing problems in the last 20 years. These have arisen from alleged fraud, careless underwriting, a disregard for the names' interests, huge claims due to pollution cases in the US and a string of natural catastrophes. This has all led to names facing huge losses.

In 1994, Lloyd's reorganised on the following lines:

❏ Allowing corporate membership with unlimited liability
❏ Setting up a system like unit trusts to pool money across syndicates
❏ Reorganising the Lloyd's Council
❏ Forming a new reinsurance vehicle called Equitas to which all claims up to the end of 1992 have been transferred; this will set a cap on names' losses.

In September 2002, Lloyd's agreed further changes:

❏ A formal franchise structure with a new franchise board to be set up
❏ Full annual accounting to be implemented from January 2005
❏ No new names to be admitted to the market from January 2003.

Lloyd's is preparing a new plan, 'Building the Optimal Platform', to meet the fierce competitive challenge from Bermuda.

Current issues affecting the market include the greater use of financial engineering, the prospects in emerging markets, increasing regulation and the massive challenge facing the life and pensions market due to demographics. In the UK, due to new regulations calling for a more precise match between future assets and liabilities, insurance companies have been selling equities and buying long-dated bonds.

The EU has passed the Third Non-Life Insurance Directive and the Third Life Assurance Directive. These provide the single passport concept that we have seen in banking but the results have been less than dramatic.

The New Tiger Economies –
China and India

16 The New Tiger Economies –
China and India

16 The New Tiger Economies – China and India

INTRODUCTION

The dominant theme at the World Economic Forum at Davos in January 2006 was the rise of China and India. Determined not to be outdone by China, India sent a delegation of 150 businessmen and politicians. Goldman Sachs is on record forecasting that, by the year 2050, the world's three top economic powers will be China, India and the US. While the usual sequence is 'China ... India', there are those who are putting their bets on India in the long term. The same Goldman Sachs has also said that, by 2015, India's *growth rate* will pass that of China. This aspect – China v India – will be examined later.

Some of the reasons for the preoccupation with these two powers will become clearer when we look at some of the facts.

The population of China is 1.3 billion and that of India 1.1 billion. China's GDP was recently revised upwards by 16.8% and is $1.9 trillion (£1.14 trillion); India's is $615 billion (£369 billion). China has been growing by 9.5% per year and India 7%, but the National Bureau of Statistics in China put first half growth in 2006 at 10.9% and forecast full-year growth at 11% or more. Over the last five years China's exports have risen by 130% and India's 110%. The US is worried about China. The US trade gap in 2005 was $729 billion, with imports from China $250 billion and exports to China just $42 billion. Thus China alone accounts for 28% of the US trade gap. This explains US pressure on China to revalue its currency. The year 2005 saw huge rows about exports of clothing from China to the US and Europe. China's foreign exchange reserves are now $820 billion, only just behind Japan's $847 billion and may well pass this by the end of 2007.

China is, of course, far more a manufacturing economy than India, with manufacturing at 46% of GDP as opposed to India's 19%. China is the biggest steel producer in the world (although India's Mittal is the biggest steel company). As a result of all this manufacturing activity, China is a huge importer of raw materials, representing 25% of global demand for copper, aluminium, tin and zinc. China is also importing large quantities of components from Asia in particular, 15% coming from Japan, 11% from Taiwan and 40% from other Asian countries. Imports of components from the EU are only 15% of the total (UK 1%).

According to the International Energy Agency, China accounts for 9% of global oil consumption (India 4.5%) but 28% of the global *increase* in demand in 2005 with all Asia, including China, accounting for 43% of the increase.

McKinsey expects China to be the world's biggest car market in 10 years – and they are already third after the US and Japan. The expansion is similar to that of the US in the 1930s. China's 17 000 kilometres of motorway in 2000 had doubled to 34 000 by 2004. China joining the World Trade Organisation in 2001 has led to an easing of barriers to imports.

The reference above to clothing exports should not lead us to believe that China's exports are all low cost, low tech goods – figures from OECD show exports in 2004 of $180 billion (£108 billion) of computers, digital phones and similar products. US international sales of such products are $150 billion (£90 billion) and China has passed Japan as the biggest exporter of IT products to the US. China's Lenovo bought IBM's PC division in 2004 and already the new models look as good or better than those of IBM.

India is perhaps better known as an entrepreneurial economy, with services 52% of GDP as opposed to China's 41% (but growing). Not surprisingly, retail services are 11% of GDP to China's 6%. Outsourcing is big business although still only 3% of GDP. Some 75% of IT services sourced outside the US go to India. Outsourcing is not just call centres but is increasingly getting more sophisticated. The wider term now is 'business process outsourcing' (BPO). This includes high value services like medical, actuarial and research, sometimes also called 'knowledge process outsourcing'. The Indian software and services lobby, NASSCOM, together with McKinsey, have produced a study estimating that outsourcing of IT and BPO will reach $60 billion (£36 billion) by 2010 from $17 billion (£10.2 billion) in 2005 – a compounded annual growth of 28%, yet still below that achieved in recent years. The biggest IT companies – Tata, Infosys and Wipro – are each recruiting 1000 people per month.

China itself is of interest to these companies. In September 2005, Infosys announced a plan to hire 6000 programmers for a site near Shanghai. Tata has signed a pact with Microsoft and several Chinese state agencies. At the time these announcements were made, each already had about 300 programmers in China.

India's population is young, as opposed to China with its 'one child' policy, which is storing up trouble for future years. Some 52% of the population of India are under 25 and have grown up with satellite TV, mobile phones and computers. India produces some 4 million graduates per year (China 3 million, the US 1.3 million). The population represented by the middle class now approaches the whole population of the US! MasterCard International forecast that China's middle class households will rise from 65 million to 650 million in the next 15 years.

Looking at the above facts, we can understand the current pressure for China and India to be admitted to the G8, making it G10.

In all this, we should not totally forget the other tiger economies – Korea, Taiwan, Singapore, Malaysia and Thailand. They had total exports in 2004 of $750 million (£450 million) compared to China's $590 million (£344 million). The non-G7 share of the world growth of 33% in 1999 is now 38%. For two centuries, Europe and the US have dominated the world economy, challenged only by Japan. Now we have China, India and the five economies mentioned above.

Of course, both China and India are poor in world terms, and the growing prosperity of the middle classes contrasts with the great poverty elsewhere. In China, 800 million live in rural areas and in India, 700 million. China's GDP per capita is only $1700 (£1020) and it is even less in India – $580 (£348). Although China's five year plan announced in late 2005 calls for a quadrupling by 2010, it would still leave a figure only one twentieth of that of the UK, for example. Urban average incomes in China are three times those in rural areas and the country's average income per head just $120 (£72) p.a. The average Indian wage is about $500 (£300) p.a. and some estimate that 28% of the population live on less than $1 per day.

Before closing this section, we should, perhaps, make mention of Hong Kong and Taiwan.

Although Hong Kong is clearly part of China, it still has some autonomy, and when people say 'China' they usually mean mainland China. This autonomy has served Hong Kong well in terms of inward investment and a stock market free from mainland restrictions and with more rigorous standards. Of the amount raised on the Hong Kong exchange in 2005, 80% was for Chinese companies and they account for 37% of the market capitalisation of the exchange.

The position with Taiwan is interesting. Officially, of course, both countries are at loggerheads and Taiwan is fearful of overdependence on China for trade. Nevertheless, the Taiwanese are the most enthusiastic investors in China, spending some £100 billion (£60 billion) in the last 15 years and about two-fifths of Taiwanese exports go to China. As this is forbidden by the government, they are all funnelled via the British Virgin Islands. The Taiwan government tries to restrict this on the grounds of national security – too much dependence on the mainland. Some 900 companies have already been punished for illegal investment and 300 others are being investigated.

Although India has not recognised the Taiwan regime officially, in January 2006, the first delegation from Taiwan visited India. In the words of the delegation's leader, Hsiao Bi-Kim, 'It is in Taiwan's interest to promote India as an alternative investment centre to China.' On 14 February, the Taiwan–India Cooperation Council was launched in Taipei intended to raise India's profile and help Taiwanese businesses to diversify away from China. Taiwan has IT hardware expertise and India software expertise which may complement this. In February 2006 also, a 24-strong delegation from Taiwan went to the annual conference in Mumbai of India's IT and outsourcing industries. At the moment, trade with India is only 0.7% of the Taiwanese total, and investment in India is small. However, the way forward will not be easy as politics intrude. On 16 February, the Chinese ambassador in Delhi issued a statement warning India 'to refrain from sending any wrong signal to Taiwan independence forces'. Given the choice between favouring Taiwan or upsetting China, India has little choice.

In the next section of this chapter, we will look at the financial markets in these countries – banking and the various capital markets. We will then look again at China and India and compare and contrast, analysing strengths and weaknesses. Finally, we will close the chapter by looking at a key issue. Much of the comment on and reaction to the facts listed at the start of this chapter is of the 'we'll all be murdered in our beds' variety, so we will finally examine the question – to what extent is Chinese and Indian growth a threat to the West?

FINANCIAL MARKETS

Banking: General

There are broad similarities between the banking systems in China and India. Both operate capital controls and are proud to have missed the financial crises which engulfed so many Asian economies in 1997. In both cases the sector is dominated by state-owned banks which control almost all assets in China, although the picture is muddied by partial privatisations and the fact that the major banks have started to list in Hong Kong offering small stakes, such as 12%, to outsiders. The state banks in India control 75% of banking assets and privatisation is opposed by the communist group who hold the balance of power in the coalition government. However, there are purely private banks and they account for 18% of banking assets. In China, this would be exceptional and, indeed, probably the only wholly private bank is the China Minsheng Bank, formed for lending to the private sector and Sino–foreign joint ventures.

Both China and India are carefully controlling foreign stakes in their banks, more so in India. Nevertheless, India has a foreign bank sector to a much greater extent than China, with 7% of all banking assets.

One point of difference is the sheer size of the biggest Chinese banks and the number of their branches. The four biggest Chinese banks have assets which total $2094 billion (£1257 billion) while the assets of the top four Indian banks total $278 billion (£167 billion). The Industrial and Commercial Bank of China has 20 000 branches, the China Construction Bank 14 250 and the Bank of China 11 230. The State Bank of India compares with 9036 branches but the next biggest in terms of branches is the Punjab National Bank with 4005. Of course, much of this can be explained by the totally different historical background of the two countries.

Banking: China

Nationalisation as a policy received priority attention in the early years of the People's Republic of China. Banking was controlled totally by the People's Bank of China. Between 1979 and 1987, restructuring took place leading to the setting up of other institutions, deposits tripled and there was an enormous increase in bank loans. By 1987, many of the existing dominant banks had been set up such as the Bank of China, the Agricultural Bank, the China Investment Bank and the China Construction Bank. Also set up was the network of cooperative banks and the People's Insurance Company of China. The People's Bank of China, which had been set up in 1948, was re-established as the central bank in 1983. The governor is Xhou Xiaochuan who was appointed in January 2003 for no specific term.

Today there are four major state-owned banks: the Bank of China, the Industrial and Commercial Bank of China, the China Construction Bank and the Agricultural Bank of China. Three other state banks are regarded as 'policy banks' – the China Development Bank, China Import Export Bank and the Agricultural Development Bank of China – they finance infrastructure projects and other long-term state-supported projects. After this, there are other state-owned banks, regarded as 'second tier' and ten joint stock banks with a mixture of state and private owners. These include the Shanghai Pudong Development Bank, the Shenzen Development Bank and the China Merchants Bank. Then there is the wholly private Minsheng Bank. Finally, there are about 100 smaller regional commercial banks. The top Chinese banks by assets are shown in Table 16.1.

Table 16.1 *Top Chinese banks by assets*

Bank	Assets $bn
Industrial and Commercial Bank	685
Bank of China	575
China Construction Bank	472
Agricultural Bank of China	422
Bank of Communications	138
China Merchants Bank	72
China CITIC	62
Shanghai Pudong Development Bank	55
China Minsheng Bank	53
China Everbright	47
Industrial Bank	41
Huaxa Bank	38
Guandong Development Bank	36
Bank of Shanghai	26
Bank of Beijing	25
Shenzai Development Bank	23
Ningbo Commercial Bank	4

Source: *Banker* magazine, July 2005.

Being a large agricultural country, of key importance are some 35 000 rural credit cooperatives and 1000 urban credit cooperatives. Many of these are in the process of merging to form a smaller number of stronger banks.

Mention should be made of a number of bank and non-bank financial services for leasing and hire purchase. There are also six auto-finance firms including VW, GM and Toyota.

For investment banking, the China Investment Capital Corporation was set up in 1995 by the China Construction Bank, Morgan Stanley (34% stake) and three smaller shareholders. The Bank of China has a record of providing investment banking services and all state banks are expanding into this field. Many foreign bankers have representative offices in Shanghai and Beijing.

Some foreign investment banks have taken stakes in Chinese firms, a move which is being carefully controlled by the authorities. Morgan Stanley's early move, mentioned in the last paragraph, was followed in 2003 by Crédit Agricole's Asian investment banking arm taking a 33% stake in China Euro Securities as part of a joint venture with a Chinese broker. In the same year, BNP Paribas took a 33% stake in Changjiang Paribas Securities as a joint venture with Changjiang Securities. In 2004, Goldman Sachs made a joint move with Fang Fenglei to take over Gao Hua and in 2005 Merrill Lynch took a 33% stake in a joint venture brokerage with Huaan Securities. An interesting move, later in 2005, saw UBS take a 20% stake in a reorganised brokerage with the Beijing City government, the World Bank private sector arm and three state-owned companies. The company is being carved out of Beijing Securities, which has some 130 offices and which has lost $2 billion (£1.2 billion). The new company picks up the best of these offices, will inherit the trading licences but will not shoulder past liabilities. In many ways this is typical of the authorities' attitude to foreign investment, as we shall see. Where local banks or brokers are in trouble and need reorganising and fresh capital, the foreign banks are welcome!

Important to the whole picture of banking is the question of post offices. China has 76 000 post offices, including 33 000 postal savings offices which handle 260 million postal savings accounts. These savings deposits are about 10% of all financial system deposits. The government intends to turn the postal savings system into a bank and separate the rest. The profit on savings subsidises a nationwide postal delivery service with countless rural routes. Most of these savings deposits are simply passed to the central bank.

One of the major features of the Chinese banking system at the moment is the gradual floating of the shares of key state banks. The Bank of Communications led the way in June 2005 with a listing in Hong Kong to raise £2.2 billion (£1.3 billion). This was followed by the flotation of China Construction Bank in October 2005 in Hong Kong raising $8 billion (£4.8 billion) for 12% of the company, and then the Bank of China in May 2005 raising $9.7 billion (£5.8 billion) for 10.5% of the company. The state is clearly intent on keeping a major share in each. Increases in the share price since have led to vocal criticisms claiming shares had been sold to foreigners 'on the cheap'. As a result, approval of some moves by foreign banks into Chinese banks have been held up. As an example of this, the Singapore bank, Temasek, wanted to take a 10% stake in the Bank of China, a move we mention later. This was cut back to 5%.

Expected to follow suit in 2006–07 are the Industrial and Commercial Bank of China, the Agricultural Bank of China, the China Merchants Bank and the China Minsheng Bank.

There is a frenzy to win mandates among the foreign investment community. The usual suspects are Goldman Sachs, UBS, Citigroup, Morgan Stanley, JP Morgan and Deutsche Bank.

There are tight controls over investments by *foreign banks*. A group of foreign banks may not own more than 25% of a state-owned bank and no one foreign bank can own more than 20%. Foreign banks can deal in local currency and provide foreign exchange. If they open branches (this needs approval) they can provide much the same service to local clients as the Chinese banks. They cannot, however, lend renminbi to corporates except as part of a syndicate of Chinese banks and may not underwrite share or bond issues.

By end September 2005, the assets of foreign banks in China were estimated to total $80 billion (£48 billion). Nineteen foreign banks had stakes in seventeen Chinese banks.

The most important among these are:

❏ HSBC 19.9% of the Bank of Communications
❏ Bank of America (9%) and Temasek (5%) of the China Construction Bank
❏ Temasek (5%), RBS, Merrill Lynch and Li Ka-shing Corporation (10%), and UBS (16%) of the Bank of China
❏ Goldman Sachs, Allianz and American Express splitting 10% of the Industrial and Commercial Bank of China
❏ Citigroup 19.9% of Shanghai Pudong Development Bank.

In February 2006, two rival groups – Société Générale and Citigroup – were trying to secure an 80% stake in the Guandong Development Bank.

This last case is interesting. Why the 80% stake when the maximum is 25%? This is because the Chinese bank is loss-making and otherwise needs state assistance to reduce its debt levels. This is where the Chinese attitude is quite pragmatic and applies to holdings in brokers too (as we shall see). If the bank is in serious trouble, foreign banks can exceed the normally permitted stakes.

The Chinese banks gain from these stakes by selling off non-performing loans and slimming down on staff, all assisted by state money and by picking up foreign bank expertise.

The foreign banks can join in underwriting and gain access to the retail market in credit cards, mortgages and savings products for the growing middle classes.

The question of *foreign exchange* received a lot of attention in 2005, with the US expressing anger at China's refusal to strengthen the renminbi rate against the dollar. China (like India) is proud to have shrugged off the currency crises affecting Asian markets in 1997–99. Capital controls have kept the currency stable and insulated to a degree from economic problems, although there are some leaks and one or two speculative inflows. The central bank has used Treasury bill sales to sterilise any excessive inflows in renminbi. There were some small relaxations in capital controls in April 2006, making it easier for individuals and companies to buy foreign currency and invest abroad, but the move fell well short of a complete opening up of China's capital account. Worry about hedge fund activity led to a declaration from the central bank in 2005 that the currency will not be fully convertible for at least five years.

Forward purchases of foreign currency are carefully controlled – there must be firm proof that they are based on genuine trade. There is no foreign exchange derivatives trading. Following earlier scandals, derivatives generally are frowned on. The exchanges trade commodity derivatives only.

In May 2005, a new foreign exchange trading system was launched, allowing traders to deal in eight currency pairs not including the renminbi, such as \$/£. Four pairs involving the renminbi were already permitted. Reuters has set up a platform for this. The new official Chinese trading system is the Chinese Foreign Exchange Trading System (CFETS) and involves 11 banks. For bonds denominated in foreign currencies, the electronic bond trading system, MTS, has signed a letter of intent with CFETS as part of a move to develop electronic bond trading.

Having pegged the renminbi to the dollar for ten years, the Chinese moved at last in July 2005 and announced a new system in which the currency would be kept with reference to a basket of currencies, announced later as those of key trading partners – the dollar, euro, yen and Korean won. Others in the basket, such as the Malaysian ringgit, have a lesser weighting. The initial permitted fluctuation was only 2.1%. This hardly satisfied the Americans, who wanted something much bigger. The Chinese price advantage is such that even a 10% devaluation would make little difference and there is clearly no chance of that. Interestingly, the Malaysians followed suit at once and announced that the dollar peg would be replaced by a basket of currencies.

When the announcement was made, the central bank governor, Zhou Xiaochuan, said that the move was only an 'initial step'. This led to hopes that it would be followed by further moves to strengthen the currency in the following months. These hopes turned out to be optimistic as no further moves took place and, by the early months of 2006, the renminbi had only risen by a further 0.8%. The US was once more banging the revaluation drum when China's trade surplus in May 2006 hit \$13 billion (£7.8 billion).

China has, of course, huge foreign exchange reserves. The central bank governor announced in January 2006 that they plan for a slower accumulation of reserves in 2006. He said that they were committed to encourage consumption and wanted to rebalance the economy away from net exports.

To aid the development of China from the 1990s onwards, huge funds have been channelled into industry by the banks. The capital markets have been too weak to share the load. Much of the lending has been extremely wasteful and has led to very high figures for non-performing loans (NPL). As a result, the government has had to inject funds into the banking sector to help – $430 billion (£258 billion) to end 2005. The official non-performing loan ratio is 3.9%, although this is received with some cynicism and there are unofficial estimates of 8%. A contrary opinion was expressed by Jonathan Anderson, the UBS chief economist in Asia, who says that his research shows that the cleanup legacy of NPLs is almost complete and that new ones are not piling up. He believes that the residual balance will be written off by the end of 2007. The government is curbing overheating sectors such as cars, steel and property. Although the Basel required capital ratio is 8%, the head of Fitch, the ratings company in Asia, has said that capital ratios of 15% to 20% are perhaps needed to combat uncertainty and reduce risk.

In 2003, a China Banking Regulatory Commission was set up. This has issued some 130 rules and guidelines on capital adequacy, large exposures and derivatives. It has helped to get the non-performing loan ratio down. To control some 120 regional and local banks and many thousands of rural cooperatives is a major task.

At a banking seminar in early 2006, the McKinsey principal in Hong Kong said that to support GDP growth of 9%, the banking sector needed to expand lending by 15% while still writing off more bad debts and increasing credit skills. Nevertheless, he forecast that the Chinese banking system would be the second largest in the world by 2014.

Banking: India

The major banks were nationalised in 1949 and the remainder between 1969 and 1991. The central bank, the Reserve Bank of India (RBI), was set up in 1935. At first a private bank, it, too, was nationalised in 1949. The present governor is Dr YV Reddy who was appointed in September 2003 for a term of five years. The top Indian banks by assets are shown in Table 16.2.

Today, the 27 public sector banks and state sector cooperatives control 75% of all banking assets. The biggest is the State Bank of India, with assets of $143 billion (£85.8 billion). Of these state banks, the State Bank of India has 9036 branches, the Punjab National Bank 4005, the Central Bank of India 3130, the Bank of Baroda 2680, the Bank of India 2551 and the Canara Bank 2519.

In the 1970s and 1980s, the banking sector was further developed to finance public spending and the investment needs of big companies and to take this financing away from the state itself. A number of banks were not nationalised and there are 21 of them known as the 'Old Private Sector Banks'. Then there are the newer private banks, of which easily the most important are ICICI, the second biggest in India in asset terms and HDFC, the ninth biggest. The whole private sector controls 18% of all banking assets.

Historically, there have always been some foreign banks, such as Standard Chartered (83 branches and 6500 employees) and HSBC. Added to these, we now have Citigroup, ABN-AMRO, American Express Bank, Bank of America, BNP Paribas, Bank of Tokyo-Mitsubishi, Deutsche Bank, Calyon Bank (from Crédit Agricole) and many others. These foreign banks control the balance of 7% of banking assets. (Post Office assets are not included in these figures). Any foreign ownership of Indian public sector banks is generally restricted to 10%.

Table 16.2   *Top Indian banks by assets*

Bank	Assets $bn
State Bank of India	143
ICICI	38
Canara Bank	25
Punjab National Bank	24
Bank of Baroda	22
Bank of India	20
Central Bank of India	16
Union Bank of India	13
HDFC	12
India Overseas Bank	12
Syndicate Bank	11
Allahabad Bank	10
India Bank	9
Oriental Bank of Commerce	9
Corporation Bank	7
Andhra Bank	7

Source: *Banker* magazine, July 2005.

Like China, also important in a large agricultural economy are 1872 urban cooperative banks and 106 919 rural cooperative credit institutions. They make loans not only to farmers but cottage industries, retail trade, small businesses, professionals and for housing purposes.

For similar reasons, again just as in China, the Post Office plays a key role and one which could be developed much further. There are 154 000 post offices, 89% outside cities. The Post Office Savings Banks have the largest bank network of all in view of the number of branches and number of accounts. These handle various types of savings deposits, a number of national savings certificates, mutual fund sales and money transfers using Western Union Financial Services. Some 840 post offices are designated as head post offices and a further 1450 others as departmental sub post offices. These are computerised for counter and back office procedures. E-mail and Internet facilities have been set up in many villages to give the locals access to these facilities. Finally, many banks, such as ICICI, seeing the value of the network, are working with post offices to help them with IT and giving them the ability to offer a range of the bank's products.

There are also bank financial institutions and non-bank financial institutions for leasing, hire purchase, general loans and investments. These include Citigroup Financial, with 250 branches and 15 million credit card users, and GE Capital with 120 branches.

According to the World Bank, some 79% of rural householders have no access to formal lending and loan sharks proliferate. There is a huge scope here but banks are prevented from charging what they regard as the proper rate for risk. Many villages have no electricity and those that do experience erratic supplies. To aid weaker sections of the economy the banks have 'priority lending targets'.

In larger villages and in urban areas there are, of course, ATMs and Internet connections. Some 87% of cheque clearing is done using magnetic ink character recognition and there is an electronic funds transfer system covering 169 centres. There are moves to cheque truncation. In March 2004, the implementation of a real-time gross settlement system started for interbank transfers. There is connectivity available at 4800 bank branches and the aim was to increase this to 10 000 before the end of 2006.

Credit card usage is increasing fast, and between 2003 and 2004 the number grew from 26.9 million to 43.3 million. The central bank announced a curb on aggressive selling and raised the risk weighting for capital ratio purposes from 100% to 120%.

A Banking Standards Board was created in April 2005 and this has drawn up a banking code of conduct.

Foreign ownership of Indian banks is restricted, as we have mentioned. Early in 2005, the RBI suggested maximum limits of 5% to 10% for investment in a state bank. In spite of this, in July 2005 Rabobank was allowed to keep a 20% stake of a new private bank, Yes Bank, which needed extra capital. In the same way, in October 2002, ING acquired a major holding in one of the old private banks, Vysya, because it was in need of restructuring.

Foreign banks can set up in their own right, as we have seen, but licences for new branches are tightly controlled. The RSB has promised to allow 100% ownership of private banks in 2009. In view of the increasing number of people in the middle classes, the prospects for consumer finance are excellent and foreign banks are champing at the bit. Citigroup's Sanjay Nayar has commented, 'Since our focus is on organic growth, we'd like three times as many branches as we get.' Société Générale has moved in and opened branches in Delhi and Mumbai and has set up private banking for the new high net worth individuals.

While the Indian banks do investment banking, generally their expertise is less than the foreign investment banks who see good prospects for underwriting, custodial services, asset management and general non-commercial banking. Crédit Suisse First Boston (CSFB) has returned after an absence of four years following an alleged price fixing scandal. They are starting equity and brokerage services but are not looking for a joint venture.

Many investment banks are moving into India, not just for banking but for outsourcing, and this includes sophisticated back office functions. JP Morgan plans the recruitment of 4500 Indian graduates over a period of two years and expects to have 9000 local staff by the end of 2007, of which one third will be in investment banking. UBS expects to have 500 local staff by end 2006 and Goldman Sachs already has 700. Finally, IBM announced in June 2006 that it intends to invest $6 billion (£3.6 billion) in India over the next three years. This is triple the sum they have so far invested in India, where they already employ 42 000 staff.

Foreign exchange   The Indian currency floats, but there are exchange controls on capital account transactions. Like China, India is proud that it survived the Asian financial crises of the late 90s unscathed. The RBI has no target for full convertibility but wants to maintain 'orderly conditions'.

In June 2000, Parliament passed the Foreign Exchange Management Act (FEMA) to promote 'the orderly maintenance of the foreign exchange market in India'. The government manages current account transactions and the RBI the capital account. Foreign investors may bring in repatriatable funds and companies may borrow on international markets subject to RBI approval. Indian residents and firms may not freely convert the rupee in order to acquire assets or lend funds overseas.

The Prime Minister of India, Manmohan Singh, has boasted that their banking system is ahead of China – more robust and sound. Others are not so sure. There are impressive savings, but the government is grabbing a major share. High deficit financing is crowding out the private sector. The combined fiscal deficit of the government and the states is about 10%. The deficit funds subsidies, capital and revenue items but interest payments are 21% of government spending, which limits the room for much needed investment in infrastructure, health and education. The banks have a statutory liquidity ratio, which means they must keep government securities as 25% of net demand and time liabilities. In practice, the figure is about 40% and reflects this excessive government expenditure.

There is poor contract enforcement, weak bankruptcy laws and a much needed credit information database (being set up). To be fair, exactly the same criticisms can be applied to China, if not more so. The end result is that public sector bank managers are conservative when it comes to private sector clients. We have already mentioned the tight grip that money lenders have over the poor who have no bank accounts. Pria Basu, a lead sector specialist at the World Bank, comments, 'The banking system has traded efficiency for stability.' Underperforming public banks are being sheltered from the full blast of competition.

Capital Markets

Equities: China   The main stock exchanges are in Shanghai and Shenzen. Shares are divided into three main classes:

- ❏ 'A' shares are quoted in renminbi and available to domestic investors, but there is restricted access only for 34 'qualified' foreign investors
- ❏ 'B' shares are quoted in hard currencies, mainly in US and Hong Kong dollars
- ❏ 'H' shares are those quoted in Hong Kong.

The stock market regulator is the China Securities Regulatory Commission (CSRC).

The essential problem is that almost all of the shares quoted are from state-owned companies and only a minority percentage has been floated. Thus, in the case of Baosteel, 22% of the shares are private but 78% are still held by the state. The end result is that two thirds of all the shares are simply not tradeable. This also gives the market an unpleasant overhang of some $250 million (£150 million). What happens when large numbers of these shares are offered for sale? Obviously, the share price will fall, to the considerable disadvantage of the existing investors. Because of these problems, the Shanghai Composite index has fallen over 50% since its high in 2001 and new flotations have been banned since mid-2004.

To compound the problem, accounting and corporate governance are weak, there is poor protection for minority shareholders and no shareholders' pre-emptive rights. The end result is that Hong Kong, with its far higher standards, has gained heavily and the quotations of all major Chinese companies have been made there.

In May 2005, the government announced plans for a trial sale of shares in some 46 listed companies. This further sale would need the approval of CSRC and two thirds of the public shareholders (usually cities, provinces or central government). Also, the buyers must hold the shares for 1 year, and a scheme to compensate existing shareholders in the event of a price fall was unveiled.

These plans for shareholder compensation were confirmed later in the year, and the way was paved for a release of the 'overhang' of some $250 million (£150 million) worth of shares, with the caveat that no more than 10% would be released in any year.

In January 2006 came the news that purchase of 'A' shares by foreigners was being eased. They must be 'strategic' investors taking a minimum stake of 10% and prepared to hold the shares for three years. The approval of CSRC is still required. There were also strong rumours of a trial programme to merge the status of 'A' and 'B' shares, but no date was given. As a result of this, there was a new feeling of optimism. Another interesting piece of news came in the following month. Air China, already quoted in Hong Kong, was seeking permission to issue new shares on the Shanghai Exchange.

The problems of weak accounting standards and low levels of corporate governance still persist. Indeed, in December 2005 Li Rongrong, chairman of the state-owned Assets Supervision and Administration Commission, said openly that state-owned companies would benefit from listing first on a market like Hong Kong (over 20 Chinese shares are traded in London) because the international exchanges had more rigorous corporate governance standards which would improve the performance of state-owned groups.

The problem of the equity markets certainly needs to be resolved. China has a looming pensions crisis and equity and bond assets are needed for investment by pension funds.

Equities: India   India has 22 stock exchanges and a National Stock Exchange in Mumbai (NSE). The NSE was set up in 1993 as the first debt market exchange for Treasury bills, government securities and corporate bonds. The Bombay Stock Exchange is really the Mumbai Stock Exchange but is still known as BSE. It is the dominant equity market, set up in 1875, and is thus the oldest in Asia (Tokyo 1878). Its main share index, the SENSEX 30, is the one that is normally quoted. There is also the Over the Counter Exchange of India for the listing of small and medium-sized companies. The regulator is the Securities and Exchange Board of India and the market is transparent and well regulated.

The BSE trades some 6000 shares and has been going through a boom time. The SENSEX index, which was 3300 in March 2003, was about 10 400 by late February 2006, although it suffered a fall in May/June 2006 like other world markets. There is a large amount of M&A activity and much foreign investment in private firms. There were record inflows of foreign purchases in 2005 totalling $10 billion (£6 billion). What is really needed is more *domestic* investment. The financial savings of the household sector are 13.7% of GDP, but shares and bonds are only 0.2% of GDP.

Securities are held in a dematerialised form and shares are traded on the BSE using their screen-based system, BOLT. Members may act as either brokers or market makers and settlement is T+2. Debt instruments are also traded on the BSE as well as the NSE. Derivatives are traded and will be covered later.

We have mentioned before that the Congress Party coalition needs the support of the communists. The latter are strongly opposed to the privatisation of state enterprises. But for this, the activity of the BSE would be even bigger than it is.

Bonds and money markets: China   The bond markets are dominated by state bonds. They are sold by auction to banks, non-bank financial institutions, insurance companies and corporates. There is secondary trading on the stock exchanges and both primary and secondary use electronic trading. China's first inflation-linked bond was in 1988, well ahead of the US in 1997. The government also issued a $1.7 billion (£1.02 billion) Eurobond on the Hong Kong Exchange in mid-2004, split into 5 and 10 year segments. There are also stripped bonds domestically. There are some corporate issues, including convertibles, but the market is small and needs developing as a source of capital for corporates. The Asian Development Bank and the International Finance Corporation (the private sector lending arm of the World Bank) became the first foreign issuers of renminbi bonds in 2005. Perhaps inevitably, they have become known as 'panda' bonds.

Following guidelines issued by the central bank, November 2005 saw the start of asset-backed bonds in China. The China Construction Bank issued 3 billion renminbi of residential mortgage-backed securities, organised by Standard Chartered Bank. The China Development Bank followed with a collateralised loan obligation issue. In each case, the collateral offered was scrutinised by the main rating agencies. The bonds were aimed at domestic investors.

There are some corporate bonds but the market suffers from poor liquidity. They tend to be short-term and face a long and difficult approval process.

As regards money markets, there is trading in Treasury bills but the markets in certificates of deposit and commercial paper are embryonic. Growth is nevertheless expected. In December 2005, Collins Stewart Tullett went into a joint venture with the state-controlled Shanghai International Group to launch the country's first interdealer broker, followed by a licence for Icap, the world's biggest interdealer broker, in July 2006. These moves clearly foresee a growth in the markets for foreign exchange, bonds and commercial paper.

Bonds and money markets: India   As usual, the market is dominated by government issues with Treasury bills from 14 days to 12 months, and 5, 10 and 20 year bonds. Trading is by order-matching screen on BSE and NSE. Some bonds have been stripped. There are also bonds issued by the Indian states. In the primary market, the RBI used to take up any bonds not sold at the auctions but this is dying as a proper system of primary dealers (17) is being set up.

Asset-backed bonds are traded. For example, the Indian Railways Finance Corporation securitised lease receivables with a 10 year issue in April 2005 arranged by Citigroup. Mortgage-backed bonds are also popular. In the year up to end March 2004 there were 90 issues of asset-backed bonds and up to end March 2005 there were 119, totalling 292 billion rupees.

In the money markets, there are repos, reverse repos, commercial paper and certificates of deposit. There has been a big increase in the latter as stamp duty has been withdrawn and the tax is no longer deducted at source. FRAs are used and the interbank reference rate is MIBOR.

Derivatives: China   Previous losses and scandals have led to the authorities taking an extremely cautious attitude to derivatives trading. For example, in November 2004, the China Aviation Organisation, an importer of fuel oil, collapsed under the weight of derivative losses. The China Securities Regulatory Organisation issued guidelines in March 2004, 'Interim Rules on the Derivative Business of Financial Institutions'. Financial derivative trading has still not been cleared but interest rate swaps and options are now being considered.

The only derivatives trading is that in commodities. There are three exchanges, in Shanghai, Dalian and Zhengzhou. The Shanghai Futures Exchange (SHFE) operates four contracts for copper, aluminium, rubber and fuel oil. They have 200 members and 250 distant trading terminals worldwide. They also have an alliance with the CME.

On the assumption that trading in financial derivatives will be allowed, Thailand and Taiwan have stepped up their derivatives trading to get ahead of the anticipated commencement in China. Euronext.liffe and the CME have also set up telephone connections in Singapore to make it easier for access.

Derivatives: India   In contrast to China, financial derivative trading is well established. There are interest rate options, futures and swaps, mainly over the counter. The main exchanges are the NSE and BSE mentioned in the Equities subsection. The BSE offers index futures and options on the SENSEX index and this began in 2000. There are stock options on the shares of 76 companies. Having sensed a demand for shorter-dated options, weekly stock options were introduced in September 2004 and offered for five companies. Bond futures and options are traded on the NSE. Both exchanges trade electronically, as for equities.

INSURANCE: CHINA AND INDIA

Emerging markets generally are showing strong growth in insurance with rates of 10.4% for life business and 7.3% for non-life. The corresponding figures for industrialised nations are 3.4% and 2.6% (Swiss Re Research).

In China and India, insurance is growing fast from modest beginnings. CSFB did a China Insurance Market Survey in March 2004. They found a 10 year average annual real growth rate of 10.8% for non-life business and 23.7% for life business. Swiss Re estimates India's growth to be 6.2% for non-life and 12.7% for life. Although growth rates are high, in world terms the market is still small. The premiums per GDP percentage is 3.3% for China and 2.9% for India against a world average of 8.1%. Total value of premiums is shown in Table 16.3.

Table 16.3   *Total premiums for life and non-life insurance in China and India, 2004*

Category	China $m	India $m
Life insurance	35 407	16 919
Non-life insurance	16 765	4 330

Source: Swiss Re Economic Research and Consulting, National Insurance Authorities.

In China, the market is controlled by the China Insurance Regulatory Commission (CIRC) set up in 1998. In India, it is the India Regulatory and Development Authority (IRDA) set up in 1999.

Both markets are emerging from a history of nationalisation but are moving toward liberalisation. China joined the World Trade Organisation in 2001 and – as part of this – promised to improve access for foreign insurers who were first admitted in 1992, the first being AIG. There are now some 11 private insurers, 19 foreign branches and 21 joint ventures in life assurance where the maximum holding allowed is 50%. The market is, nevertheless, dominated by state insurers, of whom the biggest are the Peoples Insurance Company of China, China Life Insurance and Ping Ann Insurance, all of whom are listed abroad.

In India, foreign insurers can take a holding in a local insurer of 26% (promised to increase to 49%) and there are 19 joint ventures. The first private Indian life insurer without a foreign partner was Sahara in March 2004. Again, as in China, the state sector dominates with the Life Insurance Company of India in the life business and New India, National, Oriental and the United India in the non-life business. In the life business, at least, there are three very successful private companies (helped by a foreign joint venture) – ICICI Prudential, Bajaj Allianz and Birla Sunlife.

Prominent foreign insurers in China are Allianz, Tokyo Marine and Fire, Winterthur, Liberty Mutual, Royal and SunAlliance in non-life business; and in life, Aegon, AIG, Axa, Generali, Nippon Life, Skandia and Aviva. In November 2005, Lloyd's was granted permission to do reinsurance business in China and be considered a local insurer alongside the Chinese insurers and Swiss Re and Munich Re, who were already there. An exception to the 50% rule came in the same month when the Willis Group were allowed to raise their holding in Willis Pudong Brokers to 51%.

In India, we have seen the Prudential, Allianz and Sunlife in joint ventures with ICICI, Bajaj and Birla. Other foreign companies include Allianz, AIG and Tokyo Marine and Fire in non-life and Allianz, AIG, Aviva and Standard Life in life business. Lloyd's has also opened an office in India.

Bancassurance is widespread in both markets and accounts for 25% of life business in China and 10% in India.

One problem for both economies is the occurrence of natural catastrophes – both heavily underinsured. Foreign expertise in underwriting is needed and much strengthening of capital.

Again, both markets have seen the practice of imposing price controls. In China, at least, this seems to be easing following the release of price limits on motor insurance (car usage has gone up so fast that the authorities now wish to cool this market). India still imposes price controls over 75% of the market. China set high price levels to discourage cut-throat competition. India set prices at low levels to protect the consumer, leading to cross-subsidisation over different lines of business.

Pensions is another key issue. The one-child policy leaves China with a massive future problem as the population is aging rapidly. Some 600 million workers are not covered and there is a growing demand from the better-off for private cover. There is now a new legal framework by which approved institutions can act as custodian, asset manager and fund holder for company schemes. Some tax concessions are available. The first licences were given in mid-2005 to 15 investment managers to offer new corporate pension schemes. Four out of the 15 are joint ventures with foreign companies: ING, Fortis, Deutsche Bank and the Bank of Montreal. Pension contributors are to be held in a legally distinct pension fund governed by trust law.

In India, no integral pension or social security schemes exist. The huge agricultural army of farmers and labourers is not covered. For better-off workers, there is an Employee Provident Fund Organisation and there are civil service pension schemes for central and local government. Probably 11% of the working population are not covered. New government employees are covered by a defined contribution and fully funded pension scheme. Non-government employees can join on a voluntary basis. A pension authority – the Pension Fund Regulatory and Development Authority – was set up in October 2003 to oversee pension reform issues.

Private sector suppliers clearly have a role to play in both markets. Pension products for the better-off are now available. The challenge is the large rural sector and how to reach it. The fact that their incomes are very volatile presents another difficulty.

China and India have great potential for insurance. Standards need to be raised and more emphasis placed on the insurer's asset/liability management skills. Allowing freer foreign access would help.

In order to grow, the business needs a predictable environment which includes economic stability, legal certainty, stability of institutions and enforcement of property rights.

(Readers who are particularly interested in this subject will find a complete coverage in Swiss Re *Sigma* publication No. 5/2004, 'Exploiting the Growth Potential of Emerging Insurance Markets – China and India in the Spotlight'.)

CHINA AND INDIA – A COMPARISON

China and India are home to almost two fifths of humanity and are two of the world's fastest growing economies. In terms of GDP, China is three times as big, but may not be able to keep up the current rate of growth indefinitely. Some see India moving ahead faster at some point.

In making a comparison, one of the first things that Westerners seize on is that China is a communist state and that India is a democracy.

An article in *The Economist* dated 25 February 2006 noted that India had stability, but that 'China's transition to democracy could be traumatic'. It is not very clear why it is assumed that China, in the end, will become democratic. Nor is it clear that, in terms of economic development, being a democracy is necessarily an advantage.

Within reason, if the Chinese government decides to do something, it will do it.

That's not to say that there may not be some internal dissent at government level. The fact that the share prices of some Chinese companies on the Hong Kong Exchange have gone up has led to criticism that the state's assets are being sold to 'foreigners' too quickly. This has led to a slowdown in approval of some foreign moves into Chinese banks. In addition, there is grave concern among many prominent party members that the rich–poor gap is being closed so slowly. Nevertheless, broadly speaking, the government can make a decision and get on with it. Look at the situation in India. The 2004 election saw the Bharatiya Janata party pushed out of office. The Congress party leads an alliance – the United Progressive Alliance of 19 parties including the communists and led by the Prime Minister, Manmohan Singh. Does this lead to decisive government? The communist part is naturally suspicious of foreign capitalists and capitalist ideas generally. They called a one day strike on 29 September 2004, and for a time boycotted the co-ordination committee which was attempting to negotiate policy between the coalition partners. In July 2005, they successfully prevented the attempt by the Prime Minister to sell just 10% of Bhel, a public sector electrical company. Announcing the privatisation of the Delhi and Mumbai airports (badly needed), the communist opposition called a strike of 22 000 workers. In the end, the strike was called off when there were assurances of job security, regarded by some as a victory for the government. In July 2006, the government announced modest plans to sell small stakes in two companies that would still have left the majority in public hands. Two weeks later, the plan was suspended following opposition from the DMK party. In the meantime, China has 130 airports handling one million passengers a year, has another 55 planned by 2020 and accounted for one fifth of all Boeing's orders in 2005. The argument that democracy is assisting economic development is not persuasive.

The references above, to an electrical company and to airports, highlight one of India's biggest weaknesses – infrastructure. Let us take the example of Bangalore, India's Silicon Valley. In 30 years, it has gone from a medium-sized town to one with a population of seven million. Some 55%–60% of the nation's high-tech companies (about 1500 of them) are there. One would imagine that the state, Karnataka, would be delighted at this success and, presumably, the influx of local tax revenues – instead of which it is indifferent, if not hostile. Its preoccupation is a change of name to Bengaluru, as it has less connotation of former imperialism. Meanwhile, roads are gridlocked, rubbish goes uncollected, sewage pollutes the water and bare power lines run through the slums. The big software houses, India's new 'jewels in the crown' – like Tata, Infosys and Wipro – are planning future expansion elsewhere.

Electricity is a key issue for infrastructure. Power supply is often erratic and only 56% of households have connections to the grid. Both central and state governments have a role here and government action on this and other issues can be frustrated by lack of action by the states. The Electricity Act of 2003 promised more privatisation but has achieved little. Only two states have privatised distribution and the communist party would like to see the Act weakened.

Apart from electricity, there are problems with roads, airports, phones, rail freight and ports. The World Bank is providing money to assist with 63 000 kilometres of rail track and 33 million kilometres of roads, 57% of which are unpaved. Rail freight costs are said to be two thirds higher than in China, and airport modernisation is badly needed – although a start is being made. The government is now in the process of awarding licences for private sector operators to run freight services using railway infrastructure. Finally, 100 000 villages are said to have no telephones.

That is not to say that everything in the garden is rosy in China. Both countries are enormous and face massive problems with infrastructure. One difference, however, is that India spends some 3.5% of GDP on infrastructure and China 10%. Where is the money to come from? Central and state government deficits amount to 10% as it is, and anything spent on infrastructure is not spent on anything else. Drewry Shipping Consultants estimate that India loses 1.2% of GDP due to poor infrastructures and coalition politics. Other estimates range as high as 3%, so the position is serious.

One area where India scores is graduate education. India has some four million graduates a year and China three million – both large figures. India, however, has the big advantage in a global world of the use of the English language. In spite of the growing use and teaching of Hindi, even internally the use of English facilitates communications between one part of the country and another. There is also the question of the quality of the graduates. There have been some criticisms of the quality of Chinese graduates, due to their receiving what is regarded as 'highly theoretical' training. A McKinsey report in October 2005 concluded that a shortage of well trained graduates may hinder China's development of service industries, such as IT. A study found that less than 10% of graduates had the skill to work for a foreign company, compared with 25% in India. Another report from the McKinsey Global Institute concluded that India's pool of highly qualified graduates will be twice as large as China's by 2008.

Capital markets – equities and bonds – need to be developed much further in both countries. China has laid the foundations for the recovery of the moribund stock markets but this will take time and the corporate bond market is very weak. India's stock markets are far healthier but it is foreign, rather than domestic, money which is sustaining it. While there are plenty of private companies, the corporate bond market is not strong and, surprisingly, as a percentage of GDP, less than China's – although bigger in absolute terms as the GDP is much smaller. In Malaysia, the corporate bond market is 38% of GDP and in South Korea 33%. In China it is 0.7% and India 0.4% – there is a long way to go. Finance in both countries comes overwhelmingly from a bank sector dominated by state banks.

India suffers badly from bureaucracy. On average it takes 89 days to start up a business in India, 41 days in China and 18 days in the UK, according to the World Bank. There are widespread demands for registration and licensing as well as restrictive labour laws. Any company with more than 100 employees cannot declare redundancies without approval from local labour boards. The above World Bank study ranked countries in terms of ease of doing business. India ranked 116 out of 155 countries, between Indonesia and Albania.

Clearly, China is not free from bureaucracy. For example, a host of prices are state-controlled – water, oil, power, cable TV fees, land, education, pharmaceuticals, telecommunications, gold and precious metals, air tickets and even parking fees for cars and bicycles. It is all controlled by the National Development Reform Corporation. The problem is that if you don't ration oil, for example by price, then you get rationing through shortages. This is exactly what has happened as retail prices have been kept artificially well below the world level.

China attracts far more foreign investment than India, but then China is much more a manufacturing economy – 46% of GDP as opposed to India's 19%. Even so, the attitude is different. China seems to realise that foreigners and foreign money can be useful and is prepared to accept them on that basis. We have seen in the financial area that foreign firms are allowed bigger shares in banks and brokers, where these firms are in trouble and need recapitalising. Interestingly, there is an aphorism from the Quing dynasty which says, 'Make the past serve the present, make the foreign serve China'! India puts caps on foreign direct investment in aviation, insurance, coal mining and media, and only franchises are allowed in the important area of retailing. Here overseas groups can set up *wholesaling* operations or retail for one product range only (for example, Louis Vuitton). The entry of firms like Tesco or Wal-Mart is banned, even though they would create jobs and much of what they sold would be bought in India. Wal-Mart is allowed in China and is estimated to spend $15 billion (£9 billion) there. Some 96% of all retailing in India is still done in small stores and bazaars. There are now some 100 shopping 'malls' but this is still small for such a big country.

Poverty is a major issue in both countries and a source of social discontent as the gap between the rural poor and prosperous urban middle classes grows. China has abolished direct agricultural taxes, which have existed for hundreds of years, and announced a 'New Deal' for farming in late February 2006. However, the announcement of further subsidies for unproductive farming communities is itself controversial. The Indian novelist, Arundhati Roy, says that she sees India as a land where emaciated labourers dig trenches to lay fibre optic cable by candlelight. The boom has yet to reach the two thirds who live in the country.

In summary, both countries claim to be making reforms to plug weaknesses. India feels it is tackling bureaucracy, its mass illiteracy and ghastly roads. It claims as plus factors the use of English and managers and technicians who can think for themselves. As China's working population shrinks, India's will be bigger. There are, however, critics amongst their own countrymen. Chetan Ahya of Morgan Stanley says that 'unless the government responds quickly to ensure a major increase in privatisation, foreign direct investment and infrastructure, growth momentum is likely to slow to 6.5% on the average in the next four quarters' (that is, 2006–07 fiscal year). Shankar Acharya, former chief economic adviser to the Indian government, takes a similar view. In a book (*Essays on Macroeconomic*

Policy and Growth in India, Oxford University Press), he argues that medium-term growth will remain at 6.0% and gives as India's principle needs the deregulation of labour markets, elimination of fiscal deficits and across-the-board privatisation and trade liberalisation. It's all a tall order.

In the case of China, one key problem for future years is the effect of the one-child policy. The United Nations calculates that today there are 9.1 workers for every pensioner, but in 40 years there will be only 2.1, when China will have 100 million people aged over 80. This will be an enormous demand on resources and there will come a point when India's working population exceeds that of China. Huge overcapacity, especially in automobiles and steel, is another problem and may lead to a slowing of growth for a time while things stabilise. An OECD report in September 2003 urges certain reforms – restructuring of the public sector, reform of company law (to remove barriers to the entry of new firms), better property rights, proper bankruptcy laws and further development of financial markets.

At the same time, the Chinese will claim that reforms have already started:

❏ the scrapping of farm taxes
❏ a reduction in the rate at which income tax kicks in
❏ scrapping the 11-year-old peg against the dollar in favour of a managed float
❏ the launch of market makers for currency trading and a widening of the market for non-renminbi currency pairs
❏ the launch of commercial paper and mortgage-backed securities
❏ approval for banks to trade currency swaps and forwards
❏ establishment of the first money broker
❏ the first 'panda' bonds for international borrowers in the renminbi
❏ the start of equity market reorganisation, and finally
❏ the agreement to bring its national accounting standards in line with internal rules from 1 January 2007.

It's all for the future, of course, but this is a nation with a reputation for the patient long-term view – remember: 'The journey of a thousand miles begins with one step'! There is also the no doubt apocryphal story of a modern Chinese statesman who was asked what effect the French revolution had had on the development of China and replied, 'It is too early to say.' If this view of China was ever true, it certainly seems to have changed now.

CHINA AND INDIA – A THREAT?

The growth of Asia, and China and India in particular, tends to be seen as a threat. The Americans are particularly paranoid about China in this respect. As well as the obvious fears about imports (28% of their trade gap in 2005), defence hawks worry about China's military buildup; there was a considerable overreaction to the attempt by the Chinese oil firm, CNOOC, to buy a relatively minor US firm in the same business – Unocol. Congress went into panic mode seeing Unocol as a 'strategic asset' and the Chinese withdrew. China has also made investments in steel in Brazil, has bought the TV manufacturing business of Thomson, the mobile handset making side of Alcatel and the PC business of IBM. On the other hand, the bid for the US firm Maytag failed as did bids for Canada's Norands and Pakistan Telecom. The D'Long conglomerate bought several foreign brands including Murray lawnmowers and part of bankrupt aircraft maker Fairchild Dornier before collapsing under the weight of its debts in 2004. The idea that China is 'buying the world' looks silly now. For them, it's a way of learning modern business practices – management skills, marketing, brand names and strategic thinking. It's a bit like Japanese buying in the 1980s, such as the Rockefeller Centre, and references to unfair trade practices, 'dumping money' – and even a 1991 book with the alarming title '*The Coming War with Japan*' by George Friedman and Meredith Lebard.

Of course jobs are a key worry. The UK's Chancellor, Gordon Brown, published a paper in early 2004 entitled, 'Long Term Global Economic Challenges and Opportunities for the UK'. In it he pointed out that the US and Europe will lose at least 5 million jobs to Asia over the next 10 years and that before long China and India alone will have half the world's manufacturing. In part, the paper was a wakeup call to the European Union, with its total disregard of the changed position and liking for legislation that threatens jobs and competitiveness. Those who believed that our high tech industries will continue to do well, thinking that the Asian challenge is in low wage, low tech products, will not have been encouraged by Marconi's closure of the Edge Lane works in Liverpool (builder of Britain's first automatic telephone exchange in 1912) and IBM's announcement that it is cutting 13 000 jobs in Europe.

A more optimistic view comes from Roger Bootle, MD of Capital Economics, who has published a book *Money For Nothing* (Nicholas Brealey Publishing) which has a chapter on this same subject – should we fear Asia? He prefers to stress the opportunities to sell to Asia and their rising middle classes with an appetite for cars, computers, food, drink, professional services, retail financial products, pharmaceutical products, luxury branded goods and knowledge-based services. In the case of the UK, for example, it is interesting that while exports of goods have at best marked time, our exports of services to Asia have risen by almost 60% since 1997. The new Asian middle classes want retail financial services – loans, mortgages, insurance and pensions. Other opportunities outside of finance will also increase. Roger Bootle reminds us of Ricardo's 'Theory of Comparative Advantage' which we discussed in Chapter 14. Even if the Chinese were to prove more efficient at manufacturing everything, we can still concentrate on the areas where the comparative advantage is least. In any case, as prosperity grows over 20/30 years, so the price advantage will reduce.

Roger Bootle returned to the theme in an article in the *Sunday Telegraph* of 13 November 2005. He pointed out that as China grows faster relative to the West it does not mean that we are worse off in *absolute* terms. There does not have to be a loser for every winner – the cake may grow larger.

We may lose influence but not prosperity. We must allow workers to transfer from those industries where we cannot compete to those where we can. We should also not forget that over the past 10 years prices of clothing and footwear have fallen 40%, giving a boost to real incomes.

It's a nice positive note on which to finish.

SUMMARY

China and India are home to two fifths of humanity and are two of the world's fastest growing economies. The population of China is 1.3 billion and India, 1.1 billion. China is growing at 9.5% per year and India 7%. India's GDP is one third that of China.

China accounts for 28% of the US trade gap, which explains the arguments about their exports to the US in particular.

China is a large manufacturing economy (49% of GDP) and its growth has led to substantial imports of raw materials including oil,and also imports of components from neighbouring Asian economies. Exports are not just of low cost, low tech goods but computers, digital phones and similar products.

India is an entrepreneurial economy with skilled English-speaking graduates and has a high reputation in the field of information technology. It has become a major centre for outsourcing. It is also a young economy (52% under the age of 25). China will face major future problems as a result of its one-child policy.

Both economies have massive rural populations and face the problem of the contrast between the growing prosperity of the middle classes and the extreme poverty in rural areas.

Hong Kong retains some autonomy. When people speak of China they usually mean mainland China.

Banking in both economies is dominated by state sector banks and this has led to much wasteful lending to local enterprises. Foreign ownership is carefully controlled. China's state banks are gradually going public, using the Hong Kong exchange and releasing only a minor percentage of shares for sale.

There are a large number of rural and urban cooperatives in both China and India and also many thousands of post offices which both countries would like to see playing a larger role in providing banking services.

The renminbi is kept within a tight band in a basket of currencies; the rupee floats; but both countries impose tight capital controls.

Capital markets are weak in both countries. China's stock exchanges are dormant pending implementation of changes to allow large state holdings to be floated without disruption. China's top companies float in Hong Kong. India's Mumbai Stock Exchange is flourishing. Bond markets are dominated by state bonds in both economies and the corporate bond market is weak. Banks are far too dominant as a source of finance and strong capital markets are badly needed in China and India.

Derivative markets in China only exist for commodities. In India, financial derivatives are well established.

Insurance is growing fast in both markets and many foreign insurers are represented. Financing pensions for the rural poor is a major future challenge for both countries.

The growth of China and India can be seen as a threat to employment in the US and Europe. At the same time, the influx of low cost goods reduces inflation and raises living standards. The opportunity is there to sell services, general and financial, to the fast growing, prosperous middle classes.

Trends in the Global Financial Markets

17 Key Trends

17 Key Trends

The global financial markets are still going through a period of rapid change brought about by a changing economic and political outlook. We are in a period of exceptionally low inflation and interest rates. Desperate investors of all kinds are taking on high levels of risk in the search for a higher return. Derivative markets are continuing to expand and innovate, to help investors pass on the risk. The West faces the challenge of the rise of Asian emerging markets and the high price of oil and commodities, the latter partly a consequence of the Asian growth. Middle Eastern states find themselves awash with funds due to the high oil price. A new 'Islamic consciousness' has led to a growth in Islamic banking techniques.

It is the purpose of this last chapter to highlight a number of these recent and future trends.

EMERGING MARKETS

A dominant theme at the World Economic Forum in Davos was the fast growth of emerging markets, especially China and India. Back in October 2003, Goldman Sachs had talked of the BRICs – Brazil, Russia, India and China – and argued that by 2040 they will be larger in dollar terms than the top six existing developed economies – US, Japan, Germany, UK, France and Italy. After China's upgrade of its GDP figures in December 2005, Lehman Brothers concluded that China had now shot past Italy, France and probably the UK. They argued that Germany would be surpassed in 2010 and Japan by 2020. All this is a long way into the future, of course, and there are still problems to be faced by China and India, particularly the growing gap between rich and poor. Russia and Brazil, the other BRICS, also face the usual political uncertainty.

In more general terms, the non-G7 share of world growth, 33% in 1999, was 38% in 2006. For two centuries, Europe and the US have dominated the world economy, challenged only by Japan. Now we have the four BRIC economies and countries like Korea, Malaysia, Taiwan, Thailand and Singapore.

China's expansion has been of great benefit to the other Asian economies with its need to import components made by them. Exports to China have finally helped Japan to emerge from a long deflationary spiral. The consequent rise in the price of oil and raw materials has also helped producers in Latin America.

The success of the emerging markets generally has attracted considerable investment. Encouraged by better performance in Latin America, including paying off IMF debt and Brady bonds, has enabled countries like Colombia and Brazil to resume selling bonds denominated in their own currencies. Argentina, in February 2005, restructured its debts and forced bond holders to face up to losses of 65% of the original value. Yet in July 2005, Argentina, a serial defaulter and long running economic failure, was able successfully to sell more dollar bonds. This was on the back of burgeoning exports and a fiscal surplus.

Investment banks had their best ever year in Asia in 2005, with total fees estimated at $7 billion for M&A, fixed income deals and underwriting. Equities in emerging markets as a whole returned 31% in 2005 and Jerome Booth, head of research at London-based Ashmore Investment Management, claims that cash-laden Asian and Middle Eastern central banks are poised to invest billions of dollars in emerging market debt.

Of course, the transfer of manufacturing to cheaper markets in the Near and Far East presents a challenge to Western countries. Manufacturing is 10% of GDP in the US and 49% in China. This decline is an inevitable part of economic growth and prosperity. In some cases, workers have been replaced by technology to boost productivity. They have moved from labour-intensive products to other sectors such as pharmaceuticals. Consumers have benefited from cheaper goods and, although some jobs are lost, imports create other opportunities for employment and profit. For instance, an import of some textile from China, sold in the US at, say, $10 has probably only cost the importer $1. The remaining $9 goes to the importer, wholesaler, retailer and distribution and advertising.

To pay for the imports, services must be exported – professional, knowledge-based and financial. It is interesting to note that the export of services from the US to China in 2005 went up by 20% (Bank of America estimates). McKinsey estimates that consumer spending in emerging economies is expected to increase from $4000 billion to $9000 billion by 2015. This not only means a market for services but food, drink, pharmaceuticals and luxury branded goods. Ricardo's 'Theory of Comparative Advantage' means that the West can still concentrate on products where the emerging market's advantage is not as great. Companies like Wal-Mart and Tesco are not only sourcing cheap goods from China but opening supermarkets there and doing good business. Opportunities are there to be grasped, and governments must spend on training and education and ease the transition for those who are in jobs no longer viable.

OIL

One of the key issues in global markets since the last edition of this book (2003) has been the large increase in the price of oil. This moved from figures of just over $20 a barrel in 2003 to $40 by mid-2004 and $60 or higher throughout most of 2005. Having been $67 in early 2006, it was $70 in June 2006.

Several questions arise which we will try to answer. What has caused these massive increases? Why have they not had a greater effect? Where are the extra petrodollars earned by these increases? What are the long-term prospects?

The Cause

Undoubtedly, a key reason for the increase in price has been the rise in demand for oil from Asia in particular due to fast growth. Of the increase in demand, 28% has come from China and 43% from all Asia, including China. This is against a background of high global growth generally. Crédit Suisse First Boston's global snapshot in early 2006 puts world growth at 5.1% in 2004, 4.5% in 2005 and 4.8% forecast for 2006.

An exacerbating factor has been the shortage of refinery capacity. No refineries have been built in the US since 1976, and many closed during the downturn in the 1980s. Oil needs to be turned into a range of products from petrol to plastic bags and it is a low margin business. Wood Mackenzie, the oil consultancy, estimates that the US consumed 32 million tonnes of petrol more than it refined in 2005, and faces an annual shortfall of 10 million tonnes of diesel and gas oil – all made up by imports from Europe. Building more refineries could take at least five years with the possibility of prices being much lower then. In any case, proposals to build new refineries are not popular and face environmental regulations and hostile local governments.

Finally, there is the effect of nervousness about supply – Nigeria, Iran – and large-scale speculation by hedge funds and others.

The Effect

Why hasn't this massive increase had a greater effect? Memories go back to the OPEC increases in 1973–74 and the considerable upheaval that they caused.

One reason is that the 'oil intensity' of GDP use has declined, mainly due to the fall in manufacturing in the US and Europe. Heavy industry is in retreat, replaced by a less intensive service sector. Manufacturing was 25% of US GDP in 1970 but is 10% now; it was 35% of UK GDP in 1970 but 14% now, and there are similar figures across Europe. On the other hand, manufacturing is 49% of GDP in China. Oil was 10% of the UK's total consumption in 1983 but only 5% now, according to Bank of England figures. In the last 25 years also, new-car fuel consumption has fallen by 25%.

Another factor is that world trade and growth is such that economies have been strong enough to absorb the increases. Monetary policies, too, are generally much more effective than in 1973–74. In any case, research from London's Centre for Economic Policy Research claims that oil may have made only a minor contribution to the economic dislocations of the last 30 years. We may have exaggerated its destructive effect. Policy errors have been much more important.

Where Are the Petrodollars?

Obviously, the oil price increases have put a lot of money into the coffers of oil producers in, say, the Middle East and Russia. Lex in the *Financial Times* of

16 January 2006 did an interesting analysis. According to OPEC and the US Department of Energy, members of OPEC generated $1021 billion in revenue from oil exports between the end of 2001 and the first half of 2005. Of this, 88% was spent on imports. Traditionally, a large part of oil revenues earned due to a sudden increase in prices have found their way into bank deposits or US Treasuries. After 1973–74 much of these bank revenues was lent in Latin America, and a large part of it subsequently written off. A lot has been written about 'recycling' of oil revenues. Clearly, the picture has now changed. What Lex describes as an 'amazingly small proportion' has gone into US Treasuries – just $10 billion and perhaps $25 billion on US equities and corporate bonds. It is also possible that some US Treasury purchases have been routed via London and intermediaries for political reasons. A final comment from Lex looks at 2006 and wonders quite where the petrodollars will go when domestic economies are already showing signs of overheating. It's a timely thought as other estimates suggest that, in 2007, the transfer of wealth to oil producing countries will amount to $1500 billion or 3.5% of world GDP.

Russia, at least, seems to have no problem in deciding what to do with the extra money – it is getting out of debt. Its foreign currency reserves are now $144 billion, the world's fifth largest: in January 2005, it paid off its debt to the IMF of $3.3 billion and, in May, paid $15 billion to the so-called Paris Club creditor nations.

What of the Future?

Goldman Sachs (who seem to specialise in eye-catching forecasts) produced a report in May 2005 suggesting that oil markets may have entered the early stages of a 'super spike' period which could drive oil prices to $105 a barrel. The argument is that demand from the emerging economies is growing much faster than the rate at which oil can be produced. One factor is the refusal of successive US governments to countenance any confrontation of the car lobby to reduce its usage of a commodity, a large part of the supply of which comes from potentially hostile nations.

The IMF had much the same message in April 2005, when its *World Economic Outlook* warned that oil prices would remain high, estimating a rise in global consumption from 82 million barrels per day to 140 million by 2040. For example, they estimate that today's 20 million Chinese vehicles will rise to 390 million by 2030.

On the other hand, Cambridge Energy Research Associates have carried out a field by field survey looking at the effects of current investment, and believe that today's output of some 85 million barrels per day could rise to just over 100 million by 2010.

World growth, of course, may not continue at this dizzy pace. Economists believe that interest rate rises take some 18 months to have their full effect. The US had 17 interest rate rises from 1% in mid-2004 to 5.25% in late June 2006. The European Central Bank is now putting rates up and there are prospects of the same in Japan. If growth falters (and there is heavy overcapacity in China), then so will oil price increases. Also technology may take a hand. Fierce oil price increases make alternatives more economically viable. It's hard to believe future estimates of the price of oil when estimates for 2006 vary so widely – from $45 a barrel to $75!

RISK

Introduction

Globally, we are going through a period of low interest rates and low inflation. Real interest rates (that is, after inflation) averaged 4% in the early 1990s and are about 1% now. This coincides with a rise in international liquidity due to the growth in world trade, the success of emerging economies, the oil price increases and the flow of money out of Japan due to real interest rates of near zero. Downward pressure on interest rates has come about in part because of the widespread switch of pension funds from equities to bonds for demographic and regulatory reasons. One result of this in the UK saw the yield on the 50 year index-linked gilt fall to about 0.5% in February 2006. As a consequence, investors everywhere – institutions, funds of all kinds, banks and individuals – have been seeking increasing returns and been prepared to accept greater risk. This has manifested itself in a variety of ways which we explore below.

Hedge Funds

There is nothing new in hedge funds being prepared to take risk in the search for greater return. What is new is the willingness of investors of all kinds to back them and add to the growing value of hedge funds generally. The investors have always included high net worth individuals but now we have university endowments, insurance companies and even pension funds. The US and Europe are getting very crowded so the funds are taking an increasing interest in Asia, where the hope is that not only are markets more buoyant but perhaps also more inefficient, giving hedge funds more scope to exploit this. Eurekahedge, the Singapore-based consultancy, says that hedge fund investments in Asia have passed the $100 billion mark.

Leverage

We see examples of leverage being taken to higher and higher levels. Multiples of debt to earnings before interest, tax, depreciation and amortisation (EBITDA) are steadily on the increase. Close Brothers Corporate Finance estimates that multiples in 2004 averaged 4.2 but 5.6 in 2005. There are plenty of examples of figures in excess of this. Private equity firms Blackstone and Lion Capital bought the European beverage arm of Cadbury Schweppes for €1.85 billion ($2.2 billion) in late 2005 on a multiple of seven. INEOS, the British bulk-chemicals producer, topped the debt markets in January 2006 to finance a €9 billion ($10.8 billion) takeover of some of BP's chemical assets. A presentation was made to hedge fund executives (in their hundreds) and other fund managers. Within weeks, €25 billion was offered. In the old days this would have been the province of banks, but not any longer, nor was it the older type of plain vanilla loan. There were three tranches of term loans, some mezzanine-like debt and ten year bonds denominated in dollars and euros – all of it below investment grade. In addition, most of the demand came from lenders in Europe and not the US. Standard and Poor's calculate that the volume of such highly leveraged loans in Europe in 2005 doubled to €123 billion ($147 billion), growing much faster than in the US. JP Morgan estimates that debt in the European sub-investment grade market reached a multiple to EBITDA of nearly eight times in 2005. Not surprisingly, the rating agencies foresee trouble.

Junk Bonds

Once upon a time, for a rating to be at the junk bond level was a stigma and for a firm to be rerated at the junk bond level was considered a disgrace, but not any longer. In April 1997, Doughty Hanson issued the first non-investment grade bond in the Eurobond market. Moody's reckons no less than 31% of issues today are at this level and CCC rated bonds, which were 2% in 2003, were 30% in 2005. In January 2006, NRG, the US power generator, sold $3.6 billion of high yield bonds, the second biggest issue since the heady days of RJR Nabisco in 1989. What is even more startling is a trend for companies to raise money at junk level as a matter of strategy. Rank Group sold its DeLuxe film unit and Ladbrokes sold Hilton hotels. In both cases the funds were returned to shareholders and the companies' bonds were rerated at non-investment grade level. The extra cost of borrowing between low investment grade and junk level is such that these firms don't see it as significant. In part, this is due to the success of private equity buyouts followed by leveraged borrowing at junk level. Firms not faced with any threat by private equity firms seem to be deciding that this is a route worth following. The narrowing of spreads will not last forever and one thinks of the terrible example of Marconi.

Latin America

This market is back for a variety of reasons – oil and commodity price increases have helped a lot. We are seeing trade surpluses, high foreign exchange reserves and even fiscal surpluses. Inflation generally is down, although still uncomfortably high in one or two cases. The JP Morgan emerging bond index showed a yield over Treasuries at the end of 2000 of 756 basis points. In March 2006 it was 191 basis points. In their search for yield, investors seem to have forgotten this market's chequered history and ignored the possible impact of rising dollar interest rates or a US slowdown. David Bowers of Merrill Lynch says, 'The risk is that people have fallen so much in love with the secular story that they have overlooked the cyclical risks.' Mark Mobus of Templeton Emerging Markets Fund does not pull any punches: 'The defining characteristic of an emerging market is not the level of its real income – it's the political structure and the amount of corruption.' When one reads that the risk premium for investing in Colombian bonds (this drug-ridden, unstable economy) is just 1.58% compared to US Treasury bonds, one can be forgiven for thinking that investors have lost all contact with reality. There could not be a plainer example of the market's astonishing appetite for risk at the moment.

Derivatives

Of course, if risk can be passed on, then we would expect people to be willing to take more risk. The passing on of risk finds expression in the extraordinary market for credit and asset-backed securities which is expanding at breakneck speed. We begin with a bond where the holder pays a premium for someone else to accept the credit risk. Then we develop the idea of selling the risk on a pool of bonds. We can make this sophisticated by splitting the pool into tranches according to risk. As a first cousin to this we have the collateralised debt obligation – CDO. Here we sell the risk of a pool of tranched bonds as another bond but why stop there? Why not take a group of these bonds and pool them – a CDO backed by a portfolio of other CDOs, known as CDO2. Of course, when one of the credits hits trouble, the whole structure wobbles as was the case when Dana, the US car parts maker, was put on watch for a major downgrade by Fitch. This has affected 17 tranches of six different CDOs which include Dana.

Earlier in this section we mentioned the growth of highly leveraged transactions. If the risk seems uncomfortable, why not pass it on? The use of credit default swaps (see Chapter 14) or CDOs (see paragraph above) need not be confined to bonds but used for any debt risk, including leveraged loans. As a result, we see the Investec group, from London and Johannesburg, issue a collateralised loan obligation backed by a portfolio of leveraged or high yield loans in March 2006. The buyout activity of private equity groups, typically borrowing three times their own capital, has led to large increases in CDOs of this type. JP Morgan figures show these CDOs issued in Europe in 2005 reaching $17.5 billion as opposed to $12 billion the previous year.

The easier it is to pass risk on, the more risks people will take, and this is exactly what is happening. In the past, this type of excess has always ended in tears. 'This time it's different,' they say, but then, they always do.

Hybrid Bonds

The final example of the market's current appetite for risk is the growing popularity of hybrid bonds. This is understandable from the issuers' point of view, who are raising quasi-equity capital more cheaply, but what about the investors? The bonds are perpetual, there is no date for paying them back; they are non-cumulative, if dividends cannot be paid, so be it; finally they are deeply subordinated, if the issuer goes into liquidation the bond holders are at the end of the queue, after all other debt holders. The reward – perhaps 0.5% – but enough to lead to estimates that a market worth $4 billion in 2005 may be $40 billion in 2006.

Possible Dangers

The question now is whether all this risk taking is justified and whether there are circumstances in which it might lead to some sort of crisis.

There are a number of possibilities that one could envisage.

A large-scale terrorist event, such as 9/11, would soon shatter the market's confidence. It would be a brave person who would say that it's not going to happen. The current Iraq situation is certainly not going to lessen the possibilities.

We have already mentioned Latin America, and let's remember that the Russian default in 1998 shook the financial world. Russia is now doing well and so is Latin America, but the possibility of some political shocks must remain high.

The imbalance caused by the US huge trade deficit and budget deficit combined with large dollar holdings elsewhere worries many observers. Rising US interest rates followed by a slowdown would hit world trade and all dollar borrowings. Could a US embargo on more Chinese imports cause a backlash and a Chinese sale of US Treasury holdings? It would not be in their interests, but people often forget their best interests in the heat of a quarrel. It isn't just the US. Interest rates are on the way up in Europe, and Japan's long period of near-zero real interest rates seems to be coming to an end. However, at the World Economic Forum at Davos, where these fears were discussed, Jim O'Neill, the chief economist at Goldman Sachs, argued that a slowdown in America need not lead to a significant global loss of power. There is still strong demand in Asia to partially offset an American slowdown. If it is not a slowdown but a full recession, that would be a different matter.

Finally, the Dubai Ports World debacle, which we discuss later, reveals the possibility of a backlash and a withdrawal of Middle East surplus funds from the US. Of course, a suitable alternative home has to be found for so much money but investment opportunities elsewhere are plentiful.

ISLAMIC BANKING

Events in recent years – 9/11, the bombings in London and Madrid, the Iraq war, the continuing Israel/Palestine hostility and now the Iranian crisis over nuclear plant – all have led to a new level of Islamic consciousness. It is not surprising that this should spill over into the financial sphere.

In Chapter 2, we explained the concept of Islamic banking, to conform to Sharia, Islamic law on interest, and its increase. In Chapter 6, we met Islamic bonds, designed for the same purpose. We quoted a statement from the CEO of the Malaysian bank, CIMB, regarding their Muslim customers, 'There's a realisation that they need to be investing in their own countries and in a Sharia-compliant manner.' Islamic bonds, known as sukuks, are a third of the Malaysian market. Industry projections suggest that over the next decade Sharia-compliant investments will account for 50%–60% of the savings of the world's 1.2 billion Muslims. Estimates of the size of the Sharia finance industry vary widely, but range between $300 billion and $500 billion. A further sign of growing interest is the decision by Citigroup and Dow Jones in March 2006 to launch the first index of Islamic bonds, to create a benchmark for the market.

There is already evidence that many Middle Eastern investors are routing their US investments through intermediaries in London to avoid seizure in the event of a crisis. Now the problem has been exacerbated by the Dubai Ports World debacle. Dubai is a city state with good relations with the US and the fact that their proposed purchase of the British P&O ports, which included some American ports, caused such a political storm is seen as alarming. Analysts and businessmen in the Middle East fear that this could cause lasting damage to Arab business with the US. What we are now seeing is a 'cloud no bigger than a man's hand'. Due to high oil prices the Middle East states are awash with liquidity, and a withdrawal of these dollar funds from a US with its excessive current account gap could have serious consequences. To attract more funds into the dollar, the US would have to push interest rates up much higher. This is exactly the sequence of events which could derail the current boom in world trade and stock markets which, at last, began to show signs of a slowdown in May and June 2006.

THE EU AND EMU

The high hopes for the future of the European Union which found expression in the various meetings in the 1990s, and which led to Economic and Monetary Union on 1 January 1999, seemed in the spring of 2006 far from realisation. The Union is in a new mood of nationalism, protectionism and pessimism. The rejection of the constitution by France and Holland, two of the founders of the 'six', caused a seismic shock. Faced with the accession of 12 new low-cost economies, and similar competition from the new Asian tiger economies, fear caused France to reject any opening up of the market which they regard as 'Anglo-Saxon liberalism'. The Dutch, seeing low growth and themselves one of the few to abide by the Stability and Growth Pact, seem to have lost confidence in the original ideals which lay behind the idea of 'one Europe'.

What should have happened was a determination to find out what had gone wrong and to set Europe out on a new and prosperous path. Instead of which, the following months of 2005 were spent arguing about the UK's rebate and the Common Agricultural Policy. Most countries, having postponed free entry to people of the 12 for several years, then went further in the dilution of the Services Directive to ensure that domestic services would still be protected in a variety of ways from those offered by other countries, even within the EU. The new protectionism, led by France and its list of strategic interests where foreign takeovers would not be allowed, exploded in February/March 2006. The hopes raised when Italy forced its central bank governor to resign over blatant and illegal protection of banks against foreign takeover were soon dashed. Poland blocked plans for a merger of two Polish banks by UniCredit, the Italian banking group; Spain objected to a bid by Germany's Eon for the Spanish Endesa and France hastily proposed a merger of Suez and Gaz de France to frustrate a bid for Suez by Euel of Italy. Although Germany has always been a traditional ally of France, in an interview with the *Financial Times* on 13 March 2006, Joachim Wuermeling, Germany's deputy economics minister, said, 'What we see now are attacks on the single market, which is the most successful aspect of Europe's integration.'

If we look back to the 1990s, the change in Europe is quite startling. The Amsterdam Treaty became law in May 1999 and, amongst other things, set up the Stability and Growth Pact. Today, in 2006, the pact is, to all intents and purposes, dead. Its chief proponent, Germany, is one of the worst offenders. The so-called Lisbon agenda in 2000 set up a drive to make Europe 'the most competitive and dynamic, knowledge-based economy in the world'. This is so far from having been realised today that it's almost embarrassing to refer to it. Indeed, the relaunch of the plan in 2005, known as 'Lisbon 2', was the subject of a scathing report presented by two economists to the Austrian EU president, Wolfgang Schüssel, in mid-March 2006. Their conclusion was, 'We do not consider that Lisbon 2 is on track to succeed. On the contrary, our assessment is that it will fail unless its current shortcomings are addressed as a matter of urgency.' This is symptomatic of the paralysis that has affected the EU's leadership.

The Treaty of Rome set up the famous 'four freedoms' – capital, goods, services and people. In some cases, these freedoms are not only not being encouraged but actively resisted. In Chapter 11 of this book we quoted Katinka Barysch, chief economist for European Reform, the London-based think tank, 'If we were to write a new treaty today, would we be able to get these clauses accepted? I'm not sure.' Is it possible that future historians will see the extension of the Community to the 12 new countries as a step too far? What is ironic, of course, is that any competition from the 12 is nothing to that from China, India and other emerging market economies.

This is a crucial time for Europe. Either European leaders must see the danger and promote the original ideas for a single dynamic market, or Europe will stagnate further and simply become a vague affiliation of essentially separate economies.

Recommended Reading

NEWSPAPERS AND PERIODICALS

Financial Times
Economist
The Banker
Euromoney

GENERAL

Bain K and Howells P, *Financial Markets and Institutions*, FT/Prentice Hall
Buckle M and Thompson J, *The UK Financial System Theory and Practice*, Manchester University Press
Chapman SD, *The Rise of Merchant Banking*, Allen and Unwin
Chisholm A, *An Introduction to Capital Markets*, Wiley
Coggan P, *The Money Machine – How the City Works*, Penguin
Eakins SG and Mishkin F, *Financial Markets and Institutions*, Addison Wesley
Green E, *Banking, an Illustrated History*, Phaidon Press
Knott G, *Financial Management*, Palgrave Macmillan
Lewis M, *Liar's Poker*, Hodder and Stoughton
Mackay C, *Extraordinary Popular Delusions and the Madness of Crowds*, Harmony Books
Pilbeam K, *Finance and Financial Markets*, Palgrave Macmillan
Roberts R, *The City*, Profile Books
Stoakes C, *All You Need to Know About the City*, Four by Four

MONEY AND BONDS

Bruch, *The Predators' Ball*, Simon and Schuster
Fabozzi F, *Bond Markets Analysis and Strategies*, Prentice Hall
Walsh C, *Monetary Theory and Policy*, MIT Press

EQUITIES

Burrough B and Helyar J, *Barbarians at the Gate, The Fall of RJR Nabisco*, Collins
Elton E, Gruber M, Brown S and Goetzmann, *Modern Portfolio Theory and Investment Analysis*, Wiley

Geist CR, Wall St – *A History from its Beginning to the Fall of the Euro*, McGraw Hill
Roberts R, *Wall St*, Profile Books
Rutterford J, *An Introduction to Stock Exchange Investment*, Palgrave Macmillan

HEDGE FUNDS

Jaeger RA, *All About Hedge Funds*, McGraw Hill

FOREIGN EXCHANGE

Pilbeam K, *International Finance,* Palgrave Macmillan
Sarno L and Taylor MP, *The Economics of Exchange Rates*, Cambridge University Press
Shamah SA, *Foreign Exchange Primer*, Wiley

EUROPEAN UNION

Walter I and Smith RC, *High Finance in the Eurozone*, FT/Prentice Hall

DERIVATIVES

Chisholm A, *Derivatives Demystified, A Step by Step Guide to Forwards, Futures and Options*, Wiley
Hang EG, *The Complete Guide to Option Pricing Formulas*, McGraw Hill
Flavell R, *Swaps and Other Instruments*, Wiley

CHINA

Green S, *China's Stock Markets*, Profile Books

Glossary

ABS	Asset-backed security – for example, a mortgage bond.
ACCEPTING	Signing a Bill of Exchange signifying an agreement to pay. Subsequent or alternative signature by a bank virtually guarantees payment.
ACCOUNT	For equity settlements, exchanges may have an account period, for example two weeks, one month, etc. with payment due on 'account' or 'settlement' day. The alternative is a rolling settlement system.
ACCRUED INTEREST	The interest accrued so far on a bond and payable by the purchaser. Quoted separately from the 'clean price'.
ADR	American Depositary Receipt – the form in which foreign shares can be traded in the US without a formal listing.
AIM	Alternative Investment Market – a new market for smaller companies' shares set up in the UK in June 1995.
ALPHA FACTOR	The element in a share price that reflects its individual performance as opposed to the market (which is the BETA FACTOR q.v.).
ANNUAL YIELD	See FLAT YIELD.
APACS	Controlling cheque clearing, BACS and CHAPS in the UK.
ARBITRAGE	Taking advantage of an anomaly in prices or rates in different markets – e.g. buying in one and simultaneously selling in the other.
ARBITRAGEURS	Those looking for arbitrage opportunities. Applied especially in the US to those trying to exploit takeover possibilities.
ARTICLE 65	Article of the Japanese Financial Code – prevented commercial banks from engaging in some investment banking activities (and vice-versa); now dismantled.
ASK RATE	See OFFER RATE.
ASSETS	The side of the bank's balance sheet dealing with lending.
ASSURANCE	The business of life insurance and pensions.
ATM	Automated Teller Machine.
BACK OFFICE	Accounting and settlement procedures.
BACKWARDATION	When one market maker's offer price is less than another's bid – a clear opportunity for arbitrage!

BACS	Bankers Automated Clearing Services (UK).
BANK BILL	A bill of exchange accepted by a bank on the central bank's 'eligible' list. The central bank itself would rediscount a bill of this type. Also called an 'eligible' bill.
BARGAIN	Any stock exchange transaction.
BASIS POINT	One-hundredth of 1 per cent.
BEAR	A pessimist, selling securities in the belief of a falling market, hence a 'bear market'.
BEARER BOND	A bond payable to whoever is in possession – that is, no central register.
BED AND BREAKFAST	Selling shares one day and buying them back the next – at the end of the tax year to maximise CGT allowance or claim losses against profits.
BETA FACTOR	The effect of overall market movements on a share price (see ALPHA FACTOR).
BID RATE	Rate of interest offered for interbank deposits. Generally, the dealer's buying price for equities, bonds, foreign exchange, etc.
BIG BANG	Deregulation of the UK Stock Exchange, 27 October 1986.
BILL OF EXCHANGE	A signed promise to pay by a receiver of goods or services and kept by the supplier. May be sold at a discount.
BIS	Bank for International Settlements (Basel). The central bankers' central bank.
BLUE CHIP	The most highly regarded shares. (Metaphor is from gambling casinos!)
BOBL	Short name for the short term German government bond contract on EUREX.
BOND	A certificate issued by a borrower as receipt for a loan longer than 12 months, indicating a rate of interest and date of repayment.
BOND STRIPPING	See COUPON STRIPPING.
BOND WASHING	Selling a bond prior to the ex dividend date to take a capital gain instead of receiving income.
BONOS	Bonos del Estado – Spanish government bonds.
BONUS ISSUE	A free issue of shares to existing holders.
BRADY BOND	Bonds issued as part of South American country debt reduction under a scheme devised by Nicholas Brady.
BRETTON WOODS	Meetings at Bretton Woods (US) in 1944 set up the World Bank, IMF and foreign exchange system for the period following the Second World War.

BROKER	An agent for buying/selling securities or intermediary for a loan or sale of foreign exchange.
BTAN	Bons du Trésor à Intérêt Annuel. French Government two and five year notes.
BTF	Bons du Trésor à Taux Fixe. French Government Treasury bills.
BTP	Buoni del Tesoro Poliennali, Italian Government bond.
BULL	An optimist, buying securities in the belief of a rising market, hence a 'bull market'.
BULLDOGS	Sterling bonds issued in the UK by foreign organisations.
BULLET REPAYMENT	The whole of a bond or bank loan is repaid at maturity (instead of staged payments in the last few years).
BUND	Short name for the medium-term German Government bond contract on EUREX.
BUNDESBANK	The German central bank.
BUY/SELL AGREEMENT	Like STOCK BORROWING/LENDING (q.v.) or a repo except that the seller gives up all beneficial rights in the stock.
CABLE	Shorthand for dollar/sterling rate.
CALL MONEY	Money lent by banks to other banks or discount houses which can be recalled as needed.
CALL OPTION	An option to buy a share/bond/index/interest rate contract later at a price agreed today.
CAP	An agreement with a counterparty which sets an upper limit to interest rates for the cap buyer for a stated time period.
CAPITAL ADEQUACY	The need to maintain adequate capital to cover counterparty risk and position risk.
CAPITAL MARKETS	The market for medium- and long-term securities.
CAPITAL RATIO	The ratio of a bank's primary capital to a weighted value of assets (for example cash = 0 weighting).
CAPITALISATION	Market capitalisation of a company is the number of shares multiplied by the current price.
CBOE	Chicago Board Options Exchange.
CBOT	Chicago Board of Trade.
CDS	Credit Default Swaps – selling credit risk for a premium.
CERTIFICATE OF DEPOSIT	Issued by banks to raise money – strong secondary market. (Also EUROCERTIFICATE OF DEPOSIT)

CGT	Capital Gains Tax.
CHAPS	Clearing House Automated Payments System – for electronic clearing of payments the same day (UK). Used for sterling and euros.
CHINESE WALL	A theoretical barrier between different sections of a firm to avoid conflicts of interest or insider dealing.
CHIPS	Clearing House Interbank Payments – electronic bank clearing system in New York.
CLEAN PRICE	Price of a bond not including the accrued interest element.
CLEARING HOUSE	Central body guaranteeing contracts in a traded options/futures market place.
CLOSING OUT	For futures market – taking the opposite contract, for example, having previously bought 100 tons of cocoa for June delivery, the buyer now sells 100 tons for the same delivery (or vice-versa).
CMBS	Commercial Mortgage-Backed Securities – a form of asset-backed security.
CME	Chicago Mercantile Exchange.
CMO	Collateralised Mortgage Obligations – like CMBS.
COLLAR	A combination of a CAP and FLOOR. Setting a band within which interest rates will apply, for example 10%–12%, for a given period. Also used for currency rates.
COMMERCIAL BANKING	The 'classic' banking business of taking deposits and lending money, either retail or wholesale.
COMMERCIAL PAPER	A short-term security issued to raise money, usually by corporates. (Also EUROCOMMERCIAL PAPER.)
CONCERT PARTY	A group acting together (secretly) in a takeover situation, for example three people each buy 2.9% of shares to avoid no longer being able to hide behind nominee status.
CONNECT	A computer trading system at Euronext.liffe.
CONSOLIDATION	Reorganising shareholdings so that, for example, 10 shares at 10p nominal are replaced by one at £1 nominal.
CONVERTIBLE	A convertible bond may be converted later into equity, some other bond, or even a commodity, for example gold, as an alternative to redemption.
CORPORATE FINANCE	The department of a merchant/investment bank dealing with takeovers, mergers and strategic advice to companies.
COUNTERPARTY RISK	The risk involved if a counterparty fails to settle.

COUPON RATE	The annual rate of interest on a security noted on coupons issued with bearer bonds.
COUPON STRIPPING	Detaching the coupons from a bond and selling the coupons and the principal as individual zero coupon bonds.
COUPONS	Issued with bearer bonds to enable the holder to claim the interest.
COVER	The amount of dividend paid (net) divided into the amount of profit after tax available for distribution.
COVERED BONDS	A form of asset-backed security where an SPV (q.v.) is not used.
CREATION OF CREDIT	Banks' ability to lend money, facilitated by the use of notes and coin for a small percentage of transactions only.
CREDIT DERIVATIVES	A general market where credit risk is sold for a premium.
CREDIT RATINGS	For example AAA, issued by companies like Standard and Poor's and Moody's to rate the level of security of a bond or note issue.
CREST	The new UK paperless equity settlement system which started in mid-1996.
CROSS-RATES	Rates between two currencies neither of which is the dollar.
CUMULATIVE	Applied to PREFERENCE SHARES – if dividend is missed it is still owed to the holder.
CUSTODIAN	An organisation which will store the original documentation for, say, bonds or equities and will look after settlement.
CYLINDER	Name used for a COLLAR in currency markets.
DEBENTURE	In the UK, a bond secured on assets. In the US and Canada, a bond not secured on assets!
DELTA	A measure showing how the premium in an option will change as the asset price changes.
DERIVATIVES	Products whose price is derived from the price of an underlying asset – for example if ICI shares are the underlying asset, an option to buy or sell them at a given price is the derivative. Applied to options, futures, swaps etc.
DIRTY PRICES	Bond prices including the accrued interest element.
DISCOUNTING	Buying/selling a security at less than face value.
DISINTERMEDIATION	Direct market borrowing or lending by companies without going through a bank. A bank is traditionally the 'intermediary' between depositors and borrowers.

DIVIDEND YIELD	The annual percentage return on a share price represented by the current dividend – usually gross.
DOCUMENTARY LETTER OF CREDIT	The written undertaking of a bank made at the request of a customer (for example an importer) to honour the demand for payment of a seller (for example an exporter) if terms and conditions are met.
DOUBLE	See STRADDLE.
DRAGON BOND	A Eurobond issued in Hong Kong or Singapore and targeted for primary distribution to Asian investors.
DTB	Deutsche Termin Börse, former German futures/options exchange, now EUREX (q.v.).
DURATION	A calculation used to measure the remaining risk in a bond.
EARNINGS YIELD	Earnings per share (after tax) expressed as a percentage of share price.
EASDAQ	European Association of Securities Dealers Automated Quotations – a pan-European trading system which started in late 1996.
EBITDA	Earnings before interest, tax, depreciation and amortisation.
ECB	European Central Bank.
EDSP	Exchange Delivery Settlement Price – the price at which certain futures and options contracts expire.
EFT-POS	Electronic Funds Transfer at Point of Sale.
ELIGIBLE BILLS	Bills of exchange eligible for sale to the central bank when acting as 'lender of last resort'.
EMS	European Monetary System – general agreement on monetary cooperation. Included official use of the ECU, 20% of central banks' reserves held in a European Monetary Cooperation Fund and exchange rates of member countries kept within a stated range, one to another (ERM). Set up in 1979. Replaced by EMU.
EMU	European Economic and Monetary Union – a single currency area set up for eleven European countries on 1 January 1999. Greece joined later, and notes and coins were included from 1 January 2002.
EOE	European Options Exchange (Amsterdam), now known as AEX and part of Euronext.
EONIA	Euro Overnight Indexed Average – average of overnight rates in the euro area.
EQUITY	General term for shares.

ERM	The interim exchange rate system for countries waiting to join EMU.
ESCB	The European System of Central Banks – the ECB plus the central banks of the EU, technically including those not in the euro area but who play no part in monetary policy decisions.
ESOPS	Employee Stock Ownership Plans (US).
ETF	Exchange Traded Funds – these are listed securities which mimic the behaviour of an index and can be traded just like an ordinary share.
EUREX	The futures/options exchange which combines Germany's DTB and Switzerland's SOFFEX.
EURIBOR	Interbank lending rate for the euro in the countries of EMU.
EURO	The name of the single currency in Europe's monetary union.
EUROLIBOR	Interbank lending rate for the euro in London.
EUROBOND	A bond issued in a market outside that of the domestic currency.
EUROCERTIFICATE OF DEPOSIT	See CERTIFICATE OF DEPOSIT.
EUROCOMMERCIAL PAPER	See COMMERCIAL PAPER.
EUROCURRENCIES	Any currency held by banks, companies or individuals outside its country of origin.
EURONIA	Euro Overnight Indexed Average – average of overnight euro rates in the London market.
EURONEXT	The merger of stock exchanges in Paris, Brussels, Amsterdam and Lisbon. Owner of LIFFE.
EURO.NM	The Association of junior stock markets for smaller companies started by Paris, Frankfurt, Brussels and Amsterdam but with others joining.
EURONOTE	Short-term security denominated in a eurocurrency.
EUROSYSTEM	The ECB plus the central banks of the participating countries only, not including those not in the euro area.
EXERCISE PRICE	The price at which an option can be exercised. (Also called STRIKE PRICE.)
FACTORING	Buying trade debts on a regular basis to assist cash flow – usually done by subsidiaries of banks.
FALLEN ANGELS	Bonds which were investment grade but became non-investment grade later.

FAST MARKET	When normal stock market rules are superseded due to chaotic conditions.
FCP	Fonds Communs de Placement. French 'closed-ended' fund.
FEDWIRE	Electronic payments system between Federal Reserve banks in the US.
FLAT YIELD	The annual percentage return on a bond taking into account the buying price, for example if £100 nominal worth of an 8% bond is bought for £50, the yield is 16%. Also called 'annual', 'running' and 'interest' yield (see REDEMPTION YIELD).
FLOATING RATE	A loan with the interest rate varied at agreed intervals, linked to a base rate, for example LIBOR.
FLOOR	An agreement with a counterparty which sets a lower limit to interest rates for the floor buyer for a stated time period.
FOREIGN BONDS	Bonds in a domestic currency issued by non-residents.
FORFAITING	Buying export trade debts on a non-recourse basis to assist cash flow. The debts must be in the form of a BILL OF EXCHANGE or PROMISSORY NOTE.
FORWARD CONTRACT	A contract to buy or sell a commodity or security for future delivery at a price agreed today.
FORWARD/FORWARD	1. An agreement to lend money at a future point in time for a given period of time, for example, in six months for six months. 2. A forward foreign exchange deal not dated today but at a later date.
FORWARD RATE	A rate agreed now for a future purchase or sale of a currency. Derived from the difference in interest rates in the two currencies.
FRA	Forward Rate Agreement. An agreement with a counterparty which agrees on a stated rate of interest to apply to a notional principal sum at a future time to last for a stated time – for example, in six months for six months.
FRN	Floating Rate Note. An issue where the interest is at floating rate.
FRONT OFFICE	Dealing room system to facilitate buying and selling.
FSA	Financial Services Authority – the financial regulatory body in the UK.
FTSE	Financial Times Stock Exchange – indices such as FTSE 100.

FUNGIBLE	Exchangeable – for example, a contract of one futures exchange may be identical with another. Can be opened in one and closed in the other exchange (or vice-versa). Also used for further issues of bonds on exactly the same terms (and accrued interest) as those issued earlier.
FUTURES CONTRACT	Similar to FORWARD CONTRACT but not expected to go to delivery as the position will be closed out with the opposite contract.
G7, G10, etc.	Meetings of international finance ministers – 'Group of 7', 'Group of 10', etc.
GDR	Global Depositary Receipt – a form in which foreign shares can be traded outside their domestic markets.
GEARING	Carrying out financial transactions on the basis of a deposit or borrowed money. US term is 'leverage'.
GEARING RATIO	Ratio of equity and long-term debt.
GENERAL CLEARING	Part of APACS – the normal 3/4 day cheque clearing (UK).
GILTS	Term applied to UK and Irish Government bonds. From 'gilt-edged' or virtually guaranteed. In general use for UK Government stock from the 1930s onward.
GLASS-STEAGALL ACT	Passed in the US in 1933, prevented commercial banks from engaging in certain investment banking business (and vice-versa); now repealed.
GLOBAL BONDS	Designed to be sold in the eurobond market and the US market at the same time.
GLOBALISATION	The movement to integration of world markets regardless of national boundaries.
GREENSHOE OPTION	In the event of exceptional demand for a new issue, the issuer reserves the right to issue extra securities.
GREY MARKET	The market for sales of a security before the official market opens.
GROSS REDEMPTION YIELD	See REDEMPTION YIELD.
HAIRCUT	In a stock borrowing/lending agreement, the borrower passes collateral to a value in excess of the market value of the stock (to allow for the price rising). This excess is called a 'haircut'.
HEDGE FUND	An actively managed fund that seeks an absolute return, that is, a return whether markets go up or down.
HEDGING	A technique for limiting risk. For example, if a price movement would cause loss, a purchase is made of an options or futures contract giving the opposite result; if a rise in interest rates causes loss, a position is taken with interest rate options/futures so that a rise in interest rates will yield a profit.

HYBRID BONDS	Bonds that combine features of equity and debt – perpetual, non-cumulative and deeply subordinated.
IDB	Inter Dealer Broker – facilitates deals between market makers who can deal in confidence and anonymity.
IMF	International Monetary Fund. Set up in 1946 to help nations in balance of payments difficulties.
INDICES	Like the S&P 500, the CAC40, DAX, FTSE 100, etc.
INELIGIBLE BANK BILLS	Bills of exchange accepted by a bank, but one not on the central bank's list (see BANK BILL).
INITIAL MARGIN	Initial deposit required by a clearing house (as opposed to variation margin).
INSURANCE	If contrasted with assurance, this is business other than life insurance.
INTERBANK MARKET	Bank lending/borrowing one to another.
INTER DEALER BROKERS	See IDB.
INTEREST YIELD	See FLAT YIELD.
INTERNATIONALISATION	See GLOBALISATION.
INTRINSIC VALUE	The amount by which a call option exercise price is below the market price (or a put option exercise price is above it), usually called 'in the money'.
INTRODUCTION	A method of obtaining a stock exchange quotation. No new shares are issued. Usually they are foreign shares seeking a listing on a domestic market.
INVESTMENT BANKING	Banking implying a high involvement with securities – new equity issues, rights issues, bond issues, investment management, etc. Also advice to either party for mergers and acquisitions.
INVESTMENT GRADE	A credit rating of BBB (Standard and Poor's), Baa (Moodys) or better – that is, a high quality bond.
INVESTMENT TRUST	A company whose whole business is running a wide portfolio of shares. A 'closed-ended' fund.
IPMA	International Primary Markets Association (for Eurobond dealers).
IPO	Initial Public Offering – American term for OFFER FOR SALE.
IRREDEEMABLE	Same as PERPETUAL.
ISDA	International Securities and Derivatives Association.
ISLAMIC BANKING/BONDS	Issues made to conform to Sharia – Islamic law.
ISMA	International Securities Market Association.

ISSUING	Offering a security to the market in the first instance.
JOINT STOCK	Having shareholders.
JUNK BONDS	Specifically bonds with ratings of BB (Standard and Poor's), Ba (Moodys) or less. Generally high risk, high yield bonds.
KANGAROO BOND	An Australian dollar bond issued in Australia by a non-resident.
LBO	Leveraged buyout – that is, financed by heavy borrowing.
LCE	London Commodity Exchange – cocoa, coffee, sugar etc., now part of Euronext.liffe.
LDC	Less Developed Countries.
LEAD MANAGER	Bank(s) taking a key role in a syndicated loan or issue of securities like Eurobonds.
LETTER OF CREDIT	A document drawn by the importer's bank outlining the terms on which the exporter will be paid.
LEVERAGE	American term for gearing or 'making a small amount of capital go a long way'!
LIABILITIES	The side of a bank's balance sheet dealing with borrowing – that is, deposits, formal loans from others. Also share capital.
LIBID	London Interbank Bid Rate. Rate paid by one bank to another for a deposit.
LIBOR	London Interbank Offered Rate. Rate charged by one bank to another for lending money.
LIFFE	London International Financial Futures and Options Exchange – now part of Euronext.
LIMEAN	Average of the LIBOR and LIBID rates.
LIQUIDITY RATIO	Usually a percentage relationship between a bank's liquid assets and its eligible liabilities.
LLOYD'S	The Corporation of Lloyd's provides insurance through pooling the resources of individual members (the 'names') operating in syndicates.
LLOYD'S BROKER	Lloyd's will only deal with a 'Lloyd's Broker'.
LLOYD'S REGISTER	Shipping classification society dating back to 1776.
LME	London Metal Exchange – deals in six non-ferrous metals.
LOCALS	Traders dealing for themselves as speculators.

LONDON CLEARING HOUSE	The main clearing house for exchange traded derivatives in London.
LONG	To be 'long' in shares, bonds or foreign exchange is to own more than have been sold.
LORO	Alternative term for VOSTRO.
M&A	Mergers and acquisitions.
MANAGING AGENTS	Run and administer Lloyd's syndicates on behalf of the 'names'.
MARGIN	The deposit required by a clearing house.
MARKET MAKER	The dealers in stocks and shares as principals – that is, taking the risk in their own name.
MARK TO MARKET	Valuing securities or derivatives transactions at the current market price.
MATADOR BOND	Peseta bonds issued in Spain by non-residents.
MATIF	Marché à Terme International de France, French futures exchange – now part of Euronext.
MEDIUM-TERM NOTES	A flexible facility to issue notes of varying maturity, varying currency and either fixed or floating – all within one set of legal documentation.
MEFF	Mercado Español de Futuros Financieros, Spanish futures and options exchange in Madrid and Barcelona.
MEMBERS' AGENTS	Advise members on Lloyd's syndicates regarding tax, spread of risk, etc.
MERCHANT BANKS	UK term for investment banks.
MEZZANINE	Just as a mezzanine floor is a floor in between two others, so mezzanine debt is subordinated debt lying between equity and senior debt.
MIDDLE OFFICE	A general term for risk management systems.
MLA	Mandatory Liquid Asset – the charge for a sterling loan in the UK to cover non-interest bearing deposits at the Bank of England.
MLR	Minimum lending rate – the rate at which the Bank of England will lend to the banks. Only published as an 'official' rate in emergencies, for example January 1985 during the fierce run on sterling, October 1990 when the UK joined the ERM and the ERM crisis in September 1992. Now referred to as the 'repo' rate.
MOF	Multiple Option Facility. A revolving facility from a syndicate of banks permitting the raising of finance with various options – bank loan, banker's acceptance or commercial paper.

MONEP	Marché des Options Négociables de Paris, French options exchange.
MONEY AT CALL	An interbank short-term loan which may be recalled at any time.
MONEY BROKER	Intermediary putting borrowers in touch with lenders for a small commission.
MONEY MARKET	The market for money instruments with a maturity of less than one year.
MUTUAL	A bank or insurance company not a public company but owned by the members.
MUTUAL FUNDS	General name for pooled funds, such as investment trusts and unit trusts.
NAMES	Members at LLOYD'S.
NASDAQ	North American Securities Dealers Automated Quotations – computerised dealing system for US 'over the counter' (OTC) trade outside recognised exchanges.
NATIONAL DEBT	The total of outstanding debt of the central government especially bonds and national savings.
NIL PAID	A new issue of shares following a rights issue on which payment has not yet been made. Rights can be sold 'nil paid'.
NMS	'Normal Market Size'. This is the classification concept which replaced the three classes alpha, beta and gamma. It is based on a percentage (currently 2½%) of an average day's trading. There are 12 bands and they are used to decide the minimum quote size and the maximum size for immediate publication of trades (UK).
NOSTRO	'Our' – the overseas currency account of a bank with a foreign bank or subsidiary.
OATS	Obligations Assimilables de Trésor. French Government bonds.
OFEX	An over-the-counter stock market in the UK.
OFF-BALANCE SHEET RISKS	Risks for bankers other than activities which end up as an asset on the balance sheet. For example, standby loans, standby letters of credit, derivatives generally.
OFFER FOR SALE	A method of bringing a company to the market. May be at a fixed price or by tender.
OFFER RATE	Rate of interest charged for interbank lending of money. Generally, the dealer's selling price for equities, bonds, foreign exchange, etc. Also called ASK RATE or price.
OPEN OUTCRY	Face to face trading.

OPEN YEAR	When an accounting year cannot be closed due to uncertainty about claims (the Lloyd's market).
OPTION-DATED FORWARD RATE	A forward rate (foreign exchange), but the date is more flexible.
OPTIONS	The right but not the obligation to buy/sell equities, bonds, foreign exchange or interest rate contracts by a future date at a price agreed now. 'Traded options' means the options themselves can be bought and sold.
OTC	Over-the-counter market. Dealing outside a trading exchange, for example a currency option purchased from a bank.
OVERFUNDING	The issue of government bonds or Treasury bills not for immediate government borrowing needs but as an instrument of monetary control.
PAC-MAN DEFENCE	In a takeover situation, when the company which is the subject of a bid turns round and tries to take over the bidder!
PANDA BOND	A bond issued in China by non-residents.
PAR	The nominal value of a security, for example $1000 for US Treasury bonds or £100 for UK Government bonds.
P/E RATIO	Ratio of share price to earnings after tax.
PERPETUAL	A security without time limit for redemption.
PITS	Trading areas in options, futures and commodity exchanges.
PLACING	A method of bringing a company to the market. The shares are placed with institutional investors and some private investors, that is, not 'offered for sale' generally.
PLAZA AGREEMENT	An example of international cooperation. Following a meeting in October 1975 at the Plaza Hotel, New York, international finance ministers agreed to take measures to reduce the exchange rate for the dollar.
POISON PILL	A device to frustrate a hostile takeover bid.
POSITION RISK	The risk involved in holding any financial market position (equities, bonds, currencies, options, futures, etc.) should the relevant rates/prices change.
PREFERENCE SHARES	Dividend is paid as a fixed percentage. They have preference over ordinary shareholders for dividend payment and in case of liquidation. Usually non-voting. ('Preferred stock' in the US.)
PRIMARY MARKET	Markets where securities are sold when first issued.

PRIVATE BANKING	Specialist banking services for high net worth individuals.
PRIVATE EQUITY	Raising money for venture capital for early stage companies or for management buyouts.
PRIVATE PLACING	When securities are not offered for open sale but 'placed' with institutional investors.
PROGRAM TRADING	Bulk sales or purchases of securities triggered by computer programs.
PROMISSORY NOTE	A signed promise to pay a sum of money.
PSBR	Public Sector Borrowing Requirement – excess of public sector spending over revenue.
PSDR	Public Sector Debt Repayment – excess of public sector revenue over spending.
PUT OPTION	An option to sell a share/bond/index/interest rate contract later at a price agreed today.
REDEEMABLE	Applied to a preference share or bond – may be redeemed by the issuer on terms stated at the outset.
REDEMPTION	Final payment to holders of bonds.
REDEMPTION YIELD	The gross redemption yield takes into account the gain or loss to redemption as well as the FLAT YIELD (also called yield to maturity).
REINSURANCE	Laying off the original risk with others.
RELIT	Règlement Livraison de Titres. French Stock Exchange settlement system.
REPO	Sale and repurchase agreement. Securities are sold but must be repurchased later.
RETAIL MONEY	High street deposits/borrowings.
REVERSE REPO	When the REPO deal is initiated by the buyer of the securities.
REVERSE TAKEOVER	The acquisition by an unquoted company of a company whose shares are quoted and is often larger than the new owner. The new company takes over the quotation and imposes its own name. A way of getting a stock market listing.
REVOLVING CREDIT	A commitment to lend on a recurring basis on predefined terms.
RIGHTS ISSUE	An offer of shares for cash to existing shareholders in proportion to their existing holdings.
ROLLING OVER	Renewal of a bank loan with alteration of interest rate as per the agreed formula, for example LIBOR + 1%.

ROLLING SETTLEMENT	For example 'five working days' – that is deal on Tuesday, settle next Tuesday; deal Wednesday, settle next Wednesday, instead of all deals within a given 'account' being settled on a given day.
ROOM, THE	The area at LLOYD'S where brokers meet underwriters.
RULE 144A	A rule of the US Securities and Exchange Commission (SEC) by which securities issued abroad can only be sold initially to qualified institutional investors.
RUNNING YIELD	See FLAT YIELD.
SAMURAI BONDS	A yen bond issued in Japan by non-residents.
SCRIP DIVIDEND	Offer of shares instead of a dividend (optional).
SCRIP ISSUE	Same as BONUS ISSUE.
SEAQ	Stock Exchange Automated Quotations – the system that came in with BIG BANG (UK).
SEATS	Stock Exchange Alternative Trading System. A dealing system for smaller companies' shares (UK).
SEC	Securities and Exchange Commission, US body controlling regulation of the market.
SECONDARY MARKETS	The buying and selling of a security after its primary issue.
SECURITISATION	The borrowing of money through issue of securities on international markets (in particular) instead of through a bank loan. Also, converting an existing loan into securities, for example mortgage bonds (see ABS).
SEIGNORAGE	The special profit central banks make from printing banknotes whose nominal value is well in excess of their cost to the bank.
SERIES	All options of the same class, exercise price and expiry dates.
SETS	Stock Exchange Electronic Trading System – the new UK order-driven system implemented in October 1997.
SETTLEMENT DAY	When the money for a given trade is due to be paid (and the securities handed over).
SHARES	Shareholdings in companies with reward by way of dividend – usually called equity.
SHARIA	Islamic law.
SHATZE	German short-term Treasury issues.
SHELL COMPANY	A company with few assets, profits nil or in decline, and a very low share price.

SHORT	To be 'short' in shares, bonds or foreign exchange is to have sold more than have been bought.
SICAV	Société d'Investissement de Capital Variable. French 'open-ended' mutual fund.
SIGHT BILL	A BILL OF EXCHANGE payable on acceptance.
SOFFEX	Former Swiss Options and Futures Exchange, now EUREX (q.v.).
SOFT COMMODITIES	Sugar, coffee, cocoa, etc. – as opposed to metals.
SONIA	Sterling Overnight Indexed Average – average of overnight rates.
SPLIT	Existing shares are reorganised ('split') into more shares, for example two shares @ 25p are exchanged for each one @ 50p (nominal values).
SPOT	Today's rate for settlement in two days.
SPREAD	Difference between BID RATE and OFFER RATE. More generally between one rate and another.
SPV	Special Purpose Vehicle – used for asset-backed securities (q.v.).
STAG	One who applies for a new issue in the hope of selling for a premium – no real interest in the share.
STOCK BORROWING/ LENDING	Equity and bond traders may temporarily borrow or lend stock in exchange for collateral – especially useful for a SHORT position. Although called 'borrowing/lending', the stock is legally sold in UK law but not necessarily elsewhere.
STOCK EXCHANGE BORROWING/LENDING INTERMEDIARY	Someone prepared to act as a broker in matching the stock borrower and lender (UK).
STOCK INDEX ARBITRAGE	ARBITRAGE between the options, futures and market price of an index at contract closure.
STOCKS	Fixed interest securities, for example bonds, debentures, preference shares.
STRADDLE	A traded option strategy – simultaneous purchase/sale of both CALL OPTION and PUT OPTION for the same share, exercise price and expiry date.
STRIKE PRICE	See EXERCISE PRICE (alternative term).
STRIPPED BONDS	See COUPON STRIPPING.
STRIPS	Separate Trading of Registered Interest and Principal of Securities, stripped government bonds in the US.
STRUCTURED FINANCE	Applied to pools of asset-backed securities which are tranched according to risk and sold off in parcels.

SUBORDINATED DEBT   A bond that, in the event of liquidation, can claim only after other senior debts have been met.

SUKUK   A bond issued to conform to Sharia, Islamic law.

SUPERDOT   Automated execution system on the New York Stock Exchange.

SWAP   Exchange of debt obligations between two parties, either exchange of currencies or fixed to floating rate (and vice-versa) and sometimes both. The latter applies to a notional principal sum and the agreement lasts for a stated time period.

SWAPNOTE   A contract offered at Euronext.liffe. Actually, a bond contract but the cash flows of the bond are discounted by the SWAPS YIELD CURVE.

SWAPS YIELD CURVE   Based on the appropriate interest rates for top quality non-government borrowers.

SWAPTION   An option to have a SWAP at a future point in time.

SWIFT   Society for World Wide Interbank Financial Telecommunication, the banks' international message switching system.

SYNDICATE   Managers, underwriters and selling agents of a bond or bank loan.

SYNDICATES   Organisation of the NAMES at LLOYD'S. Each of the syndicates has its own professional underwriter.

TAP STOCK   In general, in bond markets further issues of a previously issued bond.

TARGET   Trans-European Automated Real Time Gross Settlement Express Transfer – the official interbank euro payment system for the euro area.

TECHNICAL ANALYSIS   Forecasting movements of securities or foreign exchange values by follwing charts based on moving averages.

TENDER   A bank loan or new security is offered to dealers who must compete for the business. If settled on a STRIKE PRICE basis, all pay the same price. If offered on a bid price basis, all pay the price they bid.

TICKS   Smallest price movement of a contract, for example 0.01 or ¹⁄₃₂.

TIME VALUE   That part of an option premium which is not the intrinsic value.

TOMBSTONE   Formal notice in the press of a syndicated loan, bond issue, commercial paper programme etc.

TOPIC   Teletext Output of Price Information by Computer, the standardised display of SEAQ information (UK).

TOUCH PRICES	The highest bid price and lowest offer price for a particular stock or share.
TRADE BILL	A bill of exchange not endorsed by a bank and not eligible for rediscount at the central bank.
TRADE DATE	The date a trade is agreed, as opposed to settled.
TRADED OPTIONS	An option to buy or sell a share/currency/index/interest rate contract later at a price agreed today. This is a standardised market and the options can themselves be sold.
TRANCHE	Further (large) issue of an existing bond to meet the needs of the market.
TRANCHETTE	Further (small) issue of an existing bond to meet the needs of the market.
TREASURY BILL	Issued by governments to raise money. Typically, three months, six months, 12 months.
UNDATED	Same as PERPETUAL.
UNDERWRITE	When a group of financial concerns agree to subscribe for a proportion of a new issue to ensure its full subscription. The other use of the term is in insurance.
UNDERWRITER	Anyone offering insurance cover for a premium.
UNIT TRUST	A portfolio of holdings in various companies, divided into units which are bought and sold directly. An 'open-ended' fund, for example, the French SICAV.
UNIVERSAL BANK	A term for a bank that is equally engaged in commercial and investment banking, for example Deutsche Bank, UBS, etc.
VAR	Value at Risk analysis – sophisticated algorithms used to evaluate the risk in a bank's positions.
VARIATION MARGIN	Further amounts of deposit (debit or credit) calculated by a clearing house.
VENDOR PLACING	In a takeover bid, where shares are offered instead of cash, if the victim's sharenholders would prefer cash, institutions are found which will buy the shares.
VENTURE CAPITAL	Capital provided for high risks which would not normally attract conventional finance.
VOSTRO	'Your' – the domestic currency account of a foreign bank with a domestic bank.
VOLATILITY	An important term in OPTIONS, used to describe the volatility of an asset's price movements – this will affect the premium.
VRN	Variable Rate Note. A floating rate note where the margin above LIBOR is not fixed but reset at intervals.

WARRANT | A certificate attached to a bond or security giving the holder the right to buy equity/bonds later at a set price. May be issued on its own without attachment, for example gilts warrants, currency warrants, CAC40 warrants, Eurotunnel warrants, etc.

WHEN ISSUED | GREY MARKET trading in government bonds prior to the regular auctions.

WHITE KNIGHT | In a takeover situation, a more acceptable bidder may be sought – the White Knight.

WHITE SQUIRE | Alternatively, key blocks of shares are bought by friendly contacts – the White Squire.

WHOLESALE MONEY | The borrowing and lending of large sums of money – usually between banks, large companies and the institutions.

WORKED PRINCIPAL AGREEMENT | A term used in London's SETS system, when a stock exchange member agrees to dispose of a large block of shares for an institution by buying/selling them in smaller parcels.

WORLD BANK | The International Bank for Reconstruction and Development. Set up in 1945.

WRITING AN OPTION | Selling the option. A margin is paid to the clearing house.

XD | 'Ex Dividend'. If a share or bond is marked 'XD', this means that the purchaser is not entitled to the forthcoming dividend/interest payment as the cutoff point has passed.

XR | 'Ex Rights'. In rights issues, if a share is marked 'XR', this means that the purchaser is not entitled to the rights as the cut-off point has passed.

YANKEE BOND | A dollar bond issued in the US by non-residents.

YARD | Foreign exchange term for 1000 million.

YIELD | See FLAT YIELD.

YIELD CURVE | A graph showing the relationship between short-term and long-term yields for a given security or type of borrowing. Upward-sloping = positive yield curve; downward-sloping = negative yield curve.

ZERO COUPON BOND | A bond issued without interest payments but at a deep discount.

Index